Art Therapy in Australia

Art Therapy in Australia

Taking a Postcolonial, Aesthetic Turn

Edited by

Andrea Gilroy, Sheridan Linnell,
Tarquam McKenna and Jill Westwood

TUTA SUB AEGIDE PALLAS 1683

BRILL
SENSE

LEIDEN | BOSTON

All chapters in this book have undergone peer review.

The Library of Congress Cataloging-in-Publication Data is available online at http://catalog.loc.gov

ISBN 978-90-04-36825-5 (paperback)
ISBN 978-90-04-31518-1 (hardback)
ISBN 978-90-04-36826-2 (e-book)

This book is printed on acid-free paper and produced in a sustainable manner.

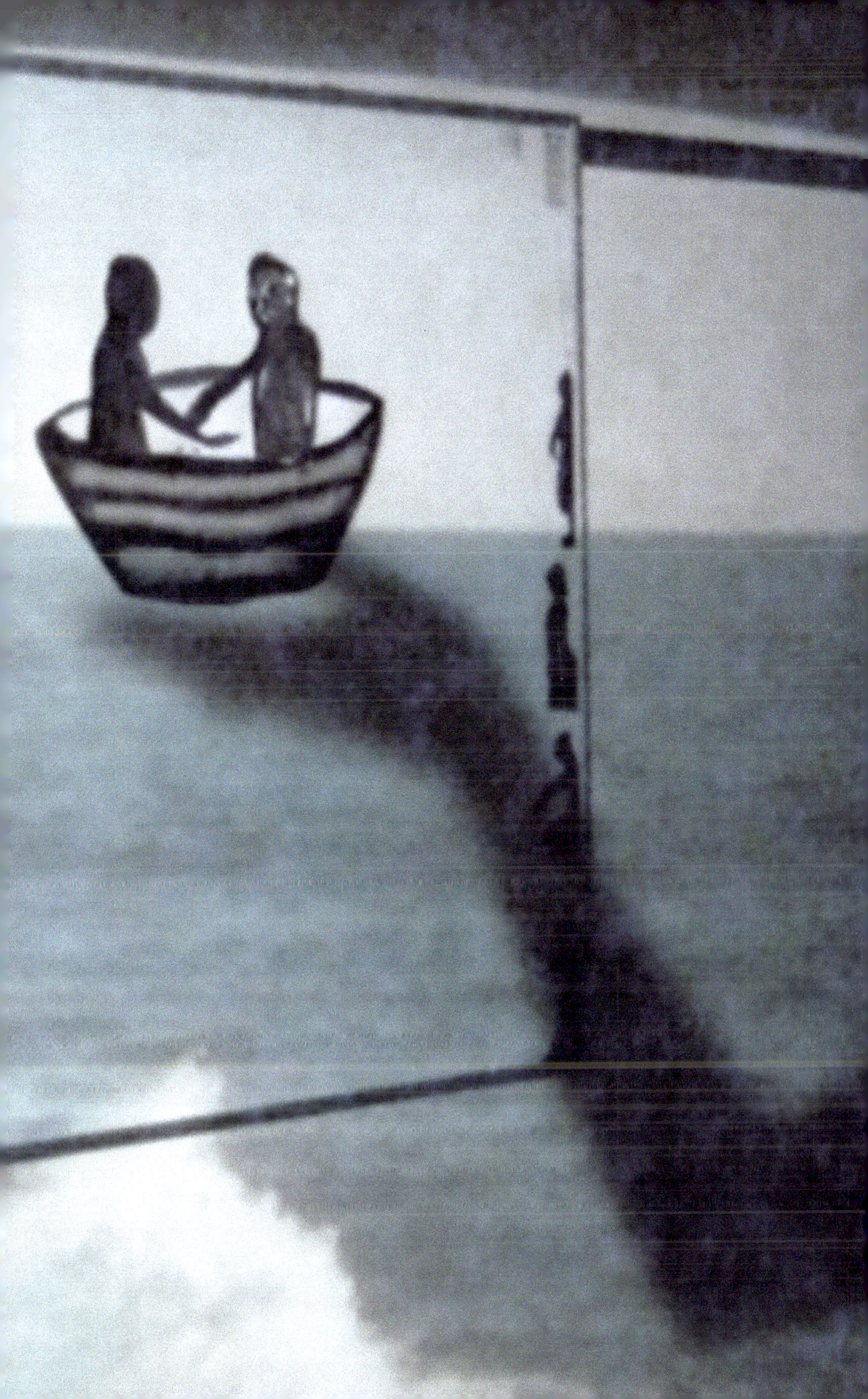

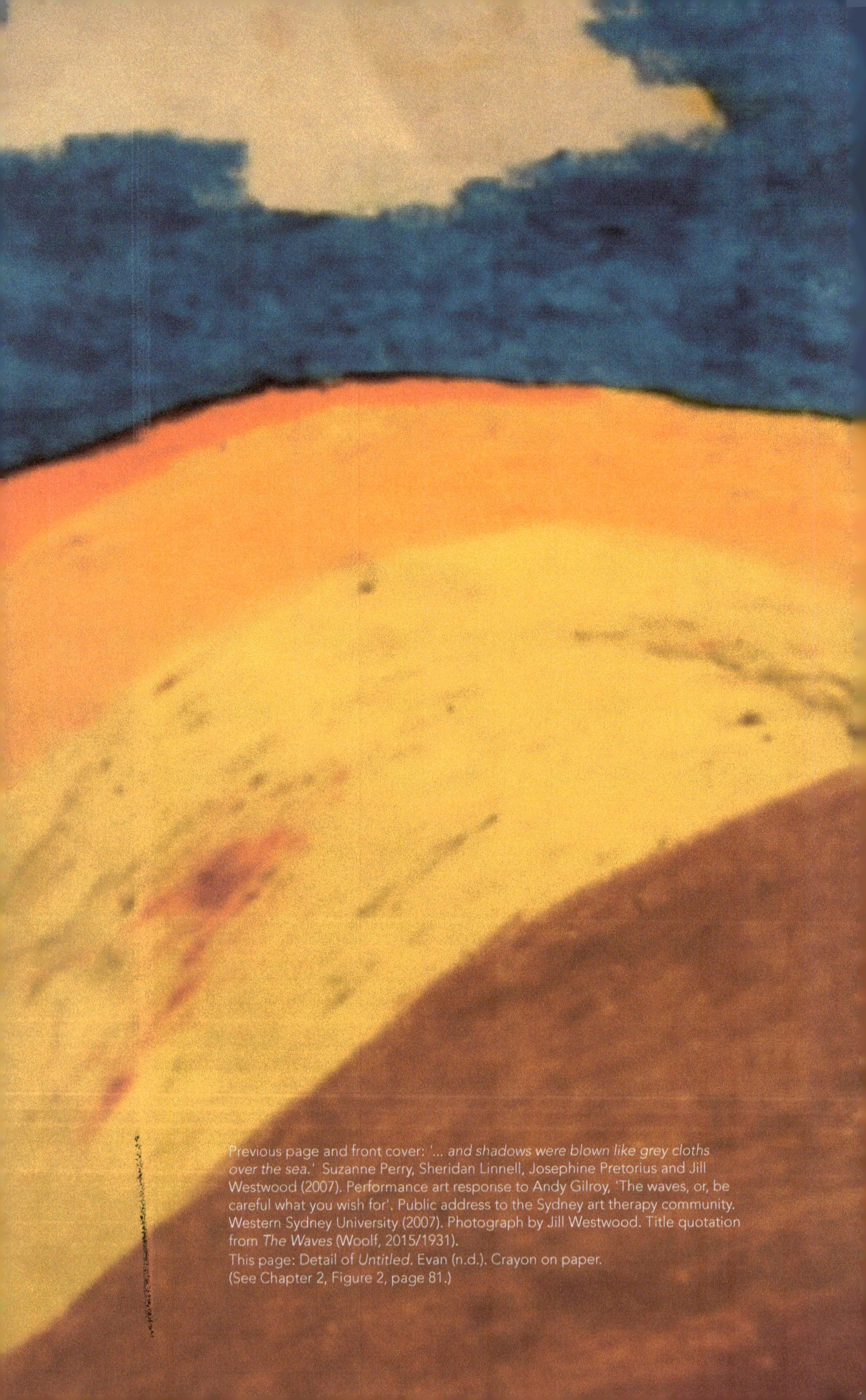

Previous page and front cover: '*... and shadows were blown like grey cloths over the sea.*' Suzanne Perry, Sheridan Linnell, Josephine Pretorius and Jill Westwood (2007). Performance art response to Andy Gilroy, 'The waves, or, be careful what you wish for'. Public address to the Sydney art therapy community. Western Sydney University (2007). Photograph by Jill Westwood. Title quotation from *The Waves* (Woolf, 2015/1931).
This page: Detail of *Untitled*. Evan (n.d.). Crayon on paper.
(See Chapter 2, Figure 2, page 81.)

CONTENTS

ACKNOWLEDGEMENTS

We acknowledge the place and land that has inspired this work. We express respect for country, for its Aboriginal custodians and for its elders past and present, recognising their strength, resilience and extraordinary capacities.

This book, a collective endeavour, has come together with the support of many people at various times. We wish to acknowledge all those who have played a part in its history and delivery.

First and foremost we are extremely grateful to all our contributing authors who have managed to sustain their enthusiasm and demonstrated immense patience whilst we brought this book to fruition.

Our friend and colleague Dr Pam Johnston, who profoundly influenced three of the current editors through her contributions towards the decolonising of art therapy education at the (then) University of Western Sydney (UWS) and who was a key participant in our early conversations with potential contributors to this book. Pam tragically died during the project before she could fully take up the role of co-editor or rewrite her iconic paper as a book chapter. We are grateful to her children and family for giving permission for us to include Pam's work in its original form.

Professor Bronwyn Davies for her long-term encouragement of this project and for a prologue that offers an imaginative point of departure for each reader's voyage through these pages. And Professor Lynn Kapitan for the epilogue – a broad, sparkling harbour of wisdom, wherein to 'dock ship' and reflect upon the journey.

We are totally indebted to Paul Manning and Julie Graves for their artistic collaboration and ground-breaking creative design of the whole book which we believe has propelled us into new art therapy territory. Chris Brown for his skill and patience indexing the book. And Michel Lokhorst, Brill | Sense publisher, for taking on and staying with this visually ambitious project.

Associate Professor Keith Bennett, former Dean of the School of Social Sciences at the UWS who enabled so much of the work of this book to happen, including Andy Gilroy's Research Fellowships. Also, Associate Professor Adrian Carr, Professor Dennis Del Favero and Ms Joanna Barnes, key founders and supporters of art therapy since the early 1990s who made space for art therapy to flourish at the UWS. To what is now Western Sydney University, and in particular Professor Kevin Dunn, Dean of the School of Social Sciences and Psychology, for his generous vision of art therapy and unstinting support of this project.

Goldsmiths, University of London, especially the former Department of Professional and Community Education (PACE) who occasionally allowed

Andy to escape, and the current Department of Social Therapeutic and Community Studies (STaCS) for their support of Jill and Andy's continuing collaboration with Australian colleagues and friends. In particular to Susan Williams in PACE, now STaCS, for her ongoing administrative support and diligent transcription skills.

With gratitude to the multiple communities of arts therapies practice, research and scholarship at Edith Cowan University and to the teachers who inhabited and continue to inhabit this and other spaces whilst passing on their knowledge in supervision, teaching, researching and art-making. Deep thanks to the many colleagues travelling the path of arts as life.

To international and Australian colleagues and friends of the arts therapies who have enabled the deepening of our understanding and given us the opportunity to expand our knowledge of the path we are all on – to the awakening of encounter! To ANATA and ANZATA, a thank you for bringing us to another space.

Each of these people, places and organisations have been navigation points in the making of this book; together they form a constellation of our guiding stars.

Andy, Sheridan, Tarquam and Jill
November 2018

LIST OF ILLUSTRATIONS

Chapter 7

Chapter 8

Chapter 9

Epilogue

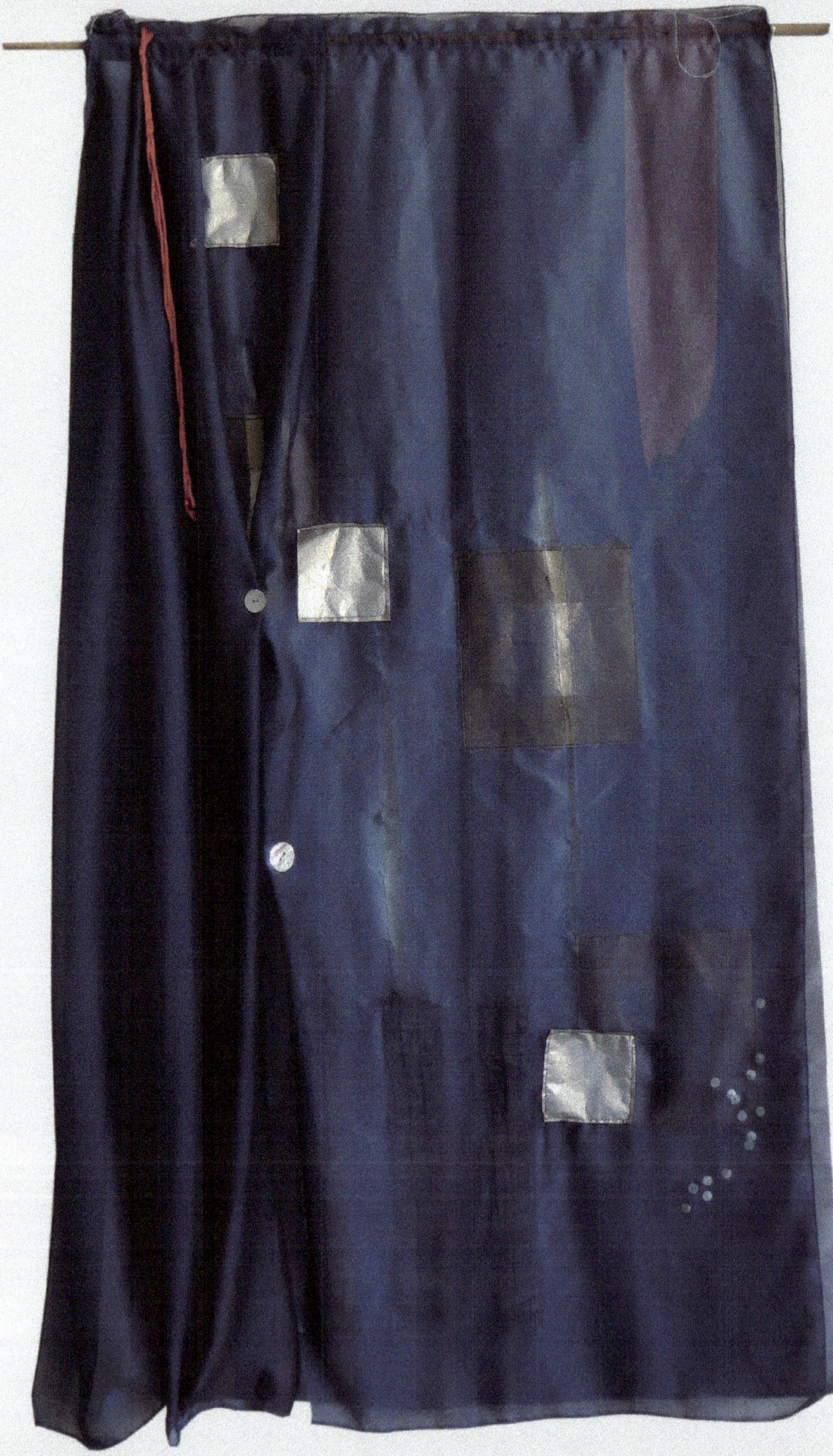

PROLOGUE

Bronwyn Davies

This gorgeous book will transport you, through words and images, across oceans, mountains and deserts of thought; it will show you, on the way how art therapists in Australia think about their work, how they practice their work. But they will not just be showing you – they invite you to travel with them in the small boat you can see on the front cover. Through words and images, the authors take you into their work as art therapists, work which is inseparable from the aesthetics of their own art-making, and inseparable from their land and its troubled history of colonisation. They will show you, and invite you to experience, not just the pain of that troubled history, but bring you inside the ways in which the postcolonial work they engage in gives Australian art therapy an edgy and exciting difference. Here is no dreary how-to-manual, but an opening up of multiple, exciting possibilities of thought and practice.

The work presented here is intra-active, revealing the ways in which each artist/writer/therapist is open to others, to affecting and being affected by the others in their work together with each other, with their clients, and with you as reader. They take you beyond the repetitive and clichéd thinking and practices of representation toward the possibilities of emergent thinking, where the new can unfold. Their work can be understood in terms of movement rather than stasis, and in terms of what Deleuze and Guattari would call qualities, speeds, flows and lines of force. The words and the images that make up this beautiful book will not bring you to "a pre-determined end-point, but through multiple encounters with emergent multiplicities" it will bring you to an encounter with something new (Bansel and Davies 2014: 41).

The aesthetics of this book, its rich materiality, its tactility, its sensual richness, the way the words and images bleed into each other, highlight each other, talk to each other, is integral to the concept that is unfolded here of *dadirri*, or deep listening. Deep listening invites you into the text – its words and images, inviting you to wait, sit, hold, wonder. It asks you to abandon preconceptions and repetitions about the way the world is or ought to be, and to open yourself to how it might be, if only you could pause in that way, and listen. After all,

> … the painter does not paint on an empty canvas, and neither does the writer write on a blank page; but the page or canvas is already so covered with pre-existing, pre-established clichés that it is first necessary to erase, to clean, to flatten, even to shred, so as to let in a breath of air from the chaos that brings us the vision.
>
> (Deleuze and Guattari, 1994: 204)

Opposite: Figure 1 *Untitled*. Bronwyn Davies (2008). Wall hanging, embroidery thread, sequins, buttons, satin and tuille on silk.

So there is necessarily a little chaos here, on the boat ride the authors take you on, and the intra-action between words and images is part of the gentle easing into chaos that the authors engage in. Having erased, cleaned, flattened, and even shredded the canvas, they bring in the fresh air that might enable, out of the ensuing chaos, a new vision to emerge – a vision of what art therapy can be – and is – in this extraordinary country.

References

Bansel, P. and Davies, B. (2014). Assembling Oscar, assembling South Africa, assembling affects. *Emotion Space and Society 13*, 40-45.

Deleuze, G. and Guattari, F. (1994). *What is Philosophy?* Columbia University Press, New York.

Woolf, V. (2015). *The Waves*. South Australia: eBooks@Adelaide, University of Adelaide Library. Retrieved from https://ebooks.adelaide.edu.au/w/woolf/virginia/w91w/

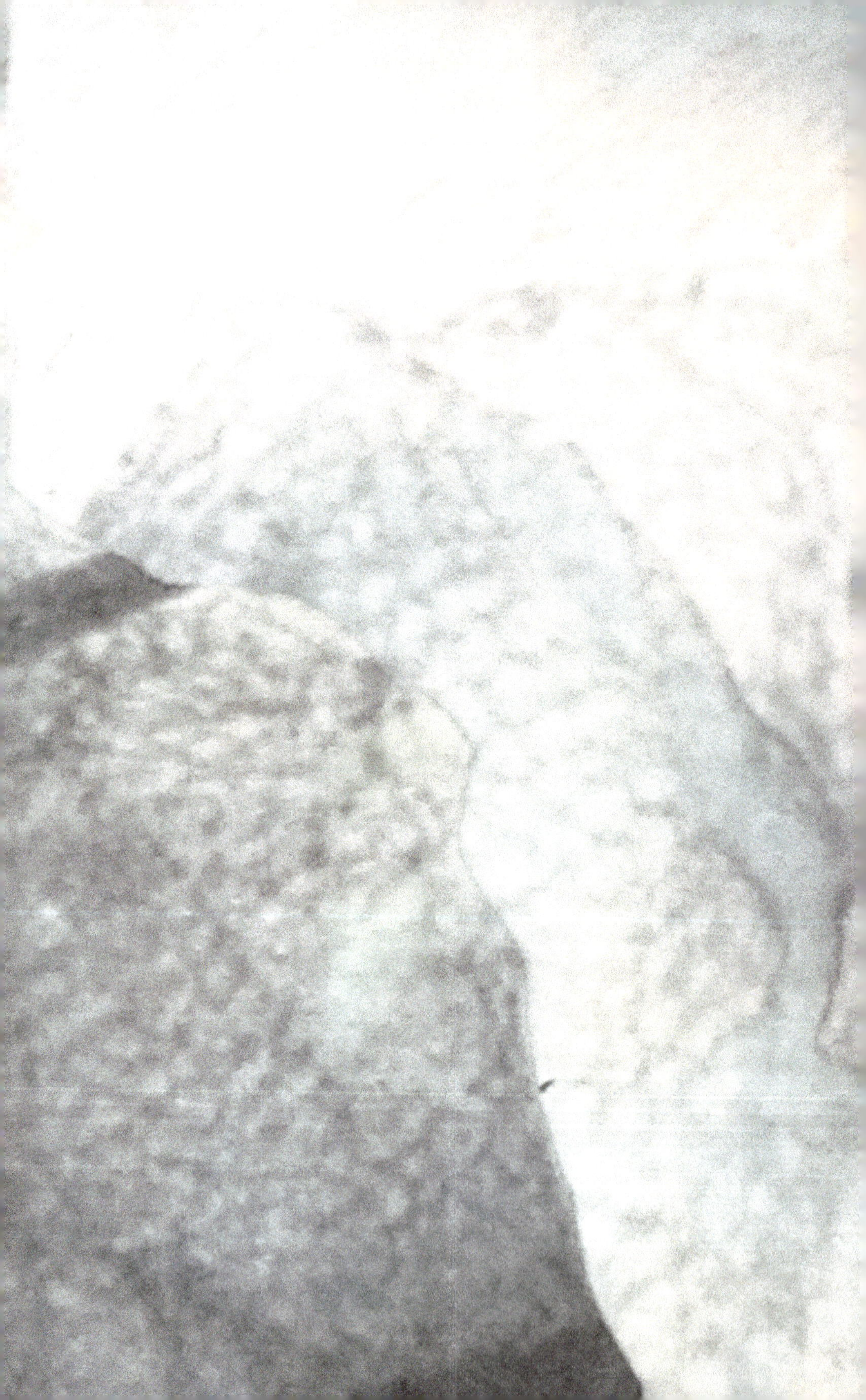

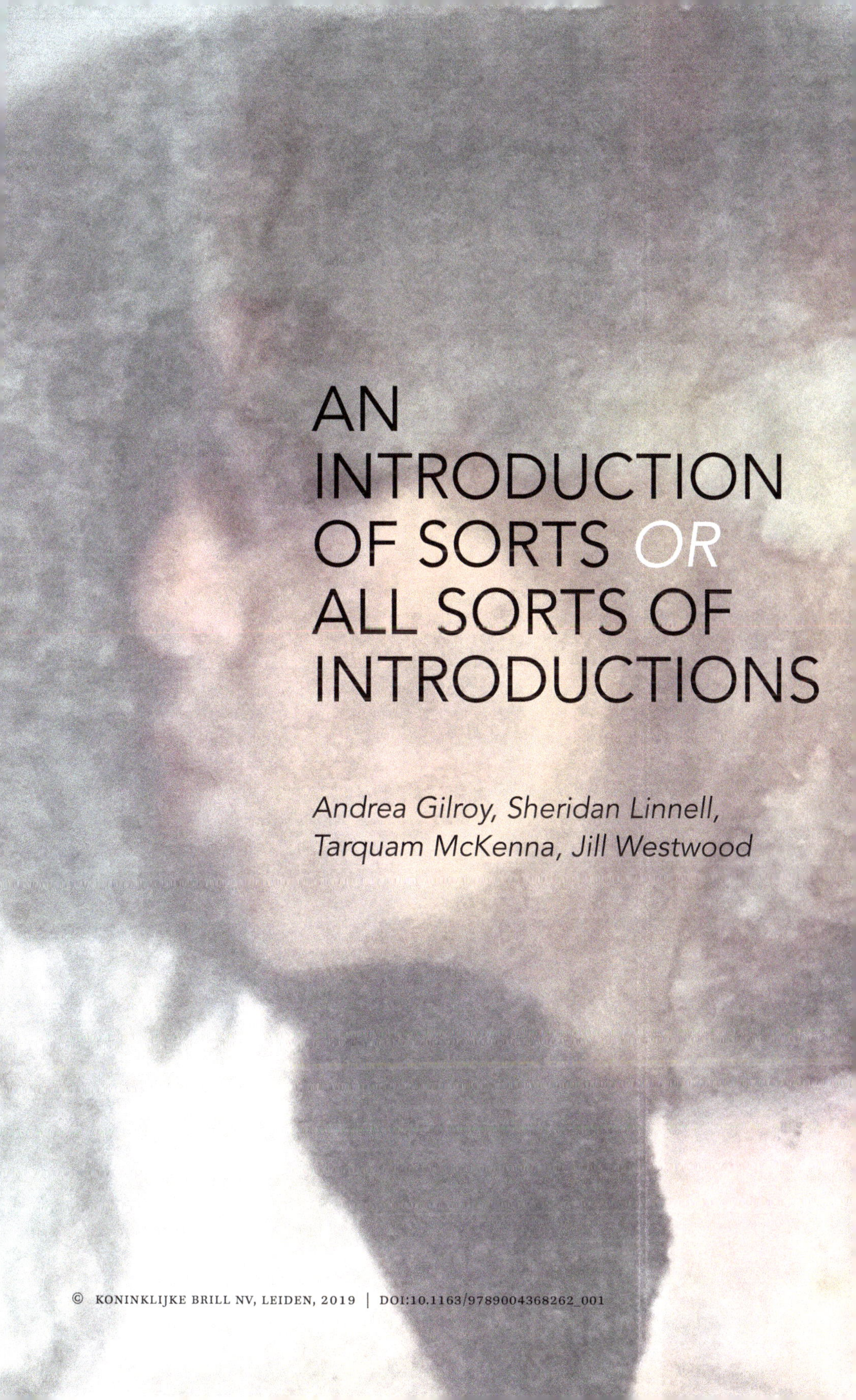

AN INTRODUCTION OF SORTS *OR* ALL SORTS OF INTRODUCTIONS

Andrea Gilroy, Sheridan Linnell,
Tarquam McKenna, Jill Westwood

 | DOI:10.1163/9789004368262_001

Placing ourselves and this project

Sheridan

Art therapy – to borrow contributor Patricia Fenner's perceptive remark about the emplacement of discourse (page 384) – always occurs some where. As to beginnings, the postcolonial theorist Edward Said (1975) suggests that it is only when we are well advanced in the journey that we can make a contingent decision about where we may have begun.

One such beginning, says John Henzell, was in the 1950s in a hospital for tuberculosis and psychiatric patients in Perth, Western Australia where Guy Grey-Smith initiated the use of 'art therapy methods' in Australia. Another was the founding of the Australian National Art Therapy Association (ANATA) in 1987, followed by the first Australian art therapy conference in Brisbane in 1989. Yet another was the establishment of Masters programmes in art therapy in Perth, Western Australia and Sydney, New South Wales in 1992 and 1993 respectively, along with Masters training in creative arts therapies at La Trobe University, Melbourne.

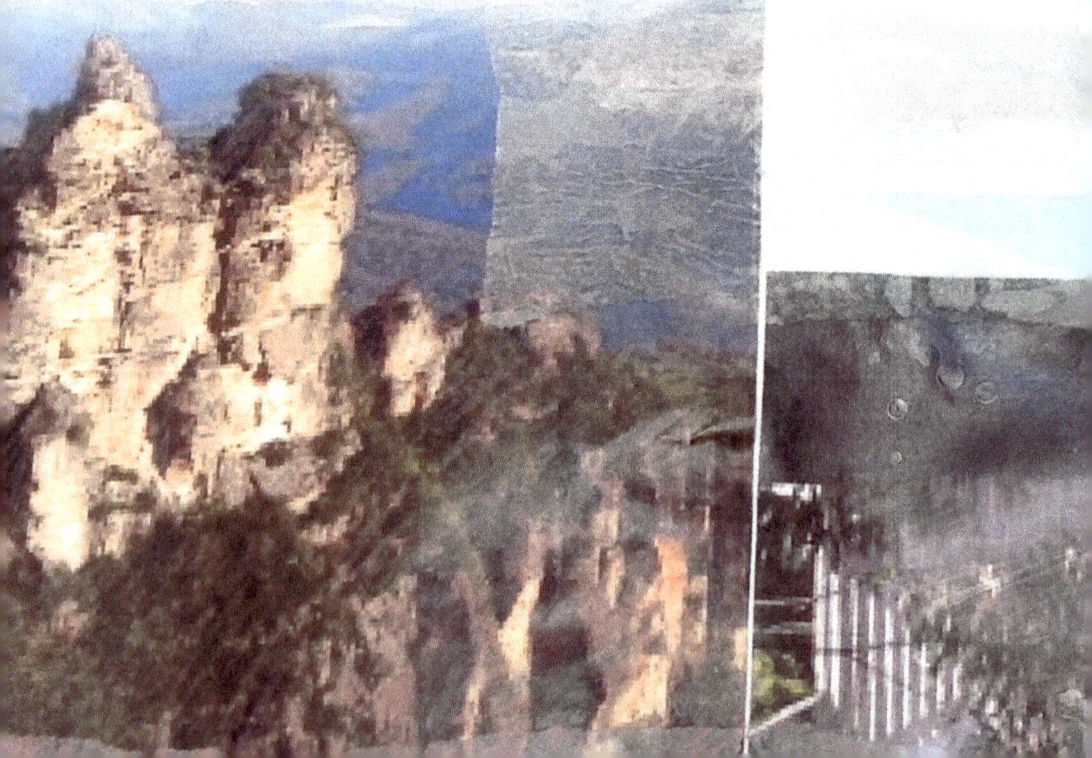

Another beginning was in 2003 in the Straw Bale House in the Blue Mountains, west of Sydney, home to the Darug and Gundungurra peoples, where a small group of wannabe art therapy researchers, including Jill Westwood and Sheridan Linnell, met for a residential workshop with Andy Gilroy and sowed the seeds for this book.

Keep going for another forty-one kilometres down that winding highway that connects the mountains to the plains and you will reach the Penrith Campus of what is now Western Sydney University. You may even discover the Art Therapy Cottage – the second of two early twentieth-century cottages that have successively housed the university's Master of Art Therapy training course during the last twenty-two years (see Figure 6.i). Travel further east and you will find, poised at the population centre of Sydney in South Parramatta, the curved edifice of the university's new Science Building. Half of its ground floor is dedicated to a huge state-of-the-art therapy studio teaching space, designed to project antipodean art therapy into an expanding future. (Meanwhile, Sheridan might be standing at the gleaming central bench, unpacking art supplies.)

We seem then to have travelled, in the space of two paragraphs, from a TB hospital in 1950s Perth to an ecologically sustainable and aesthetically enchanting space, graced with local contemporary art and traditional crafts in a native bushland setting, through cramped and hidden-away quasi-domestic, emotionally resonant and decomposing cottage rooms, into a cleanly defined public rectangle of space and light. From Medicine to Art to Science, or is it from 'art' to 'Art'? What undiscovered spaces will hold and give shelter to our memories and emotions within the smooth transparency and modernity of white studio walls and tall sheets of glass?

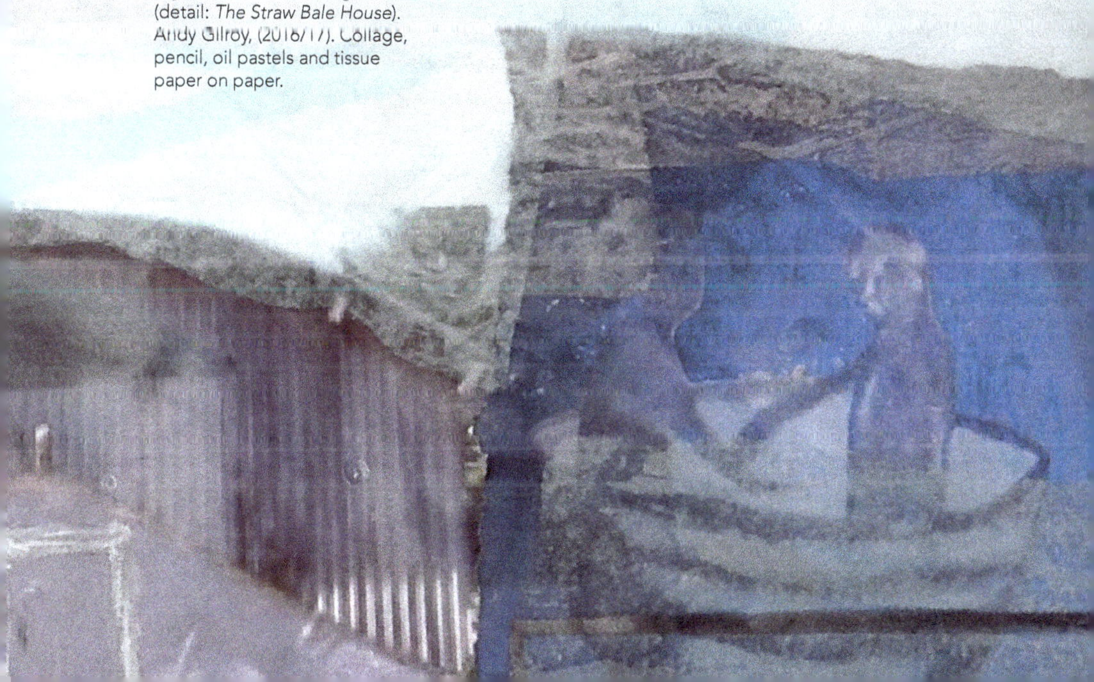

Figure 1 *It's been a long time* (detail: *The Straw Bale House*). Andy Gilroy, (2016/17). Collage, pencil, oil pastels and tissue paper on paper.

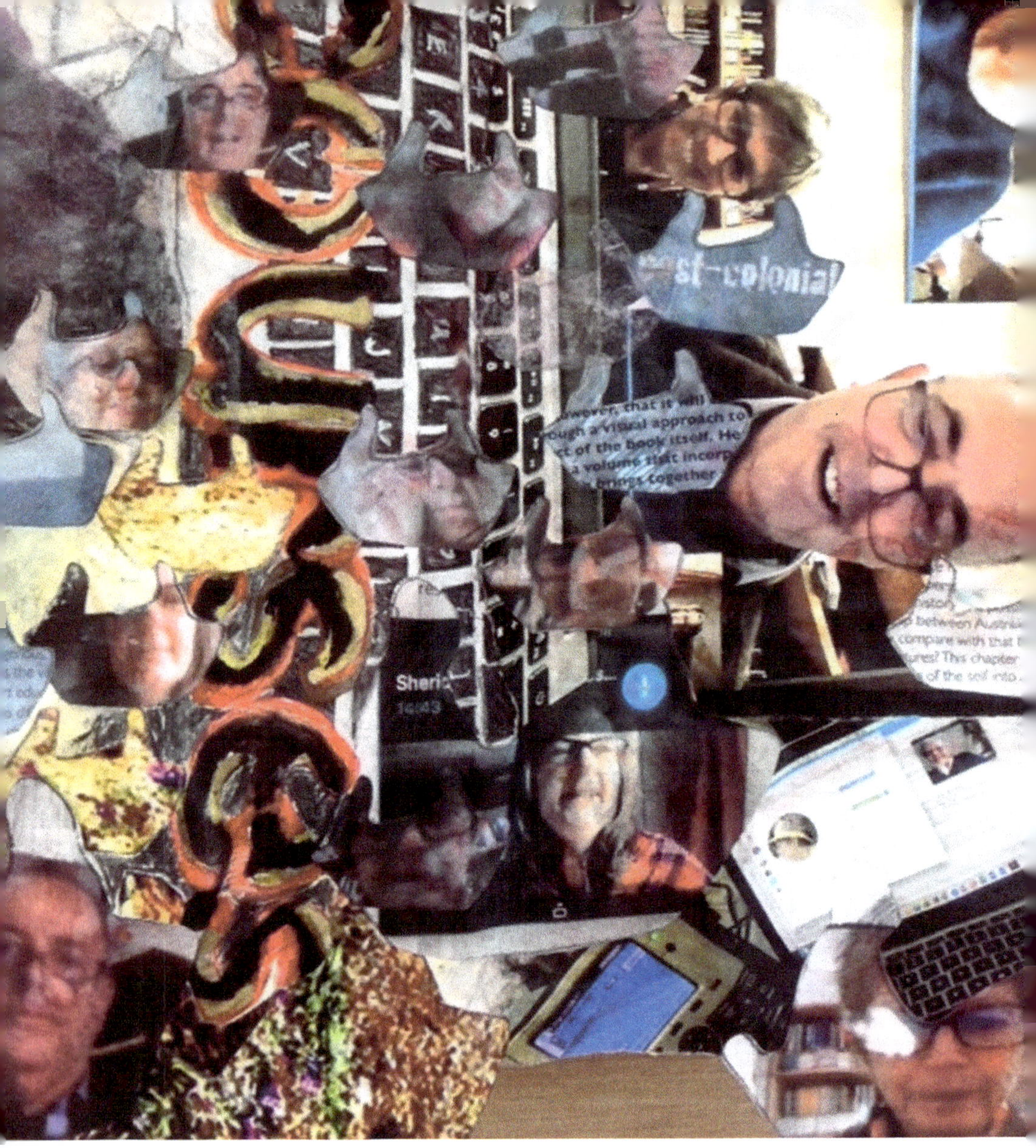

Figure 2 *It's been a long time* (detail: *We four*). Andy Gilroy (2016/17). Collage, pencil, oil pastels and tissue paper on paper.

Fly back over those mountains toward where we began and you will soon descend into an elegant, arty part of Melbourne, where Tarquam McKenna directs and teaches Indigenous Knowledges research for a regional university while keeping closely affectionate and strong scholarly ties with local arts therapies. Disappear like Alice down an endless rabbit hole, and you might emerge 'right side up' or topsy-turvy in the Victorian warrens of Goldsmiths, University of London, where the other two editors, Jill Westwood and Andy Gilroy, are now located, although Andy only notionally in these retiring and fruitful days spent writing and drawing.

How then are we four ‘placed’ to offer a commentary on the development of (visual) art therapy in Australia? What contingencies have drawn these authors and us together? We are far from representative but we wish to problematise the politics of representation in art therapy. We must situate ourselves, right here and now, stretched across two hemispheres and yet deeply connected to this drawn-out, complex project by the persistent ethical call of our relationships: to each other; to art therapy; to our colleagues and elders living and dead including our previous co-editor, Gomileroi woman, Koori urban artist and arts educator, the late Dr Pam Johnston Dahl Helm, so tragically killed during the making of this book (were we derailed? most certainly). We are indebted to the art therapy participants who are our teachers. Perhaps most of all, we are bound to the beauty, terror, pleasure and suffering of a land that claims all our hearts, even as those of us who came here uninvited would relinquish our claim – expressing sorrow, seeking forgiveness and reconciliation with the traditional custodians of country.

Figure 3 *It's been a long time* (detail: *An archaeology of shame*). Andy Gilroy (2016/17). Collage, pencil, oil pastels and tissue paper on paper.

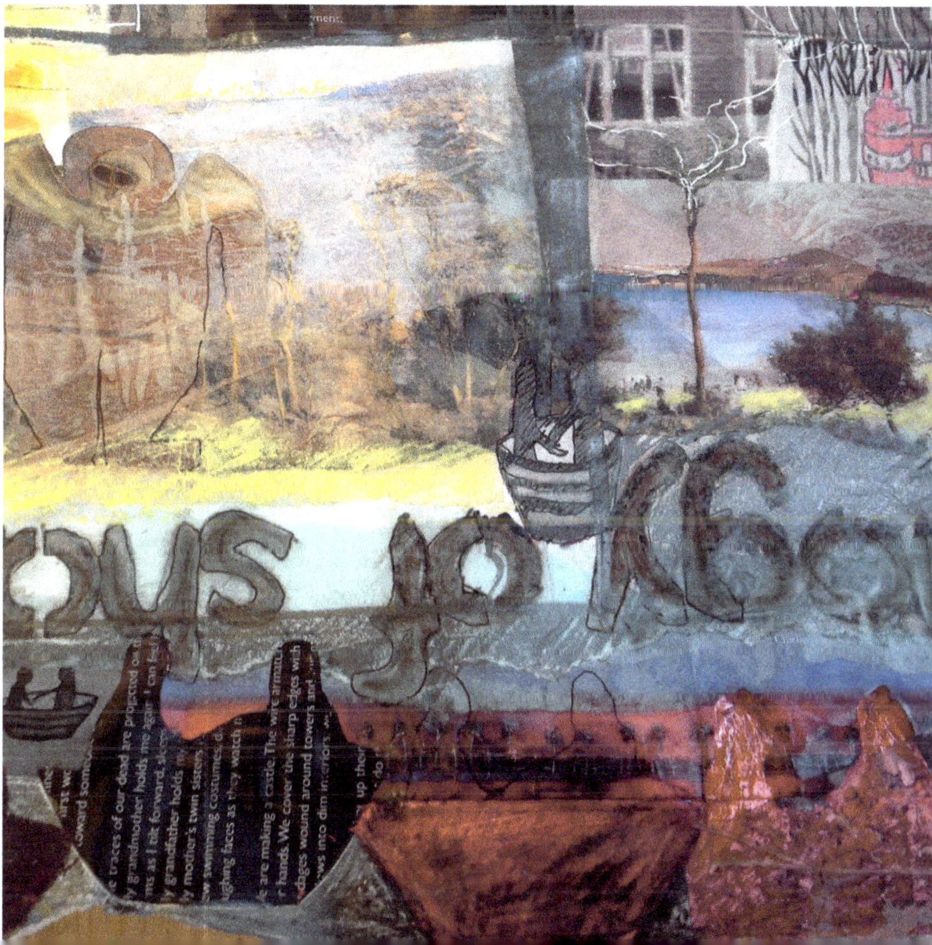

A hauntology

Andy

A between space of ocean
and then the sound of border-crossers.
Borders and oceans and tents and the land:
alive, conscious, aware.

The voices, traces and imaginings of our ancestors:
when to welcome? when to resist?
Welcomes that go wrong.

The imported and the local,
fractious in the wide, brown land
of stolen children
and the big story.
Historical injury and present injustice meet
under soft leaves and flickering shadows.
Ignored. Silenced. Oppressed.

A land that has had to roar at us
of the beauty of tangled places
and the art of letting be.
A land that has taught us
the tyranny of distance.

We subalterns in the post colony,
what do we do?
We fly in and fly out,
draw a heart on its side
and sift through the sediment
of wounds and damage and murder that are
some where, some place
in oceans of knowing
where sharks and chickens and platypus play.
We do the donkey work
of yarning knowledge, big and small.

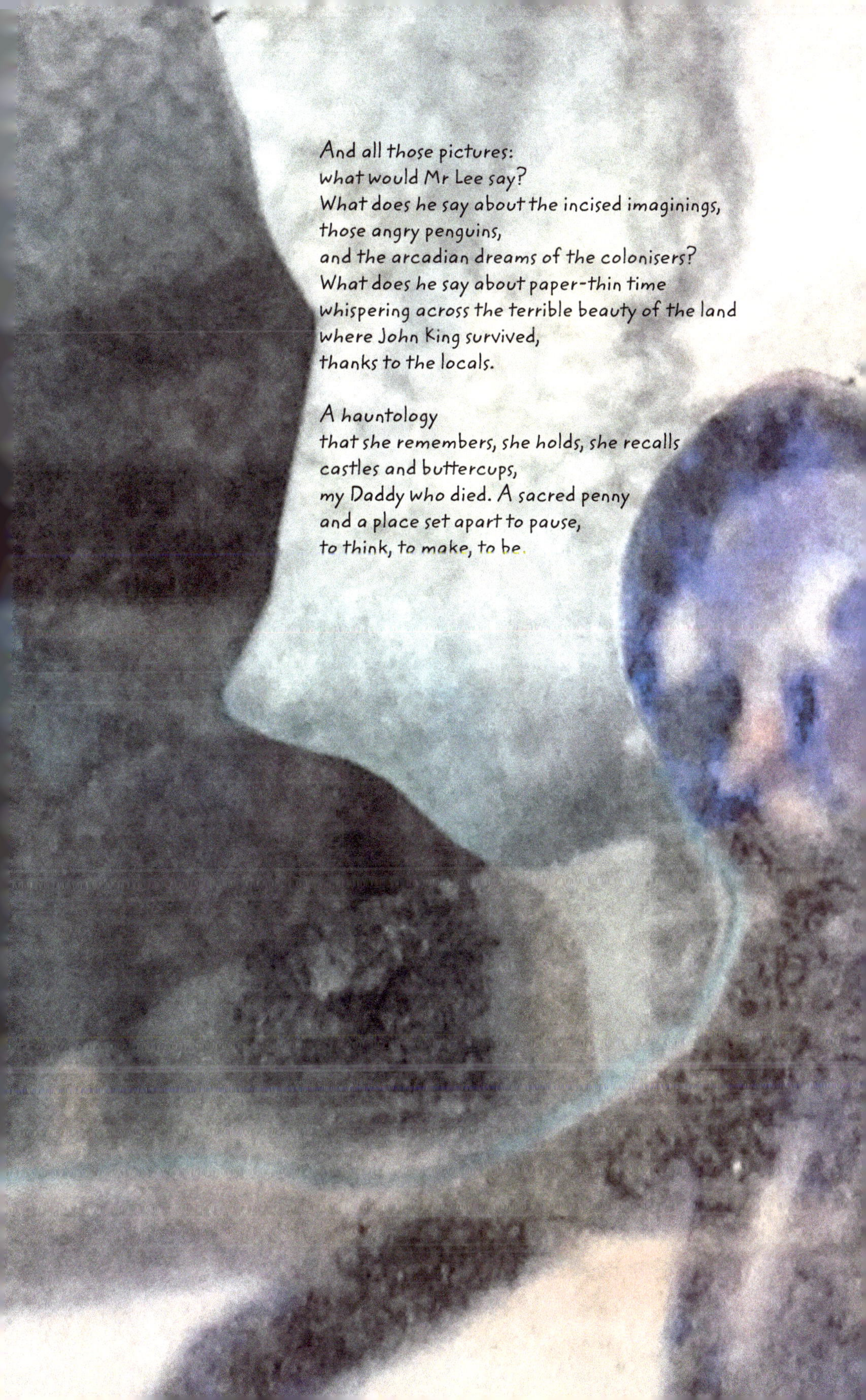

And all those pictures:
what would Mr Lee say?
What does he say about the incised imaginings,
those angry penguins,
and the arcadian dreams of the colonisers?
What does he say about paper-thin time
whispering across the terrible beauty of the land
where John King survived,
thanks to the locals.

A hauntology
that she remembers, she holds, she recalls
castles and buttercups,
my Daddy who died. A sacred penny
and a place set apart to pause,
to think, to make, to be.

Unfolding fields

Jill, Sheridan, Andy, Tarquam

The focus of this book is art therapy in Australia, exploring the themes of **aesthetics** and **postcolonialism**. It evolved through our unfolding relationships as art therapy educators in Australia and other parts of the world. It is a selective window, shaped by our partial and subjective viewpoints of what has become a diverse and changing field. It aims to embrace an ethics of difference that we consider central to the practice of art therapy in contemporary Australia. It weaves together various threads from **art and aesthetics, historical legacies, Indigenous perspectives, place and context.**

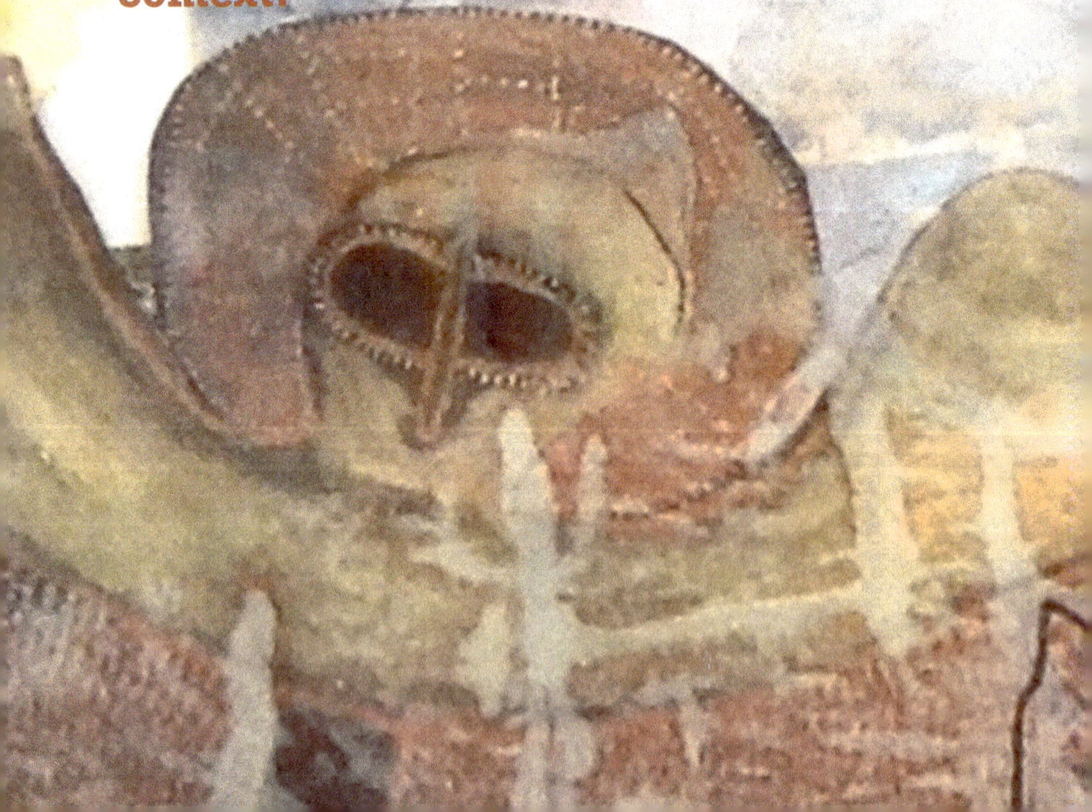

It aims to stir your interest, document practices, theories and histories and encourage further exploration of what this thing called art therapy *is* from another, Australian, perspective.

When the idea of capturing the space, place and time of art therapy in Australia comes to mind, you, our reader, might expect a chronology. However, time itself is emplaced and not necessarily linear:

> [t]he place of time references difference, embodiment and the connections between time and situation. The place of time neither forgets the critical function of mapping temporal practices nor seeks to universalise or standardise this activity ... the place of time questions the role (place) of time within an aesthetics of difference operating against the conventions of representation.
>
> Meskimmon, 2003: 168

We prefer to work with what Carmen Lawson describes (in Chapter 2) as the movement of art therapy in Australia across time. She draws our attention to chairos: the 'right time'. For Australian philosopher Moira Gatens (1996), chairos moves beyond the binary of historical time (chronos) and a rejection of history (aeon), suggesting how we "might select between a range of possible future becomings" (15). Chairos opens up possibilities for those who are marginalised in history to lead the way into possible futures (Gannon, 2016). This notion has a legitimacy and a place of being and belonging in the telling of art therapy in Australia. The threading together of the chapters of this book, the capturing of moments of being and belonging, move beyond the linearity of time. As per Said (1975), it is only through returning to the past, knowing where we were, that we know where we are now. But which past and whose story? The process of chairos is one of movement, not only back and forth but also criss-crossing the dominant and subjugated territories of art therapy, both reiterating and upending hierarchies of knowledge. It is a process of becoming, and yet we might know this 'right time' by pausing for a long moment, in the richness of a desert alive with wildflowers or on a city street where some tough, invading flower pushes its improbable green through the cracks in the concrete. Time makes itself known to us some where.

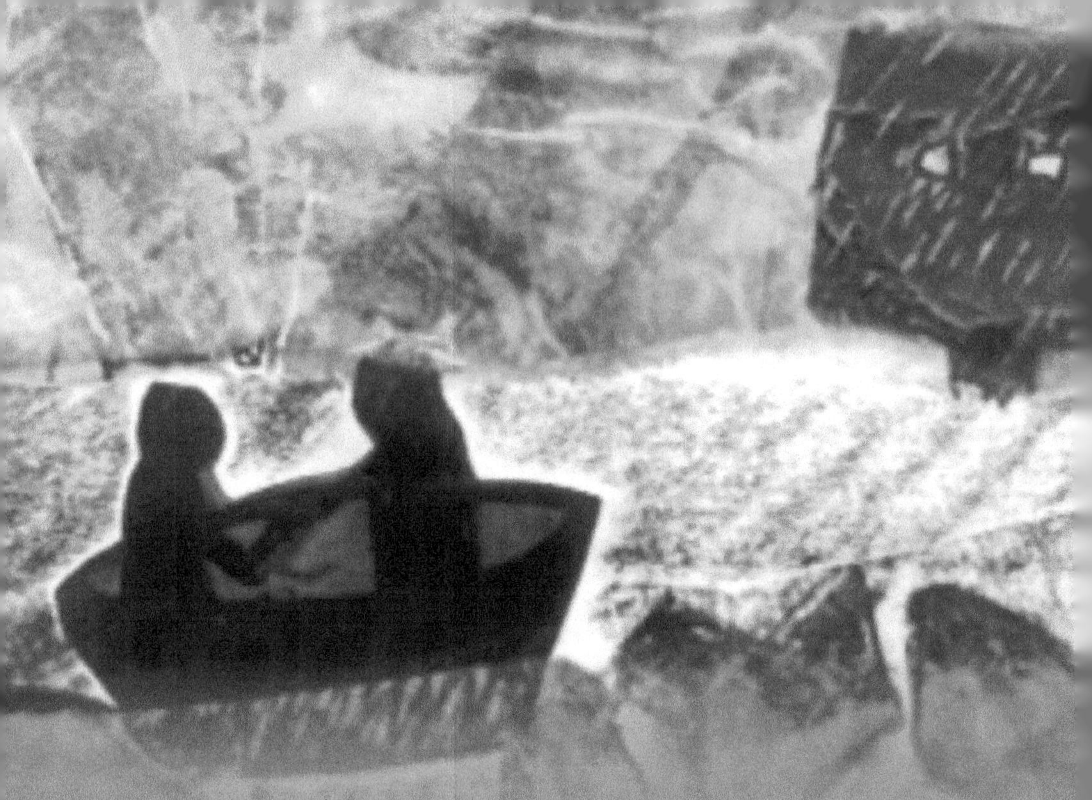

Art, aesthetics and art therapy

We have chosen to foreground the visual in this book. Why? Because in our view it embodies the potential of art therapy to open up alterity, illuminate possibilities and bear witness to the intra-psychic, relational and social realms.

It is part of the convention of our profession that the aesthetic experience of art-making in terms of both process and product is acknowledged to be fundamental to art therapy. This has been explored and discussed across the English-speaking world, beginning in the 1950s when the first accounts of art therapy were published (Naumburg, 1950, 1958; Kramer, 1958; Adamson, 1984; Hill, 1948). Since those early, pioneering days in the United States of America and Great Britain, art therapists have embraced the power of art as a way of knowing and transformation (e.g. Allen, 1992, 1995, 2001; Gilroy, 1992; Henley, 1992; Hyland-Moon, 2002; McNiff, 1981, 2009; Moon, 2006; Maclagan, 2001; Robbins, 1987; Schaverien, 1992).

Art therapy like other emerging disciplines establishes its credentials through reference to other fields of study, in particular by citing concepts from anthropology, aesthetics and psychoanalysis. Art and creativity have been explored by philosophers, psychoanalysts, psychologists, historians and artists and its value and power continues to fascinate. We have a canon of references that we draw on to support the centrality of art in human experience, some of which we reiterate and augment here. For example, Dissanayake, in *Homo Aestheticus* (1992), established how art-making is part of human evolutionary adaptation and showed how it has been used for expression, communication and rituals from the earliest civilisations. She shows how art is a way of 'making special' – an insight that makes art therapy special, too.

And so the account of our relevance continues, gathering force.

Thinkers such as Adorno (1997), a sociologist–philosopher, identified the critical role art plays in society; it allows the expression of difference and the formation of cultures counter to dominant ideologies. Psychologist Csikszentmihalyi (1991) recognised the concept of *flow*, a highly focused mental state that can occur in the experience of creative occupation such as art-making, and explored how this is connected to the state of happiness. Art theorist Bourriaud (2002) conceptualised *relational aesthetics* in the field of contemporary art. This is an art practice that concerns human relations and their social context, using these as departure points for art-making and positioning artists as facilitators of relationships. These, amongst many other thinkers show how art and aesthetic experience are powerful, complex and irreducible. This lies at the heart of the work of art therapy.

It also lies, for all our twisting and turning, our tortuous reflexivity, at the heart of this book.

Since the emergence of art therapy as a profession, the relationship and tension between *art* and *therapy* has evolved. From the beginnings of this 'uneasy partnership' (Champernowne, 1971) art therapists have researched the role of art and aesthetics in art therapy. Schaverien's (1992) seminal text *The Revealing Image*, laid down a significant foundation for the theorising of art therapy. Drawing on philosophical aesthetics, psychoanalysis and analytical psychology and working in the UK, Schaverien focused on the role of art through an in depth case study embodying an alchemical cycle of transformation. Around the same time in the USA, Robbins wrote *The Artist as Therapist* (1987), a classic text on integrating aesthetics and psychodynamics into the therapeutic process, and McNiff authored *The Arts and Psychotherapy* (1981), proposing an expressive arts perspective where all arts forms and therapies are in unity. Henley (1992) and Allen (1992, 1995) also highlighted the role of art and aesthetics in art therapy.

Then came Hyland-Moon's *Studio Art Therapy* (2002) which articulated an art-based theory and practice of art therapy, advocating a flexible approach and challenging the polarisation of the personal and the professional. Her stance encouraged the cultivation of an artistic perception of the world throughout the entirety of the work of the art therapist. Across the other side of the Atlantic, British art therapist Maclagan wrote *Psychological Aesthetics* (2001), discussing philosophical and psychoanalytic approaches to aesthetic qualities and psychological meanings. This work heightened awareness of the experience and meaning of aesthetic responses embodied in the creation and reception of works of art.

Other authors making significant contributions to the consideration of art in art therapy include Kapitan (2010) who emphasised the use of art in the art therapy research process. McNiff (1992, 1998, 2009) continued to emphasise the power of art in the work of art therapy, including its consideration as a healing force connected to shamanism (McNiff, 1979). A Western anthropological term arising from North and Central Asia origins, *shamanism* relates to Indigenous, ethnic, religious and spiritual practices usually performed by a *shaman*. This person occupies a mediating role in society with the spirit world, reaching altered states of consciousness and channelling healing energies or insights for the community. Such practices bring different ontologies into the field of art therapy other than those of the Euro-American mainstream.

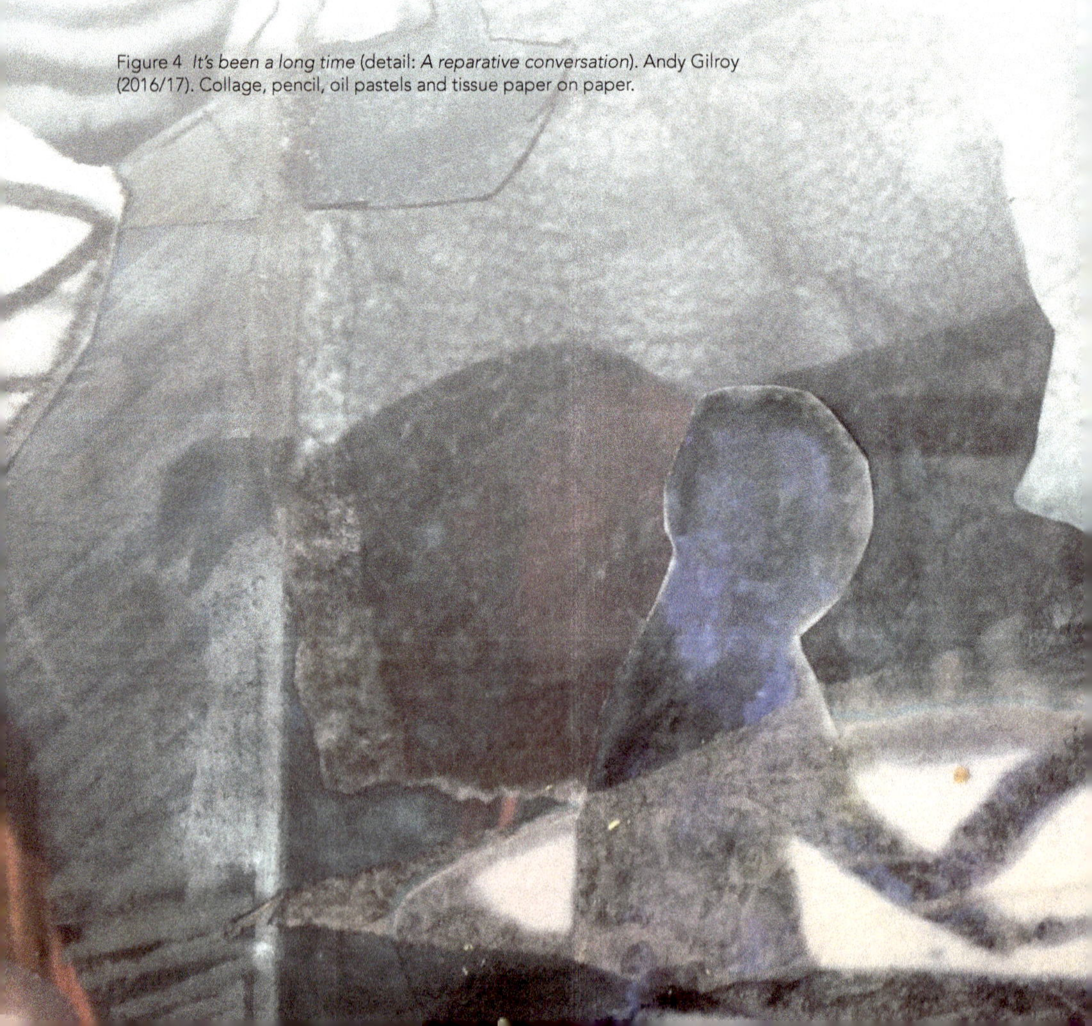

Figure 4 *It's been a long time* (detail: *A reparative conversation*). Andy Gilroy (2016/17). Collage, pencil, oil pastels and tissue paper on paper.

Yet we have struggled, in this book, with the notion of shamanism that is taken away from its specific location and accountabilities and somehow segued into art therapy. With our postcolonial hats firmly in place we worried about this being another appropriation of the culture and practices of those whom our European ancestors had already dispossessed. We did not want to be censorious, and we also did not want to abandon our editorial responsibilities.

We remembered that many in Australia are interested in the work of Miriam-Rose Ungunmerr-Baumann, Ngangikurungkurr elder and school principal from the Daly River, and the adoption and adaptation of the practice of dadirri – "inner, deep listening and quiet, still awareness" (Ungunmerr-Baumann, 2002: 1). Ungunmerr-Baumann also speaks of waiting for the "right time" (2). We wondered why this version of appropriation felt relatively OK, despite the convergence of Indigenous spirituality with Christianity being marked with a history of epistemological and physical violence. Perhaps it is because dadirri is about listening, including to the traditional custodians of country. Dadirri is located in the generous extension of knowledge from Indigenous to non-Indigenous community, whereas when shamanism is appropriated it might invest some 'one' with undue and unmediated power.

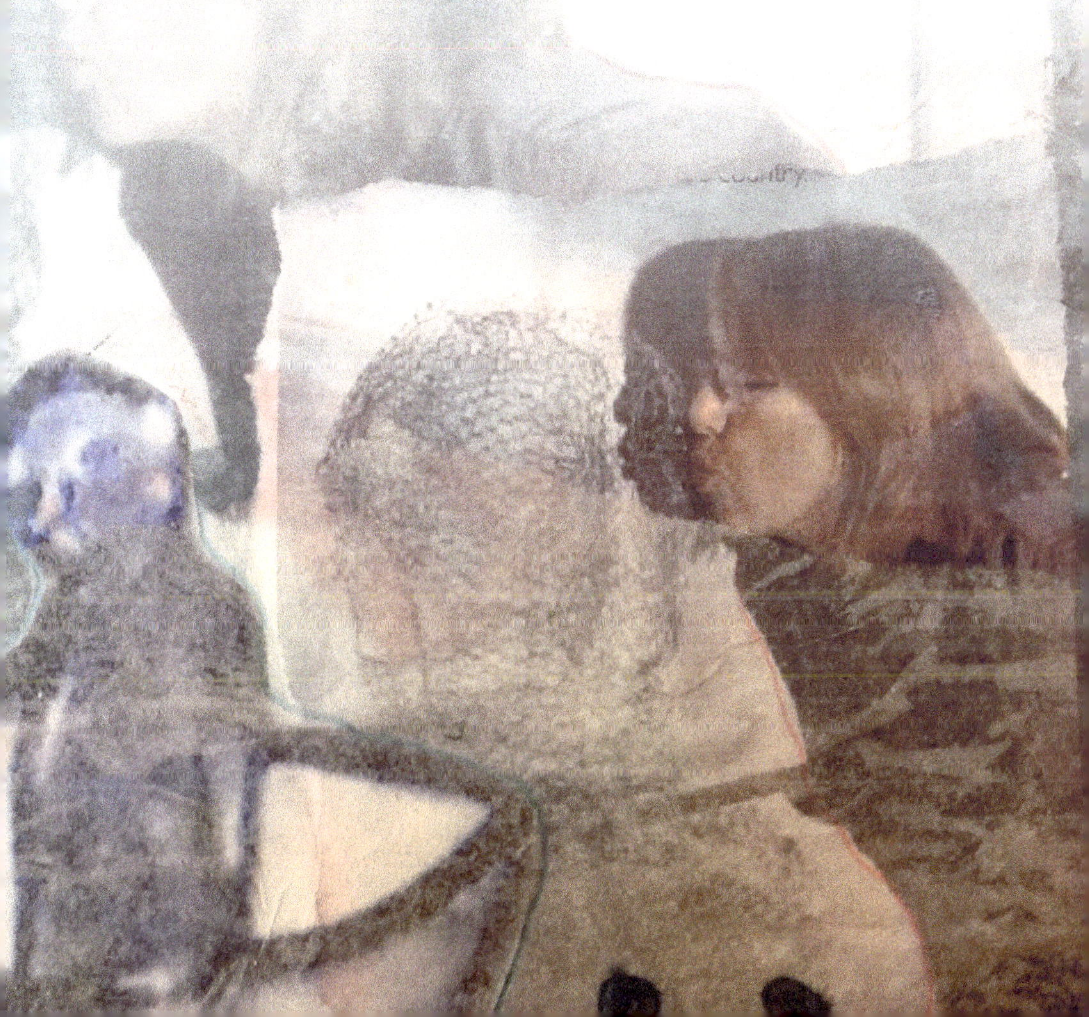

Some practices drawn from Indigenous epistemologies may be opaque to 'us' (but who are 'we'?) and/or challenge who we think we are because they are not just different ways of knowing the same reality but fundamentally different realities. Anthropologists such as Laidlaw (2012) discuss the idea of *ontological pluralism* and propose an openness to *thinking* with the materiality of the world rather than supposing that *we already know* or already have all the concepts we need with which to understand. This is not a multicultural approach but a multi-natural one that recognises alternative natural realities. Does this resonate with Deleuzian ideas concerning the relationship between identity and difference which suggest that all identities are effects of difference, and that difference cannot be reduced to difference from? These philosophical positions open up our awareness of the classifications that are used in art therapy's theory-making, leading us to a place where we wonder whether our theories and practices may not adequately address difference and might therefore create and perpetuate oppressions. This connects to us the other main theme of this book: postcolonialism.

Postcolonialism and art therapy

Colonised by the British as a penal colony in 1788 (another beginning), the theme of postcolonialism has, not surprisingly, a particular resonance for Australia. Postcolonialism is a theoretical approach concerned with the impact of colonisation and the human consequences of external control and exploitation of native peoples and their lands. It provides a way to study and analyse the politics of Western knowledge creation, control and distribution as these have been applied in order to subjugate non-Western peoples. The aim is to destabilise the cultural superiority of the colonisers and the ways that colonisers perceive, understand and know the world. Through this process it aims to establish intellectual spaces for *subaltern* peoples to speak for themselves, in their own voices and to produce cultural discourses that balance the imbalance. 'Subaltern' is a term used in critical and postcolonial theory meaning 'subordinate' or 'of lower status'. Key theorists include Bhabha (1994), Fanon (1952, 1961), Foucault (1990), Memmi (1965) and Said (1978, 1993) who, amongst many others, have led the development of postcolonial thinking and the struggle against oppressions.

Figure 5 *Art therapy has a black art history.*
Tarquam McKenna, (2016). Digital photomontage.

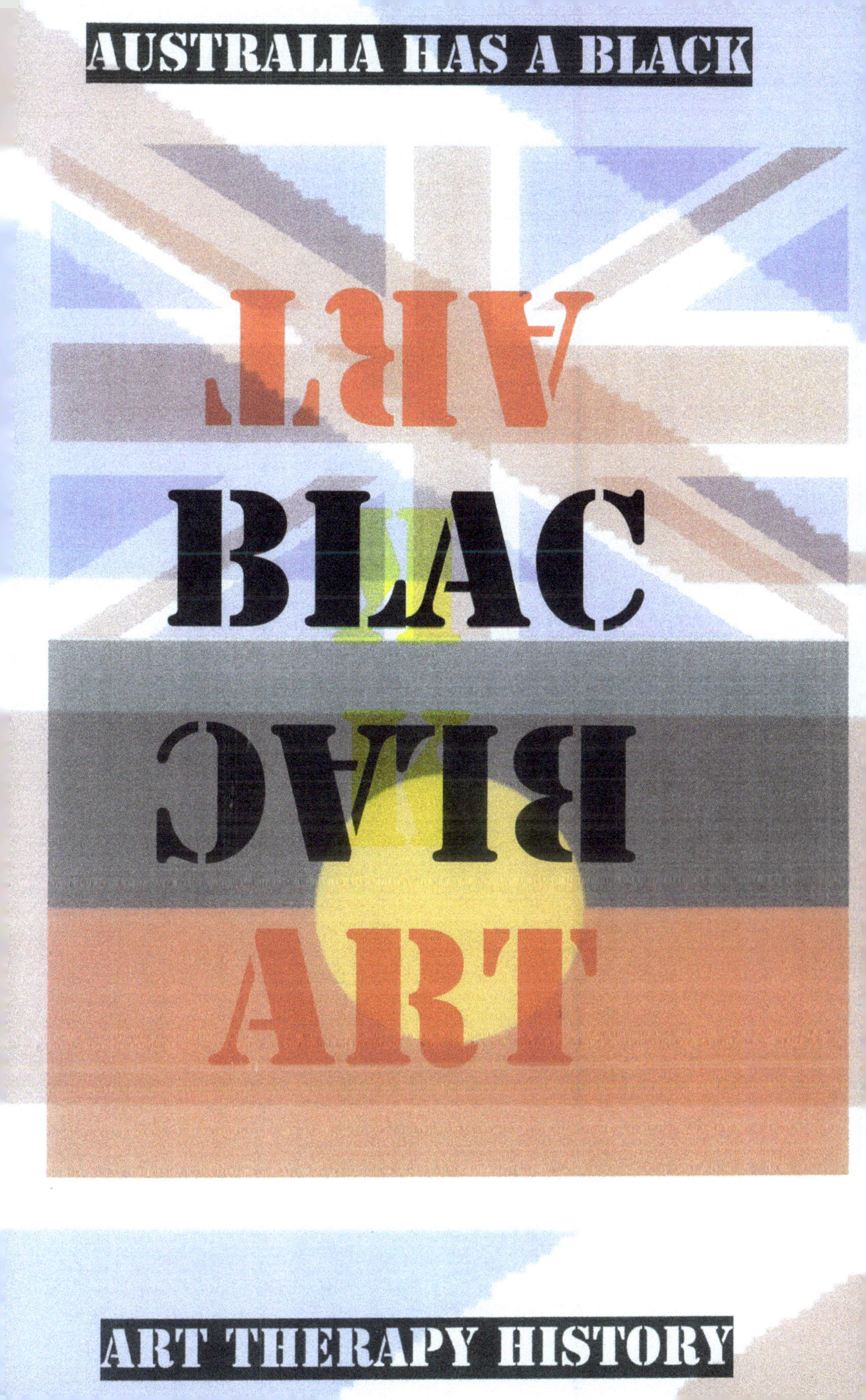
AUSTRALIA HAS A BLACK
BLAC
ART
ART THERAPY HISTORY

Fanon (1925–1961), a psychiatrist, philosopher and revolutionary, analysed the nature of colonialism as essentially destructive and a process of dehumanisation. Said (1978) theorised the 'binary social relation' with which Western Europe intellectually divided the world into the 'Occident' and the 'Orient'. Along with Foucault, he established that power and knowledge are the inseparable components of the intellectual binary relationship with which Occidentals claim 'knowledge of the Orient' and thereby control of Oriental peoples, places and things. Foucault argued that these colonial discourses provide consistent gratification of superiority. Since these ground-breaking thinkers, many more have added to the development of postcolonialism in order to claim "the right of all people to the same material and cultural well-being" (Young, 2003: 2).

Turning our attention to the English-speaking art therapy literature it soon becomes apparent that Western (Euro-American) values are both embedded and dominant in the discourses of its theory and practice. Some write from and about different places and points of view and there is an emerging literature that is beginning to take up international and global perspectives. For example, Kalmanowitz and Lloyd's *Art Therapy and Political Violence* (2004) has offered critical views of place and context, addressing culturally sensitive practice in many parts of the world such as the Balkans, the 'Middle East', the Sudan, Northern Ireland, New York and South Africa.

Of particular, local significance to art therapy in Australia is *Art Therapy in Asia* (Kalmanowitz, Potash and Chan, 2012) that brings awareness of art therapy in this part of the world. It features art therapy practices that are informed by Asian philosophical approaches and traditions, exploring the particular issues encountered in therapeutic processes where the expression of personal conflicts and negative feelings is considered to be threatening to social harmony. Simultaneously local and not local, authors and editors from Britain and Australia have recently focused on *Art Therapy in the Early Years: Therapeutic Interventions with Infants, Toddlers and their Families* (Meyerowitz-Katz and Reddick, 2017). Here practices with particular client populations in different places continue to draw on Western psychoanalytic thinking about the role of art in art therapy, seeking to extend the foundational theoretical work of Joy Schaverien (1992) by shifting emphasis from the image to the art-making.

A number of authors have examined the influence of Western culture on art therapy practice, countering its dominance and offering critical perspectives on the themes of race, culture and gender (e.g. Campbell et al. 1999; Docktor, 1998; Gilroy, 1998; Gilroy and Hanna 1998: Hiscox and Calisch 1998; Hocoy 2002, 2006; Hogan 1997, 2002, 2012; Kalmanowitz, Potash and Chan, 2012; Kapitan 2015; Kaplan 2007, 2016; Lewis 1997; Linnell 2006, 2010; McNiff 1984; Moon 2006; Sajnani 2012; Sajnani, and Kaplan, 2012; Skaife 2001; Talwar, Iyer and Doby-Copeland 2004; Talwar 2010, 2015, 2016, 2017; Westwood and Linnell 2011). These art therapists question and challenge cultural assumptions, values and constructions. Drawing on *intersectionality*, they look at how oppressive structures operate unequal distributions of power across society.

> *"Postcolonialism is a theoretical approach concerned with the impact of colonisation and the human consequences of external control and exploitation of native people and their lands"*

Intersectionality is a sociological theory about how an individual can face threats of discrimination when their identities overlap a number of areas such as race, gender, age, ethnicity, disability etc. An intersectional approach considers social, cultural and historic frameworks in order to examine how power and privilege interact in our relationships. Through the theorisation of intersectionality, these multiple intersecting sites of oppression also become the ground for critique and resistance. A prominent author in this field is Talwar who, together with others, advocates the adoption of an intersectional perspective which challenges monolithic and unitary narratives and locates difference within the specific social and cultural experiences of individuals. As Talwar says, this is in order to "empower clients rather than pathologise the realities they cannot escape" (2015: 101). Echoing this view, Hocoy (2006) discusses an 'invisible veil' that art therapists may carry in their practices which prevents them from realising how they may perpetuate oppressions. Similarly Kapitan (2015) considers *ethnorelativism* as a critical, self-reflexive approach that enables art therapists to understand and work with cultural difference and guard against collusion in oppressive practices.

Segueing now towards the specificities of art therapy in Australia, it seems wrong to put aside the persistent fact of the dispossession of Aboriginal people and the ethical call this exerts for Australian art therapists.

Sheridan remembers how she turned to postcolonial theorist Couze Venn's (2002) metaphor of 'apprenticeship to the other' to inform a collaborative approach to art therapy with Australian Aboriginal children who have been removed from their families as a consequence of transgenerational trauma. Her co-author and guide Galiindurra (Auntie Glendra) puts it this way:

> You know, Sheridan, we're working with third generation removed people. You look at the little faces of the little ones, say, in my care, and you think, "Oh God, her grandmother was in an institution, and she didn't get to parent her children, and now the third generation of these kids are in care"... I mean, what do you say to an eight year old? Can you say, "It's transgenerational grief and separation?" There isn't one person in that family who hasn't been affected, who isn't grieving. Yeah, it makes you sad.
>
> Galiindurra in Linnell, 2010: 156

[Sheridan tried to shorten this quotation but what can you take out without detracting from the enormity of the injustice?)

When we set out to explore the themes of aesthetics and postcolonialism in Australian art therapy we scarcely realised how closely this act of going out to find new intellectual and practice-led riches might mirror the colonising processes we sought to critique. How we might have mapped our desire for difference homogeneously across a complex landscape. How we might want the locals to dance their dance for us – to satisfy our yearning for the exotic. How loathe we might be to acknowledge that many of the fruits of transported art therapy might taste familiar to us after all. We would proffer the bright beads of publication while swaddling our reluctant discoveries in the infected blanket of Eurocentric theory.

But now, to the Australian literature ...

Partial perspectives on Australian art therapy

Gilroy and Hanna (1998) noted a peculiarity of Australian art therapy compared to other English speaking countries, in that the Australian profession appears to have had forerunners in the mid-twentieth century who did not in any obvious sense have followers. As noted earlier, John Henzell has described how the artist Guy Grey-Smith worked as an art therapist in a Perth hospital during the 1950s. Grey-Smith had contracted tuberculosis as a soldier during WWII and had subsequently engaged in art-making as part of his treatment under the guidance of the first, self-identified British art therapist, Adrian Hill (Henzell, 1997). Australian psychiatrist, Ainslie Meares (1957, 1958, 1960), who made extensive use of painting and modelling in his clinical work and theorised visual symbolisation as an expression of unconscious conflicts, has also been identified as a forerunner of art therapy in Australia (Junge, 1994; Henzell, this volume). However there is a relatively small body of published literature about art therapy in Australia and as yet no book-length account of its history. Perhaps there are legacies and trajectories yet to be uncovered.

Of the earlier literature, two pieces in particular, both by overseas art therapists who have taught in Australia, seek to provide an overview of the history, status and potential of Australian art therapy. There have clearly been developments in Australian art therapy in the eight to ten years since these papers were written, but they nevertheless offer a perspective both on Australian art therapy and how it is perceived by senior art therapists from countries with well-established professional and pedagogical institutions and substantial bodies of professional literature. The first was written by Michael Campanelli and Frances Kaplan (1996), both art therapy educators from the USA who taught on the Master of Art Therapy programme at Edith Cowan University in Perth, WA. The second was written by Andrea Gilroy, a British art therapist, and Margarete Hanna, a Canadian art therapist (1998), both of whom taught on the Master of Art Therapy at the University of Western Sydney (UWS) Nepean. Their chapter is based on a paper they presented at the ANATA conference in Perth in 1994, prior to the publication of Campanelli and Kaplan's article and, despite a two year gap in publication, there is a sense of dialogue and reciprocity between the two pieces. They also have in common a sensitivity to the authors' positions as influential 'outsiders' attempting to offer an overview and recommendations about Australian art therapy.

In 'Conflict and Culture in Australian Art Therapy', Gilroy and Hanna discuss Australian art therapy in the context of their knowledge of the histories of art therapy in the UK, Europe, USA and Canada. From this they conclude that art therapy, while manifesting differently in different cultures, survives and flourishes as a profession to the extent that it is able to recognise and tolerate conflict within its own ranks. Campanelli and Kaplan focus more on how Australian art therapy might challenge what the authors identify as the dominant Eurocentric tendencies of English and North American art therapies, by cultivating relationships with the diverse cultural traditions that are present in Australia by virtue of its Indigenous population and its location in Asia. They note a potential in the critical perspectives that students bring with them to their art therapy education, attributing these to both the maturity and life experience of students, and to Australian cultural scepticism about the influence of more powerful Western nations. More recently, Jill Westwood and Sheridan Linnell who, respectively, have taught and continue to teach on the Master of Art Therapy at the University of Western Sydney, have offered an historical and current perspective on Australian art therapy as a rich hybridisation of influences and practices within a postcolonial context (Westwood and Linnell, 2011).

Meanwhile Australians, both local and expatriate, have made and continue to make a vigorous contribution to the international literature, beyond the scope of what can be discussed here. (Think Susan Hogan, Annette Coulter and Julia Meyerowitz-Katz to start with, as well as some of the contributors to the current book.) There are texts released by local and international publishers that describe art therapy work that has arisen from the particularities of our local systems and context, written by authors who do not wish to limit their relevance or appeal to that context. Marilyn Dennes and Sue Gilchrist's (2005) book on art therapy with people in aged care is an early example; more recently Sonia Stace (e.g. Stace, 2016) exemplifies an Australian art therapy practitioner making a vigorous contribution to the international literature from outside academia.

The Australian and New Zealand Journal of Arts Therapy (*ANZJAT*) was first published at the end of 2006. The first issue contains Annette Coulter's historical account of Australian art therapy, a detailed and 'eye-witness' view (Coulter, 2006). Coulter, one of the first professional art therapists to have worked in Australia (having trained in the UK), has been a central figure in the establishment and development of the local art therapy association and domestic training programs. Coulter's paper responded to a need for art therapists who live and work in Australia to reflect on the profession themselves. According to Coulter, the first Australian art therapists, who were generally trained in either the US or the UK "were caught up in a silent war between their parent nations" (8). Coulter (a family art therapist) maps the dynamics of family relationships onto the early days of art therapy in Australia, suggesting through her language and guiding metaphor that Australia was positioned in a similar way to a child in a family where the parents are in conflict. Coulter describes Australia prior to the inaugural ANATA conference in 1989 as an "art therapy desert".

The metaphor of a 'desert' is compelling. One of Sheridan's memories from her training is the suggestion that Freud would not have invented psychoanalysis if he had bicycled across the Simpson Desert. Perhaps, though, he would have invented a more horizontal, less individualising, de-territorialised – dare we say 'Deleuzian'? – account of the psyche and its relations. Nonetheless desert, as a parched, inhospitable place, sits in tension with Indigenous relations to country, even with European spiritual preoccupations with deserts as places of self-testing and discovery, as in Josephine Pretorius' chapter in this book.

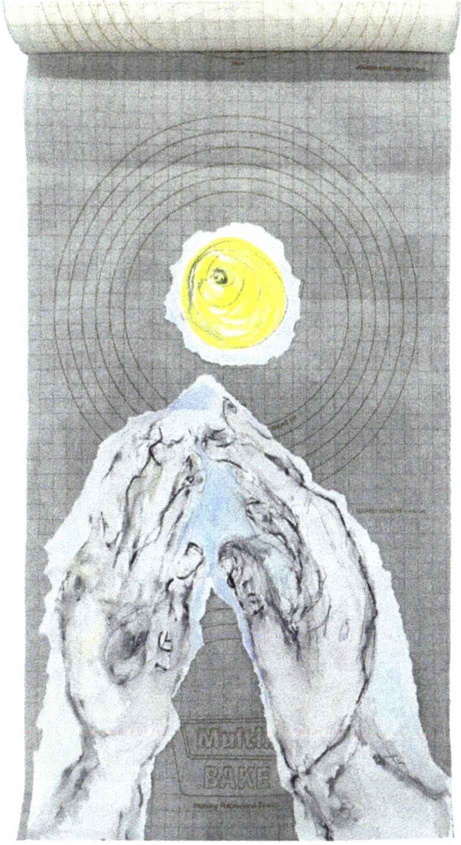

Figure 6 *Multibake*. Sheridan Linnell (2017). Charcoal and ink sketch, torn and mounted on found baking paper.

Sheridan remembers drawing and painting with Josephine Pretorius and Suzanne Perry while on retreat at the Benedictine Abbey in Jamberoo. She couldn't take Mass because she was never confirmed. Raised by agnostics she remains a disbeliever, albeit one who engages in Buddhist meditation, but somehow she prayed. White hands reaching (praying?) toward the Antipodean sun…

Desert as emptiness is perhaps the metaphorical ghost of Terra Nullius played out in the difficulty of seeing what is t/here through a Euro-centric lens.

ANZJAT is a repository of accounts of art (and more recently arts) therapy work not only from Australia but from the wider region. The editors of *ANZJAT*, it is true, have so far all been Australians, but the geographical scope of the journal is wider than that of this book. This begs a question: is an 'Australian art therapy' already an anachronism, too singular in its location and focus? *ANZJAT* editors have shared a vision of the journal as innovative, arts-based, diverse and inclusive. This is partly echoed in a recent contribution by Annette Coulter to a handbook of art therapy, where art therapy 'down-under' in Australia and New Zealand is figured as "a tale of collaborative necessity, integrative orientation, and adaptation to local culture, as art therapists promote, expand, and apply their art therapy knowledge to local networks, systems, and culture", as well as a story of struggle for professional recognition (Coulter, 2016: 710).

Yet when Nadia Balatti and Patricia Fenner (2012) conducted a systematic review of the content of *ANZJAT* 2006–2011, they found a predominance of theory-driven single case studies, with a relative absence of rigorous research methodology on the one hand and client perspectives/voices on the other. Arguably the single case study is so naturalised in the art therapy literature that it is a primary instrument of reproducing the dominant assumptions of the field (Linnell, 2010). For Balatti and Fenner, a way forward would be for Australian and New Zealand art(s) therapists (noting that *ANZJAT* has, like ANZATA, recently expanded to include Singapore and Hong Kong) to more systematically adopt mixed method research. This is indeed necessary, although not the focus of the current book. Here we are more interested in what else is marginalised when universalist assumptions prevail within largely globalised accounts and even critiques of clinical art therapy practice. Although *ANZJAT* claims to be interested in this too, it is unclear whether a systemic review of the journal 2012–2016 would reveal anything different. Perhaps we need to pay attention to the 'how' as well the 'what' – to bring those elements of publication often relegated to the category of 'production values' to the fore – an emphasis that *ANZJAT* shares with this book.

This then, is a central paradox of this book, and possibly of art therapy in Australia and perhaps in many other places too. How do we as art therapists do 'difference' as well as talk about it? Or rather, how do we notice and account in detail for the difference that we already do? How do we do this when our underlying frameworks and theoretical antecedents continue to dominate and reconstitute us as 'the same'? Not only this, but the systems and daily practices of knowledge and power, systems and practices in which professional art therapy ambivalently desires to become more embedded, require us to become more like, and prove ourselves in the same terms as, other health-related disciplines.

Meanwhile, the recent politics of art therapy in Australia circulate around a heated discussion as to whether the Australian and New Zealand Arts Therapy Association (ANZATA) should merge with the Australian Creative Arts Therapy Association (ACATA). The most heated aspect of the debate is about something that ANZATA has already decided to adopt but which is still fiercely contested by some visual art therapists. This is a membership structure for ANZATA that mirrors the structure of ACATA by including and regulating a tiered membership system, with levels of membership beginning at baseline for those with associate diplomas taught at technical colleges (short courses with no prerequisite for an undergraduate degree) and progressing through to registered professional members with accredited Masters degrees who will exclusively be entitled to use the post-nominal AThR. At the point of writing, the sheer diversity of what is known as art therapy and art therapy education in Australia has become as much a battleground as a cause for celebration. Old and new worlds collide. Meanwhile Gilroy and Hanna's (1998) warning resonates still: art therapy succeeds around the world to the extent that it can acknowledge and resolve its domestic conflicts.

This brief overview of some of the relevant art therapy literature underlines the significance and difficulty of shifting our gaze from the dominant discourses to a different place, one of mutual influence and infinite affirmation of differences. It shows the recursive relationship between difference and the reconstitution of the same, driven in both instances by necessity and desire. It shows how the struggle we have experienced as editors to compose the motley and precious assemblage that is this book is echoed elsewhere. It shows how art therapy in Australia, but not only in Australia, might open onto a number of possible futures.

One of the readers of this manuscript asked us: 'Why are you putting so much emphasis on Aboriginal Australian issues? If this is so important, you need to tell your readers why.'

One compelling reason is that we would have hoped for things to change since the late Pam Johnston wrote her paper, now a chapter in this book, but instead the gaps in the lives of the first people of Australia continue to be vast. In fact, recent statistics tell a story of largely worsening inequities. The inequalities of health and wellbeing between Indigenous and non-Indigenous Australians have not reduced; this includes shorter life expectancy, higher rates of infant mortality, poorer health and lower levels of education and employment. To put it bluntly, Aboriginal people continue to die earlier and to be significantly poorer, sicker, less educated, more frequently arrested and imprisoned, more often subjected to violence and systematically less powerful than their non-Indigenous counterparts. This is so despite the status of Aboriginal people as the original and ongoing owners and custodians of country and their extraordinary resilience, generosity and contribution to national life, including the arts. As recently as 2016, we read how Aboriginal and Torres Strait Islander people are massively overrepresented in the criminal justice system of Australia. Aboriginal people represent only three per cent of the total population and yet:

- 28 per cent of all prisoners in Australia in 2015 were Aboriginal;
- 30 per cent of all incarcerated women in Australia in 2010 were Aboriginal; of incarcerated men, 24 per cent were Aboriginal;
- 48 per cent of juveniles in custody are Aboriginal;
- the imprisonment rates of Aboriginal women increased by 58.6 per cent between 2000 and 2010; for Aboriginal men, by 35.2 per cent.[1]

These stark figures bring to the fore the gaps in the lives of the First People of Australia. We choose to again draw your attention to the life worlds of these Indigenous women and men as we struggle to respond to intrapsychic and social questions about how we can enable access to the healing arts in Australia. Key here is the concept of the relational. We offer this book in the hope that our readers will consider its relational ethic of care and our complicity in advancing, or not, the healing that we all aspire to.

1 https://www.creativespirits.info/aboriginalculture/law/aboriginal-prison-rates, retrieved 1 November 2016)

"What's Indigenous petroglyphing doing in my life?"

Carving or Engraving My Self into This Story

Tarquam

I had never intended to come out as having any Indigenous heritage and maybe I never will accept this possibility but there is a chance it still might happen for me. In early 2000s in an Art Therapy supervision session with Carmen Lawson – a joint author to the chapter in this collection – I had an awakening which changed my way of being. Carmen was around 61 when she began the Art Therapy course and always struck me as a loving and gentle kind of person. Her life had been hard and she is Murri (Queensland regional area) woman. I also taught her daughter Rihi at the same time in Perth. The family became important to me.

The boundaries are blurred as the multiple meanings coalesced in our work together. Two or three hours a fortnight we would 'yarn' about her work. It was one on one and group art therapy supervision, as mandated in the then ANATA code of supervision. I loved working with Carmen and my supervision group of eight art therapists in the Edith Cowan program. Carmen was alive and her vibrancy held the space in our one on one and in the group work and her presence made the work enriching, exciting and buoyant. We stumbled as she at times naively wove the fabric of her identity, debriefing on the art works she had brought from her clinical placements. These were around dispossession, alienation and Indigenous young people being incarcerated in WA far more than the white population. On more than one occasion there was a level of sophistication that I stumbled to accommodate. I knew she was talking an epistemology that belonged elsewhere. Then in a moment in a clinical one-on-one supervision mid-session she announced: "Nerreman knows your mother's people in Tasmania." This sentence was to change my way of knowing and the beginning of a self-discovery journey that is still being continued.

At this juncture of my life I had been living in Perth for ten or more years but was born in Tasmania. It was literally and metaphorically as far away from Tassie as was possible but it is still Australia. I was stunned by Carmen's pronouncement: "Nerreman knows your mother's people in Tasmania." The knowing of my mother's 'people' was to be my own realisation of a sort. But I was in a clinical supervision session with Carmen as she valiantly pronounced this unknown meaningfulness. We were working with her clients' needs from the Aboriginal Counselling Centre where she was undertaking her clinical placements and I had been taught to 'hold the hermetic space' – the temenos; vase bene clausum.

"Carmen, we are here to talk about the work of you with your art therapy clients," I directed in a focused and defensive manner. Again, she went off supervision: "Yes, I sent Nerrreman a picture of you and she knows your people … Nerreman is in Launceston and she is an artist." Befuddled and now feeling uncomfortable I said something like, "Let's talk about this later … when the session is over …"

That session ended and I was stunned. In a dazed manner I wandered into the tunnels of my own memories. I could not believe what I had heard. I knew the matriarchal connections between Indigenous Australian women were very rich and they shared so many stories. Davina Woods (another co-author of the chapter in this collection) and I talked a lot around that too. Yarning. I saw the picture that Carmen had shared and it was from the 'net'; and subsequently I went on to meet Nerreman and discuss this process of unfolding one's sense of who you are.

It so happened my father's cousin was living in Perth and she was from Papua New Guinea. On the first time of meeting her in forty years we went to the Queen's Hotel in Beaufort Street, Mt Lawley and over lunch Margaret Dwyer and another distant cousin were talking. Margaret was born to my father's side – she was what we irreverently called half-caste, being Papuan and having a white father and a Papuan mother. I first met her as a twelve year old in Tasmania. Sitting calmly over lunch she asked me in an assured but unannounced manner: "Did you know your mother was Indigenous?" Again I was stunned. I said I did not. She stated that when she first met my mother she knew this instantly. She was recounting her physical features and impassively asked me had I considered this? Beyond any doubt I was now seriously bewildered My mother had died a year or two before this so I had only my father to ask. Sure enough his response was: "Yes, there is some story about your mother's heritage'

Genealogical web-based processes came to the fore and I worked with family historians but we always came up to the same end of the road. Mary Brown, five generations ago was my great great grandmother and yes she was in all probability an Indigenous woman. But who am I? Who are the people that inform our world and work as art therapists in Australia? I am still to fully claim the space of belonging as a person with researchers taking the lead in the field of 'how' one is identified in Australia as Indigenous.

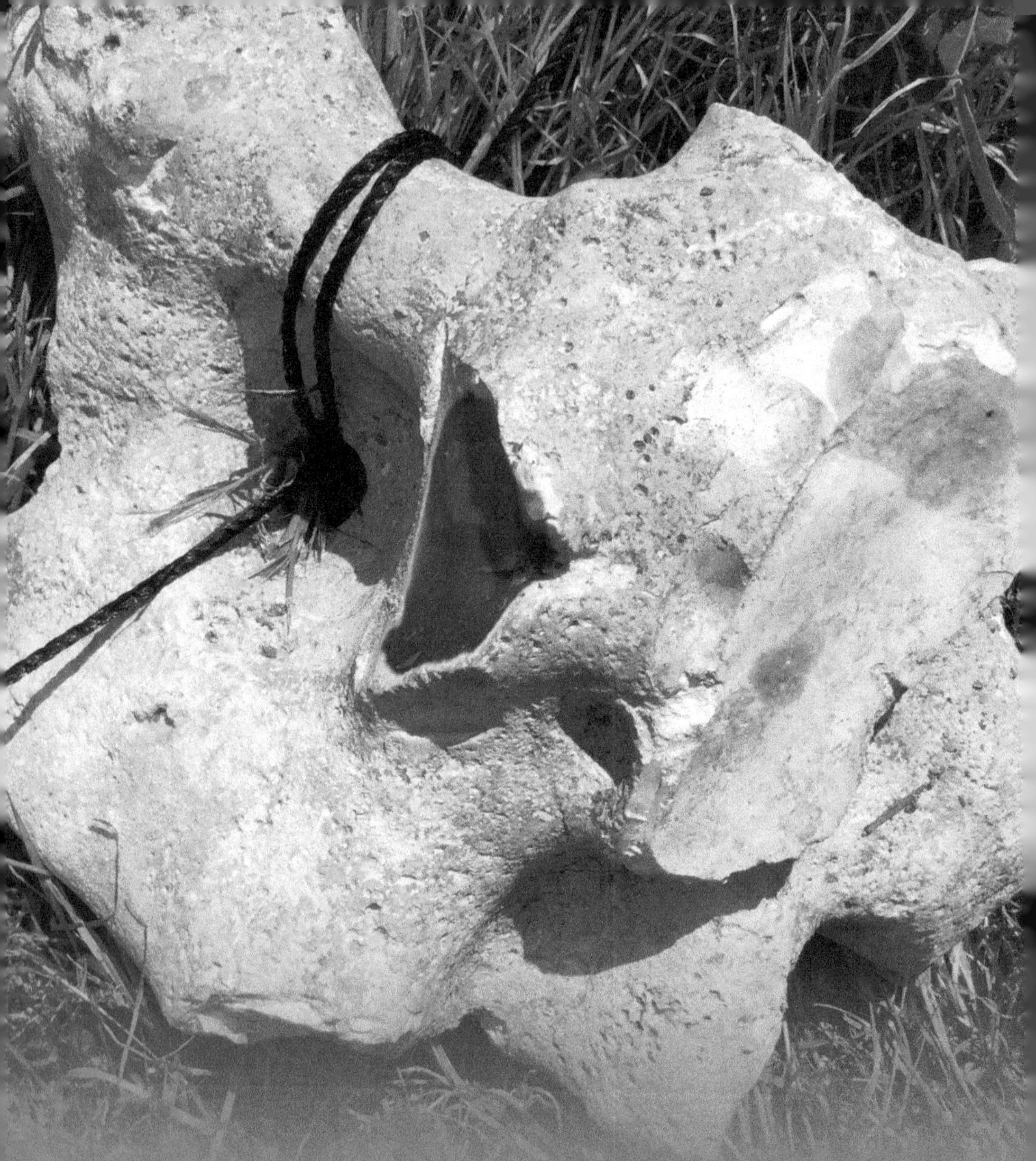

Her / his / storical legacies

Jill

Trust is at the heart of the therapeutic encounter. Trust in the relationship; trust in the process; and for art psychotherapists, trust in the art.

The evolution of this book has been complex, layered and relatively lengthy. We have followed a trail over time and at various stages have made art work in order to progress our thinking. Edging towards completion, one day in the summer of 2016 I visited Andy in her new home. I found these flints and bricks, displaced in the renovations to her house and studio and used them to grapple with the themes and content of the book. The use of text and object, construction, geology and territory became connected in this exploration in ways that resonate with the histories and legacies of art therapy in Australia.

Foucault (1986, in Foucault and Miskowiec) has influenced my thinking here when, in his work, Heterotopia – an exploration of space and time – he spoke of nets and muddles. This project has been like a well-used fishing net with all its web-like connections and entangled links that gathers together and catches materials and debris from the deep in order to develop our thinking, making and writing.

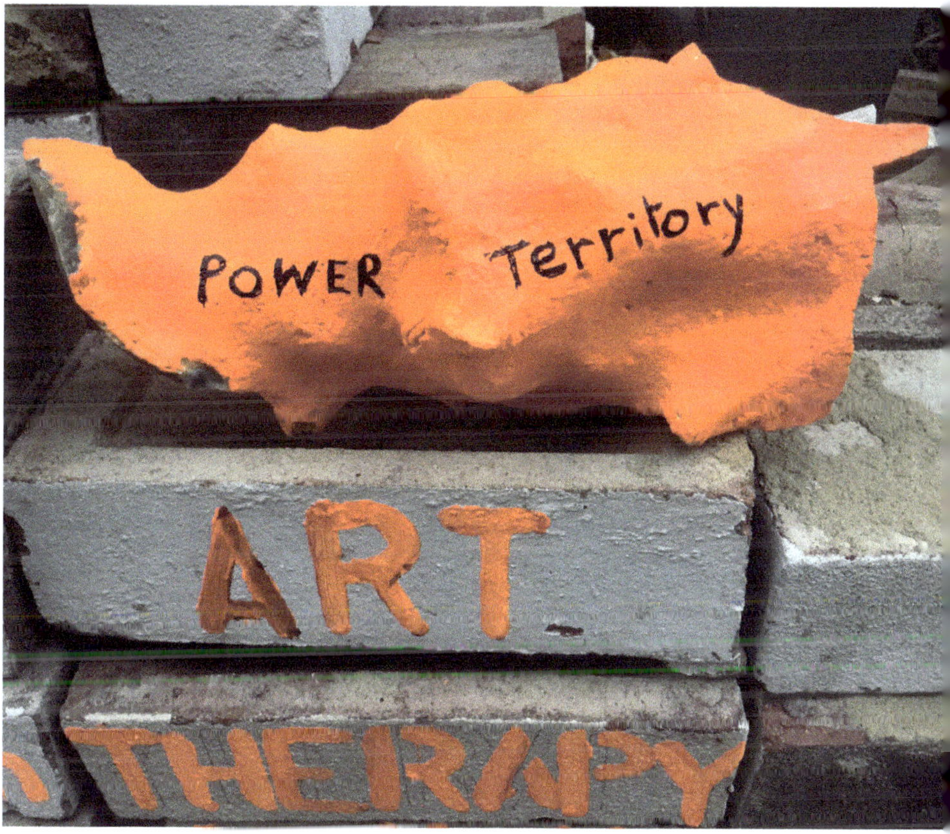

Figure 7 *Power – Territory: Art Therapy*. Jill Westwood (2016). Assemblage of flints, net and found objects on floor tiles.

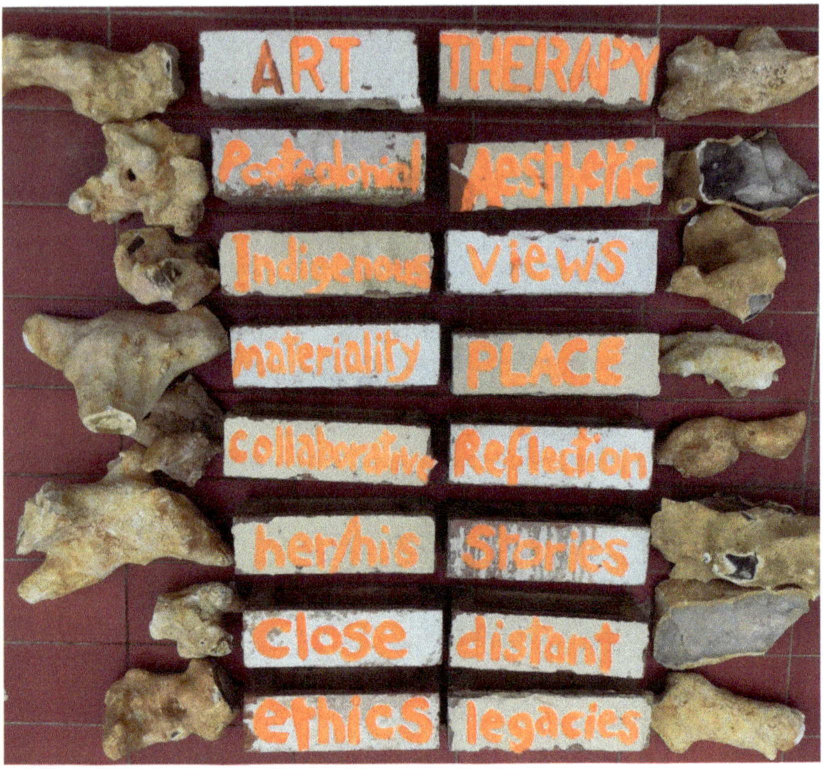

Figure 8 *Art therapy: taking a postcolonial, aesthetic turn*. Jill Westwood (2016). Assemblage of flints, bricks and paint on floor tiles.

Art therapy's histories and legacies, internationally and locally, flow and meander throughout this book but one particular thread can be found in the chapters by Henzell, Edwards, Eisdell, Thomson and by me, Jill (Westwood). These five chapters' address, in their different ways, aspects of her/hi/storical relevance and weave distinctive personal threads in the 'heterotopic net' of Australian art therapy. They reveal a genealogical flow which enables consideration of the interplay of the different discourses within Australian art therapy: the dominant ones and the other, subaltern ones that are making their rhizomatic way through the concrete.

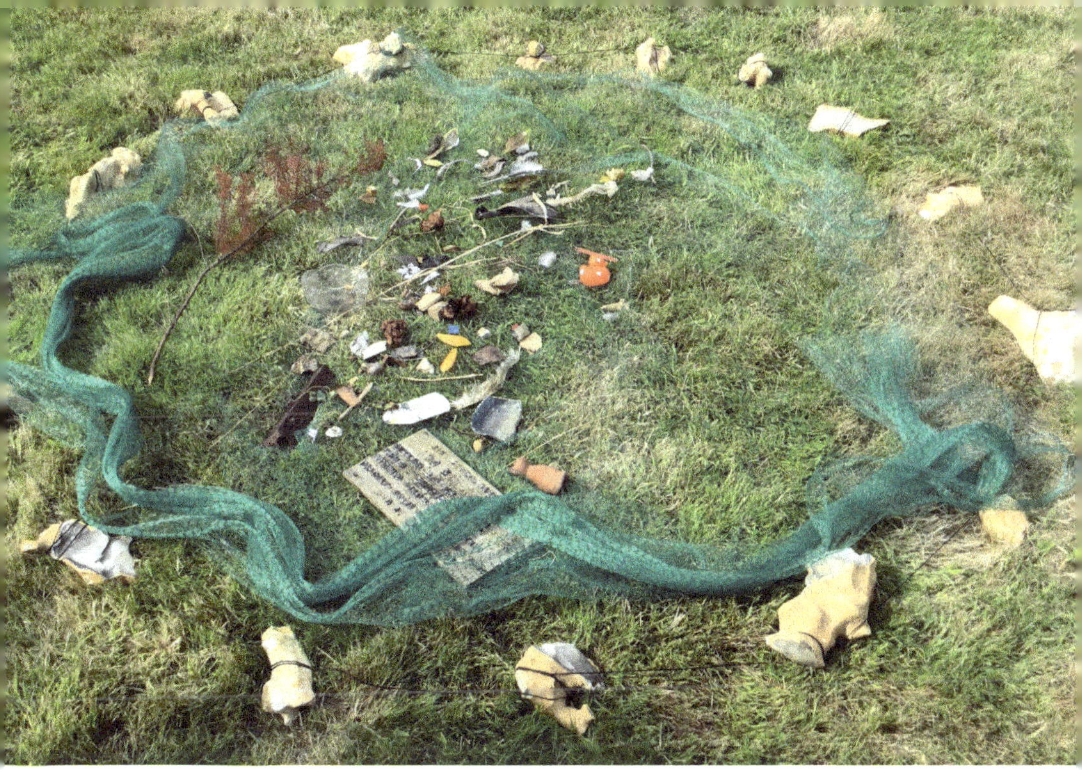

Above: Figure 9 *Heterotopic net 1*. Jill Westwood (2016). Assemblage of flints, net and found objects on floor tiles. *Below*: Figure 10 *Heterotopic net 2*. Jill Westwood (2016). Assemblage of flints, net and found objects on floor tiles.

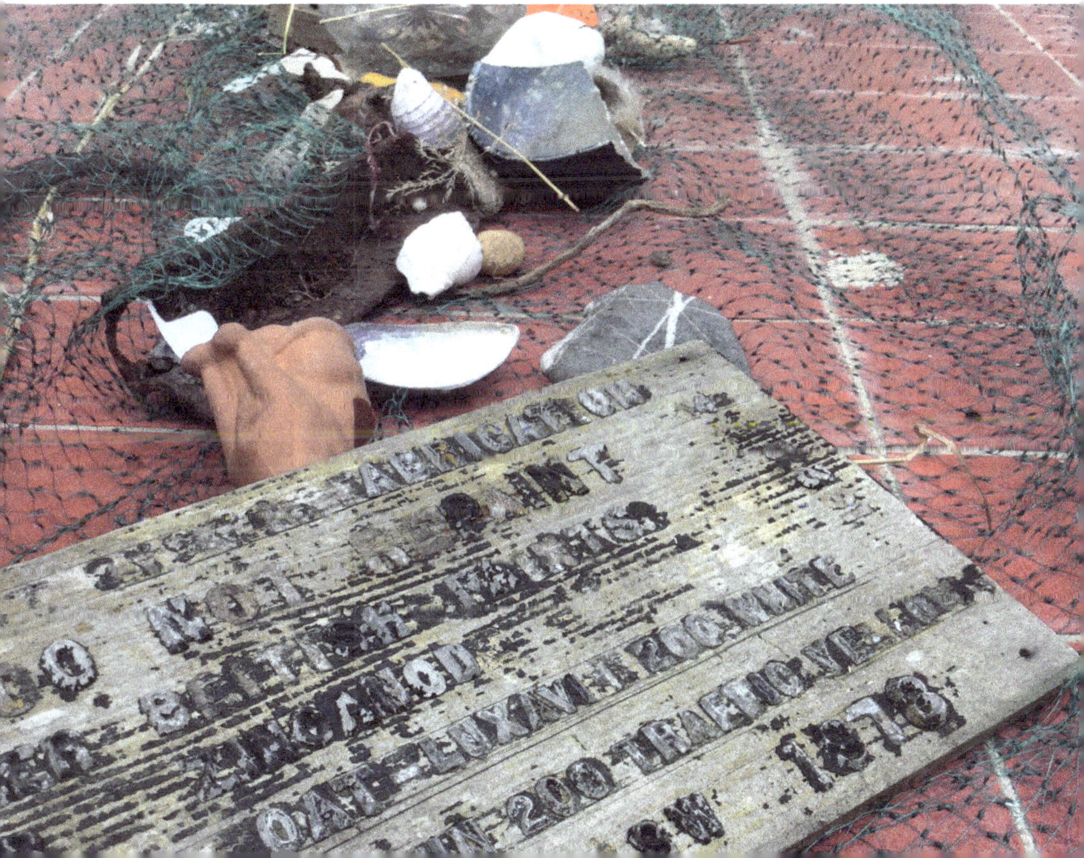

Unfolding fields continued

Jill, Sheridan, Andy, Tarquam

Reading this book is not meant to be arduous; rather, we would like it to be akin to walking into a gallery and experiencing a space – a space where your desire is awoken.

An immersion in the visual occurs not only in a gallery but also in an art therapy encounter where participants respond as images and words resonate with knowledge and experience, both personal and professional. This is the nature of the encounter we have in mind for you, our reader, as you make your way through this book – one that foregrounds the visual, one that does not always privilege text.

During our editing, writing and art-making we have taken a great deal of time and traversed many landscapes, each with its own valency that will be experienced differently by fellow itinerants travelling through these pages. We have tried to capture multiple perspectives so that the palette is neither pale nor bland, invoking a spectrum of colour and a play with and between texts and images. Tenses change, voices morph and formality gives way to informality. This bricolage or melange in a narrative style is intentional. We ask that you gambol with the pictures, savour them, and wander through the text in any way you please – knowing that you may have the whole book or merely a chapter or two in your hands – letting the voice, art and self-hoods of the writers emerge. This is a big ask of you and somewhat of a risk for us editors. Indeed, the circumscribed knowing that a more definitive, chronological account provides would be easier to navigate, and simpler to write.

This book offers a partial assemblage of perspectives and voices from Australia. It documents some home-grown theories and practices and demonstrates the assimilation of approaches developed in other places. We hope it will assist the exploration of what constitutes art therapy in Australia as it emerges from a melee of received ideas and local developments, all within the context of the deep heritage of country. We hope it also speaks to a wider, international conversation, writing and image-making as we are both with and against prevailing discourses.

At this point we feel compelled to respectfully acknowledge that the cultures, values, attitudes and stories in these chapters are located in histories that were harmful and disrespectful. Similarly, terms used to refer to Indigenous Australian People(s) or Australia's First People – our preferred terms that refer to Australia's pre-invasion history and recognise the colonising language that was and remains a vehicle for the expression of discrimination and prejudice – while they may not be appropriate now are of their time. Given that this book has been some fifteen years in the making, we have decided to retain the terms 'black', 'white' or 'aborigine' only as they serve to show the diminishing of identity that prevailed.

Many of these chapters attempt to disturb the relationship between the written and the visual in an art therapy book by overlaying words and images, foregrounding visuality in a manner that is surprisingly absent from the art therapy canon. The materiality of this book – whether digital or printed – the book as something that *matters*, is brought into focus. This is how text and image relate in contemporary art – and contemporary art, so alive in Australia, alongside and informed by Aboriginal practices of mark-making and ceremony, is for the editors of this book a central inspiration. For us, a book about Australian art therapy *matters* – not only as a reflection of the field but as a refractive apparatus through which we create new lines of flight for art therapy, both in Australia and elsewhere. We can only do this by approaching the book as material and emplaced; we cannot deterritorialise that which is not located anywhere to begin with.

As suggested earlier, our profession has talked endlessly and interestingly about the relationship between therapy and art – variously hierarchising that relationship, celebrating it, theorising it, even deconstructing it. The art therapy literature is richly discursive. All that is left to do, it would seem, is to produce a book that *does something different*. A book that decolonises the empire of the illustrated text, that does not proceed in an orderly fashion, and which releases the 'list of illustrations' from their subaltern status so that they can dance with the words in both material and virtual domains. We do this kind of thing at conferences, in galleries, studios and even in our art therapy rooms. Is there something (beyond the undoubted constraints of including multiple colour images in print media) that holds authors of art therapy books in thrall to the conventions of representation?

If a gaol break from behind the bars of the captivating discourses of realism, representation, professionalisation and the like has to come from some *where* then Australia seems well placed to do so by virtue not only of its colonial heritage but also of its strange situation of having a vibrant art therapy community that operates diffusely and almost undercover. We thought back to 2007 when Andy presented a talk – or was it a performance? – to the art therapy community in Sydney and the Master of Art Therapy students at what was then the UWS. Taking passages from Virginia Woolf's *The Waves* that were immersed in a blue wash, Andy messed with our fantasies of becoming a state-registered profession as we, a group of Australian art therapists, grew from childhood into adolescence and adulthood, warning us to be careful what we wished for. Meanwhile Jill, Sheridan, Suzanne and Josephine – editors and/or authors of the current text – drew and sculpted in response. Images of people in boats and of Josephine kissing an Australian art therapist made of chicken wire, inhabit this book and indeed have introduced you to it (the cover and pages 1, 12–13). In the background, Suzanne's unwitting choice of music added to the undercurrent of anxiety as it was brought into consciousness through a cover version of Split Enz's *'Six months in a leaky boat'*.

Yet Australian art therapy has stayed afloat without making it to, or even any longer aiming for, that shoreline (sure-line) of state registration. We do not wish to romanticise the seemingly endless emergent and uncertain condition of art therapy in Australia, where there is a nationally endorsed Framework for the Arts in Health that includes art therapy and you can find an art therapist in almost every nook and cranny across a wide range of fields, but there are still very few named and stable positions as art therapists. Yet it seems to us that this very uncertainty and lack of regulation has allowed for a rhizomatic spread of ideas and a productive diversity of practice that is under-represented in the literature to date.

We hope that you will discover some of that vigour in the pages of this book, illuminating its contents and its discontents, and animating its materiality and its flights of imagination.

We also hope – having moved beyond a desire for regulation but not for recognition – not only to put Australian art therapy on the map but to be map-makers, and even to navigate by the stars.

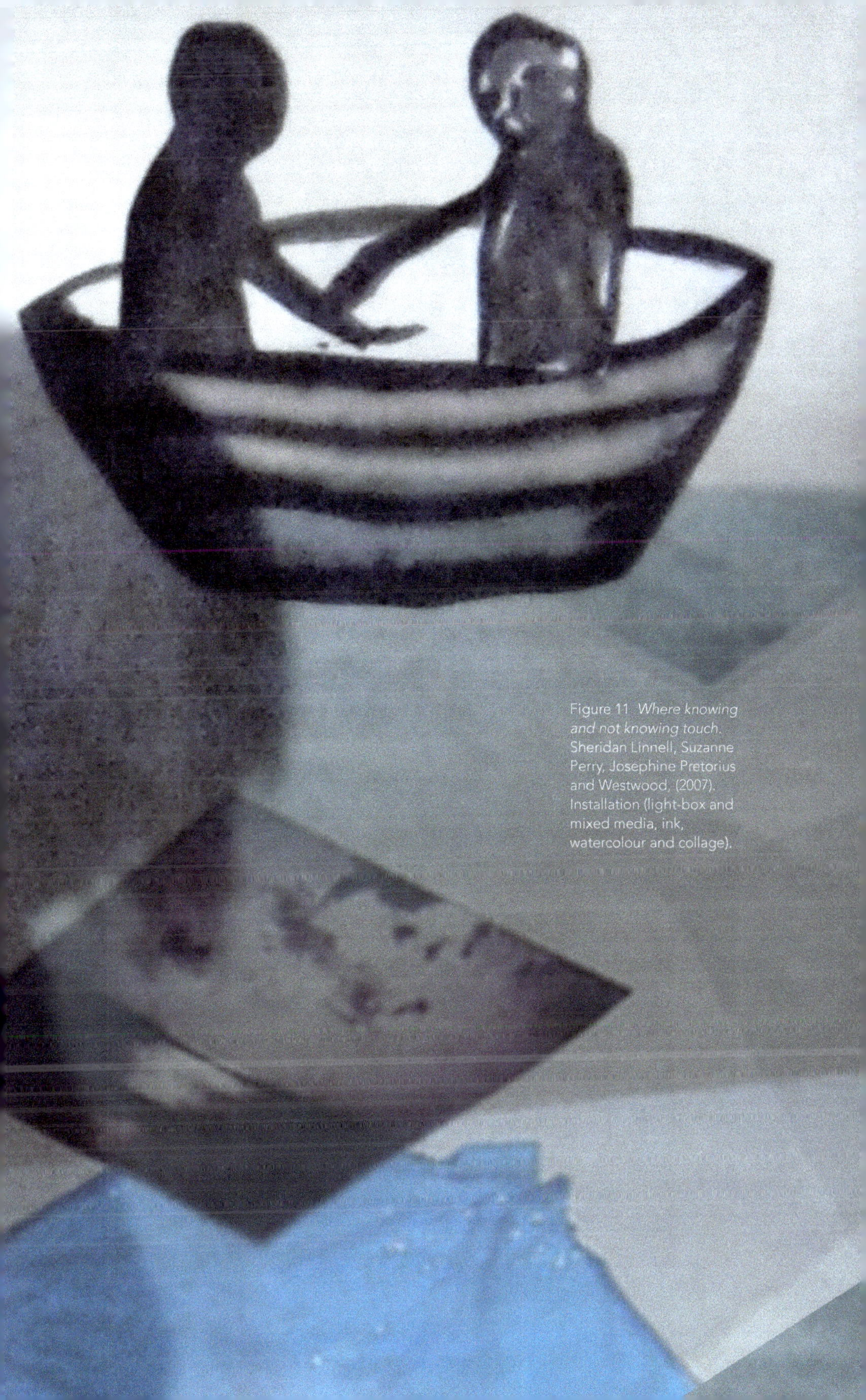

Figure 11 *Where knowing and not knowing touch*. Sheridan Linnell, Suzanne Perry, Josephine Pretorius and Westwood, (2007). Installation (light-box and mixed media, ink, watercolour and collage).

The chapters

Andy

We begin in Chapter 1 with boats and crossings, borders and welcomes, colonisers and refugees. Allen, Rumbold, Schnaedelbach, Woodford and Tann encounter each other in a visual conversation that asks who is, and who is not, an art therapist in the places of contemporary Australia.

This is wrong. So begins a yarn about art and the First Peoples of Australia, told by three therapists/artists/educators who share an Indigeneity. In Chapter 2, Lawson, Woods and McKenna wonder where and how the dispossession, loss and grief of First Peoples' separation from country and culture will be addressed. Can art (therapy?) be a de-colonising force?

The desert. The land is alive but it's a thin place where boundaries dissolve. One can be still, one can wait, but there's the call of the wild, a far horizon and being emptied out, all in Pretorius, Chapter 3.

A personal memoir and the beginnings of a profession are described by Henzell in Chapter 4. He explores the many imaginings of Australia, from their earliest incised manifestations and an immigrant's Arcadian dream to boisterous larrikinism and vivid modernism. So many stories and pictures, some in a fragile collection constrained by the clinical gloss that has colonised the psychological terra nullius of the Great Southern Land.

Bridges between some where and some place are negotiated in a journey towards a profession and becoming an Australian, so writes Edwards in Chapter 5. Take something local and something imported and mix them together; add pragmatism and a healthy dose of resilience; season with conflict, sprinkle with scepticism and add a dash of iconoclasm and you may make something uniquely Australian.

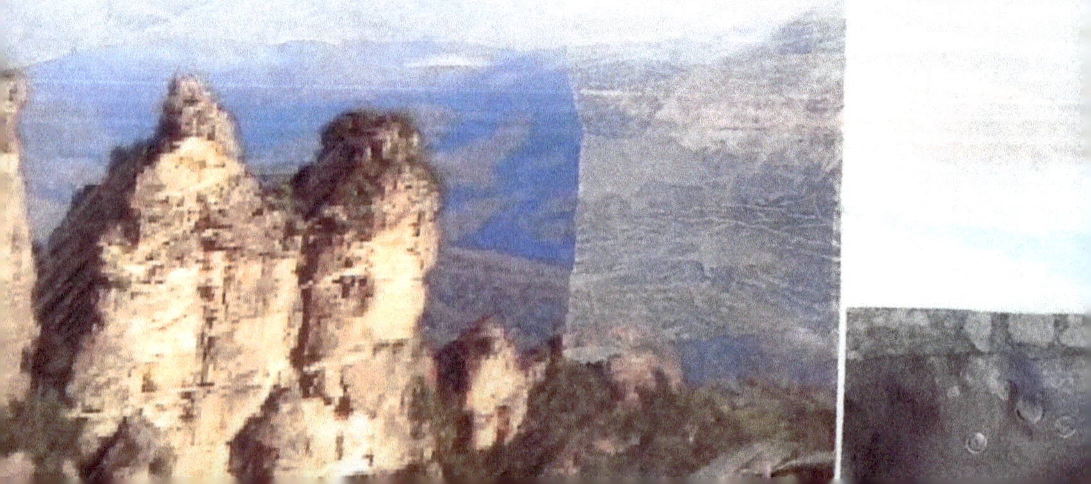

Trees and maps and creatures combine in Westwood's visual, autoethnographic account of migration in Chapter 6. Mapping art therapy education in Australia lays bare the bones of its becoming. Flesh grows on the bones but skeletons rattle in the cupboard.

Perry paints her way into the heart of theory, feeling and making in Chapter 7, encountering hybrid creatures who witness horror and do impossible things. A fairytale about nameless dread and Abject Art.

The dominant discourse of Evidence-Based Practice remains in the contemporary sites of art therapy in Australian cancer care, explored in Chapter 8. Nuanced, visual, relational and emotional, Thomson immerses her self in an airless space where time is marked and trauma is honoured.

Four white women perform and make themselves in the intersections of childhood memory and imagination. In Chapter 9, art therapy educators Linnell, Perry, Pretorius and Westwood become themselves, remembering delicate, precious things.

Broken circles and broken children. Spirit? Culture? Country? Lost. All lost. This, says Moss in Chapter 10, is what happens when Western developmental discourse dominates the care of Aboriginal children and Indigenous beliefs and practices are ignored. Extended family and community can connect and protect from the likes of Erikson but "Holy hell! Someone should probe him and tell him a different story."

Talking (about) you, (not) talking (to) me: Chapter 11 and Johnston on the dispossession and trauma of people and country by observing others who construct the history, culture and education of Aboriginal people according to another time and place. The ongoing effects of colonisation are made visible through statistics and stories of incarceration whilst imagery from some where confirms living Aboriginal identity and contemporary Aboriginal society.

In Chapter 12, Linnell bathes us in an ethnodrama of burgundy, yellow and green. This is a play within an organisation about the work of team-building: a drama and a painting that is not full of noise.

Back and forth between phantasy and reality, aliveness and deadness, father and son, painter and sitter/s, Britain and Australia: such is the route travelled by Eisdell in Chapter 13. Conversations over time are developed and drawn into a visual language of the heart. They go to prison and liberate an incarcerated man.

We end in the spaces and places of art therapy. Fenner, in Chapter 14, researches a place-attentive practice that takes account of the material and expressive assemblage that is an art therapy room. Here the lifelong search for objects and places to love is embraced through an emplaced discourse where the triangular relationship is not the only therapeutic relationship in the room.

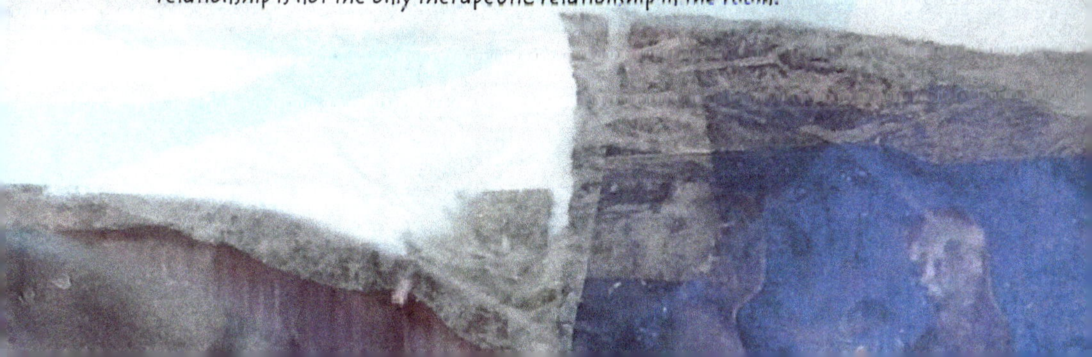

And finally

Tarquam, Andy

How do these trajectories of belonging, space and time intersect? What do you hope to learn by reading this Introduction, these chapters and our subsequent reflections? Stop. Think awhile before you read on.

The boat that sits on the cover of this book is a metaphor. It drifts until it is sailed. It waits at the whim of the weather; it waits for your hand on the tiller. Then it can be read purposefully and meaningfully and can take you from one place to another by whatever route you choose.

In the period of making this book we, in accordance with the metaphor at the heart of our art, have moved from one form of knowing to another. We have tried to capture the sense of space, place and belonging that is central to art therapy, and to the human conditions with which we work, in the particular context that is Australia. It is our hope that you are able to reach into the world of this work, in its place, and see it for yourself, threading your meaning and your yarn into its big story.

There are no certainties here and the lack of assuredness in these accounts may leave you wanting more. Some will be satisfied with an image or an allusion – as we have been – others will not. The book aims to be an evocation, one that will lead you to wonder about what we did in Australia when and as the world of art therapy emerged here and elsewhere. Not unlike the looking and listening work of the therapist, deep listening – or *dadirri*, as the First People of Australia would say – requires that we readers, viewers and editors wait, sit, hold, wonder. There may then be an insight; your insight; your meaning. The book you are reading on a screen or holding in your hands is a transitional artefact made by us but the captain of this vessel is now you. As it leaves our care it sails away with you to other places and may move you through the rabbit hole to another world view.

This work and your world coalesce here. We offer the compass, the terrain and the ocean for you to traverse, together with images and narratives that evoke then and now. It was, and is, like this for the people you are reading about. We wonder, and hope you will too, what will art therapy be like next, in this place and space that is Australia?

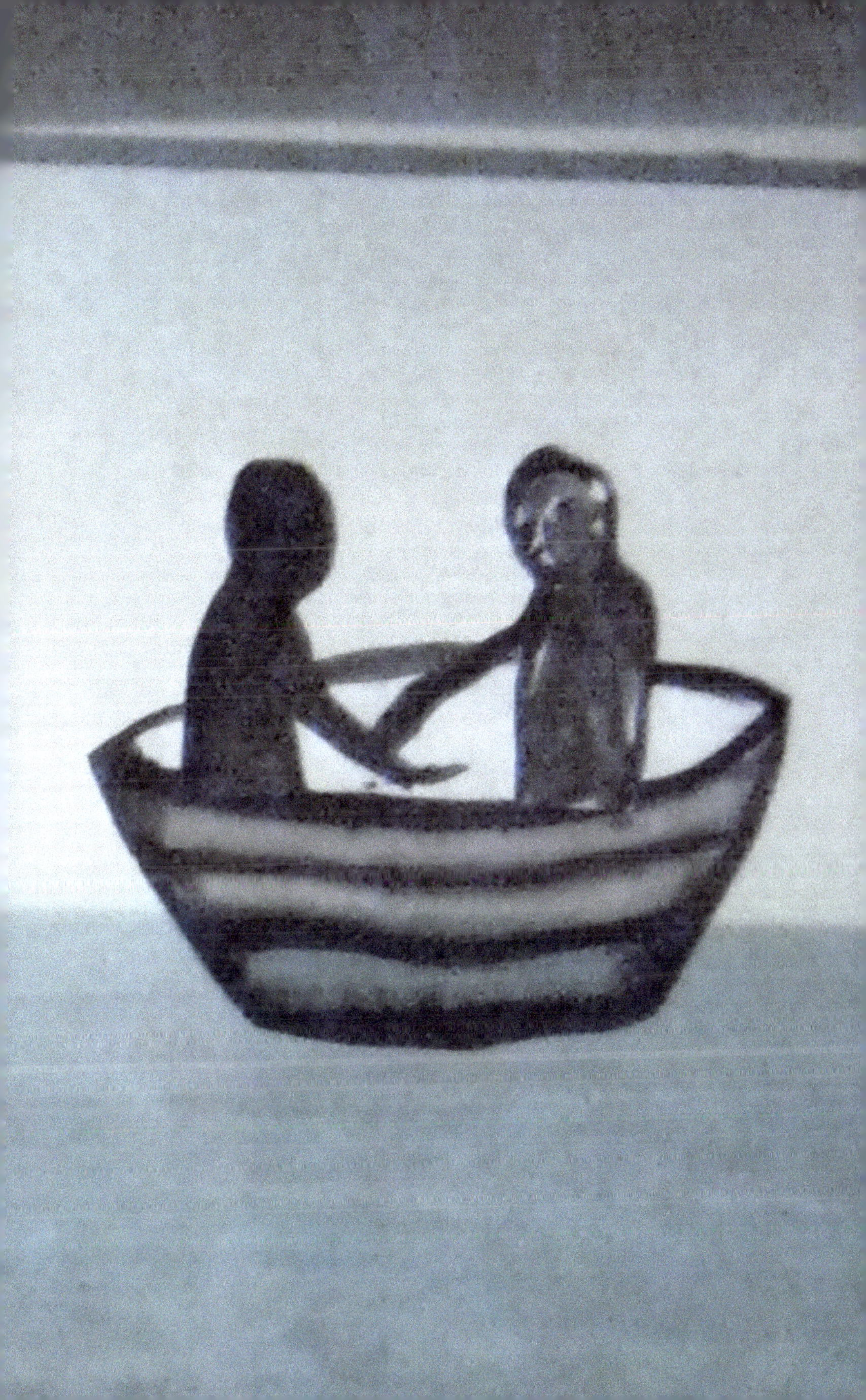

References

Adamson, E. (1984). *Art as healing.* Coventure, London.

Adorno, T. (1997). *Aesthetic theory* [R. Hullot-Kentor, Trans]. Althone Press, London.

Allen, P. (1992). Artist in residence: An alternative to 'clinification' for art therapists. *Art Therapy: Journal of the American Art Therapy Association,* 9(1): 22–29.

Allen, P. (1995). *Art is a way of knowing: A guide to self-knowledge and spiritual fulfilment through creativity.* Shambala, Boston.

Allen, P. (2001). Art making as a spiritual path: The open studio process as a way to practice art therapy. In: J. Rubin (Ed.) (2001) *Approaches to art therapy.* Brunner-Routledge, Philadelphia.

Bhabha, H. (1994). *The location of culture.* Routledge, New York.

Bourriaud, N. (2002). *Relational aesthetics.* Les presses du réel, Dijon.

Campanelli, M. and Kaplan, F. (1996). Art therapy in Oz: Report from Australia. *Arts in Psychotherapy 23* (1): 61–67.

Campbell, J., Liebmann, M., Brooks, F., Jones, J. and Ward, C. (Eds.) (1999). *Art therapy, race and culture.* Jessica Kingsley Publications, London.

Champernowne, H. (1971). Art and therapy: An uneasy partnership. *Art Therapy: Journal of the American Art Therapy Association,* 10(3): 131–144.

Csikszentmihalyi, M. (1991). *Flow.* First Harper Perennial, New York (reprinted 2008).

Coulter, A. (2006). Art therapy in Australia: The extended family. *Australian and New Zealand Journal of Art Therapy,* 1(1), 8–18.

Coulter, A. (2016). Art therapy down under: Perspectives on the profession from Australia and New Zealand. In: Gussak, D. and Rosal, M. (Eds). *The Wiley-Blackwell Handbook of Art Therapy.* John Wiley & Sons, Inc., New Jersey.

Dennes, M. and Gilchrist, S. (2005). *Halfway between everything: case material for art therapy in aged care.* Bonza Street Press, Australia.

Dissanayake, E. (1992). *Homo aestheticus: Where art comes from and why.* Free Press, New York, NY.

Doktor, D. (Ed) (1998). *Arts therapists, refugees and migrants: Reaching across borders.* Jessica Kingsley Publications, London.

Fanon, F. (1952). *Black skin, white masks.* [Trans. Charles Lam Markmann, 1967], Grove Press, New York.

Fanon, F. (1961). *The wretched of the earth.* [Trans. Constance Farrington, 1963], Grove Weidenfeld, New York.

Gannon, S. (2016). Kairos and the time of gender equity policy in Australian schooling. *Gender and Education,* 28(3): 330 – 342.

Gatens, M. (1996). Sex, gender, sexuality: Can ethologists practice genealogy? *The Southern Journal of Philosophy* 34 (Supplement): 1–19.

Gilroy, A. (1998). On being a temporary migrant to Australia: Reflections on art therapy education and practice. In: Docktor, D. (Ed.) (1998) *Arts therapists, refugees and migrants: Reaching across borders*. Jessica Kingsley Publications, London.

Gilroy, A., and Hanna, M. (1998). Conflict and culture in art therapy: an Australian perspective. In: Calisch, A. and Hiscox. A. (Eds.), (1998) *Tapestry of cultural issues in art therapy*. Jessica Kingsley Publications, London.

Henley, D. (1992). Aesthetics in art therapy: Theory into practice. *The Arts in Psychotherapy,* 19(3): 153–161.

Hill, A. (1948). Art versus illness. Allen and Unwin, London.

Hiscox, A. and Calisch, A. (Eds.) (1998). Tapestry of cultural issues in art therapy. Jessica Kingsley Publications, London.

Hocoy, D. (2002). Cross-cultural issues in art therapy. *Art Therapy: Journal of the American Art Therapy Association* 19(4): 141–145.

Hocoy, D., (2006.) Art therapy as a tool for social change. In: Kaplan, F. (Ed) (2006) *Art Therapy and Social Action*. Jessica Kingsley Publications, London and Philadelphia.

Hogan, S. (Ed) (1997). *Feminist approaches to art therapy.* Routledge, London and New York.

Hogan, S. (2001). *Healing arts: the history of art therapy*. Jessica Kingsley Publications, London.

Hogan, S. (Ed) (2002). *Gender issues in art therapy.* Jessica Kingsley Publishers, London and Philadelphia.

Hogan, S. (Ed) (2012). *Revisiting feminist approaches to art therapy.* Berghahn Books, New York and Oxford..

Hogan, S., and Coulter, A. (2014). *The introductory guide to art therapy: Experiential teaching and learning for students and practitioners*. Routledge, New York, NY.

Hyland-Moon, C. (2002). *Studio art therapy: Cultivating the artist identity of the art therapist*. Jessica Kingsley Publications, London.

Kalmanowitz, D. and Lloyd, B. (2004). *Art therapy and political violence*. Brunner-Routledge, London and New York.

Kapitan, L. (2010) *Introduction to art therapy research*. Taylor Francis Group, New York, NY.

Kapitan, L. (2013). Making or Breaking: Art Therapy in the Shifting Tides of a Violent Culture. *Art Therapy: Journal of the American Art Therapy Association*, 14(4): 255–260.

Kapitan, L. (2015). Social Action in Practice: Shifting the Ethnocentric Lens in Cross-Cultural Art Therapy Encounters, *Art Therapy: Journal of the American Art Therapy Association*, 32(3): 104–111.

Kaplan, F. (2007). *Art therapy and social action*. Jessica Kingsley Publishers, London and Philadelphia.

Kaplan, F (2015). Social Action Art Therapy. In: Gussack, D. and Rosal, M. (Eds) (2015) *The Wiley Handbook of Art Therapy.* Wiley Blackwell, Malden, MA and Oxford, UK.

Kramer, E. (1958). *Art therapy in a children's community.* Charles C. Thomas, Springfield, Ill.

Laidlaw, J. (2012). Ontologically challenged. *Anthropology of this century, 4.* Charles Stanford, London.

Lewis, P. (1997). Multiculturalism and globalisation in the arts in psychotherapy, *The Arts in Psychotherapy,* 24(2): 123–127.

Linnell, S. (2006). *Towards ethical 'arts of existence': through art therapy and narrative therapy.* Unpublished PhD thesis, University of Western Sydney, Australia.

Linnell, S. (2010). *Art psychotherapy and narrative therapy: An account of practitioner research. (Rethinking research and professional practices in terms of relationality, subjectivity and power).* Bentham Science Publishers, Thousand Oaks.

Maclagan, D. (2001). *Psychological aesthetics: painting, feeling and making sense.* Jessica Kingsley Publications, London.

Meskimmon, M. (2003). *Women making art: history, subjectivity, aesthetics.* Routledge, London and New York.

McNiff, S. (1979). From shamanism to art therapy. *Art Psychotherapy,* 6(3): 155–161.

McNiff, S. (1981). *The arts and psychotherapy.* Charles. C. Thomas, Springfield, Ill.

McNiff, S. (1984). Cross-cultural psychotherapy and art. *Art Therapy: Journal of the American Art Therapy Association 1,* 3, 125–131. (Re-published 2009, 25th Anniversary issue of *Art Therapy: Journal of the American Art Therapy Association,* 26(3): 100–106).

McNiff, S. (1992). *Art as medicine: Creating a therapy of the imagination.* Shambala Publications, Boston and London.

McNiff, S. (1998). *Art-based research.* Jessica Kingsley Publications, London and Philadelphia.

McNiff, S. (2009). *Integrating the arts in therapy, history, theory and practice.* Charles C. Thomas, Springfield, Ill.

Memmi, A. (1965). *The colonizer and the colonized.* [Trans. Howard Greenfield 1991] Beacon Press, Boston.

Meyerowitz-Katz, J. and Reddick, D. (Eds) (2017). *Art therapy in the early years: therapeutic interventions with infants, toddlers and their families.* Routledge, London and New York.

Moon, B. (2006). *Ethical issues in art therapy,* 2nd edn. Charles C. Thomas, Springfield, Ill.

Naumburg, M. (1950). *Introduction to art therapy: Studies of the free art expression of behaviour problem children and adolescents as a means of diagnosis and therapy.* Teachers College Press, New York.

Naumburg, M. (1958). *Dynamically oriented art therapy.* Grune and Stratton, New York.

Robbins, A. (1987). *The artist as therapist.* Human Sciences Press, New York.

Said, E. (1978). *Orientalism.* Penguin Modern Classics, Harmondsworth.

Sajnani, N. (2012). Response/ability: Imagining a critical race feminist paradigm for the creative arts therapies. *The Arts in Psychotherapy*, 39: 186–191.

Sajnani, N. and Kaplan, F. (2012). Editorial. The creative arts therapies and social justice: A conversation between the editors of this special issue. *The Arts in Psychotherapy,* 39: 165–167.

Schaverien, J. (1992). *The revealing image: analytical art psychotherapy in theory and practice*. Tavistock/Routledge, London.

Stace, S. (2016) The use of sculptural lifelines in art psychotherapy (L'utilisation des lignes de vie sculpturales en art-thérapie). *Canadian Art Therapy Association Journal*, 29(1): 21–29.

Talwar, S. (2010). An intersectional framework for race, class, gender, and sexuality in art therapy. *Art Therapy: Journal of the American Art Therapy Association*, 27(1): 11–17.

Talwar, S. (2015). Culture, Diversity, and Identity: From Margins to Center, *Art Therapy: Journal of the American Art Therapy Association,* 32(3): 100–103.

Talwar, S. (2016). Is there a need to redefine art therapy? *Art Therapy: Journal of the American Art Therapy Association*, 32(3): 116–118.

Talwar, S. (Ed.) (2017) *Art therapy for social justice: Radical intersections*. Routledge: London, New York.

Talwar, S., Iyer, J. and Doby-Copeland, C. (2004). The invisible veil: Changing paradigms in the art therapy profession. *Art Therapy: Journal of the American Art Therapy Association,* 21(1): 44–48.

Ungunmerr-Baumann, M. (2002). Dadirri: a reflection by Miriam-Rose Ungunmerr-Baumann. Australia: Emmaus Productions. http://www.dadirri.org.au/dadirri-meaning. Accessed 13/5/2017.

Venn, C. (2002). Refiguring subjectivity after modernity. In: Walkerdine, V. (Ed.) (2002), *Challenging subjects: critical psychology for a new millennium*. Palgrave, Houndsmills, UK.

Westwood, J. and Linnell, S. (2011). The emergence of Australian art therapies: colonial legacies and hybrid practices. *ATOL Art Therapy On Line: Goldsmiths, 1(3): 1–19.*

Young, R. (2003). *Postcolonialism: a Very Short Introduction*. Oxford University Press, Oxford and New York.

1

TAKING A TURN

An Image-Led Dialogue between Creative Arts Educators and Practitioners in Melbourne, Australia

Jan Allen, Jean Rumbold, Victoria Schnaedelbach, Amanda Woodford, Lilian Tann

© KONINKLIJKE BRILL NV, LEIDEN, 2019 | DOI:10.1163/9789004368262_002

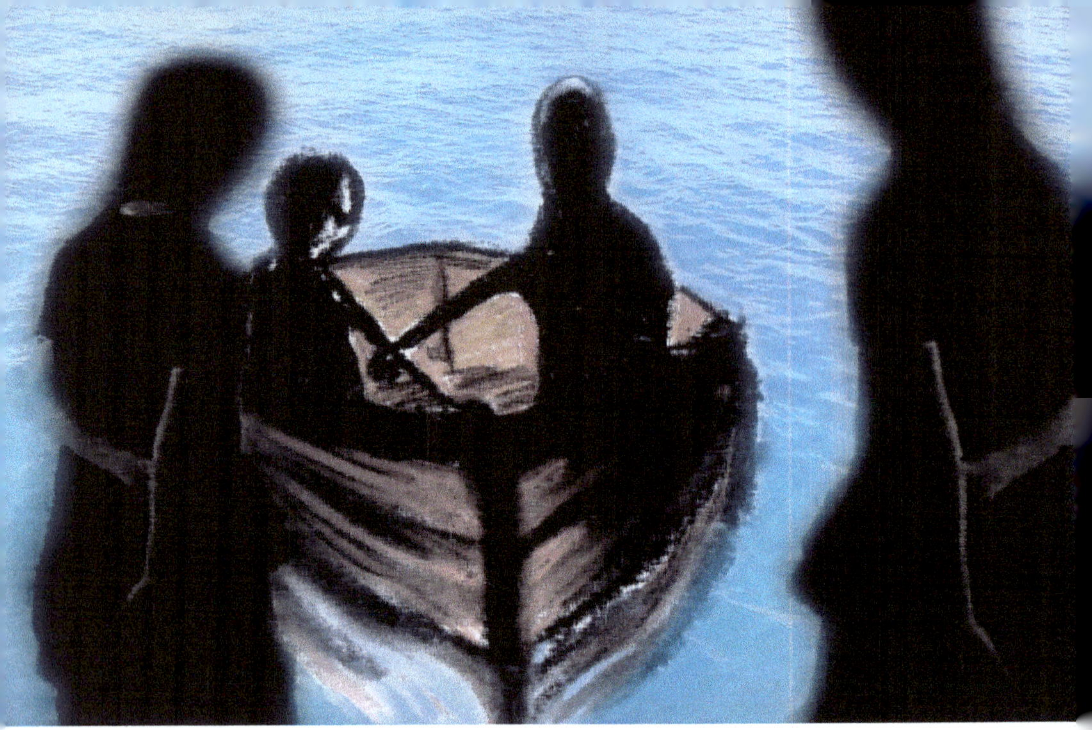

Figure 1 *Untitled postcard*. Jan Allen (2011). Pastel drawing, digital photocollage.

Dear Jean,
It is with much interest, curiosity and delight that I begin my first postcard in another of our inquiries. I was inspired by the image Jill, Andy, Sheridan and Pam displayed in their e-book proposal, and so created my version of the "boat people" and added another two – I am not sure if you and I are in the boat or are a part of the boat or looking on, or all of these. So this is a dialogue about *Art therapy: taking a postcolonial, aesthetic turn*. Both of us are mostly outside the art therapy boat although we certainly collaborate with, and sometimes teach or supervise those who might locate themselves inside it. Maybe we are in the postcolonial boat, as white, protestant arts educator/researchers from suburban Melbourne, though I wonder what this term really means, except perhaps to bring attention to the "contested terrains, global flows, and hybrid identities of a world undeniably marked by histories and legacies of colonization and decolonization" (Willems-Braun, 1997: 3). Clearly I struggle with the term postcolonial, as I wonder when the practices and ideas attributed to the postcolonial cease to be – or if they inevitably remain to permeate the present. Do we take postcolonial to mean conditions after colonialism or rather the ways in which ideas persist – the after-effects if you like? One could imagine, then, multiple temporalities and spatialities that intersect and overlap in any given moment. If we take this many layered perspective, then the postcolonial invites us to listen carefully for voices of the ancestors in those present now and look for the tracings of their and our imaginings that together form the figure and ground of our work.
I look forward to your response.
Jan

Dear Jan,
I think the context of this dialogue makes me far more aware of the people around us, and our location, than I was in our earlier postcard conversations (2004, 2008). So it interests me that you are drawn to the figures and boat, and I go at once to these shapes behind their backs. At first I saw them as sticks, as if the watchers wait to ward off the boat people. Now I see they are arms, perhaps suggesting some constraint? We are not art therapists. Will that constrain us here? Maybe you can provide the art and I the (psycho) therapy, but these days I see myself as an educator again, like you, and have shed my counselling psychologist/family therapist role. As educators with an interest in community capacity building (Ife, 2003), we may want to take the boat upstream (Baum and Harris, 2006), to encourage professionals to coach and support communities, rather than all staying downstream to provide professional services to individuals (though we certainly need that too). Most of all, though, the image speaks to me of this place, of this invaded/colonised land. For the watchers, there is the dilemma of when to welcome, when to resist. Both hospitality and resistance are strong traditions in this land. I think of the Moon Man story told me by Lardil elders, and wonder what happens when a welcome goes wrong? We believe therapy can offer mended experiences (Winnicott, 1971). Can there be a mended experience for boat people (then and now) and people of this land?
Jean

Figure 2 *Untitled postcard*. Jean Rumbold (2011). Digitally altered image.

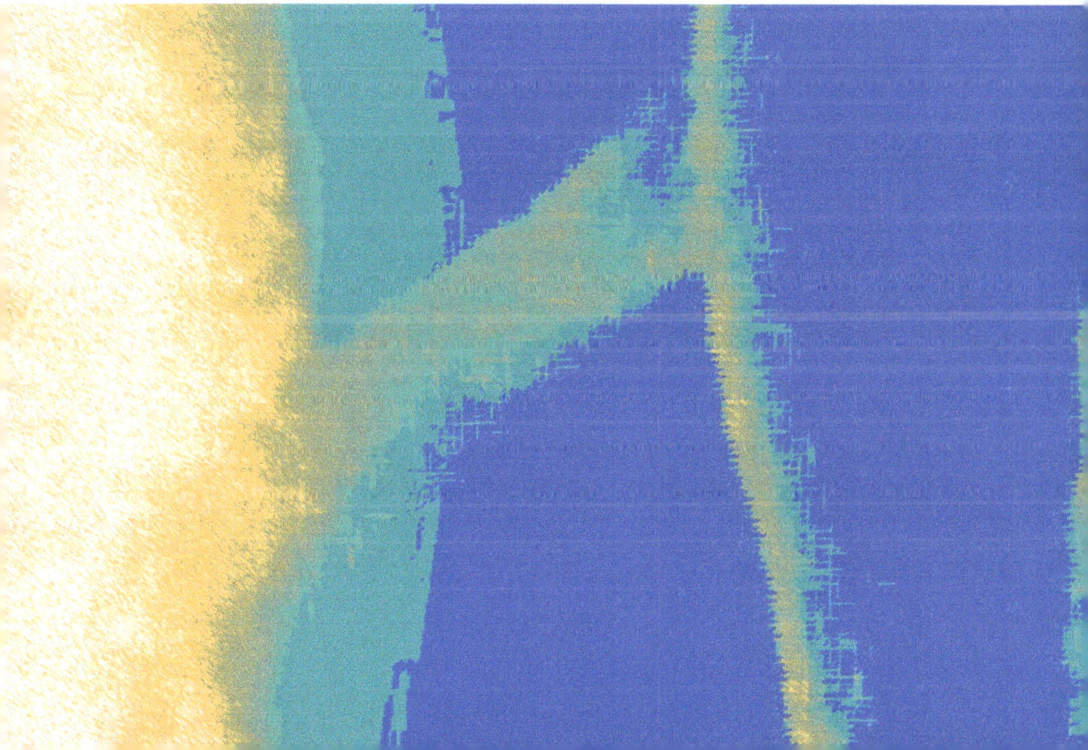

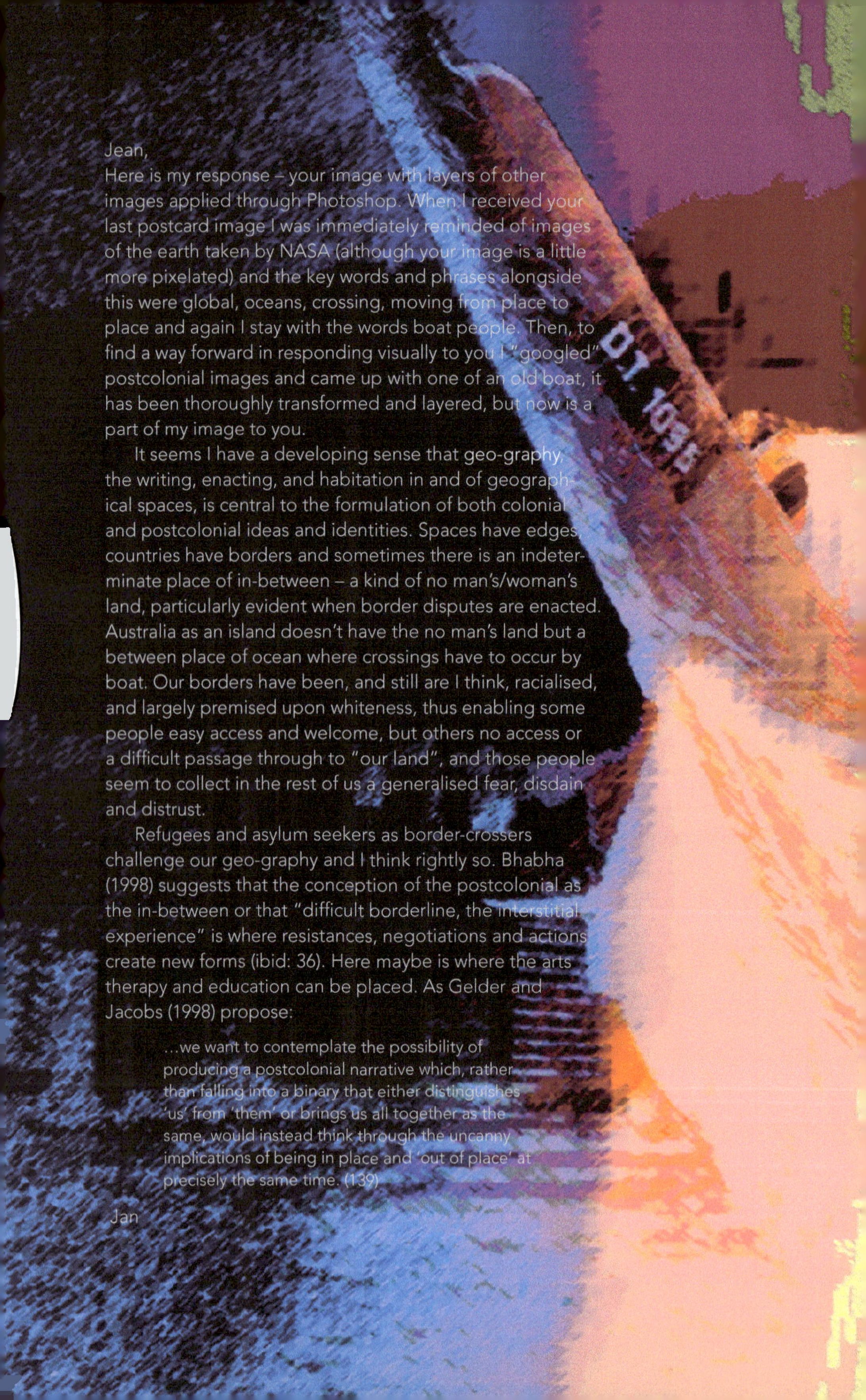

Jean,

Here is my response – your image with layers of other images applied through Photoshop. When I received your last postcard image I was immediately reminded of images of the earth taken by NASA (although your image is a little more pixelated) and the key words and phrases alongside this were global, oceans, crossing, moving from place to place and again I stay with the words boat people. Then, to find a way forward in responding visually to you I "googled" postcolonial images and came up with one of an old boat, it has been thoroughly transformed and layered, but now is a part of my image to you.

It seems I have a developing sense that geo-graphy, the writing, enacting, and habitation in and of geographical spaces, is central to the formulation of both colonial and postcolonial ideas and identities. Spaces have edges, countries have borders and sometimes there is an indeterminate place of in-between – a kind of no man's/woman's land, particularly evident when border disputes are enacted. Australia as an island doesn't have the no man's land but a between place of ocean where crossings have to occur by boat. Our borders have been, and still are I think, racialised, and largely premised upon whiteness, thus enabling some people easy access and welcome, but others no access or a difficult passage through to "our land", and those people seem to collect in the rest of us a generalised fear, disdain and distrust.

Refugees and asylum seekers as border-crossers challenge our geo-graphy and I think rightly so. Bhabha (1998) suggests that the conception of the postcolonial as the in-between or that "difficult borderline, the interstitial experience" is where resistances, negotiations and actions create new forms (ibid: 36). Here maybe is where the arts therapy and education can be placed. As Gelder and Jacobs (1998) propose:

> …we want to contemplate the possibility of producing a postcolonial narrative which, rather than falling into a binary that either distinguishes 'us' from 'them' or brings us all together as the same, would instead think through the uncanny implications of being in place and 'out of place' at precisely the same time. (139)

Jan

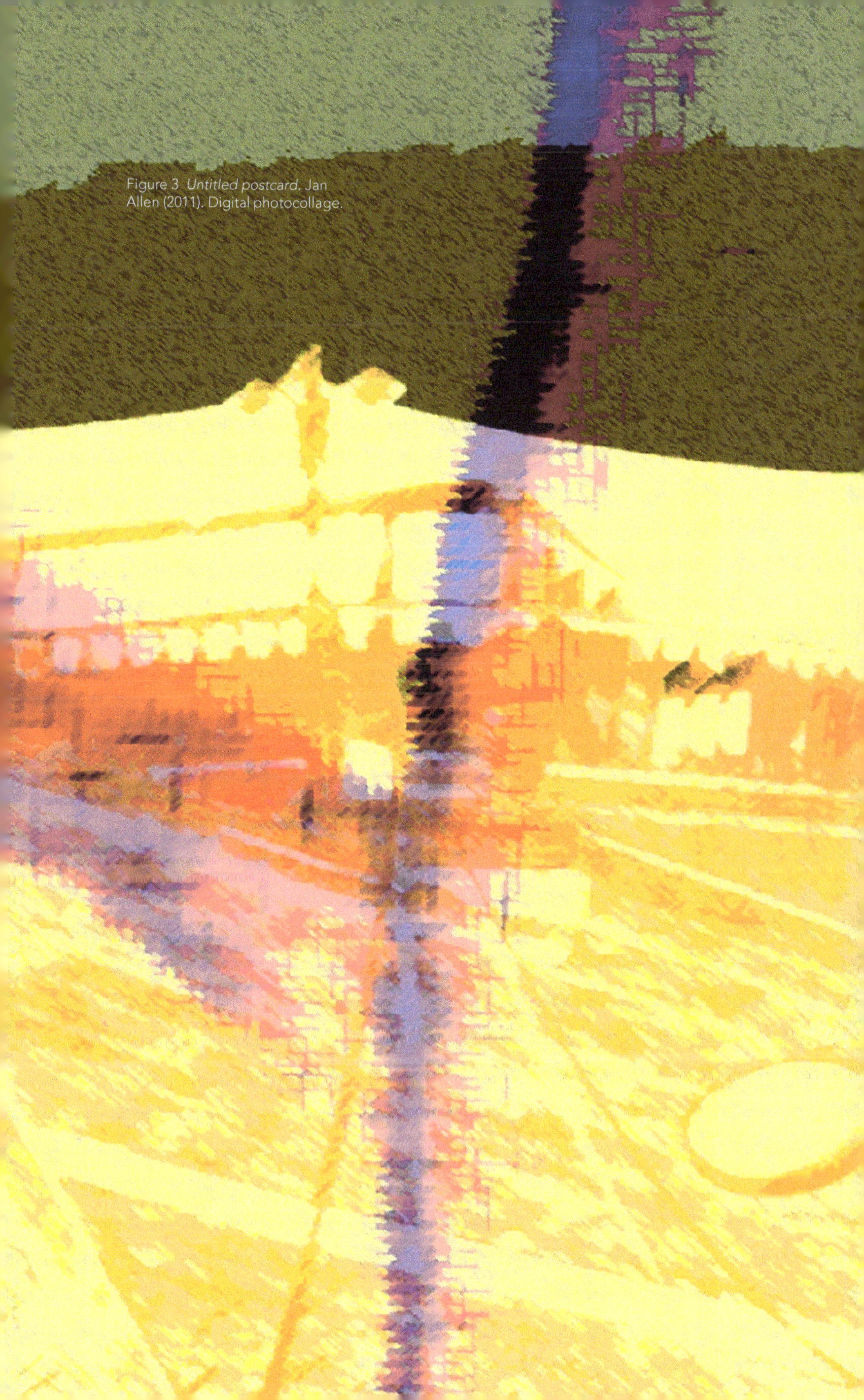

Figure 3 *Untitled postcard*. Jan Allen (2011). Digital photocollage.

Jan,
Here I managed to overlook the boat and see tents and an inland range in the distance. Maybe you characteristically head for the boundaries to test them, while I concern myself with what happens on land? So I am interested in the welcome, finding or making safe places and healthy settings (Kickbusch, 1997). To be in dialogue we will have to start in the liminal spaces, and I guess art itself and art therapy provide such places. This time I am torn between starting from experiential knowing or from presentational knowing (Heron and Reason,1997). So I could start from an experience that stays with me, a recent comment from Nellie Green of La Trobe's Narn-gi Bagora Centre for Indigenous Students. Nellie said; "We are very welcoming, though that's what got us into trouble in the first place". But I do understand something about my curiosity about 'welcomes that go wrong' already, whereas I have no idea where your image will take me. So I will follow the aesthetic prompts and see if they lead me somewhere new.

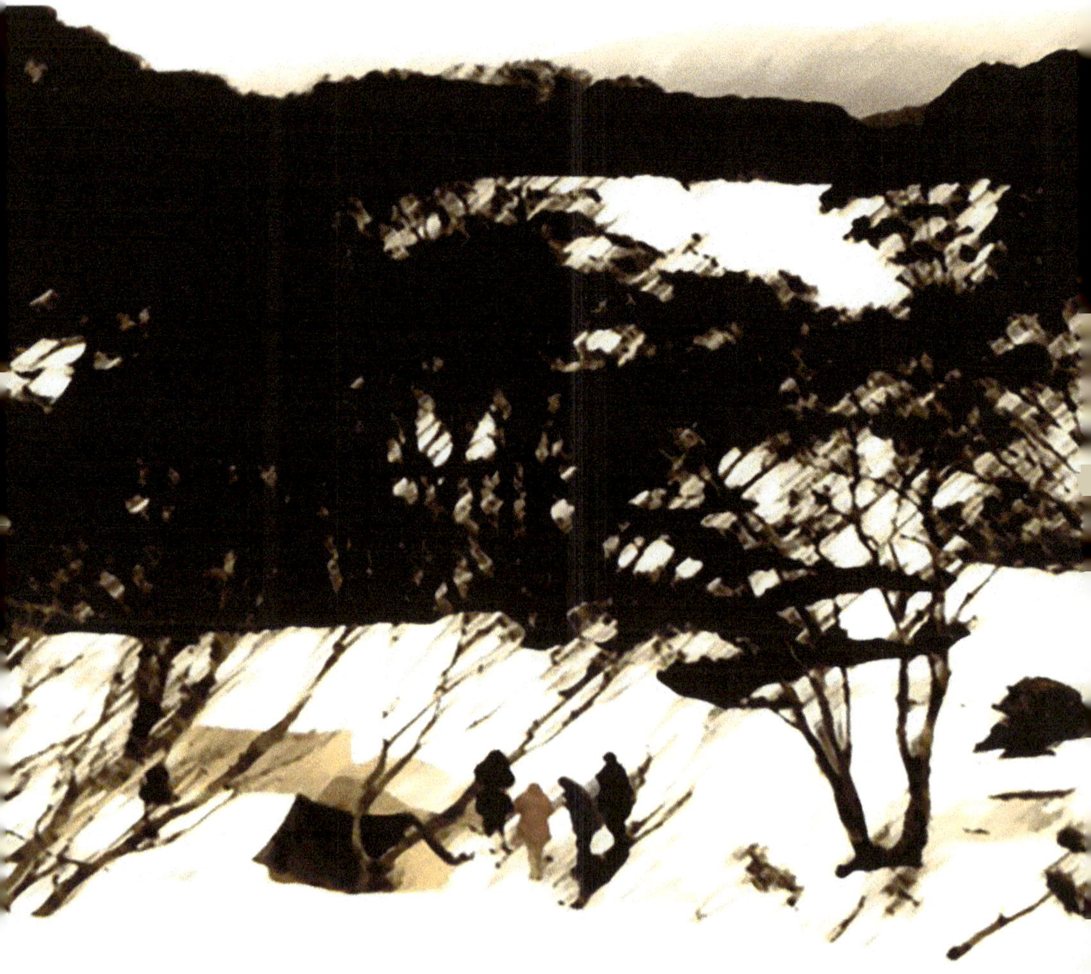

In your image, I keep going back to the tent I see here. I think of the tent in Tom Roberts' painting of The Artists' Camp, painted not far from where I live. I am surprised to be thinking about tents, such temporary, though sometimes very welcome, shelter. I remember huddling in tents in the Victorian Alps as gales roared through or snow fell. I think about all the art therapy done in tents, from refugee camps to festivals. I remember the Aboriginal tent embassy outside the Houses of Parliament in Canberra. The recent floods, earthquakes and tsunamis have made even solid buildings fragile, and forced us to look beyond our manmade structures. Yet, as I was writing this, the Victorian premier decided to discontinue, as a usual practice, the acknowledgement of country, where elders are not there to offer a welcome to country. It seems we are so unwilling to listen to the land and those who have been its custodians that the land itself has had to roar at us.
Jean

Figure 4 *Untitled postcard*. Jean Rumbold (2011). Digitally altered image.

Jean,
I began by layering an image from arts therapy with a map of the Indigenous language areas of Australia (very hard to see – probably hard to hear nowadays) and a desert photo. Then I felt this should be framed by an image from Fitzroy, which feels better although looks messier – which also feels right.

I struggle to find something coherent to write about. We have the arts, which have a rich tradition in white colonial Australia and in Indigenous Australia – I read today in the paper about the 174 Indigenous images gifted to the National Gallery of Victoria from the Felton Bequest on the Gallery's 150th birthday. We have art therapy, now present in our schools, hospitals, prisons, in communities of refugees, asylum seekers, and health centres. Psychological frameworks sometimes divide us in this work; artists occasionally pit themselves against therapists and vice versa; art forms struggle for precedence – dance over visual art, music contesting drama; goodwill and compassion struggle with oppression and patronising attitudes. It is messy, fractious sometimes, dynamic and innovative and I struggle to find a common thread except the concern and goodwill of all of us in it together. We all want to feel better, to act in ways that are healthy for us, for others and for our material world.

Jean as you know this conversation has been a bit slow to get going. This postcard has sat on my desk top for a week or two, while I have struggled to write something useful or interesting for our readers. What now seems clear is that if I write about the postcolonial or art therapy or art practice, I don't really touch the complexity of what happens in the moment to moment encounters between therapists/artists and the people with whom they work. Recently I was reading a thesis by a soon to be graduating Melbourne Institute for Experiential Creative Arts Therapies (MIECAT) student doing the MA by Supervision, Danni von der Borch, part of which really stayed with me – it follows with her permission and the permission of the woman with whom she spoke:

> I am with a mother whose children come to an inner city adventure playground and meeting place for the local community. We are talking about her home, she is from Somalia. We are outside, I am scratching the goat, behind her horns, it is late afternoon and very cold. I ask does she have any photos…and then she begins the story of her leaving:
>
> > We must leave so quickly. We must go. We take nothing. The corrupted people they take everything, all my furniture, our papers, documents. They say the farm is theirs. They sell it. I have no photos … terrible terrible day. I still remember this day … the moment the guns started.
>
> She tells me about sitting outside the house, all gathered, women, children, and family, taking afternoon tea mats spread out, drinking coffee and eating. And then the sound. Everyone stops. (She is looking around rapidly, her body moving from one side to the other, reaching and searching with her eyes.) The sound again and again. It was at about this time (she gestures at the fading light of the afternoon). By

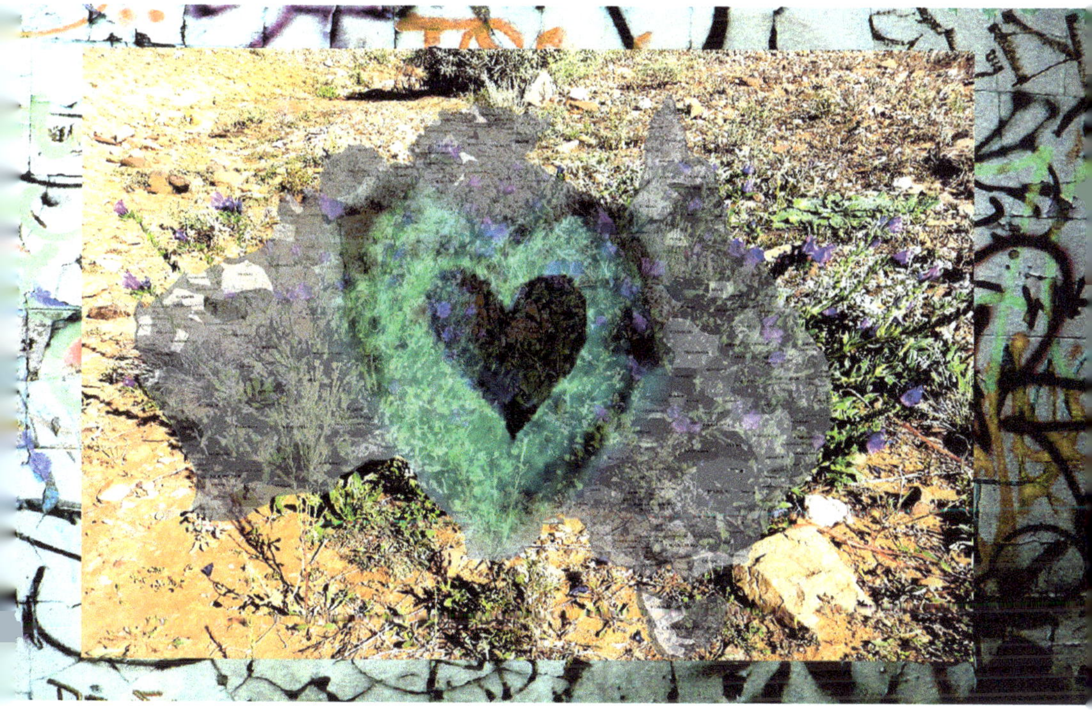

Figure 5 *Layers postcard*. Jan Allen (2011). Digital photocollage.

the morning we could see the fire and the smoke. (She gestures all around.) We all go. I could never believe I would one day come to Australia, I could never believe Kenya. You wouldn't believe here (she gestures to her head, holds it), here (gestures to her chest), I couldn't… for three years when I am here I cry and cry, for three years, I am (she slumps her body down, head down, she is leaning on the fence) couldn't stop thinking about it all.

She wants to see her mum again, but she is afraid of being killed, of her children being killed. Every time she gets close to going she speaks to her mother who says 'come come it's OK' and then 'no stop stop' (she raises her arm in the air with a 'stop' motion of her hand).

I want to surprise my children, to take them to see my home.

The longing for home and a sense of place continue to be part of our dialogue. I have not included some aspects of our exchange to protect privacy. Hearing her story was profoundly unsettling for me … I felt strongly that I was a landing place for an experience of great loss.

von der Borch, 2011

Jan

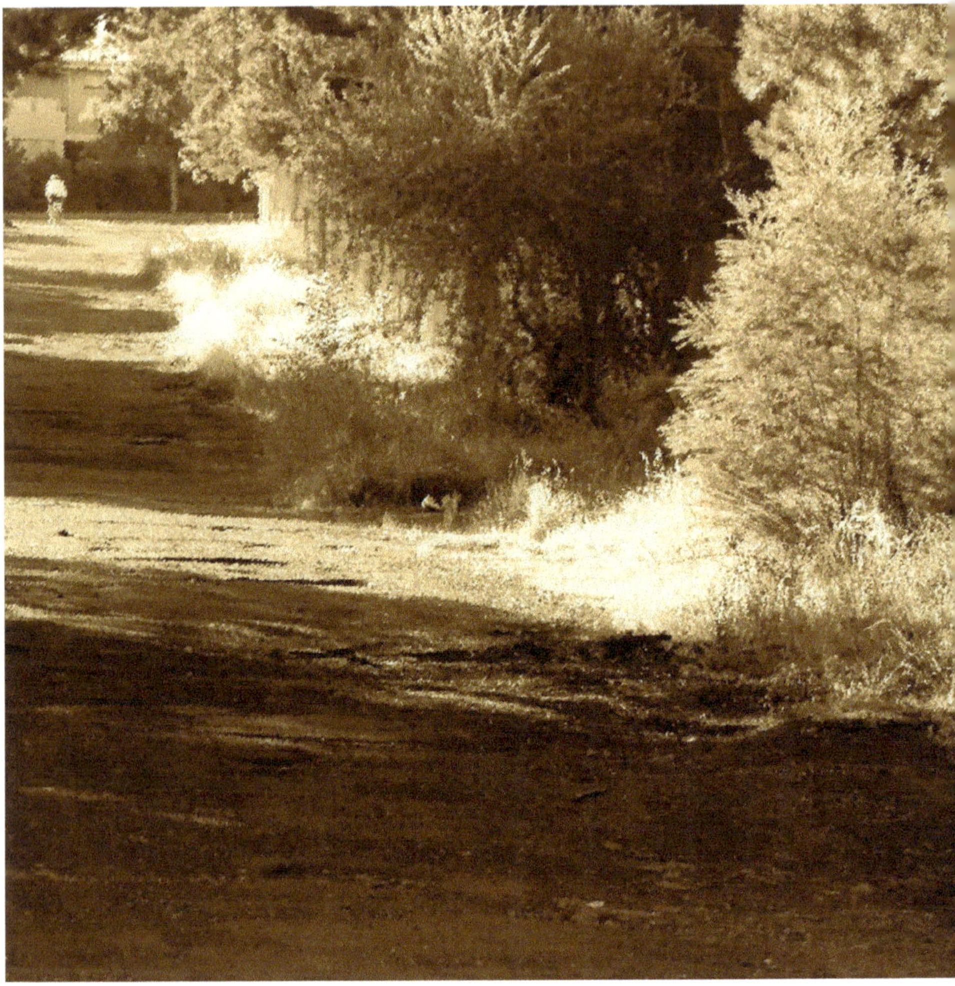

Jan,
The complexities of your last image sent me searching for this rather simple photo of mine titled *Way home*. As I read your text, you are also suggesting that in the widening possibilities of this dialogue we find our way back to the heart of our work. That seems good to me. If we are to contribute anything useful here, it is likely to be from the experience we share of helping people explore arts-based ways of working in therapy, education, community development, public health, and research. And the point of doing this is that art-making and working cooperatively allow new kinds of encounter and enable things to happen in relationships and in peoples' lives that can increase their sense of meaning and purpose, their autonomy, and their social inclusion and support. How do we show this?

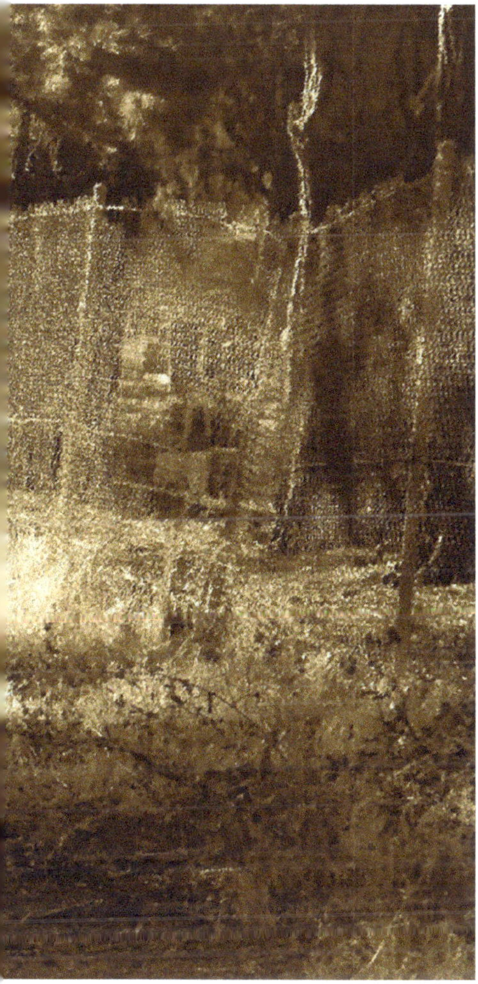

Figure 6 *Way home* postcard. Jean Rumbold (2011). Digitally altered image.

Behind the wonky fence in this photo is the old Box Hill cemetery. I do hope they never fix the fence and make the road and cut down the trees, though I fear they might as their efforts to tidy up the rest of it have left large stretches of tidy grey concrete. I want to add something here about the importance of the aesthetic, the beauty of tangled places, the art of letting be, and the need for places that make reflection and encounters possible. The adventure playground of your student's encounter, and this cemetery, are messy, friendly, liminal places. I think that at the heart of my work is making and finding such settings, and helping to facilitate the explorations that go on there.
Jean

Jean,
I have asked Lilian, a MIECAT Master of Arts (Creative Arts Therapy) student to contribute to our discussion. Lilian is currently working as an art therapist in an inner city housing estate using the arts with young primary age children from Africa, Asia and Europe. Their work focuses on exploring, documenting and expressing via stories and art work, the kids' experiences of living in the Collingwood flats – shown above. Lilian has agreed to respond to this card and briefly describe something of her work here.

Jean, returning to your image… it is interesting how your image is rustic, very rural looking for suburban Melbourne and aesthetically quite lovely. My image depicts the high rise deemed by most people living around (but not in) these 'lift-ups' and the lower rise 'walk-ups' as very unattractive. The girl portrayed here is deliberately stretched, to represent my sense of how fraught it may initially feel for people who come to these high rises from completely different, often rural, village or camp environments to find themselves in this vertical concrete city.

Here the art is not so much about letting it be, but I think about working to make this place home for people who have recently arrived in Australia. I know so much art now happens in and around these high rises, yarn bombing, stencil and aerosol graffiti art projects, lantern and moon festivals and many more – all so those participating have opportunities to improve the spaces that they use, whilst developing connections with these spaces and with others who use them through their artistic and creative contributions.
Jan

Figure 7 *The flats postcard.*
Jan Allen (2011). Digital photocollage.

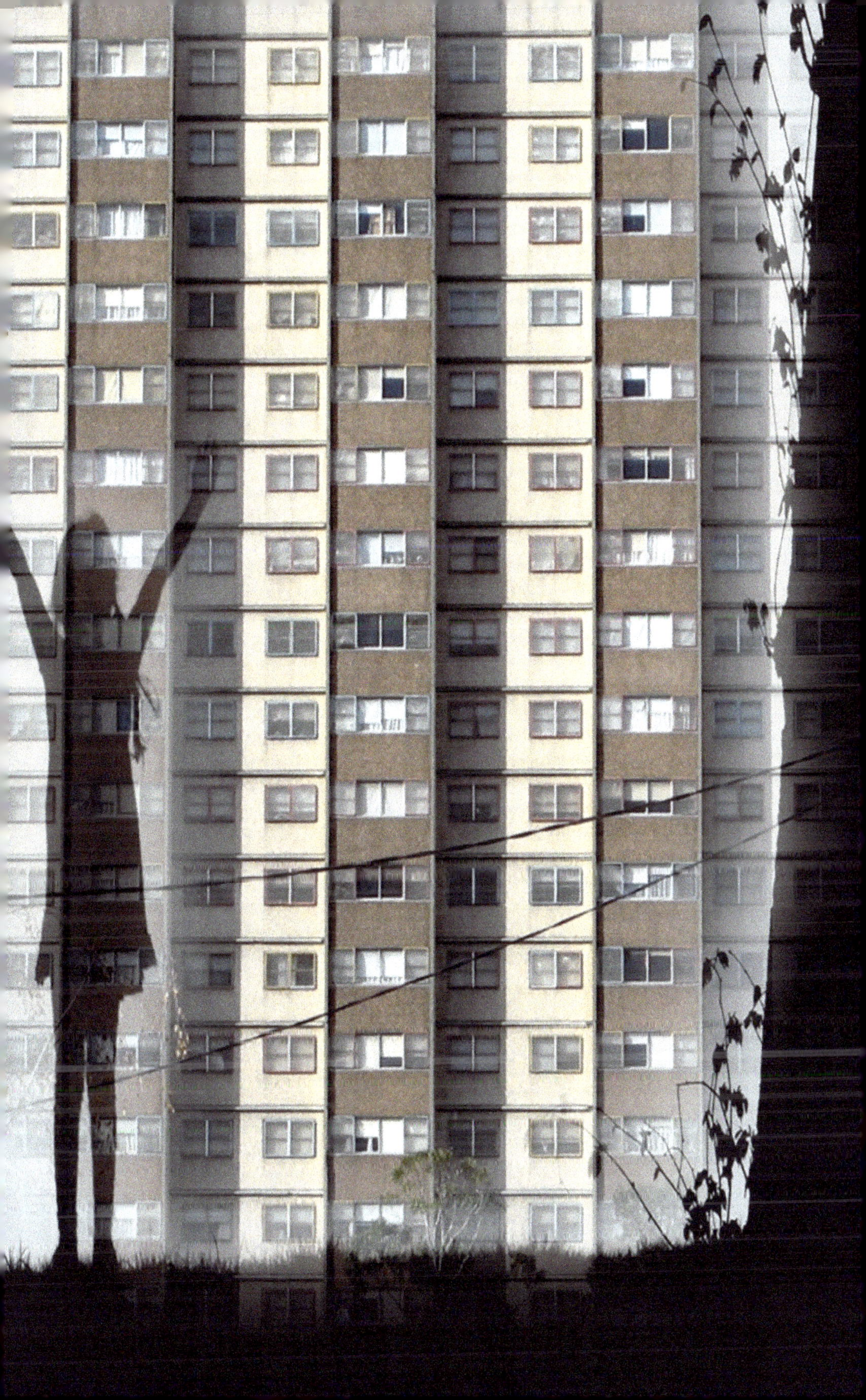

Dear Jan
Thank you for the opportunity to contribute to your postcard conversation with Jean. Your postcard is very resonant of the image I had in mind when you first asked me to participate. The repetitious box-like apartments stacked together convey a sense of limitation and a drab existence. Yet the silhouette of the child with her arms stretched upwards conveys a sense of innocence and hope.

My work with the children at the Collingwood Housing Estate commenced after a long period of engagement with them, essential as these kids see so many people come and go in their lives. Using disposable cameras, a few of the kids have captured some moments in time from their lives, and the people, places and things that mattered most to them. It gave me glimpses into lives that happen in those boxed apartments stacked together. Throughout my work with the children, I've been surprised by what I have learnt about the children and those they live with.

And this is what I have attempted to capture in my postcard to you. Despite the appearances from the outside, and the common perceptions about these housing estates and their inhabitants as being poor and lacking, there is richness beneath the surface. Their stories of how they came to live there are diverse, and details of their current daily lives vary, often weaving in and around each other. The children display a strong resilience, especially those with difficult home lives. The density and close proximity of friends and support is almost taken for granted. The children say one of the best things about living there is being close to their friends. The children also show a hunger for living and experiencing, be it new environments, new games or new art materials. They are as excited about using recycled everyday items as using brand new watercolour paints. The children share a common sense of hopes and dreams for their futures, beyond any perceived limitations.
Lilian

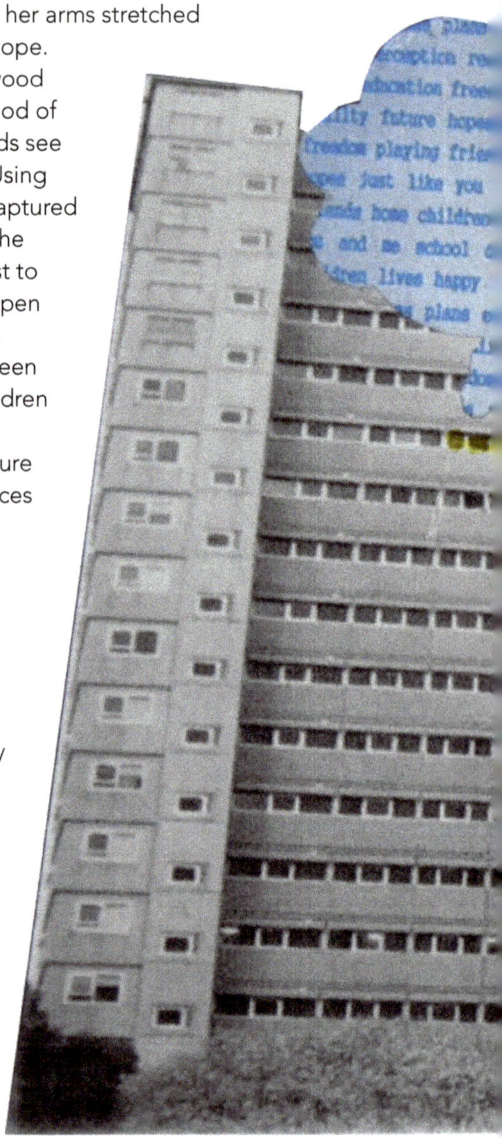

Figure 8 *Untitled postcard*. Lilian Tann (2011). Digital photocollage.

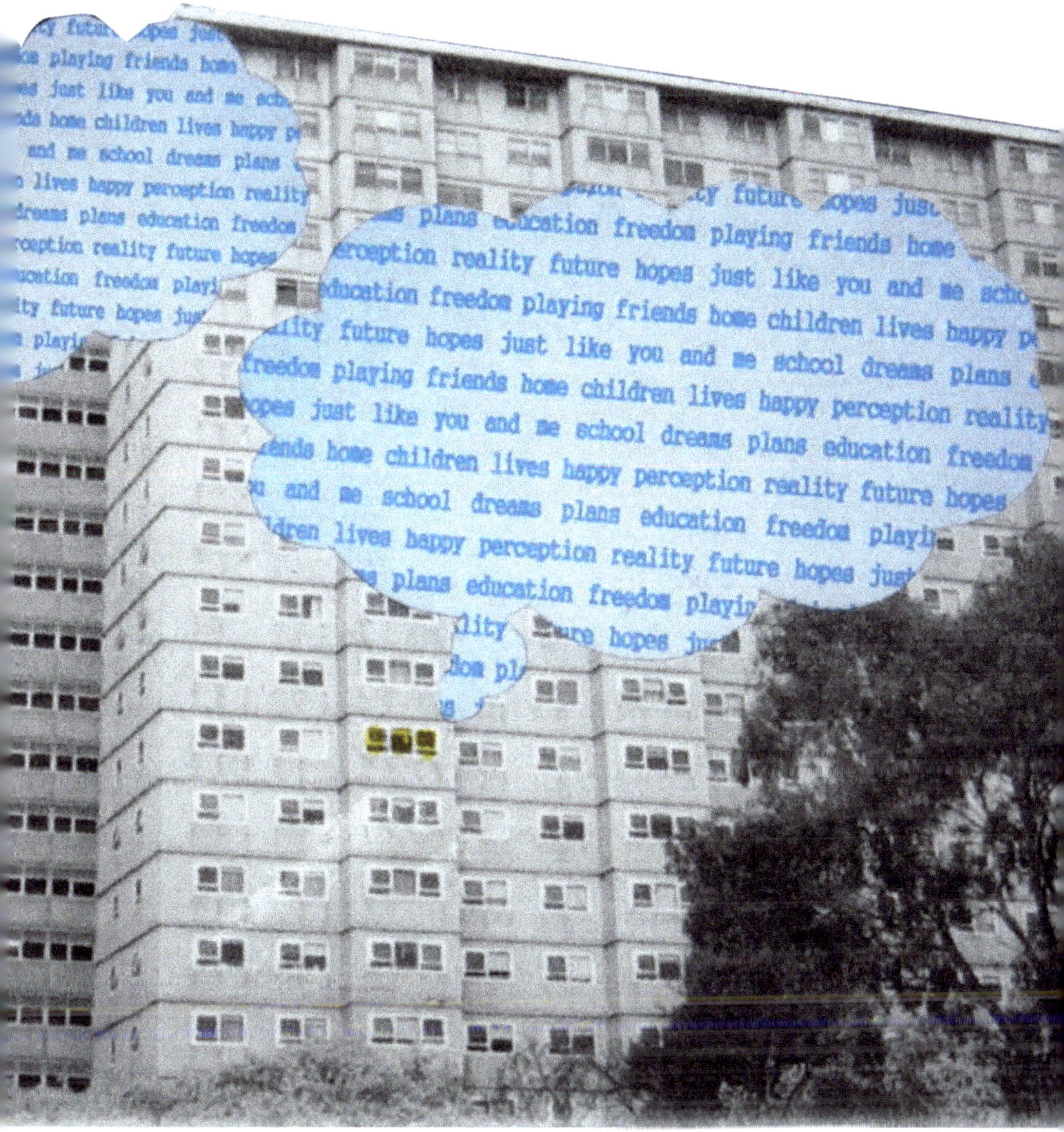

plans education freedom playing friends home
reality future hopes just like you and me
education freedom playing friends home children lives happy
future hopes just like you and me school dreams plans
playing friends home children lives happy perception reality
just like you and me school dreams plans education freedom
home children lives happy perception reality future hopes
and me school dreams plans education freedom
lives happy perception reality future hopes
plans education freedom

Dear Jan and Lilian,
This is a response to your images of the high rise flats. This underpass in Box Hill is I guess another liminal space where kids hang out. It is not a terribly satisfactory one. I think of Terence Davies' film *Of time and the city* and the loss of the Liverpool doorsteps where people sat and talked and watched kids play. The high rises that replaced them, like the ones in our inner city, did not have the same kind of private/public thresholds where people could meet. I know that those working with the arts and health, and the arts and community development in such places are intent on creating meeting places and thresholds, as are the residents themselves. Buskers play in this underpass, and there were notices about a public art project, which has since added glittery text in clouds. Designer spaces are not necessarily people scaled or friendly. Their sleekness may look good on concept drawings but some of these aesthetic forms seem inimical to safe and easy encounters. I think messiness can invite creative efforts to claim the spaces for human beings. The fact that in this postcolonial world we need to meet across barriers of visible difference and of historical injury and present injustice must add urgency to work like yours, Lillian, and to the work of others working in such ways.
Jean

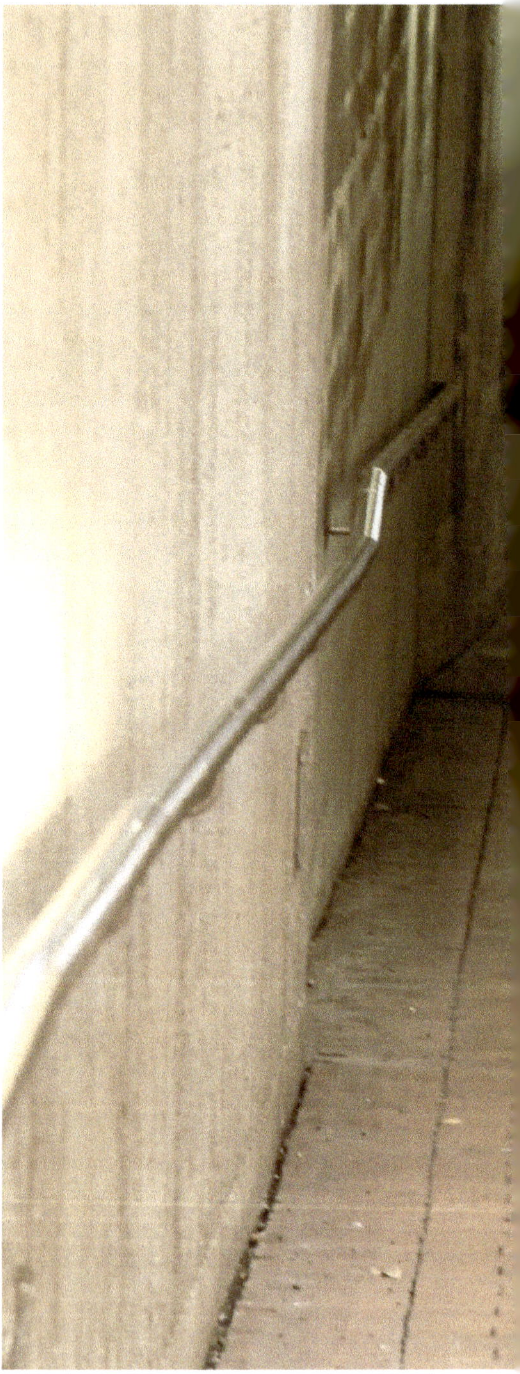

Figure 9 *The underpass postcard*. Jean Rumbold (2011). Digital photograph.

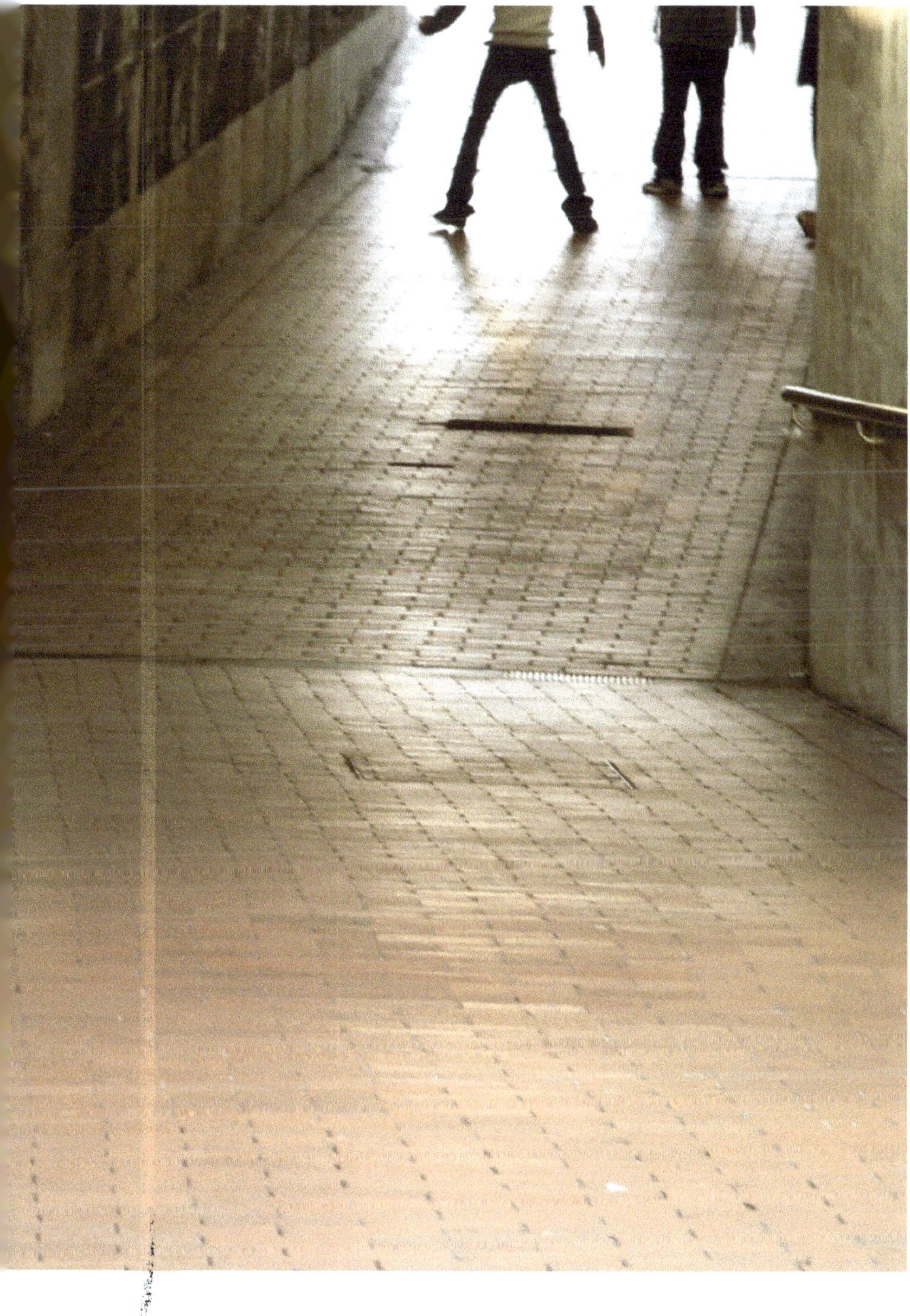

Jean,
Last night at MIECAT we had the pleasure of welcoming creative arts therapist and MIECAT MA graduate, Victoria Schnaedelbach to class. Students about to complete the Graduate Diploma in Creative and Experiential Arts Practice are participating in a series of workshops designed to introduce them to the work of practitioners in the community, and to how they have adopted the form of inquiry taught at MIECAT in various contexts.

Last night Victoria showed images, movies and told stories of her involvement in the Culture in Transit program. She, Kate Wide, a multi-cultural youth worker, and Edwina Entwistle, a MIECAT staff member, performer and film maker bought together Australian born, migrant and refugee young people to explore their experiences of before, being and becoming. They explored these experiences through the creation of symbols on suitcases (representing the past memories, stories and associated feelings), on T shirts (representing who they feel they are now), and on kites (showing hopes and aspirations for their futures).

To engage the MIECAT students in the work, Victoria invited us to watch the documentary and to attend to our experience of one child (previously 'assigned' to us by her), and to note our resonances to their story, their images or simply their presence in the project. The MIECAT students responded by creating visual responses to each child. They offered the comments [opposite] (which I have edited slightly and paraphrased) in our feedback session at the end of the evening.
Jan

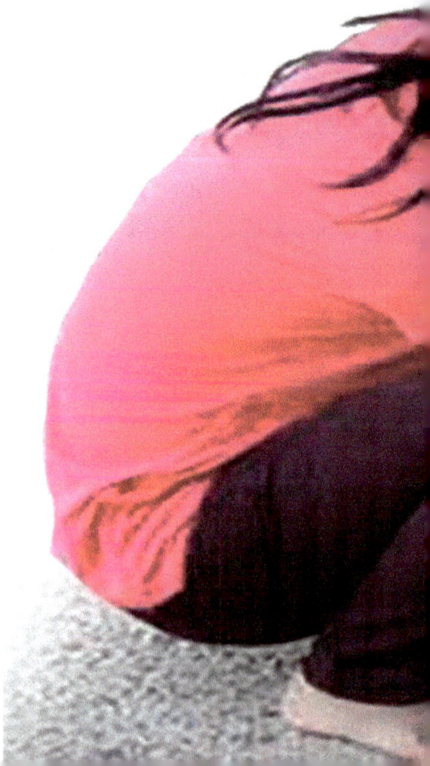

Figure 10 *Untitled postcard.* Victoria Schaendelbach (2011). Pastel drawing, digital photocollage.

I really appreciate the fact that Australian born kids were a part of this project and could experience refugees' stories first hand, not through our socially erected prejudices about refugees, asylum seekers boat people and queue jumpers!

The stories really moved me. First I thought these Australian kids had nothing to be stressed about, but as I attended closely I realized that we all have stories of joy and pain, each child's stories are in a sense their reality – what they live with – what they know.

Stories of horror and killing sit side by side with stories about the deliciousness of watermelons.

Amongst these young people, many varied threads of transition, change and adjustment were evident in their small, and humble creative storied tellings. Small tellings of courage and big journeys borne of their short lives thus far.

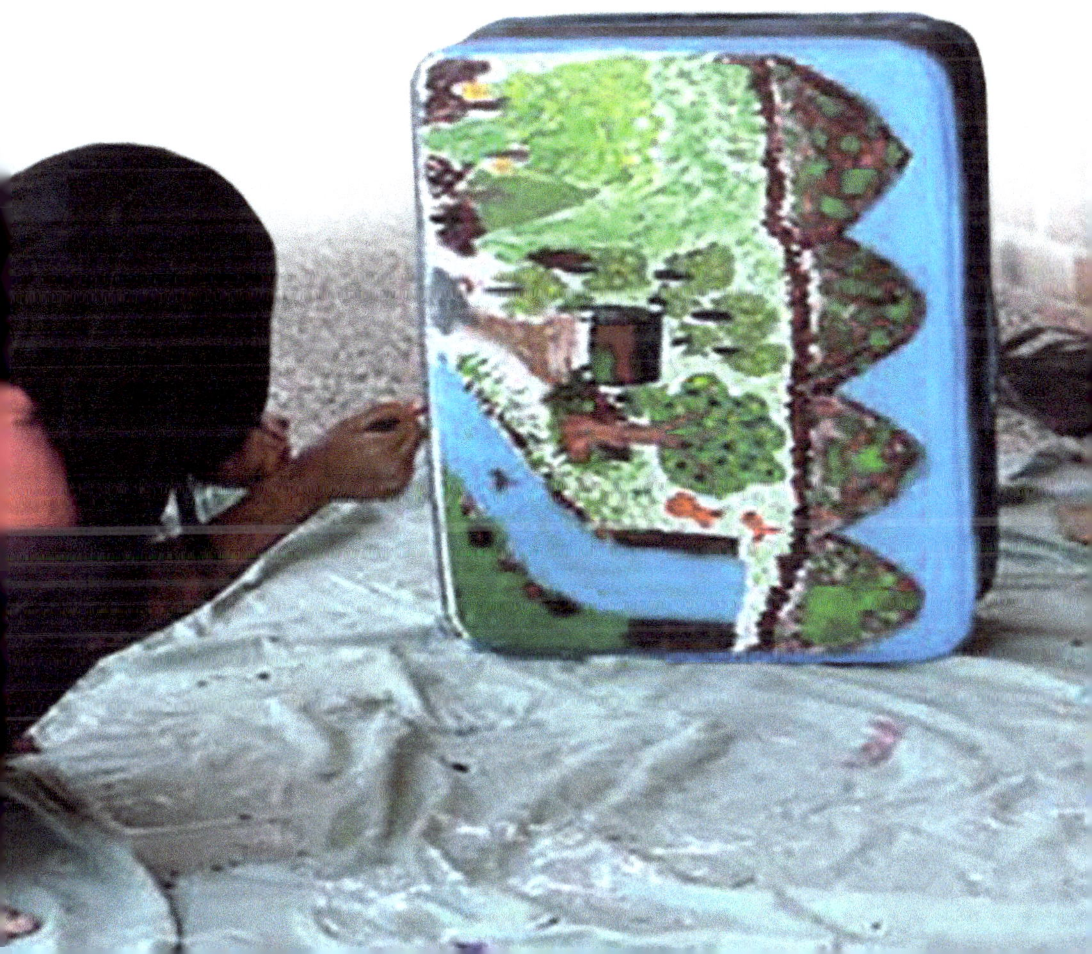

Jan,

It has been good to have you turn to the work of your students to ground this discussion in practice, and to welcome Lilian and Victoria to this conversation. I no longer run a counselling course though, and my only students now are doing PhDs and professional doctorates. However they often use these research projects to reflect on their practice or enrich it, and many of them use arts-based methods to do this.

When I looked at the image of Victoria's work, this one came to mind somehow, and I have Janine Brophy Dixon's permission to include it here and describe something of her research and her work as an art therapist. Janine's PhD project took her to New York where she explored her experience of mother-daughter separation by making postcards every day to send her mother and her daughter. She then returned to Australia and undertook a cooperative inquiry with her mother, in which the postcards led and held them through an exploration that transformed their relationship. Janine's research,

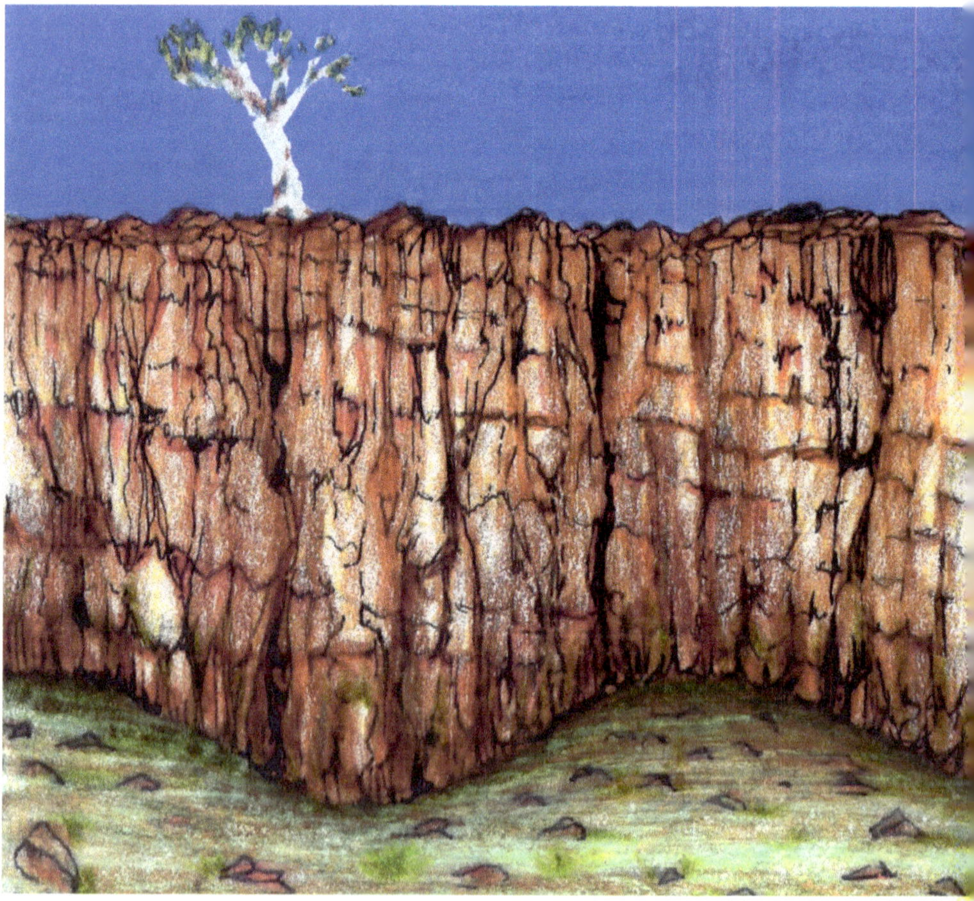

I think, does reflect art therapy's aesthetic turn, using art-making as a means of inquiry, and giving a central place to images and stories as forms of presentational knowing (Heron and Reason, 1997).

Since completing her thesis, Janine has spent some time working as an art therapist with Indigenous children in Alice Springs. While she was there, we adapted her postcard methodology to create a postcard dialogue that helped us reflect on, and debrief, our work. This is one of her postcards from that sequence. She found the land, the people and their art had a profound effect on her and it is this I see in her artwork rather than the frustrations that caused her to leave the agency eventually. Both of us I think delighted in the postcard exchange and experienced it as a source of insight and support. We haven't discussed the details of her experience, but from a few comments Janine has made, and my reading of emails from the Women for Wik, I do have the sense that, under the intervention, Australia is not postcolonial enough!
Jean

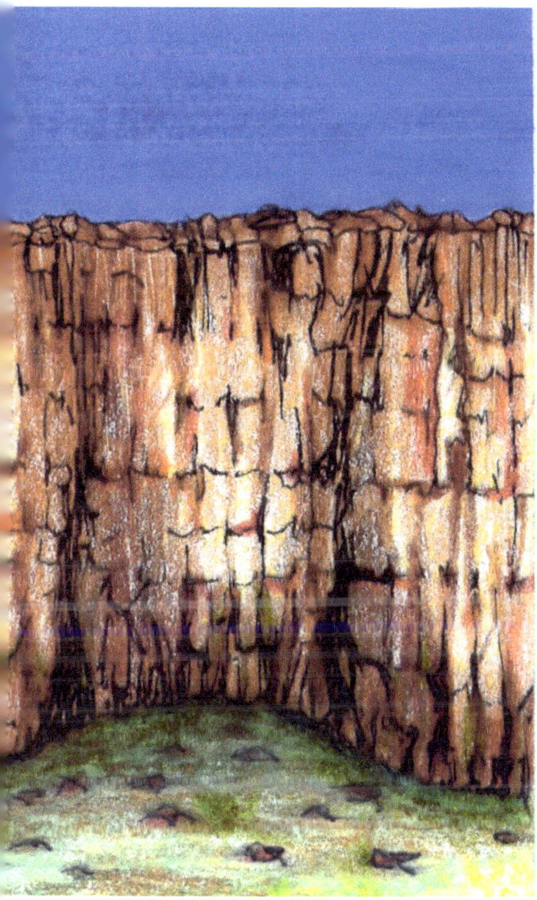

Figure 11 *One tree postcard.* Janine Brophy Dixon (2011). Pastel drawing.

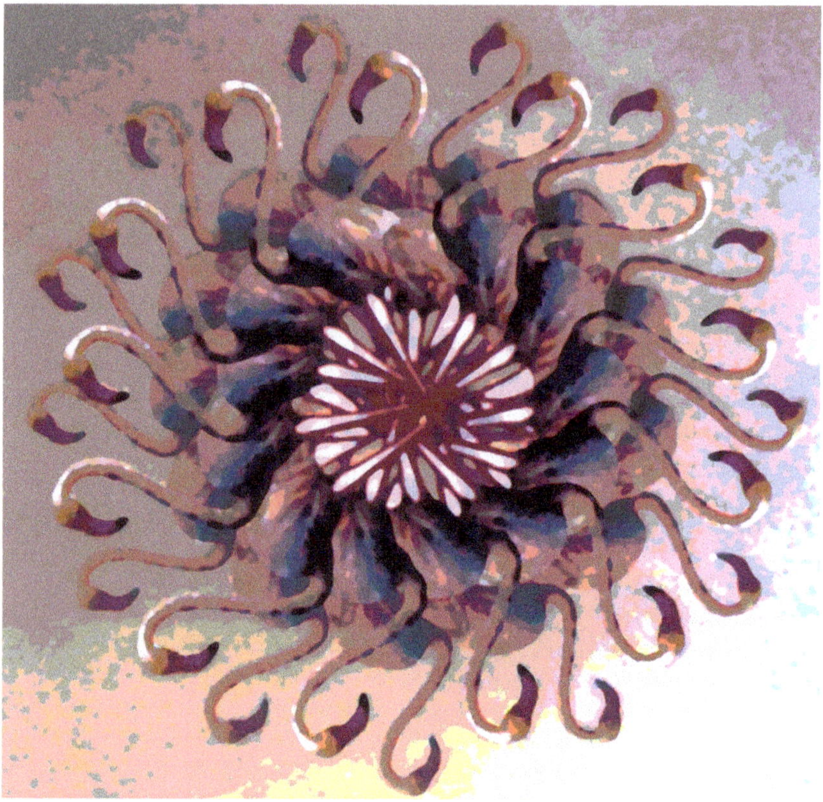

Figure 12 *Untitled image postcard* from the *Culture in Transit* project. (Undated. Reprinted with permission.)

Dear co responders,
A warm thanks for including my work. The *Culture in Transit* Project is a pretty good example of a postcolonial 'interstitial experience' in action, where resistances, contested terrains, negotiations and actions create new forms. The Maroondah City Council allocated funding for a community based Multicultural Arts project and signed on a freelance youth services team, *The Workshop*, founded by Richard Williams and Kate Wilde. The workshop also sessionally employs a social worker, a nurse educator and myself, a creative art therapist. It was set up to enable more responsive and flexible ways to work with all parts of school communities – kids, parents, teachers and administrators. Its aim is to develop partnerships with school communities to develop their capacity for local collaborative problem-solving. It is understood as an incremental and evolutionary process where work is highly intuitive and relies heavily on the quality of the long-term relationships they are able to develop.

Working with the Council for this project was a mixed blessing. The ongoing 'bureaucracies' were tempered with the great luck of a goodly, salt of the earth, council arts officer, Leanne Wilkinson and the peaceful, homely setting of old school grounds converted into a community, cultural and arts facility named Federation Estate (suitably postcolonial I must say). Here we were able to spread out, relax and make noise freely. As well as art-making we got physical and connected using interesting, fun games, some drama therapy, and BBQs. On our last day together, the not-too-tidy, suburban expanse of open, green space just across the way received us on a balmy and lazy summer afternoon and provided a perfect breeze, light enough to lift our kites and our hearts flying way up high above with ease. A number of the young lads had great kite flying skills borne of long passed-down cultural tradition and shared them with a gentle, warm teaching style. The kite flying was a definite project highlight captured superbly by Edwina on film. The generous funding available enabled us to have ample resources, people and time, and the chance to document the project with film and to use the *Culture in Transit* DVD (Wilde, 2010) we produced as a key education tool.

The young people involved thrived humbly in this rare 'rich' atmosphere with warmth, abundance, yet simplicity and ease. They took the unfamiliarity of the whole exhibition thing, and the opening in particular, in their stride. They responded to approaches by council officials, press photographers and the like with delightful raw and polite honesty. The community response was resoundingly strong with invitations to tour the show throughout the municipality as an awareness raising and education tool. We took up the council's invitation to include the show in its current *Moving* Project. This initiative aims to transform derelict vacant shop windows in central Ringwood into works of art to help deter vandalism and maintain safety after dark (*Ringwood Art in Windows* Project). Exhibiting the project's artwork at the onsite Maroondah Art Gallery pushed a few boundaries but worked well in the end. Much of *The Workshop's* success is dependent on willing co-operation, reflexive practice and the creative diplomacy staff foster. It is a bit of a specialty of ours but something we have to keep an eye on or it blows out into over extending ourselves, pushing too much uphill too often.

Better yet, the MIECAT students offered their creative responses to the young people who participated in *Culture in Transit*. They were tickled pink to receive them and I am impressed with the inventive creative generosity of people and their efforts to share and connect.

Victoria

Overleaf: Figure 13 *From migration to integration installation postcard.* Amanda Woodford (2011). Digital photocollage.

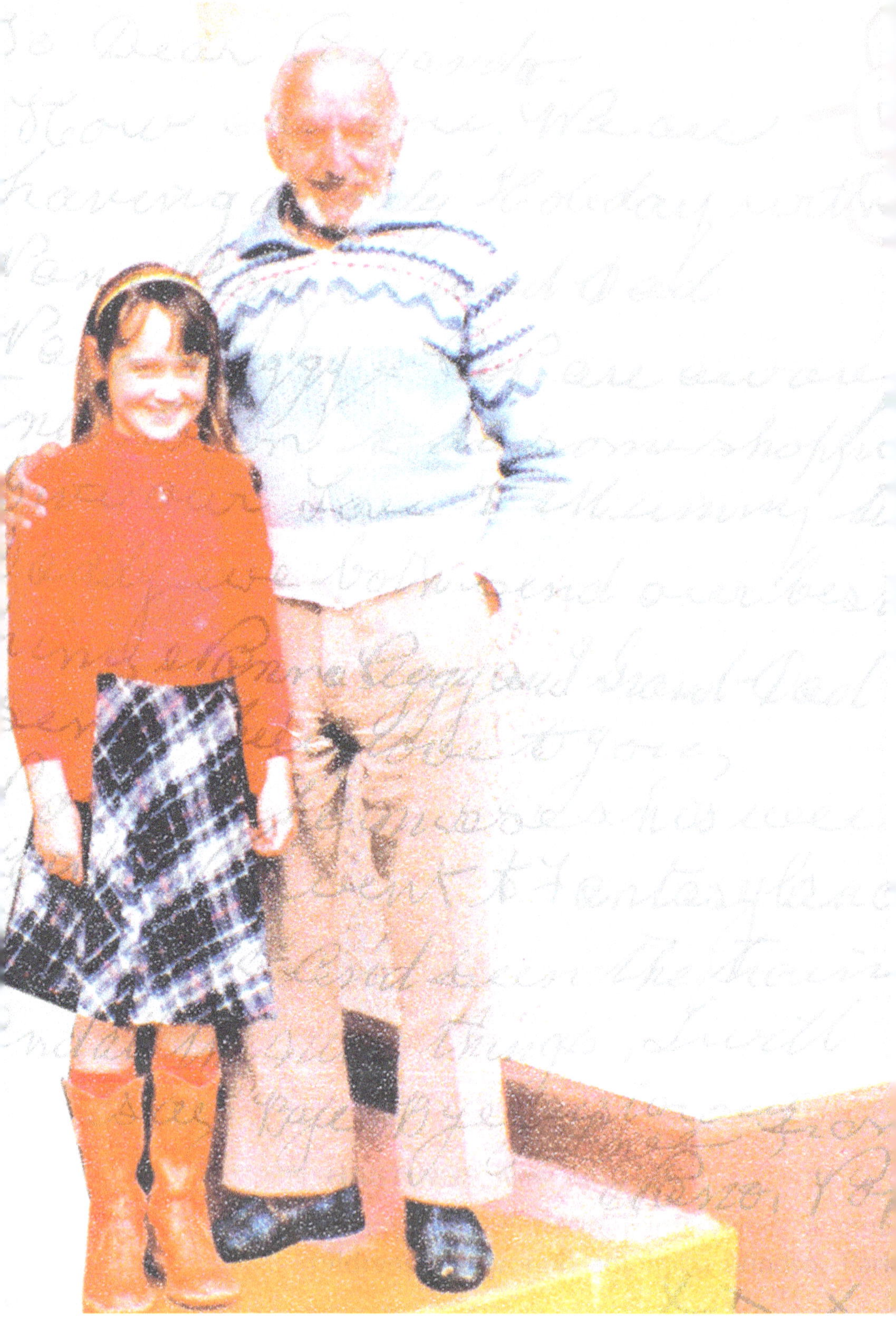

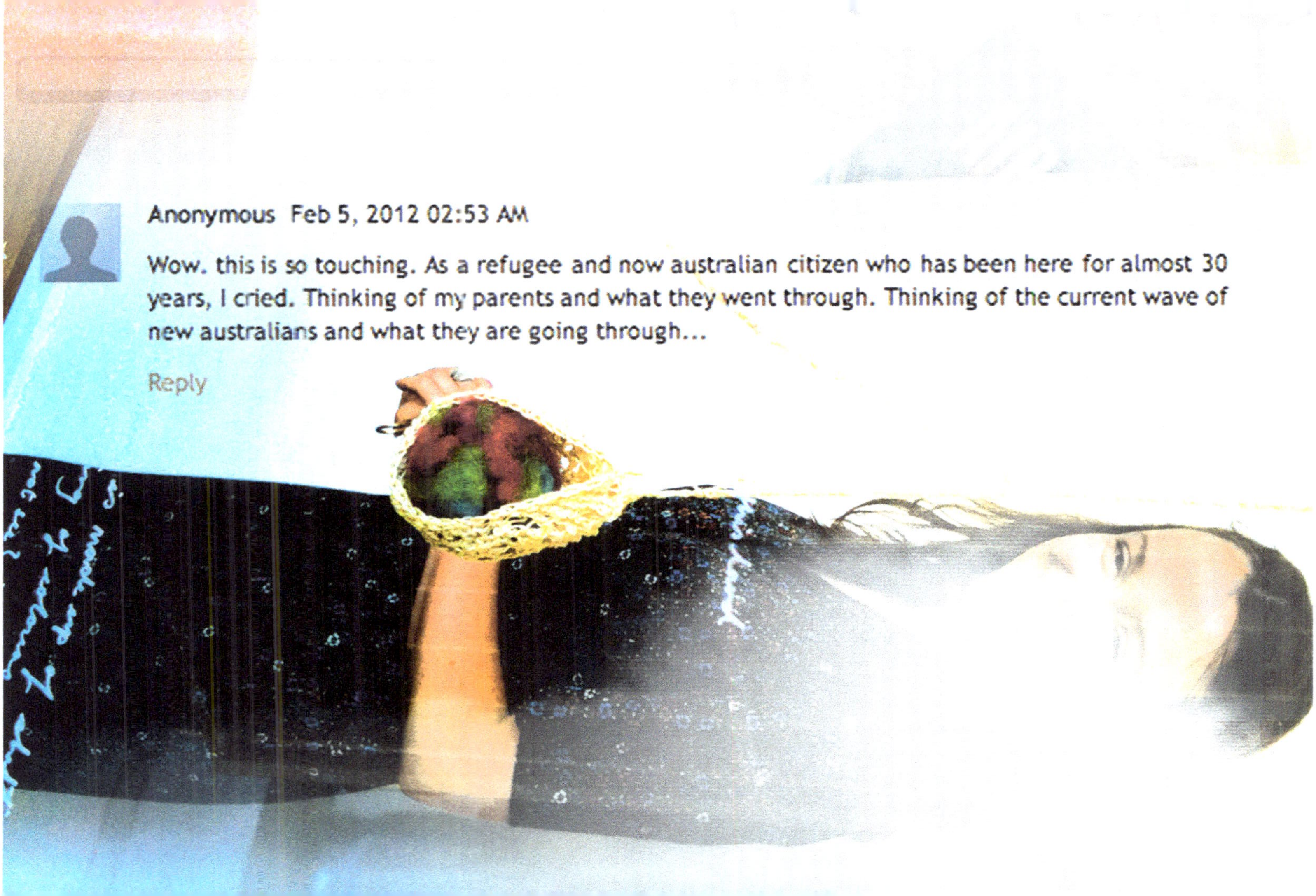
Anonymous Feb 5, 2012 02:53 AM
Wow. this is so touching. As a refugee and now australian citizen who has been here for almost 30 years, I cried. Thinking of my parents and what they went through. Thinking of the current wave of new australians and what they are going through...
Reply

Dear All,
Thank you Jan for the invitation to participate after viewing my recent artwork, *From Migration to Integration* (2011). The crochet silk-thread, wool and poetic installation (partially seen here above to the right, with me at the exhibition) explored ancestral traces in my life-story. I offer a part of my story-thread to this conversation. To the left is an image of myself as a child with my great-grandfather; he was born in Lebanon, migrating to Aotearoa/New Zealand as a small boy. Overlaid is a postcard hand-written by my great-grandmother to me. Her background was rich in Scottish heritage and tradition. My montage of images, capturing moments of time, personal memories and experiences, is in response to the 'boat people' image, at the beginning of your dialogue.

All of my ancestors were 'boat people'. However, in the early 1900s their oceanic passage and acceptance into a colonial landscape was vastly different. Those from the motherland were considered 'desirable' and, sadly, those from Lebanon 'undesirable'. I am left wondering if your image captures 'my desirables' watching 'my undesirables' for the first time? Possibly. I sense an air of fear, distrust and un-sureness between the two, despite both tracing forward to me. These are quite confronting and confusing thoughts, but not unfamiliar. They connect directly to an ongoing search for understanding around my own (cultural) identity and of cultural acceptance in our communities.

To respond further, beyond image, I searched for and found key words and phrases within your postcard conversations that 'connected' with me and grouped them into 'clusters'. Lett (2011) describes the clustering of key words/phrases/images as occurring "on the basis of their sensed connectedness to shared meaning" (279). I had five distinct clusters I could 'pin-down' and one more fluid cluster in the middle. Their physical placement on the page also became important. The first cluster I titled 'the past informs the present', the ancestors, tracings, those present now. Moving on to 'me', a hybrid of identities, overlaps, edges and relationships. To the right, still connected to 'me' but divided with a dotted line, the cluster 'passage of rights' including crossings, difficult passage, negotiations. Sketched arrows link these to 'no man's land', the phrase 'being in place and out of place at the same time' center stage. A place of difficulty, unsure of its position, unclear definitions – a tangled place. Farry (2005) speaks of the shifting nature of identity, as being continually on the move, always under construction. To me this space is where a search for autonomy exists, as the different cultural identities overlap, shift and sometimes jolt like tectonic plates without warning. A solid line separates 'being in place and out of place at the same time' from the words beneath, welcoming/intersect/resist, mending and autonomy.

Below sits the clusters 'art-making' and 'seeping beyond me'. They create a solid base to what has become more like a map, than groupings of words. Reflection, meaning and purpose, support, individual, easy access and tangible, sit within the 'art-making' cluster. Using the arts to explore a personal narrative, in *From Migration to Integration*, as I knotted threads, matted wool and explored poetic verse, I came to know more about my identity as an individual whose ancestral traces reside in both 'colonial and non-colonial camps'. I gained a greater sense of ownership, clarity, and acceptance of the shifts and changes of being 'a part' of cultural differences. I also came to see 'patterns of being' which thrived 100 years ago, actions and behaviour directed at 'difference', shockingly still present today. It is with the last cluster, 'seeping beyond me', new encounters, social inclusion, support, communities, co-operatively, that I hope these patterns can be altered as we tell and listen to our own and others' stories, to define identities and open possibilities, towards greater understanding.

From Migration to Integration, my arts-based, story-thread has moved beyond me, to connect to others. It has nurtured discussions, companioned similar stories – 'that is my story too' – and brought others' stories into awareness. I have included one response emailed to me, which sits on the top layer of my postcard to you, from 'Anonymous' (2012) who comments:

> Wow. This is so touching. As a refugee and now Australian citizen who has been here for almost 30 years, I cried. Thinking of my parents and what they went through. Thinking of the current wave of new Australians and what they are going through…

Safe travels.
Amanda

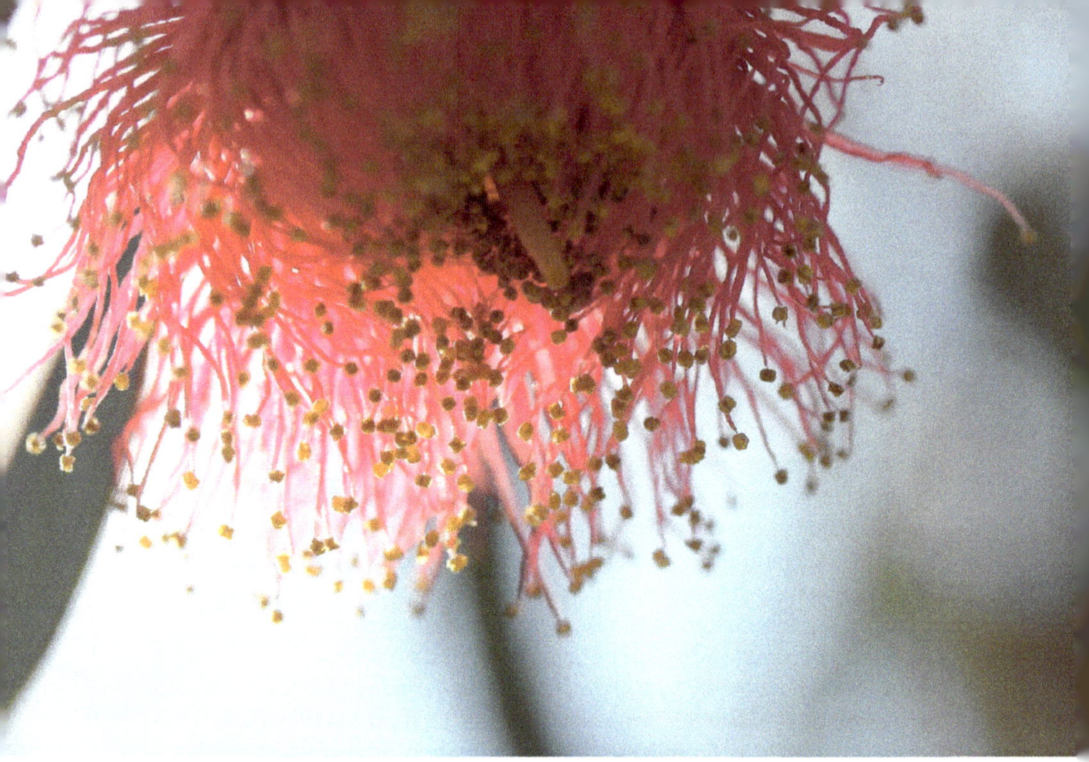

Figure 14 *Eucalyptus Caesia postcard*. Jean Rumbold (2011). Digital photograph.

Dear Jan, Lilian and Victoria,
This is the image I am choosing to bring my part in this postcard conversation to a close – a eucalyptus caesia blossom recently taking its turn in our garden. There is something here to me of the energy and warmth I see in the work you three and Janine do. This tree is nearly falling over our neighbour's fence, but the gum blossoms dance in the wind. John Heron and Peter Reason (1997) think all our work, even research, should serve human flourishing. Others prefer to speak of human thriving. This photo makes me think about flourishing even in harsh environments, and about the idea of resilience as challenged thriving (Ryff and Singer, 2003). The art-making you facilitate for children and adults in difficult places offers individuals the autonomy of creating and the social inclusion of joining group projects. That seems to me to promote resilience, understood as individual agency, but also I think can contribute structurally to more resilient communities (Norris, Stevens, Pfefferbaum, Wyche and Pfefferbaum, 2008). Since materials and places seem particularly important for art therapists (Fenner, 2010), perhaps it is no surprise that as creative art therapists you naturally help to create healthy settings?

Jan, it seems that in taking a turn in this conversation with some art therapy practitioners, we have found ourselves welcoming new aesthetic inputs, as well as hearing from people working with those most affected by the wash up from our world's colonial pasts. I want to finish by saying to you all that 'what you are doing matters!'
Jean

Amanda, Jean, Lilian, Victoria,
I have collaged a final card reproduced twice, to bring this postcard exchange to a close. From Jean and I, to all of you as arts therapists, and/or arts practitioners, thanks for participating in our conversations and bringing your practitioner voices to our dialogue.

My final image began with a gathering of bits and pieces of magazine cut outs collaged together and then filtered and photographed differently in each case through my iPhone apps. The paper cut outs were a direct response to your postcard Amanda, the process of filtering and layering and changing orientation more to do with exploring the ideas of how we are placed, the lenses through which we view the world and construct our ideas and theories and how these change the 'original' so much and at the same time are differently evocative.

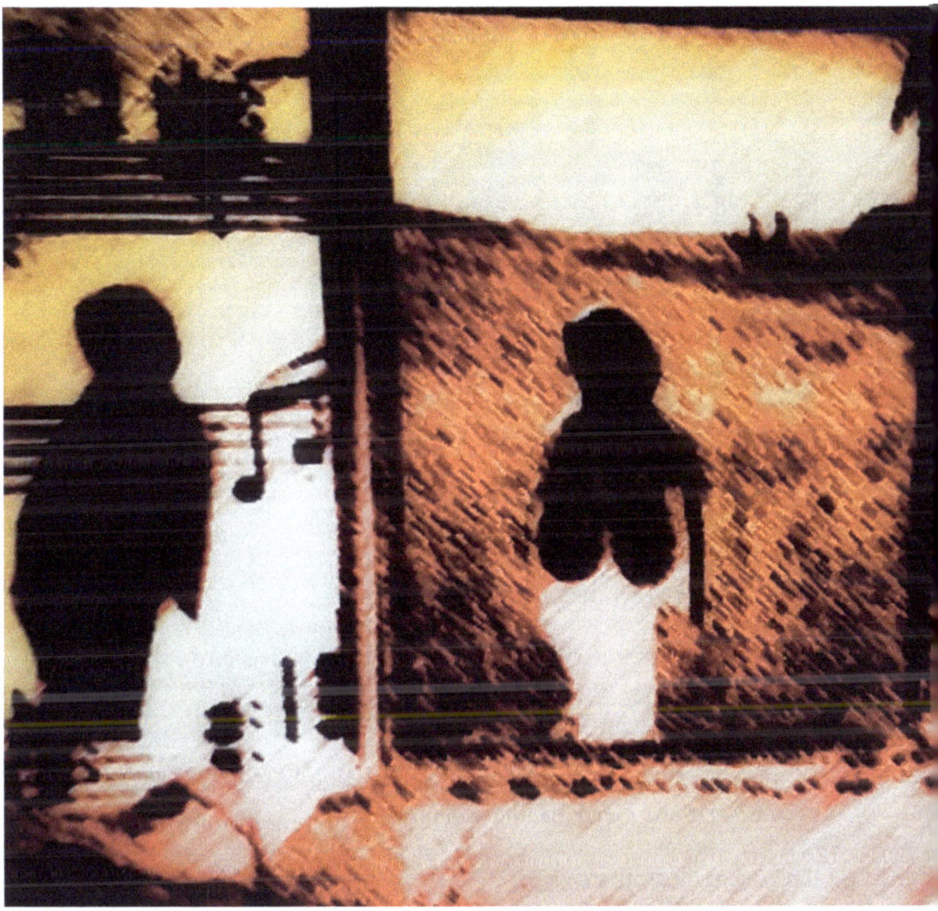

Figure 15 *Untitled postcard 1*. Jan Allen (2011). Digital photocollage.

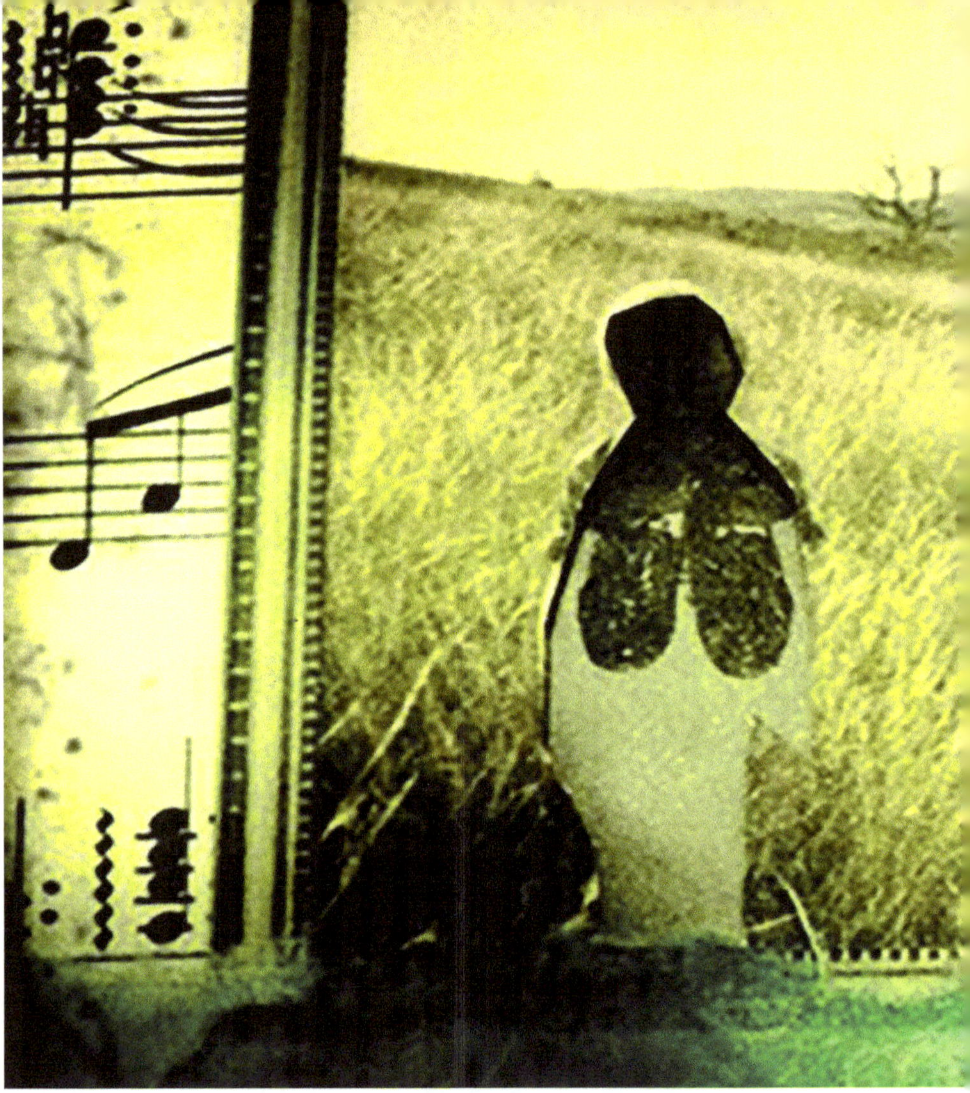

This version shows the young boy leaning towards, but outside the frame. He was cut out from this place and replaced by the feet of another figure. The boy's features are obscured, as he stands in a somewhat brooding landscape that I think would texture his world so differently from the wheat fields inside the frame. The feet that stand in the place of the figure of the boy appear here to be those of a man; I imagine the man in a dark suit with an umbrella on his way to the office.

Through this lens the boy's features are visible and he smiles. The filter evokes hope and nostalgia; the feet of the man no longer seem to be the feet of a businessman but those of an older, less well dressed man (white sox aren't the go in the corporate world!). I am reminded of the sepia photographs taken as the European immigrants disembarked at Station Pier in Melbourne in the 1950s, and of family slide shows we all sat through, feigning interest in all the photos that weren't of us kids, and laughing at those that were.

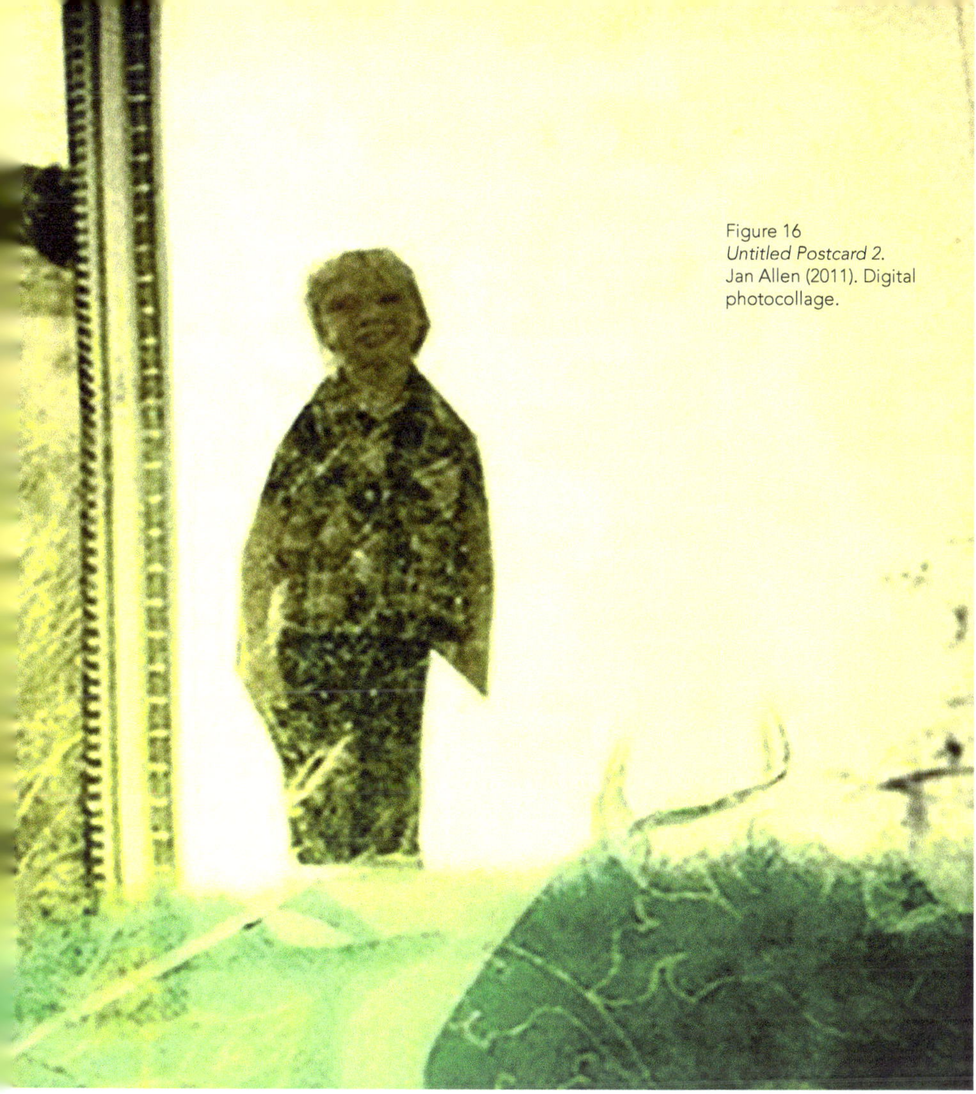

Figure 16
Untitled Postcard 2.
Jan Allen (2011). Digital photocollage.

In both versions of my photographed collage place, where we are placed – inside or outside the frame – and how we are oriented to the otherness appears really important. All this seems to be about relationship; ours to each other and to the material world.

I will finish this conversation with words from Kenneth Gergen (2009: 391–5) who writes:

> [r]elations between groups – religious, political, tribal, ethnic have bought untold misery in the history of civilisation, and the future hangs in the balance…Dialogic practices that restore the flow of productive meaning are vitally needed. Similarly honored are practices that bring humans and their environment together into a mutually sustainable world.

References

Allen, J and Rumbold, J. (2004). Postcard conversations: a dialogue about methodology, Qualitative Research Journal, *4* (4): 100–142.

Anonymous. (2012, February 5). Re: Holding spaces [Web log message]. Retrieved from http://www.amanda-creativearts.com/p/holding-spaces_07.html.

Baum, F. and Harris, L. (2006). Equity and the social determinants of health. *Health Promotion Journal of Australia, 17* (3): 163–165.

Bhabha, H.K. (1998). Culture's in between. In: Bennett, D. (Ed.) *Multicultural states: rethinking difference and identity.* Routledge, London.

Culture in Transit DVD. (2010) k.wilde@theworkshop.id.au

Farry (Fakhry), M. (2005). Shifting identities among second and third generation Lebanese living in Aotearoa/New Zealand. In: Tabar, P. (Ed.) (2005). *Lebanese diaspora: history, racism and belonging.* Chamas, Beirut.

Fenner, P. (2011) Place, matter and meaning: extending the relationship in psychological therapies, *Health and place,* 17(3): 851–857.

Gelder, K. and Jacobs, J.M. (1998). *Uncanny Australia: sacredness and identity in a postcolonial nation.* Melbourne University Press, Melbourne, Victoria.

Gergen, K. (2009*). Relational being: beyond self and community.* Oxford University Press, New York.

Heron, J and Reason, P. (1997). A participatory inquiry paradigm. *Qualitative Inquiry, 3* (3): 274–294.

Hooley, G. (2002). Two-way enquiry learning: exploring the interface between Indigenous and non-Indigenous knowing. Victoria Institute of Technology, Melbourne, Victoria.

Ife, J. (2003, April). People, place, partnerships. Keynote address presented at the Strengthening Communities Conference, Sydney, Australia.

Kickbusch, I. (1997). Health-promoting environments: the next steps. *Australian and New Zealand Journal of Public Health, 21* (4): 431–434.

Lett, W. (2011). An inquiry into making sense of our lives. Rebus Press, Eltham, VIC.

Norris, F.H., Stevens, S.P., Pfefferbaum, B., Wyche, K.F. and Pfefferbaum, R.L. (2008). Community resilience as a metaphor, theory, set of capacities, and strategy for disaster readiness. *American Journal of Community Psychology,* 41: 127–150.

Ringwood Art in Windows Project. http://www.alexmakin.com.au/2009/08/ringwood-art-in-windows-project/

Rumbold, J., Allen, J., Alexander, L. and van Laar, C. (2008). Knowing together differently: intersubjective responding. In: Liamputtong, P. and Rumbold, J. (Eds.) (2008). *Knowing differently: arts-based and collaborative research.* Nova Science, New York.

Ryff, C. and Singer, B. (2003). Flourishing under fire: resilience as a prototype of challenged thriving. In: Keynes, C. and Haidt, J. (Eds.) (2003) *Flourishing: positive psychology and the life well-lived.* American Psychological Association, Washington, DC.

Tascón, S. M. (2002). Refugees and asylum-seekers in Australia: border-crossers of the postcolonical imaginary. No 21, May. http://www.arts.uwa.edu.au/MotsPluriels/MP2102smt.html

Von der Borch, D. (2011). Memory needs a place to rest. Unpublished MA thesis, MIECAT, Melbourne.

Willems-Braun, B. (1997). Buried epistemologies: the politics of nature in (post) colonial British Columbia. *Annals – Association of American Geographers.* 87(1): 3-31.

Winnicott, D. (1971). *Playing and reality.* Tavistock Publications, London.

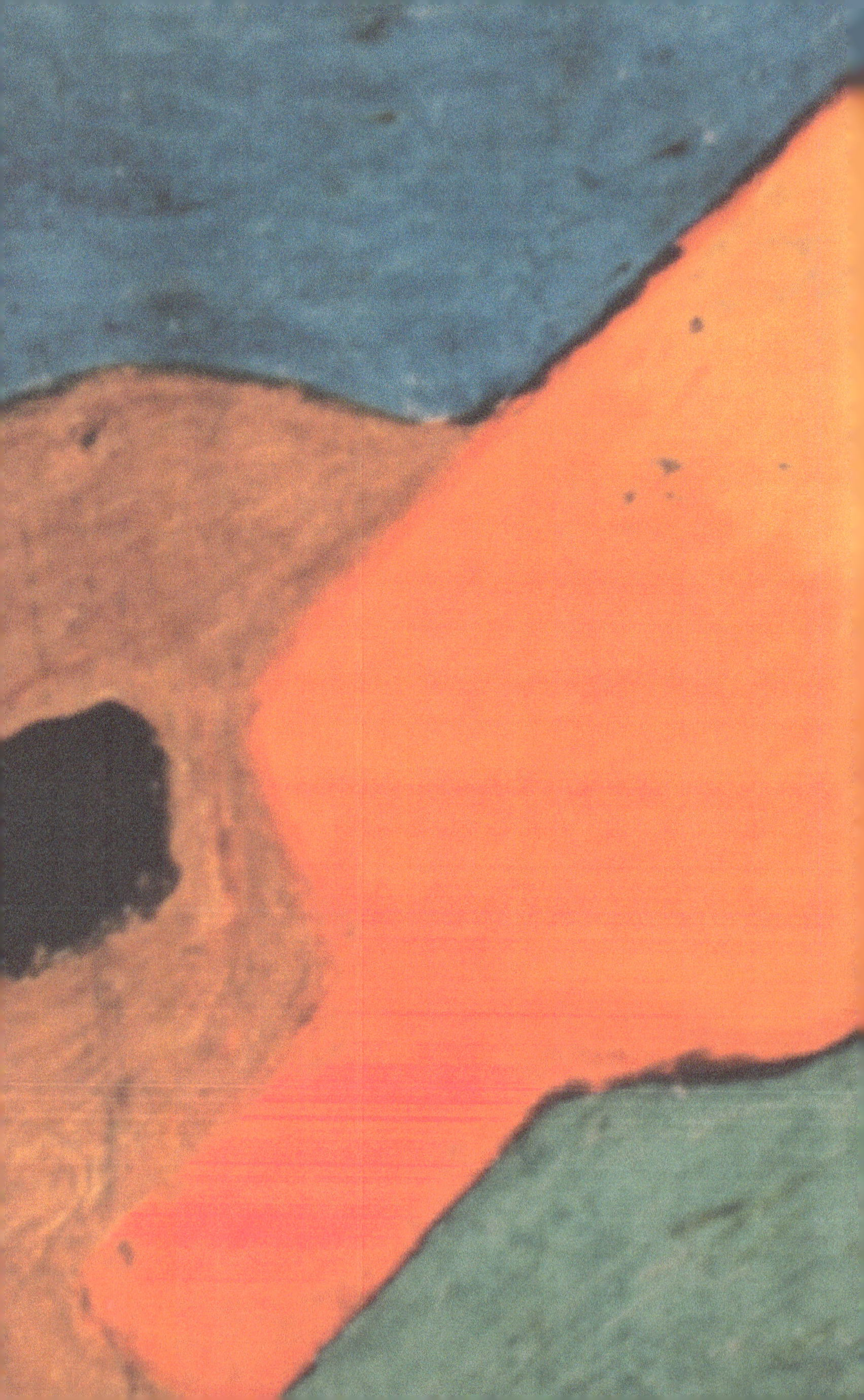

2

TOWARDS INDIGENOUS AUSTRALIAN KNOWING

Carmen Lawson, Davina Woods, Tarquam McKenna

 | DOI:10.1163/9789004368262_003

The Aboriginal flag was designed in 1971 by Harold Thomas, an artist and an Aboriginal. The flag was designed to be an eye-catching, rallying symbol for the Aboriginal people and a symbol of their race and identity. The black represents the Aboriginal people, the red the earth and their spiritual relationship to the land, and the yellow the sun, the giver of life.

In the late 1960s, Aborigines stepped up their campaign for First Peoples of Australia land rights through protest marches, demonstrations, banners and posters. The protests increased in the early 1970s. Harold Thomas noticed they were often outnumbered by non-Aborigines with their own banners and placards. He decided they needed to be more visible and the idea of the flag was born.

The Aboriginal flag was first raised in Victoria Square in Adelaide on National Aboriginal Day in 1971 but was adopted nationally by Aborigines and Torres Strait Islanders in 1972, after it was flown above the Aboriginal 'Tent Embassy' outside of the old Parliament House in Canberra.

Mr Thomas has often been asked to design a new Australian flag but he says the design of the Aboriginal flag 'sprung from passionate times' and that his inspiration could not necessarily 'be repeated' for a new Australian flag. Mr Thomas says he would prefer to see something different for a new Australian flag.

Mr Thomas is also uneasy about suggestions that the Aboriginal Flag could replace the Union Jack in the current Australian flag to create a new national flag. Mr Thomas says: 'Our flag is not a secondary thing. It stands on its own, not to be placed as an adjunct to any other thing. It shouldn't be treated that way'.

The Aboriginal flag is increasingly being flown by both Aboriginal and non-Aboriginal people. In view of its increasing importance in Australian society, the Government initiated steps in 1994 to give the flag legal recognition. After a period of public consultation, the Government made its own decision in July 1995 that the flag should be proclaimed a 'Flag of Australia' under section 5 of the Flags Act 1953. The flag was so proclaimed by the Governor General of Australia, William Hayden, on 14 July 1995 (http://www.ausflag.com.au/aboriginal_flag.asp).

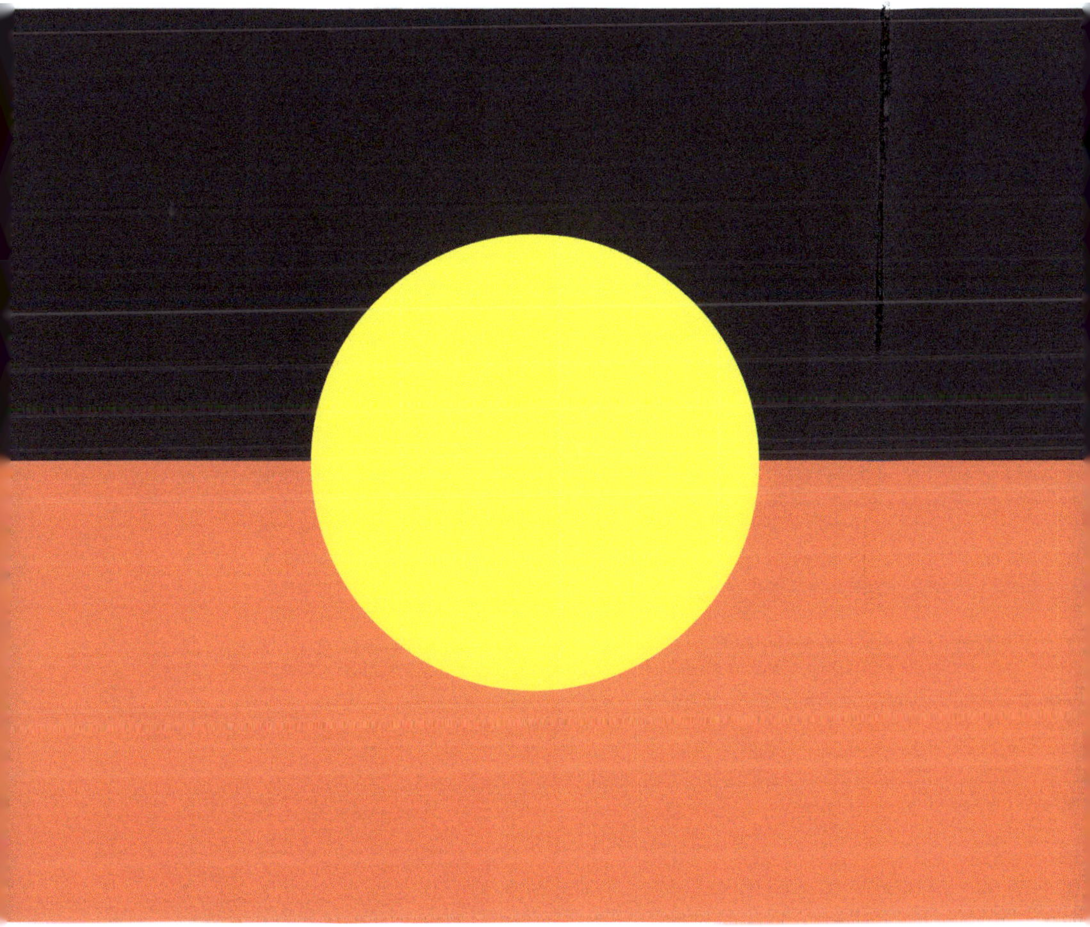

Figure 1 *Australian Aboriginal flag*, Harold Thomas (1971)

Artists, writers and performers should desist from unauthorised incorporation of Indigenous heritage in their works. Instead they should support the artistic and cultural development of Indigenous peoples and participate in public awareness campaigns to promote Indigenous art and culture.

Joseph Wambugu Githhaiga, 1998

The Australian Aborigines speak of jiva or guruwari, a "seed power" deposited in the earth. In the Aboriginal world view, every meaningful activity, event, or life process that occurs at a particular place leaves behind a vibrational residue in the earth, as plants leave an image of themselves as seeds. The shape of the land – its mountains, rocks, riverbeds, and waterholes – and its unseen vibrations echo the events that brought that place into creation. Everything in the natural world is a symbolic footprint of the metaphysical beings whose actions created our world. As with a seed, the potency of an earthly location is wedded to the memory of its origin. The Aborigines called this potency the "Dreaming" of a place, and this Dreaming constitutes the sacredness of the earth. Only in extraordinary states of consciousness can one be aware of, or attuned to, the inner dreaming of the earth.

Robert Lawlor, 1991: 112–114

There is information that is restricted, that our children cannot learn about, there is information that is restricted even to adults, there is information that is of a secret or sacred nature that many people have no knowledge of or access to. That knowledge is only there for certain people to have access to.

Gularrwuy Yunupingu, 2003, cited in Graham, Mason and Nayling, 2013: 107

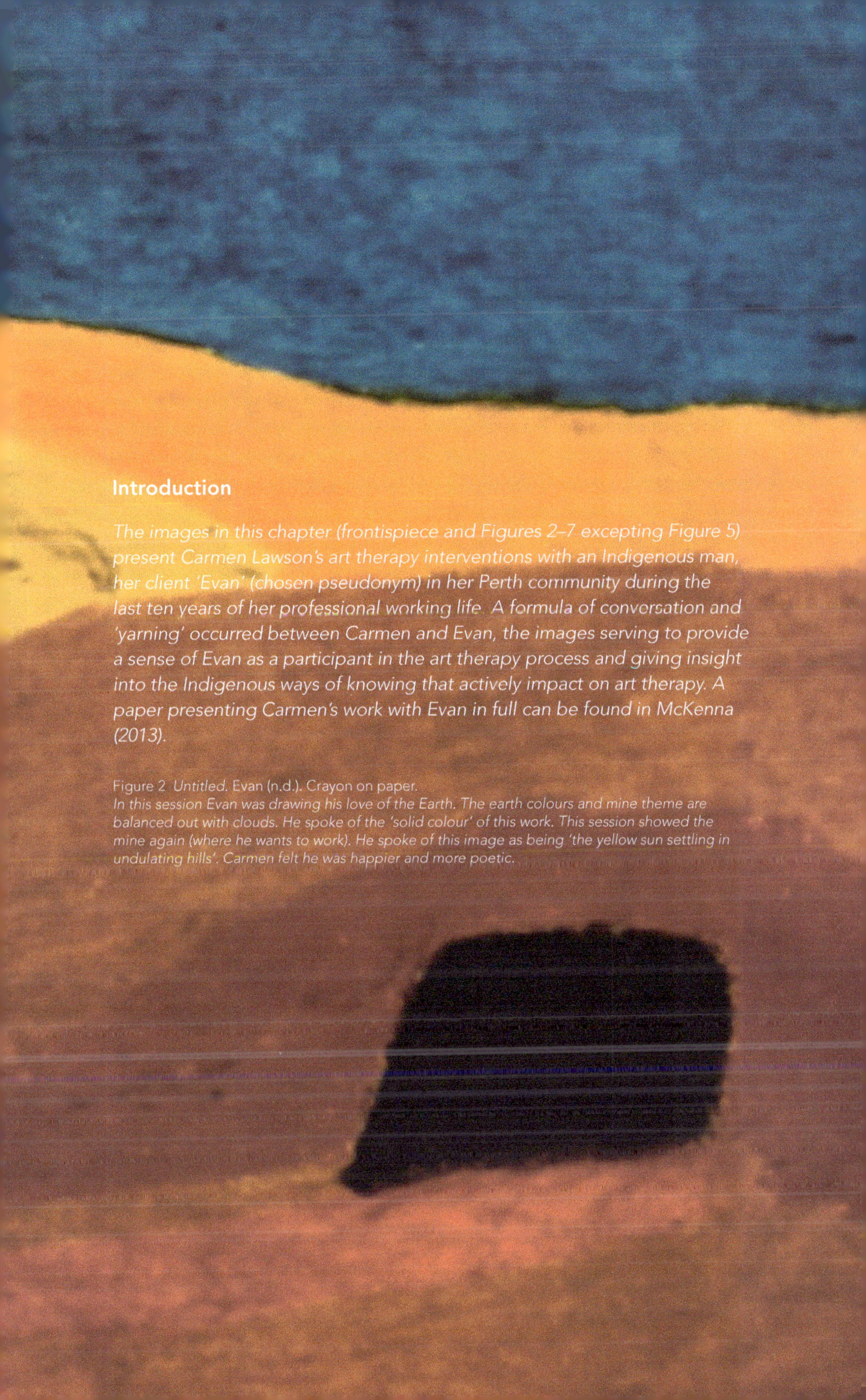

Introduction

The images in this chapter (frontispiece and Figures 2–7 excepting Figure 5) present Carmen Lawson's art therapy interventions with an Indigenous man, her client 'Evan' (chosen pseudonym) in her Perth community during the last ten years of her professional working life. A formula of conversation and 'yarning' occurred between Carmen and Evan, the images serving to provide a sense of Evan as a participant in the art therapy process and giving insight into the Indigenous ways of knowing that actively impact on art therapy. A paper presenting Carmen's work with Evan in full can be found in McKenna (2013).

Figure 2 *Untitled*. Evan (n.d.). Crayon on paper.
In this session Evan was drawing his love of the Earth. The earth colours and mine theme are balanced out with clouds. He spoke of the 'solid colour' of this work. This session showed the mine again (where he wants to work). He spoke of this image as being 'the yellow sun settling in undulating hills'. Carmen felt he was happier and more poetic.

For millennia, the First Peoples of Australia have passed on their Indigenous laws through lore and knowledge acquired through experience and historical anecdotes passed on through stories. Living in twenty-first-century Australia, the lore, with its various levels of complexity and significance, is synonymous with 'yarns'. These may range from a simple tale of an everyday incident retold for humorous reasons or the sharing of intimate details of life. Yarning, the act of sharing stories, keeps culture and collective memory alive and, at the same time, allows space for the inclusion of new stories, new yarns to build the database of collective knowledge. Our chapter is a shared story, a yarn that weaves together the thoughts of three people considering the way art heals, particularly art therapy. Working in a variety of arts-based practices, we, the authors, offer a series of insights as speculations on the meaning of art and therapies in the lives of the First Peoples of Australia, particularly focussed on their emotional and social wellbeing.[1]

Background

Carmen Lawson is a qualified Art Therapist and Counsellor. She completed her Master of Arts in Art Therapy at Edith Cowan University in Perth, Western Australia. Davina is the descendent of a Murri baby stolen from the area of the Kuku-Yalanji/Kuku-Djungan peoples of the Atherton Tablelands in far north Queensland. She has lived on Kulin country, Melbourne, Victoria for over twenty years and worked at Victoria University as a lecturer in the College of Education. A Professor at Deakin University, Melbourne, Tarquam McKenna is a teacher and art psychotherapist. Tarquam's own interest in the history of his family's Indigeneity is his personal life-search. This is informed by the belief that his mother's people may have travelled from Victoria or have been Pallawah, the First Peoples of Tasmania, Australia's island state.

Tarquam and Carmen met through the Masters of Arts training in Art Therapy, which Carmen completed at Edith Cowan University, beginning in early 2000. Tarquam was her supervisor. Davina approached Tarquam to supervise her PhD focused on yarning, connecting and self-healing. Based on Tarquam's past work as a researcher in 'evocative' ethnographies, Davina chose him to work with her on her inter-textual autoethnographic study. Autoethnography was chosen as a decolonising research method.

The three quotes opening this chapter illustrate that there are issues of inappropriate use and understanding of Indigenous art among Non-First Peoples of Australia. This brings to the fore the fact that sacredness is central to all of the First Peoples of Australia's art-making processes; this is also the case for their art therapy and art that heals. Carmen and Tarquam met together once a week for nearly two years and in that time, several themes emerged around decolonisation and the use of art therapy for the First Peoples of Australia. Over several years, they shared stories of new births, with grandchildren, and of loss and grief.

1 'Social and emotional well-being' is the phrase preferred by the First Peoples of Australia when referring to what is generally known as 'mental health'.

Whilst now retired as an art therapist, Carmen endorsed the writing of this chapter and welcomed the opportunity to co-author the work in order to reflect on our shared ideas and values. Carmen's words interweave throughout the chapter. Together Davina and Tarquam have engaged with other First Peoples of Australia and 'critical' friends have assisted in the construction of the work. Importantly, the authors highlight the fact that the chapter is generalist. It is not an overarching perspective of knowledge that is relevant to all First Peoples of Australia. Quite the contrary. The chapter is woven around relationships, connecting, disclosure and intimacies of encounter as expressed through three people's perceptions of yarning and the arts. Each author has their own epistemological and ontological understanding of life as First Peoples of Australia.

All three authors have witnessed how the political and cultural movement called 'Australia' continues to grow. While Australia expands, only occasionally are the issues of representation, power, and control critiqued from the perspective of Australia's First Peoples. These Indigenous Peoples are those descended from the colonised original inhabitants of the continent and nearby islands known since 1901 as Australia. The lack of critique is not because Australia's First Peoples fail to comment on the performance of those who have authority. Ignored, silenced and suppressed, only those who have always listened and are prepared to continue to hear our comments ultimately matter in this conversation. An objective of this chapter is to bring the voices of the First Peoples of Australia to a wider audience by yarning loud and clear around wellbeing.

Healing

In some sense an ethnographic work, our chapter gives power to the voice, particularly the voices of Australia's First Peoples, with powerful descriptions of healing. The descriptions include the emerging sense of the

> *vulnerable selves, emotions, bodies, and spirits; (that) produces evocative stories that create the effect of reality; celebrates concrete experiences and intimate detail; examines how human experience is endowed with meaning; is concerned with moral, ethical, and political consequences; encourages compassion and empathy; helps us to know how to live and cope; features multiple voices and repositions readers and "subjects" as co-participants in dialogue ...*
>
> Ellis, 1999: 17

In our roles as therapists and educators and through our research, we have engaged with, listened to and expressed the voices of the First Peoples of Australia. Reflected in our chapter are the yarns and the process of yarning that became the basis for Carmen's therapeutic supervision work. We hold to the idea that yarning is the act of reflecting and revisioning the past and the future, which may be simultaneously conducted. For there is no end, there is no beginning, there is only being, the never-ending spiral of being.

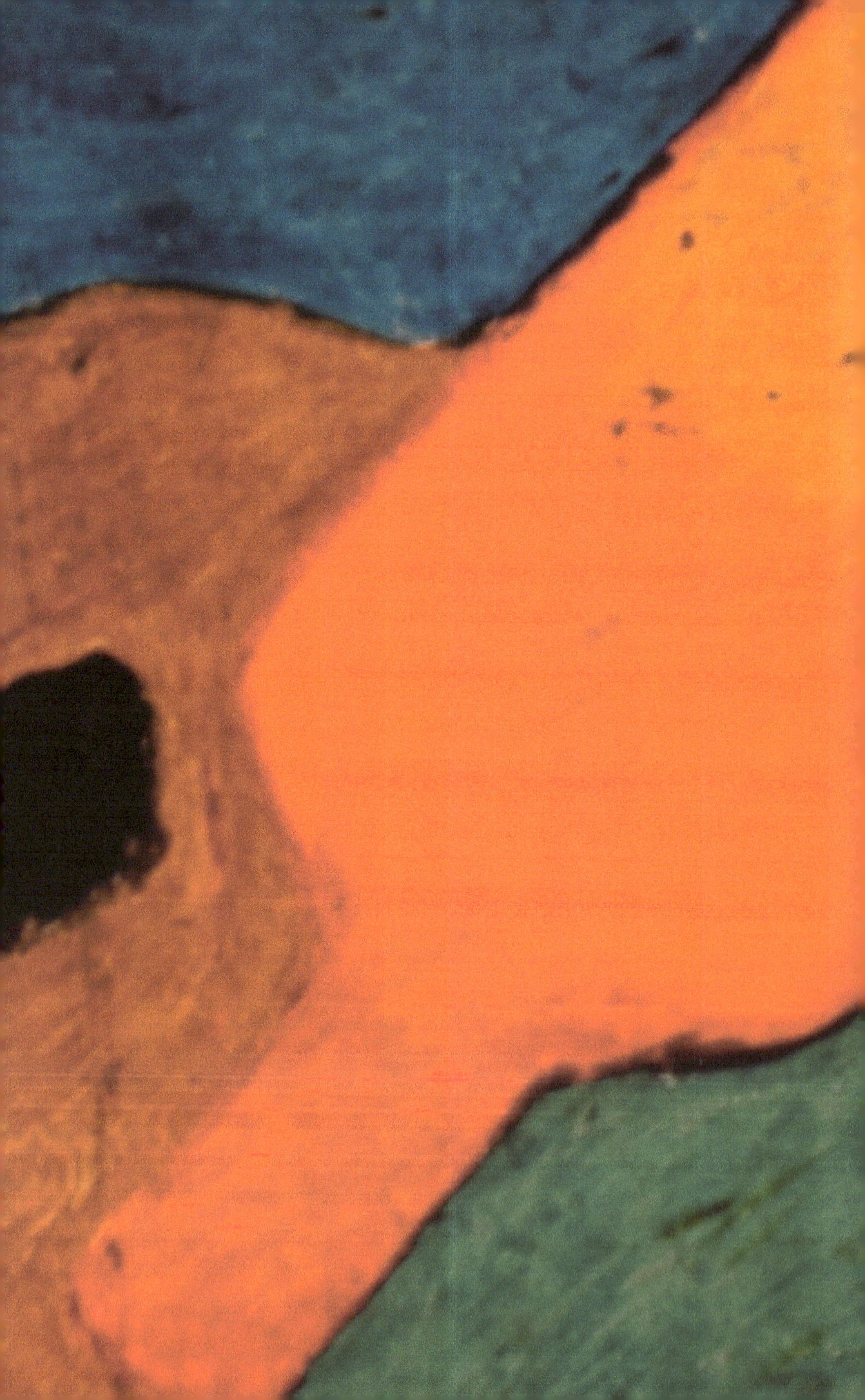

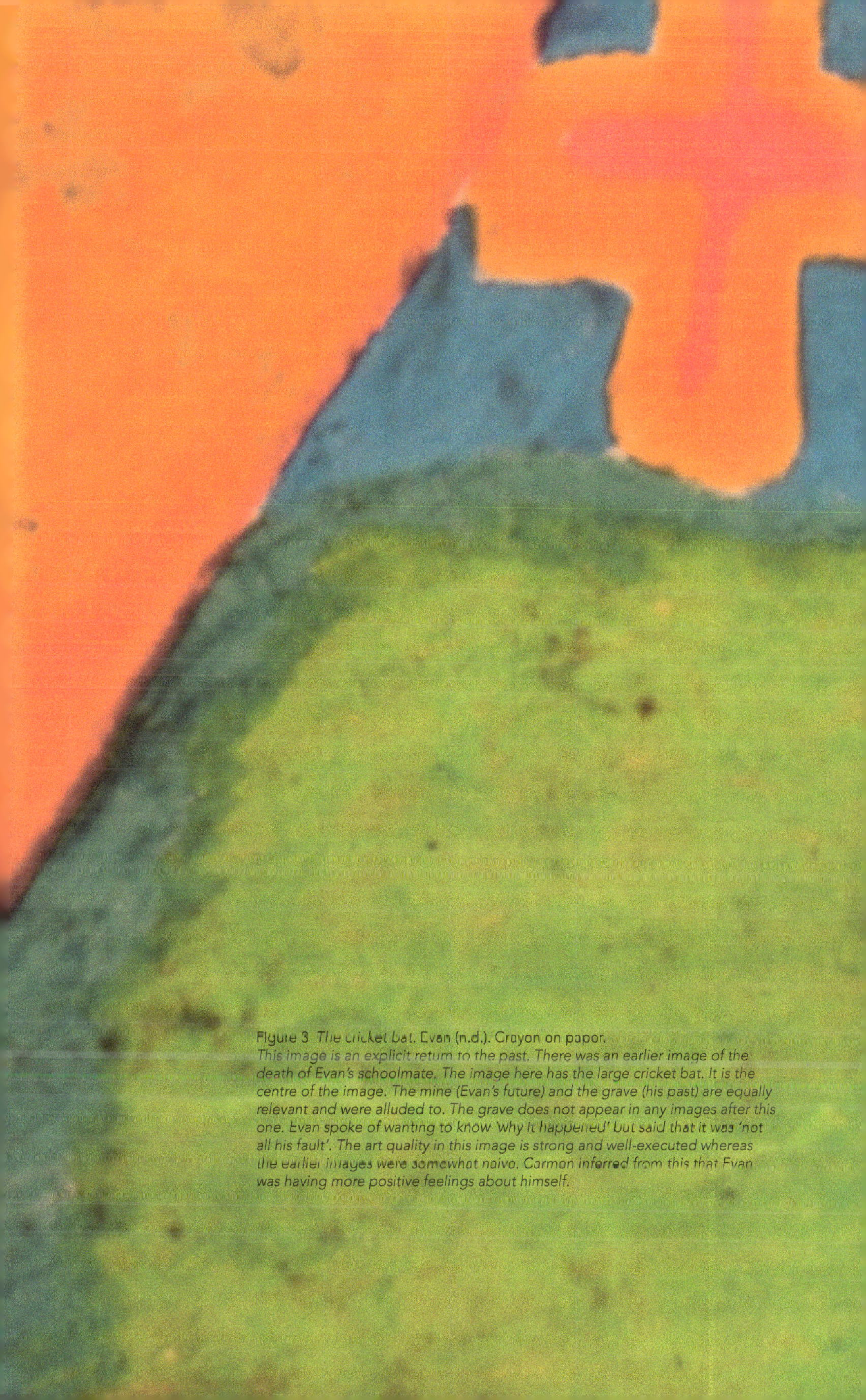

Figure 3 *The cricket bat*. Evan (n.d.). Crayon on paper.
This image is an explicit return to the past. There was an earlier image of the death of Evan's schoolmate. The image here has the large cricket bat. It is the centre of the image. The mine (Evan's future) and the grave (his past) are equally relevant and were alluded to. The grave does not appear in any images after this one. Evan spoke of wanting to know 'why it happened' but said that it was 'not all his fault'. The art quality in this image is strong and well-executed whereas the earlier images were somewhat naive. Carmon inferred from this that Evan was having more positive feelings about himself.

Largely neglected on a global scale, the social and emotional wellbeing of the First Peoples of Australia has only recently been identified as a matter of serious concern for both Australia's First Peoples and Non-First Peoples (the descendants of the colonisers and the newly-arrived alike). Often the stigma attached to illness and the many cultural misunderstandings still prevail for both Non-First Peoples of Australia and Australia's First Peoples when considering mental health and social and emotional wellbeing. Rarely considered, relegated to the edge of deliberations on approaches to social and emotional wellbeing healing for the First Peoples of Australia, the lack of access to art therapy perpetuates the legacy of past failures in social and emotional well-being engagement for both Non-First Peoples of Australia and Australia's First Peoples. The field of art therapy is still a fringe therapy.

Holism – creative approaches that afford recognition

As art therapy advocates, our work emphasises the need for cultural appropriateness in services that in the past may have not respectfully acknowledged Australia's First Peoples' notions of wellness. We hold to the ideals that the impact of loss and separation (often traumatic) affects strongly the health needs of Australia's First Peoples. Yet, the physical, social, and emotional impact of dispossession and displacement from country, culture and community on Australia's First Peoples has yet to be addressed adequately. In addition, the role of art therapies and creative arts in this area is not well understood by many mental health and social and emotional wellbeing managers and other allied health workers in Australia. Engagement in holistic arts-based practice in western medicine is often conflicted. In our chapter, we present art therapy as a form of psychotherapy that addresses the mental, spiritual, psychical and emotional needs of an individual, their family and their community. We emphasise that social and emotional wellbeing and physical health cannot be separated from the spiritual sense of the person.

The sense of holistic, collaborative and community arts practice that we propose addresses cultural identity, feelings of hopelessness, unhappiness and powerlessness. Davina notes later in the chapter that the majority of the First Peoples of Australia now live in city suburbs; that said, there are art therapist workforce shortages in Australia's First Peoples communities with art therapy and social and emotional well-being services still inadequately funded. Part of the challenge is that art therapies and art practice are specific workplace roles that perhaps are viewed by other health working professions as 'less valid' as a way to redress the spiritual, social and emotional needs of Australia's First Peoples. In Australia, there is still a resistance to the recognition of art therapy. Afforded limited recognition of their workplace roles, a lack of career development and professional opportunities along with a lack of recognition of art therapists' value and skills by other health professionals leads to limited funding for art therapists in the First People's community. Art therapies can and should be used 'outside' the regular clinical context of client-therapist to address Indigenous cultural, familial and social issues.

Australia's First Peoples' Elders who work as healers are utilising a unique epistemology that deals with the spiritual, emotional and social wellbeing issues of individuals and communities in their local contexts. The publication from Queensland, *Protocols for the Delivery of Social and Emotional Wellbeing and Mental Health Services in Indigenous Australia Communities* articulates clearly the significance of traditional healing. Traditional ways of knowing bring meaning which is a 'source of guidance, strength, comfort, particularly in times of illness' (Haswell, 2009: 34).

The role and knowledge of the First Peoples of Australia's healers, prevalent prior to colonisation, still exists today. These traditional healers are known by many names, but while we respectfully acknowledge these people it is not the purpose of this paper to name all varieties of healers. Haswell writes of *Ngangkari*, a term used mainly in central Australia, as healers who are able to 'capture negative energy inside the body and expel it, mostly by using the mouth, hands and breath.' These women and men can also 'touch the spirit of people who are sad and depressed, or feeling not quite themselves. They might be feeling a displacement of their spirit, or believe that their spirit is missing. These traditional healers can locate a lost spirit or reposition dislocated spirits making a person feel whole again.' Ngangkari work in ways and at levels that 'other healing providers cannot' with the law for all Ngangkari having its origins in 'the Dreamtime and they have practiced their healing powers ever since. For centuries, Indigenous people have consulted traditional healers, including the Ngangkari, for their ancient healing treatments. They are considered to be doctors, in much the same way that mainstream society views medical practitioners' (Haswell, 2009: 36).

Colonisation, dreaming, citizenship and the power of art

At the time of first contact between the First Peoples of Australia and the colonisers, differences in views and values and ontological clashes arising from differing epistemologies prompted not only physical violence but also psychological violence. The technology that enabled the colonisers to win governance over the First Peoples of Australia did not leave space for understanding or acceptance of the principles and worth of the Dreamtime and the Dreaming. This centres on the ongoing spirituality and philosophy of existence that began in the Dreamtime when the Ancestral Beings created the world and the country of each group of First Peoples. Colonialism tried unsuccessfully to replace all belief in the Dreaming with belief in Christianity.

Dreaming in our chapter is the translation of the word *alcheringa* from *Arunta/Aranda* (Stanner, 2009: 57, cited in Martin, 2010), a Central Australian language. We acknowledge that Australia's First Peoples share concepts that are similar but slightly different in specific translation. For example, alcheringa is more commonly known than *bulurru*, the Far North Queensland *Djabugay* word, which translates into Story-Time – the time of the world's making (Bottoms, 1999: 1). Another example is the translation from *Pitjantjatjara* and *Yankunytjatjara* of *tjukurpa* (Eickelkamp, 1999: 88) into the Dreaming, enlivened through the retelling of stories via the arts. In this concept, ceremony is important as both a process of reflection and a series of lessons for life. In our work, the foundation principles that keep the Dreaming, the Story-Time alive, is lore. We equate this to the art practice of storytelling or yarning, which we deliberate on in our work.

Although for us yarning includes story sharing via the arts, it traditionally uses language and voice. However, another signifier of colonialism has been the silencing of Australia's First Peoples' voices (Nabobo-Baba, 2004: 17; Ashcroft, Griffiths and Tiffin, 1998: 175; Stanner, 2009: 182, cited in Martin, 2010) and language – 'the political condition of colonized people is bound up with language' (Ashcroft, Griffiths and Tiffin, 1998: 83). The taking of 'Aboriginal languages away from Aboriginal peoples in the name of a process toward a universal English language [being] the initial step' (Battiste, 2000: 264), when accompanied by restrictions on access to the learning of English, produced silence.

Baldwin states that 'Story told to inform – inspire – activate -... [as] an act of citizenship ... [which] invite[s] the listener or reader to reflect and act' (Baldwin, 2005: 226) acknowledges story as a process of reflection and something experienced not just through reading but also through speaking and listening (ibid: 222). Terszak argues that 'Yarning and the engagement in story in therapy is the way oral-based cultures use stories and conversations as a process of making meaning, communicating and passing on history and knowledge ... relating and connecting' (Terszak 2002: 90). Yarns and the process of yarning for us incorporate what Judy Atkinson recognises as *dadirri*, meaning 'inner deep listening and quiet still awareness' (Atkinson, 2002: ix). An individual needs dadirri to be able 'to reflect and act' (Baldwin, 2005: 226). It is only after achieving the listening and awareness of dadirri that we know to which stories and yarns to attend.

Storytelling, yarning and story writing are forms of the arts; the therapeutic engagement of story is central to the First Peoples of Australia and the work of educators and therapists alike. When working with Carmen and her communities, multiple arts approaches were used. The use of song, dance, story and visual images intersect to make meaning. Women of the First Peoples of Australia who live in Central Australia from Ernabella use 'Textile art ... which reflects the common artistic experiences of Aboriginal and non-Aboriginal ... while at the same time allowing for the expression of cultural and individual idiosyncrasies of style' (Eickelkamp, 1999: vii).

Therapeutic work and training requires that we see the yarn as a way of threading together the lives of the First Peoples of Australia. As researchers, we hold to the notion that it is through sharing our experiences by yarning that we find our connection to one another. We are reminded that it is by following the threads woven in the yarn that the stories of Stolen Generations and their descendants have found a place to be seen and heard. The fabric of lives is complex and it is clear that the intersection of stories is more than the warp and the weft; there is a tangled web of interactions beyond analysis. The Australian consciousness that permeates the work of therapy is built on the Dreaming, the Story-Time, the place where alignment with the Dreaming emphasises that we are all connected. In the First Peoples of Australia's models of consciousness we, you, and I are now forever after – will be and are (Stanner, 2009: 58) – for this is the behaviour of Aboriginality (Woods, 2010).

Aboriginality in Australia and the diverse reflections of identity as demonstrated through art therapy require an acceptance that the First Peoples of Australia are engaged in therapy that 'is a social and political activity as well as a psychological one...embedded in a cultural and historical context' (Boud, Keogh and Walker, 1988: 17). Art therapy and art-making are built on the telling of the yarn of our interwoven lives. Art therapy links disparate and dispersed peoples across place, time, being and non-physical-being. Through deep, thoughtful reflection about significant events in our lives, art therapy encounters incorporate knowledge of Australia's social, cultural and political movements at the times of crucial life-making events. In therapy using art, the individual and community alike deliberate on the impact of these movements on their lives, physically, philosophically and psychologically, and of their lives within the bigger yarn, that is the story of Australia, for without the small yarns, there is no big story.

Trauma, Indigeneity and identification

Judy Atkinson's *Trauma Trails – Recreating Song Lines: The Transgenerational Effects of Trauma in Indigenous Australia* (2002), describes the scope of work concerning the effects of trauma in the families and communities of Australia's Indigenous peoples between and across generations. Focusing on developing a better understanding of the impact of colonisation, the origin of contemporary trauma upon Australia's First Peoples and the invasive colonisation, therapeutic engagement enables a better understanding and explanation of the impact that colonisation still has on Australians, both the First Peoples and Non-First Peoples of Australia. Here we must pause to consider the complex and important question: 'But what is it to be a First Person of Australia and Australian?'

After the significant 'yes' vote in the 1967 referendum, where Australians voted unanimously to amend the constitution to include Australia's First Nation people in the census and allow the Commonwealth to create laws for them, the Australian Commonwealth Government was compelled to recognise the necessity of seeking the opinions of Australia's First Peoples on issues. Attesting to this fact was the establishment of First Peoples of Australia-led government agencies in the following decades which, in various publications, stated their own understandings of Indigeneity. In a 1975 letter to Dr McKinnon, Chairperson of the Schools Commission, relating to a report, the Aboriginal Consultative Group (ACG) recognised:

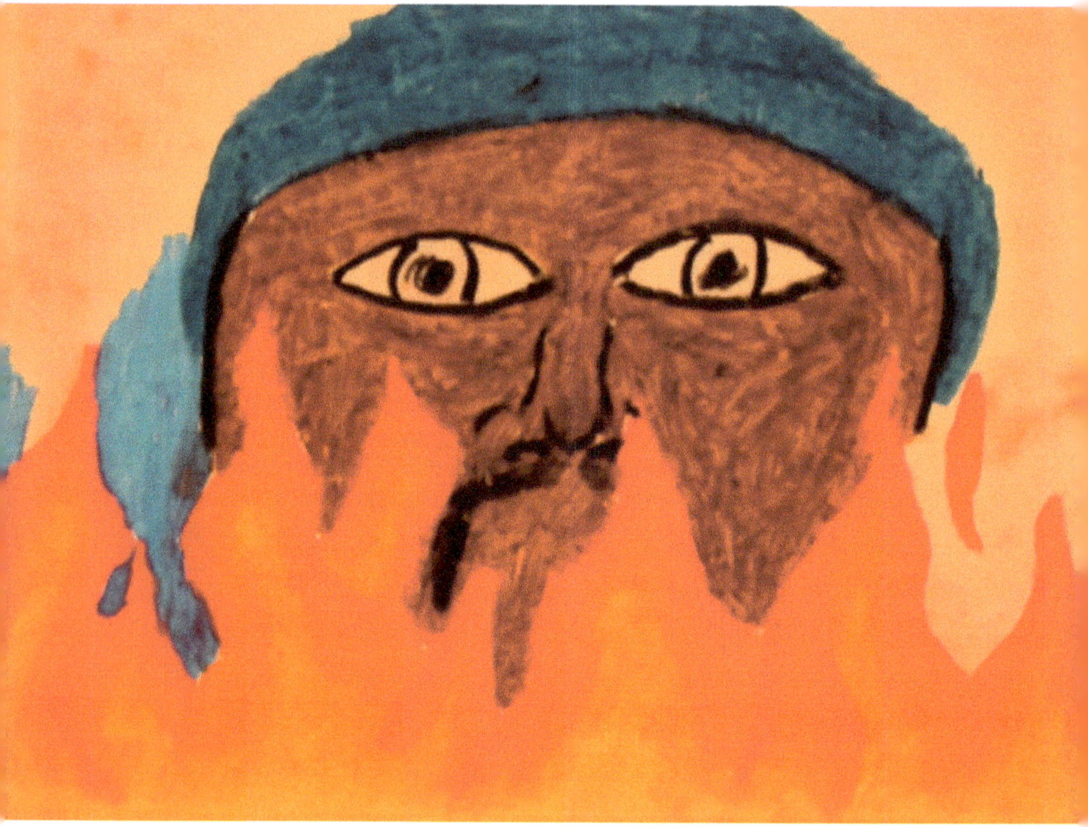

Figure 4 *Looking over the hell fire*. Evan (n.d.). Crayon on paper.
Evan spoke of this as 'hell fire' and a 'sad thing' that had happened. He spoke of not being in the fire but staring outwards. The self-portrait is clear and strong and yet this image was completed over a five week period. The re-working of images could be considered as Evan 'dealing with something', given that after five weeks he said that he was happy with the 'finishing touches' he put to the complete image. There was a 'that's taken care of that' quality to the re-worked, final image.

> … the existence of an Aboriginal people consisting of many diverse communities and individuals … But we see a common cohesion of cultural values and aspirations that identify us as a distinct people, with aspirations often quite different to that of the non-Aboriginal community.
>
> ACG, 1975, covering letter

A decade later, the National Aboriginal Education Committee (NAEC) stated 'that there exists a common feeling of "Aboriginality" among all the descendants of the Indigenous people of Australia, both traditional and non-traditional' (NAEC, 1985: 4).

The complex and often-contentious concept of Indigeneity is contingent on many facts and in our chapter, we will only touch on the shared history of Australia's First Peoples – which is a history of colonisation that has had profound, disastrous repercussions across generations of Australia's First Peoples (Sanson, 2008: 126; Atkinson, 2002: 35). Listening to and retelling story is a part of the Dreaming, a part of the Story-Time with each cultural group having an essential connection to country. All of Australia's First Peoples hold to the belief that lore pervaded and in many cases still pervades every aspect of life. Related to his or her country through linkages outlined in the stories of creation, each group and each individual, both in everyday and ceremonial life, mirror the ways outlined by the Ancestors (Bottom, 1999: 3; Bell, 1998: 16; Trezise, 1969: 10; Mattingley, 1998: 72-73; Marika, 1977: 8-25; Edwards, 1998: 81). The realm of sacred story and Dreaming comes into the work of knowing through the worldview of the First Peoples of Australia.

Australian Bureau of Statistics (ABS) data and reports of psychiatrists suggest that, in general, the First Peoples of Australia lack self-esteem: i.e. a sense of personal worth, social recognition and accomplishment. A report in a 2007 psychiatric journal emphasised that 'Aboriginal women were more likely than non-Aboriginal women to screen positive for symptoms of psychosis ... they also had higher psychological distress scores' (Butler et al, 2007: 431). A Commonwealth of Australia publication stated that '… psychological distress data showed that 27 per cent of Indigenous adults had experienced a high to very high level of distress, compared with 13 per cent of non-Indigenous adults' (Steering Committee for the Review of Government Service Provision, 2007: 49). It is thus unsurprising that the report further stated that '… from 2001-02 to 2004-05, Indigenous people had higher rates of hospitalisation for mental and behavioural disorders than non-Indigenous people' (ibid). The report also stated that '… growing up in very remote communities, where adherence to traditional culture and ways of life are strongest, may be protective against emotional and behavioural difficulties in Aboriginal children' (ibid). The Steering Committee's report supports our assertion that many of the First People from Australia's Stolen Generations and those who are the descendants of the Stolen Generations, lack emotional and social wellbeing because of dislocation from family and country.

It is important to note that although most of the First Peoples of Australia live in urban areas, '…the majority of Indigenous adults (60.1 per cent) recognised an area as their homeland or traditional country' (Steering Committee for the Review of Government Service Provision, 2007, Figure 9.5.1). Inferred within the ABS and psychiatrists' reports is the assertion that, despite many generations of colonisation and the accompanying dispossession of communities from country and children from communities, there is a strong identification with traditional country that we refer to as ancestral country. Thus, the right of return to ancestral country is necessary for the emotional and social wellbeing of the First Peoples of Australia, whether they be Stolen Generation members or the descendants of the stolen babies and children.

Coming home – reclaimation

The idea of personal story or yarn as 're-claimation' (McKenna and Woods, 2009) to help connect with the personal and the cultural story formed the foundation of Carmen's work in supervision and training as an Art Therapist. Carmen's work then and now, along with other First Peoples of Australia, illustrates that the First Peoples of Australia are 'coming home' to their identities after a period of loss of self. The return to the self is the basis of Carmen's work in the field of 're-claimative' arts therapy practice. Like all psychotherapy, 're-claimative' art therapy is profound and is a most intimate form of encounter. It seems to us that, in our supervision and discussion times together, we have come to understand and use art and ideas on art therapy to develop a notion of what it is to be an 'Australian', but especially to focus on the mind-set that is unique to the First Peoples of Australia. We have had to look at the fundamentals of the First Australian's ways of knowing and the many models of knowledge or epistemology. We began to link this with the use of art therapy as a way of giving voice back to the First Peoples of Australia.

In the typical art therapy supervision relationship, Carmen worked with images from her sessions with clients and we co-created work together and separately. The works were embodied and performative as she used drama and action as a way of illustrating her sense of the First Peoples of Australia's interconnectedness and the sacredness of the shared story and yarn. It is easy to forget that the First Peoples of Australia dance and sing their life stories and have done so for 60,000 years, or for at least 2,400 generations.

The melding in our discussions has led us to the notion that the use of arts practice, story and wellbeing all intersect. We also recognise the need for a hermetic healing space in which introspection and reflection can necessarily occur. In the sessions of supervision, training and social encounter, it became clear that here we were yarning and with the centrality of the meta-narratives or the deeper level of the stories beneath and inside the story emerging.

The idea that story and 're-claimation' can move beyond re-traumatisation was always driving this work. It has become clear to us that we are all working to heal the collective wounds of the First Peoples of Australia when we work and listen to each other. We have told many stories, many yarns of our cultural heritage and the wounds and the damage done to us. However, we have also recognised that we are always investigating the social construction of our self, by the self, particularly the self of individuals whose multifaceted identity incorporates that of a colonised art therapist or patient. In training and supervision, Carmen often came to examine ideas around how story and art therapy allow us to engage with representations of our lives. In our work, Davina and Tarquam are constantly returning to the resiliency that characterises the work of any 're-claimative', restorative and transformative journey (McKenna and Carpenter, 2009). The quality of this is always reflexive and qualitatively enriching for the individual and the community in which we locate ourselves. As Abdian (2006: 11) reminds us:

> We like to make meaning out of everything that happens to us, and thus we create stories to try to explain why things have happened to us. Even after an awful experience ends, the story and meaning we make of that experience remains long after, channelling our thoughts back to the experience. Therefore, even when something horrible happens to us only once, we do not just experience it that one time. We recreate the experience through our stories, and in those stories we live it again. We can begin to see, then, how story-telling and meaning-making are not always benign or benevolent. Our underlying narratives have the power to magnify or to ameliorate the effects of a stressful event. Sometimes we make meaning in less than productive ways and tell ourselves stories that perpetuate pain, false entitlements, and cycles of violence. These are toxic narratives that hold us back and keep us from healing. However, if the narrative helps us solve our real problems, then the narrative is adaptive. Depending on the tone and content of our narratives – the way we make meaning – they can be more or less toxic, more or less adaptive.

A 2001 paper by Hawaiian epistemologist Manu Aluli Meyer, *Our Own Liberation: Reflections on Hawaiian Epistemology*, influenced the work Carmen and Tarquam did together and gave them a way of mapping the First Peoples of Australia's models of knowing using another cultural context. Meyer refers to Indigenous themes as 'oceans of knowing'. Carmen and Tarquam set out to further understand and tentatively demonstrate how the Aboriginal people in Australia have used art to sense the oceans of their knowing, both in the old ways and now in 'modern' ways. Their encounters have, at the core, a belief that the First Peoples of Australia have always used their art to bring their people to their own centre. Paradoxically they emphasise and place great importance on the belief that artwork has now been politicised and used to serve the First Peoples of Australia in opening up all other people to understanding their marginalisation.

An example of politicised artwork is the yarn Davina presented in the form of a poem (pages 94–95). Written in 2006, it reflects the emotional, social and political concerns of many First Peoples of Australia before the 2008 National Apology to the Stolen Generations. On 13 February 2008, First Nation people across Australia were deeply inspired when, with many in tears, the then Prime Minister of Australia, Kevin Rudd, finally apologised to the Stolen Generations and said 'sorry'.

Beyond causality

Modelling on Manu Meyer's paradigm, through a series of respectful meetings and encounters, we assumed that together we could explore how First Peoples of Australia could use art and art therapy, embracing spirituality as the most central component of Aboriginal people's cultural contexts of knowledge. Many times we have reflected on how art-making 'feeds us and gives us a place and a way of knowing' whilst being deeply embedded in the cultural legacies of Australia's First Peoples. We hold to the idea that art builds a relationship with the sense of self, as well as the community of others, whilst allowing the First Peoples of Australia to see beyond utility to

Urban songlines

In 1938 our Elders; statesmen and women of high degree
Cooper, Patten, Briggs and Tucker, working for us to be free
Along with others like Ferguson, organised and set a date
January 26, Australia Day they did redesignate
No longer commemorating British invasion
Now a day for Aboriginal political persuasion
A Day of Mourning it was called
A day supported by those appalled:
At Black soldiers not yet citizens
Although their families for generations were called denizens
Elders denied the old age pension
And to add to the tension
Our most precious resource
Not land nor sea, but our children of course
Stolen, forced into domestic servitude
Taken to be raised as non-First Peoples of Australia in someone else's brood

In other cities, towns and States
Prohibitions people did hate:
Included bans on walking city streets
Wages less than others each week
Children not taken were not to be educated
And this was never allowed to be debated
Children were not even allowed in schools
And definitely not in the local swimming pools

That date in 1938 was then sown
Moved in the calendar year, and grown
Now we call it NAIDOC Week!
It is a time to gather, celebrate and speak
Speak of the Elders and their fights
Speak of the Elders how they achieved our rights.

On the Friday of NAIDOC Week we celebrate NAIDOC Day.
Each year our communities gather at the beginning of the way
The beginning of the path, we travel celebrating our urban Songlines
Each knows what others think and outcomes the chanted lines
"Extra! Extra! Read all about it!
This is our land and there's no doubt about it!"

Along city streets passed parliament and the mall
We step out, a gathering of people walking tall
We do this every year rain or bright sunlight
Community; Black, Brindle and family Whites
Following our songmen and women with their megaphones
We march, we chant, we make no bones

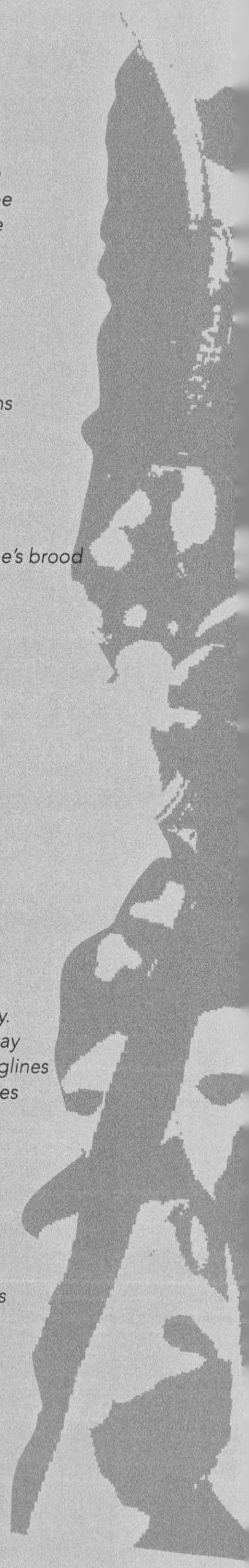

Figure 5 *Actress Shareena Clanton speaks at a protest in Melbourne organised by Aboriginal rights activists to mark Australia Day, January 2017.* Asanka Brendon Ratnayake/Anadolu. Photograph (2017).

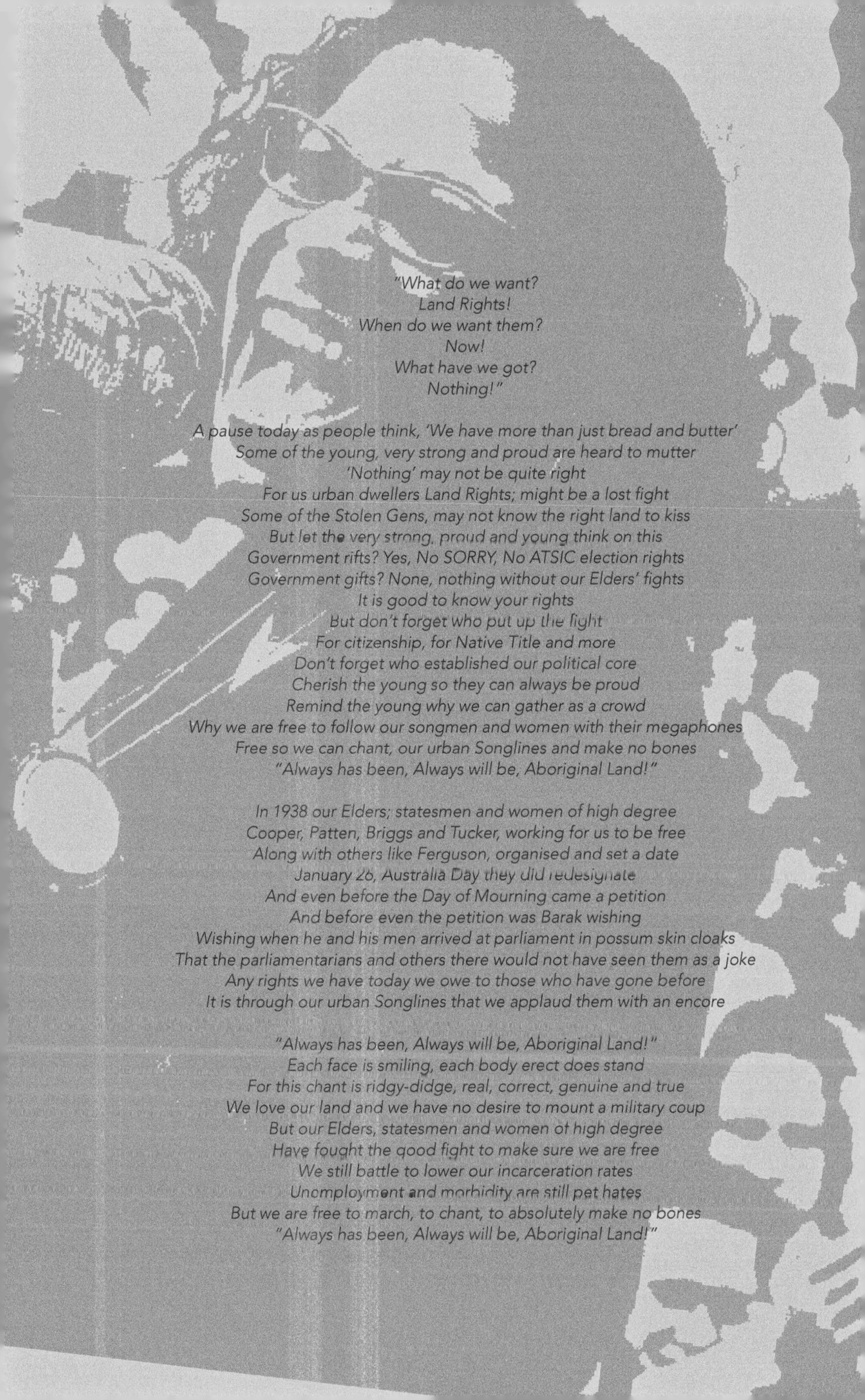

"What do we want?
Land Rights!
When do we want them?
Now!
What have we got?
Nothing!"

A pause today as people think, 'We have more than just bread and butter'
Some of the young, very strong and proud are heard to mutter
'Nothing' may not be quite right
For us urban dwellers Land Rights; might be a lost fight
Some of the Stolen Gens, may not know the right land to kiss
But let the very strong, proud and young think on this
Government rifts? Yes, No SORRY, No ATSIC election rights
Government gifts? None, nothing without our Elders' fights
It is good to know your rights
But don't forget who put up the fight
For citizenship, for Native Title and more
Don't forget who established our political core
Cherish the young so they can always be proud
Remind the young why we can gather as a crowd
Why we are free to follow our songmen and women with their megaphones
Free so we can chant, our urban Songlines and make no bones
"Always has been, Always will be, Aboriginal Land!"

In 1938 our Elders; statesmen and women of high degree
Cooper, Patten, Briggs and Tucker, working for us to be free
Along with others like Ferguson, organised and set a date
January 26, Australia Day they did redesignate
And even before the Day of Mourning came a petition
And before even the petition was Barak wishing
Wishing when he and his men arrived at parliament in possum skin cloaks
That the parliamentarians and others there would not have seen them as a joke
Any rights we have today we owe to those who have gone before
It is through our urban Songlines that we applaud them with an encore

"Always has been, Always will be, Aboriginal Land!"
Each face is smiling, each body erect does stand
For this chant is ridgy-didge, real, correct, genuine and true
We love our land and we have no desire to mount a military coup
But our Elders, statesmen and women of high degree
Have fought the good fight to make sure we are free
We still battle to lower our incarceration rates
Unemployment and morbidity are still pet hates
But we are free to march, to chant, to absolutely make no bones
"Always has been, Always will be, Aboriginal Land!"

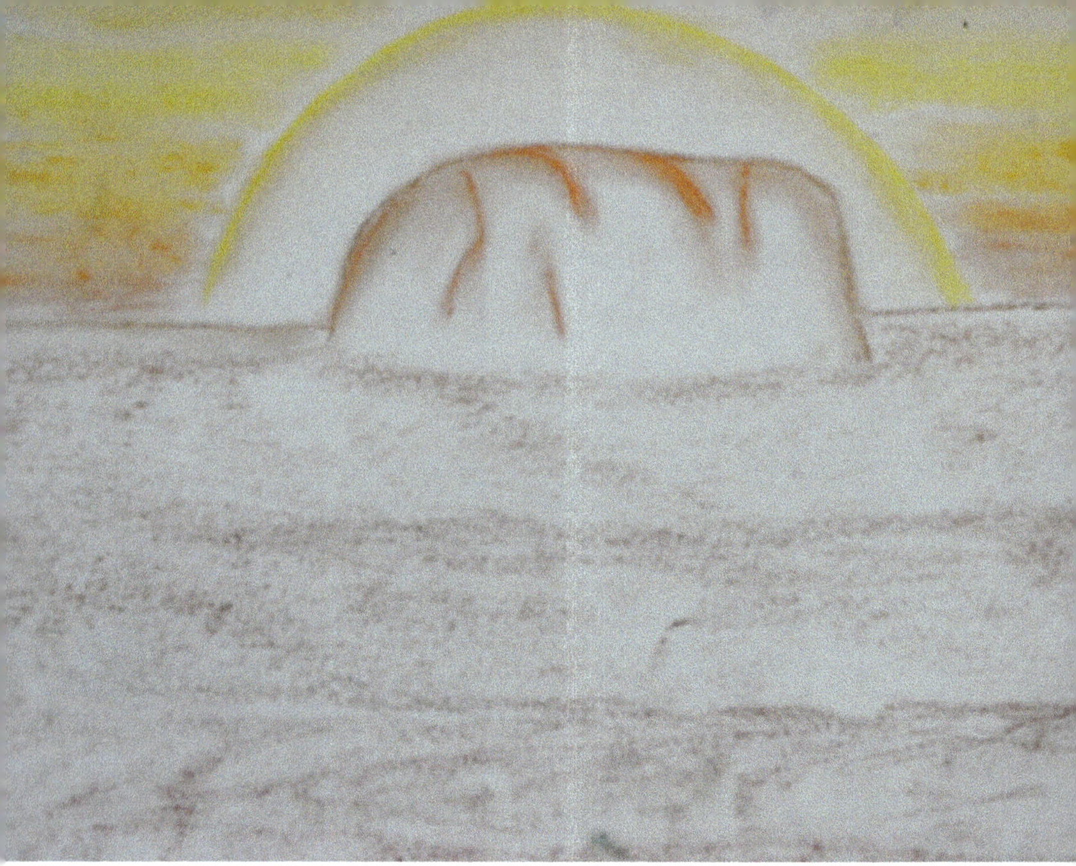

Figure 6 *Uluru*. Evan (n.d.). Crayon on paper.
Sometimes referred to as Ayers Rock and sometimes called Uluru by Evan, he spoke of this image as being his 'spiritual home and the heart of things'. There was a sense of security about this image.

the place of ideas of wealth and usefulness beyond pragmatic ideals. In many moments during our group encounters the concept of art therapy highlighted that art was, and is, beyond words that have, at their core, an over-emphasis on causality. Of course, many of our moments and meetings also emphasised how the critical separation of the body-mind question is for the First Peoples of Australia an illusion of separation with which they were yoked from the various moments of first contact with the Non-First Peoples of Australia.

It is important to recount that in the work with Carmen she was at pains to emphasise the guides and mentors that informed her learning. These people included her Elders: Uncle Joe Davidson from the Jagera people around Ipswich, in Queensland; Nugget Dodds, also from Ipswich; and Nerreman from Tasmania. Carmen and Davina always speak from their life, retelling stories and reflecting on ideas from the viewpoint of women, whether mothers, grandmothers, activists, teachers or artists.

In her work, Carmen emphasised that '…until the ideas are brought to fruition they are "ideals" which I aspire to as an art therapist working with people who are my people'. In the training work, Carmen was at pains to point out that art therapy provided an opportunity to develop and outline an emergent Australian Aboriginal philosophy of art that expands, invigorates, and redefines ideas of culture as put forth by Indigenous practitioners of art-making. Art-making within the work of art therapy gives hope for the future, as Carmen states:

> Any art therapy program has to have a strong building on self-esteem. I believe in the potential of all people and my people need to have these positive sorts of feelings so that more creative ideas can come into being. I see this program as hope for their future. It is not about whacking out enough art work to feed yourself or to make lots of money. It is about pride, about dignity, about a sense of achievement, a sense of value.
>
> I don't want to spend a lot of effort attempting to use art to diagnose what is 'wrong' but I want to use art to 're-create' ways that belong with the art-makers so that the Australian Aboriginal people can return to themselves as individuals and communities. The people I hope to offer this program to may be 'ill' or dispossessed but I hold that all art-making is healing and whilst not always art therapy it is powerful in redressing wrongs that have happened.

Carmen emphasised that maybe the use of art therapy could also become a way to critique the current colonisation that came through the colonisers' systems. It might also bring back the sense of spirituality that has been lost to many people. Carmen explains:

> Our Spirituality is the most central component of Aboriginal people's cultural contexts and knowledge. Mythologies and Indigenous traditions speak of another time – this is the time of myth, legend and fairy tales. The Indigenous people's way attends to the great time and the Dreamtime. The unconventional notion of time is quite unlike conventional time. The idea here is that Kairos time is as important, if not more important to Indigenous knowing than Kronos time. Mystics, poets and artists have a similar response to time as they have reminded us not to spend too much time attending to the clock but to spend time in meditation, in escaping the bonds of ordinary time, and using art to do so.

There is in the First Peoples of Australia's ways a large body of evidence for the existence of alternative ways of knowing. The conventional senses, like conventional time, are not involved in this way of knowing. There is something unconventional in this way of knowing. In the west, these ways of being and knowing might be called paranormal or psychic functioning, like clairvoyance, extra-sensory perception and intuition. The sciences of the west have excluded these ways of knowing. That said, the work of modern quantum physics through Bohm, Fritjof Capra and Brian Staendahal Ross, seem to indicate that new ways are being engaged to draw on our continuing and enduring wisdom as Australia's First Peoples. There are instances in which direct knowing appears to transcend time – as we usually conceive it. There are, again, large bodies of evidence supporting accurate knowledge of future events (precognition, premonitions), and there is a smaller, but intriguing, evidence base for a direct experiencing of the past (retrocognition). Carmen's sessions highlighted how precognition could be interpreted as the mind reaching into the future and bringing back information about what has not yet occurred, or it could be understood as a future event somehow working backward in time to influence the mental contents or actions of persons in the present. In either case, precognitive phenomena are inconsistent with our usual views of time and of causality (since the 'effect' precedes the 'cause' (Braud, 1989). Carmen says:

> The white-fella has everything in order … programmed to the *n*th degree … Our way of knowing is not about linear time. The effect happens first in our ways and we consider why after the event often. We have a knowing of events and people although it may not have already happened. Compared to Western ideas, Indigenous science collapses both time and space with the result that our fields of inquiry and participation extend into and overlap with the past and present. To me this is the idea that the story is directed by a series of relationships rather than a set order. There is story that is not always totally traditional but when we tell stories we are transcending time and space. It is not a matter of when did it happen to telling it chronologically. The story is told as a review of the past time or the now.

Carmen often alluded to her belief that the First Peoples' ways feed her and give her both a place and a way of knowing. So, when psychoanalytic or psychodynamic models of the mind are compared to Aboriginal ways of knowing, it is clear that there are both similarities and differences. The web of connectedness seems to be one main difference. The healer is central to her people's way and as she alludes to the fact that both traditional and conventional medicine are practiced for healing to occur. The mystical specialist or healer in her First Peoples of Australia communities does not engage in what Carmen referred to as the 'dominant scientific, materialistic' ideology as might be happening in Non-Indigenous contemporary Australia. She was calling for a return to the First Peoples' systems of cultural, gender and political employment. Carmen consistently states that the First Peoples' contexts have not been carried forward in time and her people have suffered psychological distress because their ways of knowing have been denied. She goes on to comment that:

> … This has been largely because the white ways and culture are politically preferred. The healer in our world holds views that differ to white ways as these men and women have usually undertaken deep personal journeys. The journey of the healer and individual is acknowledged as central to our identity: our way of political knowing is not easily understood.
>
> … all that I know indicates that Aboriginal people have got a different view on relationships and things … even if I am doing a letter I might talk about one thing and there might be something that is related time wise – from a different place in time. The white fella way is a rigid path of boundaries and I find that really constricting ... even so-called well educated Aboriginal people will still use the traditional healer and I don't leave myself separate to that ... the healer role is handed on and it is not just learned …

In attending to the psychopathology of wellbeing, Carmen would often suggest that some differences exist between the ways First Peoples of Australia and Non-First Peoples of Australia see 'illness' and 'wellness'. First Peoples of Australia ways of knowing physical, mental and spiritual illness reflect deeply on connectedness. She says:

> … The white fella doctor might say 'we need to check your liver' but there are other organs of the body that are connected and especially your psyche that needs to be taken into consideration. You cannot fix a leaf on the tree when there are other things in the tree that need attention. We see the whole body thing as related.

The preference in the First Peoples of Australia's ways of knowing is to see wholeness rather than separateness.

> If you dissect something and take one organ out of the person how are you going to recognise from examining only that organ who that person is? It is like taking a page out of a book and then trying to understand the whole book. The emphasis in our ways of knowing is on wholeness and community connectedness. We hold to a belief that sees connectedness. My people have a life based on being rather than doing. Whereas in Western culture the world can be manipulated and controlled through 'doing' in our worldview we see ourselves fed by quality of relationships.
>
> Because you will hear the white professors say that my people will whack it out cheaply. The therapy is about restoration of pride and 'stirring' up of the spiritual things so that these people believe in their inner self. It is coming from the inner source, with a story attached to it and it is not a dollar thing. There has to be a belief that they are taking part in creation itself.
>
> … as far as white fellas are concerned for me they are pretty keen on diagnosing and medicating which only deals with the symptoms. It does not cure the illness … a lot of Aboriginal people will still go to traditional healers, even if they are going to doctors. This gift that these people have for healing is handed down or handed on from somebody. These people are approaching the person with a whole body–mind–spirit approach. It is absolutely no good to give someone pills for a rash if the rash is caused by something inside … like an illness of the spirit requires that the spirit be in touch. That the patients get in touch with that part of him or herself. The traditional healers are called … and they combine all ways of knowing …

Carmen notes that First Peoples' ways of engagement build relationships with the self as well as with the community of others and it would seem that their sciences are holistic and draw on all the senses, including the 'spiritual and psychic ways'. Western and First Peoples of Australia's motivations for inquiry vary significantly. First Peoples' healers conduct

Figure 7 Detail of *Uluru*. Evan (n.d.). Crayon on paper.

'research' to increase the integrity and wholeness of their communal fabric. The benefit to the individual is important as part of the community as a whole. Carmen explains:

> In the West the researchers who came to work with our people seemed to rarely benefit the community. The Western healing paradigm is too driven by diagnosis, medication and there is limited attention to the inner world. The outside body of the person may be seen but the inner world is not really looked at. Then of course the individual is not seen in the West as having such a strong sense of community or connectedness.
>
> If we can re-connect with our own Indigenous minds then healing may come through our understanding of the Indigenous science, which went into the ceremony that precluded the use of the herb. The spiritual part of the illness is honoured. What heals is more than just the beneficial chemical.
>
> Aboriginal knowledge is based on observation, not theories to be proven. This makes a big difference ... when you theorise you can be abstracting out of the place of observation.

The idea is that activities in art-making and art therapy can bridge generational divides and generate a sense of community through the arts.

Carmen was eager that a client (or group) and an Elder or a 'mentor' would make art together. In some ways she was hopeful that the Elders, as 'professional artists', could work with young or old people alike in a shared experience in communities to transform their lives. The sharing at the subliminal level is special to her people. These stories maybe transformed into dramatic, literary, and visual presentations that would ideally explore social issues, shed light on history and, drawing from their artistic imagination, would answer community issues and conflicts. It is the sense of connectedness that the art therapy process would anticipate.

In the work with Carmen, discussion often centred on the way in which a community of mentors and clients would share the positive ideas of who we are now as well as our history. Carmen spoke of her role as a therapist who would facilitate building a sense of the 'Community Tree'. She says:

> The tree is a great idea as the roots are down into the ground. It is all part of the connectedness. Racial memory is part of who we are. We are all there and it is there for us to connect into … The things that we recall in this work are the greater spiritual memory that is shared by all of us. It is the tree that we can tap into. The tree symbolises nature as BIG and strong. The connectedness with the land is implied in the Living Tree.

Carmen noted that art-making, mask-making, fabric works and other art-making processes should be used by mentors and the community of people, sharing in a sense of collaboration. This would develop a relationship where each could consider where they had come from and what they had brought with them from that place. Homeland stories or 'my country' yarns might be different to the country these people are in now. Carmen also noted that it should be possible to offer a process where families could work with art therapists and artists, as well as individuals, to address their sense of country and place.

In previous therapeutic training undertaken by Tarquam with the Danila Dilba Biluru Butji Binnilutlum Health Service (Darwin), First Peoples of Australia began seeing yarning and telling stories of their identity as a positive way of moving towards healing the pain and suffering of the Stolen Generations and their descendants. Work undertaken in Danila Dilba was designed to explore art as a healing practice where the needs of community are addressed through innovative and mainstream therapeutic approaches; people use art therapy as a 'ritual' or rite to remedy alienation, loss and dispossession. Aboriginal tales are fluid, not fixed or set in concrete but almost always returning to themes of loss, alienation and dispossession. The use of arts therapies is a way of reparation of the impacts of colonisation. There are also many tales that told of the way in which people from the First Peoples' communities were deeply connected to their families, their land and the mythologies that surpassed chronological time and the pain of not being recognised. The respect for the heritage and cultural needs is played out through the therapeutic relationship. Resilience is part of the identity of all people who have suffered a wounding. The dispossession of Australia's First Peoples is real, the tales of murder of our own people, the alcohol and drug misuse and the family violence indicate that our identification with pain is almost always a projection into ourselves as a reply to being oppressed, dispossessed, colonised. The self-hate caused through the oppression of colonisation is referred to as 'internalised colonialism'. When the oppression is repeated and directed towards those who will not retaliate and are easily silenced because they are members of the perpetrators family and/or community, this is known as 'lateral violence'. Art-making and art therapies bring a reply to the silences by seeing and sharing these stories of pain and joy.

Whilst images of community and history are implied above in permanently recording these important moments, and the embedded feelings captured within them, personal art works become 'bridges' for accessing, exploring, and communicating feelings and memories (including unconscious ones), as well as the related psychotherapeutic issues these evoke. The art therapy sessions are an occasion to address both the individual and group needs. The art-making process anticipates a sense of shifts in understanding. The creative arts occur in such a way that understanding occurs because of shifts in knowing. This process of apperception will occur in the art-making, art-doing, art-being and the witnessing of this.

The Indigenous sense of knowing that Meyer alludes to, as outlined earlier in this chapter, could address the invisible aspects through art and image work. It is as if art therapy sets out to make visible the ongoing stories of the life of the First Peoples of Australia, serving as 'Songlines', marking where we have been or may perhaps be going, leading us toward better understanding of the non verbal components of our conscious and unconscious life.

Conclusion

The First Peoples of Australia are the most disadvantaged population group in Australia. Art therapy could help to close the 17-year life expectancy gap between First Peoples of Australia and Non-First Peoples of Australia. In closing, it could be suggested that the western world has failed to honour the notions of knowing of many First Peoples. It seems to us that the ideal world will decolonise the western mind so that the healers who attend to community and spirituality will be seen as a real power. The driving force of spirituality should be honoured in art therapy. Bringing spirituality back into the lives of individuals, the lives of communities and the systems of institutions is crucial. Transpersonal psychology and arts therapies can act as a way of decolonising the minds of the First Peoples of Australia, a community whose members have a shared heritage of colonisation beginning in 1788 and of mores and values passed on through the lore of the Dreaming dating back at least 60,000 years. It is clear that the First Peoples of Australia have always seen art as a way of cleansing, connecting and healing themselves. However, the sense of self-reflection that is part of the cult of individualism in the west is vastly different to the community notion of self that the First Peoples of Australia share. Carmen writes:

> There is not this separateness … there is community art where several people will work on one piece there is indeed community art and art-making community. Of course there are artists who work alone but they are still connected to the community. Urban Aboriginals like Uncle Joe mentioned earlier are engaged in primitiveness. He gets on with his art as an individual but still has a sense of purpose for community.

Ideally, art therapy and creative arts should be used with Australian Aboriginal people themselves, through their own way so they can address health issues within their communities and families. There is *no literature concerning best practice art therapy approaches to meeting the psycho-emotional needs of the First Peoples of Australia* who are suffering from grief and trauma as a result of separation and other emotional challenges. There have been many undesirable and severe consequences of removal in Australia on Aboriginal people's SEWB (Social Emotional Well Being), including loss, trauma, grief, criminal behaviour, adverse life outcomes, substance abuse, higher rates of mental health problems, suicide and violence, parenting problems, and inferior physical health. These effects and consequences are trans-generational i.e. they impact not only on those directly removed but also on their children, families and communities (Human Rights and Equal Opportunity Commission, 2003).

The process of art therapy would ideally create community and build trust. It has been used to address unspoken issues that inhibit psychological growth and emotional and social wellness. We hold to the idea that art therapy, with the use of traditional healing approaches alongside mainstream social and emotional well-being services, can and should be envisioned. Art therapy services should be provided to Aboriginal people by Aboriginal people.

References

Abdian, S. (2006). Cultural healing: when cultural renewal is reparative and when it is toxic. Presentation at Healing Our Spirits, World-wide Conference.

Aboriginal Consultative Group (1975). *Education for Aborigines: report to the Schools Commission*. Australian Government Printers, Canberra.

Altbach, P. and Kelly, G. (1978). *Education and colonialism*. Longman, New York.

Ashcroft, B., Griffiths, G. and Tiffin, H. (1998). *Key concepts in postcolonial studies*. Routledge, London and New York.

Atkinson, J. (2002). *Trauma trails, recreating songlines: the transgenerational effects of trauma in Indigenous Australia*. Spinifex Press, North Melbourne.

Baba, T. (2004). Researching Pacific and Indigenous peoples: issues and perspectives. [Auckland, NZ] : Centre for Pacific Studies, The University of Auckland

Baldwin, C. (2005). *Storycatcher: The power of story to change our lives*. New World Library, San Francisco.

Battiste, M. (Ed) (2000). *Reclaiming Indigenous voice and vision*. UBC Press, Vancouver.

Bell, D. (1998). *Ngarrindjeri Wurruwarrin: a world that is, was, and will be*. Spinifex Press, Melbourne.

Bin-Salik, M-A. (2000). *Aboriginal women by degrees*. University of Queensland Press, Brisbane.

Bottoms, T. (1999). *Djabugay country: an Aboriginal history of tropical North Queensland*. Allen and Unwin, St Leonards, NSW.

Boud, D., Keogh, R. and Walker, D. (1988). *What is reflection in learning?* In: Boud, D., Keogh, R. and Walker, D. (Eds.) (1998). *Reflection: Turning experience into learning*. Kogan Page, London.

Boud, D., Keogh, R. and Walker, D. (1988). *Promoting reflection in learning: a model* In: Boud, D., Keogh, R. and Walker, D. (Eds.) (1998). *Reflection: turning experience into learning*. Kogan Page, London.

Braud, W. (1989). A methodology for the objective study of transpersonal imagery. *Journal of Scientific Exploration*, 3(1): 43–63.

Butler, T., Allnutt, S., Kariminia, A. and Cain D. (2007). Mental health status of Aboriginal and non-Aboriginal Australian prisoners. *Australia and New Zealand Journal of Psychiatry*. 41 (5): 429–35.

Cook, T. (1995). *Black on white: policy and curriculum development in Aboriginal education*. Human Factors Press, Sydney.

Department of Administrative Services (1995). *Australian Flags*. Australian Government Publishing Service, Canberra.

Duara, P. (Ed) (2003). *Decolonization: Perspectives from now and then*. Routledge, London.

Duguid, C. (1978). *No dying race*. Seal Books, Hong Kong.

Edwards, B. (1998). *Living the Dreaming* in: Bourke, C., Bourke, E. and Edwards, B. (Eds.) (1998). *Aboriginal Australia: an introductory reader in Aboriginal*. University of Queensland Press, Brisbane.

Eickelkamp, U. (1999). *'Don't ask for stories ...' The women from Ernabella and their art*. Aboriginal Studies Press, Canberra.

Ellis, C. (1999). Heartful autoethnography. *Qualitative Health Research*, *9* (5): 669–683.

Gardiner, G. and Bourke, E. (2000) Indigenous populations, 'mixed' discourses and identities. *People and Place*, 8 (2): 43–45.

Githaiga, J. (1998). *Intellectual property law and the protection of Indigenous folklore and knowledge*, 5 (2) Accessed http://www.murdoch.edu.au/elaw/issues/v5n2/githaiga52nf.html.

Graham, H., Mason, R., and Nayling, N. (2013). The personal is still political: Museums, participation and copyright. *Museum and Society*, 11(2): 105.

Grant, S. (2002). *The tears of strangers: a memoir*. HarperCollins, Pymble, NSW.

Haswell, M., Hunter, E., Wargent, R., Hall, B., O'Higgins, C. and West, R. (2009). *Protocols for the delivery of social and emotional wellbeing and mental health services in Indigenous Australia communities*. University of Queensland and Queensland Health, Queensland.

Horton, D. (Ed) (1994). *Encyclopaedia of Aboriginal Australia*. Aboriginal Studies Press, Canberra.

Human Rights and Equal Opportunity Commission (2003). Bringing them home. a human rights education resource developed by the Human Rights and Equal Opportunity Commission. (2003). [Sydney]: The Commission.

Lawlor, R. (1991). *Voices of the first day: awakening in the Aboriginal Dreamtime*, n.p.: Rochester, Vt.: Inner traditions, Victoria University Library Catalogue, EBSCOhost, viewed 25 March 2016.

Loomba, A. (2005). *Colonialism/postcolonialism*. Second edition, Routledge, London.

MacQueen, N. (2007). *Colonialism*. Pearson Longman, London.

McKenna, T. (2013). Towards an Indigenous knowing: a personalised perspective on art therapy – Carmen Lawson talks with Tarquam McKenna. *Australian and New Zealand Journal of Art Therapy*, 8 (1): 15–26.

Marika, W. for the Australia Council (1977). *The Aboriginal children's history of Australia*. Rigby, Melbourne.

Martin, J. H. (2010). W.E.H. Stanner: The Dreaming and other essays [book review]. *Australian Aboriginal Studies*, (1), 124.

Mattingley, C. (Ed) (1998). *Survival in our own land: 'Aboriginal' experiences in 'South Australia' since 1836 / told by Nungas and others*. Wakefield Press, Adelaide.

McKenna, T. and Bett, R. (2001). *Report on creative arts therapies*. Danila Dilba Biluru Butji Binnilutlum Medical Service Aboriginal Corporation, Darwin.

McKenna, T. and Carpenter, C. (2012) *Exploring.* In: Pryor, A., Carpenter C., Norton, C. and Kirchner, J. (Eds.) (2012) *Emerging insights: International perspectives on adventure therapy.* Proceedings of the 5th International Adventure Therapy Conference, University of Edinburgh, Scotland. European Science and Art Publishing, Prague, Czech Republic.

Meyer, M-A. (2001). Our own liberation: reflections on Hawaiian epistemology, *The Contemporary Pacific*, Spring, 13 (1): 124.

Morrissey, P. (2003). *Aboriginality and corporatism.* In: Grossman, M. (Ed) (2003). *Blacklines: Contemporary critical writing by Indigenous Australians.* Melbourne University Press, Melbourne.

Nabobo-Baba, U. (2004) Talanoa and Indigenous Pacific research: Some reflections. Paper given to the Second Pacific Graduates Symposium, Fale Pasifika, The University of Auckland.

National Aboriginal Education Committee (1985). *Philosophy, aims and policy guidelines for Aboriginal and Torres Strait Islander education.* Australian Government Publishing Service, Canberra.

National inquiry into the separation of Aboriginal and Torres Strait Islander children from their families (1997). *Bringing them home.* (Sir Ronald Wilson, president). Human Rights and Equal Opportunity Commission, Sydney.

Partington, G. (1998). *Perspectives on Aboriginal and Torres Strait Islander education.* Social Science Press, Katoomba, NSW.

Rabinow, P. (1977). *Reflections on fieldwork in Morocco.* Quantum Books, University of California Press, Berkley.

Russell, L. (2002). *A little bird told me.* Allen and Unwin, St Leonards, NSW.

Sanson, A. (2008). Insight 11: Development psychology and Indigenous children and youth. In: Garvey, D. (Ed) (2008). *Indigenous identity in contemporary psychology: dilemmas, developments, directions.* Thomson, Melbourne.

Smith, L. (2003). *Decolonizing methodologies: research and Indigenous peoples.* Sixth Impression. Zed Books Ltd., London.

Stanner, W. (2011). *The Dreaming and other essays.* ReadHowYouWant.com.

Steering Committee for the Review of Government Service Provision. (2007). *Overcoming Indigenous disadvantage: Key indicators report.* Productivity Commission, Melbourne.

Sydney Morning Herald newspaper (1995). Aboriginal flag a symbol of reconciliation, *The Sydney Morning Herald.* 6 July 1995: 13.

Terszak, M. (2002). *Orphaned by the colour of my skin: A stolen generation story.* eContent Management Pty Ltd., Malony, Queensland.

Trezise, P. (1969). *Quinkan Country: Adventures in search of Aboriginal cave paintings in Cape York.* A.H and A.W Reed, Sydney.

Winks, R. (Ed) (1963). *British imperialista: gold, God and glory.* Holt, Rinehart and Winston, New York.

Wolfe, P. (1999). *Settler colonialism and the transformation of anthropology: The politics and poetics of an ethnographic event.* Cassell, London.

Zahar, R. (1974). *Frantz Fanon: colonialism and alienation – concerning Frantz Fanon's political theory.* Translated by Willfried F Feuser. Monthly Review Press, New York.

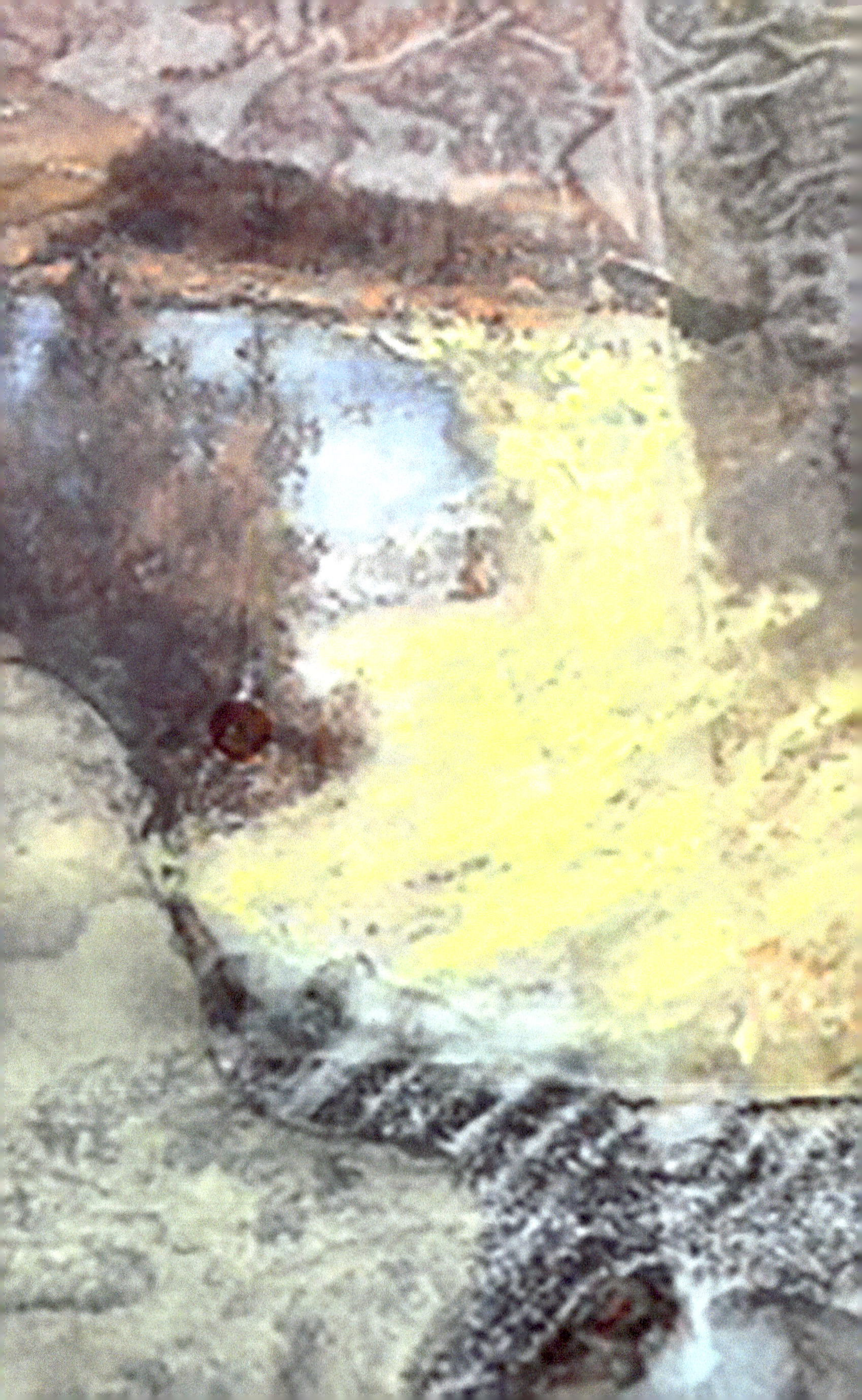

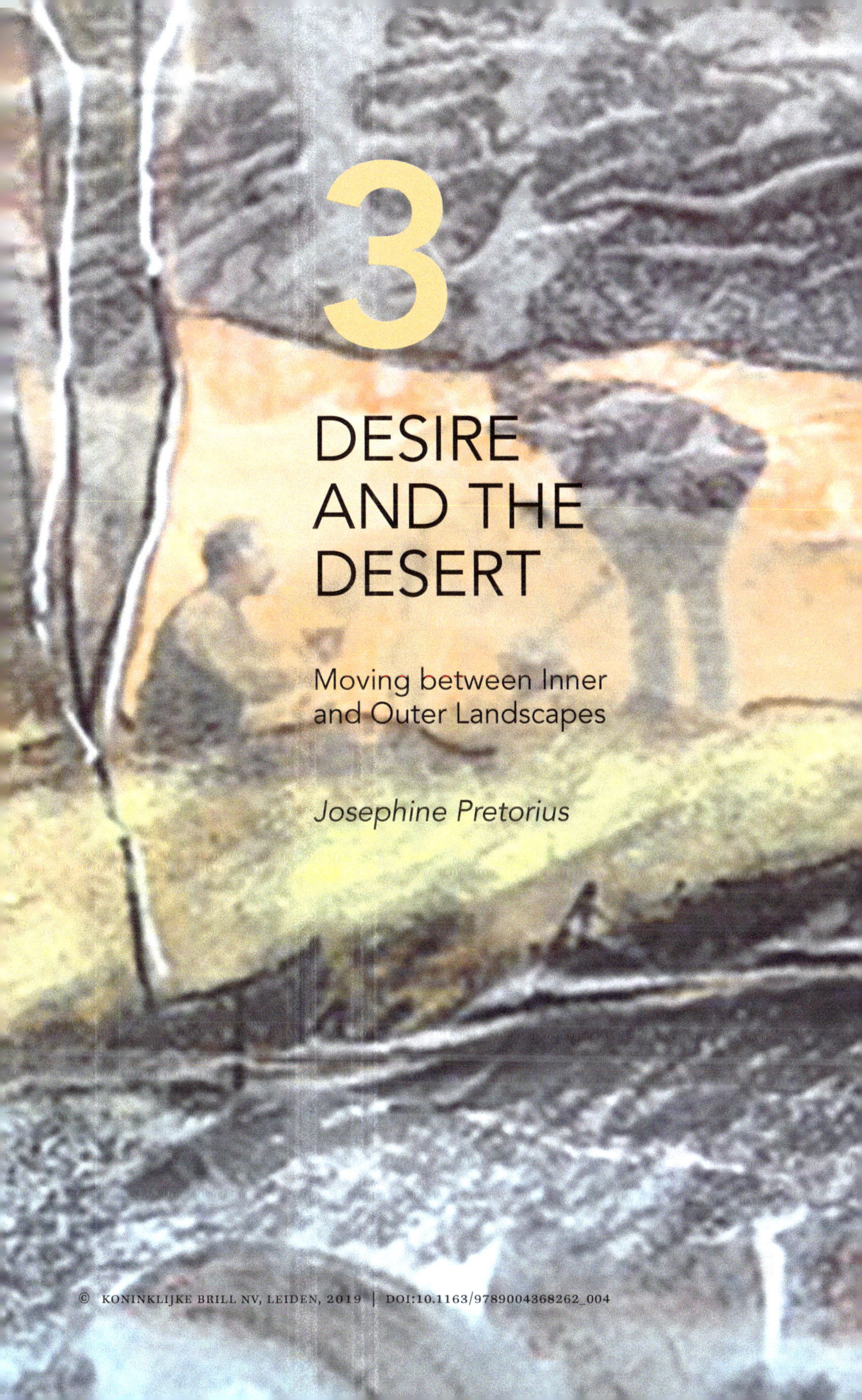

3

DESIRE AND THE DESERT

Moving between Inner and Outer Landscapes

Josephine Pretorius

 | DOI:10.1163/9789004368262_004

As I move towards writing this chapter I awaken one night from a dream in which I am returning to the desert with the same people as before. They are travelling with me to support me in my quest to spend three nights out in the ocean, alone in a small rowing boat. The ocean is vast yet encircled by an infinite horizon of rolling hills of desert sand. I don't want to disappoint them. I am afraid to tell them that I don't have the courage to do it.

In contemplative traditions hermits seek out deserts as a place of *kenosis*, or emptying out, which allows space for a more profound engagement with life. It is not only hermits who seek out such experiences, but perhaps we all do within the ordinary circumstances of our lives. Richard Rohr, Franciscan monk, quotes Francis as having said "Wherever we are, wherever we go, we bring our cell with us. Our brother (sister) cell is our body and our soul is the hermit living in the cell" (2015: 47–48.) As we enter our cells through the door of our attention we find there a wisdom alluded to by the early desert fathers and mothers of the fourth century. Abbott Moses, in response to a request for a "good word", replied: "Go, sit in your cell, your cell will teach you everything" (Merton, 1960: 30). Cells can be found anywhere where time has slowed enough so that we can enter the necessary spaciousness that enables us to see. Art-making is one such place. Retreating into nature is another. So too the cell of therapy, it being a place where external and internal landscapes meet. Our lives and relationships outside therapy are brought into life in the here and now of the therapeutic relationship. This chapter is an attempt to draw together such disparate threads and link them within the crucible of nature which has the capacity to provide a form of universal holding.

Lake Caroline in the Simpson Desert in outback Australia is a place that draws one into the necessary silence, stillness and simplicity. I was there some years ago and wandered out into its centre, crunching over the glazed cracked pottery of its surface, where fish and water had once flowed and would again. As I glanced back over my shoulder I noticed that my companions had shrunk in size to mere specks in the distance. I turned slowly, seeing clear to the horizon in all directions. I was reminded of Dennes (2001) who has spoken about how the space within us seems to expand as the space between ourselves and the horizon opens up in an unimpeded landscape. It was only after I returned to Sydney that I realised that the sense of space expanding within me was only possible because the space within and the space without were, and are, the same space. Bachelard (1994: 184) says: "… immensity is within ourselves. It is attached to a sort of expansion of being that life curbs and caution arrests, but which starts again when we are alone."

Miriam-Rose Ungunmerr- Baumann, an Aboriginal elder from Nauiyu (Daly River in the Northern Territory) speaks of *Dadirri* as that inner deep listening which recognises the spring that flows within each of us:

> We call on it and it calls to us. This is the gift that Australia is thirsting for. It is something like what you call 'contemplation'… Our Aboriginal culture has taught us to be still and wait. We do not try to hurry things up. We let them follow their natural course – like the seasons. We watch the

> moon in each of its phases. We wait for the rain to fill our rivers and water the thirsty earth. When twilight comes we prepare for the night. At dawn we rise with the sun ... We own our own grief and allow it to heal slowly.
>
> About Dadirri: www.miriamrosefoundation.org.au.

It seems to me that our Western culture is impoverished by our separation from such profound interconnectedness to the natural world. Such separation enables us to use nature as a resource without due regard to its own innate rhythm of growing and adapting and dying. It calls to us but we are not always listening. Children hear the call and they respond to it. They enter spontaneously and unselfconsciously into relationship with the natural world.

This brings to mind the central role that a natural bush garden played in my work with May, a young girl with language delay following early childhood abuse and trauma who was referred to me years back. I was working for the first time in a studio that overlooked this garden that I ventured into almost by accident as a way of containing the mess that was spilling out of the studio. I had moved the sand tray and the paints to a small table on the garden's edge and May soon colonised the entire garden, discovering in it a sense of joy that she drew me into with her. There was a difference between what was dealt with in the studio and the spontaneous play that occurred without, in the garden, and yet the two were inextricably linked. In the studio dolls were bound and gagged and had ribbons tied around their necks. They were left in various states of dishevelment and undress as May emerged from the studio into the dappled sunlight filtering through the trees. In May's imagination, low-hanging tree branches became horses upon which she galloped, mulch was cooked up in a pot and served and bushes became hiding places where I had to pretend I could not see her, despite her being quite clearly visible. Her antics made me laugh and this seemed to catch her by surprise. On one lovely, warm, winter afternoon a sudden gust of wind set flurries of autumn leaves dancing around us. She called out to me "Run! Run!" and we did, with arms stretched out wide.

I felt at the time that we were inexplicably held in the healing embrace of the garden. It was a garden that had survived despite my benign neglect. I had often watched the garden through the kitchen window as it ebbed and flowed in rhythm with the seasons. Birds would sit and observe me back. Aboriginal Dreamtime wisdom tells us that "Trees observe us as we move towards them" and that "The land and all that is in it is alive and conscious and aware" (Stockton in Shailer, 2007: 32). Annie Dillard similarly writes of the joy she feels "... knowing that the creek runs all night, whether we wish it, or know about it or even care" (Shaller, 2007: 69). Reflecting once more on that warm, winter afternoon as I write it seems to me now that together we entered a state of play – the child, the wind and I.

During my time in the Simpson Desert I was acutely aware of a particular melodic whistling quality to the wind that wrapped itself around us unceasingly. Laurens van der Post, in *The Heart of the Hunter*, set in the Kalahari Desert in Africa, writes that the relationship of Bushmen to the wind is so intimate that they feel it to be both "inside as well as outside" themselves (1961: 204). He recalls a conversation sitting around the campfire when an elderly man noticed a feather with a few drops of blood on it, born aloft by one of those sudden small whirlwinds, and related the following:

> This little feather falls down out of the sky, it having whirled around, falls down. It goes into the water, it becomes wet in water, it is conscious, it lies in water, it becomes ostrich flesh, it gets feathers, it puts on wings, it basks in the sun upon the edge of the water because it is still a young ostrich. Its feathers are young feathers because its feathers are little feathers. They are black for a little male ostrich he is. When his little feathers are dry, he may walk, unstiffening his legs.

Van der Post describes how this tale "… trembles with the Bushman's quick love and delicate concern for the small young first things of life." (ibid: 205). Of relevance here is the way the Bushman links the eternal and the ephemeral. The wisdom underlying the simplicity of his words enables us to see something we might otherwise have missed. The poignancy of this tale stirs up within me a love and a yearning for Africa, the land I was born in, and left behind.

The ability of place to frame and form us was brought vividly to life in a documentary I happened upon when I was watching Message Stick (Australian Broadcasting Channel, 2009 http://www.abc.net.au/tv/messagestick/stories/s2635673.htm.) It was about the making of an exhibition of Emily Kame Kngwarreye's work in Japan (Neale, 2008.) The program included archival footage of Emily Kngwarreye 'singing' her country in front of her last major painting *Big Yam Dreaming* (1995.) I was instantly captivated by Emily, slight in stature, wearing a headscarf, long dress, joggers and socks. She was flanked by assorted art world glitterati. As she sang her hand moved rapidly backwards and forwards over the huge canvas and the cadence of her voice rose and fell in rhythm with her movements. Drawing from the "immensity within her" (ibid: 184) she held her audience lightly in the palm of her hand.

Similarly, Rudy Talmacs (1994) recalls an incident in a Sydney Gallery in 1992 where he witnessed Emily engaged in what he called a 'visual prayer':

> She bowed her head and with her left hand she covered her eyes. As her outstretched hand pointed to the picture she quietly began to intone a thin, droning song at the harder edge of the voice… Gloria Petyarre, Emily's niece and fellow artist, began to drum with her finger on a board at hand in a steady supporting rhythm. With soft voice, Gloria entered Emily's song … shortly, Emily half looked up at her painting, pointed to another region and started another song. After another brief interval, they changed again to a new song, both given over to the utmost awareness and concentration, the drone of their voices hard, harmonious and completely encompassing their awareness.
>
> Talmacs, 1994, quoted in Neale, 2008: 224

Her ability to 'sing' the connection between inner world and country glowed with luminosity and yet remained anchored in the everyday. Laurence Freeman, Benedictine monk, has written that "we are the desert we enter." It is a journey we ultimately make alone and yet we may find ourselves "alone in the presence of another" (Winnicott, 1990: 30-34). Winnicott's notion of being alone whilst someone else is present develops in a particular way out of early caregiving relationships and may be impeded or enhanced by such experiences. The environment is protective when someone is present and oriented towards the needs of the infant, whether the infant is consciously aware of it or not. It is only when alone but in the presence of someone, that the infant can discover whom they are. He suggests the infant is able to enter that state of unintegration, which in an adult world we would call relaxing, where they may simply exist without being intruded upon, abandoned, or called upon to respond. After some moments an impulse may arise from within which will feel real and be a truly personal experience. The link between having the spaciousness within which to discover who we are is made possible by being held in someone's thoughts and feelings. That experience of being held is internalised within us. It forms a potential space, a cell, in which we may come into being in a new way. It becomes part of our inner world, a womb of our becoming, as we grow in self-knowledge.

When we meditate we work to let go of well-worn patterns of thinking and may find ourselves dropping into the space between our thoughts where divisions between self and other disappear. In a paradoxical way we connect more truly to whom we are when we let go of ourselves. When Emily 'sings' her country, she and her country become one. In Western parlance her singing could be described as something like chant or a sung meditation. She holds her country in a gaze of love. Raimond Gaita, whose parents migrated to Australia, wrote a memoir honouring his parents and their courage in facing the battles of their ordinary lives and everyday traumas. He writes that we often learn something is precious only when "we see it in the light of someone's love" (1999: 24). When such noticing deepens into the work of attention it "creates sacred space" (Weil, 1951: 54–65).

As therapists we wait with our clients on the cusp of the sacred. I had the opportunity to wait with one particular man in his dying. He was admitted to the palliative care unit in a large hospital. The social worker told me that he was numbered among the 'socially dissociated.' He was tall and fair and of slender build, probably in his late thirties. He gave a name that did not exist in taxation records and he had no social security number. He was brought to the hospital by ambulance from a boarding house. The manager there had no further information beyond the scant details the man proffered on admission. He never spoke of family, friends or life outside the hospital.

At the first Art Therapy group he chose a large sheet of white paper and gathered a few tubes of nearly spent watercolours. He soaked the dried out ends in water and used them as one might a paintbrush. He produced a simple image with an horizon line and what appeared to be a large and vibrant bushfire burning along the length of it. As the weeks passed his images reduced to increasingly faded, geometric shapes. At one unusually busy group session, where patients had to move in close, he folded his image down to a small square so that he did not take up too much room. The only comment he ever made in the three months we worked together was that "there were many kangaroos in that area." In his memory the kangaroos and perhaps bushfires from 'that area' found their way across the miles and over time to where we met together in the studio. He took great care with his final image, a distant horizon line stretched across a landscape that was barely there.

This man's process of painting out his inner landscape is reflected in Maeinrad Craighead's description of her experience among the sandstone flats and underground kivas of the Pueblo Indians:

> When I came to New Mexico in 1960 I found the land which matched my interior landscape. The door separating inside and outside opened. What my eyes saw meshed with images I carried inside my body. Pictures painted on the walls of my womb began to emerge.
>
> Craighead, 1986, in Lane, 1998: 67

My dying client's artwork traced a slow emptying out and articulation of the landscape within him. Thin places, in the Celtic tradition, are those places where the membrane of the earth is stretched thin and immortal forces may be more strongly felt. Times of birthing and times of dying are such places.

I went to see him as he lay on his back in bed with his eyes closed. Not talking. We sat for a period quietly together. I noticed some of his paintings stacked neatly on the bedside locker that formed a sort of trinity of healing: image, self and other. When the time finally came the social worker, a Buddhist nun and myself went to pay our last respects. There was a mix up and his body passed into the flames without anyone who had ever known him being present. Woebegone, we sat on a bench outside until a kookaburra's sudden shrill cackle in the trees above returned us to ourselves. He had eluded us in death as in life and yet managed to leave a profound impression on each of us. Smiling ruefully we trudged together back towards home. The social worker made enquiries afterwards but was never able to locate his artwork.

In *Love Dogs*, a poem by the Sufi poet Rumi (www.goodreads.com/quotes/109002-love-dogs-one-night-a-man-was-crying-allah-allah), a man is interrupted as he calls out to Allah. A cynic mocks him by asking him if he has ever gotten any response. The man falls silent but in a dream he sees Khidr, the guide of souls who tells him:

The longing you express
is the return message
The grief you cry out from
Draws you toward union

Artists, clients, therapists: we are all allured into the spacious places of our lives by yearning. We seek in our lives and at times in our dreams, to find the courage to cast off from the shore. I have learned to trust this yearning, to trust most those voices that speak of mystery and unknowing. The emptiness of the desert is what keeps desire alive. May it ever be so.

References

Bachelard, G. (1994) *The poetics of space*. Beacon Press, Massachusetts.

Craighead, M. (1986) The mother's songs: images of God the mother. In: Lane, Belden C. (1998) *The solace of fierce landscapes*. Oxford University Press, New York.

Dennes, M. (2001) Art therapy lecture. Master of Art Therapy program. University of Western Sydney

Dillard, A. (1974) *Pilgrim at Tinker Creek*. HarperCollins Publishers, New York.

Gaita, R. (1999) *A common humanity*. The Text Publishing Company. Melbourne.

Kame Kngwarreye, Emily. (2009) Message Stick on ABC Television. *Emily in Japan part 2: Big Yam Dreaming*, 28.2.08 to 13.4.08, National Museum of Art, Osaka, Japan (1330: 2.8.09.)

May, G. (2006) *The wisdom of wilderness*. HarperCollins Publishers, New York

Merton, T. (1960) *The wisdom of the desert*. Penguin Books, Canada.

Neale, M. (2008) (Ed.) *Utopia: the genius of Emily Kame Kngwarreye*. National Museum of Australia Press, Canberra.

Rohr, Richard. (2015) *Eager to love*. Hodder and Stoughton Ltd., London.

Shailer, J. (2007) *Wildflower journey prayers: a collection of prayers and readings with photographs*. David Lovell Publishing, Kew East, Australia.

Ungunmerr-Baumann, Miriam-Rose. *About Dadirri*. www.miriamrose-foundation.org.au.

Van der Post, L. (1961) *The heart of the hunter*. The Companion Book Club, London.

Weil, S. (1951) *Waiting for God*. HarperCollins Publisher, London.

Winnicott, D.W. (1990) *The maturational processes and the facilitating environment*. Karnac Books, London.

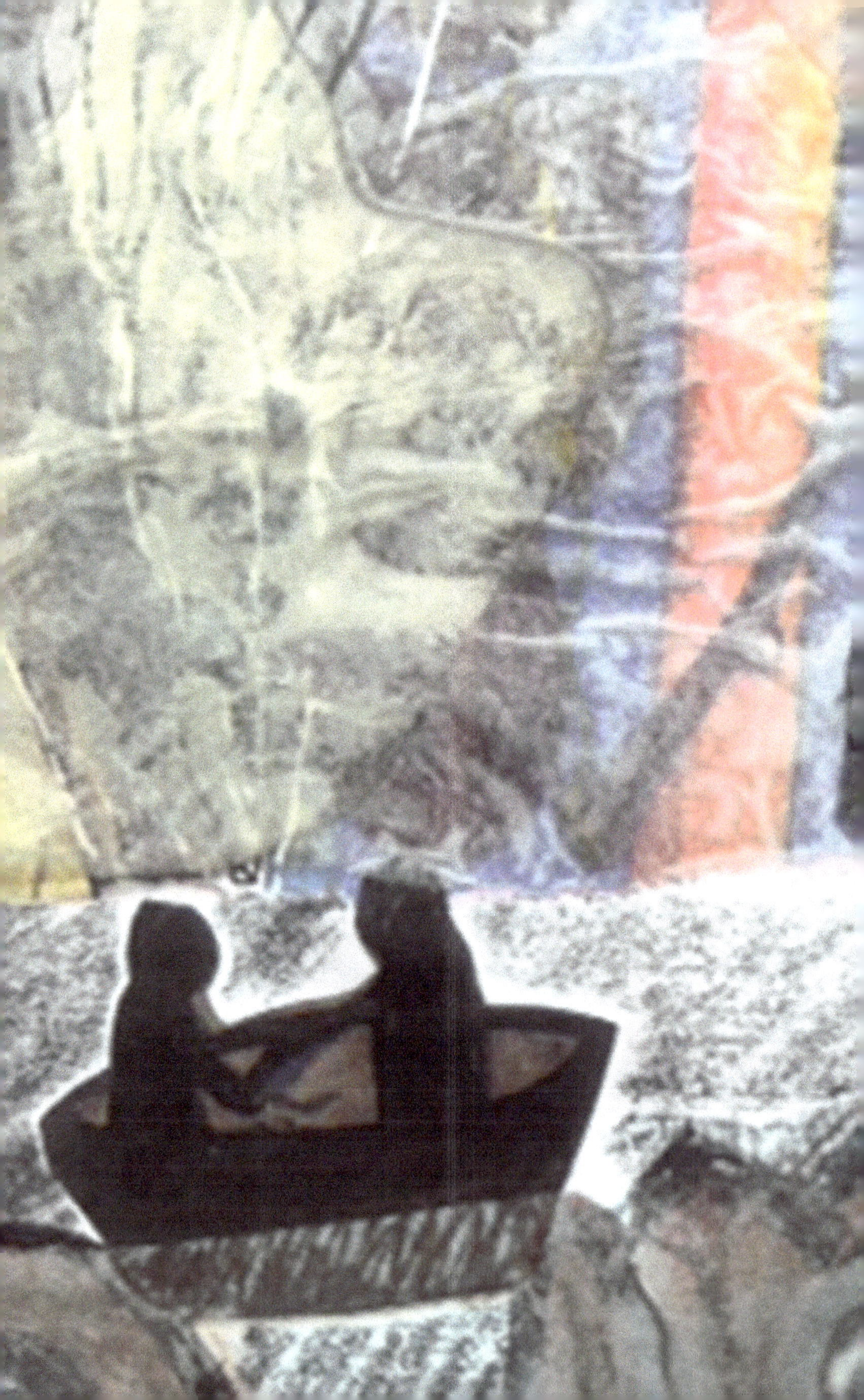

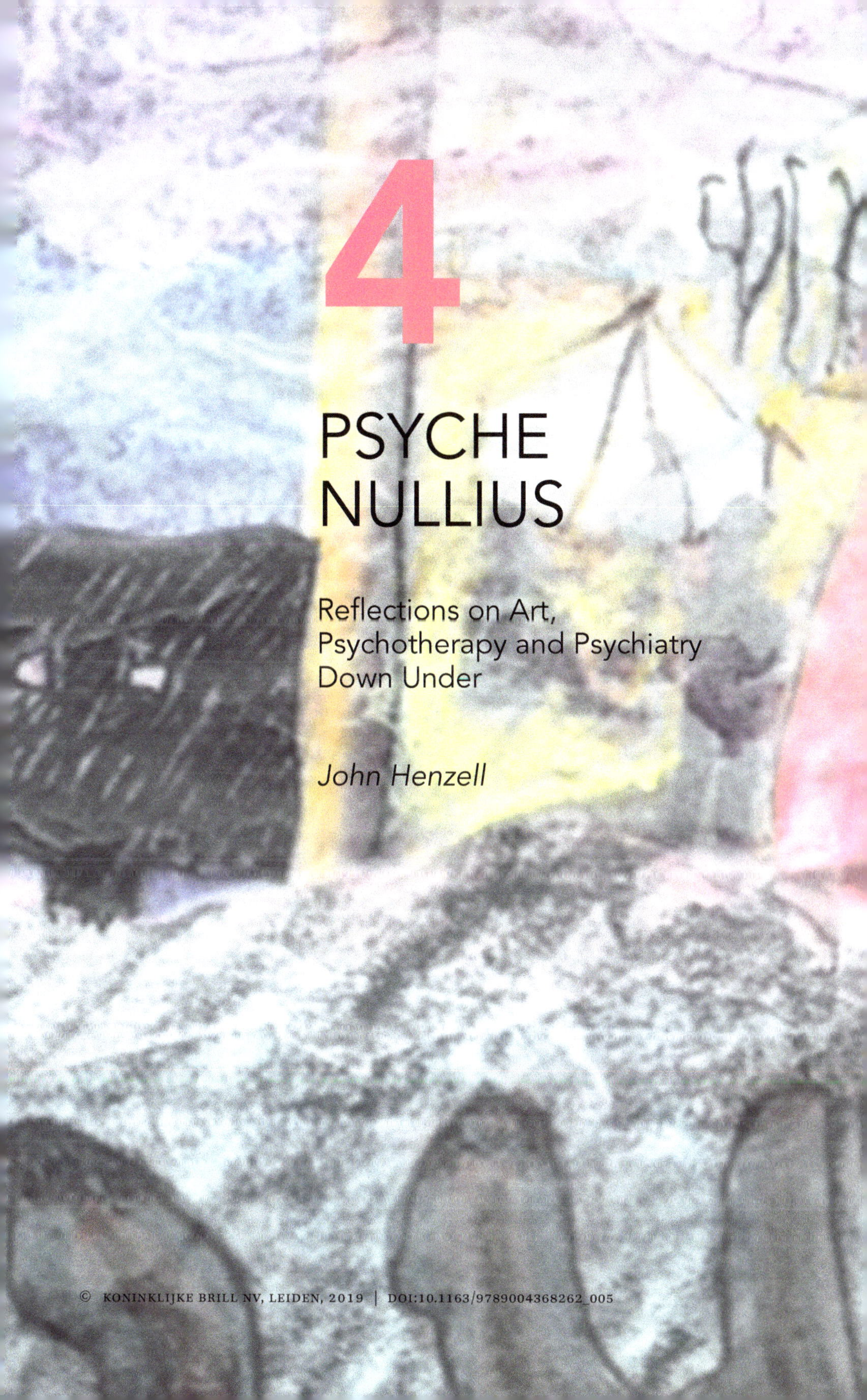

4

PSYCHE NULLIUS

Reflections on Art, Psychotherapy and Psychiatry Down Under

John Henzell

 | DOI:10.1163/9789004368262_005

In initial discussions about my contribution to this book a suggestion was that I write about 'the Australian imagination'. My first reaction was to wonder what this might be. Why should imagination differ in Australia from imagination elsewhere? The puzzle evaporates if we stop thinking of imagining as a thing, which an expression like 'the imagination' tempts us into. By not objectifying it we can more easily see how imagining is communal as well as personal and furthermore how there might be different, even conflicting imagining, or speaking, or how we actually see, like dialects or styles within languages, ways of speaking, that provide conduits for different kinds of experience. We can then see too how certain ways of imagining, thinking, speaking or how we look at situations and people in them can become privileged as a right and claim themselves to be factual and correct, just how things *are* rather than could be if we were more curious: the objectified view is severed from its origins in personal experience and losing its bold force becomes a dogmatic husk that dutifully follows orders.

Much of what follows will be concerned with the making of visual images by those receiving psychotherapy or by psychiatric patients in Australia and Britain. Imagination, the imaginary and imagining are all of course involved in this – as is sometimes their absence. In the eighteenth and early nineteenth centuries in Europe many forms of mental distress or madness were actually called 'disorders of the imagination'. More recently, just over a century ago, psychoanalysis starts with a form of oral imagining Freud called 'free association', say whatever comes up in your mind; then roughly two decades later Jung used what he called 'active imagination' in his analytic work and encouraged his patients in Zurich to bring drawings and paintings to their analytic sessions. He was I believe the first art therapist. Both Freud and Jung insisted that such psychotherapeutic work was absolutely always within a personal relationship.[1]

In the years following World War I psychologists of a more medical frame of mind began to design 'projective' diagnostic procedures in which they provided the images, the most popularly known of which is the Rorschach Test whereby subjects are asked to give their associations to symmetrical ink blots printed on nine cards with a tenth left blank, these responses to be scored against tabulated psychological criteria. Although the idea of projection was borrowed from psychoanalysis, the idea that you could 'score' these results, or imaginative activity and the subject's unconscious preoccupations, via a pre-formed set of images was a far cry from unconstrained free-associating or active imagining. Another test using pre-made standardised images was the Thematic Apperception Test in which printed cards showed vague shadowy depictions of people set against ambiguous backgrounds. There are also a number of similar tests in which the subject is requested to make a drawing of a situation, for example the House Tree Person Test, just these three, or as a gauge of someone's ability to cope with difficulties, the Draw a Person in the Rain Test, in which umbrellas may figure.

1 Robert Hobson called it a 'special form of friendship'. Robert F. Hobson (1981) *Forms of Feeling: The Heart of Psychotherapy*, Routledge.

The cards and score sheets were often kept secret as it was believed that only someone with the correct training could interpret the patient's or client's responses and if the cards were publicly available this could contaminate their clinical use. The relationship element is excluded to make the tests supposedly 'scientific'. The problem with such projective tests is that we judge such things all the time in our ordinary lives, we don't need as it were to peek through some kind of periscope into ourselves and find out what we're feeling like, whether jovial, serene, in love, sad, fearful or furious. We just are these things, they are immediate and sometimes more than one of them at once so that shadows and reflections are cast in our mind where there may be an internal politics going on, desire versus conscience.[2]

The way in which our imagination is shaped and coloured arises from our background, social customs, history, language and our own location in an endless human conversation, both literally and figuratively about our place or places in space and in time – where and how we live our lives and who with. In contrast to imagining, which is a necessary fiction, a 'what-if-ness' or 'seeing-into' of possibilities, is opposed a bureaucratic official consciousness in which everything is settled and located, that what meets the surface glance is just what it is. We are capable of both – of freeing up imagination and of closing it down by literalising – by letting it lead us wherever or pigeonholing its destinations in advance. We only notice the imaginative by its standing out in relief from its defensive shadow. But the distinction I am making oversimplifies, for the denial of our playful images – often a very serious play indeed, that might take us too far for comfort into unknown regions and perils, must itself play at the same game in an upside-down way in the interests of suppression. We shouldn't think of the imagination as a unitary single directional thing, but rather of many imaginations contesting our lived experience, opening or shoring it up in different ways and for a variety of human reasons and interests. Hence sometimes someone might be told *You're just imagining it* and indeed we do sometimes imagine what is not there. But sometimes there is sense in the mistake, like the young woman in a mental hospital where I worked who said *There's a bad smell in the room*; none of us others there could detect this, thinking because of her diagnosis she was having an olfactory hallucination until we realised she meant the social atmosphere in the room *stank*. We had at first assumed the wrong thing. Furthermore, when

2 The psychologists who devised such tests were if you like post-positivists, that is they followed the nineteenth-century quasi-religious belief that quantifiable empirical science should be the favoured methodology in absolutely all fields of knowledge. In the 1940s and 50s aestheticism tests were devised (a strange form of beauty contest) by Eysenck in Britain, and a recent PhD was awarded by a UK university psychology department for a candidate who devised a method of dividing drawings and paintings into a grid of squares within each one of which the quantities of pictorial ingredients, shapes and colours, were rated on a scale leading to an overall 'psychopathology rating'. The tragic brain surgery epidemic in psychiatry which swept through the 1930s, 40s and 50s is another example.

we call someone imaginative we are also referring to something in addition to circumstantial conditioning; we mean something innate, a native wit or soul, like the seemingly inherent abilities of good athletes or musicians.

There have been people imagining in what we now call Australia for countless millennia, right back to the ice age. During relatively recent geological time since then, but vast in terms of individual life, the map of this southern land has been redrawn by climate change and other natural forces, its northern extension to Papua and Asia and its southern to Tasmania have been below or above the sea, and changes too in the flora and fauna existing within the edges of this fluctuating coastline, for example giant kangaroos and marsupial lions. All seen by human beings. Engraved in the rock surfaces of Australia are traces of what its inhabitants over countless generations thought, felt, imagined and believed of their existence in the changing land which some amongst the first European navigators with an eye to staking a claim dubbed *terra nullius* – 'land belonging to no one'. These incised imaginings, there are vast numbers of them, might be the very oldest records of human expression.

There are differences between ways in which an imaginative capacity is passed on to us from previous times and lives, one being the immediacy of oral transmission by the living, from older to younger over succeeding generations in our 'mother tongue', another by the permanency of marks, images or objects left by our predecessors[3] which may leap-frog over many generations as is the case of the rock art left by those living in Australia tens of thousands of years before the first fleet arrived just over a paper-thin two centuries and a bit ago. It may have seemed to much later Indigenous generations that many of these ancient signs left embedded in the rocks by their ancestors were deposited by dreaming spirits. Before modern palaeontology Europeans as well spoke of fossilised forms encased in stone as God's handwriting or perhaps even creation designs.[4]

Since the initial forced settlement of convicts by the British at Port Jackson, and the many subsequent waves of more voluntary immigration, different metaphors, languages and images from other shores and histories have implanted themselves in our consciousness and there have been, as one would expect, running battles between them. Different nationalisms revisiting European conflicts, boisterous larrikinism against wowserism and protestant respectability, and the attempt to impose a sentimental and foreign landscape upon what is actually here. The prevalence of the suburban lawn in a country short of water is an everyday instance. The landscape is one key to this imaginative struggle. Not only did it take time for the newly arrived

3 And in some cultures by writing which is a later development of drawing.

4 It is interesting to think that hidden knowledge of this kind might be spread out laterally, even lost, in the great distances of continental Australia, whereas signs of the past tend to be more vertically hidden, buried beneath the constantly ploughed, disturbed, built on and densely populated surface of agrarian cultures in the Middle East, Europe and Asia.

white immigrants to see that Australia was not *terra nullius* at all but the artists amongst them found it hard to perceive the place as it was; their narrowed pupils allowed the bright hot light onto their retinas but there was nowhere for it to register or develop. It was mistaken at best for an Arcadian dream, a kind of picturesque hallucination forested with oaks and elms, as if it was still Blighty in spite of the sharply contrary visual evidence, and at worst an alien wilderness. A strangely distorted map of Great Britain and Ireland could be made from the British and Irish place names dotted around Australia. As well as these place names European notions of ownership and the right to do as we wish in and with our property were applied on a vast scale to Australian land. Many of the convicts had been sentenced for stealing property, like the swagman in *Waltzing Matilda*, and chose transportation in place of hanging.

At a conference in Albany in 2004 Brenda Croft, an Aboriginal artist, photographer and writer who grew up in Western Australia, drove across the Nullabor from Melbourne to present her paper and spoke of what she called the 'terrible beauty' she saw and photographed when she entered the wheat belt, stretching out east from the western seaboard for hundreds of kilometres, at a guess the size of France. Terrible because it was a vision of a catastrophe, the almost total destruction of the pre-existing habitat as far as you can see hour after hour from the highway. I know these roads well, how every now and then they duck down to cross a river or creek bed for brief relief in mallee and eucalypt shade, relief as well from the interminable roadside wire fences enclosing properties, before re-entering the endless expanse of wheat fields as the road rises again. It goes without saying that more than trees were removed, so were people. The clearances of the Scottish highlands in the 18th and 19th centuries are comparable. Her images of this landscape arise from her position within its past and present, how else could she imagine it?

One of the first Europeans to really respond to what he was seeing was the artist John Glover. An established and largely self-taught artist in Britain, born in the English midlands from a farming family, he arrived in Tasmania, then Van Diemen's Land, in 1831 on his sixty-fourth birthday. Many of his British paintings are in the manner of Turner or Claude Lorrain,[5] yet he was able to change the perceptual habits of a lifetime's work and really *see* what was spread before his eyes. No mean feat! In a series of magnificent paintings and many sketches made during the following eighteen years of his life he was possibly the earliest European artist to capture something of the sheer vastness of the landscape with its endless horizons, the activities of Aboriginals, their social lives, and, strikingly, the distinctive serpentine branching of native Australian trees. All of this in Tasmania, the most compact piece of Australian geography.

Notoriously, what many white settlers also found hard to see, or tolerate seeing, were the existing black inhabitants of this landscape. If the short-hand *terra nullius* was employed prior to colonisation to indicate that the southern continent belonged to nobody, that is no one considered as fellow human

5 He had been referred as the English Claude.

creatures having a right to the land, then post-settlement, Aboriginals with their many languages and knowledges were often brutally cleared from the land much as the trees were for pastoral development – though there were some whites who strongly objected to the horrors of this.[6] The greater the moral and ethical issues became apparent, the more many whites wished the problem, the fact that there were Aboriginals at all, would disappear – if only there had been really no one here, especially not black, to complicate white settlement. I stress black and white because this crude binary opposition forms the harsh virus that infects a colour prejudiced imagination. In a speech given in 1937 the Commissioner for Native Affairs in Western Australia, A.O. Neville, asked rhetorically: 'Are we going to have a population of one million blacks in the Commonwealth, or are we going to merge them into our white community and eventually forget that there were any Aborigines in Australia?' His question, arising from an imagined future trying to avoid a troubling present, became the intention which led to the stolen generation of *Rabbit-Proof Fence* fame, though as Aboriginal children had been forcibly removed from their families since the nineteenth century we would better call it stolen generations in the plural. Nevertheless it is Neville's question that crystallises the notion of wholescale elimination rather than piecemeal clearance. Who is to say he wasn't imagining too, his own 'as if'? Yet others were appalled then and are now by his hopes and the acts that they led to.

There are disputes about this, the 'history wars', Keith Windschuttle in one corner Henry Reynolds in the other, John Howard's castigation of a 'black arm band' view of Australian history versus Kevin Rudd's apology – or to go back to landscape, bitter disputes about the meaning of the land and its resources. I raise them as instances of, depending on one's point of view, imagination not being the exclusive property of the good guys or any one way of seeing things. It is the single limited one way vision that is the stumbling block. If Neville had somewhere in himself been able to think – *Maybe the blacks are just like me and my own white kith and kin, with our grandparents, mums, dads and kids, our language, feelings, memory, customs and faith, but there is a complicated problem between us and much wrong has been done, a real dispute about whose place this is and how we should conduct ourselves from now on* – and then go on to imagine further and enter this dilemma, then his place in Australian history wouldn't be as ignominious as it has become.

One can think of imagining as a richly figured rhetoric that occurs inside and between us, replete with shapes, movements, sounds, scents, metaphors, thoughts, dramas and speech, a play we may choose to realise via all the difficulties of translation into an external incarnation available to others. Because of this, imagining occupies a virtual space inside as well as outside our skins, sometimes an outside in the sense of an unconscious projection that, because we are unaware we are engaging it to solve some problem of our own, forces itself on others against their will. These 'others'

6 See Henry Reynolds (1998), *This whispering in Our Hearts*, Allen & Unwin.

can be readily summoned up, not only Aboriginals but Asians, refugees, Muslims, the chattering classes, gays, and so on. Driving around Australia some years ago, sitting around a proverbial Aussie campfire in the Pilbara in the north west, having a chat and a beer with other travellers, we were discussing south east Asians in Australia, maybe wishing there was a deli nearby, when someone suddenly interrupted, 'Hitler had the right idea!' adding that they should be sent back to where they'd come from, ignoring that he himself was a European immigrant and, of course, white. It was like he was trying to belong to two clubs at once.

In 2007 I attended a conference in Melbourne. Because the conference was about art, therapy and psychiatry we visited the Cunningham Dax Collection in Parkville, a short walk from our venue. According to its publicity the collection exists to foster art, creativity and education in mental health. Our friendly host was Dr Eugen Koh, then Senior Lecturer in Art and Psychiatry in the Department of Psychiatry at the University of Melbourne. The parts of the collection on display were well framed and hung, clearly lit and made a crisp showing against the white walls of the exhibition space. As I walked around looking at the images I felt in very familiar territory. For I knew the older parts of the collection well and their darkly contentious history of which my fellow visitors seemed quite unaware, as was possibly Dr Koh himself. The ruminations stemming from this visit lie behind much of what follows.

The first real instance of art and image-making forming an integral part of psychotherapy was in the 1920s in Zurich where C.G. Jung encouraged patients to bring paintings and drawings to analytic sessions; there is an archive of several thousands of these images. If psychoanalysis, the talking cure, begins with free association in words, what we say and hear, then this work in Zurich widens free association to include images, what we make and see. One feature of this is that paintings, drawings and sculptures persist in time and space whereas words, except for those that are written or recorded, do not, they vanish in the air – but of course leave different traces in personal memories. From the 1940s in the English speaking world either side of the Atlantic the use of art in psychotherapeutic work came to be known as art therapy. This early history as it occurred in the UK and USA is perhaps broadly understood. What is little known is the same period in Australia after World War II when relatively unrecognised forms of therapy were happening which, perhaps because they were so little recognised, failed to take root as they could have done in more favourable circumstances.

At present there is a small art therapy profession in Australia and it seems, I think, to many involved in it that things started here in the 1980s when a number of art therapists, either Australians who had trained in Britain or the United States, or nationals of those countries, decided to live and work in Australia. Towards the end of the decade postgraduate training in art therapy started in Australia and now several universities in Australia and New Zealand offer training courses.

But the practice of art therapy here has an interesting but largely forgotten Australian background which goes back further than is thought and connects with what were contemporary developments in Britain and America. I would locate this around two people, one a psychotherapist and psychiatrist, the other a painter, though I'm sure there must be others. The first was the psychiatrist, psychotherapist and hypnotherapist, Ainsley Meares, who worked in Melbourne from the 1950s to 1970s. He wrote *The Door to Serenity* (1958) which I read in the early 60s in Britain. It deals in detail with a patient diagnosed with psychosis for whom art was a part in her psychotherapy with him. Later on he became best known for his popularisation of self-hypnosis, or one might say attention control, as a method of relieving severe pain. Famously he had a wisdom tooth pulled without anaesthesia to demonstrate his method and the courage of his convictions. Interesting as this is, his earlier work could have been a potential beginning of greater public awareness of art and psychotherapy in Australia which might have formed a basis for practice by others.

A second potential beginning, with which I have a personal connection, arose from the Western Australian painter, Guy Grey-Smith. The son of a farmer in the Western Australian wheatbelt he served in the RAF in Europe during World War II. He was shot down and incarcerated in a German prisoner of war camp, subject of *The Wooden Horse* and *Great Escape* movies, along with another Western Australian, Howard Taylor, who helped make the decoy wooden horse at Stalag Luft III and later became a prominent artist in W.A. Grey-Smith's way out of captivity however wasn't to be by means of the wooden horse; providentially as it turned out he contracted tuberculosis and was repatriated back to Britain in exchange for a similarly ill German prisoner of war. He became a patient at King Edward VII Hospital at Midhurst in Sussex where he benefited from meeting Adrian Hill who encouraged him to paint and draw as part of Hill's novel 'art therapy' work at the hospital (Hill 1945, 1951). As far as I know it was Hill who originated the term 'art therapy'. After his recovery Grey-Smith went to art school in London before returning with his English wife, the artist Helen Grey-Smith, to Western Australia. He then suffered a brief recurrence of tuberculosis and on his recovery continued to paint and helped financially support this by using Hill's art therapy methods with tuberculosis and psychiatric patients in Perth. This was with the assistance and encouragement of my father, Linley Henzell, who was a specialist in the treatment of tuberculosis and held a government position making him responsible for the management of chest illnesses in WA where he played a part in the world movement which culminated in the eradication of tuberculosis in the developed world which until then was still an epidemic and usually fatal illness.

As far as I know Grey-Smith was the first person to be called an art therapist in Australia – all this was in the 1950s. He was ideal for the task with his combination of enthusiasm for art, talkativeness, perceptiveness and personal warmth. Through being a patient of my father he became a family friend and after I finished art school in 1957 he offered me some of his hospital work with TB patients so he could devote more of his time to painting. He became well known for his vivid modernist paintings of the bush and, alongside Howard Taylor and Bob Juniper, one of the most prominent Western Australian artists then. He died in 1981. I have vivid memories of that early work, my first paid employment. It was in a military repatriation hospital for army veterans suffering from tuberculosis, some of them terminally ill. I was still a teenager and wheeled my trolley with art materials from bed to bed and got to know some of the men, old enough to be my dad or uncle. I would help them make images of their life and interests, often very ordinary and some would say sentimental, their wife or girlfriend, an idealised homestead, a sunset, a horse, the bush or a favourite car – but seldom of their military life. We would have conversations arising from these images, I was aware of how important and emotionally laden they were – then one day I would arrive to an empty bed and be told by staff that the man I had got to know had 'passed away'. I had never previously known anyone who had died. It was an introduction to human mortality and the fragility of existence.

As a young man I hardly realised at first the full importance of the work Guy had introduced me to, fascinated as I was by it, and left for England in 1959 where I began working with psychiatric patients and immersed myself in the experimentation and rich events of the 1960s and later years in Britain (Henzell, 1997). That I had this opportunity is in large measure due to Guy and my father who furnished me with the introductions I needed to find my first appointment in a large psychiatric hospital. I had little idea then of how close I had been to people and events that could have been an antipodean parallel to events elsewhere in the world.

There were other wider Australian influences in the background. Post-War Australia became a centre of richly narrative figurative painting, particularly the work of the 'angry penguins' in Melbourne and others, that stood out from the dominant non-figurative art schools of Europe and Abstract Expressionism in the USA. Prominent amongst these artists were Sydney Nolan – who re-invented Ned Kelly as an Aussie icon – Arthur Boyd, Albert Tucker, Russell Drysdale and Fred Williams, but also significant was an increasing awareness in Australia and beyond of Aboriginal art and of individual Aboriginal artists. Part of this was a propensity in some Australians for accounting in one way or another for their past in stories and images – to be expected given the emotionally and socially powerful events these narratives and depictions dealt with: forcible transportation, the persecution of Indigenous people and their view of their own history, far longer than anything European, rebellions and languages on the verge of extinction, the redemption of a convict past, stories about wrecked Dutch navigators, immigration, the great treks of white explorers like Burke and Wills, Gallipoli and the World Wars, asylum seekers, the 'stolen generation', and, for Europeans, the seemingly strange, to recent immigrants, nature of Australia's ancient geography – its compelling, or to some repelling, infinities of space.[7] Here was a deep well of communal experience and images, both starkly beautiful and tragic, which could not help but inform the narratives and images that constitute important parts of the Australian landscape in both its geological and psychological registers, or for some lead to a laconic style of speech or silence, which I discovered is often true of returned war veterans.

Two years ago while walking through the permanent collection of Australian painting at the Art Gallery of Western Australia, mostly European Australian, I walked into a gallery space and encountered a truly breath-taking spectacle, an encounter with Australia in full voice, Sidney Nolan's vast painting, seven adjoining panels each 152.3 cm high x 122 cm wide (5 x 4 feet), called *Desert Storm*. A singular masterpiece. It made me shiver, it's hard to know whether in fear or exultation, not only by seeing what's happening on such a panoramic scale but hearing the searing wind and feeling the smarting whip of its driven sand. An eighth panel had somehow escaped to Sydney. It should be rejoined with its siblings and permanently mounted in an arc like Monet's *Water Lilies* were at the London Tate in memory of another great artist's visions.

What prevented Meare's and Grey-Smith's work, and the burgeoning imagery of those Australian artists contemporary with them from forming deeper and more lasting connections with psychotherapeutic work? A complete answer to this question may be impossible given the myriad circumstances bearing on it, even if it were possible the research required to give it in the fullest sense would be of a scope far beyond this short chapter. I cannot do more here than make some educated guesses which I hope will not be too wide of the mark.

First let us look briefly at the state of psychiatry and psychotherapy beyond Australia in the period I have been discussing, especially in the United States and Britain in the years immediately after World War II. Like the USA, Britain had become the host country for psychoanalysts escaping from fascist persecution in continental Europe before and during the war, the most famous being Sigmund Freud. Indeed both countries became the primary homes of psychoanalysis. After Freud's death, Ernest Jones, Anna Freud and Melanie Klein, together with Michael Balint from Hungary, were formative influences in the development of psychoanalysis and psychotherapy in the UK. Of the British born psychoanalysts, Marion Milner and the paediatrician Donald Winnicott both used the making of pictorial work in their clinical work and theoretical writing. Jung's deep and personal interest in the arts also exerted great influence on psychotherapy and progressive education in these years. Michael Edwards, an artist, jazz musician, Jungian analyst and friend once remarked to me that Jung's way of thinking came about in an important sense because '..he was good with his hands'. He made and built things, houses,

7 Driving in the outback one comes across many traces of European immigrants' struggles with this unforgiving environment with its great distances between neighbourhoods: ruins of abandoned homesteads, hotels, cemeteries, mines, rusting machinery, even whole settlements.

sculptures, paintings, was a calligrapher (see the Red and Black Books), sailed boats on Lake Zurich and so knew at first hand how we actually make what we mean as well as speak it. Michael trained in Zurich and while doing so helped archive the collection of drawings and paintings in Zurich made by patients of Jung and his colleagues. Jung's ideas were influential in the 'Education Through Art' movement which held great sway in Britain as well as internationally between the 1950s and 80s and still exists. Its major figure was the British poet and philosopher Herbert Read (1967)[8]. As well as this there was a growing interest in 'outsider art' and the art of the mentally ill of which collections began being made in the 19th century and have continued since.

This was the intellectual and social milieu in which a number of artists, psychoanalysts and psychiatrists in Britain, including Homer Lane, Adrian Hill, Arthur and Marianne Segal, Edward Adamson, Marion Milner, E.M. Lyddiatt, and Irene Champernowne, devised ways of placing art and image-making within psychotherapy. It was at this time that the term 'art therapy' became established in Britain as a distinct form of psychotherapeutic practice. There is no doubt that art therapy could not have developed as it did without its connections with psychotherapy in general, and with psychoanalysis and analytical psychology in particular. Irene Champernowne, for example, had created a therapeutic community, the Withymead Centre in Devon, specifically structured around a working alliance of Jungian psychotherapists and artist therapists.

A further factor helping non-medically qualified people to practice psychotherapy was the influence in Britain of what were known as the "Balint groups". Michael Balint, a Hungarian émigré psychoanalyst with his wife Enid Balint, and other psychoanalysts, including Donald Winnicott and Colin Woodmansey, realising that psychoanalysis in its pure and maybe dogmatic form was simply impractical and misguided within a mass health service free at the point of delivery as the British NHS was, decided to disseminate psychotherapeutic ideas and ways of working amongst key groups of health workers. Essentially this involved discussion in a trusting relationship. These groups included GPs, nurses, midwives, psychologists, psychiatrists, paediatricians, social workers, managers and ancillary staff (Balint, M. 1957, Balint, E. 1993). The more experienced people became at working in this way so they could repay their debt to the process by supervising others, and so on; a "benign chain reaction" as Woodmansey called it. As a legacy of this when I first worked in Sheffield people suffering from acute psychological distress but without the money to purchase private psychotherapy were able to access skilful psychotherapy from many NHS and social services staff who in turn were supervised by their peers. Once too this was of enormous benefit to art therapists and trainees who could position themselves within these psychotherapeutic networks and receive the supervision they provided and then in turn become part of the same network without endlessly worrying

8 See Herbert Read (1967), *Education through art*, Faber and Faber. This movement and related ideas of 'child centred education' were significant factors in the creation of the art therapy profession during the post-war years and later in Britain.

whether they could afford it. Art therapists were on the same footing as other psychotherapists. I fear decades of post-Thatcher economics have degraded some of this communal and collegiate generosity.

In the early 1950s there were three psychiatric advisors to the Minister of Health in the UK concerning the role of the ancillary professions in the revolutionary new National Health Service, created in 1948 after the landslide election of Clement Attlee's post-war Labour government. Cunningham Dax was one of these, together with Doctors Guttman and Maclay. They had begun a collection of 'psychiatric art' at the Maudsley and Bethlem Royal Hospitals in London, now called the Guttman-Maclay Collection. They were determined to encase this body of work in what they thought of as a proper medical and 'scientific' framework. Their collection continued a psychiatric history of collecting art made by patients, Cesare Lombroso was one of the progenitors of this in late 19th century Italy. In 1888 he published *l'uome di genio in rapport alla psichiatrica*, (published in 1891 as *The Man of Genius* in English) – a study of 'psychiatric art'. He was also the founder of the 'Italian School of Positivist Criminology'. Lombroso's idea was that madness was linked to genius and many what now seem comical comparisons are adduced to 'prove' this. One typically brief example: in 1705 J.S. Bach walked 400 kilometres from Amstadt to Lubech to hear the famed Buxtehude playing the organ. We all know, Lombroso writes, that 'vagabondage', wandering, was a 'mattoid' (psychotic) symptom, Bach was therefore without doubt mad, but also undeniably a genius. There are many other anecdotes concerning the eccentric habits of 'men of genius', writers, artists, statesmen and so on, 'proving' that they were mattoids and consequently geniuses. Lombroso's writing often reads as if it was a series of Monty Python skits.

Of the work increasingly being done by artists in National Health Service hospitals, particularly mental hospitals, the conservative advice of Dax, Guttman and Maclay to the Minister was that this work should be an entirely diversional activity for patients, that it must be supervised by occupational therapists and that actual therapy through pictorial work, or any discussion of it, should absolutely only be undertaken by psychiatrists or clinical psychologists. However, given the extreme resistance to this by those directly involved in the work, and strong support received from influential psychiatrists and psychotherapists, as well as from the National Association for Mental Health, this advice was disregarded by the 1960s (Waller, 1991).

Eric Cunningham Dax (1908-2008) had experimented with physical treatments for mental illness in the 1930s and became Medical Superintendent of Netherne Hospital, a large asylum in Surrey, south of London, in 1946. He continued his biological orientation and made use of brain surgery and electroconvulsive therapy (ECT) at Netherne. A fellow psychiatrist at Netherne was Francis Reitmann, Director of Clinical Research, who shared Dax's enthusiasm for physical approaches to the causes and treatment of mental illness and like him experimented with, and carried out, leucotomy and shock therapy. Dax wrote a book, *Psychiatric Experiments in Art* (1953), about art produced by patients at Netherne. A few years earlier Reitmann had published his *Psychotic Art* (1950). In fact much of their 'research' arose from work with patients by the artist and pioneer art therapist in the psychiatric field, Edward Adamson who had been appointed at Netherne in 1946 to run an art studio for patients to produce the art that Dax and Reitmann required for their 'research'. Before this appointment Adamson had given talks on art to hospital patients as part of a scheme run by the Red Cross Picture Library after the war and had met Adrian Hill. His first introduction to Netherne was an evening journey from London to this large Edwardian mental hospital, being led down a seemingly endless dark corridor to a big hall in which was seated a large audience of patients several of whom had bandages wrapped around their bruised heads as they recovered from lobotomies.

The working conditions in which he was offered his job at Netherne were ring fenced with extraordinary restrictions. The patients referred to him would produce their artworks in a setting and with materials that were strictly standardised so the artistic work they produced would be, according to Dax and Reitman, 'scientific'. Each individual would be given the same range of colours in their paints or pastels, the same range of brushes, pencils, same easels, even chairs, all work made on paper 22 x 18 inches (55 x 45 cm), and Adamson would keep his advice to a bare minimum. In fact the environment Dax and Reitman wanted was a laboratory rather than a studio, in which the art works were as it were excretions, or diagnostic specimens like blood or urine samples, something like biopsies of madness. Looking back on this now I wonder how Adamson could have accepted the situation rather than just burst out laughing.

Dax writes as if Adamson was no more than incidental to the interpretations and diagnoses of psychiatrists like himself, as does Reitmann. Adamson's role seems little more than a footnote, just two or three sentences in the whole book by Dax in fact, though he obviously had the ability to somehow enable the powerful expressive work of the patients who worked in his studio, which in turn formed an important basis of Dax's and Reitman's books. To Dax, Adamson seemed an orderly or medical instrument. I have heard anecdotal evidence of weekly medical meetings in the hospital's Management Committee room where Adamson would be asked to bring some of the most recent examples of patients' pictorial work and lay them out on the table for all to see, that is the medical staff. There would then follow a discussion of what psychiatric diagnoses might be applied to the patients whose pictures were displayed. Adamson would not be asked for his opinions of the work, the task was to infer an expert diagnosis of psychopathology from the evidence of the pictures alone, akin to a connoisseurs' 'blind tasting'. That this was a misguided activity has been pointed out in the particular case of the pictures in the Guttman-Maclay collection by its curator in later years, the art historian Patricia Allridge in conversation with me. She felt that in spite of what might have been their often sympathetic concern for their patients, these medical interpretations of their art works and other patients in the past, were quite mistaken. That forms of artistic depiction were at least as conditioned by the individual artist's knowledge of style, whether popular or sophisticated, as by any psychopathological determination. For example a painting by the artist Richard Dadd, who had been a patient a century before, showing a knife pointing over a table edge toward the viewer was described in the Guttman-Maclay commentary as evidence of the artist's homicidal tendencies. It is true Dadd was confined in Bedlam after stabbing his father to death – the first murderer in British law to successfully plead diminished responsibility in a case of homicide. Allridge's point was that Dadd was a young and successful artist trained and practised in early 19th century genre painting where still life scenes would often include an implement inclined in such a way to show off the artist's skill in painting and foreshortening and that his practical knowledge of this was not necessarily evidence of repressed parricidal inclinations. The psychiatrists were simply unaware of the conventions and technicalities of artistic depiction in which Dadd would have been trained, their epistemological assumptions were quite naive. One should say too that fervent psychoanalytic interpretations of everything imaginable in terms of favoured Freudian, Kleinian or Jungian symbols often seem too like jigsaw pieces pushed into spaces they don't really fit.

Messianic protagonists either side of this body mind split share a similar hubris, whether on one side the ages of psychoanalysis required for a 'cure' by an analyst who has in turn been similarly analysed for years on end, or on the other with typical American entrepreneurial savvy driving around the USA in the 1950s as Walter Freeman and James Watts did in their 'lobotomobile' charging institutions or families $25 per icepick lobotomy on thousands said to be suffering from schizophrenia in half the states of the USA.

In 1952 Dax came to Australia under the auspices of the Victorian Institute of Mental Hygiene and subsequently became Chairman of the newly formed Federal Mental Health Authority and remained in that post until 1969. A tenure of 17 years. During this time and later he built up his collection of 'psychiatric art' along the lines of the Guttman-Maclay Collection at the Maudsley in Britain. Some of these art works had been produced in Adamson's studio and there were added works by Australian psychiatric patients. These were collected together in an archive at Melbourne University which was housed in Carlton before the collection moved to its present home in Parkville where I encountered it again in very different circumstances in 2007. I had visited its previous venue in the early 90s which was amazing, but not really in the sense which Dax intended. There were several treasures if one looked behind the simplistic diagnostic spin put on the archive's contents. A star in the collection when I saw it then were the loosely woven and knitted garments made by a woman patient from Ballarat diagnosed as psychotic. Coats, blouses, dresses of such loose and free-form construction they seemed more like coverings for an imaginary world than everyday wear. Suspended on coat-hangers inside the front door they made an unearthly impression as you entered the building, as if the house and entrance hall where they hung belonged to the mystery woman who had made and wore them. All the other works I saw after these were collected in plan chests, drawings and water colour paintings, all classified in the manner of specimens in a medical museum. So the drawers of art works were pulled out, each of them according to generalised clinical labels, psychosis, hebephrenia, schizophrenia, paranoia, mania, depression, neurosis, psychopathy, and so on. Dax wasn't inclined to engage in any conversation about these pictures with me in spite of my interest and obviously knowing much about the same field; perhaps this was why.

Dax was an old man when I met him in Melbourne and the management of the collection was left to a retired occupational therapist. It was like opening the doors of a house locked up half a century ago and seeing furniture, place settings and ways of doing things from the past, but here I mean preserved remnants of a bygone psychiatric practice overlaying images and imaginings that in themselves sometimes spoke of bitter predicaments and outlandish dreams rather than symptoms and syndromes. I do not know how Dax used his administrative posts in Australia in relation to psychotherapy and art therapy in the public sector, but I doubt that it was especially helpful to those who wanted to use art psychotherapeutically or respond to those who requested or needed it – precisely because the message of the collection is that artistic creativity is beneficial only in the vague sense of well-being, while the real clinical, diagnostic and therapeutic work should be left to medical experts. Certainly his imprimatur is to be felt in a number of Australian mental health settings where staff employed as art therapists are employed essentially as art instructors and discouraged from engaging in real explorative work with patients or clients. I feel his influence was at least one of the reasons why the enthusiastic potential of Grey-Smith's initiative in Perth, and of the work of Meares in Melbourne and very possibly others, may have failed to make the wider connections they could have done. But whatever part Dax played in this, the ideology of much psychiatric and clinical psychology practice in Australia would not have encouraged it. Psychotherapy, certainly in-depth psychotherapy, which in other countries is the ambience in which art therapy fits, has tended to operate on the sidelines of Australian public sector health care, remaining largely confined to private practice. In spite of this however the main body representing psychotherapy in Australia is a broad church pleasingly free of pecking orders.[9]

It has often been said that the medical profession has created one of the most powerful guilds or trade unions ever. Undoubtedly amongst the compelling reasons for this is our immediate dread of death, disfigurement, bodily or functional impairment and pain. For those who offer relief from these threats, from the signs of their presence whether real or alleged, we trade and offer great rewards of privilege and wealth. These signs are least conclusive and harder to establish in psychiatry as they further depart from physicality, that is as they enter the psychological domain. To put this another way, how do we move from quantities to qualities? Psychiatry lives in a no man's land between these

9 Anyone professionally practising psychotherapy or counselling, including art therapists, psychologists, psychiatrists, psychoanalysts, or counsellors can belong to the Psychotherapy and Counselling Federation of Australia (PACFA) which makes available a national list of accredited practitioners.

territories and discourses. What kinds of pain or suffering live here? Perhaps anguish rather than agony – is that right? In the months immediately before the British NHS was finally created psychiatry, being in this indefinable and in-between territory, was about to be left out of this great experiment and administered by the Home Office. Alarmed at being out of pocket, via their exclusion from the lucrative 'merits' scheme,[10] the most influential consultant psychiatrists lobbied the government successfully at the last moment to be included.

Finally there was an obvious logistic difficulty in Australia preventing psychotherapy and art therapy developing as fully they did in Britain and the USA – compared to now the difficulty, time and cost of travel as well as communication between one end of the world and the other. When I travelled to England in 1959 it took me five weeks by sea and the single passage cost the equivalent of a good part of an annual salary; you used the phone sparingly, carefully costing the minutes, and postal communication involved a turnaround of several weeks. There was no Australian television, no cheap air travel, or the immediacy of email and the internet. At the time Perth was especially isolated in these respects, additionally separated from Australia's more populous and cosmopolitan Eastern cities. Inter-state travel was and still is much more than an everyday undertaking in a huge country like Australia with a handful of major cities widely spread around the coast. A wry joke is that when God was handing out continents he gave a whole one to Australia. UK friends sometimes ask me whether I see much of a friend or relative who lives in Melbourne or Sydney, not realising that they are as far away from Perth as Athens or Casablanca are from Britain and misses out the endless stretches of Australia's interior between its cities.

A closely related problem in Australia is the thin spread of population in such a large place. In a country of 60 million like the UK factions or minorities and their interests are much bigger than in a population a third the size, especially when this third is so spread out. When I was at school in Western Australia an oddly proud and often repeated boast was that you could fit Britain into WA sixteen times over. The downside of this boast was that you could have easily fitted WA's population into any one of many British cities. Those with common interests are bigger and can more easily be in touch in the UK, at most just a relatively brief journey to meet in person.

The issue in much of the foregoing is that psychiatry and its junior partner clinical psychology have as it were colonised the psychological territory of Australia much as the early white settlers had the actual place. As if they

10 The merit scheme was operated by a medical freemasonry. After several years as a consultant a doctor might receive a letter declaring he had been recommended to the lowest level of the merit scheme, but with a large salary increase and the right to cast a vote for doctors to be included like he had been, and it was mostly 'he', to the scheme. All this of course should be confidential. The same scheme continued for a further two levels of the scheme, three in all, by which time enormous salaries were being paid by the NHS. This was the bribe that the Minister of Health, Aneurin Bevan, paid to gain support for the NHS from the medical profession. Those in the merit scheme were mostly male consultants and surgeons in fields like thoracic surgery, very few from psychiatry.

thought of this psychological territory as also a *terra nullius*, of which they presumed themselves the first explorers with few rivals to take seriously. A sign of their political adroitness and its success is that whenever there are issues or events causing public concern the names of the experts that automatically spring to mind in politics and from the media are 'psychiatrist' or 'psychologist' and comment is then called for a member of one of these guilds. In this sense they have a monopoly. This is odd in a country that has and continues to produce so many discerning psychological observers in literature, art and general commentary out of all proportion to its small population. But of course it will be said that these are not 'experts'; their views may be entertaining but are not backed by evidence or research. But what is the 'evidence' requested here? It is this question of what evidence is that is so important, yet the politician or manager with a crowded schedule full of political complications reaches for a quick fix, just like the French newspaper typesetters used a *cliché*, an already typeset heading or phrase which could be used without wasting time. So the clichéd or usual view of evidence is that it involves statistics, is supported by experts, can be sought quickly, and doesn't complicate things too much.

The confusion in their approach is that quality and quantity, mind and body, are a paradoxical continuum like a Mobius strip. Psychoanalysis half realised this but, having professional ambitions, hedged their bets with a clinical gloss. So Freud or Klein or Jung are said to have 'discovered' the unconscious, the Oedipus complex, the Id, the mechanisms of repression, the depressive position, the archetypes, and so on,[11] as if they were African explorers like Livingstone and Stanley, not seeing they more resemble Australia's Burke and Wills wandering tragically around *Terra Nullius*. If only they had asked someone familiar with the place, and in the end it was the Aboriginal locals who rescued John King, the only survivor. If Burke and Wills made mistakes about equipment, the professions with psychological ambitions make them about assumptions; their epistemology is shaky no matter how much the language of positivism or scientism tries to be scientific, as physicists or astronomers in the physical sciences can quite rightly be. Hence the restrictive equipment prescribed in the Netherne art studio that tries to snare the wrong meaning in a web in which nothing can stick. Many of the assumptions of psychiatry and clinical psychology are radical category mistakes, mistakes about how we speak our experience – or at Netherne paint or draw it. At a conference a psychiatrist asked me what colours were contraindicated when working with psychotic patients, he wasn't joking. Michel Foucault says of positivist psychiatrists faced with their case material endlessly leaking through their theories that '..they would increasingly confine themselves in positivism, the more they felt their practice slipping out of it.' Clinical language, because it is being made to operate in the wrong field, cannot naturally listen to the vernacular speaking inside our heads, or to each other,

11 The terminology of psychoanalysis is really redescription or metaphor misunderstood to be discovery.

because it is caught up in professional ambitions which cannot hear Yeats's '... now my ladder's gone, I must lie down where all the ladders start, in the foul rag-and-bone shop of the heart'.

Clinical language in its rightful areas, the world of the body with its physical infections and diseases, damaged limbs and organs, cancers, and other physical symptoms is of value to us because it models causation and helps prevent pain, bodily impairment and can save our life. I am thankful I live in a time and place where there is pain relief, antibiotics and little chance of contracting tuberculosis. If we break a leg we want it restored to its normal state, or as near as we can get to that. But if we are unhappy, confused or frightened we might need someone to help us ask questions about these states of mind and to keep us company through them. A large part of this may be patiently hearing or witnessing them in exactly the way in which they may say or show their feelings if they can, it may not be easy for them and it could be hard to listen to. It's their story not ours. If we use our work to push a theory or doctrine neither we or they might hear each other – and if we charge too much they may be unable to afford it. The world is a great emporium of experiences, ideas and feasts, and also of puzzles and if you're unlucky, terrors and agonies. There is no need to be dogmatic or shy in choosing how we work with others' distresses and flights of imagination and then respond to how these echo within ourselves – providing of course our employers will permit us. But that becomes an unavoidable political business.

References

Balint, E. (1993). *The doctor, the patient, and the group: Balint revisited.* Routledge, London.

Balint, M. (1957). *The doctor, his patient and the illness.* Churchill Livingstone, London.

Dax, E. C. (1953). *Experimental studies in psychiatric art.* Faber and Faber, London.

Foucault, M. (1967). *Madness and civilization: a history of insanity in the age of reason.* Translated from the French by John Howard. Tavistock Publications, London.

Henzell, J. (1997). Art, madness and anti-psychiatry: a memoir. In: Killick, K. and Schaverien, J. (Eds) (1997) *Art, psychotherapy and psychosis.* Routledge, London.

Hill, A. (1945). *Art versus illness: A story of art therapy.* Allen and Unwin, London.

Hill, A. (1951). *Painting out illness.* Williams and Northgate, London.

Hillman, J (1979). Image-sense, *Spring: An annual of archetypal psychology and Jungian thought.* Spring Publications, Dallas.

Hillman, J. (1970). An imaginal ego, *Inscape*, 2: 2–8.

Hobson, R. (1981). *Forms of feeling: the heart of psychotherapy,* Routledge, London.

Laing, R. and Esterson, A. (1964). *Sanity, madness, and the family: families of schizophrenics,* (Second edition, 1970). Penguin Books, London.

Lombroso, C. (1891). *Man of genius.* (English edition of the Italian original, published 1889.) W. Scott, London, and C. Scribener's sons, New York.

Meares, A. (1958). *The door to serenity: a study in the therapeutic use of symbolic painting.* Faber and Faber, London.

Milner, M. (1950). *On not being able to paint.* Heinemann, London.

Read, H. (1967). *Education through art.* Faber and Faber, London.

Reitmann, F. (1950, republished 1999) *Psychotic art.* Routledge, London.

Reynolds, H. (1998) *This whispering in our hearts.* Allen and Unwin, Sydney.

Waller, D (1991) *Becoming a profession: the history of art therapy in Britain 1940-82.* Routledge, London.

Yeats, W. (1963). The Circus Animals' Desertion. *The collected poems of W.B. Yeats.* Wordsworth Editions, Ware, Hertfordshire.

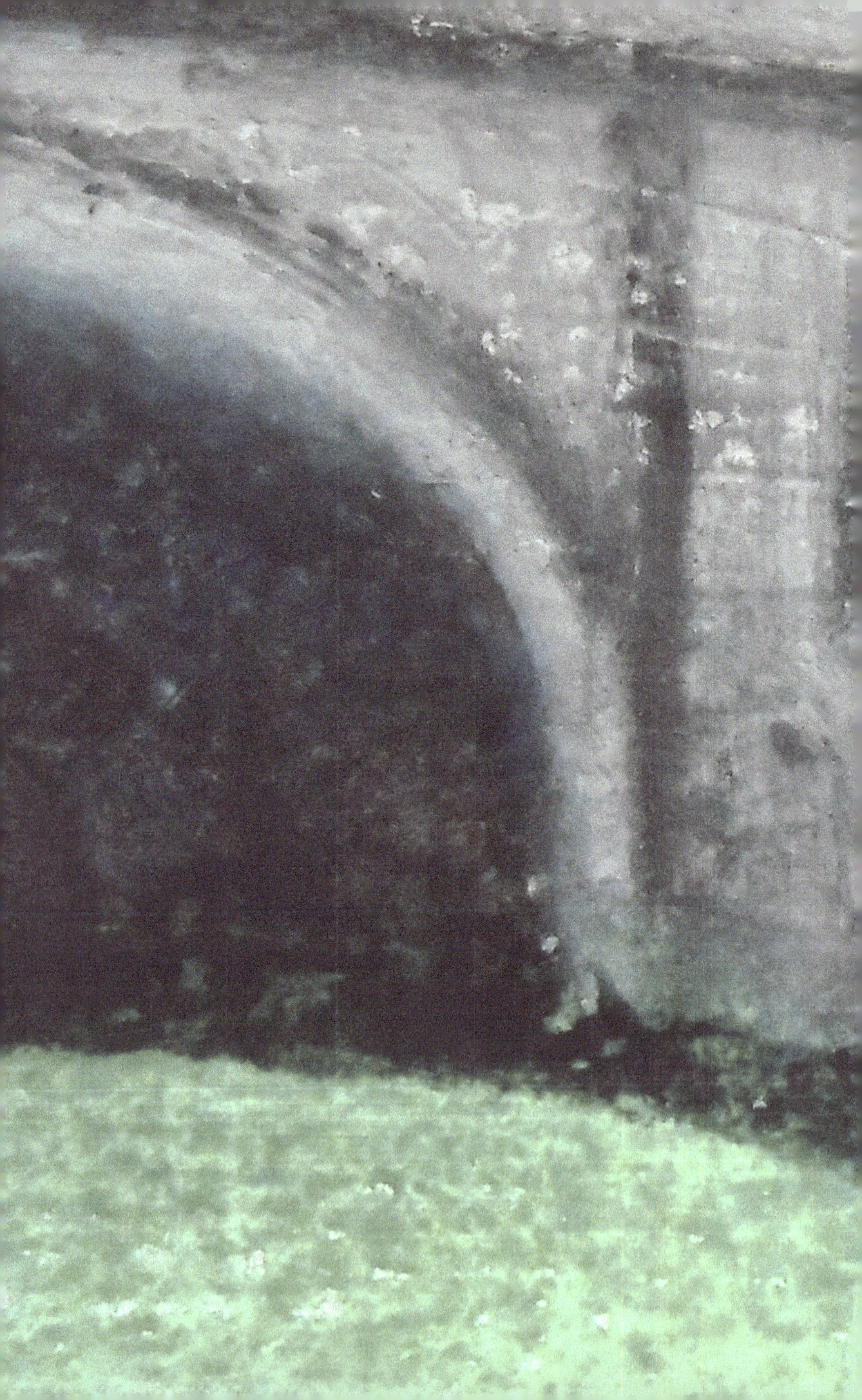

5

CROSSING BRIDGES, SOWING SEEDS

Becoming an Australian Art Therapist

Claire Edwards

 | DOI:10.1163/9789004368262_006

'Draw a bridge between somewhere and someplace. Draw yourself on the bridge.'[1]

I was born, grew up and trained in England, and yet I identify myself as an Australian art therapist. The story of my journey to the other side of the world, both physically and culturally, is described in this chapter. Drawing on my experience of migration from Britain to Australia at the end of 1989, five years after completing my art therapy training, I investigate the notion of an Australian art therapy identity.

1 Hays and Lyons, 1981

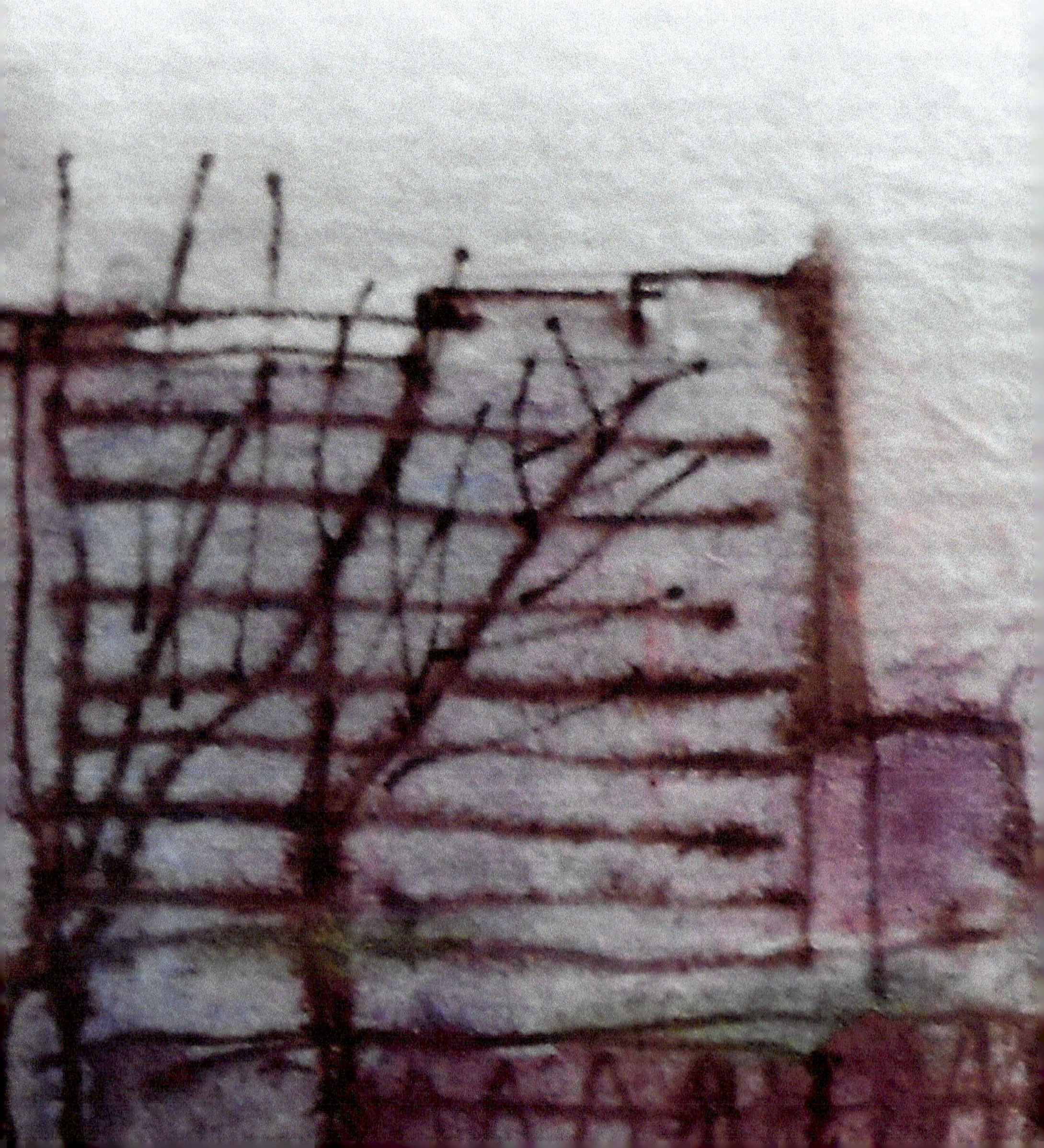

In order to explore what it means to be an Australian art therapist, I will address the question from both professional and personal perspectives that are interwoven through the text as a dual narrative, highlighting parallel processes. On a personal level, I will explore experiences of the migration process, and the ideas and imagery that have helped me to identify with this 'wide brown land': in other words, how I have 'become Australian'. I am indebted to Gilroy and Hanna, whose chapter *Culture and conflict in art therapy: an Australian perspective* (1998), provided the starting point, and suggested many of the key concepts, or sowed the seeds, cultivated in this chapter.

Figure 1 Detail of *University of Essex, view of the residential towers.* Claire Edwards (2016). Pen and ink on paper.

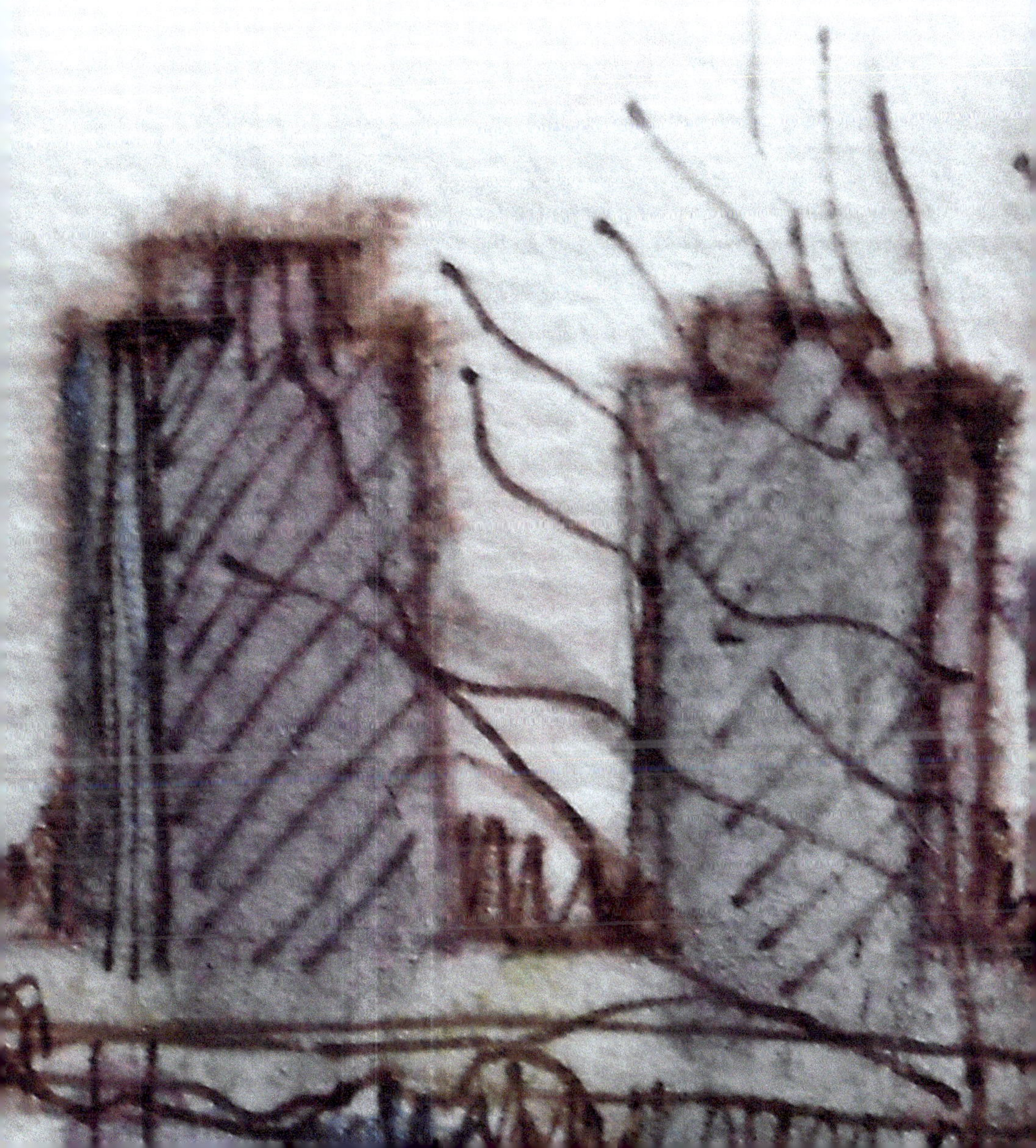

Crossing bridges

1980–1989, London: 'growing up'

In 1980 I was twenty-two years old. I had an arts degree in Literature and Art History, I lived in a squat, had casual work and friends from school as well as university. I underwent various social experiments, such as open relationships, and was often insolvent and irresponsible, as many of us are in our early twenties.

A decade later I was in a stable relationship, I had a baby son, a mortgage, a steady job in mental health rehabilitation, and a professional qualification in art therapy. Having just achieved all these stabilising elements my life, my new family and I threw caution to the wind, and decided to migrate to Australia.

I have reflected previously on my experience of migration and how this influenced my approach to art therapy (Edwards, 2007). I described the effect of migrating to Australia as "liberating. I felt an expansion of opportunities to practice as an art therapist" (ibid: 91). This expansion of opportunities culminated in my being involved in developing and teaching on an art therapy Masters program at the University of Queensland, with a group of colleagues. I attributed the freedom I experienced to "being in a new environment, and feeling less constrained by the rules and expectations instilled in me during my initial training. Here, perhaps I could do art therapy "my way", and there would be no one to tell me it was the "wrong" way" (ibid: 91).

It seemed I needed to escape the orthodoxy of British art therapy practice, through the process of migration, in order to feel free enough to grow into the kind of art therapist I wanted to be. In order to explore this further, I will first make a detour through the landscape of my childhood.

1957–1976 Devon, England: my 'inner island'

I grew up in the South West of England, halfway between the scenic South Devon coast and the barren wilderness of Dartmoor where granite outcrops or 'tors', 'clapper bridges' and bronze age stone circles create a dramatic landscape steeped in ancient history.

I lived for most of my childhood in a four-storey, Victorian terraced house in a suburb called Bridgetown, on the rural edge of the small Elizabethan town of Totnes. From my attic bedroom window I could see Dartmoor and the river Dart. The bridge, which gave Bridgetown its name, spanned the river, sprang from the wilds of Dartmoor and flowed into the sea at Dartmouth. The metaphor of the bridge became a strong connecting force between the high inland wilderness of the moors and the sea, between the rural and the urban, and between the town and me. The bridge resonates as a more personal symbol as my parents separated when I was ten, and I felt perpetually torn between the two.

I crossed the bridge to walk to school, to the shops, to the library and to the park. Ironically, the metaphor extended to incorporate my future life in Australia. Close to the library, in an open area called 'The Plains', stood the Wills memorial, dedicated to William John Wills, (1834–1861), born in Totnes,

Right: Figure 2 *Wills Memorial, the Plains, Totnes, Devon*. Phil End (2013), photograph.

Below: Figure 3 *View from the Island towards Bridgetown, Totnes, Devon*. Claire Edwards (2016). Oil pastels on paper.

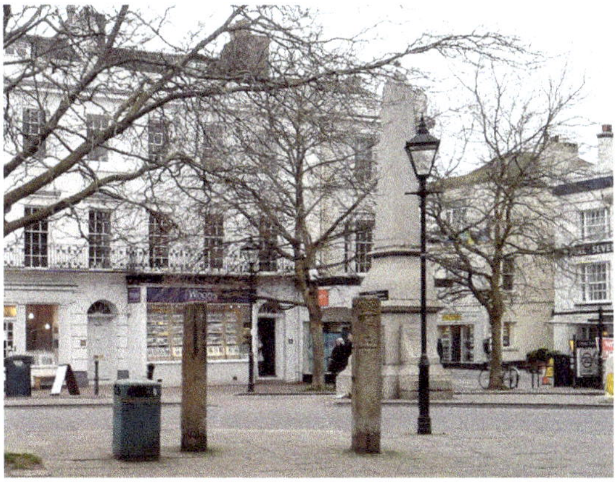

a surveyor and Australian explorer. Wills was a member of the ill-fated Burke and Wills expedition which attempted to reach the Gulf of Carpentaria in the North from Victoria in the South. Wills died en route at Cooper Creek while still only in his twenties (Macinnis, 2007).

One of my favourite places in Totnes was 'the Island', a small piece of parkland situated in the middle of the river and only accessible from the bridge. There were ducks, swans and horse chestnut trees – plus it was an ideal vantage point for viewing the boats on the river and its surrounding banks. Somehow, my 'inner island', to use another metaphor, helped me stay grounded, through the loneliness and storms of my childhood.

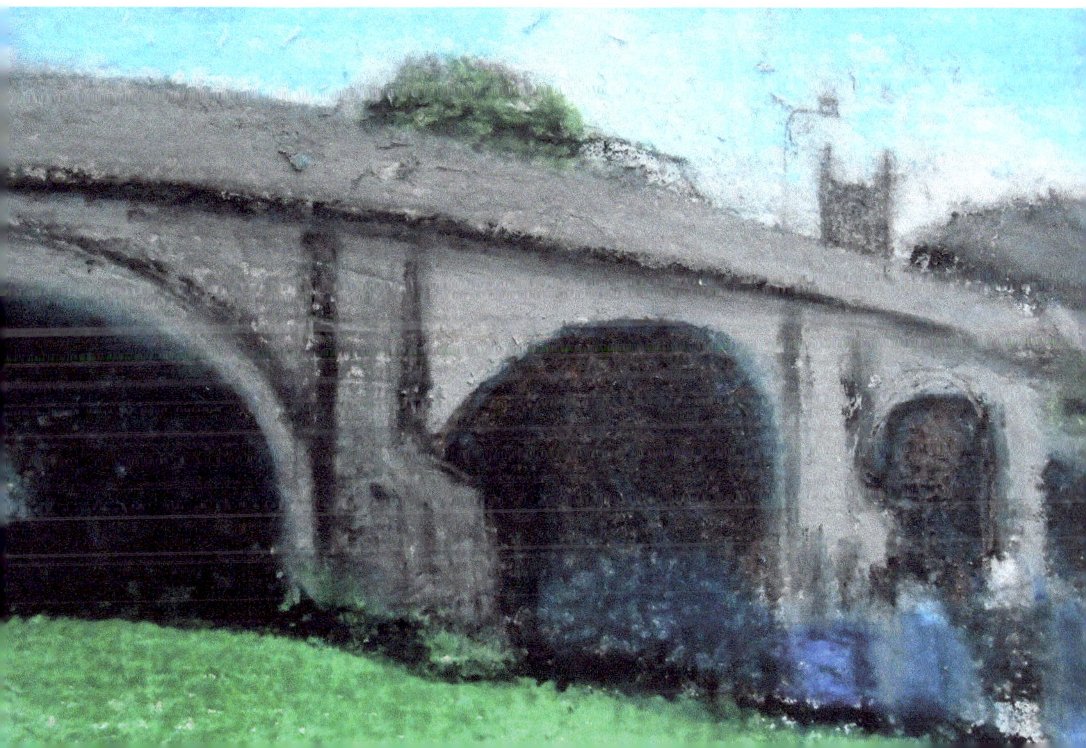

1977–1980, South-east England: study in a cold climate

For three years, as an undergraduate student studying English and Art History, I lived in Colchester, Essex, before moving to London. Cold winds from the North Sea were tunnelled between the sixties-built concrete campus towers, named after dead English and Irishmen. My studies bridged two related fields of study, Literature and Art History, and although I did not realise it at the time, this was a continuation of the personal theme of feeling split in two, being unable to choose, and deciding to do both.

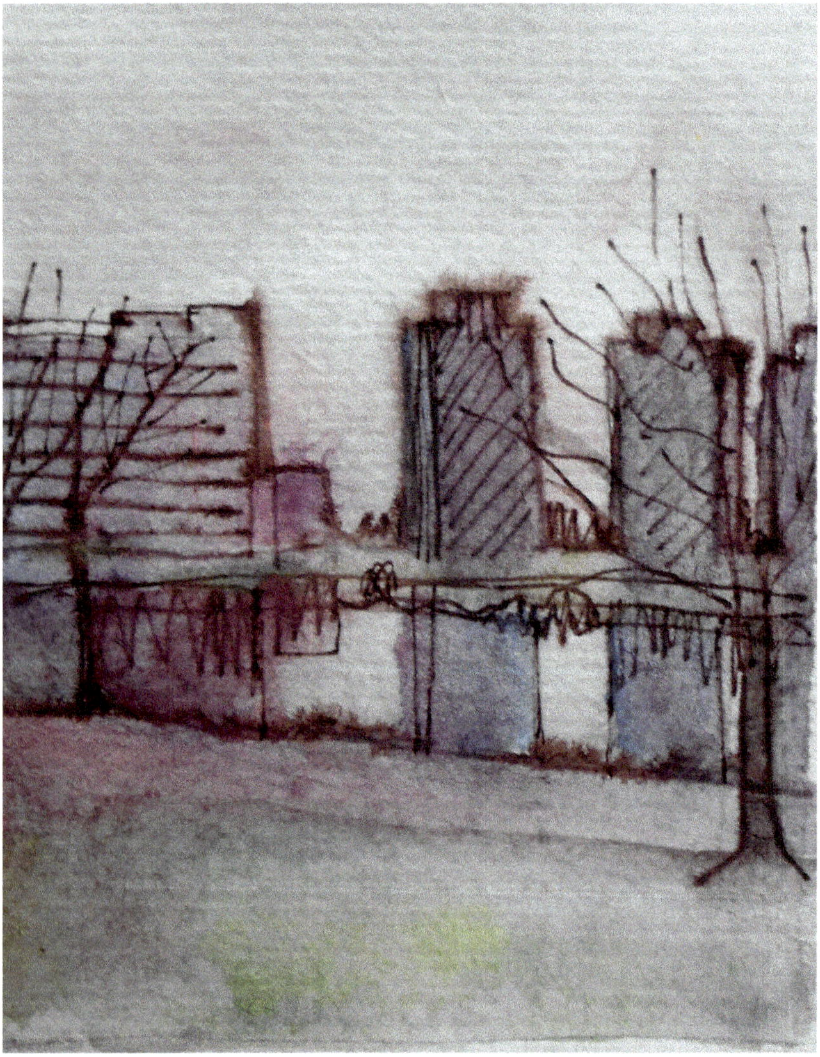

Figure 4 *University of Essex, view of the residential towers.* Claire Edwards (2016). Pen and ink on paper.

I will now consider some of the physical and historical characteristics that have contributed to an Australian identity.

Geographical and spiritual relationship with the land

The physical landscape has to be the starting point in exploring this question of Australian identity. Gilroy and Hanna (1998) acknowledge the importance of the unique Australian landscape when they quote Parker's (1991) question: "… would Freud have discovered psychoanalysis if he'd biked across the Simpson Desert?" (Gilroy and Hanna, 1998: 266). The question hints at the issue of how vastness, wildness and aridity are perceived by humans, especially contemporary urban dwellers, and how we make sense of the physical realities of this country.

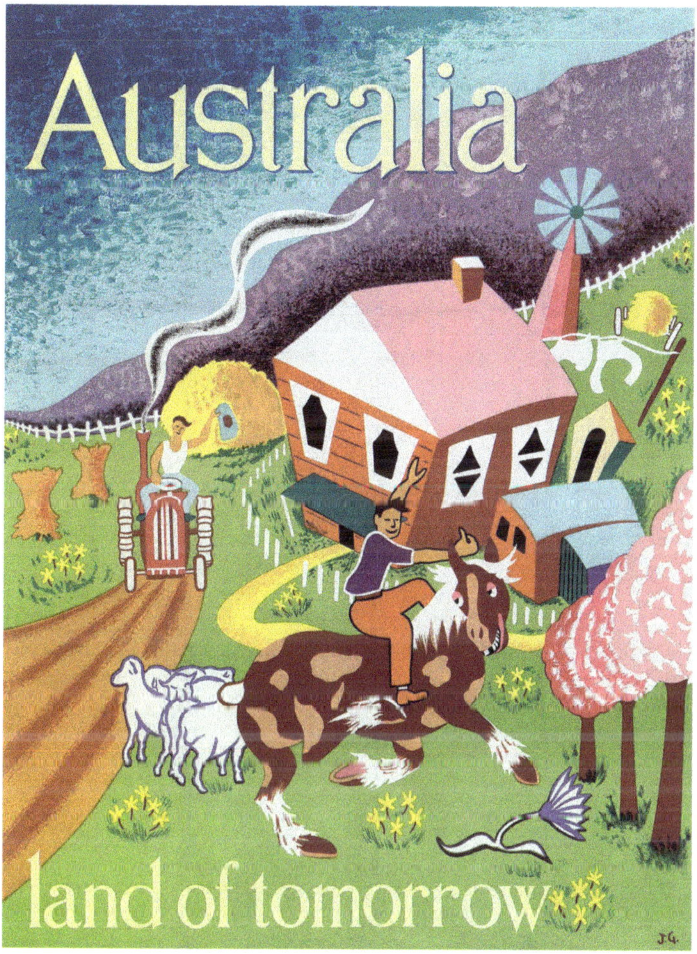

Figure 5 *Australia: land of tomorrow.* Joe Greenberg, (1948). Migration poster, Museum of Victoria.

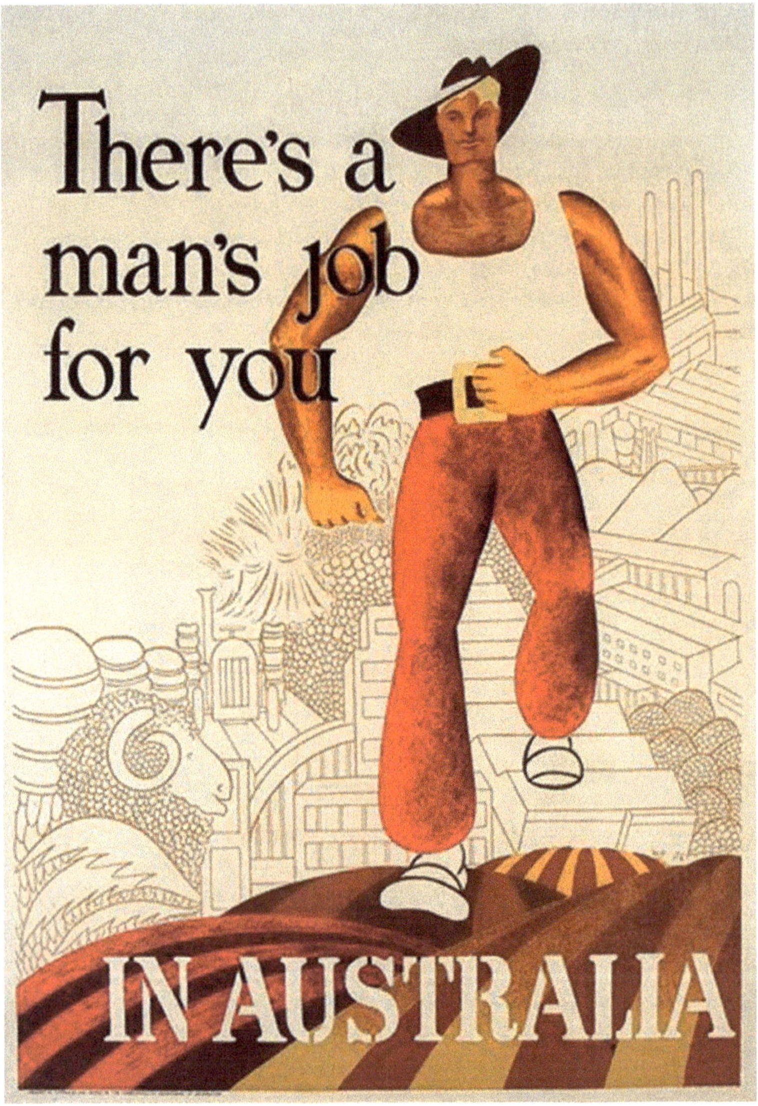

Figure 6 *There's a man's job for you in Australia*. WP and JG. (1947). Migration poster, National Library of Australia.

Aspects of human interaction with the Australian landscape have contributed to its unique culture, such as the experiences of early white settlers and Aboriginal Australians' spiritual relationship with the land. Physical characteristics of the land, which influenced this interaction, include the extremes of climate and geography, the relative 'emptiness' of the interior, and the tyranny of distance (Gilroy and Hanna, 1998).

Aboriginal and Torres Strait Islander people and the land

For Indigenous people everywhere the land is of spiritual and cultural importance in a way that migrants may never completely understand or experience. Indeed to have spiritual and ancestral links to a specific place, which go back thousands of years, could be seen as the antithesis of migration[2] a process which inevitably creates dislocation, ambivalence and a sense of being split, or torn, in two. Ironically, however, the experience of being Aboriginal in contemporary Australia may not be that different from that of being a migrant. Misguided past actions and fatal 'mistakes' by governments and charitable organisations such as the development of missions; racist notions of 'assimilation' and the so-called 'White Australia policy' which encouraged migration by White English speaking people; the removal of Aboriginal children from their families, referred to as the 'Stolen Generation'; as well as the rapid transition from hunter-gatherer to urban dweller, have all had huge impacts on the identity of Aboriginal Australians (Grant, 2016).

Like migration, forced separation from land and culture can result in trauma and grief on spiritual, political and psychological levels. Many contemporary Aboriginal and Torres Strait Islander Australians have experienced being displaced and feeling split. Inevitably the national psyche is still affected by these historical events. This was finally publicly acknowledged in 2008 when then Prime Minister, Kevin Rudd, apologised to Aboriginal and Torres Strait Islander Australians for the harms caused by previous government policies.

Dislocation can also lead to resilience as it provides a unique perspective, like my vantage point on the island, of seeing both points of view and providing a bridge between them. This concept, referred to as post-traumatic growth, is becoming recognised more widely as a positive outcome of trauma (Calhoun & Tedeschi, 2006).

Experiences of early white settlers

White settlement of Australia commenced after the arrival of Captain Cook in 1770, in part through the implementation of the policy of importing British convicts to populate and cultivate the 'wide brown land'. The difficulty of this task is unimaginable to contemporary Australians but it is likely that only the fittest and strongest survived in a country so different from the one the convicts and free settlers left behind. As previously discussed, the country features extremes of climate and geography, including the relative 'emptiness' and infertility of the interior, scorching hot summers, droughts, bushfires, floods, and vast distances between settlements, which in the days of the first settlers were far less easily accommodated than they are now in this era of cheap plane travel, mobile phones and the internet.

Qualities that sustained the settlers were youthfulness and physical strength, stoicism, pragmatism, and the ability to make do with what is available, qualities which would have also assisted the Aboriginal population to survive. Collabo-

2 Although of course at some stage all early humans migrated from the African continent.

ration with others outside the social group was not always so strongly pursued. However in some instances, strong alliances were formed to fight against injustices (such as the Eureka stockade, World War One, especially Gallipoli, and the Vietnam War) and the perception of a threat from external forces.

Multiculturalism: 'New Australians'

After World War Two, the White Australia policy was officially abandoned and migration was encouraged, particularly from Southern and Eastern European countries such as Italy, Greece and former Yugoslavia. Labour was required on projects such as the Snowy River scheme, and (as was the case in post-war Britain, when mass migration from the West Indies was introduced) this was the main motivation behind this new migration policy.

Subsequent 'waves' of migration included Vietnamese refugees (the original 'boat people') in the 1970s and 1980s, and more recently those from Afghanistan, Iraq, Sudan, Congo and other war-torn countries. English-speaking migrants still remained the majority, however. Until recently, Australia was noted for its ability to accommodate ethnically diverse groups without significant racial conflict and who were able to co-exist in relative harmony. More recently there have been outbreaks of intolerant, racist behaviour, often fuelled by prejudice against refugees and negative perceptions of non-Anglo migrants, created either by politicians or the popular media.

I will now consider several commonly identified Australian traits and cultural factors, which may provide us with a starting point for mapping an Australian art therapy identity.

Pioneer spirit, pragmatism

There is a tradition in Australia of action rather than contemplation. In the early days of white settlement, daily life involved hard work and the ability to cope without a great deal of support. This is reflected today in a culture of pragmatism and 'getting on with it', and a dislike of theory and pretention.

Scepticism, iconoclasm

There is an element of Australian culture that is deeply irreverent and suspicious of authority. Teasing your mates as a way of showing affection is a significant aspect of this. Alongside this is importance of not taking yourself too seriously. 'Tall poppy syndrome', which involves bringing people who dare to stand above their comrades down to size, is an Australian take on egalitarianism.

Larrikinism

'Larrikinism', that characteristic of laconic male Australian charm combined with mischief, immediately calls to mind both the late Steve Irwin, aka the 'Crocodile Hunter', and the main character played by Paul Hogan from the movie *Crocodile Dundee*. It is perhaps best encapsulated in the iconic figure of robber and police killer Ned Kelly, who has been adopted by Australians as a national hero and is the subject of many of Sidney Nolan's paintings. Again themes of irreverence and dislike of authority are paramount.

'Un-Australian' behaviour

The adjective 'un-Australian' is often applied to behaviours that are being publicly condemned in the media or by politicians, for example racism or corruption, (although interestingly, its converse, 'Australian' is rarely used to mean anything other than nationality). This sometimes has a darker, and ironically racist aspect, whereby those displaying 'un-Australian' behaviour could be advised to return home from whence they came; however, the implication is that by be(com)ing Australian, one has taken on board values such as egalitarianism, and democracy, and giving everyone a 'fair go'. This seems to me to reflect a shared national vision of what is decent and just, and reflects an optimistic and positive view of human nature.

In a sense these characteristics are stereotypes and bear little relationship to the diverse lives of actual Australians. Arguably, however, some of these qualities have contributed to the Australian character, and indeed to the developing Australian art therapy profession to which I will now turn. Before discussing Australian art therapy, however, it is necessary to consider the influence of British and American art therapy schools.

Transatlantic influences

Given that the two dominant forces in art therapy, the British and American schools, are both represented in Australia, it seems likely that both schools would be expected to exert an influence on the development of Australian art therapy (Gilroy and Hanna, 1998). It may therefore be useful to reflect on some of the differences and similarities of these approaches, and how they interact. American art therapist Maralynn Hagood (1990) writes about her visit to Britain to investigate the possibilities for completing her doctoral dissertation in the UK. She met with several prominent British art therapists and made the following comment. "…(we) spent a very enjoyable, albeit sometimes frustrating time attempting to understand each other's professional jargon. We jokingly concluded that perhaps, in some instances, we weren't speaking the same language after all" (ibid: 75).

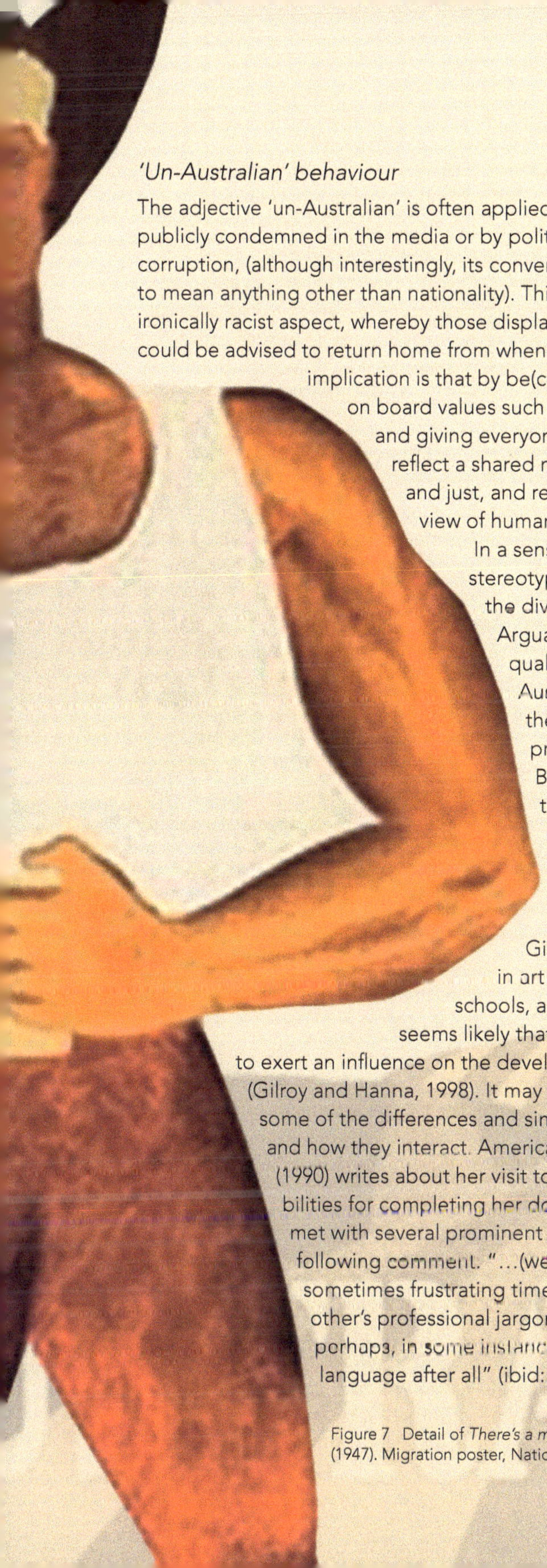

Figure 7 Detail of *There's a man's job for you in Australia*. WP and JG. (1947). Migration poster, National Library of Australia

In her article, Hagood (1990) represents the views of a number of British art therapists, and accepts their criticism of their American counterparts with good grace. These include the focus (in America) on interpretation and diagnosis, and a tendency to be 'superficial and simplistic at times' (ibid: 78) due to a lack of awareness of the historical roots of psychoanalysis, amongst other things. Hagood provides her own critical commentary on some aspects of British art therapy as she perceives them, such as a lack of awareness of systemic family therapy approaches, strong adherence to object relations theorists and ambivalence towards conducting empirical art therapy research, and concludes that both schools have something to learn from the other.

In a publication dedicated to comparing art therapy traditions on both side of the Atlantic (Spring, 2007), American art therapist and author Marcia Rosal (2007) relates how coming to Australia, again for the purpose of doctoral studies, provided her with the opportunity to meet several British trained art therapists and to be influenced by their approach. In particular she cites the work of Gerry McNeilly (1983), whose advocacy of non-directive art therapy groups challenged what she calls her "American beliefs" (ibid: 35).

Rosal's PhD studies aimed to show that directive art therapy groups, using a cognitive behavioural approach for children with behavioural problems, were more effective than groups using a non-directive approach. Her outcomes, which compared both styles of groups, showed that both approaches were equally effective (Rosal 2007). Rosal's results are a salutary lesson for those of us who may cling to a particular way of doing things when, in fact, doing it another way can be just as effective. How appropriate that she conducted this research in Australia!

We could conclude from these examples that cross cultural exchange (and, by extension, migration) can be an enriching, helpful and positive phenomena, which shows us a different way of doing things. This may compensate for the limitations of our original approach, and open up new possibilities, not just for the migrant, but also for their adopted country. Between Britain and America there has been a tradition of cross-cultural exchange, as I have described. However, there has possibly been until now a lack of a sense of a unique Australian art therapy identity, which I will now address. Initially personal and professional perspectives remain separate, but they become increasingly entwined.

Sowing seeds

April 1989, London: 'born in the UK, 100% Australian'

Referencing Bruce Springsteen's iconic and ironic 1980s rock anthem 'Born in the USA', the poster of the blond boy in his school uniform in the dusty Australian bush, immediately caught my eye. The slogan 'Born in the UK, 100% Australian' was particularly poignant. Despite the subtext, which was dodgy in the extreme (a throwback to the White Australia policy?), I imagine this was my son, now one year old, going to primary school in a dusty outback town somewhere in the Australian bush, instead of inner city London.

I was in Australia House in London, lodging my visa application for migration. The poster perpetuated the myth that Australians mostly live in the bush and reassured us that they are mostly 'like us' i.e. from an Anglo background. I was seeing my young son, not myself, as the family member who would 'become Australian' as a result of our migration. However, over 20 years later, I now think of myself as Australian in a way I never imagined, as my previous identity as a British citizen seemed so deeply entrenched. My (now fully grown) son has trained to be a teacher of English as a second language to refugee and migrant children.

On one level 'becoming Australian' involved attending a formal citizenship ceremony but on another level it has been a slow process of letting go of the past and re-orientating myself to a new continent and, almost, a new and somehow 'improved' identity. It is interesting how much more positively I have been able to identify with this new country, perhaps since it is one I chose to belong to.

Professional perspectives

Art therapy has been described as a "hybrid profession", derived from art and psychotherapy (Davis, 2003: 32). In Australia, art therapy could arguably be described as the 'hybrid of a hybrid', since the majority of art therapists who pioneered art therapy in Australia in the 1980s and 90s were generally either British or North American trained (Gilroy and Hanna, 1998; Westwood, 2010). Hybridisation in biology is generally thought of as producing a healthy 'hybrid vigour', but there is perhaps the inevitable outcome that the newly created individual has less of an established identity than its 'pedigree' parents.

Art therapy developed virtually simultaneously in the UK and the USA in the 1940s (Waller 1991, Gilroy and Hanna, 1998). The nature of, and differences between, British and North American art therapy traditions has been the subject of much healthy discussion and debate in ensuing decades (Hagood 1990, Gilroy and Hanna, 1998). Since its inception, art therapy has spread to many countries in the world, and Masters level art therapy training is increasingly available, in Europe, Asia, and South America for example. This suggests that creative, therapeutic processes are applicable, and beneficial, in a wide range of ethnic and socio-cultural environments.

When professional art therapy training was first established in Australia, in the late 1980s, the art therapists who were employed to deliver art therapy education were inevitably trained overseas, and at times even 'imported' specifically for this purpose. As Gilroy and Hanna (1998) acknowledge, their prior experiences in Britain and North America respectively, undoubtedly influenced their approach.

Despite art therapy engaging clients in non-verbal processes, art therapists still rely largely on the written word, whether for communicating with clients, colleagues and other professionals on the one hand, or for teaching, researching and professional development on the other. Much of the published writing in art therapy, at least in English, still emanates from either the UK or the USA. Even in contemporary Australia, where art therapy has been practised for over 25 years, there have been until recently very few significant 'Australian' art therapy publications, apart from newsletters and a professional journal (ANZJAT, 2006)[3]. This means that when teaching art therapy, or consulting the literature for our own reference purposes, Australian art therapists often have to refer to material published in the UK and the USA. As a result, a uniquely Australian art therapy identity has remained largely underdeveloped and, more significantly perhaps, undefined.

In a thoughtful exploration of her own racial identity as a White Australian art therapist of British origin, Holloway (2009) comments on this gap in the literature and how this became obvious to her whilst working with young African and Polynesian clients in Western Sydney. This topic ultimately became a major focus of her art therapy training. She writes: "A fundamental roadblock I faced…was the lack of relevantly contextualised literature… that recognised and explained the process I was going through" (ibid: 62). Holloway's journey involved exploring her own racial history and questioning the assumptions she had about 'being Australian', such as egalitarianism and becoming aware of the power and privileges that being White actually conferred. She also comments that discussion of these issues was "noticeably absent: from her art therapy training (ibid: 65).

November 1989, Brisbane: 'arrival in Oz'

On arriving in Australia at the end of 1989, (just after the fall of the Berlin Wall so anything seemed possible), Brisbane was the hub of the art therapy scene in Australia (Gilroy and Hanna, 1998). I had just missed the first national art therapy conference, held in Brisbane in October 1989. I soon became aware that this conference had brought to a head some of the tensions within a small existing core group of overseas trained art therapists. My impression was that the split was between those trained in Britain and those trained in North America. This was somewhat alarming. Would my presence be seen as a way to gain an ally for the 'UK team'? I tried, at times less than successfully, to distance myself from this conflict (Edwards 1991, Gilroy and Hanna, 1998).

As the parent of any adolescent knows very well, conflict is an inevitable part of developing identity. Gilroy and Hanna suggest that: "indeed it seems to be necessary to have an energetic debate about identity where difference, even divergence, is acknowledged but contained and through which separation from allied professions is achieved." (ibid: 269). In Gilroy and Hanna's example, the conflict within the art therapy field is seen as an inevitable part of the developmental process of identity formation. As with parenting, however, understanding the reason for the conflict does not always make it easier to negotiate.

3 Since this article was written, *Creative Arts in Counselling and Mental Health* (2015) edited by Neilsen, King and Baker, largely describing the practices of arts therapies in Australia, was published by Sage.

1989–2004 Brisbane: 'cultivating the wilderness'

Due to the difficulties this conflict created but with a growing interest in the field from artists and allied health professionals, there was an immediate dilemma: how to cater for the demand for information and support whilst somehow working through these philosophical differences which had, inevitably, due to the small number of individuals involved, become personalised? At least the former task, which I had more motivation for, gave a welcome external focus.

I took on the job of ANATA (Australian National Art Therapy Association, now ANZATA, incorporating New Zealand and the other Arts Therapies) Newsletter Editor for a while; one of the first things I wrote was an editorial on the somewhat patronising theme of 'Exploring the Wilderness' (Edwards, 1990). The wilderness was a metaphor for the conflicted professional environment I had found myself in, perhaps also reflecting my personal sense of dislocation and alienation at that time. I had left my familiar life behind and, like other new migrants, I was somewhat homesick and anxious about what the future held. Noting the high level of interest in art therapy, however, one of my more memorable comments in the same editorial was that "the seeds of art therapy will not be sown on barren soil" (Edwards, 1990: 1). The fact that I was writing about sowing seeds suggests that it felt like being back at the beginning, daunted by the huge task of pioneering art therapy, a task which had already been started decades earlier in Britain and America. The fertile soil, however, was clearly full of promise, even then.

Within a year I had a full time job as an alcohol and drug counsellor in a residential rehabilitation centre. My art therapy qualifications and mental health experience were recognised as being equivalent to that of other allied health professionals. This has been my common experience in the community or non-government sector, if not in the better resourced but more regulated public sector. Run as a therapeutic community, which I had both experience and training in, I felt immediately at home in the rehab centre whilst at the same time finding it strangely unfamiliar.

As Hagood (1990) had described the language in particular was different, especially as I was working with clients from a drug using sub-culture whose slang I did not know. Even the staff used a different jargon, reflecting the dominant role of cognitive behavioural therapy (CBT) in Australia compared to Britain (Edwards 2007, Gilroy and Hanna, 1998). Despite this difficulty, I found my feet, and stayed for seven years, working as both a counsellor and an art therapist until I was made redundant after a restructure. My employment history has continued through Child Safety and Child and Youth Mental Health Services and expanded into art therapy education in 2004. I currently work as a private practitioner in a children's therapy clinic.

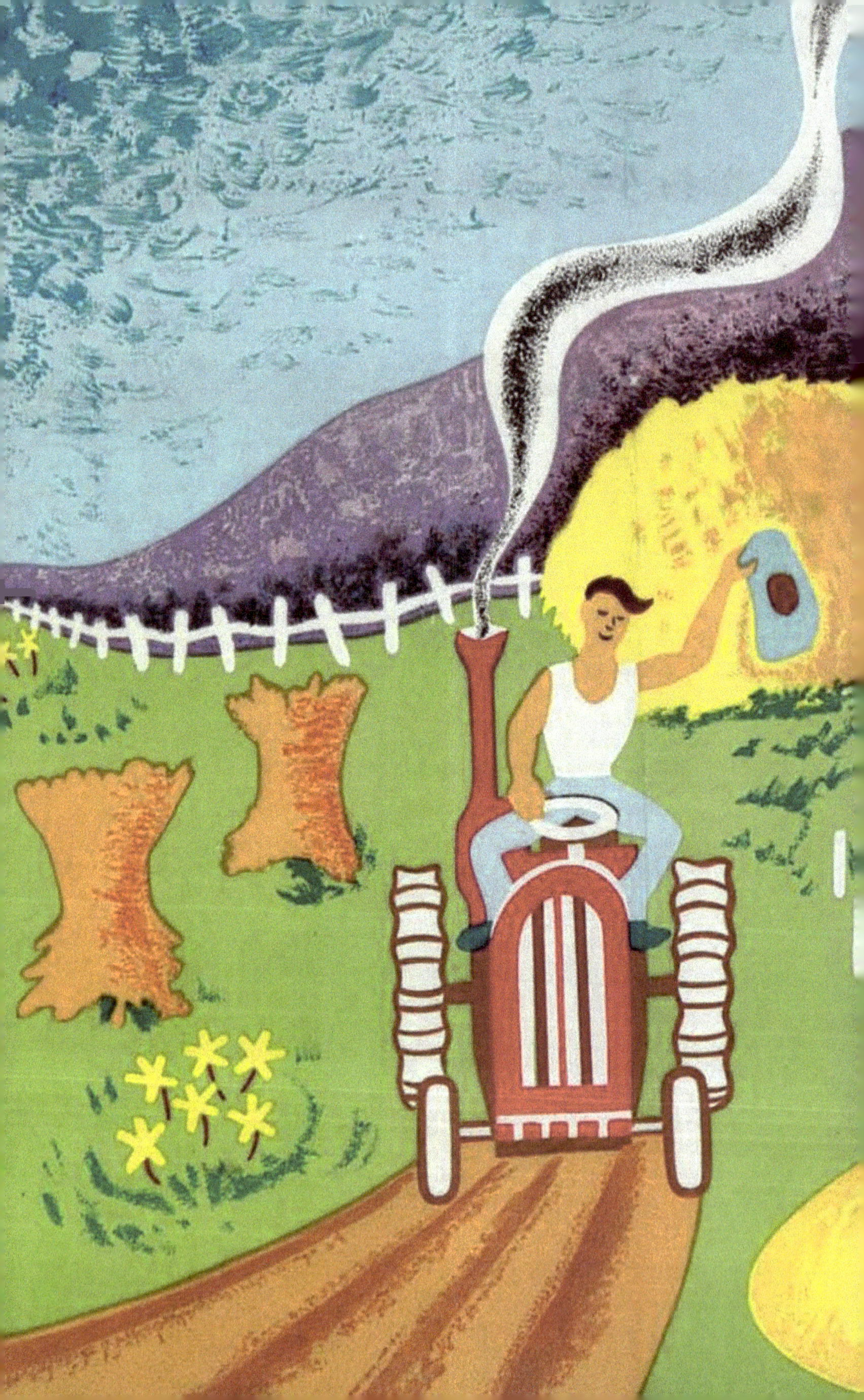

Australian art therapy

Just as Aboriginal and Torres Strait Islander Australians and migrants alike have struggled to maintain and develop their own sense of identity in a changing and at times hostile environment, so too have Australian art therapists found it difficult to develop a sense of themselves as uniquely Australian. In the following section I focus on the development of art therapy training in Brisbane at University of Queensland since 2004. I try to determine whether particular aspects of Australian culture can be seen as influential in the development of Australian art therapy, based on this experience.

Migration of art therapists

All except the Aboriginal Australian population have been migrants of one kind or another, either voluntary or involuntary, or descendents of migrants. The experience of migration can in itself be a process of dislocation and disorientation, as previously highlighted. Since clinical art therapy training has only been available in Brisbane since 2004, and the first cohort of graduates emerged in 2007, it is not surprising that prior to this, the small handful of art therapists, who became the art therapy educators in this locality, all had similar experiences of dislocation.

In order to achieve our current status, my art therapy colleagues and I had travelled thousands of miles, overseas or interstate, either in order to seek training outside of our home state or country, or as I did, to migrate here post-training. Our experiences of such personal dislocations, has been reflected in our work with marginalised populations, including refugees, other migrants, the homeless, children at risk, and those experiencing trauma, grief and loss.

The tyranny of distance: mapping the interior

One of the challenges for Australian art therapists is the small population coupled with the tyranny of geographical distance (Gilroy and Hanna 1990). Initially, when the national association, ANATA, was formed in 1987, there were only 11 professional members (ibid: 267) within a country which is a vast island continent the size of Europe. A few years later in 1990/1, this number had only increased to 14. These members moreover were scattered across the country, with thousands of miles separating them. Technological advances such as email and the internet, cheaper plane travel and improved telecommunication systems have undoubtedly played a part in enabling contact between art therapists across the distance. It is still possible to feel very isolated, however, not only from Australian colleagues but also from the rest of the art therapy world. This is particularly true for those working in regional and remote areas. I recently spoke to one art therapist who is employed by the Royal Flying Doctor service in Longreach in remote Western Queensland. To meet with another art therapist face-to-face, for peer supervision or support, she would need to fly to Brisbane, a distance of several hundred kilometres.

Figure 8 *Detail of Australia: land of tomorrow.* Joe Greenberg, (1948). Migration poster, Museum of Victoria.

Medical model

A feature of Australian mental health care identified by Gilroy and Hanna (1998), and Gilroy (1998), is the lack of influence of psychoanalytic ideas and processes compared to USA and Europe. The Australian mental health care system is much more heavily dominated by the medical model, and cognitive behavioural therapy, which Gilroy and Hanna relate to the possible influence of Australia's penal origins, since they see them largely as systems of control.

2004–, Brisbane: built using local material

The Masters of Mental Health (MMH) Art Therapy program was established at the University of Queensland in 2004. The art therapy field of study was introduced into the broader program as a new stream; this incorporated some existing elements and introduced new art therapy specific ones. The original aim of the overall MMH program was to provide higher degree level training for a broad spectrum of already qualified and experienced mental health professionals such as social workers, psychologists, occupational therapists and mental health nurses. Art therapy was a totally different kettle of fish as applicants were generally visual arts graduates, albeit with some experience in mental health and with basic counselling training, rather than experienced health care professionals. In addition, the influence for the program was the ANATA training guidelines, themselves an amalgam of UK and US standards, which supported the case for elements such as 750 hours of supervised placements, experiential art therapy workshops, and a substantial independent research project.

We were able to demonstrate a demand for art therapy training and so, despite these differences, the art therapy stream was incorporated and some of these specialist art therapy elements, such as the placement and the independent project, were subsequently introduced into the broader program after a major restructure in 2009. This indicated that there has been a healthy two-way cross-fertilisation of ideas and processes.

The Brisbane UQ program is unusual in being located within a medical school. The existing program was part of the discipline of psychiatry. Teaching has since been transferred to the Royal Brisbane and Women's Hospital (RBWH) site so that the program is not just symbolically and administratively part of the medical school, it is taught in a medical rather than academic environment.

Prior to moving to the RBWH, the program was delivered at the Mater Hospital. The Mater Child and Youth Mental Health Service, now part of Queensland Health, has close links with the University of Queensland and four of our art therapy teaching staff, including myself, have been employed in this service at various times in the past fifteen years. The program itself arose from one of my supervision sessions with Tom O'Brien, senior psychotherapist at the Mater and also a lecturer on the MMH in group psychotherapy, during which we discussed the need for art therapy training in Queensland.

In terms of our theoretical orientation, students are exposed to a range of psychodynamic, humanistic, cognitive and systemic approaches to art therapy. Most of them veer towards humanistic, client-centred approaches, although my evidence for this statement is anecdotal. Other graduates may be strongly influenced by Jung or are advocates of a studio-based approach. In general, they seem to favour non-directive and non-interpretive approaches in theory but they may actually be quite directive in practice. My own practice is constantly evolving but my current influences are Acceptance and Commitment Therapy (ACT) and other mindfulness-based approaches, neurobiology, trauma theory and strength-based approaches. I incorporate textiles into my practice and I have also been known to combine CBT and art therapy.

Art-making continuously infuses the program and gives our students the major point of difference from the other MMH students. Their presentations are more visual and their placement supervision groups often involve art-making as part of the reflection process. Each year all art therapy students are brought together into a large group art-making workshop. Topics from lectures are explored in experiential art workshops, including Aboriginal and Torres Strait Islander perspectives on art therapy, also referred to as 'art as healing'.

2000 Brisbane: reconciliation march

The Reconciliation Marches in 2000, crossing bridges in all major cities in Australia, sent a strong message to the then Howard government about the need to apologise for past harmful policies to Indigenous Australians, and was an emotional response to the Bringing them Home report on the Stolen Generation. Crossing the bridge from North to South also symbolically involved crossing boundaries which Indigenous people were at one time forbidden from crossing.

Aboriginal and Torres Strait Islander art

One aspect of Aboriginal and Torres Strait Islander culture which appears to have been maintained throughout these dislocations, and has indeed provided a bridge between Indigenous experience and mainstream culture, is the practice of art. Aboriginal art is now highly sought after and revered throughout the Western world. By combining Western media, such as synthetic paints and canvases, with traditional motifs, designs and symbolism, Aboriginal artists have the possibility of lifting themselves and their families out of intergenerational trauma and economic disadvantage. As one Aboriginal musician, with a history of criminal offending argued, "art and music draw you out of trouble like a magnet." (*Wide Open Road*, ABC Radio National 2008).

June 2010, Brisbane: the Go-Between Bridge

In Brisbane the new Go-Between Bridge over the Brisbane River opened, named after the eponymous 1980s Brisbane band, the Go-Betweens. The bridge crosses the river not far from the Mater Hospital where we established our art therapy program. The name is evocative, not just of 80s music, but of a youthful and irreverent style and straightforwardly states its function. Art therapy, like the bridge, links two 'sides', whether art and science, images and words, inner and outer worlds, mind and body, theory and practice. Art therapists are also go-betweens.

Conclusion

I started writing this chapter by attempting to explore the question: What does it mean to be an Australian art therapist? I have combined personal and professional narratives to explore the question. I have to ask myself in conclusion, am I any closer to answering that question? In a similar vein, Kathleen Noonan comments on an interview with writer Hilary McPhee, which was broadcast on Radio National on the topic of Australian writing. She stated: "there is an Australian voice" but (McPhee argues) it is more about:

> *Our perspective … a way of looking at the world, a freedom our writers have … There was a time ten years ago when we were bending over backwards to define what it was to be Australian. Remember? It was ghastly. What it means to be Australian? Who knows? Who cares? It's not a big question any more for our writers.*
>
> McPhee, *The Book Show*, Radio National, July 2010

Noonan continues that despite living in a global culture "local writers build their own universe, constructed using local material." (Courier Mail, 24.7.10). I like to think that, with a slight adaptation, this is also the case with Australian art therapy: that it is built by local and imported art therapists, using local and imported material. We have the freedom to create it anew. That is what makes it uniquely Australian.

References

Calhoun, L. and Tedeschi, R. (2006). The foundations of post-traumatic growth: an expanded framework. In: Calhoun, L. and Tedeschi, R. (2006) (Eds.) *Handbook of posttraumatic growth: research and practice*. Erlbaum, Mahwah, NJ.

Davis, N. (2003) Feminist art therapy: Contributions from feminist theory and contemporary art practice. In: Hogan, S. (2003) (Ed) *Gender issues in art therapy*. Jessica Kingsley, London.

Edwards, C. (2007) Thinking outside the frame: a systems approach to art therapy with children. In: Spring, D. (2007) (Ed.) *Art in treatment: Transatlantic dialogue*. Springfield: Charles Thomas.

Hays, R. and Lyons, S., (1981) The bridge drawing: a projective technique for assessment in art therapy, *The arts in psychotherapy*, 8: 207–217.

Gilroy, A. (1998) On being a temporary migrant to Australia: Reflections on art therapy education and practice. In: Doktor, D. (1998) (Ed.) *Arts therapists, refugees and migrants: reaching across borders*. Jessica Kingsley, London.

Gilroy, A. and Hanna, M. (1998) Conflict and culture in art therapy: an Australian perspective. In: Hiscox A. and Calisch, A. (1998) (Eds.) *Tapestry of cultural issues in art therapy*. Jessica Kingsley, London.

Grant, S. (2016). *Talking to my country*. HarperCollins, Sydney.

Hagood, M. (1990) Art therapy research in England. Impressions of an American art therapist. *The arts in psychotherapy*, 17: 75-79.

Holloway, M. (2009) British Australian: Art therapy, white racial identity and racism in Australia, *Australian and New Zealand Journal of Art Therapy*, 4 (1): 62–67.

Human Rights and Equal Opportunity Commission (HREOC) (1997) *Bringing them home: Report of the national inquiry into the separation of Aboriginal and Torres Strait Islander children from their families.*

Neilsen, P., King, R. and Baker, F. (2015) *Creative arts in counselling and mental health*. Sage Publications, London.

Macinnis, P. (2007) *Australia's pioneers, heroes and fools: the trials, tribulations and trick of the trade of Australia's colonial explorers*. Sydney: Pier 9.

McNeilly, G. (1983) Directive and non-directive approaches in art therapy. *The arts in Psychotherapy* 10 (4): 211–219.

McPhee, *The Book Show*, Radio National, July 2010

Neilsen, P., King, R. and Baker, F. (2015) (Eds.) *Creative arts in counselling and mental health*. Sage, London.

Noonan, K., (2010) *Courier Mail*. 24.7.2010.

Parker (1991) The Australian contribution to psychiatry. In: Copolov, D. (1991) (Ed.) *Australian psychiatry and the tradition of Aubrey Lewis*. The Mental Health Research Institute of Victoria and Monash University, Melbourne.

Rosal, M. (2007) A comparative analysis of British and US group art therapy styles. In: Spring, D. (2007) (Ed.) *Art in treatment. Transatlantic dialogue*. Charles C. Thomas, Springfield.

Waller, D., (1991) *Becoming a profession*. Routledge, London.

Wide open road, ABC Radio National, Broadcast January 2010.

Westwood, J., (2010). Hybrid creatures: Mapping the emerging shape of art therapy education in Australia. Unpublished PhD Thesis, University of Western Sydney.

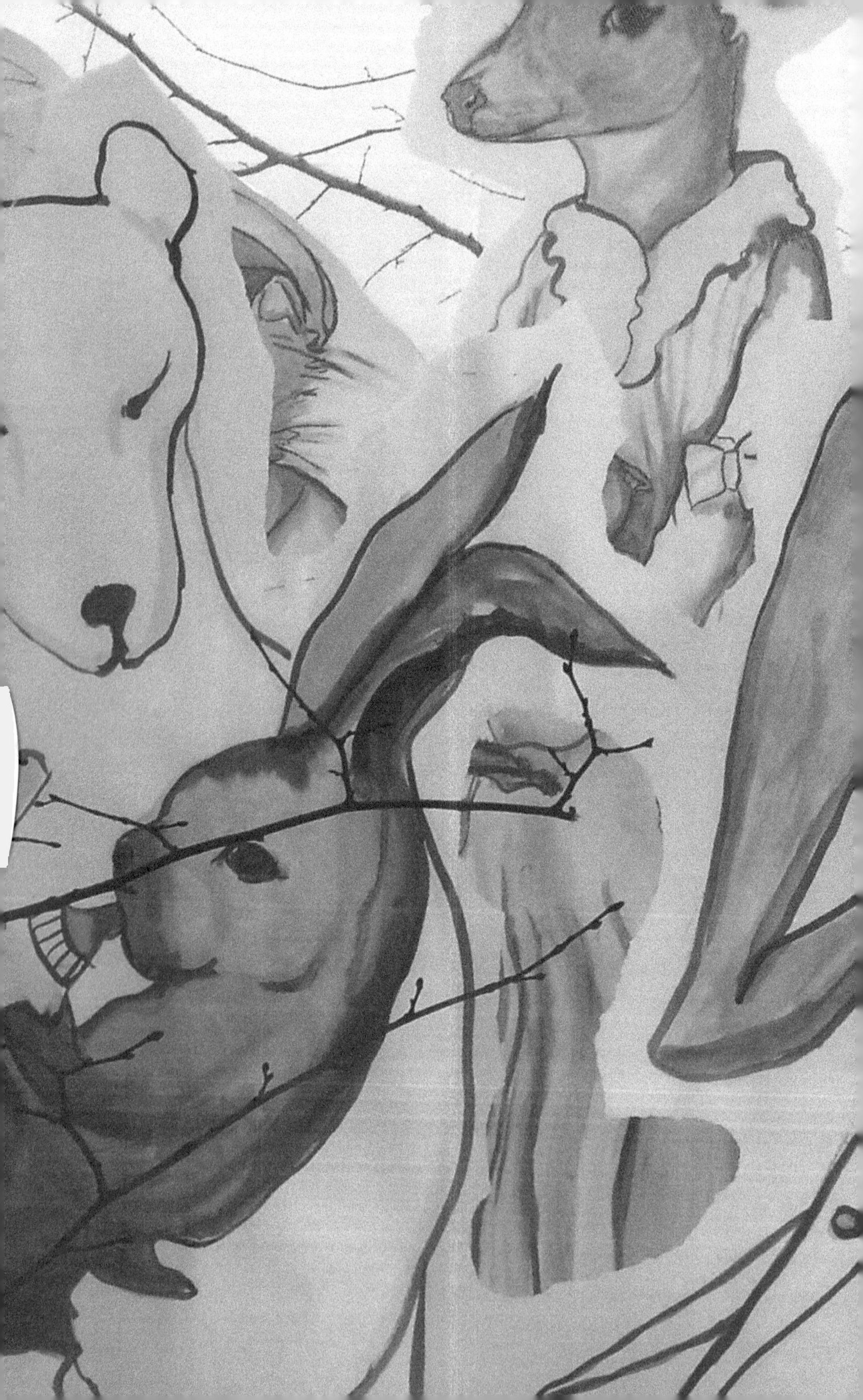

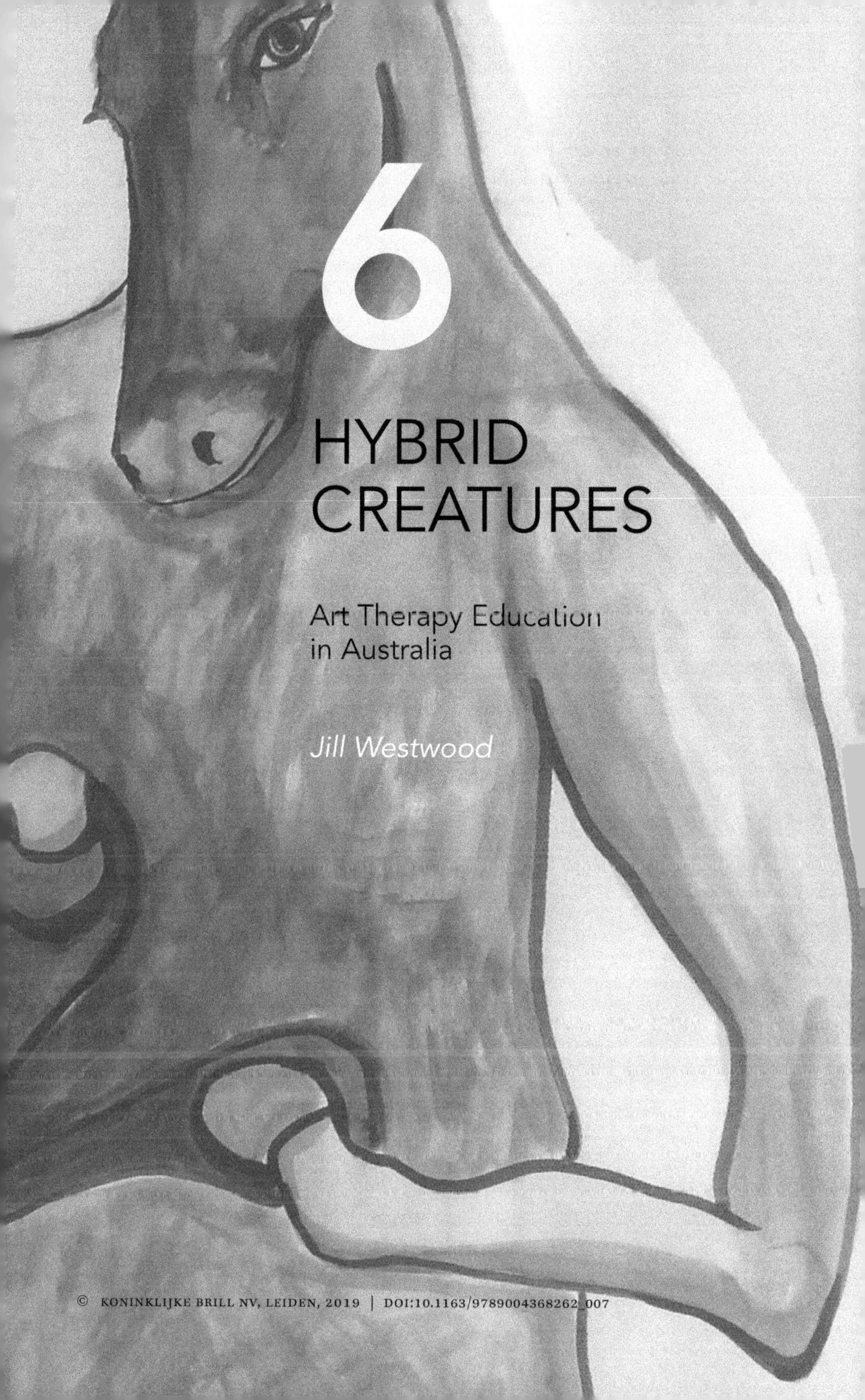

6

HYBRID CREATURES

Art Therapy Education in Australia

Jill Westwood

 | DOI:10.1163/9789004368262_007

Memory foam – re-tracing and re-searching my steps – from there to here and back again …

It is now 2016 as I retrace my steps back 21 years to 1995. It was then that I arrived as a migrant, nascent art therapy educator from Britain to Australian shores for the first time, to a new-found family of art therapists 'at home' in an early settler's cottage on a university campus in the westerly reaches of greater Sydney. It was a scene from a bygone era of pioneering in the outback. From this place the spark of a PhD research project evolved and this piece is a development of it, in the form of a visual essay.

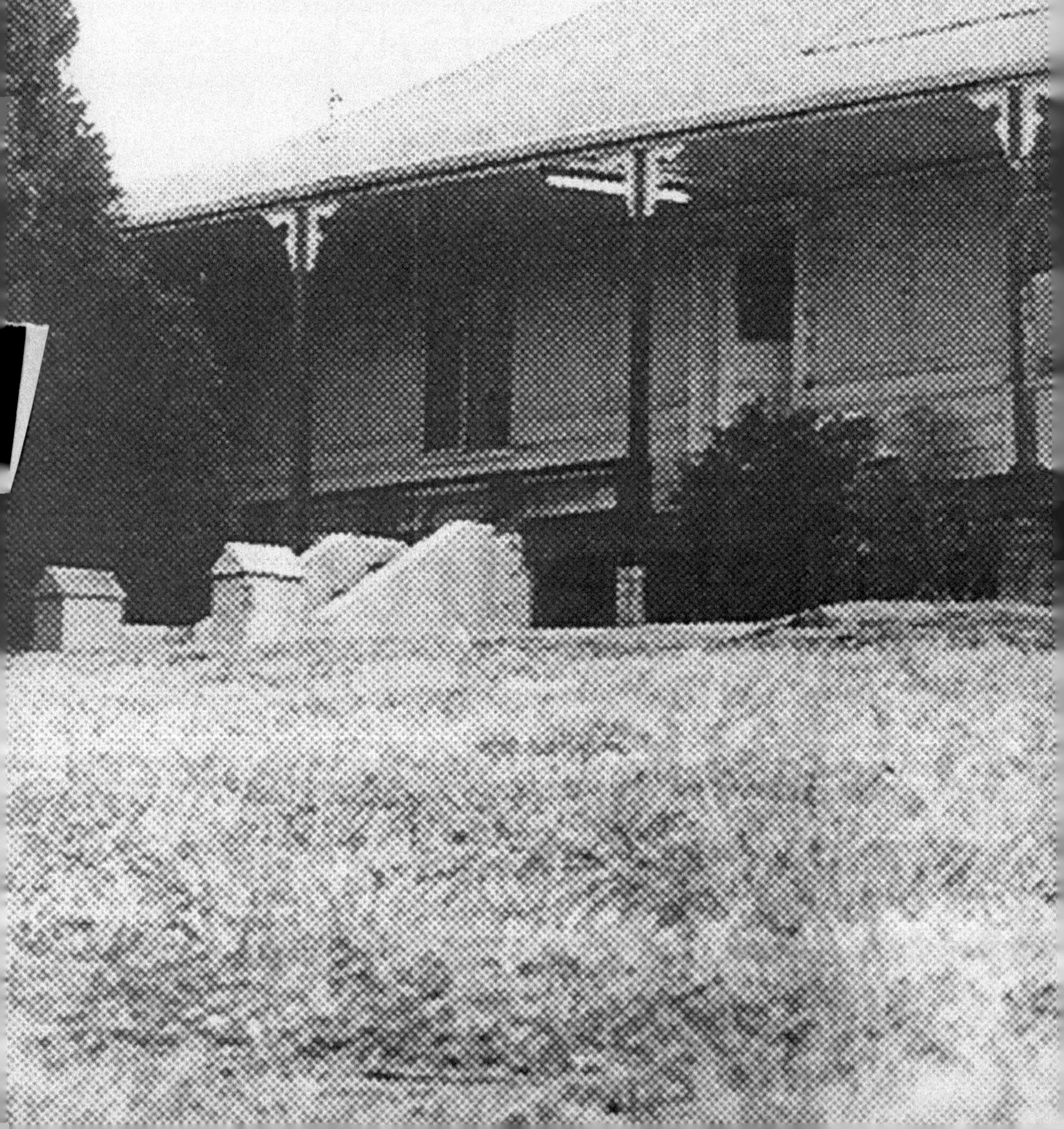

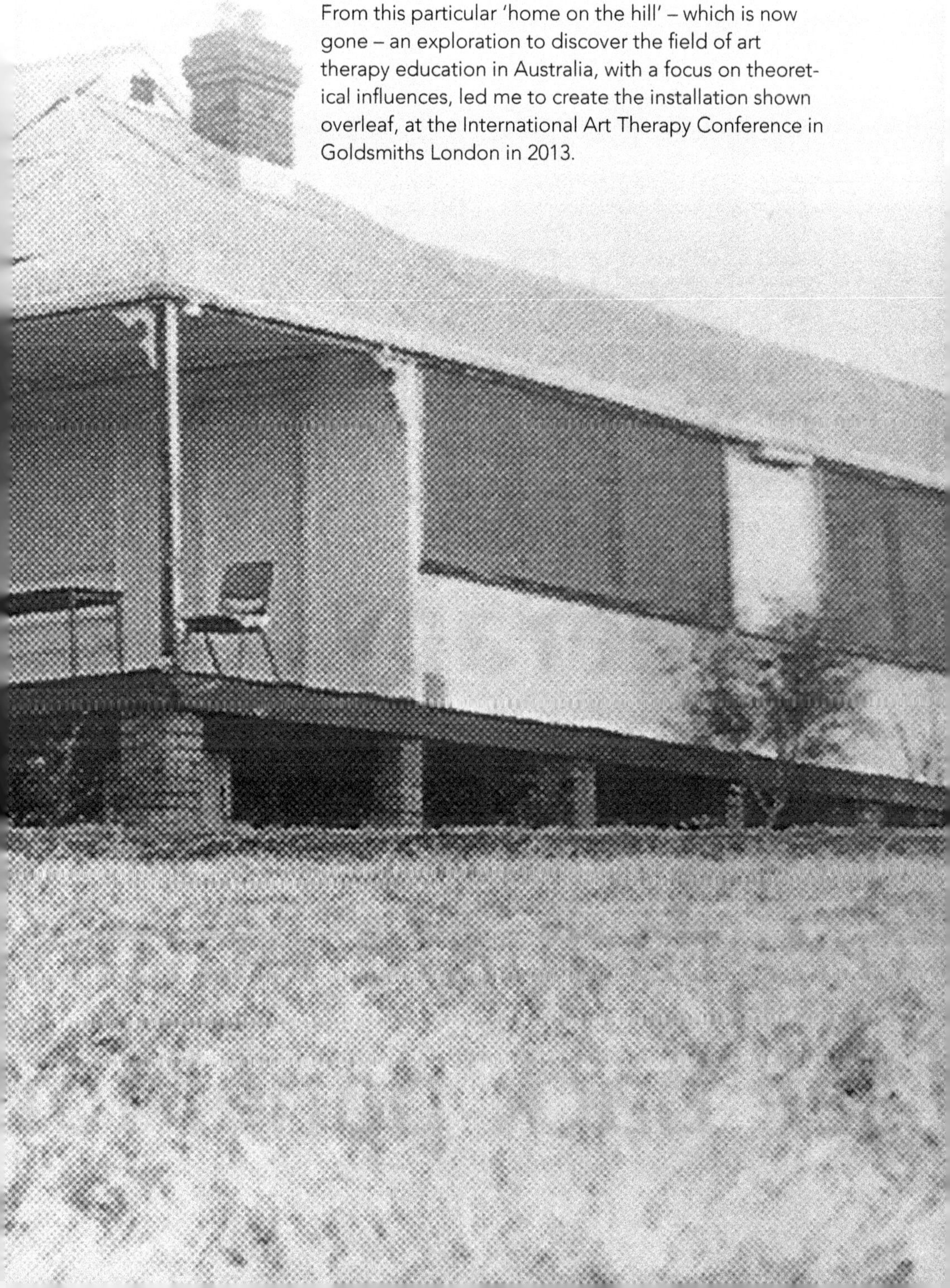

Figure 1 Detail from MA Art Therapy brochure, University of Western Sydney (UWS) (1995). Photograph.

From this particular 'home on the hill' – which is now gone – an exploration to discover the field of art therapy education in Australia, with a focus on theoretical influences, led me to create the installation shown overleaf, at the International Art Therapy Conference in Goldsmiths London in 2013.

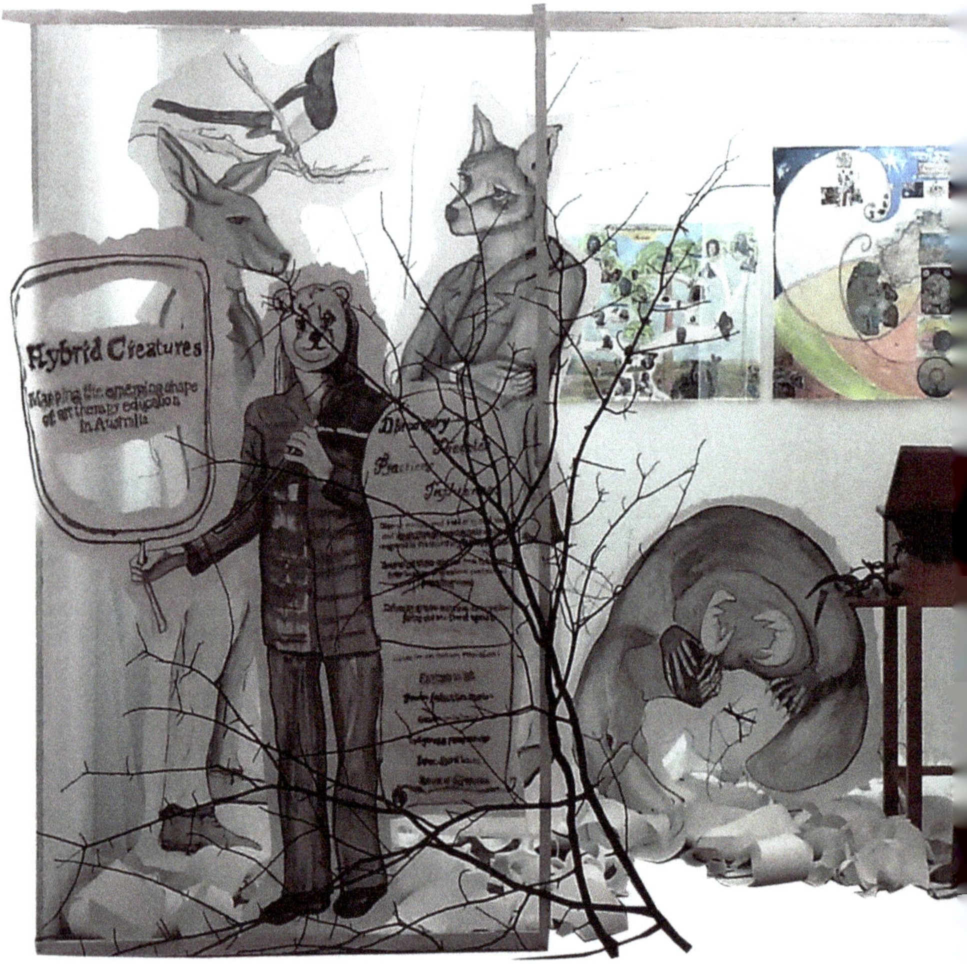

Figure 2 *Installation*, Jill Westwood (2013). Mixed media.

From immersion to reflexivity, the process from the cottage to the installation unfolded like a thick, foggy, saturated, detailed, layered, embroidered, memory-foam fabric in the images and reflections that follow.

To help you enter into this flow it is relevant to state this was a qualitative research project, located in the paradigm of personal knowledge and subjectivity. The information is based on accounts of subjectivities and lived experiences of a particular time and context; it is therefore temporary, incomplete, complex and layered. Using a bricolage of methods (McLeod, 2006), information was gathered from several sources (literature, institutional sources, and key educators, including myself) and then analyzed. This included investigating other places and educators in the world shown to be

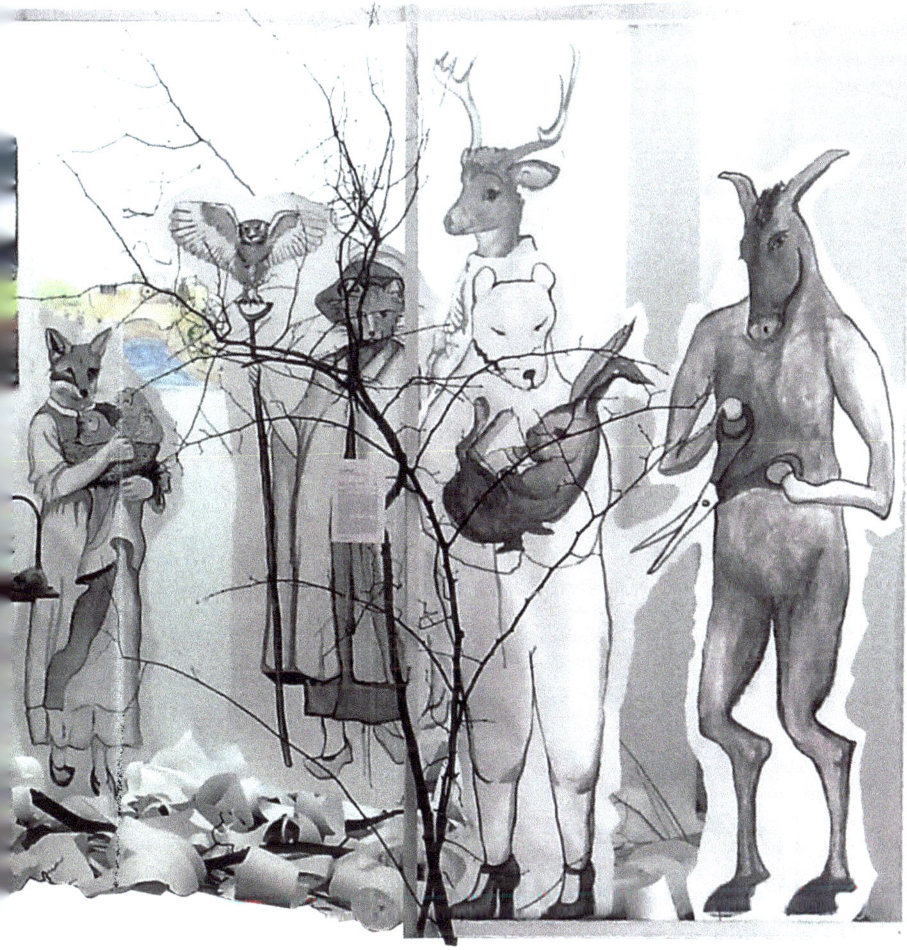

influential (USA and UK). (See Westwood (2010) for a full account and related articles: Westwood, 2012; Westwood and Linnell, 2011.)

As a migrant who has boomeranged from Britain to Australia and back again I have a view from outside and within Australia. My biases have evolved towards experiential, arts-based learning and progressive psychodynamic and group systems perspectives, including post structural and critical, race, feminist viewpoints. These preferences have influenced my use of visual processes to explore and develop ideas. This chapter foregrounds these preferences and the visual, heuristic auto-ethnographic aspects in order to open up meanings and develop understanding relevant for the field and for the region. It also embodies the visual emphasis alive in this book of collected works.

From the city by the sea to the mountains …

Here I stand in the grounds of Taronga Zoo, Sydney, which overlooks the iconic harbour and bridge, in the Australian winter of 1995. I am a new arrival making my way in a different world, strangely familiar but unknown.

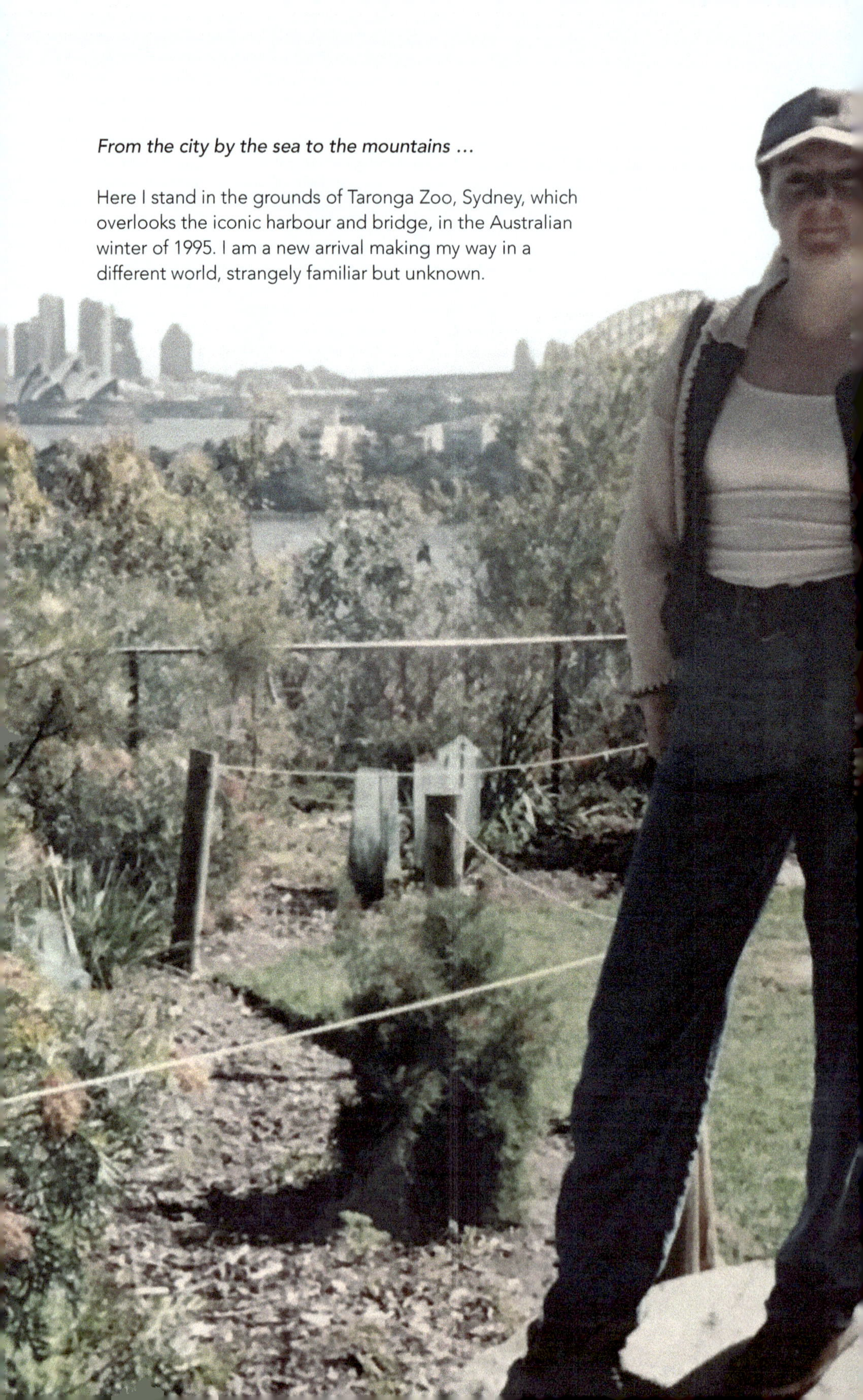

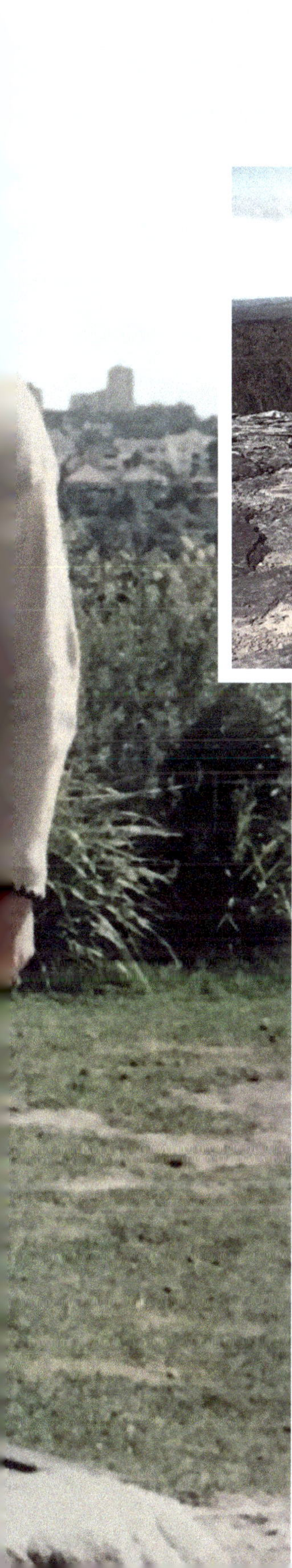

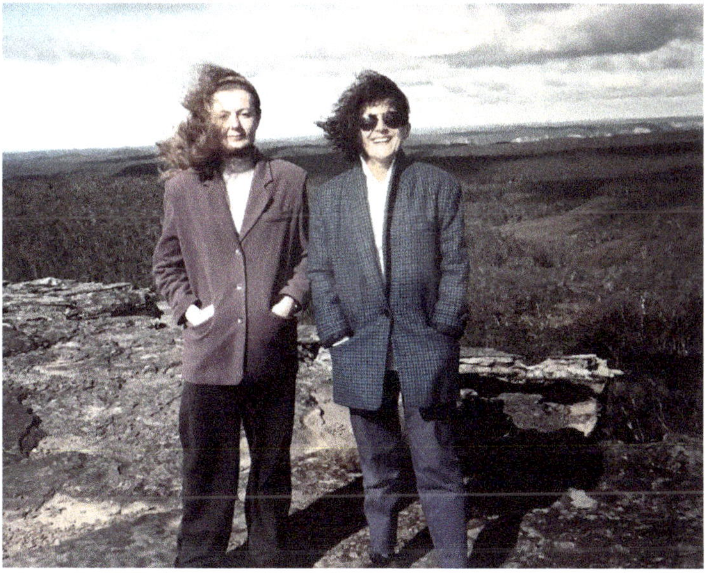

Here in the Blue Mountains around the same time I am standing with my art therapy educator colleague, Marga Hanna from Canada, looking out and back towards Sydney, the most densely built and populated area 100 kilometres away. It is almost invisible on the horizon.The vastness is enveloping as I encounter the scale of this place.

Left: Figure 3 *Taronga Zoo*. Jill Westwood (Winter, 1995). Photograph. *Above*: Figure 4 *Jill Westwood and Marga Hanna and in the Blue Mountains*. Jill Westwood (Winter, 1995). Photograph.

Going forward to the following year 1996 and long before I began the formal research process I made the image on the right.

I was invited to give a presentation at the Network for Exploring Creativity in Therapy through the Arts (NECTA) conference in Sydney on an international view of art therapy. I made this image to explore what I knew about art therapy around the world and to share my experiences and thoughts. The image is structured as a view of the world with the centre being my consciousness. It is like a global map structured around night and day with four cardinal directions on the points of a compass. In the lower half is the world I came from in Britain, symbolised by a giant well-established yew tree in the darkness of night but lit by a full moon. Opposite is the daylight of Australia with two slender white ghost gum trees, hardly visible in the glare of the midday sun. To the west, North America: a cluster of great redwood pine trees, relatively unknown to me. And to the east a Boab and some palm trees of Asia, also an unknown region to me. This was an attempt to imagine and explore the differences between places and perspectives and, by looking through 'my' eyes, to raise the idea of what different eyes and different viewers might see.

(Post)colonial ghosts begin to whisper…

Figure 5 *Map of art therapy around the world.*
Jill Westwood (1996). Acrylic paint on paper.

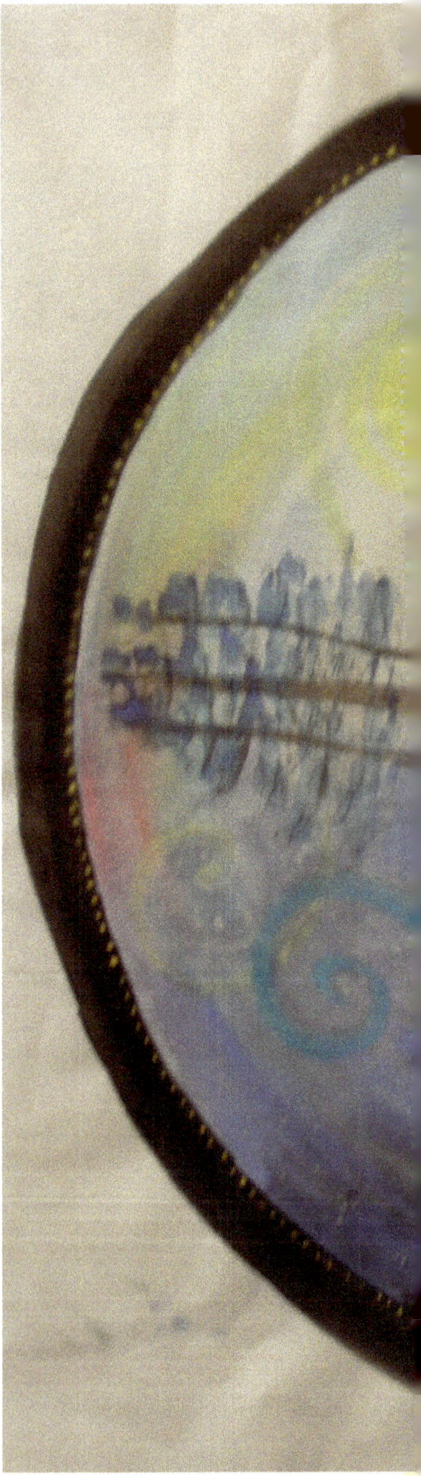

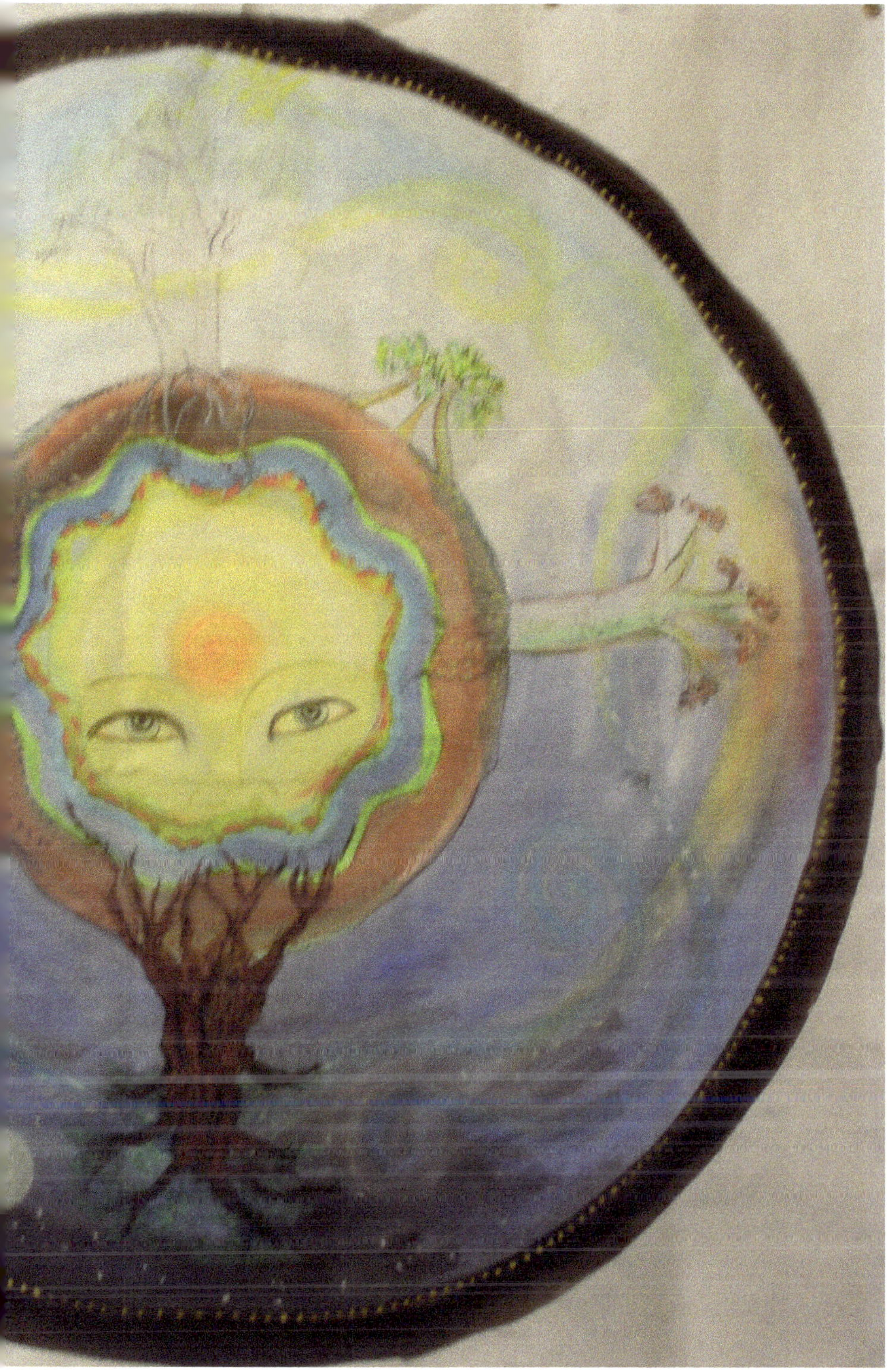

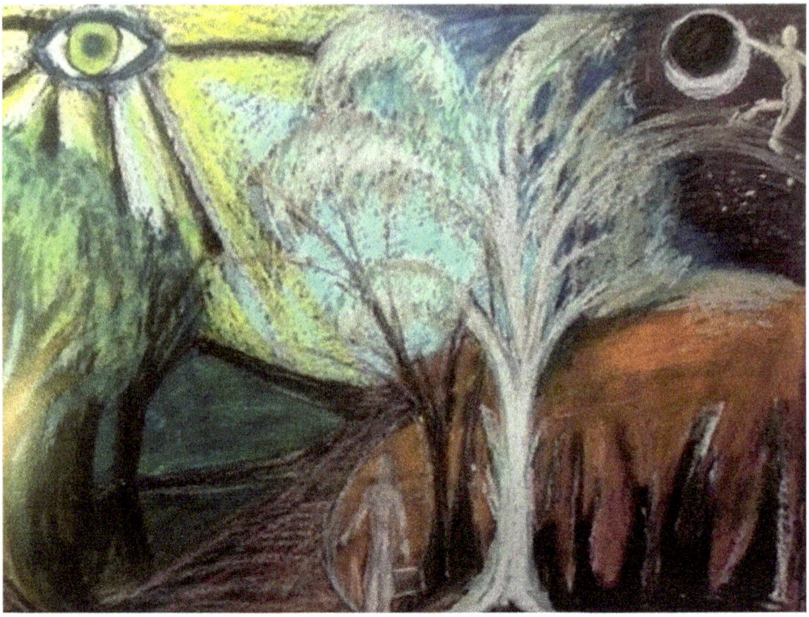

Figure 6 *A view of the landscape of the study.* Jill Westwood (2003). Oil pastel on black paper.

Fast forward to 2003. I was embarking on the PhD project to explore the field of art therapy education in Australia. At a research retreat held at a converted dairy in Leura in the Blue Mountains, facilitated by Andy Gilroy, I made the image shown in Figure 6 above.

Using the principles of art therapy processes involving image-making and group discussion, we explored our research interests. I located myself in the landscape on a path dividing the image into two parts, an Australian landscape on the right and an English landscape on the left. The Australian scene is of a harsh, burnt, desert landscape with broken charred trees. There is one silvery ghost gum, reminiscent of the trees in Figure 5 (pages 164–5). The English scene is contrastingly verdant. The sun and moon are present, echoing themes of the conscious and unconscious. The sun-god-like eye looks like it is seeking to become more conscious and see things from a bird's eye view; this contrasts with the crescent moon and a wispy, striding figure heading off to the edges.

Making these images helped me begin to question my context and how I might be limited and blinkered inside my university experience, coming as I was from the land of the old colonial power. Shortly after, I made the images above and facing page, top, during a Christmas holiday that followed the retreat.

I had a frustrating start using the materials and did not know where to begin. The chalks were dusty, dry and dirty. This led me to think about the Australian land of desert and dryness. A tree formed, a kind of hybrid English-Australian tree, a blossoming oak-gum with magenta flowers. Then a desert leading to a sea, washed out and vague. In an attempt to resolve the image, I included something that I thought would acknowledge an Aboriginal perspective in the landscape. Something I felt was missing. A circle with a black hole in the centre formed – eye-like – a different perspective. Then a swirling blue question mark – like a rainbow serpent coming out of the hole (Figure 7).

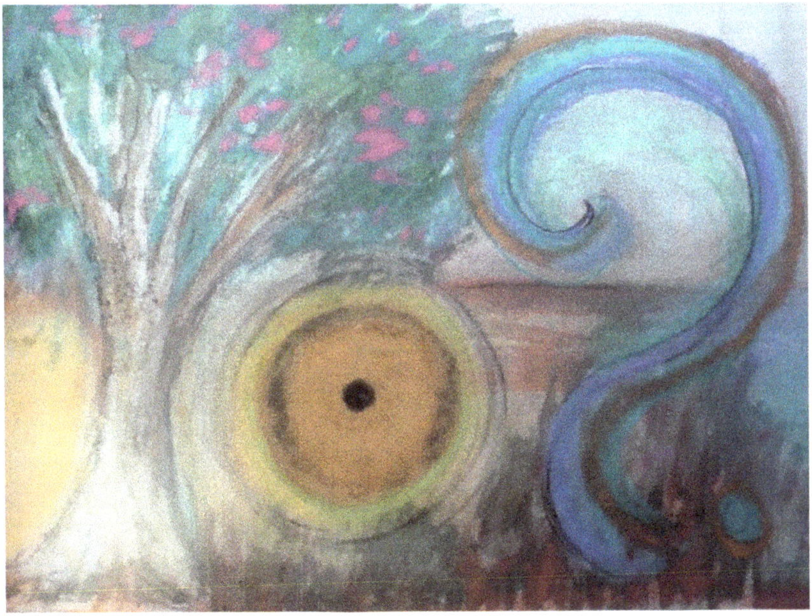

Figure 7 *Explorations into the centre?* Jill Westwood (2003). Chalk pastel on paper.

In the preceding years I'd taken a trip to the Northern Territory and been deeply impressed by the experience. Travelling to the centre of the continent and encountering Aboriginal culture directly had a profound and ineffable effect on me. I hadn't known how to actively tap into this reservoir of knowledge but it surfaced in the images and discussions. This struggle belies hidden histories and the need to take a postcolonial turn.

Figure 8 *At the base of Uluru.*
Jill Westwood (c.1998). Photograph.

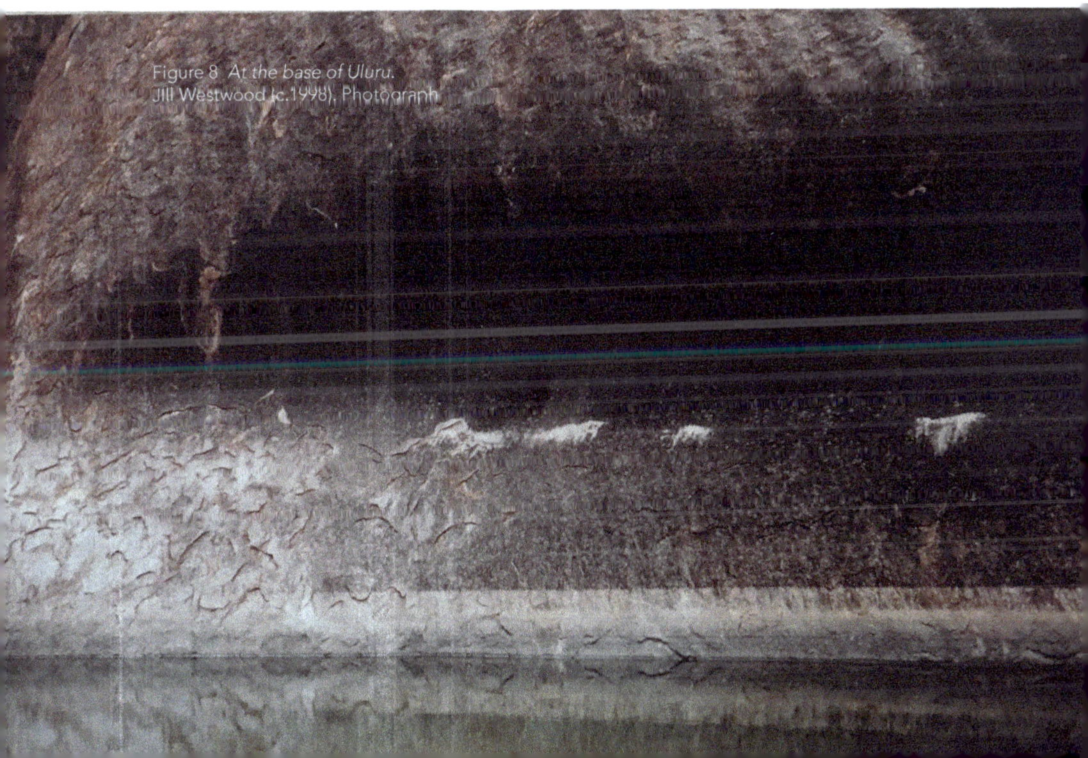

Two years later in 2005 I had been in Australia and in the role of an art therapy educator for ten years. To mark the occasion I created a 'Sistine Chapel'-inspired piece to capture and chronicle the process and achievements (Figure 9, below).

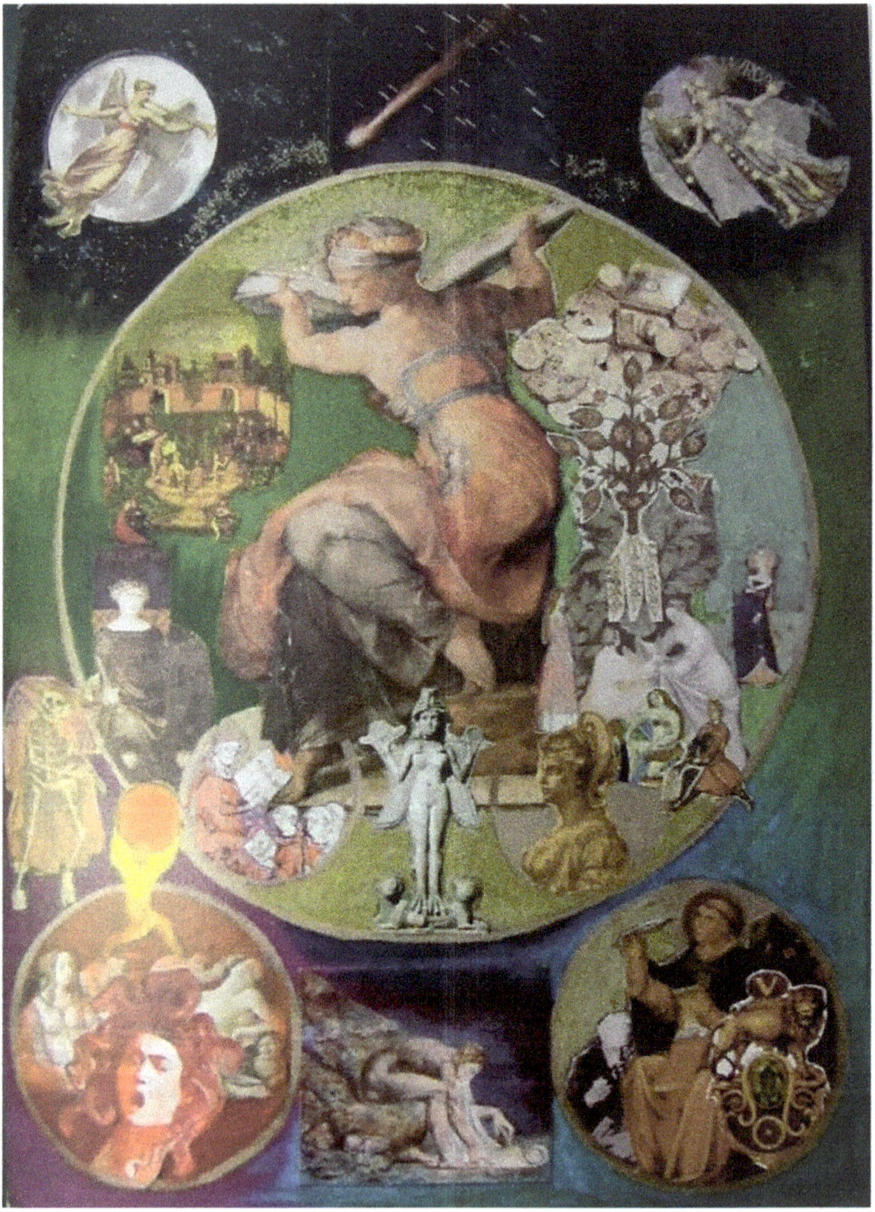

Figure 9 *A decade 1995–2005 as an art therapy educator at UWS, Australia.* Jill Westwood (2005). Collage and oil pastels on card.

It is built around the iconic Michelangelo masterpiece and the figure of the Libyan Sibyl, as well as the works of other great artists of the Renaissance. Dominated by European art and historical references I unfolded my professional experience of struggle, growth and relationships in the sphere of art therapy training at the UWS. The image is a kind of a map or cosmology of the enterprise of the programme in the university context. It was also a testament to the efforts of many people working together with a shared purpose. Although this image was not made directly about the research, it captured something of the quality of the work of an art therapy programme and the nature of the experience of being an art therapy educator. It was also relevant to observe how the imagery referenced European art history so strongly, with some links to ancient mythology from the Middle East. Significantly, there were no Australian images.

In 2007 the project was progressing. Another image (Figure 10 below and pages 170–1) was made to look more closely at the landscape of the project and my experience of the research process. Using collage, the image is structured around a mighty river which cascades through the terrain, cutting into and creating the geography with a strong perspective. There is one horizon covering a range of lands with settlements and farming.

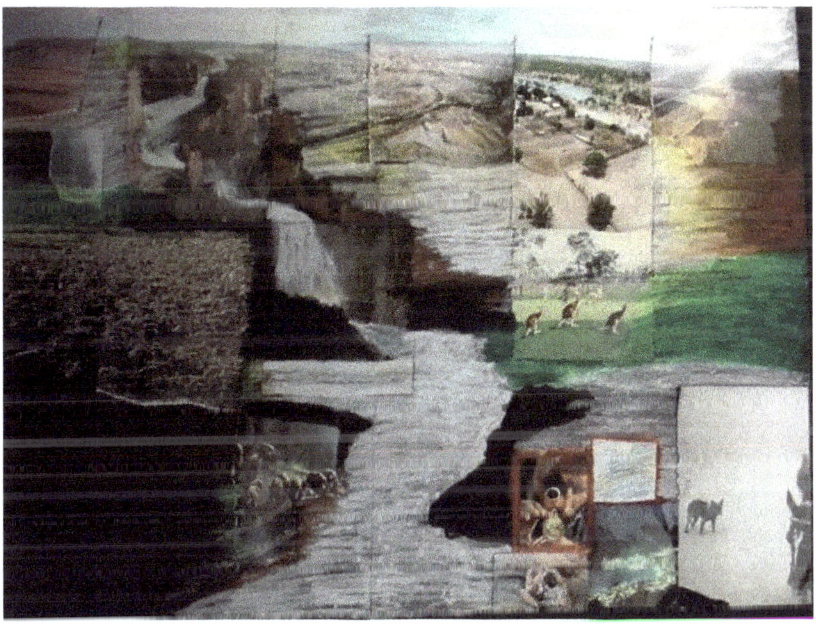

Above and overleaf: Figure 10 *Landscape of the research project.* Jill Westwood (2007). Collage and oil pastels on black paper.

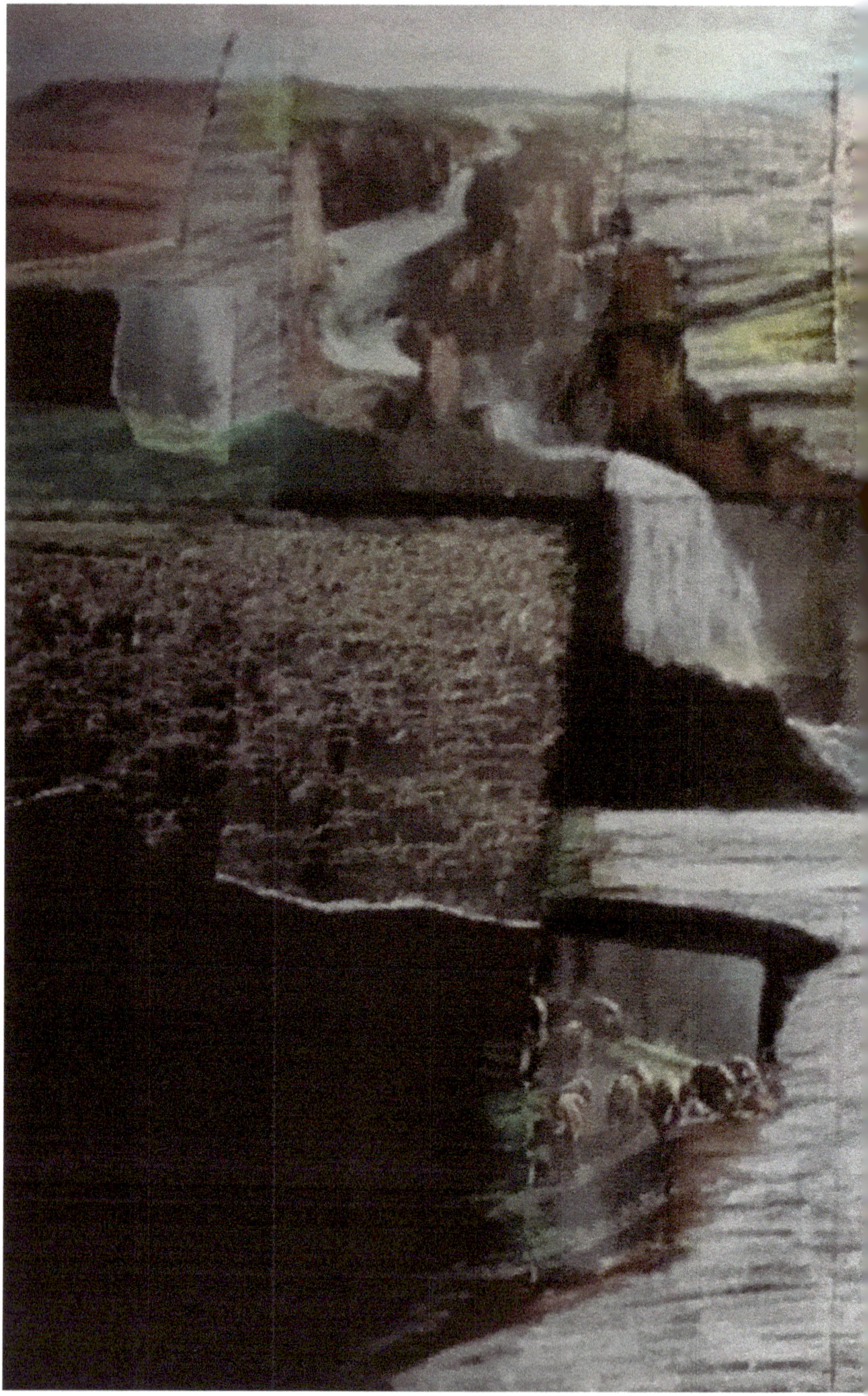

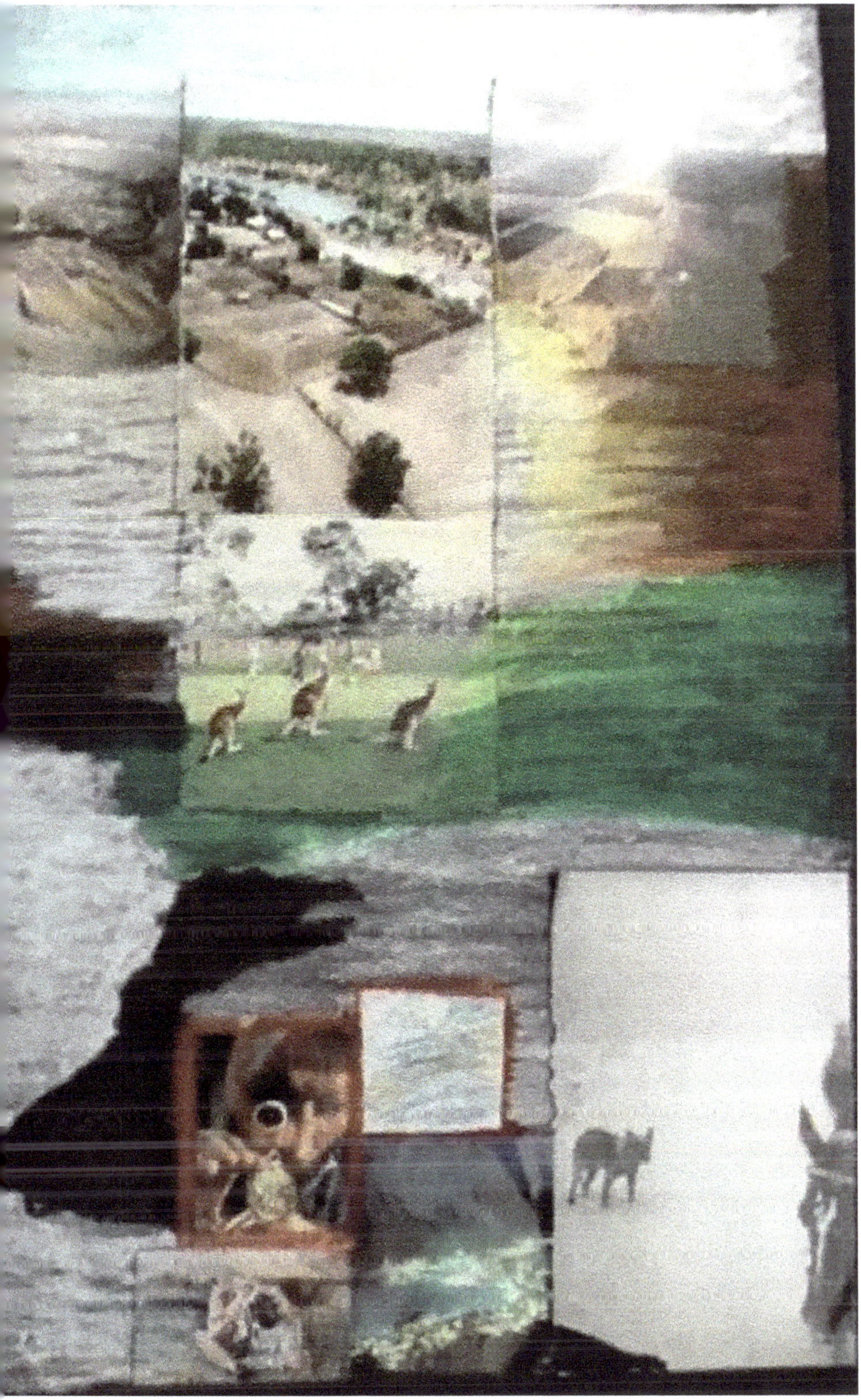

On the left side, flocks of livestock are herded and on the right, three kangaroos look out from a highly cultivated golf course; this leads to the foreground where some other scenes unfold. In the bottom right area, a man looks through a magnifying glass to inspect something very close up. A person is washed in the white foam of the cascading waters and is completely immersed. Next to them is a winter landscape which features a lone dog and a horse, right on the edge of the image. They are braving the icy terrain. On the other side the page is left vacant and undeveloped.

I saw this image as an attempt to hold in view a panorama of the project's landscape. It contrasted the herding masses of animals for farming with the wild and Indigenous kangaroos of Australia. However these kangaroos are located in a highly cultivated urban environment of a golf course. This captured some of the free and natural spirit I found in Australia coupled with the tension of fitting into an imported and cultivated environment. The theme of contrasts and opposing positions and their reconciliation spoke on many levels. In a broad sense it referred to the political process of Aboriginal reconciliation and colonial invasion. Parallels could also be found at the level of art therapy programmes which have evolved through the importation and adaptation of different educators who were from different places and who had brought different perspectives with them.

Other aspects of the image spoke about my experience of the research process. I saw the river as symbolic of the journey of the research, coursing and cutting through the landscape and having a powerful momentum that carried me along but which could wash me up in a place I had not expected and could not control. The person immersed in the foamy waters echoed my experience of being engulfed by the process. This dynamic of moving between expanded exploratory spaces to focused attention on some tiny detail also captured something of the process. The presence of the dog and the horse I associated with travelling in a lonely, harsh environment and needing companionship on the journey.

In 2008 I embarked on a series of research interviews and found that I dreamt about the research several times. Figure 11 is a visual sketch that tried to capture one of those dreams and the converging ideas I was grappling with.

I had found the process of doing the interviews profound. I was talking with people, some of whom I had never met before, who held important knowledge about the field. I heard about their experiences and views which included personal stories and sometimes difficulties and conflicts. These meetings allowed me to join up pieces of information that shifted my perception and knowledge and gave me a new overview of the field. I became highly sensitised to my role and the effects of the research process. It caused me to think more about what it was I was asking of people. I noticed, without exception, that I left each interview with a feeling of exhilaration and privilege, and that the information that had been shared with me was precious, like gold.

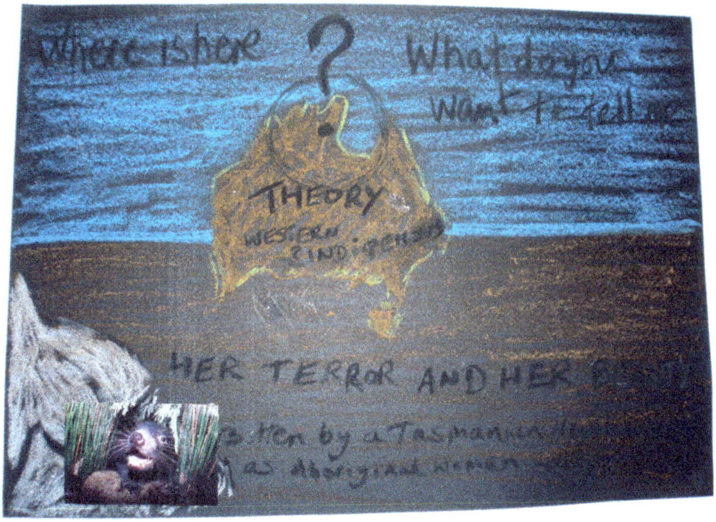

Figure 11 *Research Dreaming*, Jill Westwood (2008). Collage and oil pastel on paper.

In the dream I was to interview a participant but I could only ask one question. The question that came to me was: *"What do you want to tell me?"* In the dream this question was like an epiphany. It was as if this was a key to unlocking the research. However, ironically, this did not ask anything specific about the research I was undertaking. This made me think about the power relationship between a researcher and a participant when in pursuit of a research question. In this dynamic, the researcher is taking up a receptive function to hear what is shared.

In another image from the same dream, I was suckling a Tasmanian devil[1] as some Aboriginal women watched. The animal suddenly bit me and it was shocking and painful. I wondered about the aggressive forces involved in the rearing of an animal (art therapy / programme / research project) and of the inter-species relationship of a human and a Tasmanian devil (mixing between cultures, perspectives and theories). I also thought of the rivalry and competition that is part of the struggle of life and growth.

The other elements of the image refer to ideas about migration and the history of Australia. The question of: *"Where is here?"* sits alongside the question: *"What do you want to tell me?"* A question mark hovers above a map of Australia with the word *'theory'* plus sub-titles, *'Western'* and *'Indigenous'*.

The words of the famous poem about Australia, *'My Country'* by Dorothea Mackellar are etched below: *"Her terror and her beauty"*. This echoes the essence of the country and the context. However I had unconsciously switched the order of the words, which in the poem are *"Her beauty and her terror"*. The force of terror was pushing closer into the foreground.

1 The Tasmanian devil is the world's largest carnivorous marsupial found only in Tasmania, an island state of Australia. It is now an endangered species.

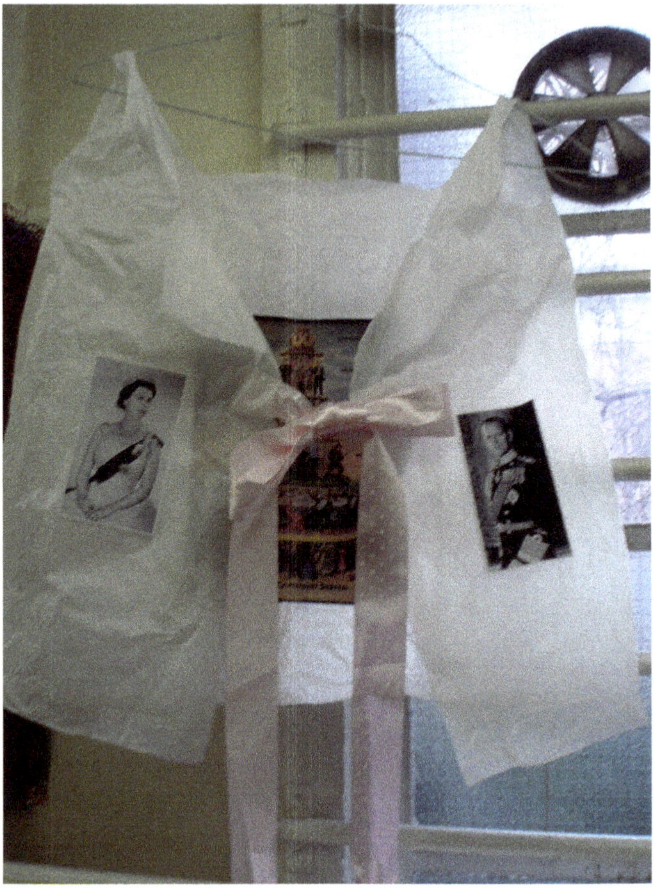

Figure 12
Artwork (Plastic bag robe featuring Queen Elizabeth II). Jill Westwood (2009). Mixed media including; paper, ribbon, plastic carrier bag.

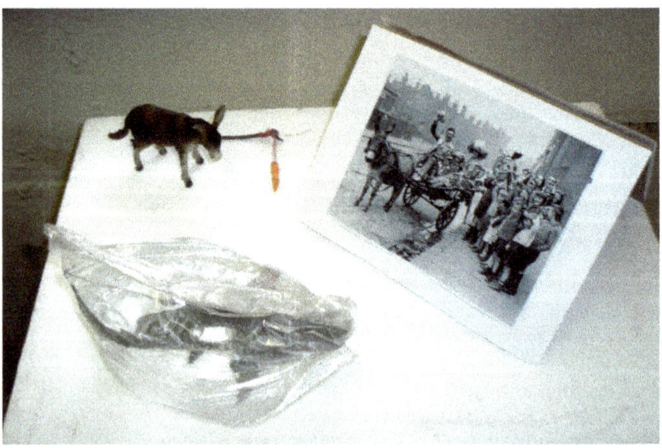

Figure 13
Artwork (Shark, Donkey, Pearly Kings and Queens). Jill Westwood (2009) Mixed media including; paper, found objects, plastic, water.

In January 2009, following changes in my circumstances I returned to Britain. I was now working at Goldsmiths, University of London, where I had trained 20 years earlier in 1988–90. I was catapulted back into a previously known context but I came to it with a different awareness and also a recognition that this place had evolved. I was confronted with the need to develop new relationships, afresh. At a workshop on identity and difference on the theme of 'class', I made a piece referencing the famous Goldsmiths alumni Damien Hirst's artwork of a shark,[2] the Royal Family and the Pearly Kings and Queens of London.

I was back inside the places and home of bygone colonial power. Swallowed up by sharks, doing the donkey work and reflecting on systemic and cultural inequalities.

2 *The Physical Impossibility of Death in the Mind of Someone Living*, 1991.

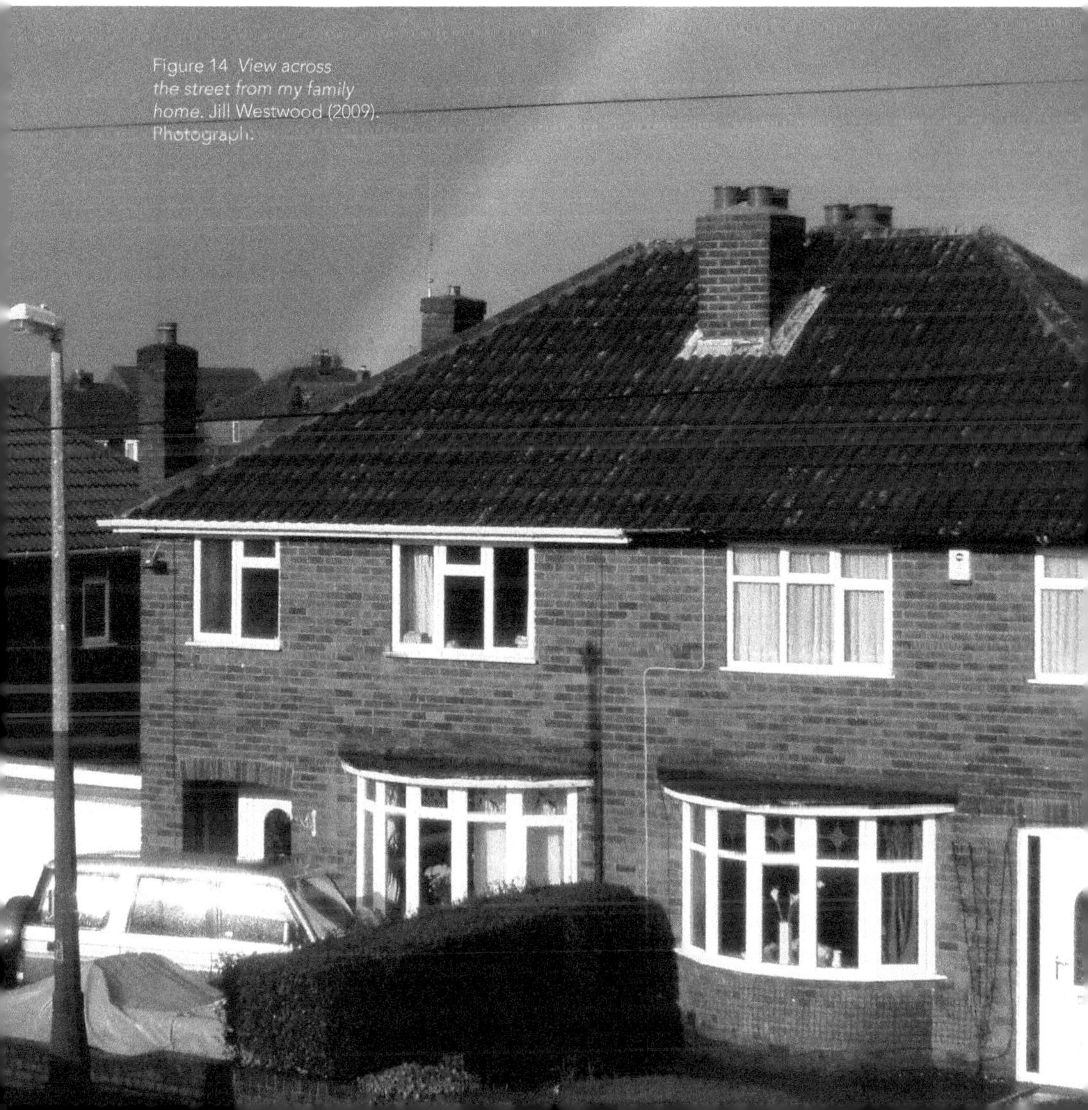

Figure 14 *View across the street from my family home.* Jill Westwood (2009). Photograph.

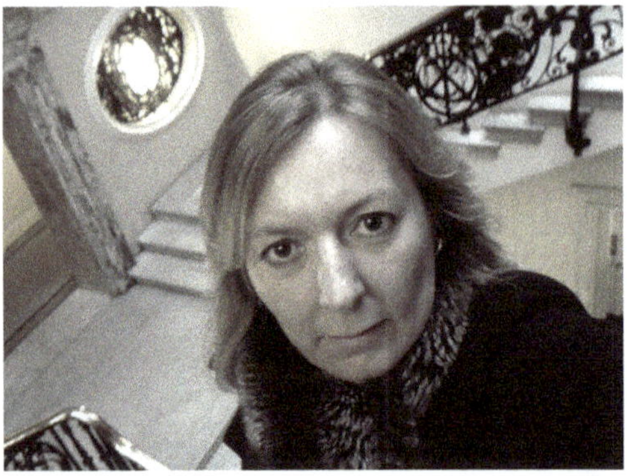

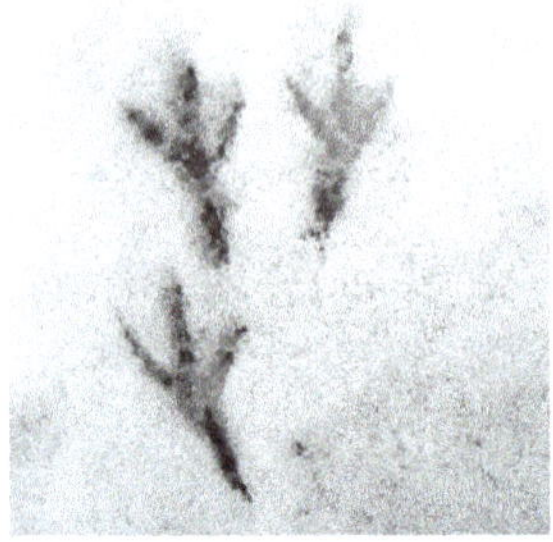

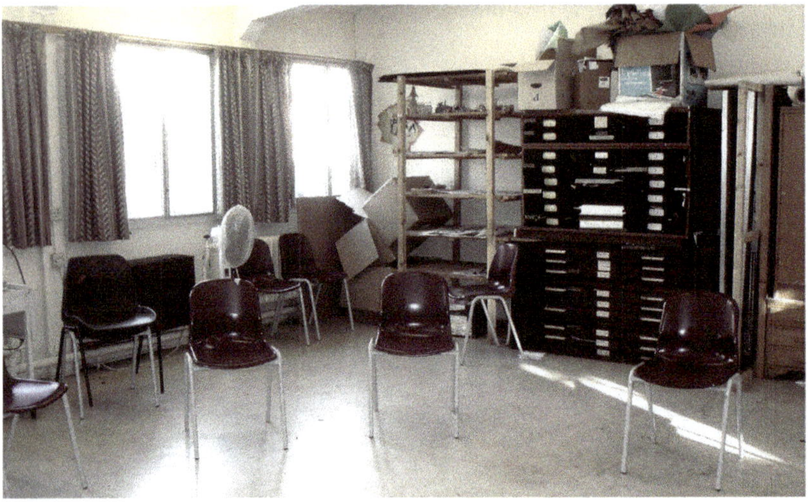

Top left: Figure 15 *Inside the Town Hall building, Goldsmiths, University of London.* Jill Westwood (2009). Photograph. *Top right:* Figure 16 *It was a cold snowy winter, the footprints of birds.* Jill Westwood (2009). Photograph. *Above:* Figure 17 *Inside one of the art therapy studios at Goldsmiths.* Jill Westwood (2009). Photograph.

By July 2009 all the interviews were completed and I was about to begin the data analysis and writing up of the study. In some designated research-based studio time I made the very tightly constructed, densely referenced image shown in Figure 18 opposite.

My aim was to try to contain all the interviews that had been done in Australia and think about them as a whole. An imaginary family or bestiary[3] of hybrid creatures is pictured on the map of Australia with a re-visited image of 'explorations into the centre' (Figure 7, page 167) located in the middle, like

3 A bestiary is a compendium or summary of illustrations of beasts or animals which are usually accompanied by a moral lesson. Bestiaries were popular in the Middle Ages.

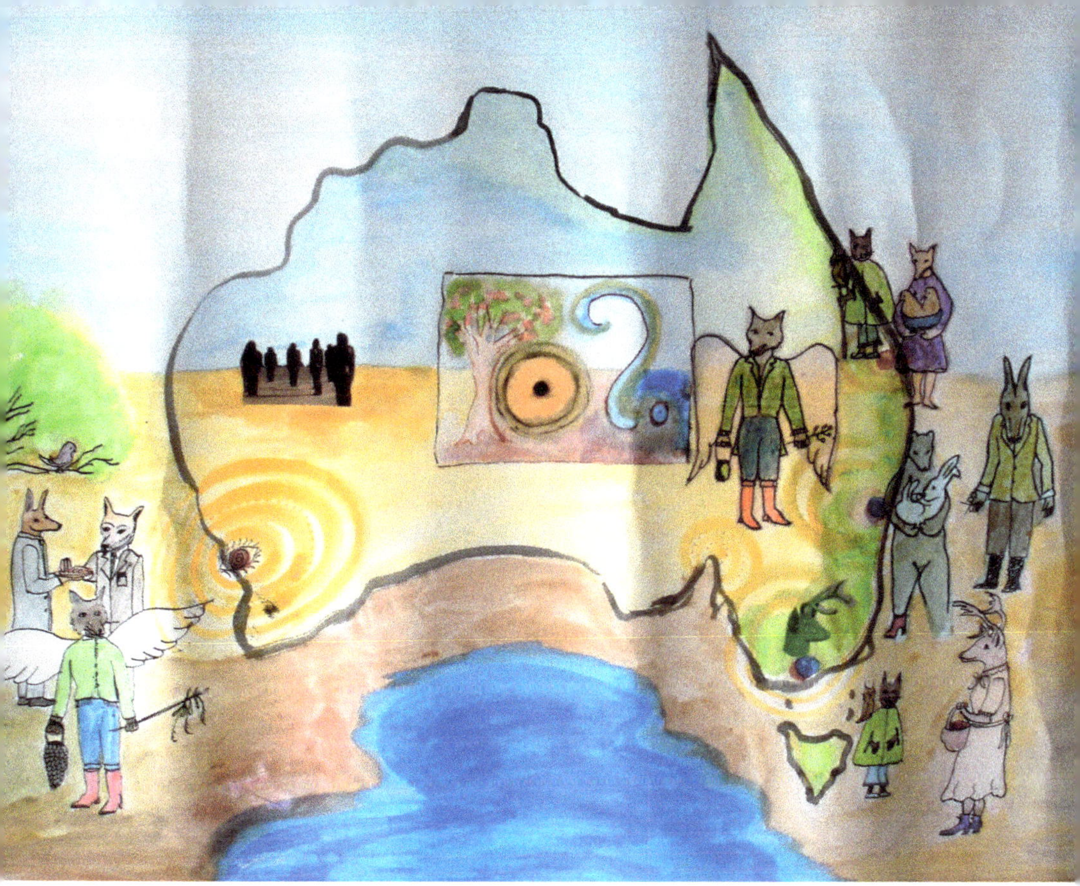

Above: Figure 18 *A bestiary of art therapy education in Australia*. Jill Westwood (2009). Collage and ink on cartridge paper.

Right: Figure 19 *Platypus*. Jill Westwood (2009). Found fabrics and sponge. Shortly after completing the 'bestiary' in Figure 18 I realised that I had inadvertently missed out the programme at Royal Melbourne Institute of Technology (RMIT); in response to this I made a soft sculpture in the form of a duck-billed platypus. This completed the 'bestiary' of art therapy creatures.

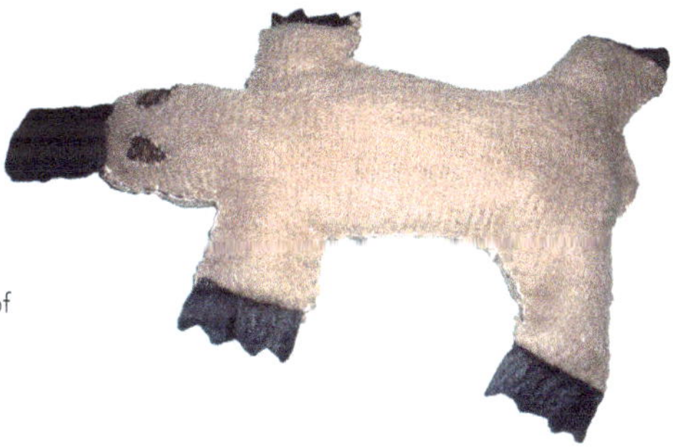

a window set on the horizon. The creatures were loosely based on the seven different programmes in the public university (five) and private (two) sectors in Australia and the art therapy educators in this field. (University sector: Edith Cowan University, University of Western Sydney, La Trobe University, Royal Melbourne Institute of Technology, University of Queensland; Private sector: IKON, Melbourne Institute for `Expressive Creative Arts Therapies (MIECAT)). The process of the interviews had produced new connections and understandings for me, stimulating a desire to link and be in relationship with all the participants, rather than be rivalrous or oppositional, the process being common to groups.

In parallel to this bestiary I began to map the influential relationships in a genealogy of programmes and educators, as can be seen in Figure 20 (opposite and pages 180–1). The image is of a large and well-established Australian gum tree with a tall palm tree in the background. It features the educators and their various connections to each other through the branches, leading to the programmes that sit in the boughs. These connections were revealed through the interviews. The left fork and branch of the gum tree holds more of the influences from UK and leads to the programmes at the University of Queensland (UQ), the University of Western Sydney (UWS) and Edith Cowan University (ECU). However, ECU sits in the centre and mingles with the right hand branches, representing the educator influences from the USA. The right hand fork in the trunk represents influences from the USA, the major branch leading to the Royal Melbourne Institute of Technology (RMIT), La Trobe University and the IKON Institute of Australia programmes. The separate, tall palm tree that grows close by in the background represents the MIECAT programme which has its own unique view and purpose, closely related but distinct from what might be considered the 'species' of the other programmes. Both trees are filled with various flora and fauna showing the rich variety and cross-fertilisation of ideas, views and practices in Australian art therapy. It also alludes to the migration of ideas and influences and how these travel from different places.

Following this I used image-making to map the entire project in 'A Cosmology of Art Therapy Education in Australia' (Figure 21, opposite and pages 182–3). A map of Australia is at the heart of the scene and a curving horizon arcs across the image. Swirling lines, reminiscent of songlines[4], suggest paths between areas. Words are used to name important factors in the context of the project and to trace the interconnected and multilayered dynamics between places, histories, cultures, literature, programmes and professional and theoretical horizons.

In this image I attempted to map out the overall project in order to process the material and progress the findings in an organised way. It shows the complexity of a diverse and multi-layered field of different views and innovative approaches within the seven art therapy programmes in Australia. I discovered that theories and practices were closely linked and that approaches to art therapy education had evolved from the educators, their background experiences, the location of the programme within the university, professional contexts (health, arts, education, social, community) and the prevailing views within these contexts which are driven by economic, socio-political forces and neo-liberal agendas.[5]

4 Songlines are part of an Australian Aboriginal Indigenous belief system. They are sacred paths across the land or sky followed by 'creator–beings' during the Creation or Dreaming. The paths of the songlines are recorded in traditional songs, stories, dance and painting.

5 Neo-liberalism can be described as an ideological paradigm that seeks to maximise the role of the private sector and shift risk from governments and corporations on to individuals.

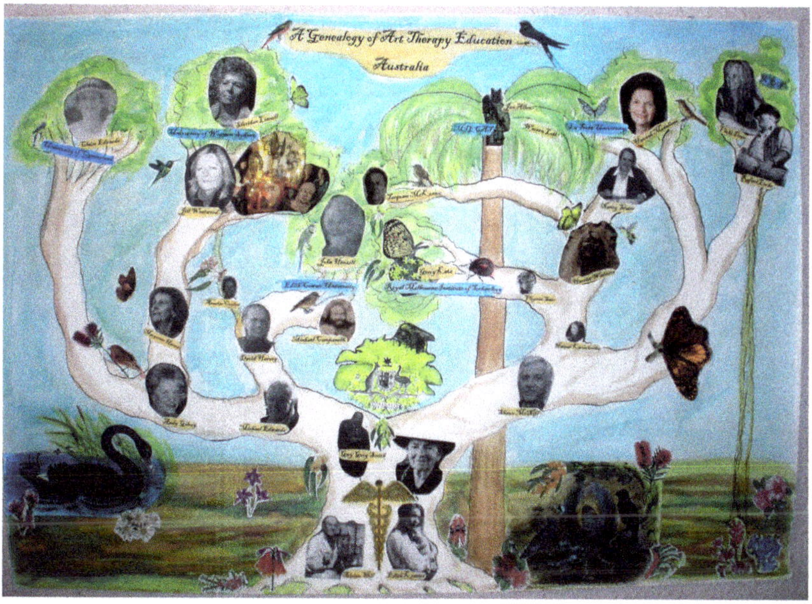

Figure 20 *A genealogy of art therapy education in Australia*. Jill Westwood (2009). Collage and ink on cartridge paper.

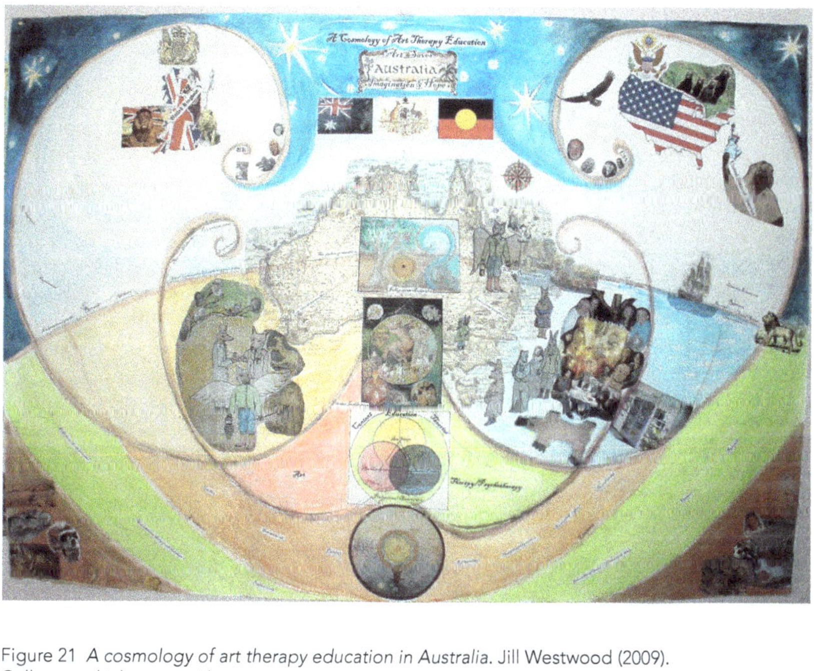

Figure 21 *A cosmology of art therapy education in Australia*. Jill Westwood (2009). Collage and ink on cartridge paper.

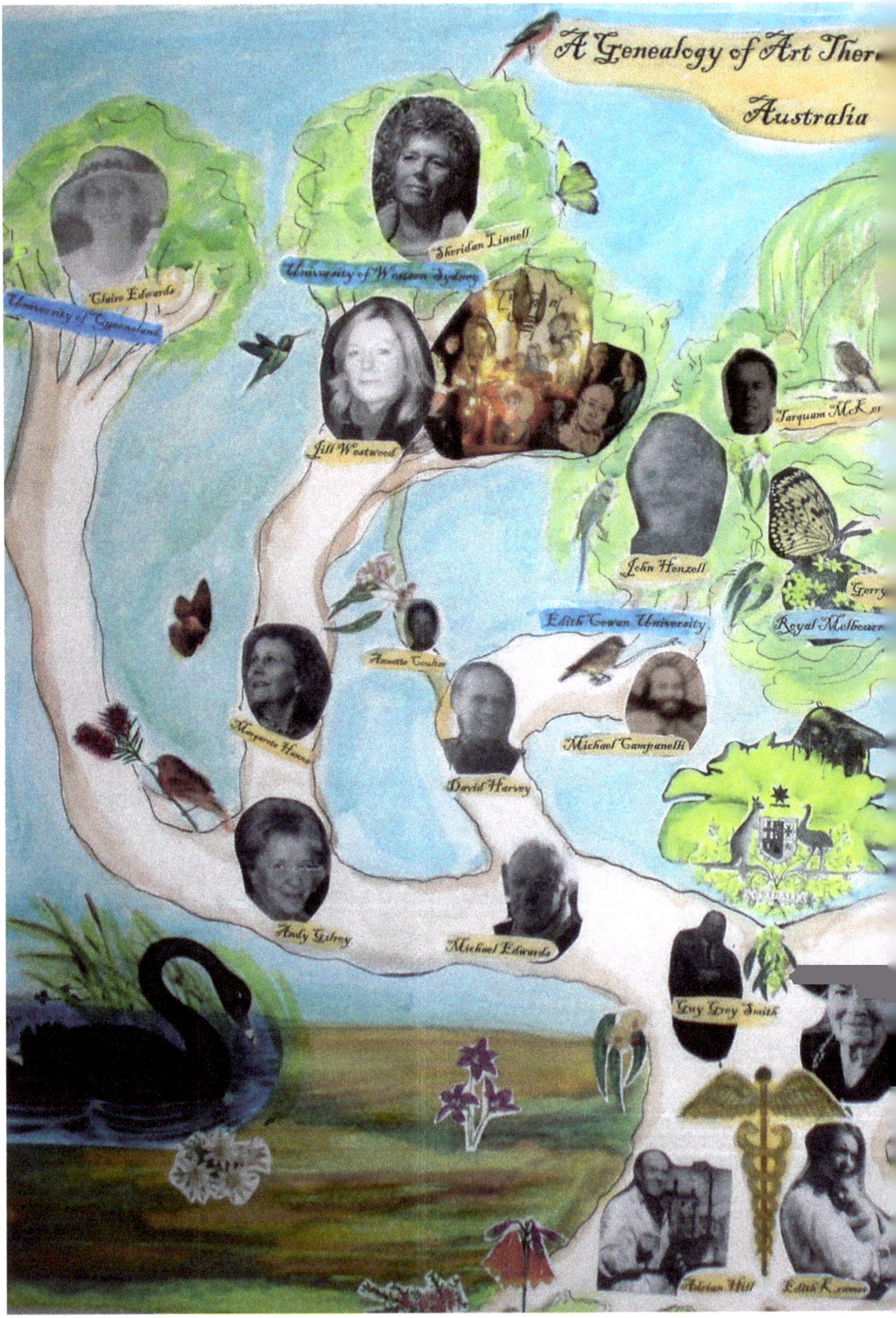
Australia
Sheridan Linnell
University of Western Sydney
Claire Edwards
University of Queensland
Jill Westwood
John Henzell
Edith Cowan University
Annette Coulter
Michael Campanelli
David Harvey
Andy Gilroy
Michael Edwards
Guy Gray Smith
Adrian Hill

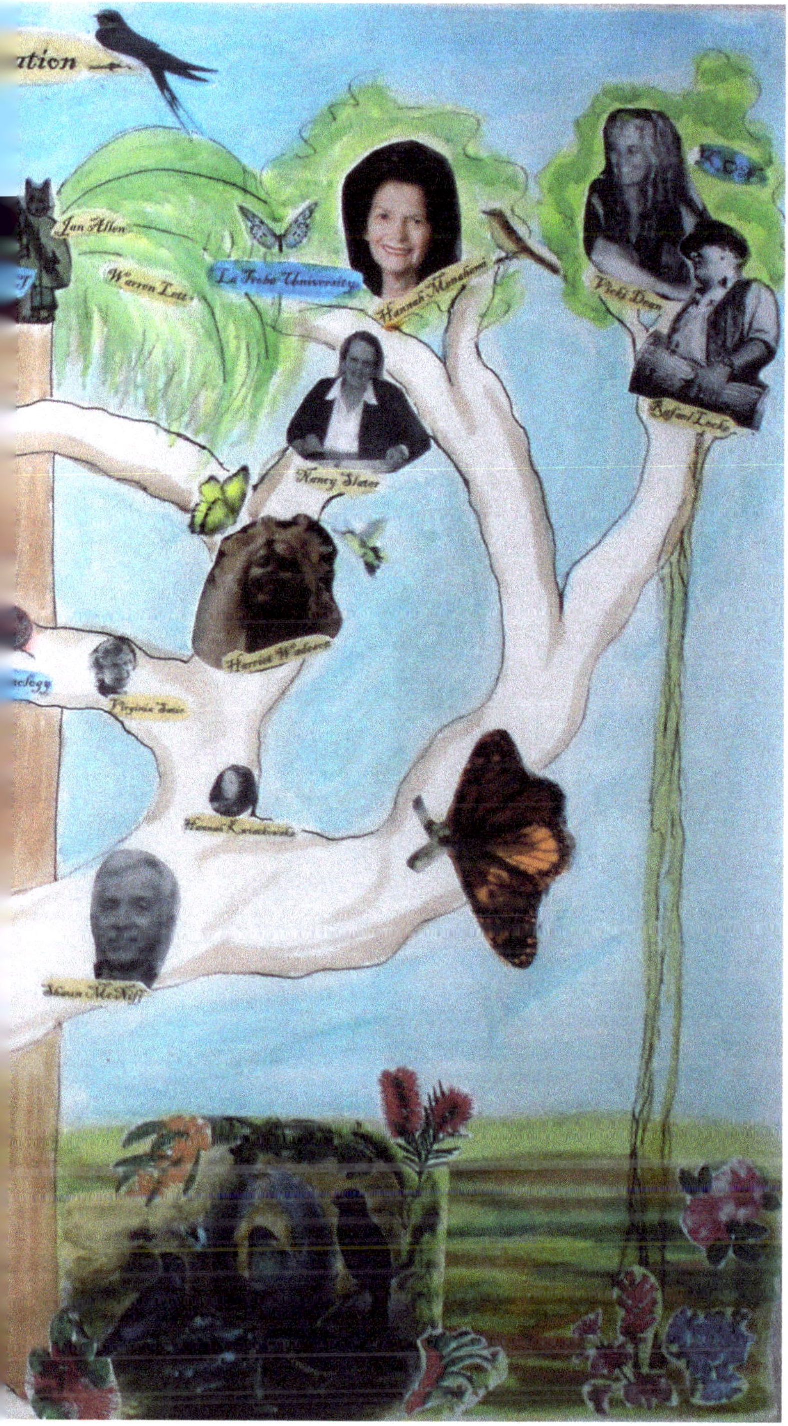

Figure 20 *(bis)* *A genealogy of art therapy education in Australia.* Jill Westwood (2009). Collage and ink on cartridge paper.

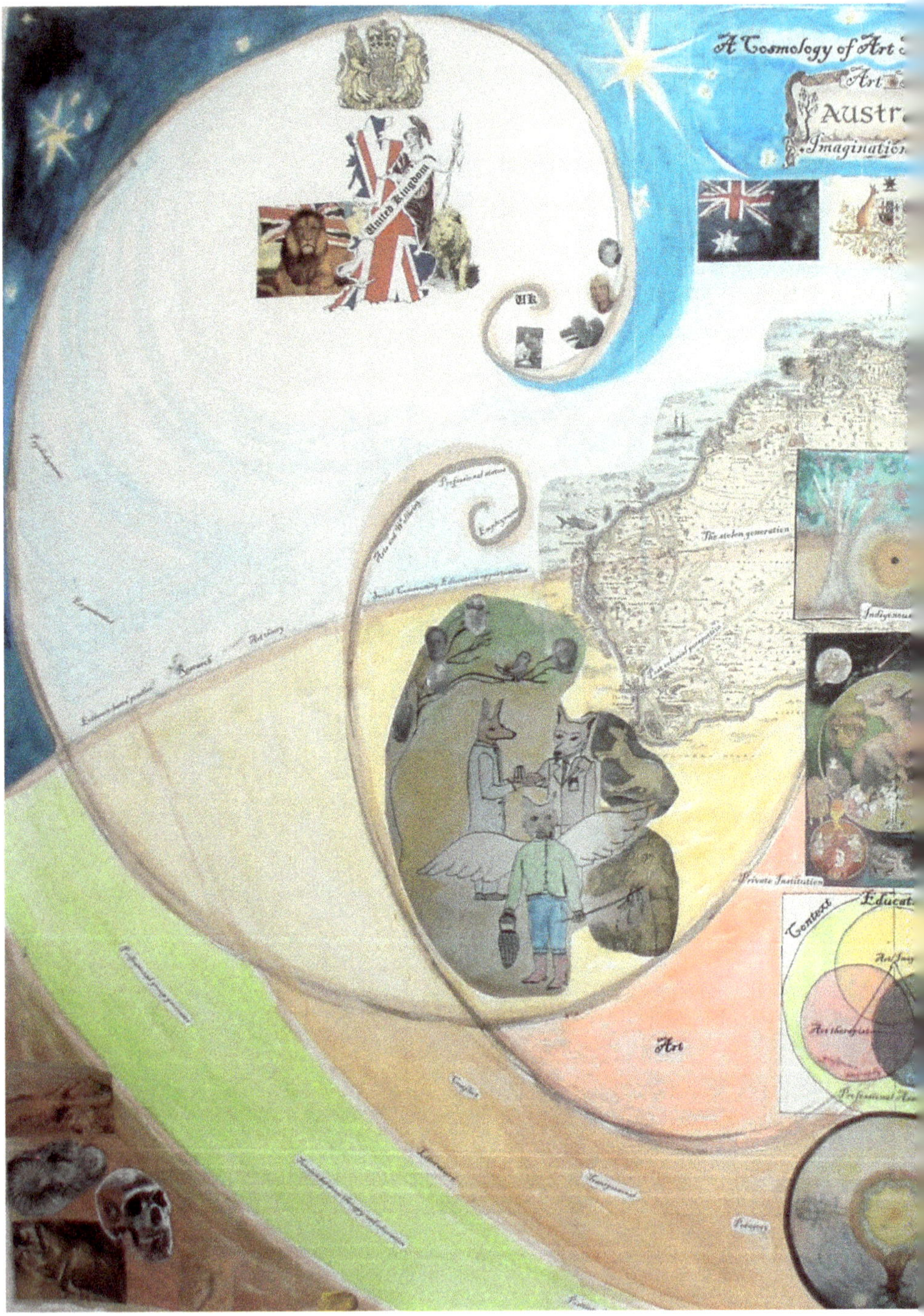
A Cosmology of Art
United Kingdom
UK
The stolen generation
Private Institution
Context
Art

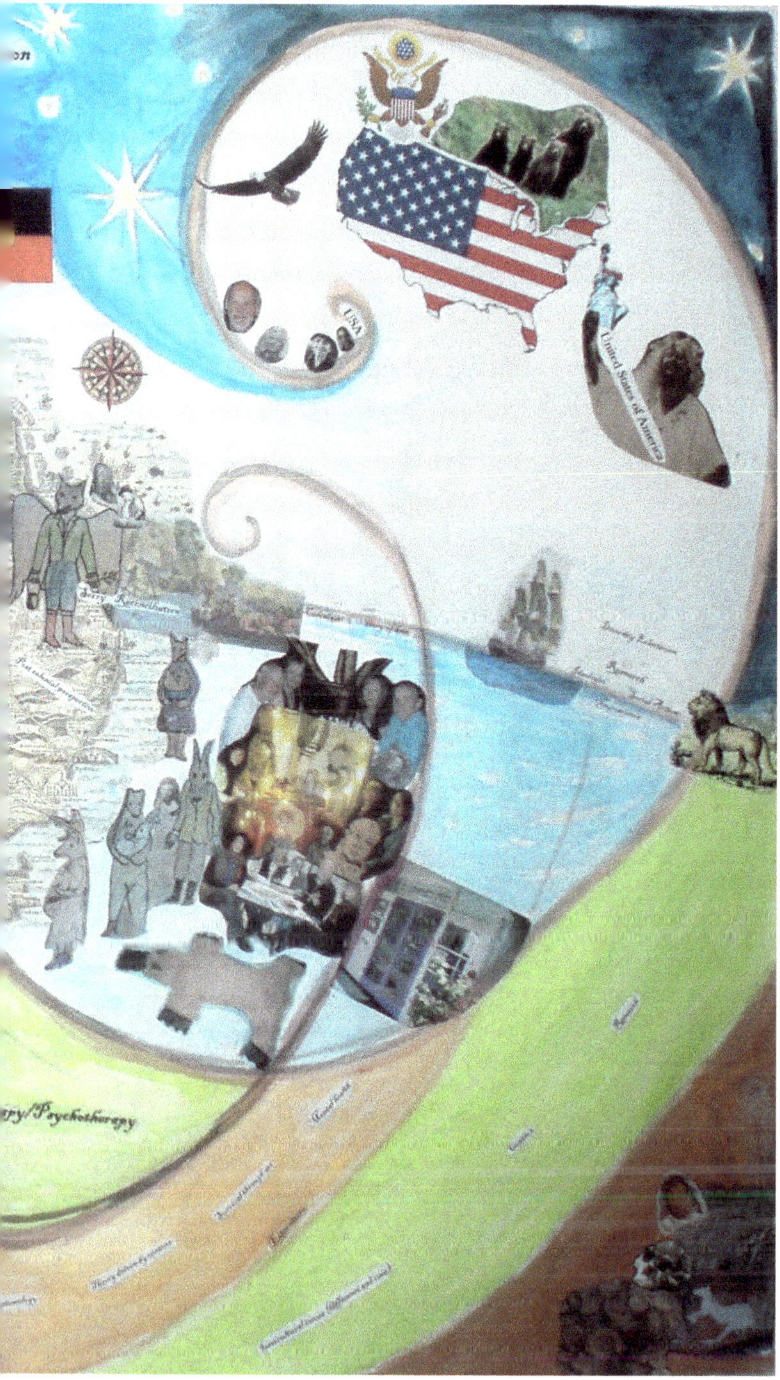

Figure 21 *(bis)*
A cosmology of art therapy education in Australia.
Jill Westwood (2009). Collage and ink on cartridge paper.

The university programmes generally taught a range of the major theories of psychotherapy, underpinned with a psychodynamic or humanistic perspective, although movement towards a more integrative and eclectic approach was also found. This was linked to being part of more general masters programmes, driven by economic forces. The private sector programmes were more distinctly grounded in a particular theoretical perspective or philosophical view.

The 'uneasy partnership' between art and psychotherapy resonates as an enduring and continual dynamic (Champernowne, 1971). This echoes in the theme of the bestiary and hybrid-creature images which owed much to my creative collaboration with colleagues at the UWS (Perry, Linnell, Pretorius, see Chapter 9, this volume). From this, more related artwork was spawned which culminated in an installation at an International Art Therapy Conference at Goldsmiths, University of London in April 2013.

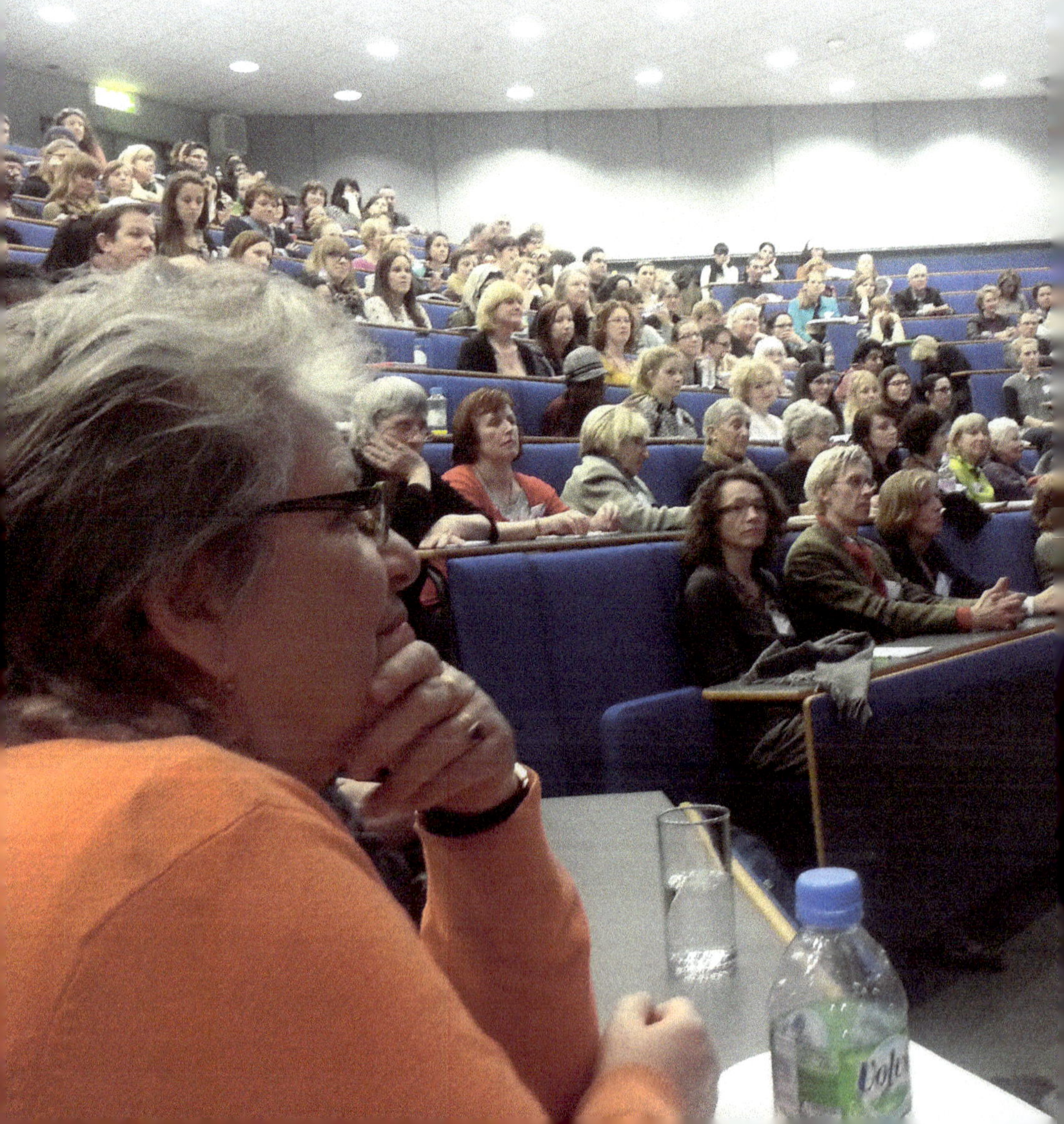

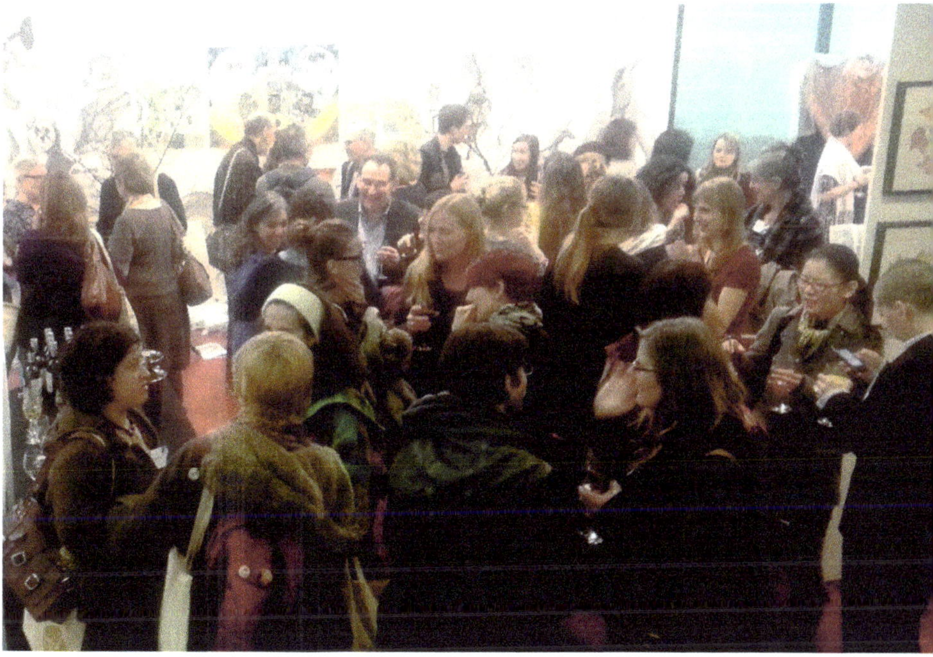

Facing page: Figure 22
Andy Gilroy in foreground and conference delegates. Jill Westwood (2013).

Above: Figure 23
View of the installation at the Conference. Jill Westwood (2013). Photograph.

Right: Figure 24
Finding a voice, making your mark. Goldsmiths, University of London (2013). Poster of the International Conference. Photograph.

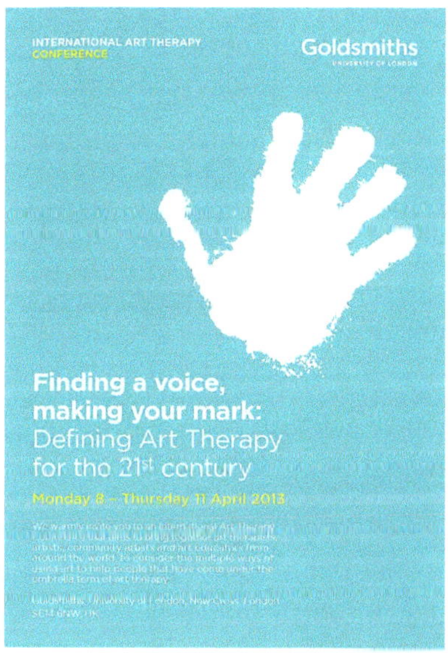

To give you, the reader, an overview of my research findings and observations about each programme, I will now interweave the content of the installation with its images and with the narratives collected from the interviews.

Edith Cowan University (ECU) 1992–2007

> *Conflict between approaches and cultures, method versus dynamic orientation, UK perspective versus USA perspective, Jungian influence, dramatherapy. Later phase: movement towards art, influences from UK, USA, Australia.*

On the Western side of Australia in Perth, the first University-based MA Art Therapy programme at Edith Cowan University was developed in 1992 and ran until 2007. This is featured on the left side of the installation.

Figure 25 *Installation.*
Jill Westwood (2013). Mixed media.

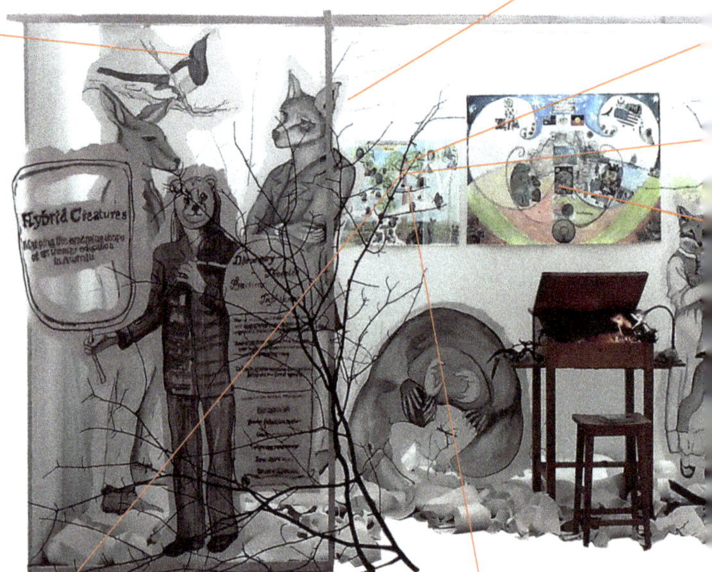

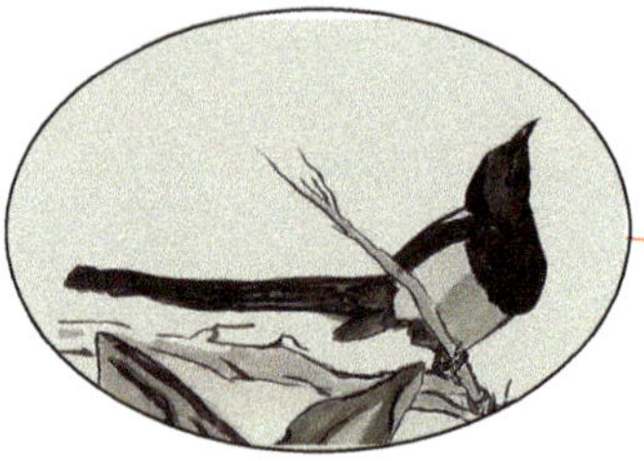

Figure 26 Magpie – detail of installation connected to ECU.

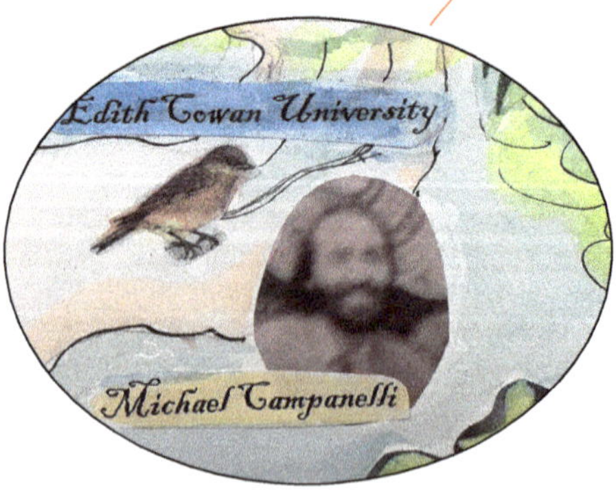

Figure 27 Detail of *Genealogy* image, Michael Campanelli.

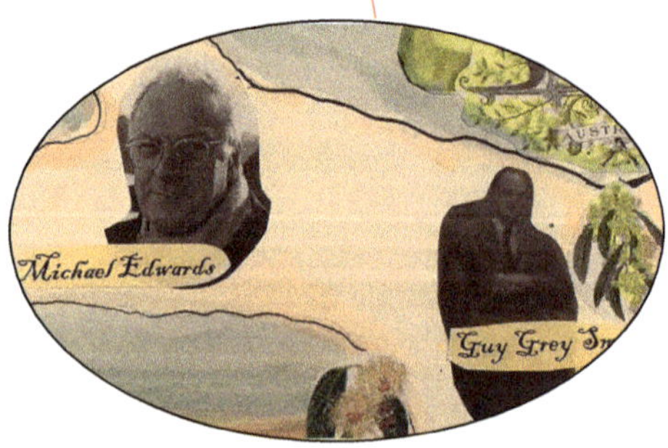

Figure 28
Detail of *Genealogy* image, Michael Edwards, Guy Grey-Smith.

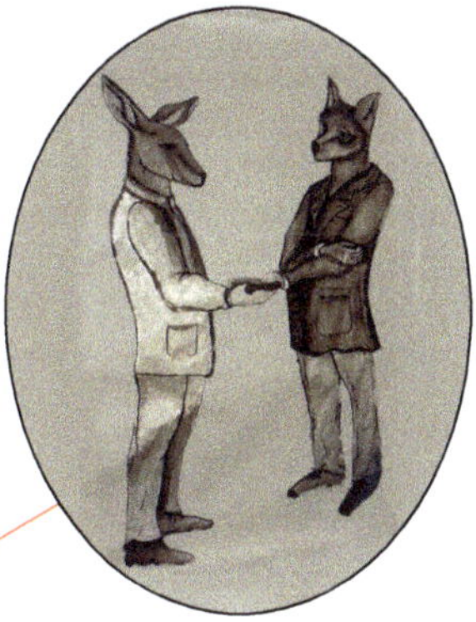

Figure 29 Figures that became part of the installation.

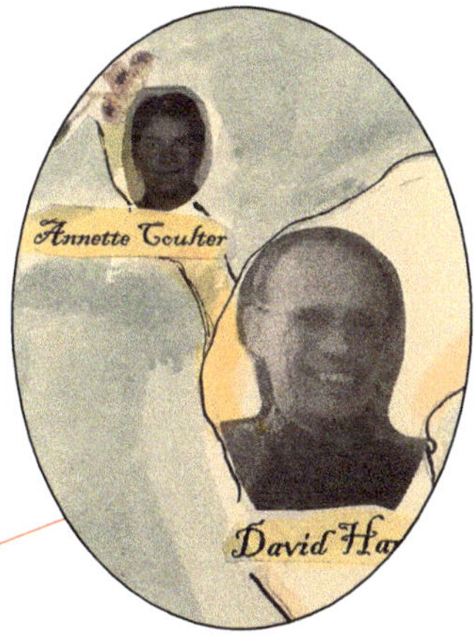

Figure 30 Detail of *Genealogy* image, David Harvey, Annette Coulter.

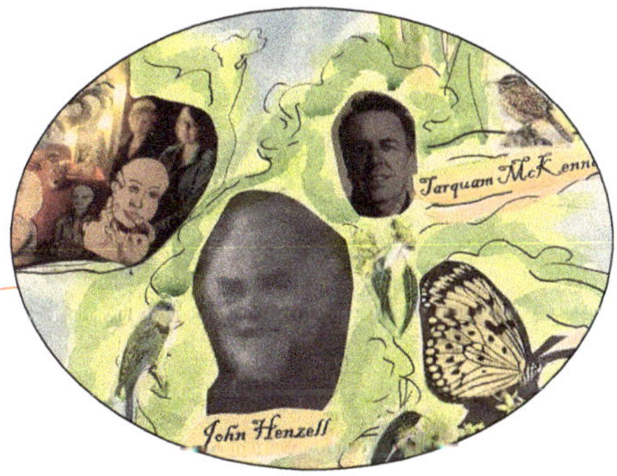

Figure 31 Detail of *Genealogy* image, John Henzell, Tarquam McKenna.

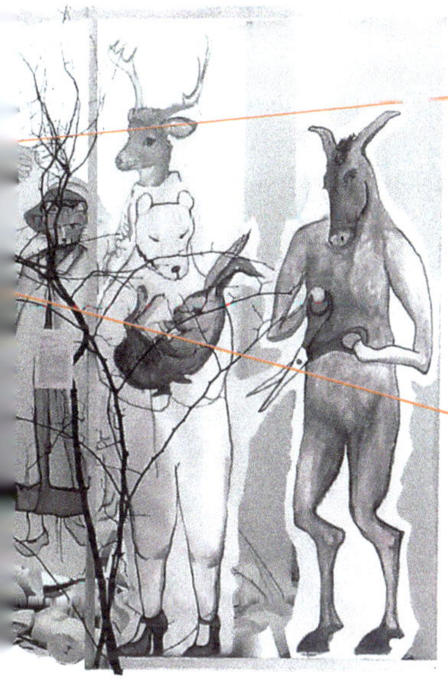

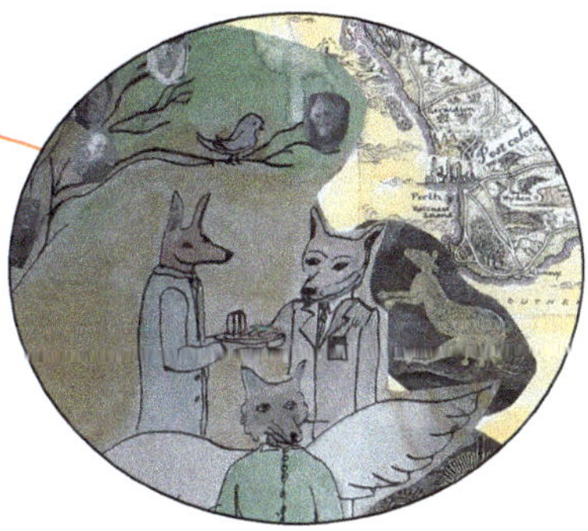

Figure 32 Detail of *Cosmology* image referencing Bestiary image of ECU/IKON programmes.

These images feature associations to the ECU programme, its educators and the themes. There is a notable lineage that runs between UK and Australia and the founding of art therapy in both places. The educators at ECU came from Australia (John Henzell, Tarquam McKenna), the UK (David Harvey) and the USA (Michael Campanelli). I first came to know this programme through meeting Michael Campanelli at conferences in the mid to late 1990s. These encounters opened up my awareness of the different views of art therapy and the ways they can be linked to the different systems of health care found in the UK (social model) and the USA (private insurance model) (Gilroy and Skaife, 1997). As this interplay of viewpoints developed between different educators from different places, it gave rise to a conflict between a 'methods' versus a 'dynamic' orientation and, to some extent, a clash between cultures and people. This echoed the complex issues of dispute often found in the beginning of professions' development in their struggle for definition and recognition (Gilroy and Hanna, 1998). While these conflicts were lived through during the period of its existence eventually, due to institutional, managerial and economic changes, the programme closed in 2007.

It was only after the ECU programme closed, and as part of the PhD research, that I spoke with David Harvey, and began to piece together the background history and his role in its evolution. This was a sensitive conversation about a period of struggle that contained the possibility of reparation through my witnessing his contribution. Born in the UK, David Harvey specialised in art education and in 1975 migrated (as an adult) to Perth, WA. He completed an MA Art Education at the (then) School of Art Education at Birmingham Polytechnic, England, (now the University of Birmingham[6]) which included the first postgraduate option in art therapy run by Michael Edwards. Several figures who were taught by Edwards at Birmingham went on to influence the field in Australia (Harvey, Henzell, Gilroy). Harvey began working at Edith Cowan University and, notably, developed the first university based art therapy programme in Australia. It started as a Postgraduate Diploma in Art Therapy 1989–1991 and was a precursor to the MA Art Therapy that commenced in 1992.

As the ECU programme developed, Michael Campanelli from the USA was appointed in 1994. Campanelli arrived shortly after Harvey went on sabbatical to do further training on the MA Art Psychotherapy at Goldsmiths, University of London in the UK. Campanelli brought a strong North American approach to the programme and took it to a more didactic 'methods' and research-oriented approach, i.e. as distinct from the experiential, psychodynamic perspective Harvey had established. Harvey returned and found the character of programme changed and his position displaced. Due largely to these differences and the struggles that ensued, he left his post in 1997. It was a difficult transition, one that was compounded by Michael Campanelli's illness and subsequent untimely death in 1999. Not surprisingly, the programme entered a period of traumatic loss. The absence of Michael Campanelli's voice leaves a gap in this research.

Following the loss of Michael Campaneli, John Henzell was appointed in 2001. My interview with John in 2008 revealed an interesting series of connections which gave impetus to my tracing the genalogy of art therapy education in Australia. John started life in England and came to Australia when he was 2 years old. He trained as an artist-painter in a technical college in Perth which later became part of ECU. As John describes in Chapter 4 (this volume), he first encountered art therapy through a family friend, Guy Grey-Smith who had worked with Adrian Hill in England. This connection was through Henzell's

6 In 1992 the binary line between polytechnics and universities was abolished. See https://www.theguardian.com/education/2012/sep/03/polytechnics-became-universities-1992-differentiation.

father who was a doctor and specialist in tuberculosis (TB). Grey-Smith, an Australian, was a survivor of a World War Two Prisoner of War camp where he contracted TB. He was repatriated to the King Edward VII Sanatorium in Godalming, Surrey, England, where Adrian Hill was introducing art therapy. Here Grey-Smith became involved with art therapy, first as a patient and then as a practitioner. Grey-Smith returned to Perth and introduced art therapy into hospitals in Western Australia and later, in 1958, shared his knowledge with John who was 19 years old at the time. At 21 John went to England and became involved with the emergence of art therapy in the UK, undertaking an MPhil with Michael Edwards at Birmingham Polytechnic. Henzell was also involved with the development of art therapy education in the UK at the Universities of Hertfordshire and Sheffield. He returned to Australia to take up the post at ECU in 2001 until its closure in 2007.

Figure 33 Detail of *Genealogy* image, tracing the origins of influences from UK (Adrian Hill) and USA (Edith Kramer). Hill and Kramer are the earliest named influences found in art therapy education in Australia.

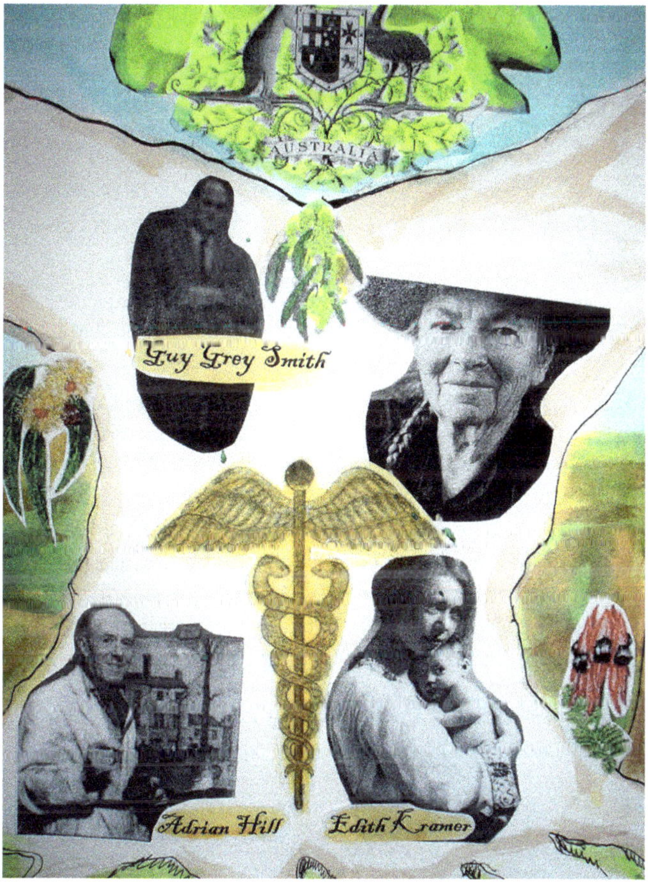

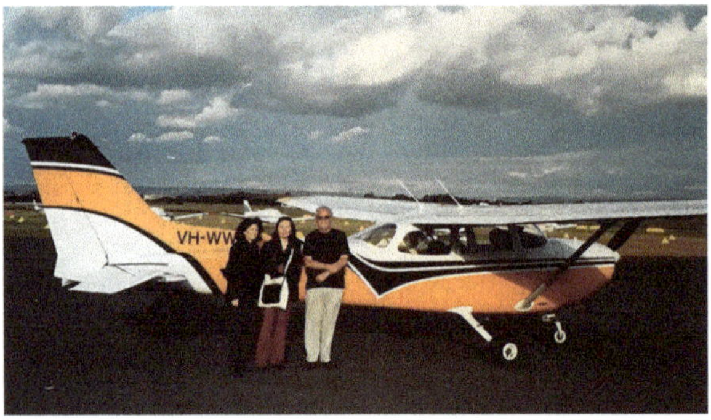

Figure 34
Hannah Menahemi, Jill Westwood and John Henzell in Perth. Jill Westwood (c2001). Photograph.
I was about to fly to Rottnest Island on a two-person plane… me and the pilot! That's not unusual in Perth!

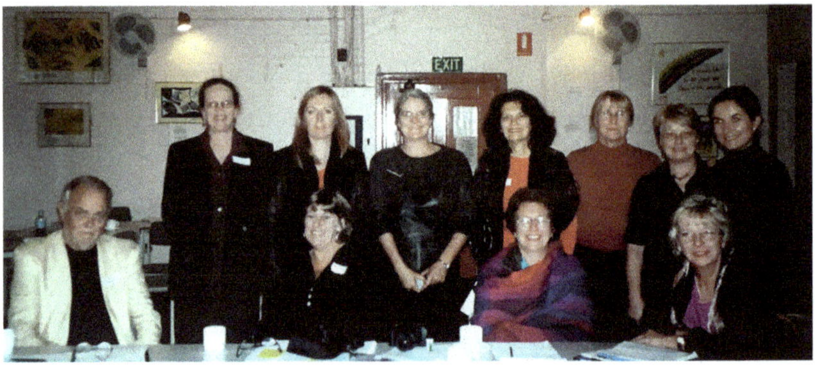

Figure 35 *A gathering of ANZATA and many of the art therapy educators at a conference in Perth.* Back row, left to right, standing: Nancy Slater, Jill Westwood, Annette Coulter, Hannah Menahemi, unknown, Joy Schimdt, unknown. Front row, left to right, sitting: Lindy Belitho, Amanda Hasenkam, Pauline Marsden. Jill Westwood (c. 2001). Photograph.

Another significant figure associated with the ECU programme was Tarquam McKenna. An Australian from Tasmania, he was one of the first cohort of students of the programme. From a background in education and special education and with particular interests in dramatherapy, psychodrama and Jungian perspectives, he went on to work part-time on the programme in its various eras. He was also active in the professional association, the Australian and New Zealand Art Therapy Association[7], holding several key positions including President, Vice President and Treasurer. McKenna studied both art therapy and dramatherapy in Australia, the USA and the UK. He brought together a range of views and perspectives that enabled different ideas, theories and views to come together. This was pivotal in the development of a more inclusive view within the profession and a drive towards greater integration.

7 Australia and New Zealand Arts Therapy Association

IKON: Transpersonal paradigm, neo-Jungian, art therapy, influences, Australia, USA

IKON, featured as a winged fox–coyote, reflects the transpersonal and psycho-spiritual approaches that were found in this region of Perth.

Pictured standing apart and independent, IKON arose from the private sector as an institute in 1988 concurrently to ECU. It began offering training in transpersonal art therapy in 1995, at diploma level, through projects with Indigenous Australians in Western Australia. The transpersonal view calls upon spiritual traditions and their healing practices, and includes Indigenous perspectives. This was in contrast to the mainstream medical/health paradigm where the university-based programmes were seeking to gain ground. Therefore significant differences concerning approaches, levels of training and outcomes between IKON and ECU (and other university-based programmes) were found.

The fox–coyote also had a strong presence elsewhere as IKON offered art therapy training in other states of Australia (SA, VIC, NSW and QLD). After the closure of the programme at ECU, IKON was the only provider of art therapy education in WA.

My interviews with Rafael Locke and Vicki Dean in 2009 facilitated a sensitive and useful conversation about these differences, shedding light on experiences of exclusion and marginalisation directed towards the programme and its graduates in the field. Our conversations seemed to open up the possibility of shifting this hidden, uncomfortable undercurrent and developing connections. But by 2016 a controversy concerning allegedly unethical practices and false claims cast a shadow over the IKON enterprise and its founder (The Australian Newspaper, 2016). However a Bachelor of Arts Psychotherapy has since been developed and is now offered through IKON (IKON Institute website, 2016).

Figure 36 Detail of *Cosmology* image referencing Bestiary image of IKON programme.

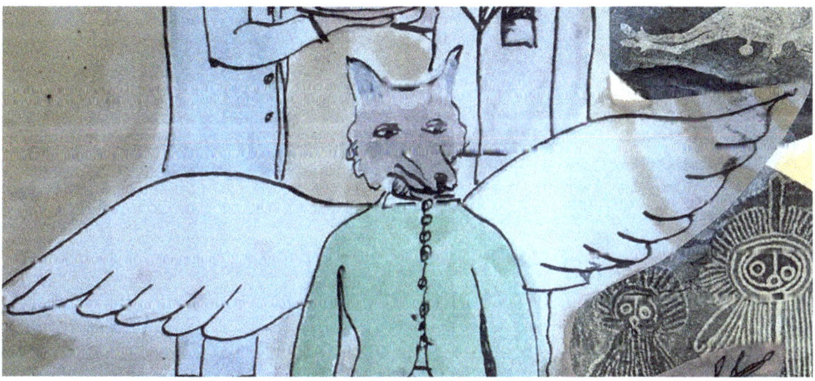

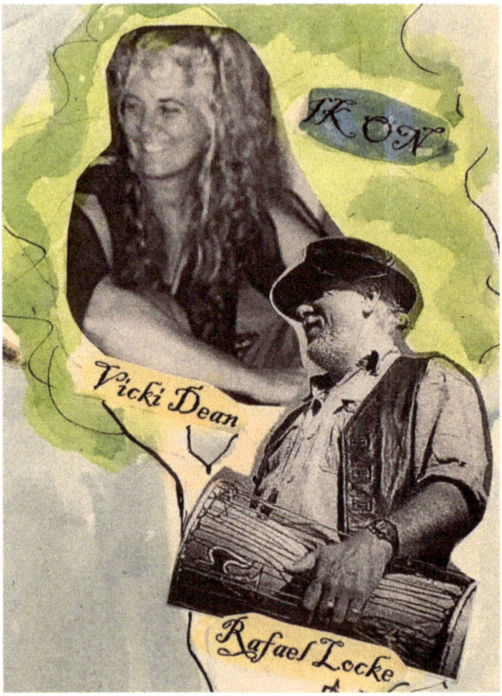

Figure 37
Detail of *Genealogy* image: Vicki Dean and Rafael Locke.

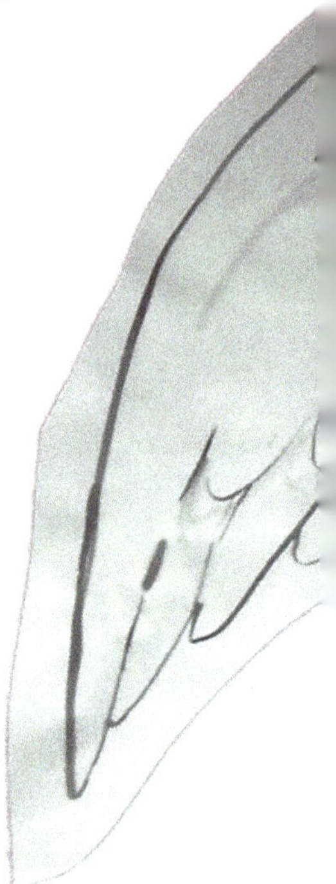

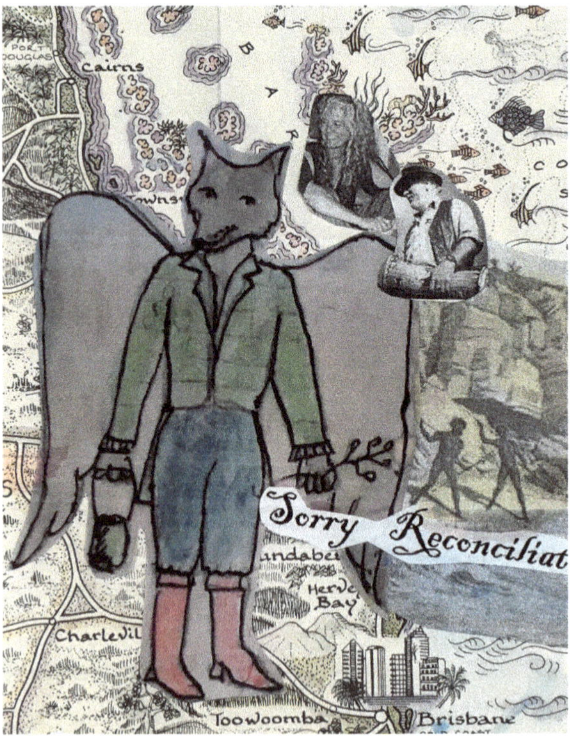

Figure 38
Detail of *Cosmology* image referencing Bestiary image of the IKON programme on the Eastern side of Australia.

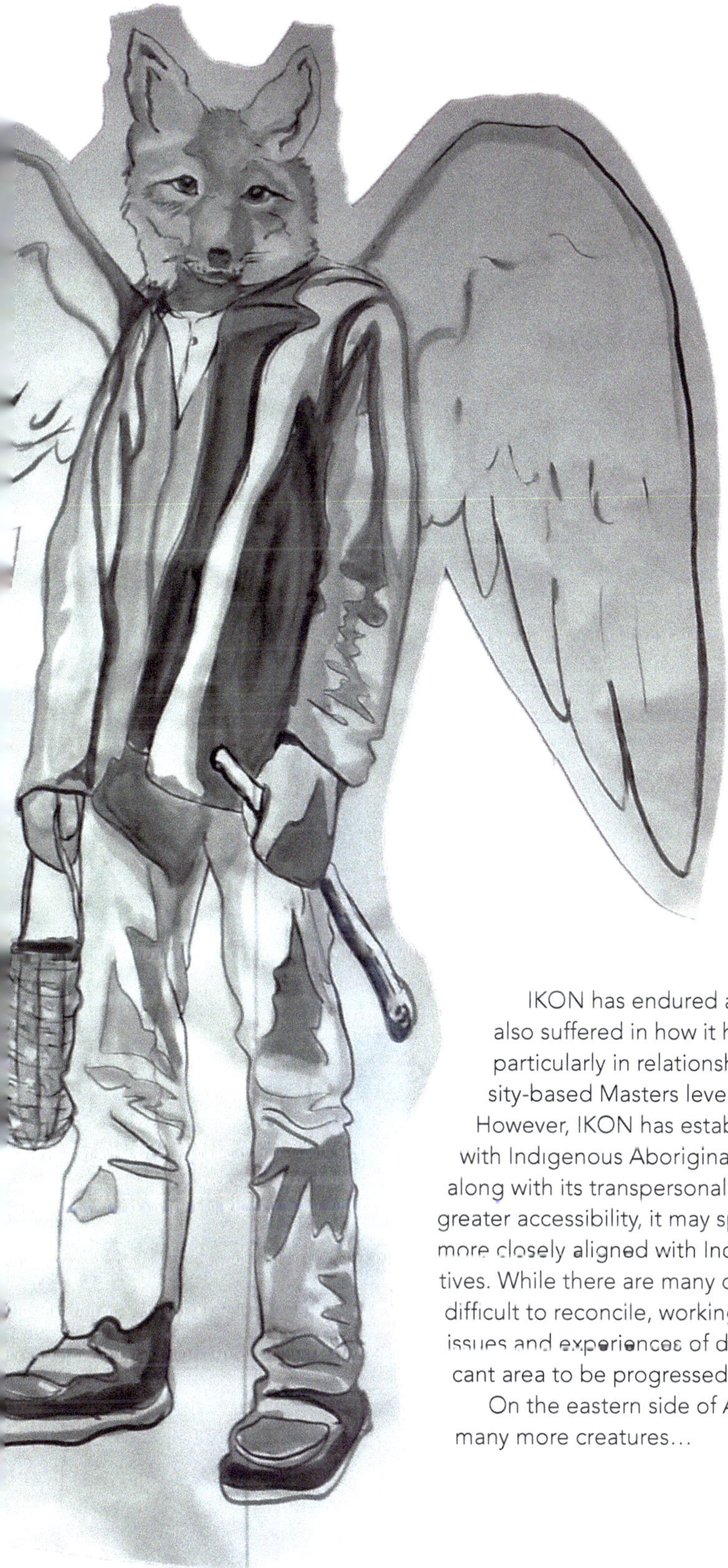

Figure 39
Fox–coyote image from installation. This was positioned away from the main tableau.

IKON has endured and grown but it has also suffered in how it has been perceived, particularly in relationship to the university-based Masters level programmes. However, IKON has established relationships with Indigenous Aboriginal communities and, along with its transpersonal perspective and greater accessibility, it may speak a language more closely aligned with Indigenous perspectives. While there are many contested concerns difficult to reconcile, working with intercultural issues and experiences of difference is a significant area to be progressed.

On the eastern side of Australia there were many more creatures…

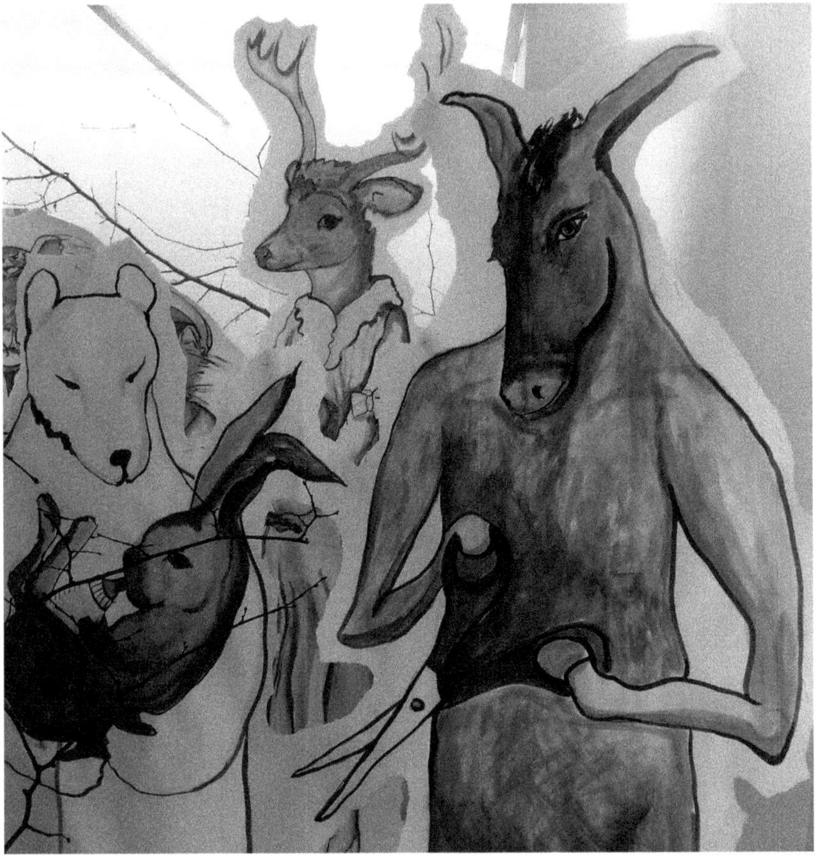

University of Western Sydney (UWS)[8] 1993–

Survival through art, art-based learning, metaphor of practice as performance/installation art, move from psychodynamic to integrative-narrative post-structural perspective, move from separate degree to shared degree with counselling and social science, expressive therapies, influences UK, Canada, Australia.

The programme at the University of Western Sydney began in 1993 and is symbolised by the family group of the bear, rabbit and donkey. This is the programme I was immersed within and these images are personally saturated. The donkey is holding a pair of scissors and has ambiguous qualities related to the dynamics within the university system: will this creature be helpful and protective or will it snip away and disturb the mother and baby? Here the importance and position of art within the educational process and the role of institutional allies were highlighted.

8 Now known as Western Sydney University (WSU)

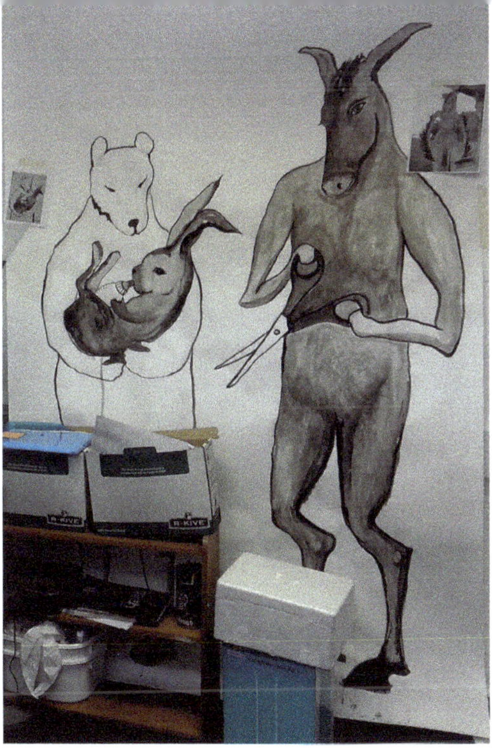

Left and facing page: Figures 40 and 41. Details of Installation referencing UWS programme.

Below: Figure 42 Detail of *Cosmology* image referencing key background figures related to the UWS programme: Keith Bennett, Andy Gilroy, Jill Westwood, Adrian Carr.

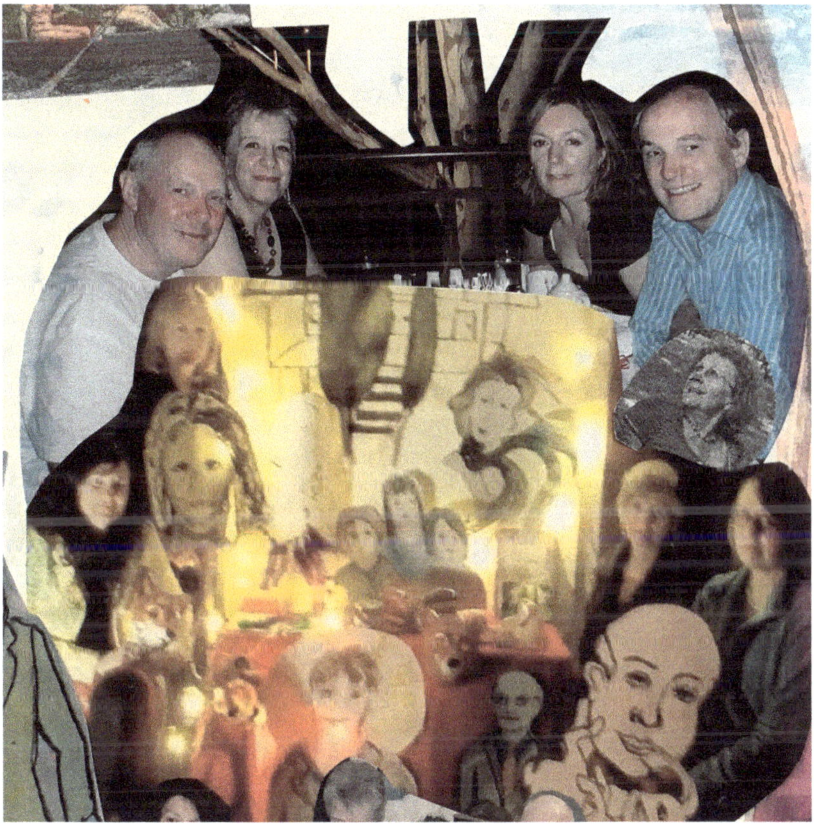

The theoretical flavour of UWS was summarised as moving from a psychodynamic to an integrative-narrative, post structural perspective. This shift was influenced by ongoing institutional, managerial and economic changes alongside different educators' backgrounds and preferences. Turbulent beginnings with early educator influences from the UK, Australia, Canada and USA were present that paralleled the issues found at ECU.

The programme almost stalled within the first few years; however, experienced educators from the UK and Canada (Gilroy and Hanna) managed to steer the program forward and think about the implications of the migration of ideas and the dangers of academic imperialism and neo-colonial practices (Gilroy and Hanna, 1998; Gilroy, 1998). The influence of Gilroy's

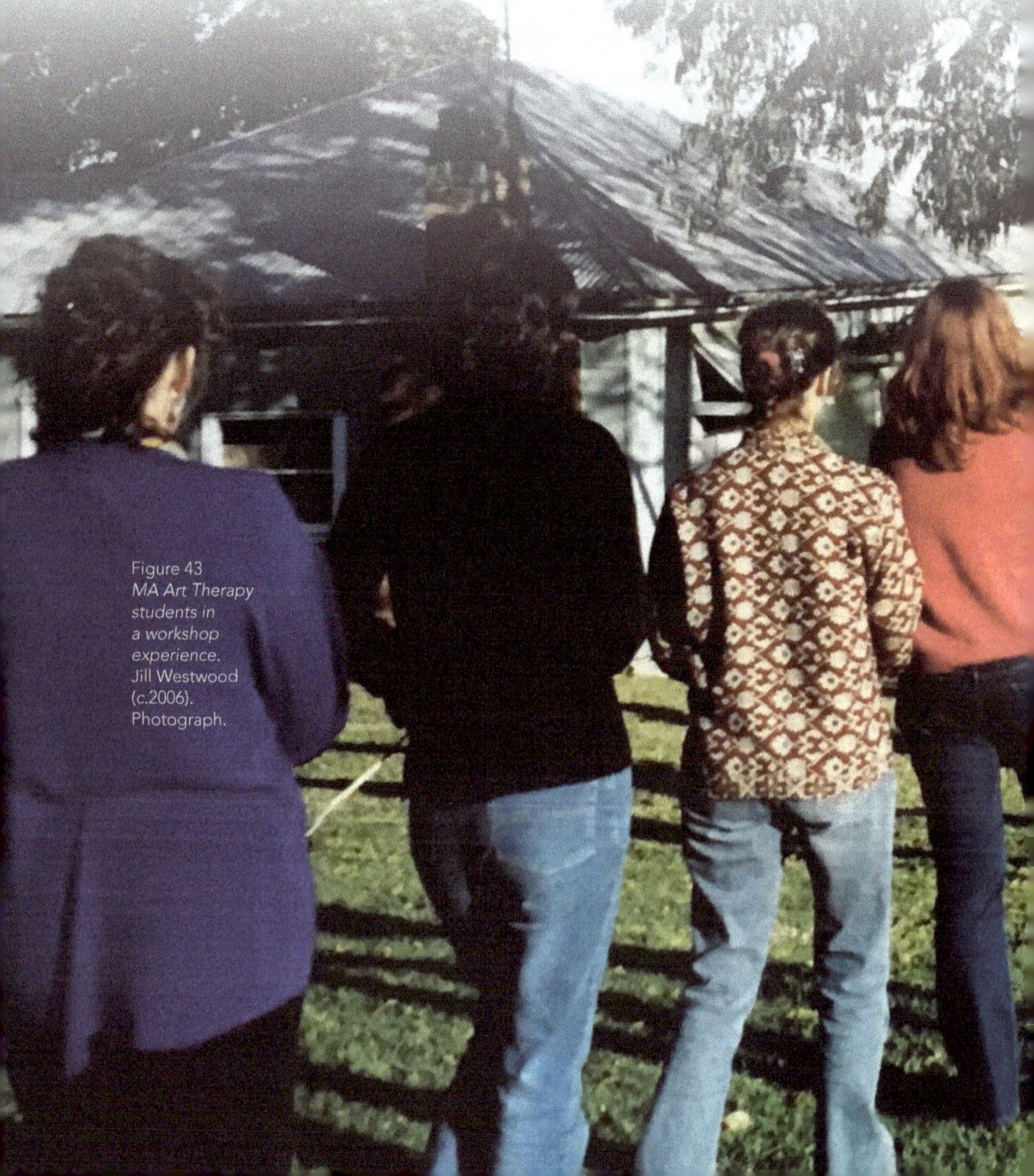

Figure 43
MA Art Therapy students in a workshop experience.
Jill Westwood (c.2006). Photograph.

critical thinking continued through my presence for many years (Westwood 1995–2007), as did the psychodynamic and systems theory view absorbed from the UK. Also during this time fortunate opportunities resulted in influential experiences with Harriet Wadeson from the USA. This opened up the possibility of bringing theories and practices together from both UK and USA perspectives and, significantly, of putting art in the centre of the education. This created the enduring flavour of the programme that was echoed in the development of the Graduate Diploma in Expressive Therapies (1999–2007). This saw a range of arts therapies being considered alongside each other and, to some extent, being integrated.

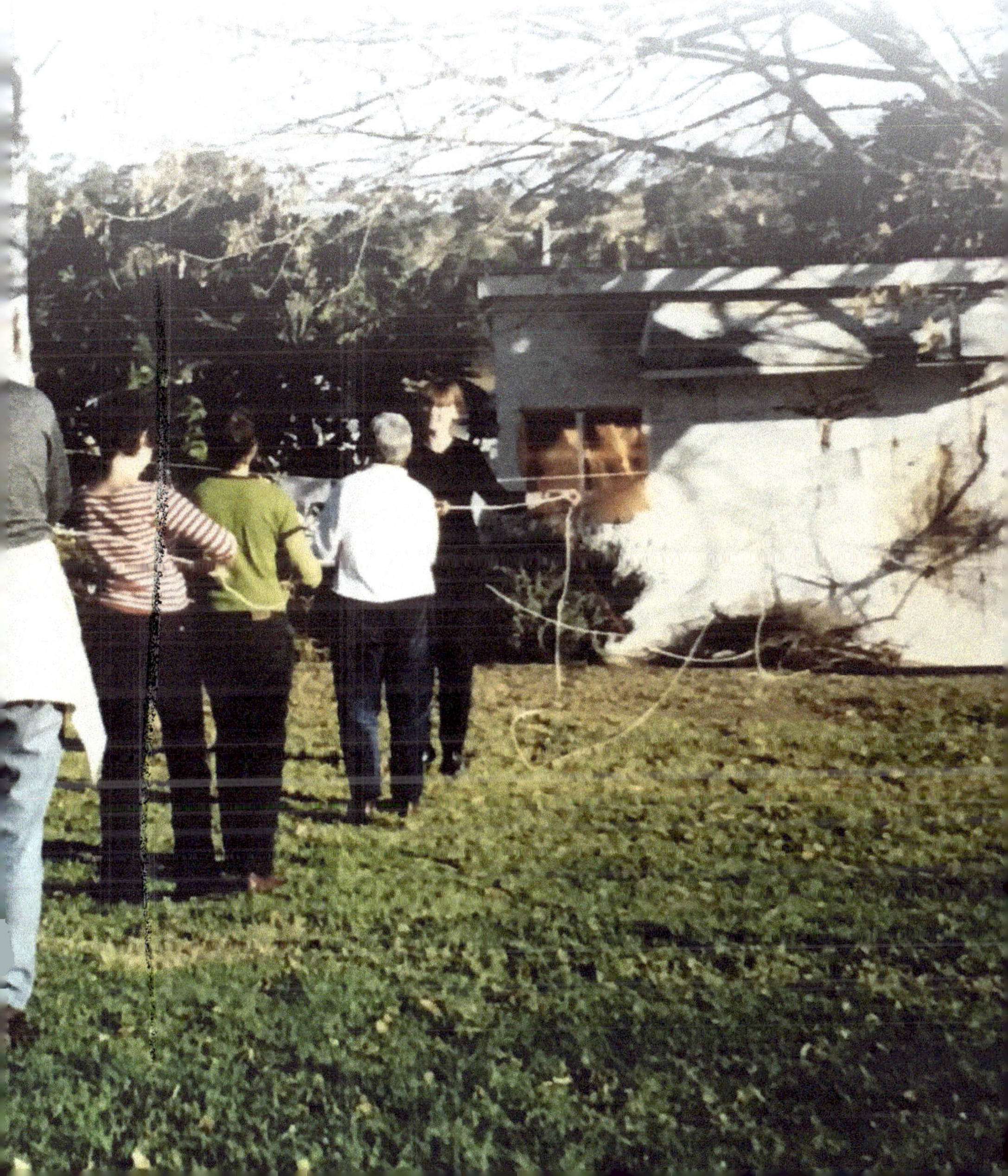

This family group holds some of my experience as I was carried through a phase of consolidation during which I sought to marry and adapt my background (UK) with the different views I encountered. Since 2008, my valued colleague and co-editor, an Australian (UWS) trained educator Sheridan Linnell has taken the leadership and the programme has become closely linked with a Master of Social Science (WSU website, 2016). The programme was described as "*surviving through art*", the development of art-based learning methods leading to a guiding metaphor of the practice and the programme being 'installation and performance art' (Linnell, Perry, Pretorius & Westwood, 2007, 2011). The foregrounding of art in the training is seen as a way to keep re-invigorating awarenesses of power relations and intercultural issues to counter conservative values and/or the re-enactment of colonising practices. This 'intercultural mix' has also been at the heart of several of the programmes.

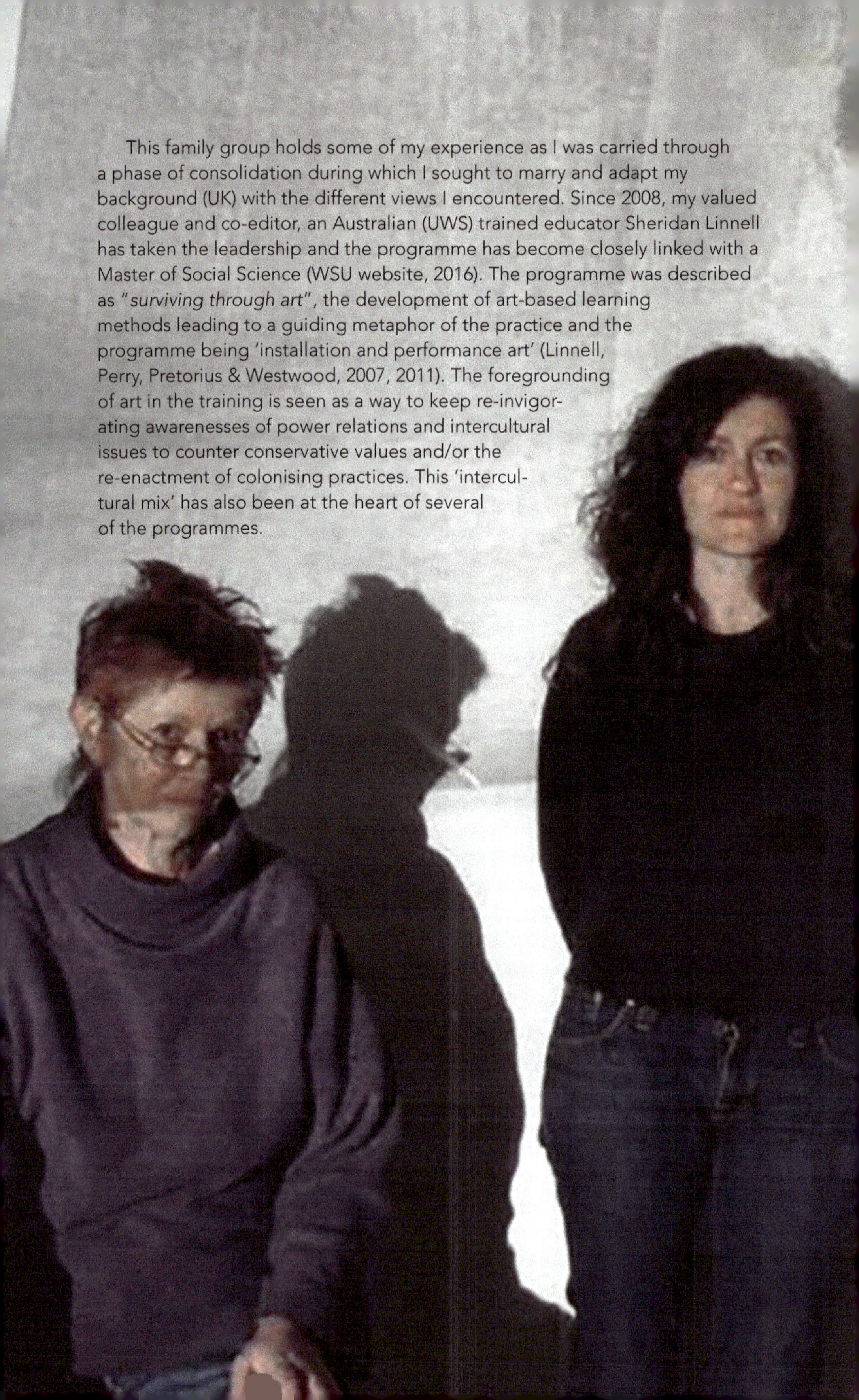

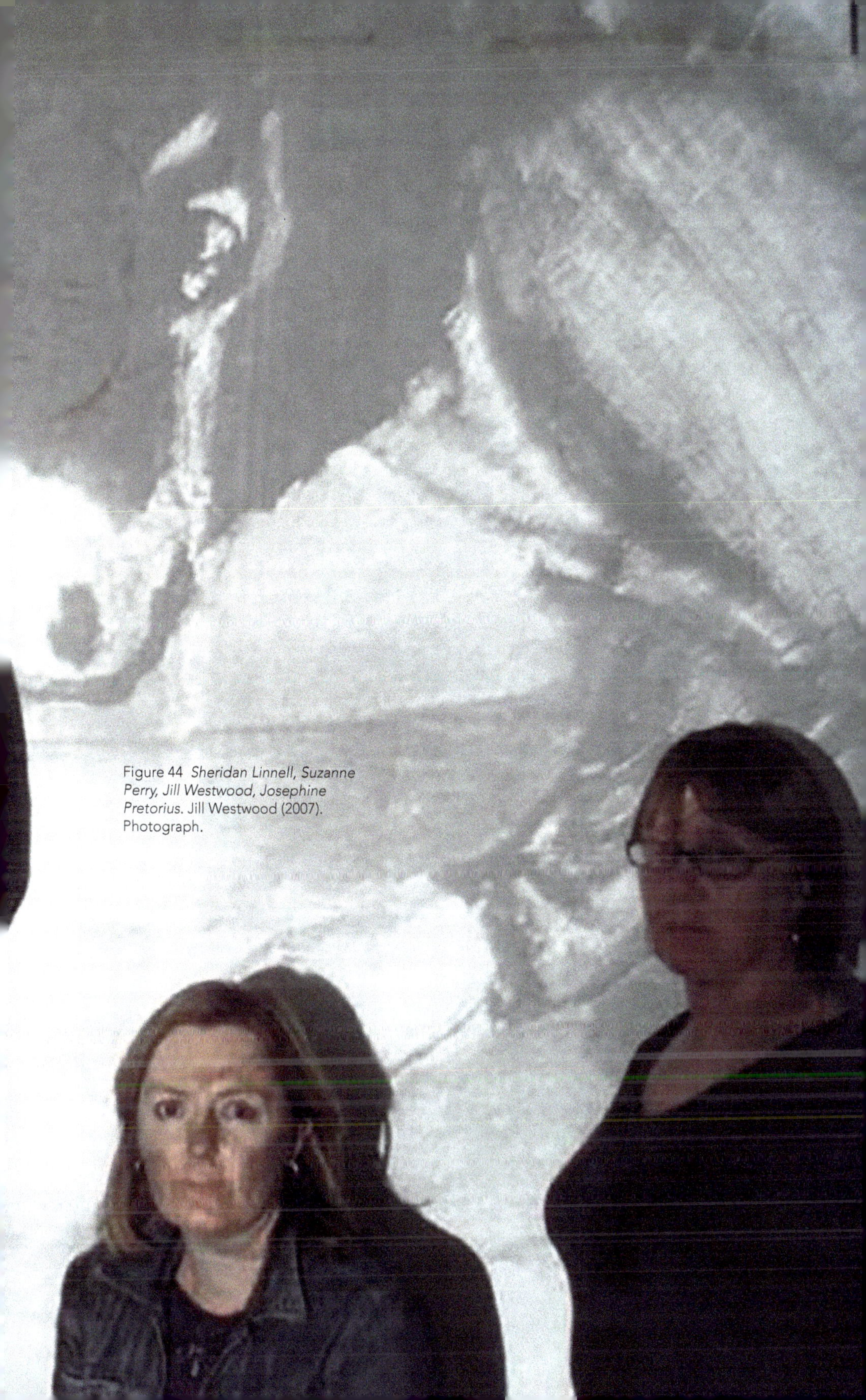

Figure 44 *Sheridan Linnell, Suzanne Perry, Jill Westwood, Josephine Pretorius*. Jill Westwood (2007). Photograph.

Melbourne, Victoria: La Trobe University 1998–

Theory driven by context, humanistic, psychodynamic, Jungian, arts-based learning, cohort model, influences, Australia, USA, Israel, Germany

The origins of the programme at La Trobe (deer with antlers) arose near to the time when IKON (1988), ECU (1989) and UWS (1992) were also emerging. At that time it was a Masters of Counselling: The Arts in Therapy (1991–1996). It became a Masters of Art Therapy in 1998 after the founding academics (Warren Lett, Jan Allen, Jean Rumbold, Andrew Morish) moved into the private sector to form MIECAT and pursued an educational practice and programme based on small group experiential learning which was not sustainable in the university context. It was in 1998 that Nancy Slater, an educator from the USA, was appointed to develop the programme at La Trobe. Later, in 2000, Hannah Menahemi, who was originally from Australia and who had studied and worked in USA and Israel for many years, was recruited to work alongside Slater. Slater returned to USA in 2001.

Menahemi's experience has some parallels with John Henzell's; first, that she was in the USA as art therapy was emerging there and returned to Australia with these experiences in mind and second, that she had a background knowledge of Australia. I recall how John Henzell, Hannah Menahemi and I would often connect by phone conference during our time as course leaders for mutual support and comradeship. Patricia Fenner, an Australian, has made a long-standing contribution to the programme at La Trobe as a lecturer; she became the programme leader when Hannah retired. She studied art therapy in various parts of the world including Germany, and also at MIECAT in Australia. The approach of the La Trobe programme is now one that can be distilled as theory driven by context within a humanistic and psychodynamic framework, teaching a variety of theoretical perspectives. Educators with experiences from the USA, Israel, Germany and Australia have shaped the evolution of this programme and developed a training which aims to produce art therapists who are also well-rounded mental health professionals (La Trobe website, 2016).

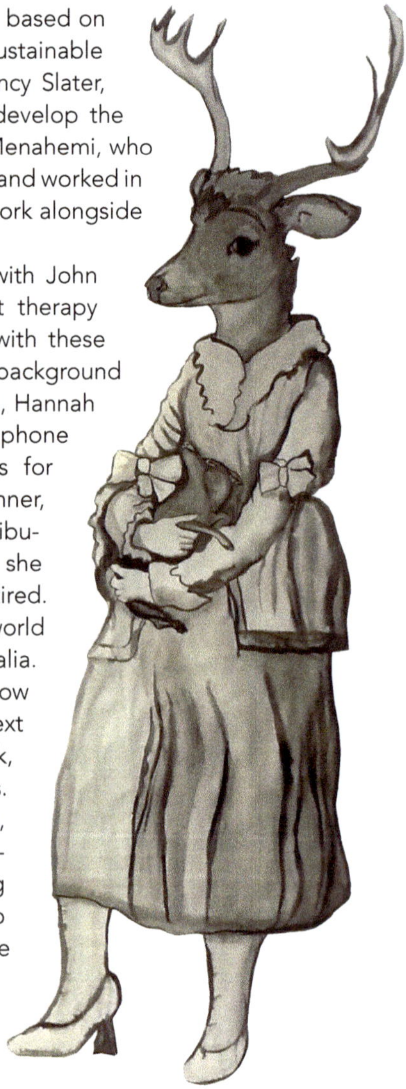

Figure 45 Detail of Installation referencing La Trobe programme.

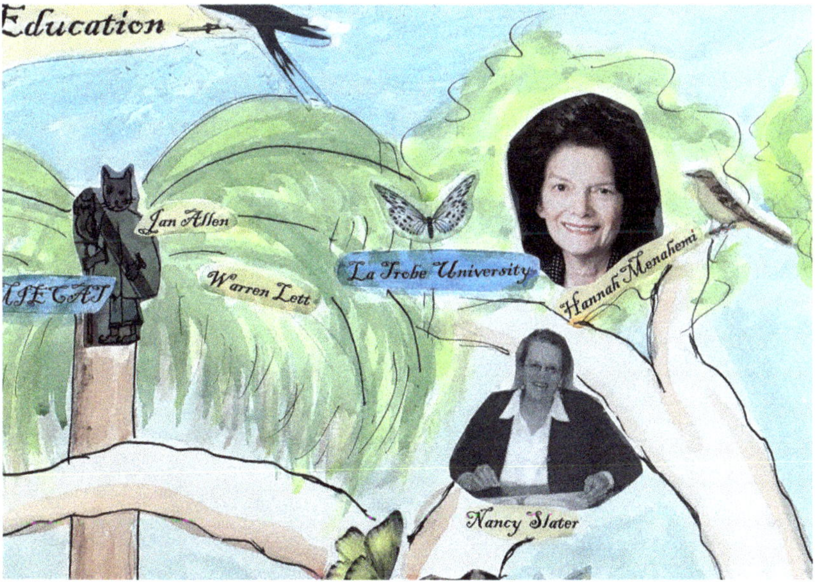

Figure 46 Detail of *Genealogy* image, Hannah Menahemi, Nancy Slater.

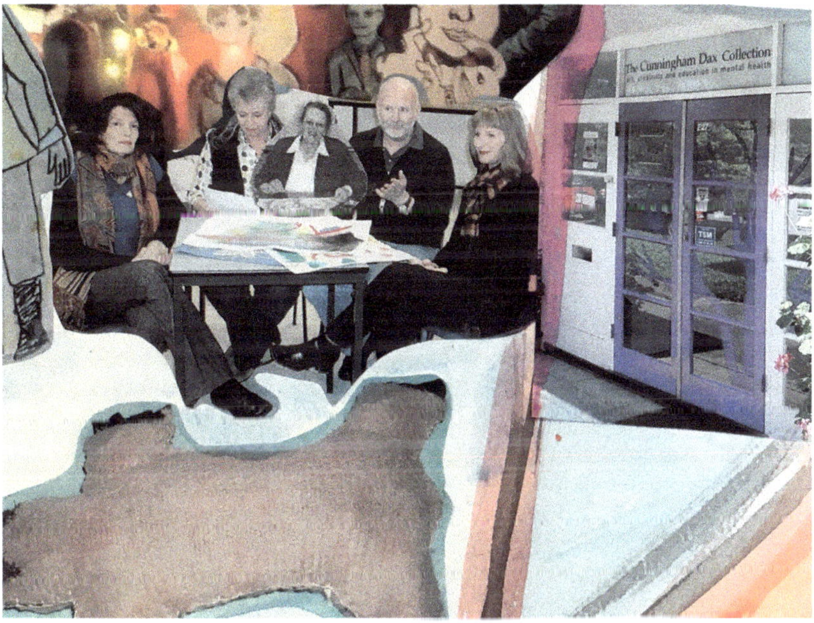

Figure 47 Detail of *Cosmology* image. L to R: Hannah Menahemi, Andy Gilroy, Nancy Slater (collage) Lawrie Moloney (Head of Dept of Counselling and Psychological Health), Patricia Fenner, Cunningham Dax – Psychiatric Art Collection.

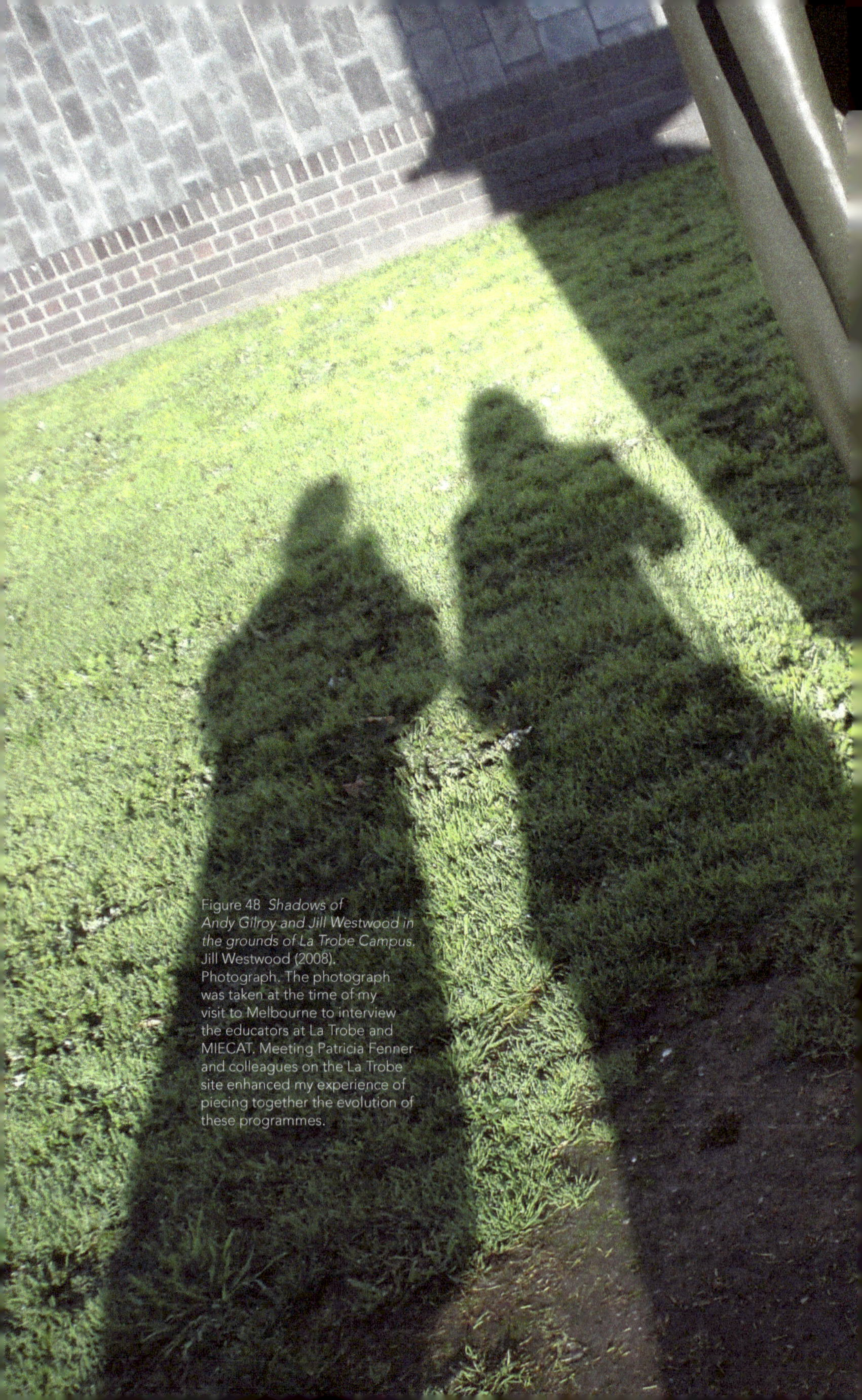

Figure 48 *Shadows of Andy Gilroy and Jill Westwood in the grounds of La Trobe Campus.* Jill Westwood (2008). Photograph. The photograph was taken at the time of my visit to Melbourne to interview the educators at La Trobe and MIECAT. Meeting Patricia Fenner and colleagues on the La Trobe site enhanced my experience of piecing together the evolution of these programmes.

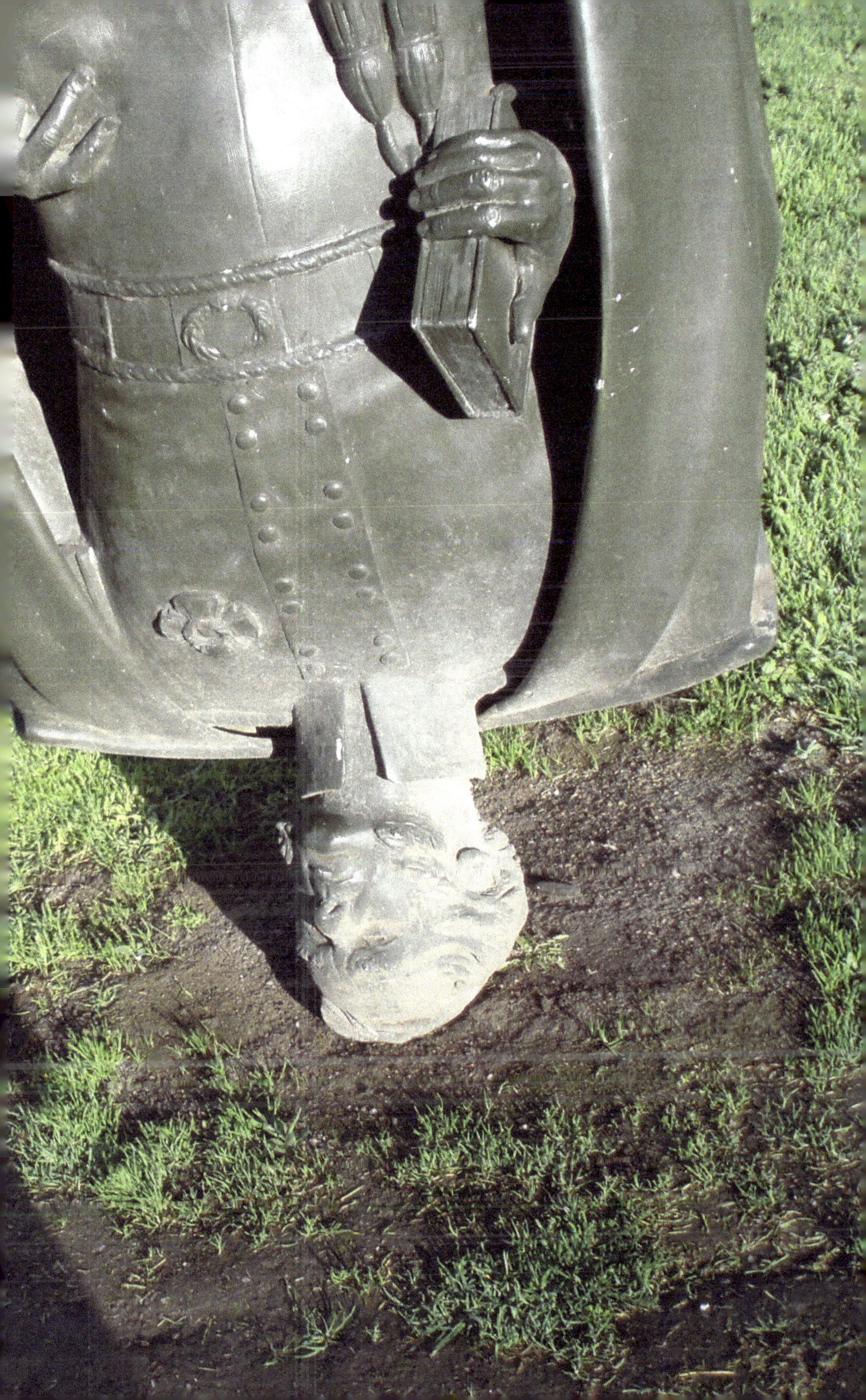

MIECAT 1997–

> *Epistemology, experiential, multi-modal arts, post-modern inquiry, phenomenology, inter-subjective, co-construction, relational – not aiming for a specific professional outcome, influence Australia*

There are two programmes that align with a multi-modal view: one is the MIECAT Institute Inc.; the other is RMIT (see below). MIECAT, formerly known as the Melbourne Institute for Experiential, Creative Arts Therapies, was initiated in 1997 by academics from the La Trobe Masters in Counselling: The Arts in Therapy (MIECAT website, 2016). This is a unique programme in the private sector concerned with arts-based inquiry. It began with a focus on a phenomenological approach to the arts and evolved alongside postmodern inquiry methods. It has developed an inter-subjective, co-constructed practice and is distinct in that it is not aligned to a professional discipline. In fact the links to therapy have been changed within the programme title which is now a Masters of Arts by Supervision in Experiential and Creative Arts Practice. The approach of MIECAT is epistemologically rather than theoretically led, the theory of knowledge being the prevailing framework rather than a particular psychological theory. It is pictured in the Genealogy of Art Therapy Education image as a tall palm tree. It is a different and particular species of education, unique to the Australian context.

Figure 49 Detail of Installation referencing MIECAT programme

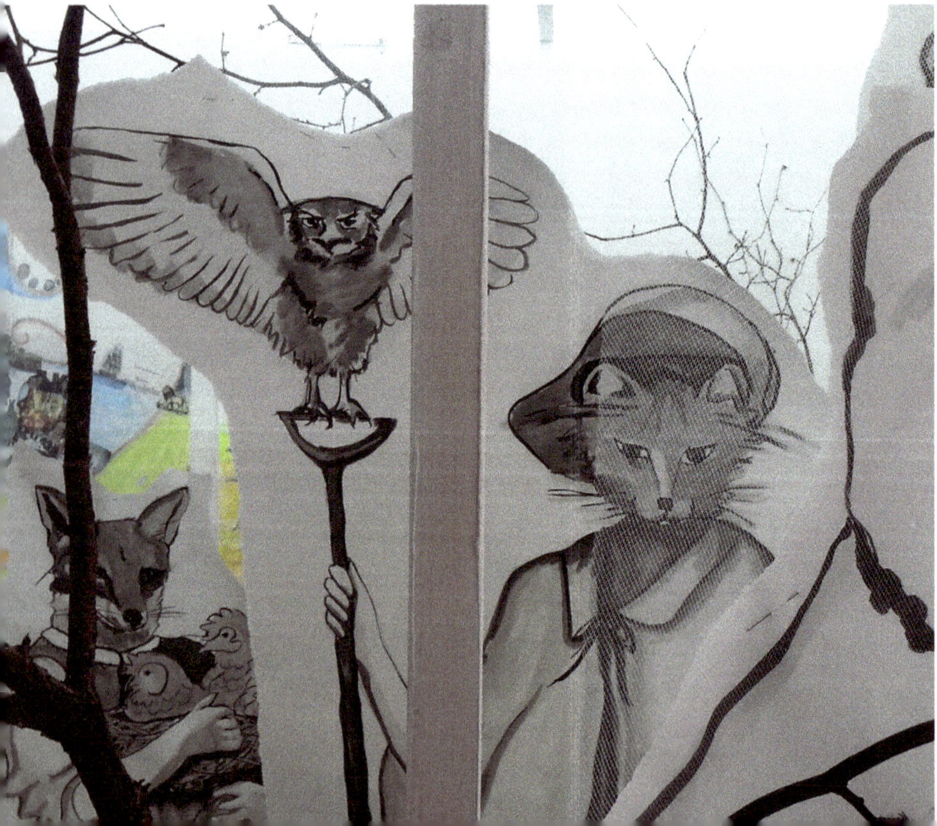

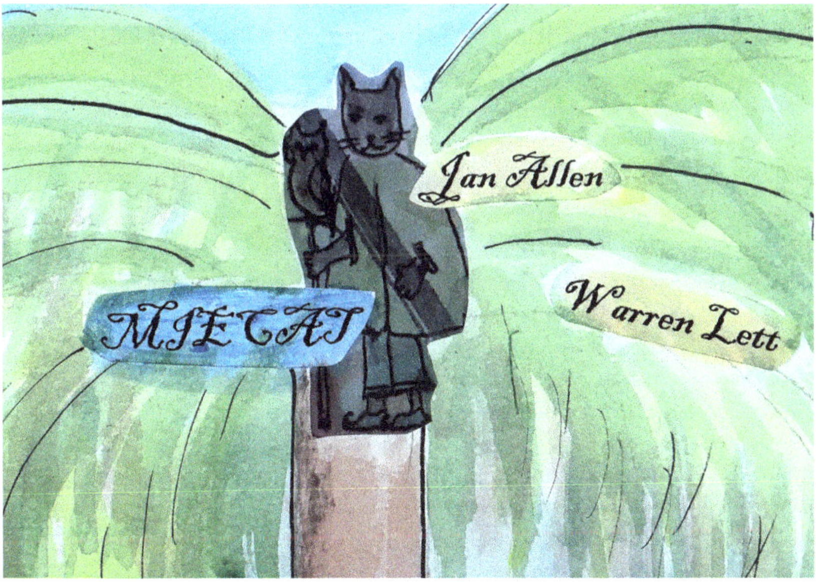

Figure 50 Detail of *Genealogy* Image, MIECAT programme with Jan Allen and Warren Lett.

By taking up their particular position MIECAT provides a counterpoint to the mainstream view of art therapy practice positioned in frameworks of psychological theory. This allows consideration of different views and understandings of the complexities of working with people and arts processes. It also brings attention to the significance of grappling with understanding the epistemology of the various practices and views of art therapy education.

On the same visit to Melbourne I interviewed Jan Allen, the director of MIECAT at their premises. I'd met Jan 10 years earlier when she had come to stay with me for a conference in Sydney. I've always found our conversations refreshing and the approach of MIECAT a progressive alternative.

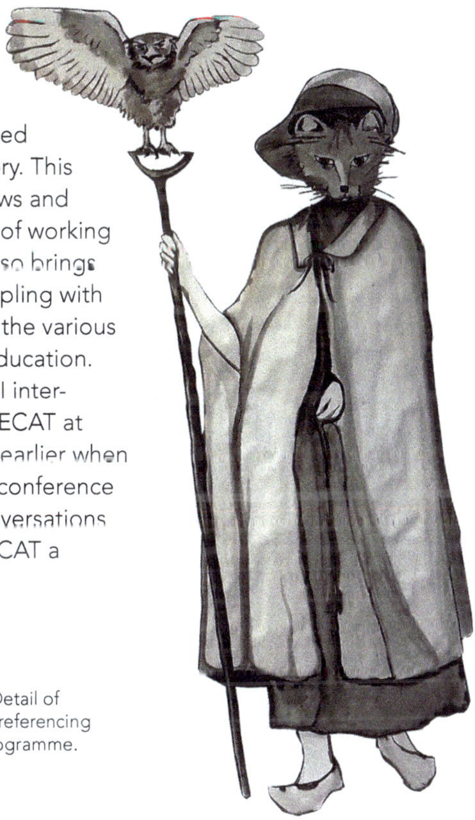

Figure 51 Detail of Installation referencing MIECAT programme.

Royal Melbourne Institute of Technology (RMIT), 1996–2007

> *Pedagogy, arts as therapy, multi-modal arts, humanistic paradigm, problem-based/collaborative learning, experiential/arts-based learning, influence Canada.*

The other programme aligned to a multi-modal approach was RMIT which is signified as the platypus.

The platypus is a native creature and an important species in evolutionary biology; it is a semi-aquatic mammal and the only one that lays eggs and produces milk. This is related to the multi-modal, arts as therapy focus of the RMIT programme. This programme was grounded in a humanistic, experiential approach and, through the vision of the educators, significantly Gerry Katz, they developed an innovative arts-based pedagogy. It began in 1996 in an environment where single art practices were being established as the norm (art therapy, music therapy etc). This surfaced tensions in the field around the requirement of less clinical placement hours than other masters programmes. Also, the multi-modal view was

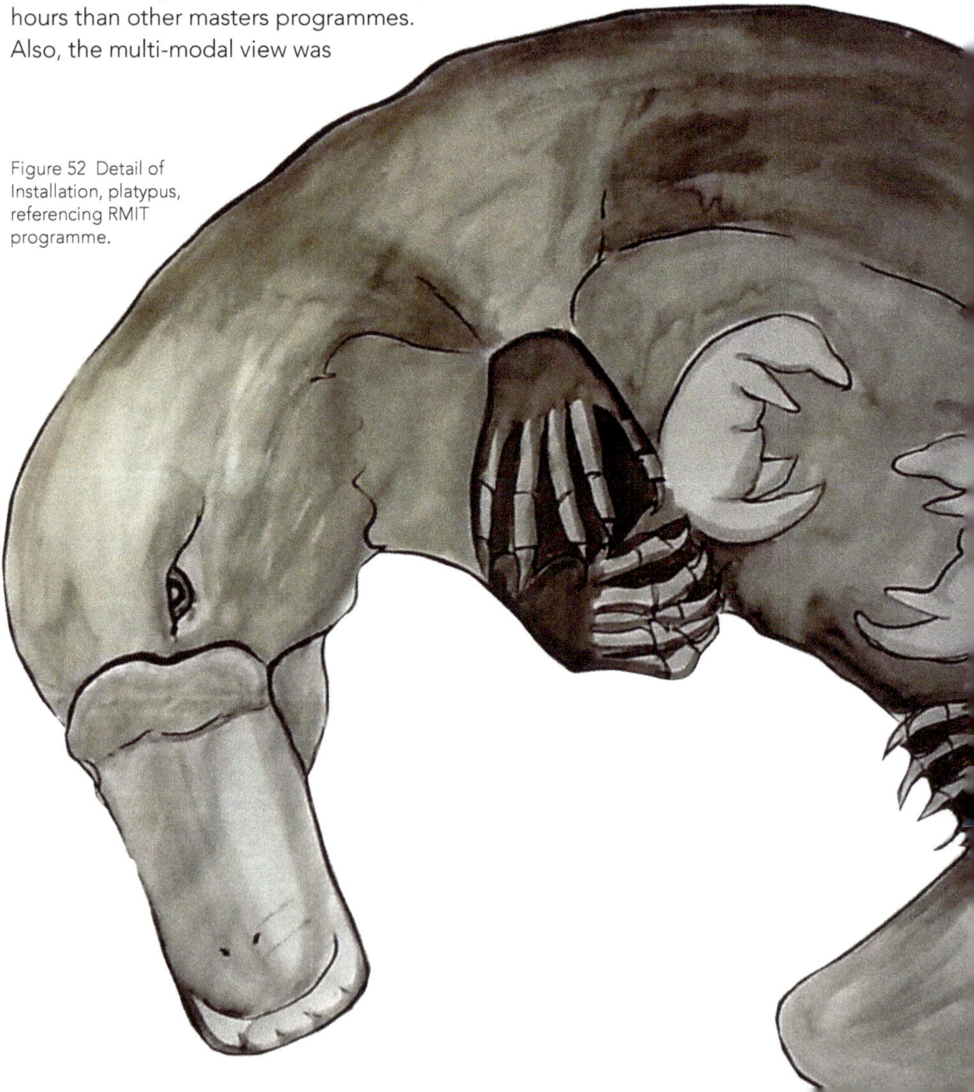

Figure 52 Detail of Installation, platypus, referencing RMIT programme.

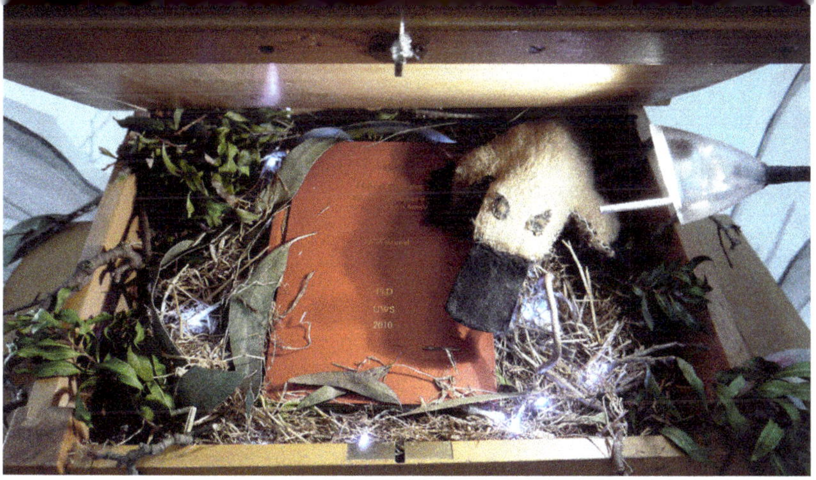

Figure 53 Detail of Installation, Platypus and PhD.

not included in the Australian National Art Therapy Association.[9] Graduates of RMIT responded by forming their own association (Australian Creative Arts Therapy Association – ACATA). This reflected a gap in the professional field where there was no existing place or association that represented multi-modal ways of working. By 2006 changes in the university organisation and financial processes resulted in the closure of the programme. However, processes of alignment, inclusion and conflict have continued to play out within the professional association.

Led by an educator who had not undertaken specific training as an arts therapist, the RMIT programme is reminiscent of the apprenticeship model of learning through doing, found in the early days of art therapy development in both the USA and UK. There are several distinguishing features of this profile: the emphasis given to pedagogy, particularly arts-based learning processes, and the various teaching and learning frameworks that were used in the education. This programme was developed from a process of discovery and exploration strongly grounded on these creative and problem based, collaborative learning frameworks. Another distinguishing feature is the emphasis on the arts process itself. This is somewhat in contrast to the other masters programs that give equal or more weight to psychotherapeutic studies. Grounding the education in the arts processes could be regarded as inspired and this emphasis on pedagogy and arts brings these areas to special attention. Gerry Katz's PhD (2013) illuminates much of the creative spirit that is embodied in taking such a view of education and practice.

At the time of writing (2016) Melbourne was the only place in Australia where four different programmes of art therapy have co-existed (La Trobe, MIECAT, IKON, RMIT). The graduates of all these programmes share the field most closely in this region. The need to work with issues of difference have therefore been apparent more strongly in this place.

9 Now known as Australia and New Zealand Arts Therapy Association. https://www.anzata.org

University of Queensland, 2004–

> *Mental Health, psychodynamic, broad view of psychotherapy theory, art therapy as a specialism within a Master of Mental Health, influences UK, Australia, USA*

The programme at the University of Queensland (UQ) is referenced in the fox-mother holding three chickens in a basket. This captures a view of the character of this most recently developed programme in Australia (2006). It is under the wing of a Masters of Mental Health within the School of Medicine (UQ website, 2016). In the natural world there is an antagonism between chickens and foxes which suggests something of the relationship between the programme and its position in the university. This programme was initiated by a group of art therapists trained in the UK (Claire Edwards, Maggie Wilson) and USA (Jane O'Sullivan) and draws on psychodynamic and expressive therapies perspectives. There is also a generic component of the programme that covers a broad range of mental health theory. However its theoretical flavour was summarised as a basic psychodynamic foundation with a pragmatic and pluralistic orientation.

A significant genealogical feature is the presence of the programme leader, Claire Edwards, who is the daughter of Michael Edwards, a founding art therapy educator from the UK who has emerged as a significant influence and link to many of the educators found in Australia (ECU – Henzell, Harvey; UWS – Gilroy, Hanna; and through Gilroy to Westwood and Linnell). Claire and I have been involved in several ways: as fellow migrants from England and graduates of the Goldsmiths art therapy training; as researchers at the UWS where Claire completed her MA(Hons) Art Therapy; then as fellow art therapy educators; and now as contributors to this book.

Figure 54 Detail of Installation referencing UQ programme.

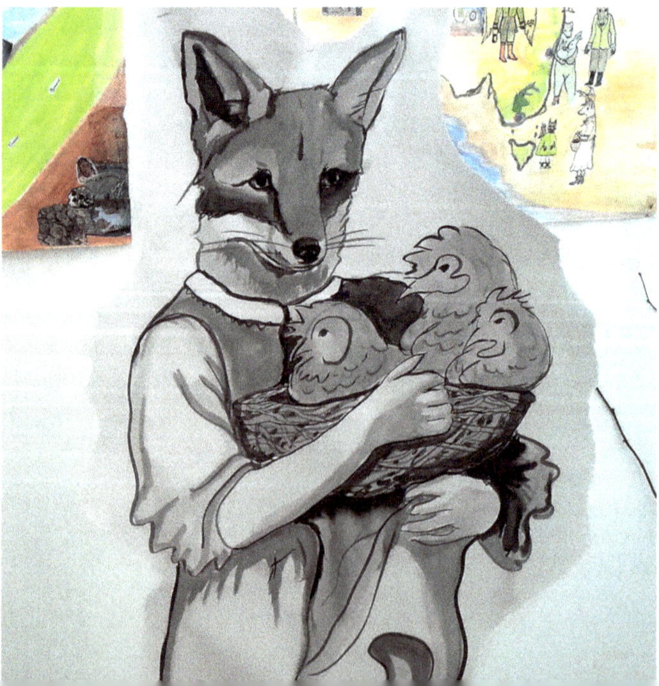

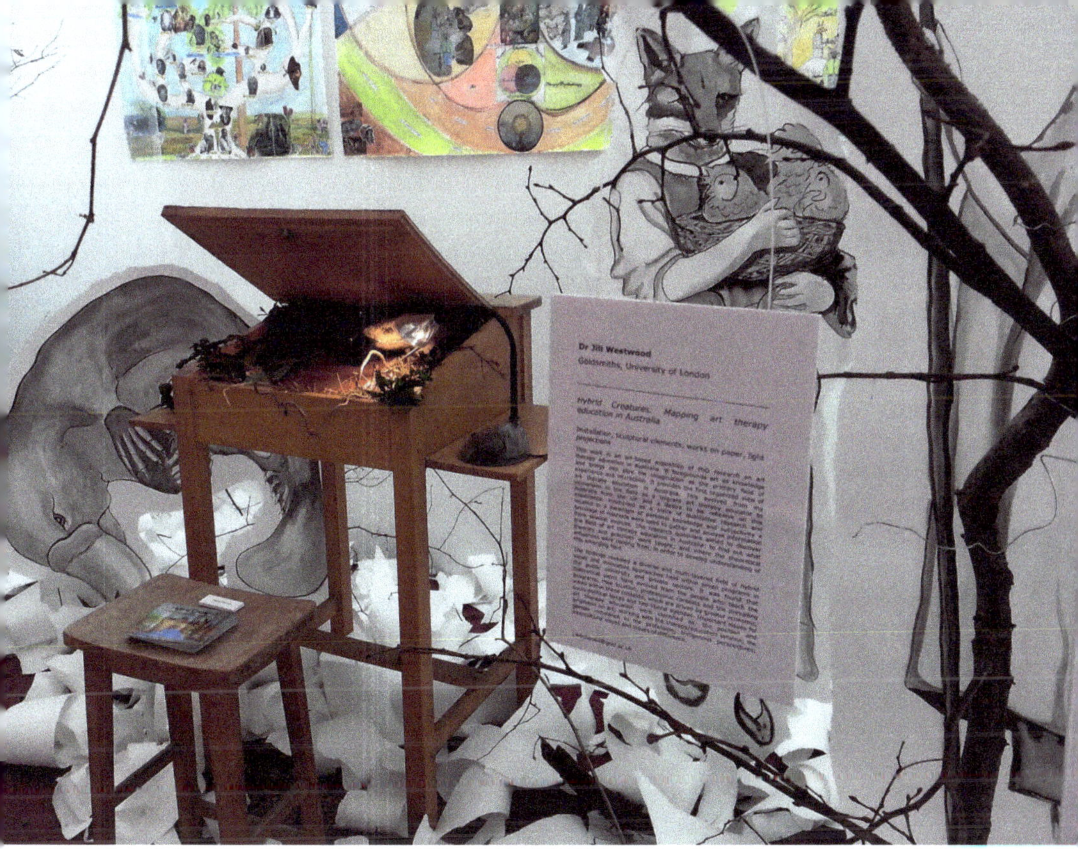

Figure 55 Detail of Installation referencing UQ programme.

Through our conversation, attention was brought to the politics and the resources for health in the different States of Australia. Queensland is not as well resourced as New South Wales and Victoria, and some disparities between the rural and city regions also play into the professional field and the opportunities available to graduates. The importance of research was discussed as a means of developing understanding of differences and the equity of services.

It emerged that art therapy's alignment with mental health within a school of medicine at UQ could enhance the status and understanding of the qualification and profession in the field. It may also enhance employability. However, it may also mean there is less specialist input about art therapy, an effect of which may be that it steers graduates towards a more generic and broad view of professional practices in mental health care.

Reflections

As I look back at my art work in all its forms and at the process of its making it seems to me that it has both embodied and guided my analysis and understanding of the research material. It reveals my subjectivity as the researcher (Eurocentric, White) and makes this influence more transparent. It generates a recurring dynamic of opening up and closing in, and of immersion and distance. It expresses the relational nature of the field, shaped by the educators and their contexts. To some extent it gives voice to their experiences and view points. It also shows how the migration and adaptation of people and their ideas are key to Australian art therapy education's evolution and development. The metaphors of trees, hybrid-creatures, geographies and maps directed my attention to the country that is Australia, to its histories and to the presence and importance of Indigenous Australian Aboriginal people and their perspectives. It revealed the microcosm of the worlds inside different art therapy programmes, their aims, struggles and triumphs, and the hostile and benign forces that they faced. It also revealed the impact of neo-liberal agendas in higher education and the developing field of art therapy in Australia.

The prevailing metaphor of 'hybrid' holds an essence of the complexity of the field and the variety of views that have been brought together in Australia (Westwood and Linnell, 2011). Hybrid can mean that the new hybrid forms are stronger and more adapted to the context. The variety of hybrids may also bring new ways of thinking that contribute back to the places from where they originated. Another view of hybrids suggests that eventually the pure species may be lost. This metaphor has challenging connotations in relation to Indigenous Aboriginal Australia and the threats posed to their survival.

Retracing and researching my steps back and forth between Australia and Britain I found that images were like memory foam insoles; the images cushioned and remembered the shape of my feet and enabled me to feel the tacit messages vibrating over time and place. It has led me to a postcolonial place in art therapy education, one where attention is given to acknowledging and understanding the impacts of the prevailing Euro/Ameri-centric viewpoints, White privilege and the effects of power differences and how this is repeated and enacted not only by the 'colonisers' but also by new elites that develop in the post-colony (Young, 2003). A resonating discovery was how the homegrown Australian programmes of IKON, MIECAT and RMIT have drawn substantially on arts-based processes, pedagogy and epistemologies and this has permeated into other programmes such as that at Western Sydney. This intermingling, exploration and emphasis on the power of art-making and imagination shifts away from dominating psychological discourses, opening up spaces where a taking a postcolonial view of art therapy education, and the use of art in immersive experiential learning, has the capacity to resist limiting, erosive forces and enable the excavation of long lost, buried bones which reinvigorate this specialised and complex field.

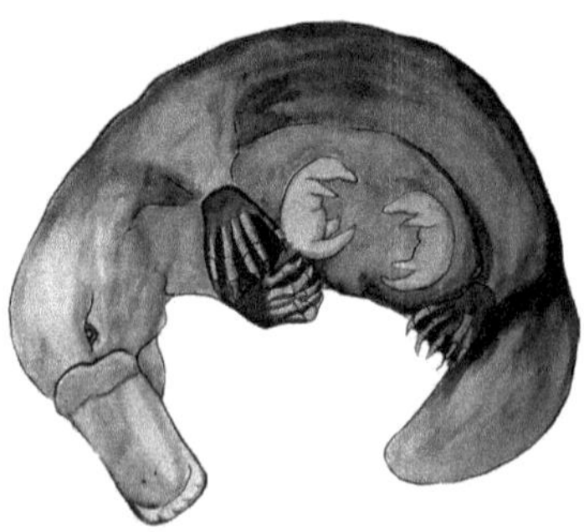

References

Champernowne, I. (1971). Art and therapy: An uneasy partnership. *American Journal of Art Therapy, 10*(3): 131–143.

Gilroy, A. (1998). On being a temporary migrant to Australia: Reflections on art therapy education and practice. In: Docktor, D. (Ed.) (1998). *Arts therapists, refugees and migrants: reaching across borders* (pp. 262–277). Jessica Kingsley Publishers, London, UK.

Gilroy, A., and Hanna, M. (1998). Conflict and culture in art therapy: an Australian perspective. In: Calisch, A. and Hiscox. A. (Eds.) (1998). *Tapestry of cultural issues in art therapy.* Jessica Kingsley Publishers, London, UK.

Gilroy, A., and Skaife, S. (1997). Taking the pulse of American art therapy: A report on the 27th Annual Conference of the American Art Therapy Association, 13–17 November 1996, Philadelphia, *Inscape 2*(2): 57–64.

IKON Institute: http://ikoninstitute.edu.au/courses/bachelor-arts-psychotherapy/ accessed 26 Oct 2016.

Katz, G. (2013) Picture this… An inquiry into the experiences, the qualities and the meanings of arts-based learning in an Australian creative arts therapy postgraduate education program. Unpublished PhD thesis. Royal Melbourne Institute of Technology, Victoria, Australia: http://citeseerx.ist.psu.edu/viewdoc/download?-doi=10.1.1.826.245&rep=rep1&type=pdf. Accessed 25 Jan 2017.

La Trobe University website: http://www.latrobe.edu.au/courses/art–therapy/postgraduate. Accessed 26 Oct 2016.

Linnell, S., Perry, S., Pretorius J., and Westwood, J. (2007) *Where knowing and not knowing touch (Art and the unconscious).* Exhibition and catalogue: at The Vanishing Point Contemporary Art, Newtown, Sydney, NSW, Australia (27 Sept–7 Oct).

Linnell, S., Perry, S., Pretorius, J. and Westwood, J. (2011) Where knowing and not knowing touch (Art and the unconscious). Film and statement. *ATOL: Art Therapy On Line, 1(3).* Goldsmiths: UK. Http://ojs.gold.ac.uk/index.php/atol/article/view/283

McLeod, J. (2006). *Qualitative research in counselling and psychotherapy.* Sage, London, UK.

MIECAT website: https://miecat.edu.au/masters–in–therapeutic–arts–practice. Accessed 26 Oct 2016.

The Australian newspaper: http://www.theaustralian.com.au/higher-education/shaman-training-courses-given-5m-funding-for-education-loans/news-story/27123677bdb-144f7ee4000968212cf99. Accessed 26 Oct 2016.

University of Queensland: https://www.uq.edu.au/study/plan.html?acad_plan=ARTTHX5151. Accessed 26 Oct 2016.

Western Sydney University website: https://www.westernsydney.edu.au/future–students/postgraduate/postgraduate/postgraduate_courses/therapeutic_studies_and_counselling_courses/art_therapy. Accessed 26 Oct 2016.

Westwood, J. and Linnell, S. (2011). The emergence of Australian art therapies: Colonial legacies and hybrid practices. *ATOL: Art Therapy On Line*, 1(3). Goldsmiths UK. http://ojs.gold.ac.uk/index.php/atol/article/view/282/307

Westwood, J. (2010). Hybrid Creatures: Mapping the emerging shape of art therapy education in Australia. Unpublished PhD thesis, University of Western Sydney, Australia. http://researchdirect.uws.edu.au/islandora/object/uws%3A11151/datastream/PDF/view.Westwood, J. (2012). Hybrid Creatures: Mapping the emerging shape of art therapy education in Australia, including reflections on New Zealand and Singapore. *The Australian and New Zealand Journal of Art Therapy,* 7(1): 15–25.

Young, R. (2003). *Postcolonialism. A Very Short Introduction.* Oxford University Press, Oxford.

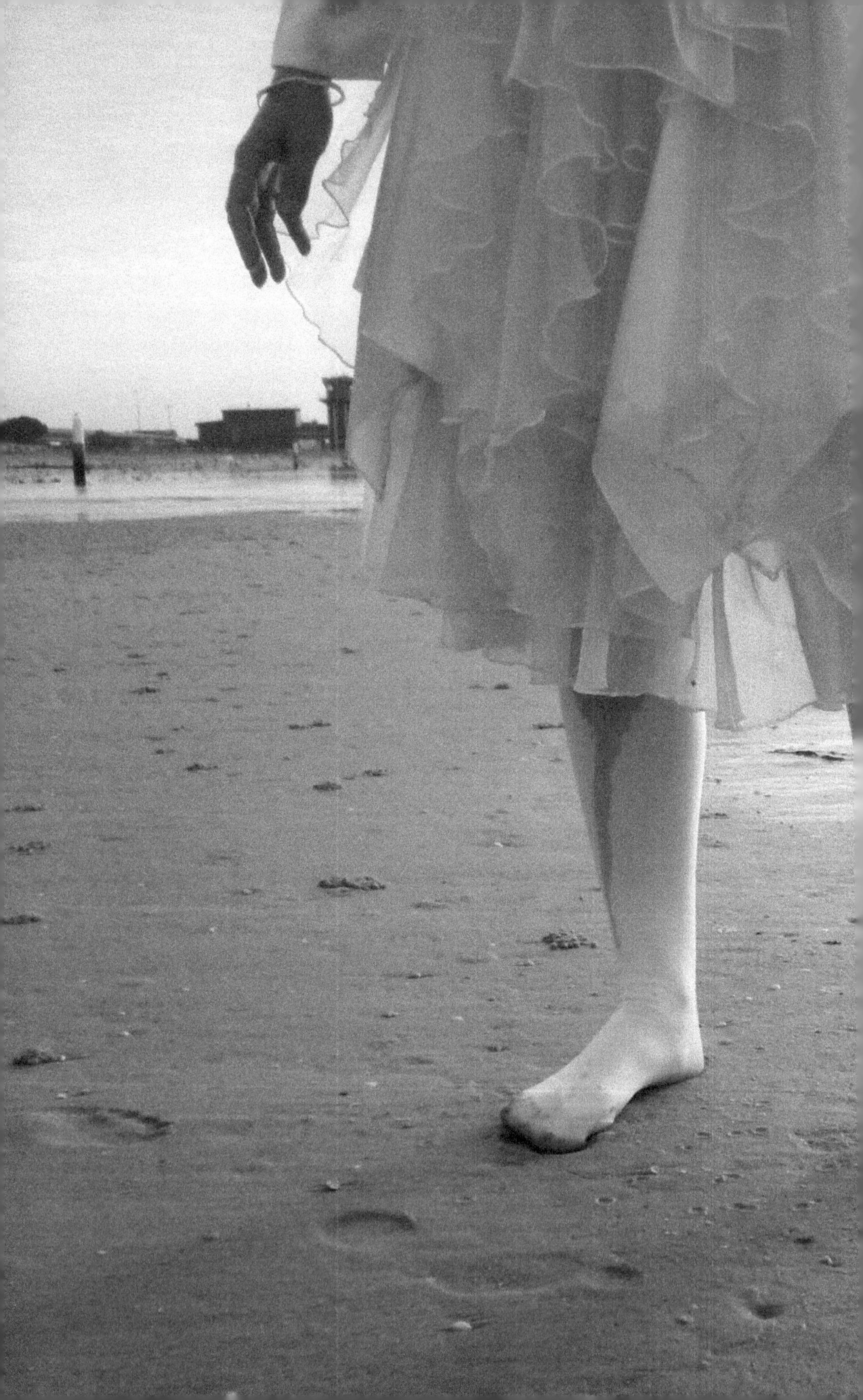

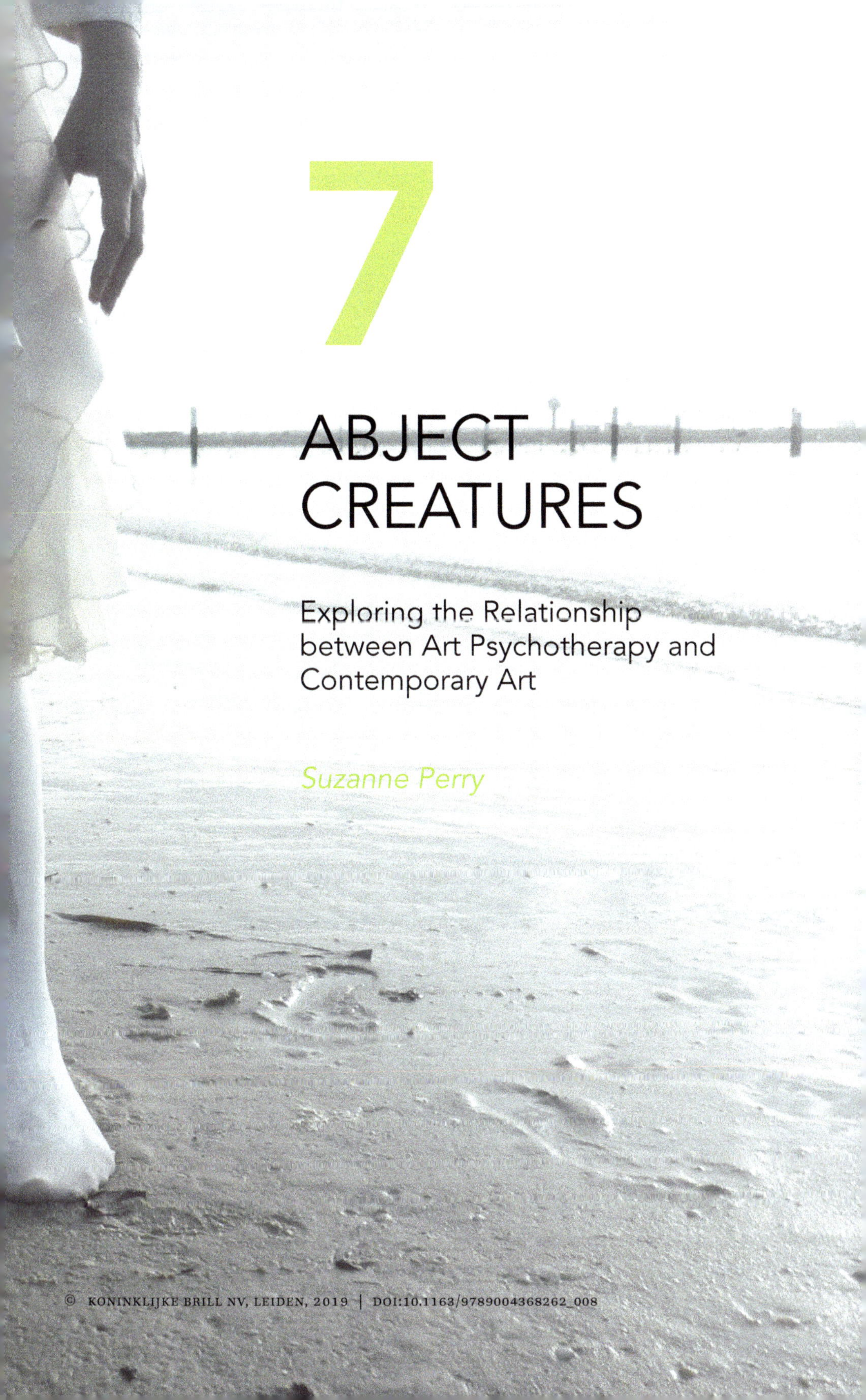

7

ABJECT CREATURES

Exploring the Relationship between Art Psychotherapy and Contemporary Art

Suzanne Perry

 | DOI:10.1163/9789004368262_008

To experience the abject is described by Julia Kristeva as being drawn into a place where constructed meaning collapses as we encounter such feelings as horror, misery, repulsion, humiliation and desire (1982: 4). In this chapter I will explore theories of the abject and art psychotherapy to reflect and shine light on the symbiotic relationship between art psychotherapy and contemporary art practices, using my own art-making as a process of exploration to further understand this relationship.

In Julia Kristeva's seminal text *The Powers of Horror* (1982) she considers the function and qualities of the abject, describing abjection as a form of the rejected experiences of horror, repulsion, misery, violence, fear and loathing. She also considers these emotional experiences as "being drawn into a place where meaning collapses, it is neither object or subject ... it disturbs identity, system and order." (1982: 4).

As I spend more time thinking about these profound psychological states felt in both body and mind, I begin to wonder about Kristeva as a child. In my search I discover she was born in 1941 and grew up in Bulgaria with her sister, attending a school run by Dominican nuns whilst her father worked as a church accountant (http://en.wikipedia.org/wiki/Julia_Kristeva#Life). I decide to paint Julia as a small child (Figure 1) as a way of trying to imaginatively enter into her theories of the abject and explore how they illuminate the ways in which I make sense of the relationship between art therapy and contemporary art.

> My mind is inhabited by an image of small girl about the age of seven; she has dark brown hair and her eyes are almost black. I am with her in a dark but magical Bulgarian forest. I watch her walk along a path holding a cross that looks as if it may be her only form of protection as she walks alone with a menacing red wolf behind her. She keeps feeling as though deception, mistrust and the threat of an attack are behind her but every time she turns around she sees nothing ... slowly she begins to doubt her own feelings.
>
> Along her pathway is an obstacle of a black bottomless pit with a formless, unidentifiable shape of nameless dread lying by the side of the black hole. She stops in her tracks, wondering if she should quietly tip toe around the black hole, trying ever so hard not to wake this formless shape of nameless dread. She looks to her left and sees a young girl about her age wearing the same dress as her, burning in a fire. She is screaming but no sound is coming out so no one can hear her; she wonders if she is invisible and if anyone has ever truly seen her. At that same moment in time a large bear with the tail of a fox and human hands walks past on its back legs, creeping ever so quietly down the path. The girl hopes this hybrid creature will stop and try to save this child but the creature is frightened and unsure what to do.

Figure 1 *Wearing the same dress.*
Suzanne Perry (2011). Acrylic paint and ink on paper.

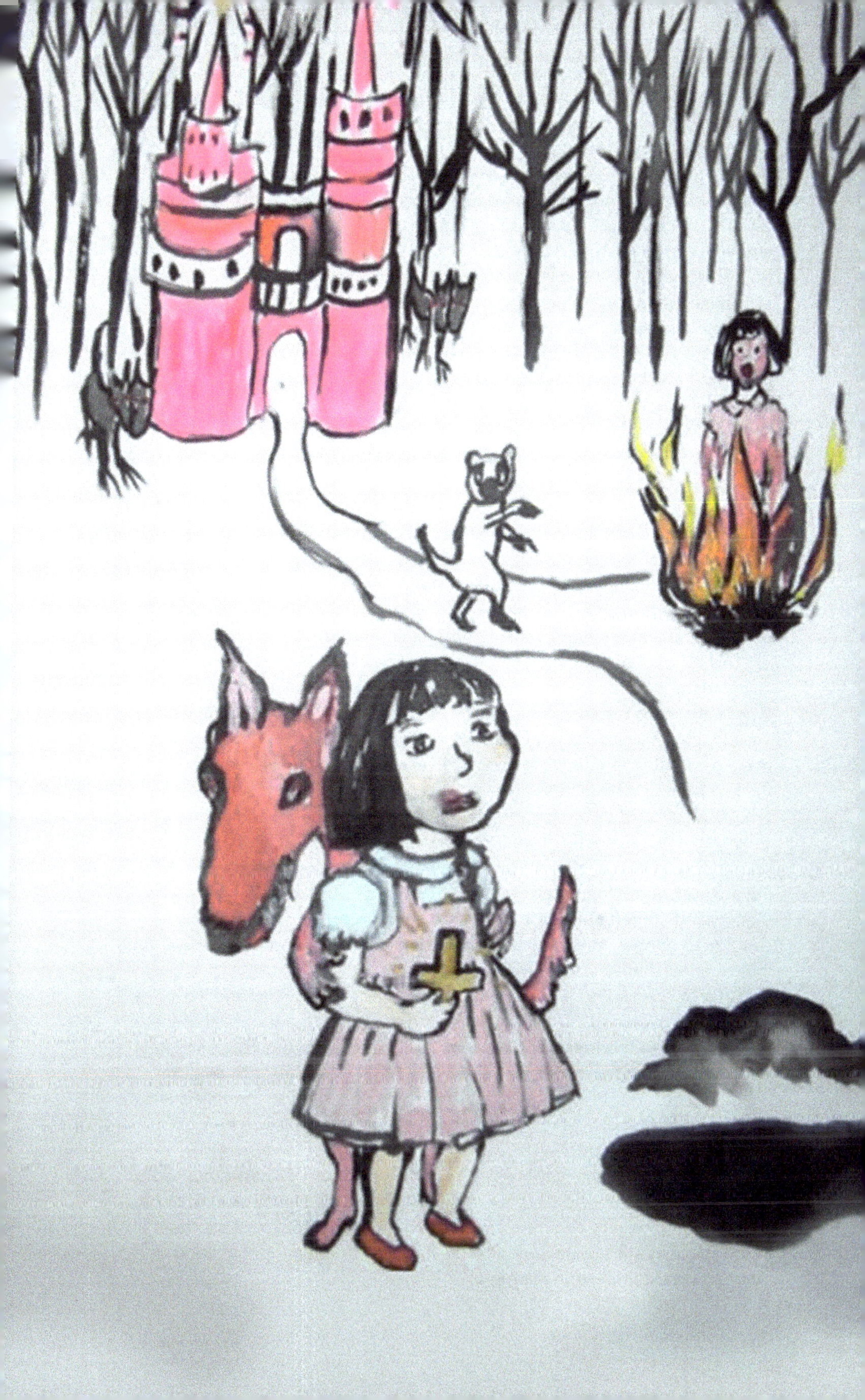

I stare at a manifestation of feelings that are painful (Figure 2). I watch in my own reflection the public expression of abjection, horror, and painfully feel the intimacy of my own abject suffering (Kristeva, 1982: 140). Through this creative process I gain a sense of my boundaries dissolving and my self being altered; I am, as Kristeva describes, neither object nor subject. My constructed boundaries of self have collapsed but through the creative process I gain the experience of safely exploring an otherness that is both me and not me.

The creative process facilitates an exploration of the unexpected and at times frightened and frightening aspects of the self. Art psychotherapist David Maclagan, in his seminal text *Psychological Aesthetics* (2001), succinctly describes this as "various kinds of leakage between subjective and objective realities, and that are often almost beyond the reach of language" (40). He considers part of the relationship between psychoanalysis and aesthetics as having to deal with the life and consequences of the unconscious. Maclagan's consideration of the psychological aesthetic is not just "concerned with judgements of beauty or ugliness" (ibid: 10), often associated with the more personal subjective taste of the physical way in which something appears. His theory is far more concerned with what he terms the "undeniable inner dimension" (ibid: 11) of aesthetics that can express a far wider range of emotional states.

This concept of psychological aesthetics has been an anchor for me as I navigate my way through my practice as an artist and as an art therapist. At times early in my career as an art therapist I wondered if the aesthetic qualities of art were welcome in art psychotherapy as I focused on the process of making and the therapeutic relationship yet, as I sat alongside clients through their creative process of making, I would often experience a quiet and embodied state of reverence towards their art objects and mark-making that conveyed a raw aesthetic gesture and expressed despair, uncertainty, rage, horror, disgust, loss and love. This was the bridge that supported and held me as I discovered for myself the deep emotional bonds between art psychotherapy and contemporary art and in particular Abject Art. This gave me courage to deepen my practice as an artist in exploring these abject psychological states that exist within all of us.

Art-making requires a process of play, where defences relax and we move into what psychoanalyst Donald Winnicott describes as a transitional space (1971, cited in Lieberman and Van Horn, 2011), a space that is not completely within us nor completely outside of us but a third, in-between space. Both artists and children inhabit this space, when it is safe to do so, getting down to the serious task of play to make sense of, reshape and explore their external worlds through their own inner reality.

Engagement in creativity holds a powerful space and process that enables us to inhabit this transitional space which is not completely inside of us nor completely outside of ourselves but the space in-between. There is a freedom in this space as it is not governed by the laws and boundaries of either our internal and external values or rules.

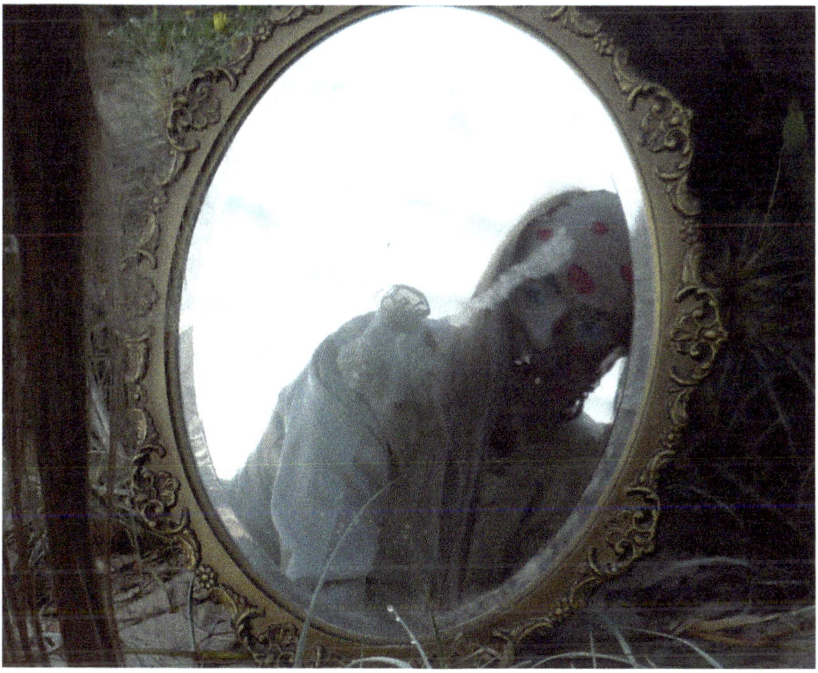

Detail of Figure 2 *Is that you?* Suzanne Perry and Jeff Allan, 2013. Digital Media

This transitional space is where our most abject feelings can be safely explored through the creative process. Children will often play out their most unspeakable fears and fantasies through the process of play and art-making with an urgency of repetition until a feeling of horror has been resolved, or at the very least given a place of expression and mobilisation. I have been the witness during numerous therapy sessions where children who have experienced family violence have played out or created scenes whereby the main protagonist experiences numerous deaths or the potential rescuer is almost at the scene in the hope of providing safety but on the way they crash the car and never make it – and so the child invites you into the terror and helplessness. The temptation is to quickly provide the child with assistance to change this scenario and bring in additional help that can provide safety but my young clients have taught me about their need to stay with the helplessness and terror until they are ready to recreate an alternative ending. Children may explore these abject states of fear, anger and vulnerability through the creative process of art-making and play. They know that they need to play out those frightening or confusing feelings in order to process and reorganise feelings and real or imagined consequences (Gil, 2013; Leiberman and Van Horn, 2011).

Overleaf: Figure 2 *Is that you?*
Suzanne Perry and Jeff Allan (2013). Digital media.

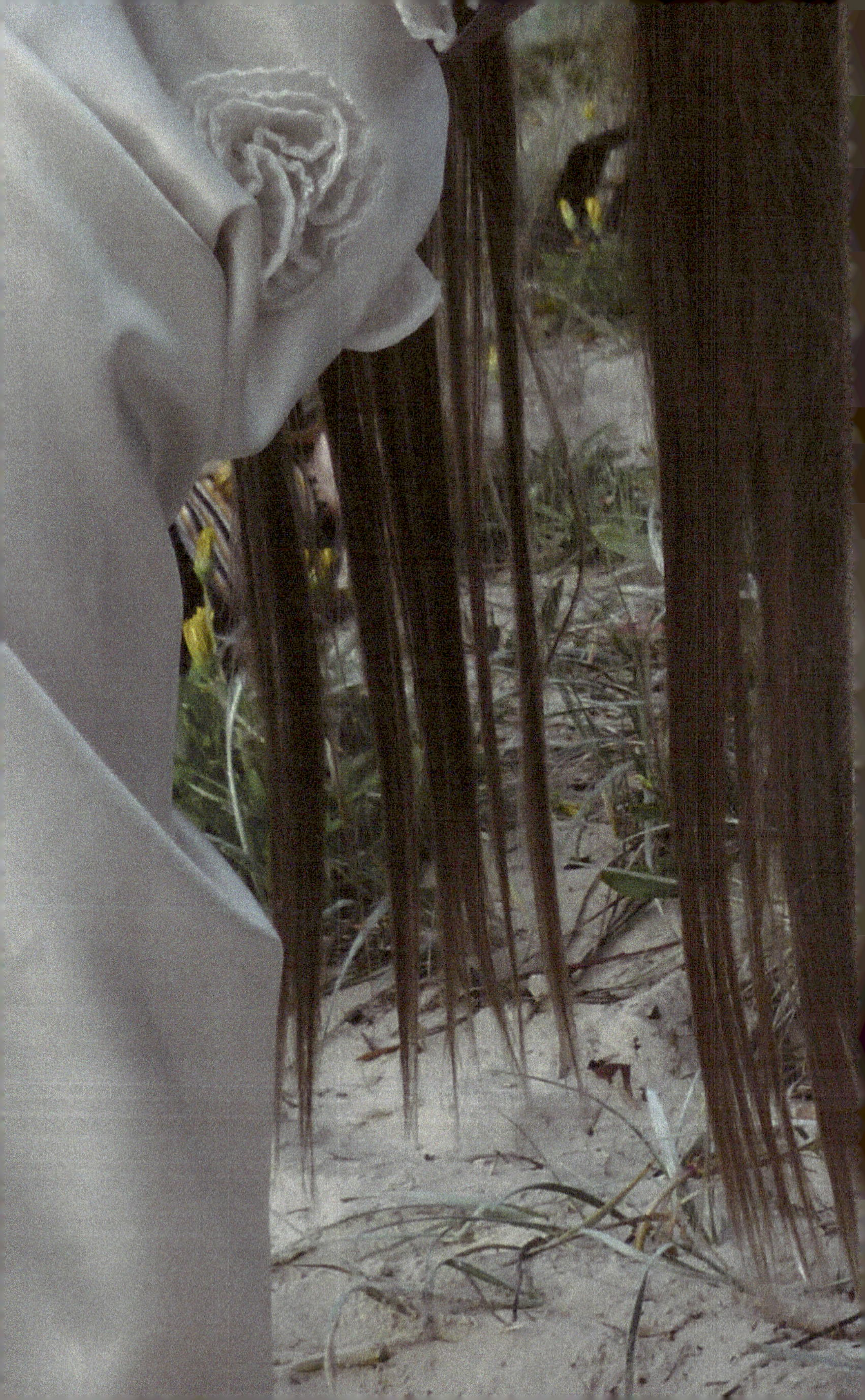

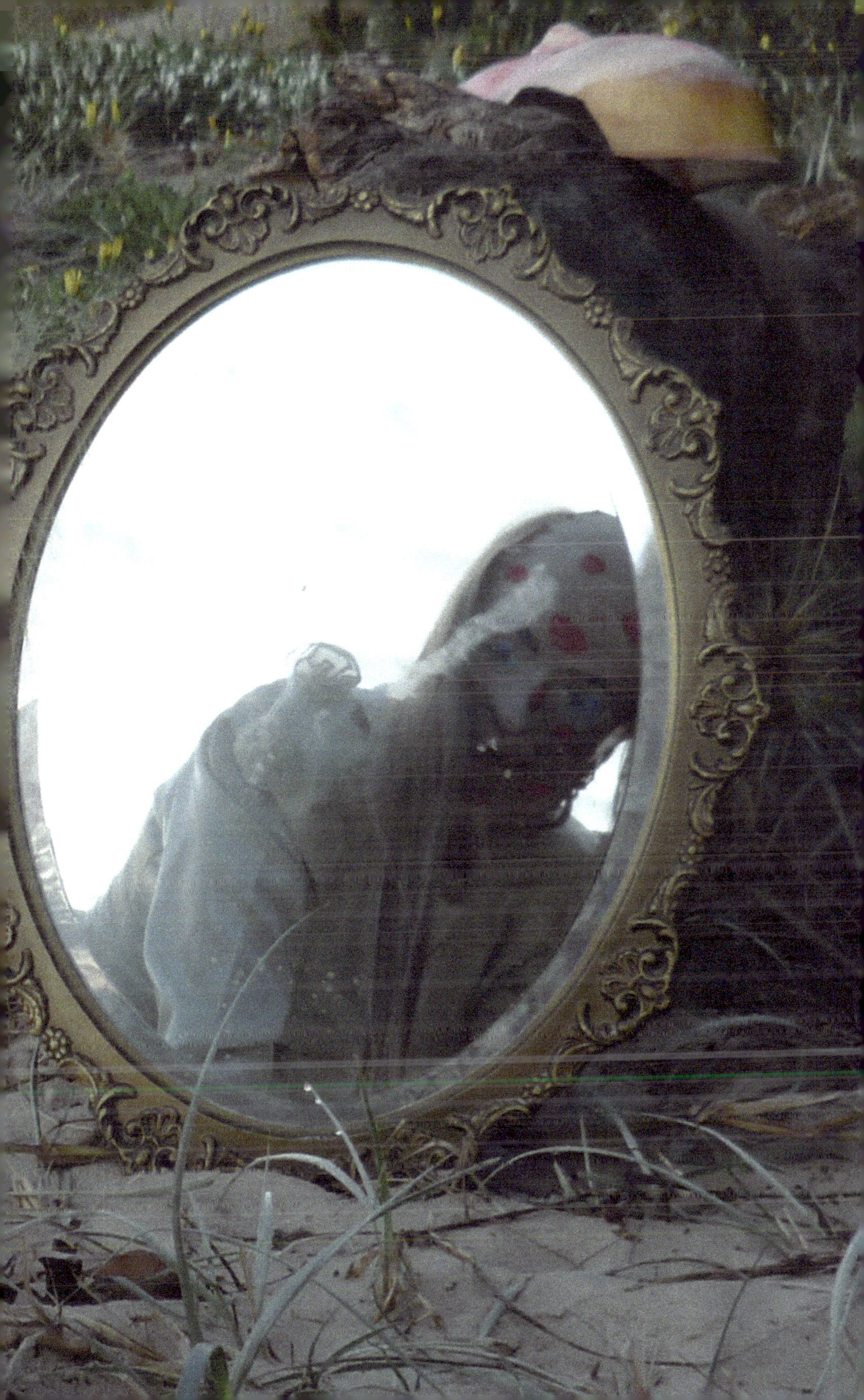

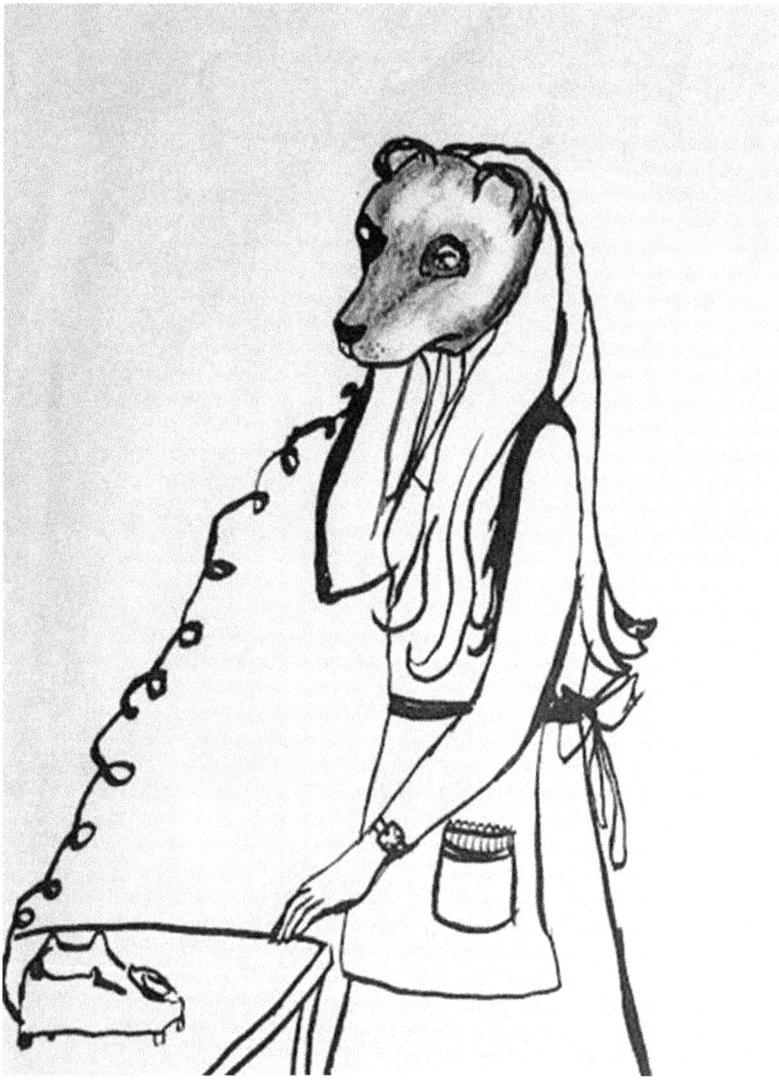

Figure 3 *Bear girl calls her father.* Suzanne Perry (2009). Ink on paper. 'The bear that can make the telephone call when missing feelings are so deeply painful.'

In my clinical practice with children who have experienced complex trauma as a result of child abuse and family violence, I have become fascinated by children's capacity to create hybrid creatures through art and play. These creatures have human capabilities and emotions and at the same time transgress boundaries of the human; they can also embody the qualities of animals.

Children know the value of creating hybrid creatures in play and of telling the stories held within their art which explore their suffering and experience of violence and, when needed, the ability to summon special powers to protect, rescue or destroy (Figure 3).

The hybrid creature has existed throughout centuries of cultural mythology. It is a creature that transgresses boundaries and is difficult to define. In these cultural stories the hybrid creature plays an important role in the expression of the abject that sits deep within the universal human psyche. It is a creature that expresses violence and desire beyond human capabilities. It evokes horror but it is also a creature that can provide insight and protection to humans, or it can incite danger and fear; at times it possesses the possibility of all (http://www.mythencyclopedia.com/Am-Ar/Animals-in-Mythology.html).

Art therapy has been considered as a hybrid discipline (Westwood, 2010) which traverses the cultural landscapes of both psychotherapy and art history and their respective practices. The art therapist must become familiar and fluent in both fields of language and practice in order to communicate and be understood. However this transgression of boundaries from both the arts and psychotherapy creates a creature which is difficult to define and can arouse binary feelings of desire and fear from both within those who practice art therapy and those who watch from the side. This very abject quality of art psychotherapy also contributes to its potency as it has the capacity to disrupt identities, systems and order (Kristeva, 1982: 4) as it gives tangible expression to often unspeakable and disowned aspects of the human psyche.

The relationship between my work as an artist and an art therapist has taken the form of a hybrid creature. It has had many guises and has been shaped by the courage of the people I work with and the places I have entered and explored within their psyche and my own. This shared experience of embodied states is sometimes understood through the lens of intersubjectivity . British art therapist Sally Skaife, in her article *Making Visible: Intersubjectivity and Art Therapy* (2001), acknowledges that the term 'intersubjectivity' has its roots in philosophy and states that "An intersubjective understanding of our relations with others has it that from the beginning we are only ourselves in relation to another." (2001: 42). She goes on to say that our individuality is dependent on others and unfolds and shifts within these relationships. Hybrid creatures give expression to these binary and yet deeply connected feelings of desire and fear, and to the ambiguous spaces in between: the domesticated bear mother who is both benign and potentially attacking; the tender, awkward, cross-dressing bear in high heels who holds her giant baby rabbit whilst it feeds from the milk of a cow; and the ghost of a donkey with human hands who feels that which cannot be spoken of (Figure 4).

Overleaf: Figure 4 *Crying Donkey*.
Suzanne Perry, (2007). Acrylic on hardboard.

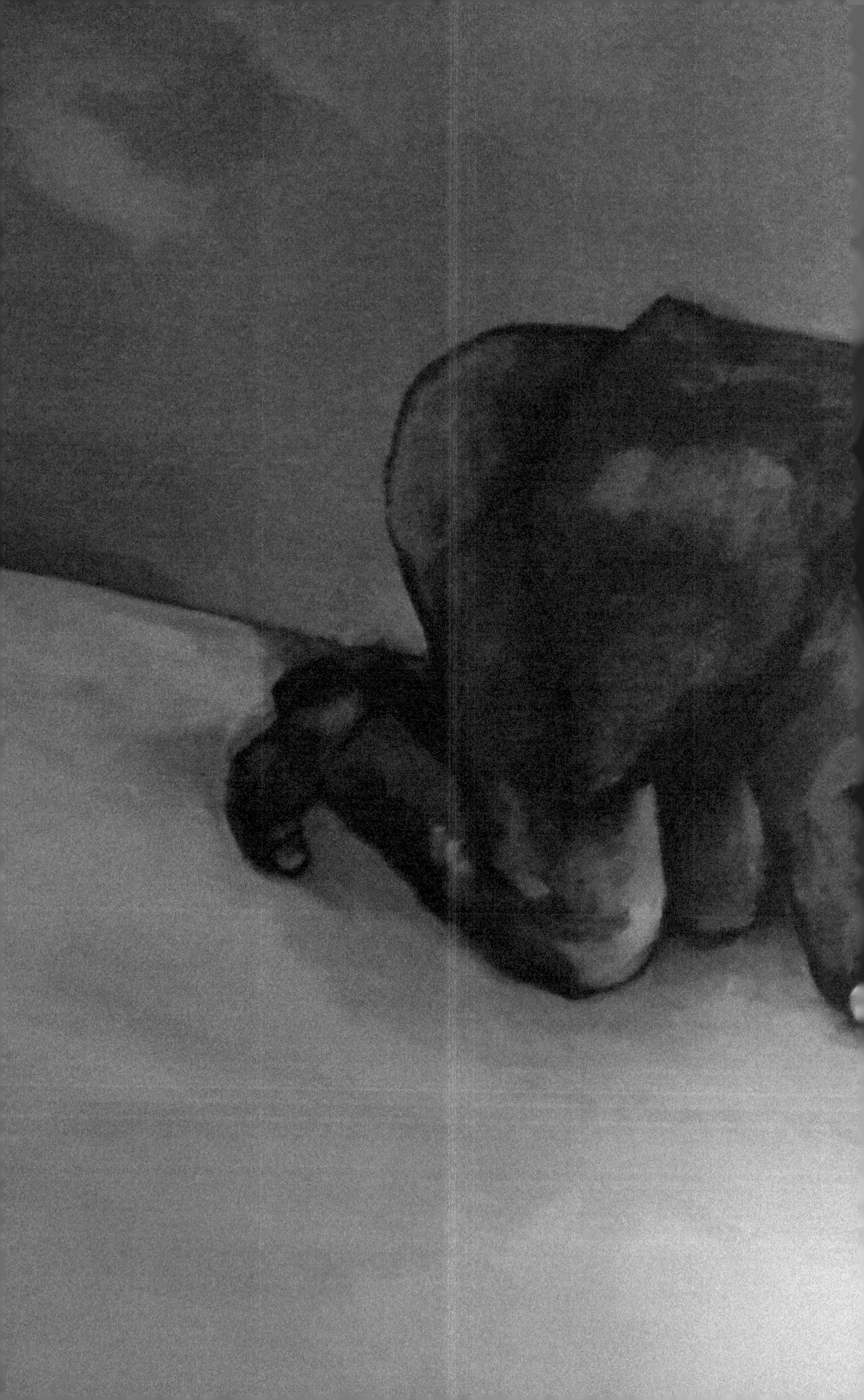

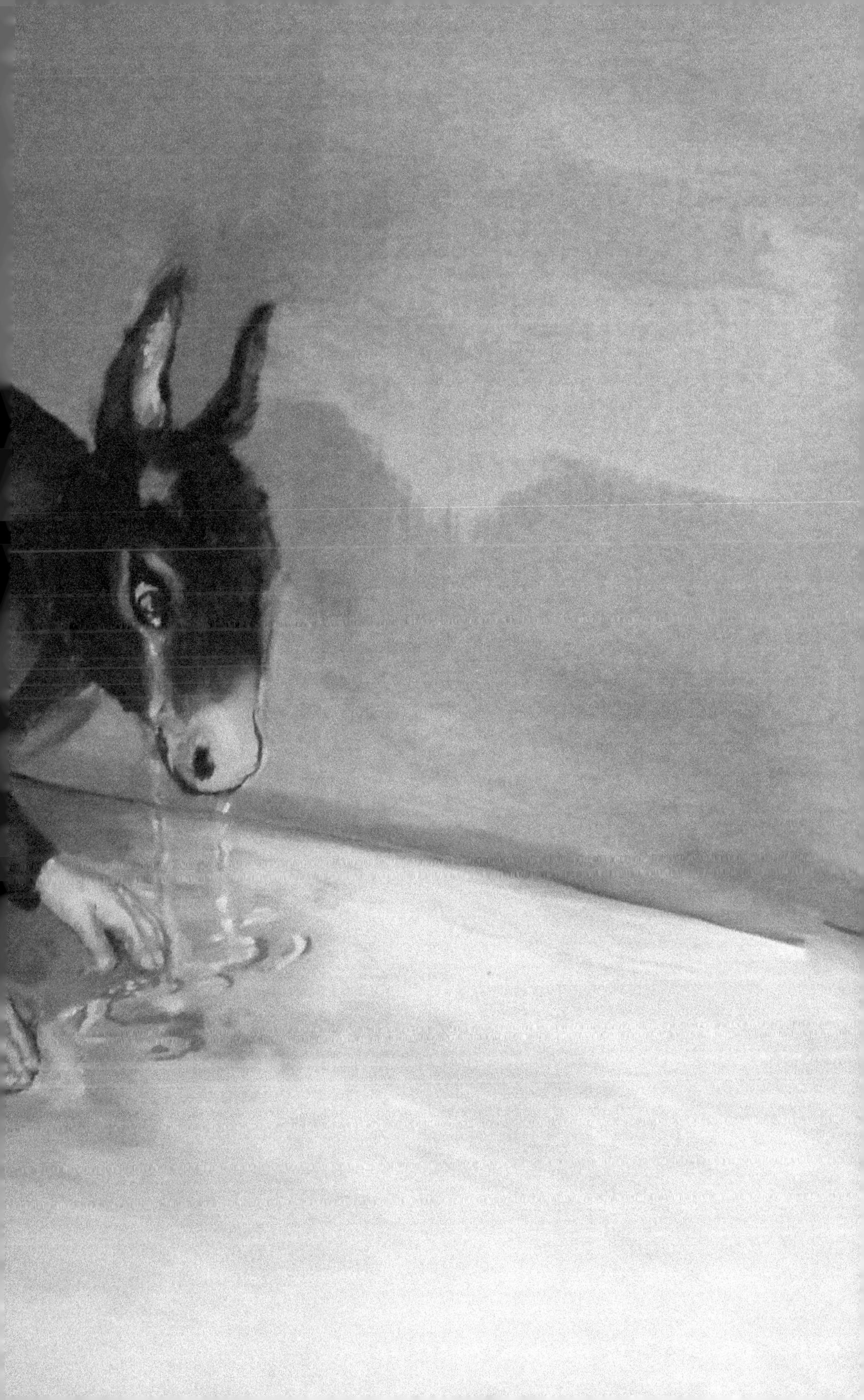

The presence of the werewolf bride and the place she inhabits begins to take hold of a space in me and elicits an exchange of relational questions, responses and feelings between myself and others. The abject sits just below the surface of each reaction: "Is that you … ? What is that … ? Why did you do that … ? Was anyone else watching … ? Are you mad … ?" Do I say I am exploring gender and sexuality, belonging and not belonging, or do I stay fleetingly suspended in relationship with feelings of desire, repulsion and shame? I think all these reactions and responses need to exist together, but it is the abject feelings that are both expressed and felt in both the other and myself that is of greater significance in the exploration of the relationship between art psychotherapy and contemporary art.

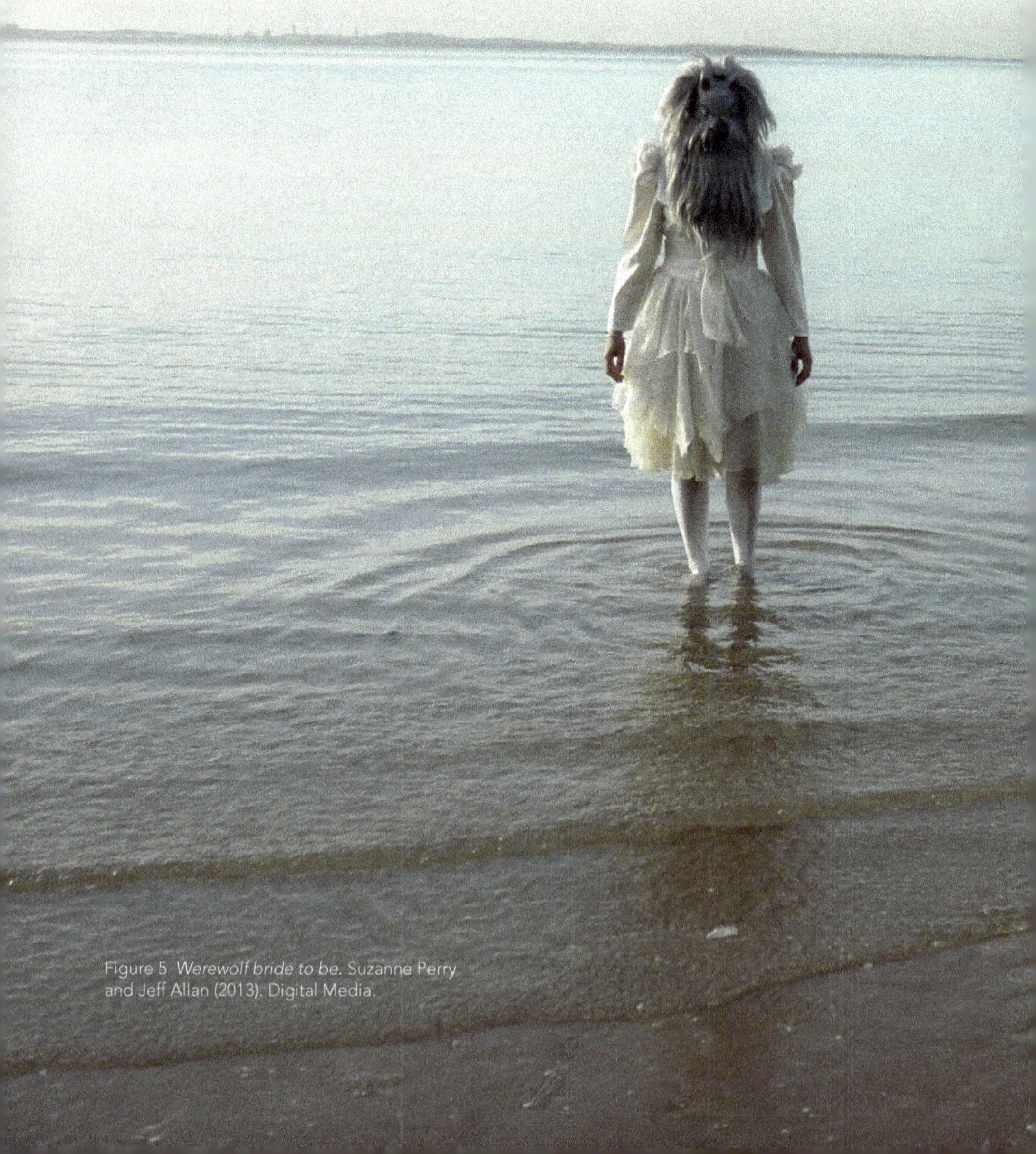

Figure 5 *Werewolf bride to be*. Suzanne Perry and Jeff Allan (2013). Digital Media.

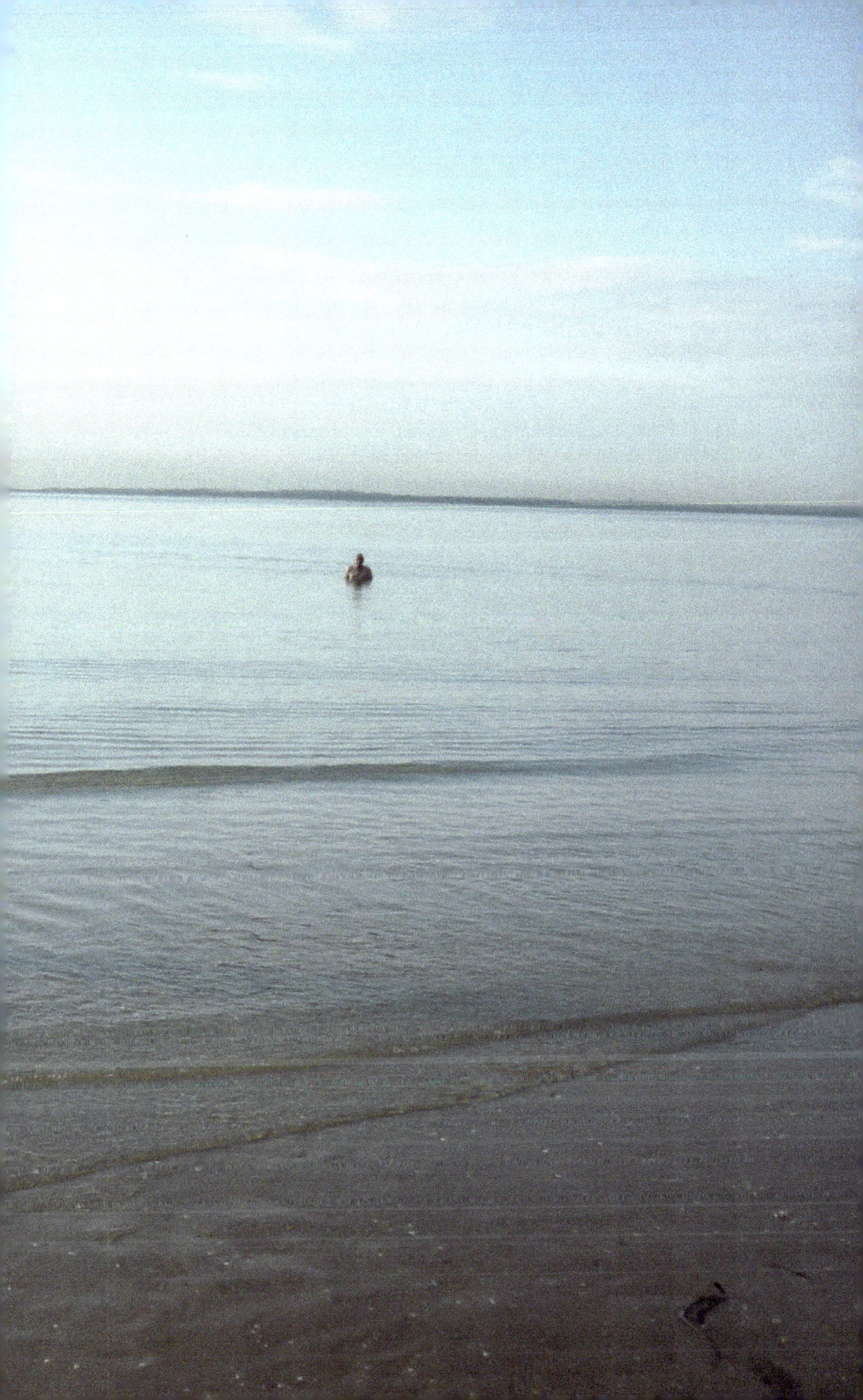

In Rina Arya's text, *Abjection and Representation* (2014), she notes: "The concept of abjection, which provoked new ways of thinking about art and aesthetics, came into prominence in the visual arts in the late twentieth century, particularly in the 1980s and 90s with '[t]he postmodernist return to the body" (Ross, 2003: 281 as cited in Arya 2014: 82). During this time the Whitney Museum of American Art curated an exhibition of contemporary artists who were exploring in some way theories of the abject through challenging and transgressing boundaries. After leaving art school I moved into my first studio and purchased the book of this ground-breaking exhibition: *Abject Art: Repulsion and Desire in American Art* (1993) at the Whitney Museum of American Art in New York. This was one of the first major exhibitions that began to form and define the concepts of Abject Art. It was written in response to an exhibition that showed the work of contemporary artists who were responding to and exploring the idea of abjection through the use of, and reference to, bodily fluids and familiar objects that transgressed and challenged their boundaries of what was the norm and what was expected. The text focused on artists and art that explored objects and subject matters as devices for challenging and expanding upon constructed and restrictive notions of sexuality, gender and culture.

Simon Taylor in his chapter in the exhibition catalogue, *The Phobic Object: Abjection in Contemporary Art* (1993: 59), looks at the function of the abject in contemporary art. He discusses an influential artist in my own art practice as a therapist and artist: Cindy Sherman. He considers her work in relation to the way in which art:

> … assaults the totalising and homogenising notions of identity, system and order … confronts and transgresses social prohibitions and taboos, re-enacting psychic traumas, personal obsessions, and phobias.
>
> (1993: 60)

Cindy Sherman more often than not places herself as the object, turning the gaze upon herself so that we, the viewer are held in the position of the onlooker, the voyeur. At times she appears ambivalent and awkward, whilst we look at her masquerade of the feminine. Dressed in fake breasts, wigs and prosthetic body parts, using vomit, blood and saliva, Sherman explores the social construct of women as the abject (ibid: 61). Sherman also artfully uses deception through her use of disguise, transforming her appearance to make us believe, if only for a moment, that she is someone else. This use of deception is at the same time being used to expose the deception behind the constructs of female gender and sexuality.

Sherman's work has been described as "… disrupting constructs of existing meaning within a culture that operates within such strict moral and religious principles." (http://www.jca-online.com/sherman.html). I think this understanding of Sherman's work can also be applied to thinking about the art that is made within the context of art therapy. This is necessary when attempting to understand the importance of the social and political inter-

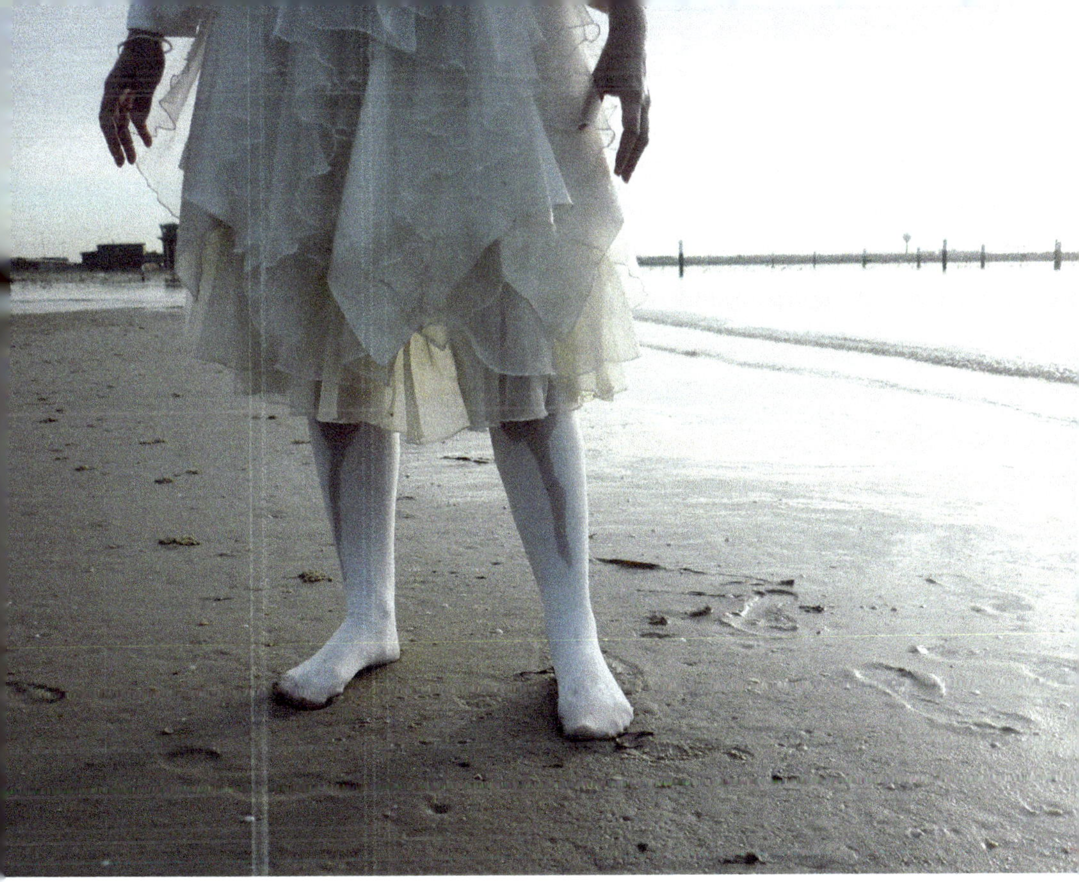

Figure 6 *What happened?* (2013). Suzanne Perry and Jeff Allan. Digital media.

vention that is art therapy and its relationship to contemporary art practices. It is my belief that political and social disruption is core to the practice of art therapy and that this disruption creates spaces for alternative realities to be created. The art process and object become a visual, tangible object of stories and experiences that perpetrators of abuse try to silence: suffering, betrayal and terror as well as courage, survival and transformation.

Contemporary artists that explore the abject have deep bonds with the practice of art therapy. Each time a client makes an art work in response to an experience of abuse and explores the associated abject feelings of both body and mind, they are on one level creating the most subversive contributions to the canons of Western art and, in doing so, are on another level often on the cutting edge of contemporary art practices. The very nature of abuse and violence is to oppress, control and silence and then use the abuse as a way to locate feelings of disgust, shame and terror within the other. Through the creative process these art works give voice to experiences and feelings that have been silenced and have remained unseen by others, instantly challenging the very structures of the abuse. The art and its maker are in dialogue with the oppressor and finding and reshaping their experiences through the creative process.

The following quote is from Ayra's research on the abject and its role in contemporary culture:

> Artists would often employ various methods to rupture the outer so that the inner would come seeping through, thus blurring the boundaries and giving rise to an experience of abjection.
>
> (2014: 86)

Whilst art psychotherapy may not be working towards rupturing the outer, I think there is a significant relational bond with art psychotherapy's concept of engaging the client in art-making within the therapeutic relationship in order to support an exploration of the inner world, making it visible through the art-making process and the object (Case and Dalley, 1999; Maclagan, 2001). This expression is felt and witnessed in clients' art work as they are either bravely or compulsively driven to connect with their creative process in the safety of the therapeutic relationship and challenge the very nature of abuse through recreating and reshaping the stories of shame, despair and violence. Ayra (ibid: 84) reflects on this process in abject art as being central to its power to disrupt, saying that when art expresses states and experiences that are usually confined to secrecy or are privatised and then witnessed by others, the art-making becomes a powerful device for disrupting identity and dominant constructs. This consideration is paramount to the work of art therapy as we continue to support the people we work with, both emotionally and politically.

In conclusion I think it is my own creative process and the creative process I bear witness to in others that that has given me the understanding of how feelings of abjection have deepened my understanding of this complex and deeply relational bond between art psychotherapy and contemporary art. Winnicott's (1971) theory of play and the transitional space that is not completely within us nor outside of us was also an important link to Kristeva's (1982) concept of self-boundaries dissolving, leaving the individual as neither object nor subject and in a place where new meanings can emerge. I think there is a deeply important relationship between art psychotherapy and the contemporary practice of abject art that are linked through their very nature in making spaces for abject feelings so often associated with trauma, enabling them to be seen, expressed and reshaped. This will continue to grow in unexpected ways, made possible through their relationship with each other.

References

Arya, R. (2014). Abjection in the visual arts. In: *Abjection and representation*. September: 82–117. [Online] Available at: http://www.palgraveconnect.com.ezproxy.uws.edu.au/pc/doifinder/10.1057/9780230389342.0007.

Case, C. and Dalley, T. (1999) *The handbook of art therapy*. Routledge, London.

Kristeva, J. (1982) *Powers of horror. An essay on abjection*. Columbia University Press.

Lieberman, A. and Van Horne, P. (2011) *Psychotherapy with infants and young children. Repairing the effects of stress and trauma on early attachment*. The Guilford Press, New York.

Maclagan, D. (2001) *Psychological aesthetics. Painting, feeling and making sense*. Jessica Kingsley Publishers, London.

In: Arya, R. (2014) Abjection in the visual arts.

In: *Abjection and representation*. September: 82–117. [Online] Available at: http://www.palgraveconnect.com.ezproxy.uws.edu.au/pc/doifinder/10.1057/9780230389342.0007.

Skaife, S. (2001) Making visible: art therapy and intersubjectivity. *Inscape*, 6, 2: 40–50.

Taylor, S. *The phobic object: abjection in contemporary art*. In: Whitney Museum of American Art, (1993). *Abject art: repulsion and desire in American art*. Whitney Museum of American Art, New York.

Westwood, J. (2010) Hybrid creatures: mapping the emerging shape of art therapy education in Australia. Unpublished PhD thesis, University of Western Sydney, Australia. Http://researchdirect.uws.edu.au/islandora/object/uws%3A11151/datastream/PDF/view

Whitney Museum of American Art (1993). *Abject art: repulsion and desire in American art*. Whitney Museum of American Art, New York.

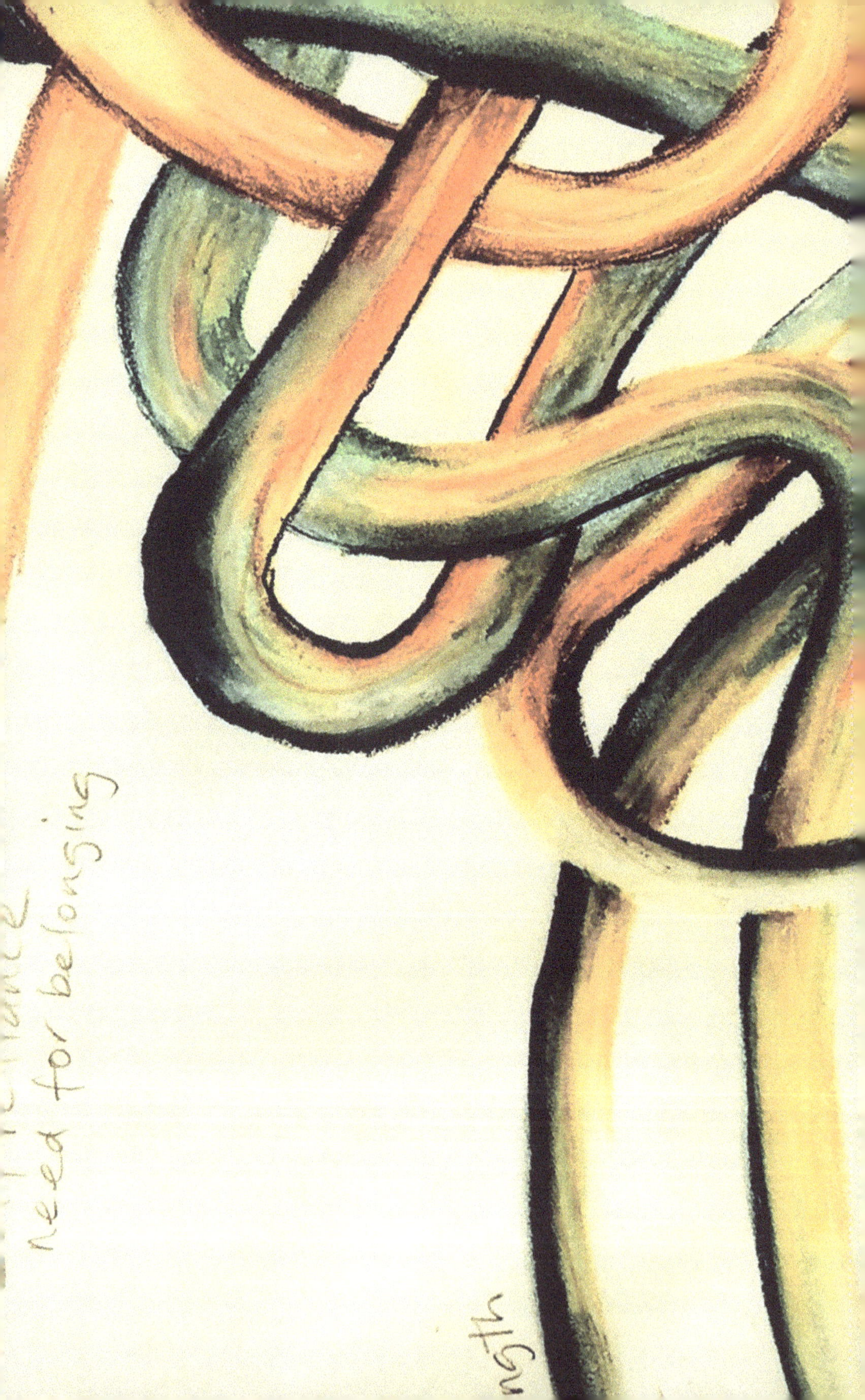
need for belonging

8

THE WORK OF ART THERAPY

An Immersive Visual Analysis

Jody Thomson

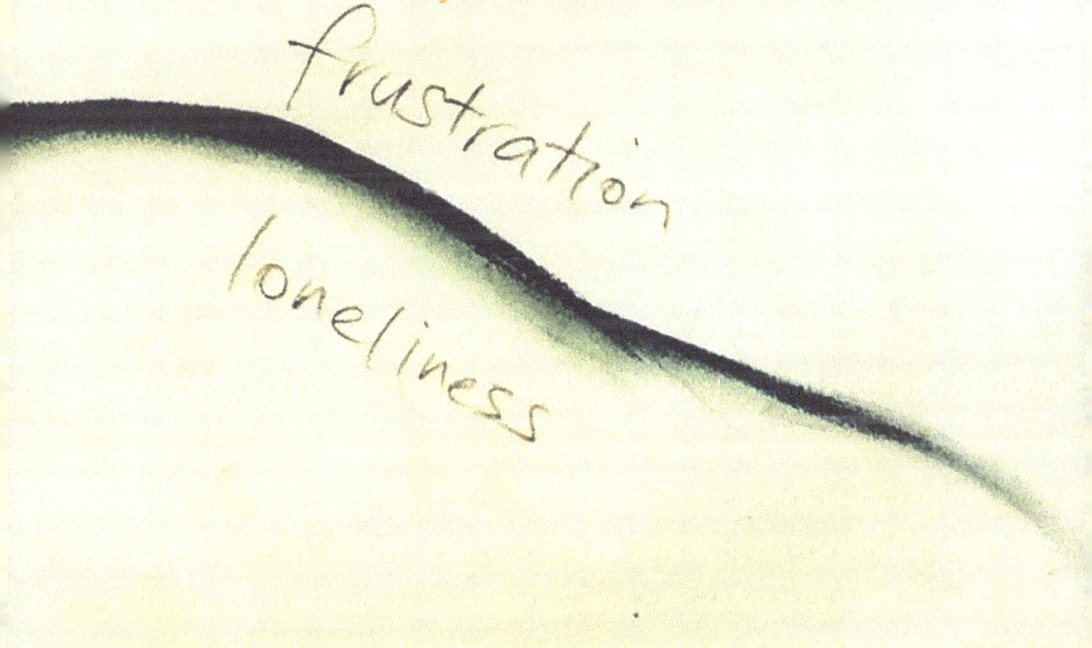

 | DOI:10.1163/9789004368262_009

This chapter describes a practice-led exploration of visual art therapists' experience of working with people living with, or dying from, cancer. My study was inspired by clinical work over many years as an independent art therapist, positioned at the intersection of psychotherapeutic practice and the Australian medical world of cancer and palliative care. With four experienced therapist-participants I explored the potential of art-making to go beyond and at times fold back into dialogue, as a powerful way to access knowledge lying outside conscious thought. A novel analytic method emerged organically, using image-making *in response* to the therapist-participants' data that I call *immersive visual analysis*. In this method, the image functions simultaneously as primary data, the method of enquiry and as a point of dialogic and analytic focus. Adopting a phenomenological, heuristic approach made it possible to explore the participants' stories and being-in-the-world, using their own 'text', as a different way of looking at the phenomenon of art-focused work with people experiencing cancer.

Whilst a growing body of international research explores the use of art therapy in cancer care focused on client perception and evaluation, little research exists that investigates the therapist's experience. Most is contained in three seminal texts (Connell, 1998; Pratt and Woods, 1998; Waller and Sibbett, 2005). Apart from a handful of auto-ethnographic studies by art therapists and art therapy educators (for example, Sibbett, 2005; Thorley, 2005; Wadeson, 2011; Zammit, 1999, 2001, 2008), to my knowledge there is no art-focused research that explores the experience of the visual art therapist working with this client group. Art therapist and cancer patient Caryl Sibbett (2005: 240) had posed what was for me, an important and relevant question – "What is the impact on humans taking on such a role?" Rather than providing an answer, Sibbett, amongst others (for example, Duesbury, 2005; Wood, 2005) argued that self-care, supervision, team support and training are vital, and that 'black humour' is often a defence mechanism that helps practitioners face-yet-manage clinical work in psycho-oncology.

I was drawn to the research by a passionate commitment to cancer work and to the potential of art making to "open liminal spaces for discovery" (Finley, 2014: 532) in therapy and research. My research aims were twofold. Firstly, I was intrigued by how art therapists experienced working with cancer patients: how they positioned and imagined their work as valuable; the ways they sustained their practice; what motivated and impelled them; and how therapists responded to and managed the impact of this difficult work.

My second research aim, and what fascinated me most, was exploring the ways in which art-making, in addition to traditional interview methods, might open up different pathways to explore the therapists' experience, and my own as a researcher-art therapist, enabling a more nuanced "route to ethnographic knowing" (Hogan and Pink 2012: 230) in a way that parallels art therapy practice.

The study drew together my own experience and training with the combined knowledge and life experience of four therapist-participants, each familiar with the artistic process as a method of enquiry. It explored the potential of using the therapist's art-making and my own, as a form of "artistic evidence" (McNiff, 2014) and as such, is research *with*, rather than research *about*. I found that keeping images and image-making fundamental to the interviews and my analysis opened a space for the therapist-participants and myself as therapist-researcher not only to think differently but to respond differently. It is based on what Patricia Leavy termed *aesthetic knowing*, which pushes the borders of inductive research further in being open to the "spontaneous and unknown" (2015: 20), thereby creating and conveying meaning and communicating the emotional aspects of social life in ways that may be otherwise inaccessible (Barone and Eisner, 2012; Leavy, 2015).

Method

In designing the study, I found myself wrestling with what constitutes *good* knowledge. My dual subjectivities as a social science researcher and an art therapist were in conflict over the desire to 'know', and my ethical and professional stance of 'witness' and 'not knowing'. To resolve this, I went back to the art, by keeping the image, and the process of image making central to the research, as it is in clinical practice.

As therapists, the art we make in response to our work is a different way of knowing (Allen, 1995) – of exploring, re-viewing, researching and making sense of our clinical work. Shaun McNiff described image-making by therapists as:

> a method of inquiry which uses the elements of the creative arts therapy experience, including the making of art by the researcher, as ways of understanding the significance of what we do within our practice.
>
> (1998: 13).

The method and rationale of my research was framed as a critical art-based social science inquiry (Finley, 2014; Pink, Hogan and Bird, 2011; Rose, 2012). I chose a bricolage approach (McLeod, 2001) – a collage[1] put together from hermeneutic phenomenology (Heidegger, 1962) and heuristics (Moustakas, 1994), semi structured interviews, response art (Fish, 2012), and a visual art-based analytic method that I call *immersive visual analysis*. This method is ontologically grounded in the aesthetic creative process, through an *immediate dynamic visual inter-play* between myself as artist-art therapist-researcher and the data.

This (bri)col(l)age provided a richly nuanced landscape, epistemologically located in a paradigm that values subjective experience, creativity and reflection as a way of knowing. I argue that this method of visual research holds the potential for discovery of deeply nuanced and intimate insight "… for the maker, researcher, co-researchers and readers" (Rumbold, Fenner, and Brophy-Dixon, 2012: 73).

The four interviews began with a simple opening question: "Can you tell me about your art therapy work with cancer patients?" This open, participant-led method generated an enormously rich and contoured landscape

1 An art method that uses various media or materials together in a single piece of work

of interview transcripts, art responses made by each participant during the two- to three- hour interviews and additional narrative and visual reflections post-interview. My aim was to remain open not only to the surface dialogue but to discover the sediment or the meta-narrative of what lay beneath.

Immediately following each of the four separate interviews, I made an image while listening to the audio-recorded dialogue and immersing myself in the photo-documented images. This subjective art-making allowed me to engage in a vital creative process by getting out of my head, and into a more intuitively alert state of "flow" that is characterised by complete absorption (Csikszentmihalyi, 2002). I tried to listen *differently*, not only to the overarching content but for the digressions, diversions and avoidances. My responsive image-making allowed colour, line, texture and shape to surface the latent feeling states underlying the information-loaded semantic themes. As my image flowed down the page, I responded with imaginal dialogue (McNiff, 2008), noting words and phrases drawn from my in-the-moment experience of art-making. These were named, counted and prioritised by repetition and divided into two sections: firstly, those that arose during the *interview alone*, and secondly, those that emerged during the *art-making and image reflection*.

I discovered that in the initial interviews, the participants shared their thoughts or 'out-sights' about working with cancer patients. Image-making opened a space to express their 'in-sights' and feeling states.

I experienced being physically and emotionally present during the *process* of art-making with three of the four participants as warm, intimate and

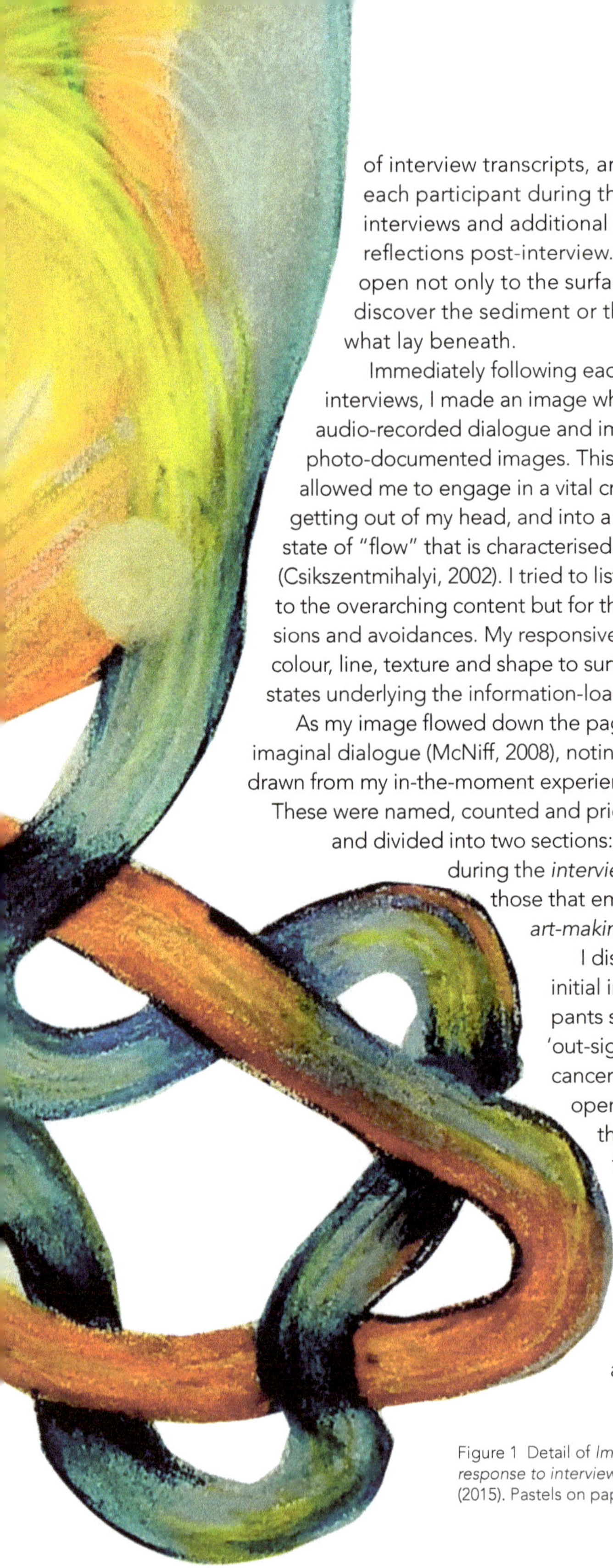

Figure 1 Detail of *Immersive visual analysis in response to interview with Poppy.* Jody Thomson (2015). Pastels on paper.

companioning. I observed an altered state of artistic flow and was made privy to the participant's soft verbal meanderings. My impression was that participating as a witness to the *process* of image-making created a bond that allowed more intensely felt subjective information to be conveyed. I was part of the process – the *phenomenon* – as witness, co(researcher), and – in my immersive visual analysis – as (co)participant in the study, which fostered more intensely felt subjective information being expressed and communicated in a tangible and concrete way. In this intimate and liminal space, insights emerged about the impact of this work on the therapist and how the creative process, as a form of self-care, helps sustain practice when confronted by the inevitable experience of death and dying. The therapists spoke around and through their images, telling stories of loss and sadness; of frustration in witnessing patients' lives not fully lived; and the loneliness of dying. Contrastingly, reflecting on the image made by the participant who brought a *completed* image to a follow-up interview, the talk felt fractured and descriptive, and I found the insights embodied in the artwork difficult to grasp.

The following section presents the research findings. I first discuss the themes that emerged in the initial interview dialogue (excluding the art-making section) with all four participants as they correlate with, and diverge from the existing literature. These themes are illustrated using interview data with participants' voices *in italicised text*. Following this, to best answer my research question about the ways that using the art-making *process* might provide more nuanced insights, I have chosen to explore in greater detail my immersive visual analysis and narrative response to the first and last interviews, with Poppy and Byron.[2] The analysis, discussion and insights drawn from the other two participants art-making is published elsewhere (Thomson, 2016).

The interview data

The therapist–participants clearly perceived socially and family inclusive art therapy as a valuable and beneficial psychotherapeutic contribution in a variety of cancer care settings. Together, these four therapists have worked in hospitals, home hospice palliative care agencies and in the community with those re-establishing their lives after cancer treatment. The breadth of experience of these therapists highlighted the flexibility of art therapy in meeting the needs of clients experiencing different stages of cancer, and in different therapeutic environments.

The existing literature explores the quality of the therapeutic relationship and the qualities and role of the therapist as a companion, guide, or witness (Connell, 1998; Kerr, 1998). The data showed that a direct approach was integral to the therapeutic relationship: "I'm a great believer in going straight to what the problem is … whether it's denial or resignation or their anger, grief

2 Pseudonyms chosen by the therapist–participants

or acceptance … and to offer them the opportunity to explore their existential situation". The relationships formed with people who are physically suffering and trying to express their experience of facing, and making meaning of a heightened possibility of dying, are intimate and poignant (Duesbury, 2005). But one must: "tell it like it is, and sometimes it's bloody awful ... and they don't get a chance to do that with family … (who) sometimes leave and say when you're over your cancer get back to me."

In this intimate therapeutic space, boundaries may become blurred (Skaife, 1993), even in short-term interventions: "what's important to understand here is the intimacy and closeness of working with a terminally-ill person ... You can become extremely important to them … so the relationship can become very close and warm, almost a friendship". In longer-term therapeutic relationships, professional boundaries may become even more flexible and the role of the art therapist may extend beyond the client's death to facilitate their wishes.

> He talked a lot about wanting to have some of his works displayed at the hospital … he was very keen to have some sort of legacy, these were his words … I remember him saying I want to leave something of myself behind ... So I went down the track of taking on the hospital system and getting permission to put something on the wall … I really care for this gentleman and I am happy to put in lots of my own time to make a difference for him and for his family.

The art therapist can offer supportive therapy both verbally and by facilitating an alternate means to express their experience though image-making. Art-making in therapy was seen as a physical, tactile, multi-sensory process that allows a non-threatening 'breathing space' from verbal dialogue by providing an additional method of communication "when there are needs and complexities that 'go beyond talking'". The ability of this external object was seen to offer a distancing relief from the trauma of illness:

> There is 'disguise' and safety … in the artwork, and the art making process … it softens the hardness of (what is) being expressed … yet in a really useful way due to the distancing experience of putting the feelings 'outside' of the self. Purely by making marks, art therapy allows us space from the experiences that may be felt to be 'too much' in reality … (it) gives these people that little bit of space from having to be so medically treated and 'too feeling' or 'raw'.

Further, the physicality of the art product provides an opportunity to create a tangible object or image to leave behind as a legacy (Connell, 1998). Legacy images or objects allow the possibility to make 'concrete'; to share; and to have witnessed the lived experience of cancer and dying; and the legacy of loss: "they wanted to keep some sort … of tactile object to do with this [two week old] child's feet. We did feet printing … with the Dad and his sibling with his tiny baby's golden feet printed on top".

From initial diagnosis, though treatment, living beyond cancer, or in palliation, patients' lives may become limited by incremental physical losses: "a lot of things are taken away from them – that's a lot of what the work in cancer care that I've found is dealing with the losses". The art therapist is responsive in providing choices: the choice to participate; of manageable materials; and of what is verbally shared or expressed:

> When people become physically diminished due to whatever reasons, then the choice of their materials will be dictated by what they can actually physically do.

Whether part of a multi-disciplinary team or as independent practitioners, therapists working in cancer and palliative care must face loss, suffering and death as a central aspect of their work (Waller and Sibbett, 2005). They bring to the work their own experiences of life, loss, relationships and resilience as a way of connecting and relating to clients, while remaining responsive, resilient and able to survive the uncertainty of the clients' threatened future. The data showed that the suffering, illness and repeated losses of these intimate relationships have an inevitable impact on the therapist working with clients' "illness in all its' guises including nasty, vengeful, 'take people out way' guises".

> When you work in palliative care, death goes home with you at the end of the day, because you are experiencing, whether you want to or not, what is going to happen to you one day.

Denial, avoidance or defensiveness in response to the uncertainty around death and dying appears in the literature (for example, Duesbury, 2005, Hardy, 2005; Yalom, 1980) and in the interviews: "It's really interesting, palliative care - no one actually talks about the actual idea of death … how we feel about it, fear it, how it affects our personal and cultural lives." This sense of existential insecurity and not knowing (Bocking, 2005: 222) similarly affects the way therapists approach their work in cancer and palliative care by "the very nature of knowing … that there is going to be a finite time of how long they live".

> I've been challenged and shaken up by this work and it's been very hard at times and very difficult but the gift for me is being mindful of my own mortality on a very frequent basis.

To be fully present and compassionately resilient when working with clients who are ill, suffering pain, trauma or who are dying and not 'burn out' or collude in denying the intensity of the work (Hardy, 2005), therapists adopt various self-care practices. They may engage in rituals to aid in 'letting go' of particularly intimate relationships. All the participants found professional supervision important (Duesbury, 2005; Sibbett, 2005; Wood, 2005): "I know I need good supervision and I treasure it". However, supervision is not always been adequately provided or accessed: "I've done it mostly alone frankly and that's been fine, that's been okay … at the hospital there was in fact no one qualified to give it to me." The art therapist has another method of self-care to process the many losses, loneliness and frustrations in this work by using their skills and knowledge of art-making and creative processes for "guidance, clarity and stress reduction". Therapeutic response art, as demonstrated during the interviews, was seen as a way of acknowledging, exter-

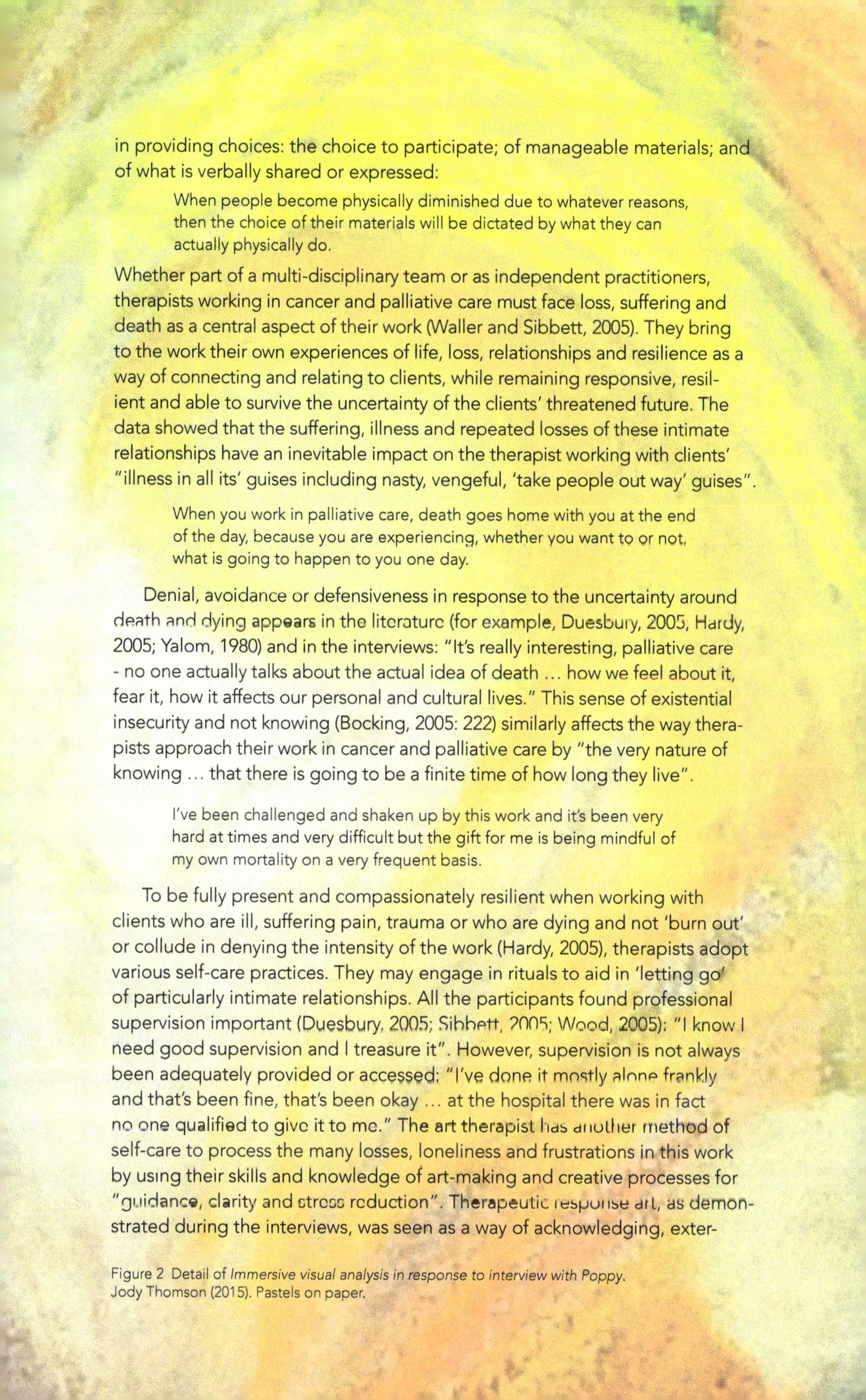

Figure 2 Detail of *Immersive visual analysis in response to interview with Poppy*. Jody Thomson (2015). Pastels on paper.

nalising and making tangible their embodied experience and is an important facet of how the art therapist sustains their practice. Making art was viewed as a way of managing the transition between clients through an "energetic release". Response art may also be used more purposefully to pay tribute to, acknowledge, and process the intensity of clinical engagements:

> I can pay homage, I can pay respect and … honour what I have just witnessed, experienced, maybe meant with a person, in their life and the preciousness of that. So it's pretty special. To me that's charmed and just feels amazing.

However, the degree to which therapists engaged in art-making or other creative processes for clinical processing, supervision or within his or her own professional art practice, I found varied widely among the participants.

The art therapists in this study were variously motivated to *begin* working in cancer care and three had worked in oncology for over ten years. The choice to work over the long-term with cancer patients was inspired by many circumstances: student training placements; as an accompaniment to nursing, social work, counselling or other allied health care; or the availability of employment. As reflected in the literature (for example Duesbury, 2005; Wood, 2005) all the participants spoke of various work-based frustrations, professional loneliness and isolation (Duesbury, 2005; Wood, 2005, Westwood, 2010), even when working within a multi-disciplinary team. These sentiments are reflected in the literature (Duesbury, 2005; Wood, 2005) and in my own experience:

> When I think about what I do, there's a sense of isolation working in this field … So while it is amazing it's still got its own drawbacks, and part of that is that isolation of being specialised.

What was remarkable was the passion, sense of personal satisfaction and motivated commitment that inspired these therapists' to continue with this client group:

> What I find quite inspiring … just seeing people do growth … it makes for a better death.
>
> I'm driven to hang out with people, and to use art to do that hanging out and particularly at the end of their life when a few options have receded from view.

Where the data diverged from, and contributes to, the existing literature related to the perception of value and accessibility of art therapy in psycho-oncology; the struggle for professional acknowledgement of the Australian art therapist working in medical settings; and the work of the independent therapist.

Whilst the value of art therapy was seen as well understood by other members of multi-disciplinary health teams in hospice and community care, the knowledge and understanding of art therapy by hospital management and non-government agency staff was perceived as limited, and a key determinant for accessibility:

> If I kept terming things as 'complementary' it wasn't truly describing what my work was or what client's were receiving. For me, the word 'psychotherapy' needed to reach the table.

The adoption of art therapy within these settings relied on motivated individual mentors and, in some settings, influenced by the therapist having additional and relevant qualifications. Amongst the participants, there was considerable discrepancy:

> … The management people liked the look of something like art therapy and music therapy on their brochures – so we're window dressing really – we're nice dummies to put in the window … The rhetoric of palliative care is holistic and biopsychosocial, but the reality is far more biomedical and the rest is more about image.

> I'm one specialist, working with a team of other specialists …

> I think they value having an art therapist particularly when there are needs and complexities that 'go beyond talking' (using) a process that is tangible for the client (and) recognisable to the team.

Relatedly, professional identity and the struggle for accreditation or professional agency was reflected in various nomenclatures used, and indicative of individual therapeutic approaches. Having a broader skill base in counselling, psychodrama or nursing in addition to art therapy was seen to be of value and had an impact on professional status.

Also absent from the literature is research into the work of the independent art therapy practitioner working with cancer patients in the community and for non-hospice or hospital-based providers. Art therapy in this setting spans the care spectrum from psychotherapeutically focused individual or group therapy, to professionally facilitated art-as-therapy. Therapy in this setting addresses the psychotherapeutic and psychosocial needs of clients for whom the immediate threat of death has receded, yet the physical and psychological impacts and risk of recurrence remains. The latter provides an opportunity for ambulatory patients, carers and those living beyond cancer to find a sense of belonging "through art and being inspired" and feeling understood by others who are facing similar challenges.

The perceived value of art therapy in this setting was difficult to gauge: "If I were to ask (the service providers) specifically what they thought was valuable about it I think they might be hard pressed to answer". Employment relied on the individual's entrepreneurial efforts (Westwood, 2010) and "years of building relationships" with other allied health professionals.

This work is transient and potentially isolating without the supportive framework of a multi-disciplinary team: "I fly in, I fly out … delivering a service, evaluating, giving feedback … but at the end of the day, I take responsibility for the work that I deliver". Interestingly, psycho-education with this client group was seen as "an important adjunct" in group interventions, and was discussed by two of the participants. This facet of practice demonstrates the flexibility of art therapy in providing not only the creative process but on-going skills and information to cancer patients and their families.

The first interview. Poppy: relationship, connectedness and compassion

In a tiny, windowless, book-filled space deep inside a quaint old city building, Poppy spoke with enormous enthusiasm, compassion, empathy and a profound respect for human suffering. She told a story about the mutual affection and intimacy of a long-term therapy relationship she had with a cancer patient and his family. She spoke about her intersecting roles as a nurse and an art therapist and about the lasting legacy work made by her client, supported by an inspired mentor.

Figure 3 is the image Poppy made towards the end of the interview. The following text is an excerpt of her narrative response to the artwork.

> 'Till we Meet Again' which was perfect – because I was feeling quite sad that my (client) is dying – yes I felt some loss about that and the ending of our work together and the ending of his life, so I just tore the paper and actually wanted to get rid of the straight edges. I needed it to line up, and as I was doing it I thought oh yeah the frame, I needed to contain it. So I continued with the tearing and the sticking and the water colour pencils, following the line and then a tree emerged to the left hand side with roots – I use trees as a symbol of resilience with some of my clients and my roots are fairly long and grounded and my trunk has music and strength but has got many sides to it. At the top of the page there are three almost mountains ... sort of like undulations and now I think it's the sort of ups and down of our practice in art therapy and when you get close to a client and you feel there is some connection … they colour your life but … there is a letting go … you know right from the start that there will be sadness – there's loss on many levels … I think for people that know they are dying … it can be very lonely.
>
> From her ocean and his, a revealing of intertwinement flowing and encircling immersive spaces, until the intimate bond of the lemniscate is broken at the death of one, and yet his colours remain, blending on the palette with her life-path, building deep water intensity, then ebbing and re-turning in witness of his legacy.

When I began my immersive visual analysis (Figure 4) after Poppy's interview, hearing again her voice alongside her image, I was taken back to that airless space. I sensed a shift in her tone and remembered the weightiness in her posture as she massaged and smoothed her image. Poppy spoke slowly and softly of her sadness about working with a terminally ill patient; of the loneliness of dying; of resilience and boundaries bent under the weight of a client's finite time to live when the marking of time, like the beat of music, takes on a new meaning. Her story was about therapeutic 'love' and the struggle to stay contained and grounded through loss when needing to let go. In finishing, I was left exhausted, and very moved.

Figure 3 *Art response to interview.*
Poppy (2015). Collage and watercolour.

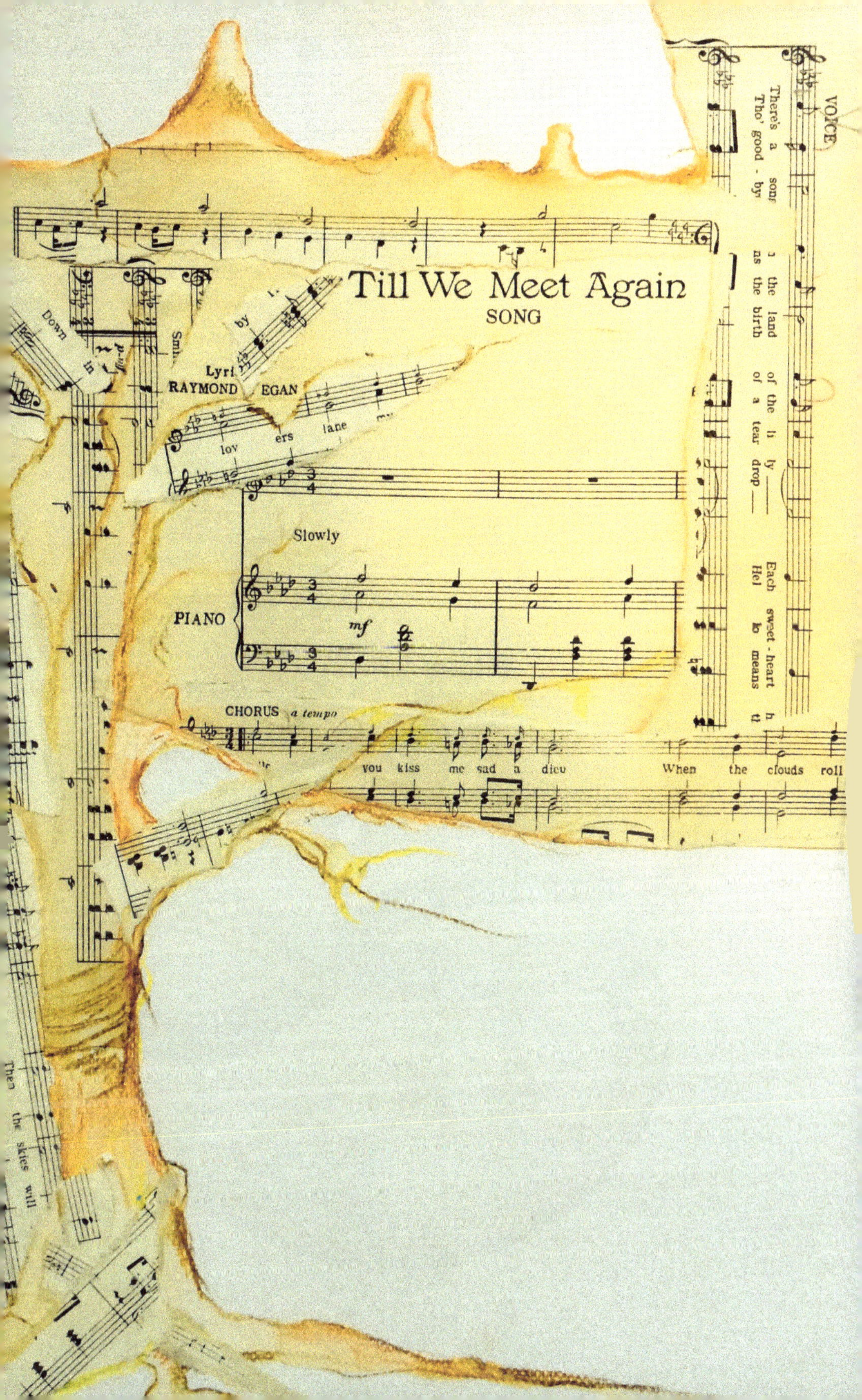
Till We Meet Again
SONG
Lyri
RAYMOND EGAN
Slowly
PIANO
CHORUS a tempo
you kiss me sad a dieu
When the clouds roll
lov ers lane
VOICE
There's a song the land of the li ly
Tho' good-bye the birth of a tear drop
Each sweet-heart
Hel lo means
Down in
Then the skies will

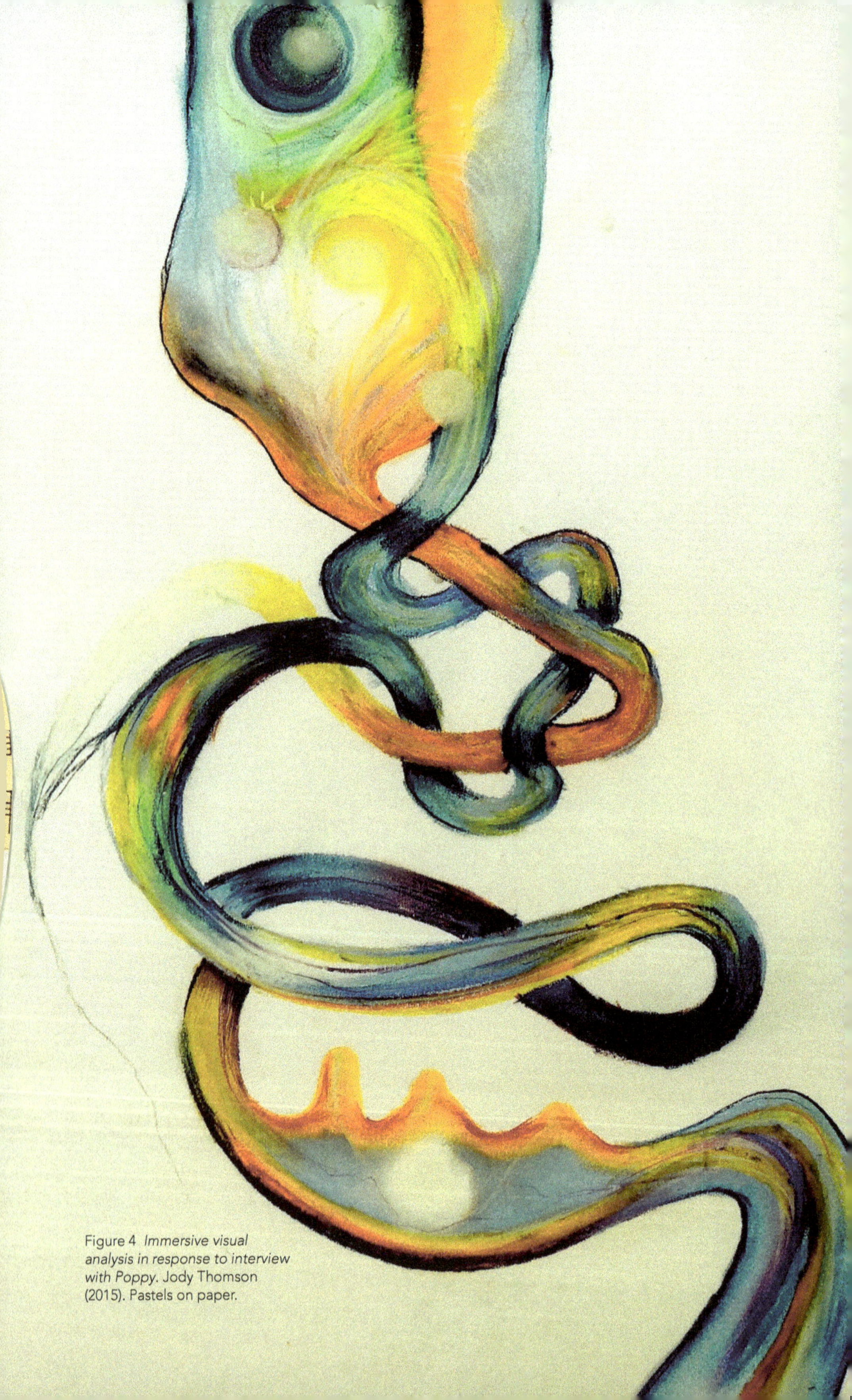

Figure 4 *Immersive visual analysis in response to interview with Poppy.* Jody Thomson (2015). Pastels on paper.

The last interview. Byron: reality – trauma, intimacy, loneliness and denial

In another tiny windowless room next to a raucous group of women, Byron spoke philosophically of intimacy, danger, frustration and of poignant loneliness, and of his personal and professional experiences around dying and death. He is a poet who finds solace in words. At the end of our conversation Byron made an image (Figure 5, speaking slowly and curiously in a dual role as self-therapist. I was largely silent, an observer, as Byron narrated his image as he was making it: about fear, danger, barriers and perspective, and of the line between witnessing and participating.

> Words are very white aren't they … and they seem to float through the air. They're very insubstantial words aren't they – they kind of float – so it seems to me that they're safe - something very, very safe about words – everyone is comfortable with words. I think we've got good control over the meanings we wish to convey with words, but boy we lose that with imagery don't we … So we identify … some sort of focus that we create an image from. I think this is about perspective - gaining perspective through insights that come up through talking about an image … I will say to people, 'where are you' in the image? That … brings me to the notion of being on the stage … I'm inviting them to place themselves on the stage in a particular position. I'm backstage, I never get in the spotlight – I'm out the front but I can't speak because I've never had a voice to speak with something like that … that's what the person would say in response to me … because I think when we start talking about pictures in a certain way you're talking directly to the unconscious … All we know is that when you investigate images, you find stuff, that you didn't know was there …
>
> I might ask about this picture here – 'I'm wondering why that black needs to be – does that black need to be around that? Or is it just there'? 'No – it needs to be around that?' 'Oh – so why does it need to be around that? Because that mustn't get out! … so then you can come to 'what is it in you that mustn't get out' and it can be something … people have been holding onto … I know it looks angry doesn't it? Hmmm, yes, I think I know what that is … I didn't plan on that! – don't you hate images?
>
> I see myself reflecting on something – I'm the observer of … the life I could be leading. And it's very alive and quite sharp … I'm in the audience looking at it – and there's something, a very safe barrier there – that barrier is keeping me safe yes – but, I'm absolutely held within this - I'm spellbound by it … I'm observing what can't get out … that has to do with fulfillment and living a fulfilled life … I always get people to do is title their pictures … [Byron titles his image] "safety". Because if we don't create we stay safe and creativity is dangerous … that blue makes this orange feel calmer … so it relieves the pressure … from the focus somewhat. So then you could ask a question like … 'what's the focus that needs pressure taken off?' … To be honest with you, I don't feel much pressure in the work, to be honest.

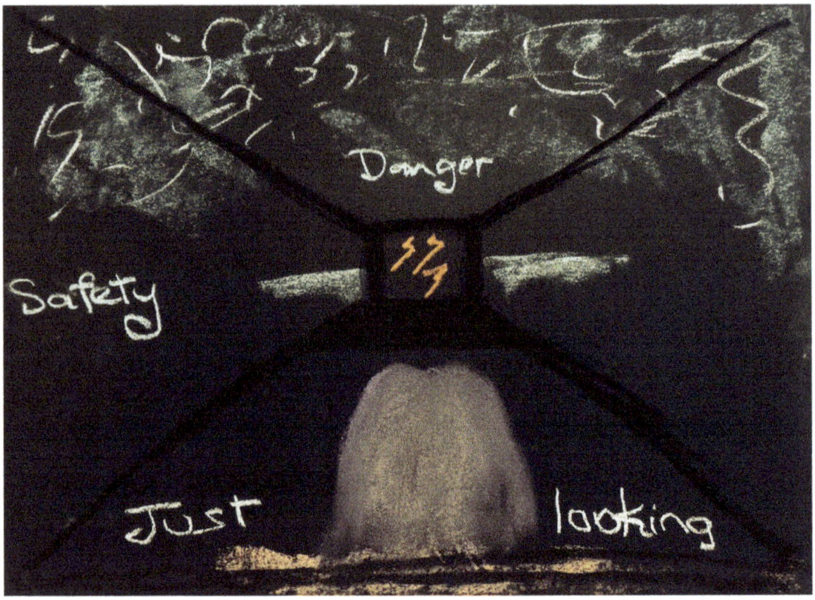

Figure 5 *Art response to interview.* Byron (2015). Pastels on paper.

The dragons eye.
The denial of death filling the sinus
And in it's gaping maw,
finding beauty and delight in warm connections
born of mutually honoured trauma.
It is a story about danger,
And of ultimately walking alone.

As my immersive analysis of Byron's interview (Figure 6, *opposite*) wound down the page, I became aware of how colours unconsciously took on themes, and how the many tangents and diversions in the spoken interview were mirrored in the turnings and changes of direction in my image. There was an unspoken colour of denial, moving around and enclosing the shapes and colours of anger and frustration. Other colours became loneliness, yearning and humour – dark at times, though not uncomfortably so. Mostly, there was compassion and gentle kindness. I left the interview, and my image-making, with a sense of loneliness, of having ended too soon with much more to say, and feeling that I had missed something.

Figure 6 *Immersive visual analysis in response to interview with Byron*. Jody Thomson (2015). Pastels on paper.

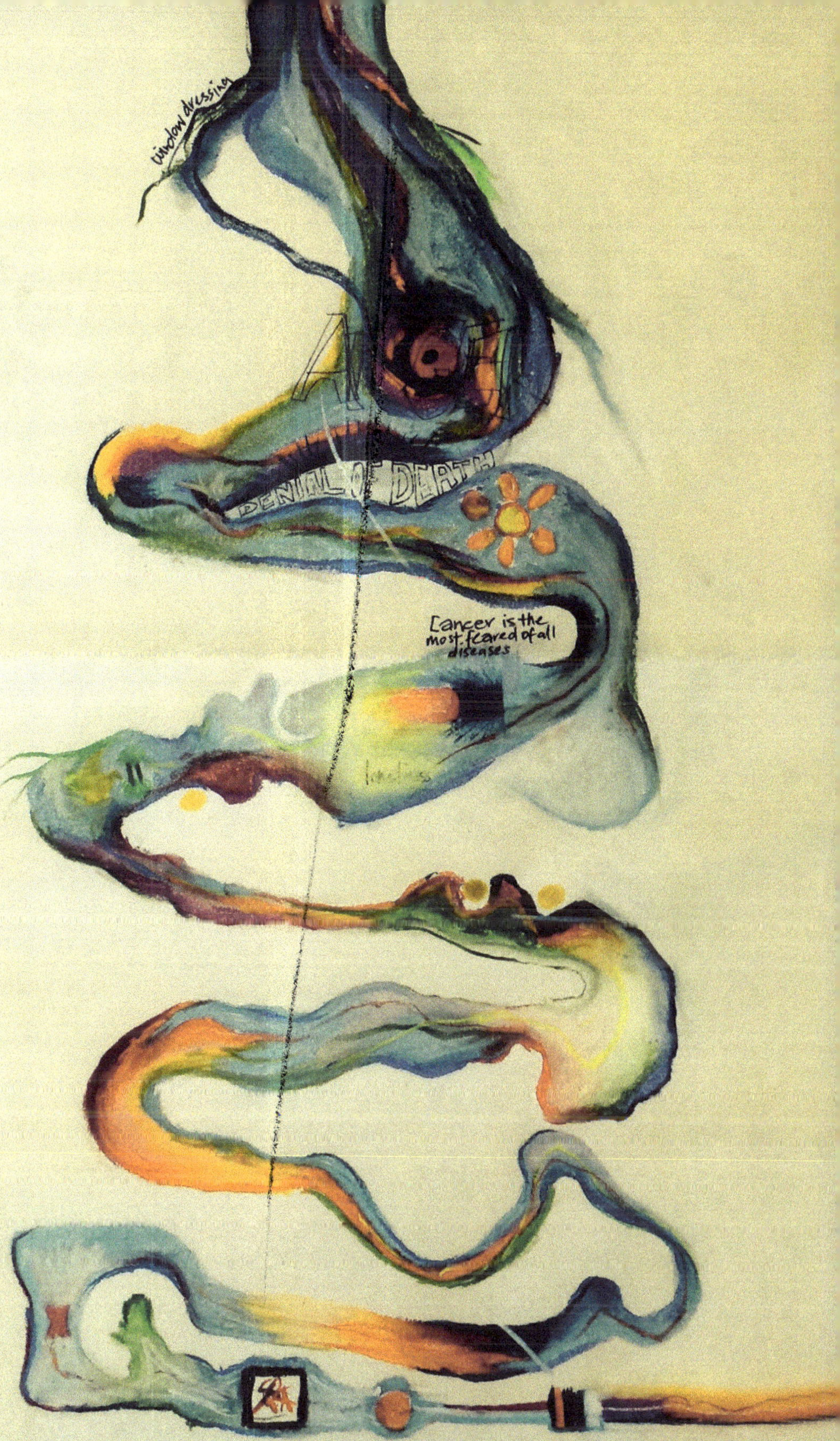
window dressing
DENIAL OF DEATH
Cancer is the most feared of all diseases

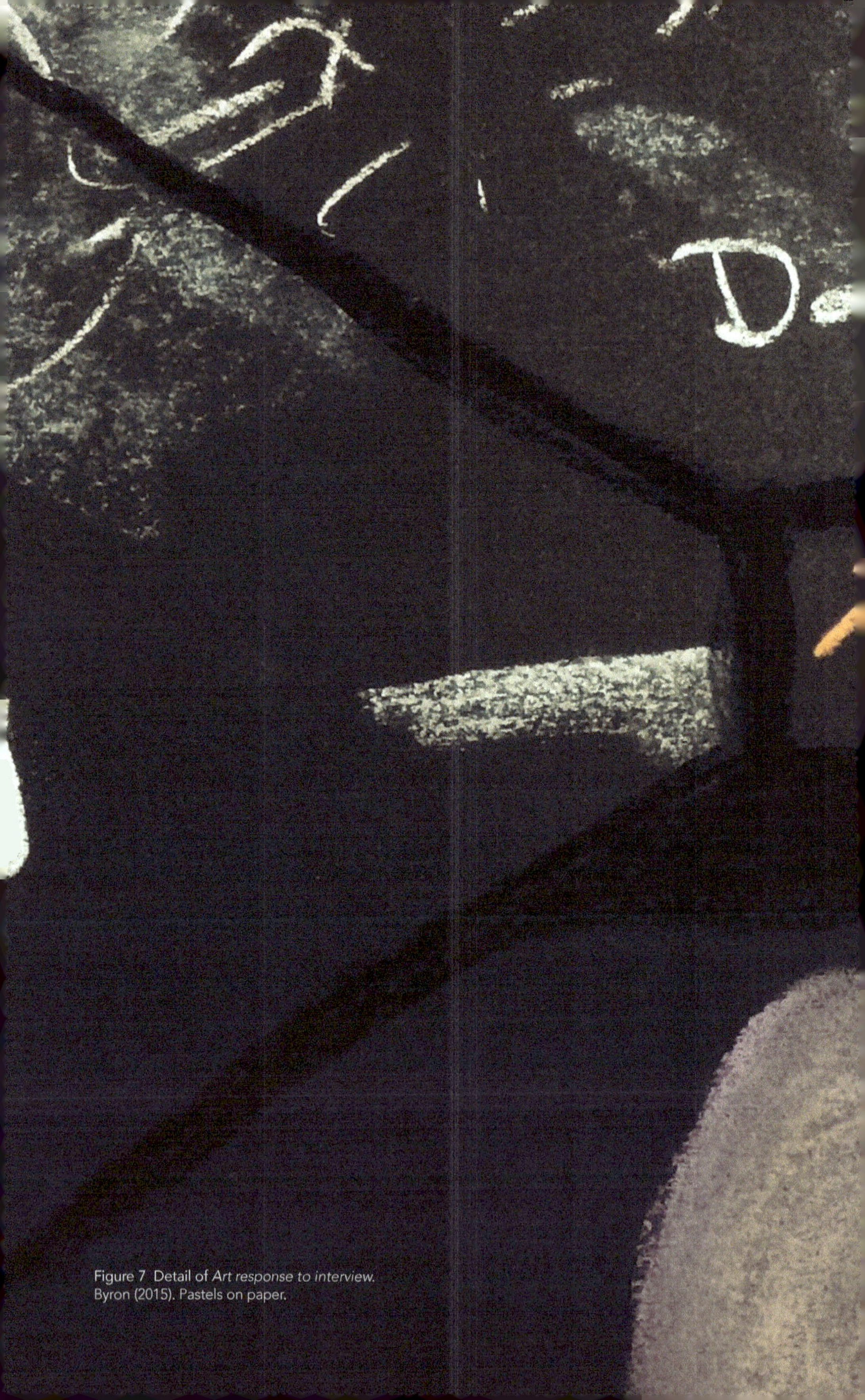

Figure 7 Detail of *Art response to interview.*
Byron (2015). Pastels on paper.

Discussion and conclusion: drawing it all together

In this chapter I have presented the method and product of a recent study[3] with four visual art therapists, exploring their professional and lived experience of working with cancer patients in Australian allied health. Informed by my own clinical work in psycho-oncology, my research aims were firstly to investigate how art therapists perceived the value of art therapy with cancer patients in various settings; what motivated them and the ways in which they sustained their practice; and how they responded to, and were affected by working with this client group. Secondly, I was intrigued by how incorporating art-making by the participants in addition to semi-structured interviews *as data*, and my own *in response* to the data might generate more nuanced insights.

My methodological '(bri)col(l)age' emerged in response to the research. It opened a space for the participants to express not only their professional knowledge but to access through art-making their subjective, lived experiences in a tangible and observable way. Participating as a witness to this creative process, and responding with my own perspectival immersive visual analysis, opened a pathway to a different quality of understanding that I used to guide an inductive analysis of the data.

Insights emerged through the semi-structured verbal interviews that *outwardly* addressed my research questions, confirming and diverging from the limited research that exists on the experience of the art therapist in the following ways.

As reflected in the literature, the therapists in my study perceived that the value of art therapy is its provision of a genuine, direct and companioning relationship. This relationship was perceived as more intimate, poignant and time-pressured with people suffering trauma, pain or existential distress caused by the experience of cancer. Witnessing the art-making and reflecting on the art product were seen as integral to this relationship in providing an alternate or different way of communicating, externalising and understanding the client's 'unspeakable' experience of cancer and possibly facilitating personal growth, even at end of life. Further, with this client group, the art images created in therapy may become 'legacy' pieces, not only of the therapeutic relationship but also as lasting gifts of memory, or of a life-in-memoriam made concrete.

The therapists in my research work as specialists on psycho-oncology and have made a long-term commitment to this client group. The data showed that this work involves cumulative losses, reflexive existential concerns, sadness and work-based frustrations. In order to bear and carry on their work with cancer patients the therapists utilised their skills in art-making and other creative self-care processes in addition to, or aiding, professional supervision to varying degrees. Most remarkable was the passion and commitment that I heard and sensed and how the participants experienced the work as an inspiring, meaningful privilege.

3 Thomson, J. (2015). From the therapist's brush: painting a picture of the art therapist's experience in Australian cancer care. Unpublished thesis: Western Sydney University.

This research makes a contribution to the existing literature in three areas. The first relates to the perceived value of art therapy and the art therapist's professional identity in Australian psycho-oncology in various medical settings. Accessibility and the value placed on the flexible and systemically inclusive approach by art therapists working with those living with, or dying from, cancer was seen as largely determined by the knowledge and understanding of individual mentors or service managers. Similarly, the art therapists' agency within these settings was seen as compromised by a lack of well-articulated information in a form valued by the positivist world of medicine. Secondly, the research contributes insight into the challenges and practices of the independent art therapist in cancer care. Intriguingly, the loneliness and isolation that may be experienced by cancer patients finds a parallel in the work of the independent art therapist, without the framework and support of a multi-disciplinary team.

Finally, the study provided an answer to my research question of the ways in which visual art-making might facilitate a more nuanced view. I found that *including the art-making process* within the interviews enabled an emergent possibility of knowing differently (Liamputtong and Rumbold, 2008), *inwardly*, opening another pathway for generating insight into the art therapists' lived experience and the ways in which the work affects them. Further, my research demonstrated the capacity of art to contain and work with the apparent contradiction of, or *productive tension between*, the idea of illuminating experience and meaning-making, which was simultaneously *truthful* and faithful to the participants, and *perspectival* in my response as researcher. As in art therapy practice, my art-informed research resulted in tangible objects born of conversation, art-making and reflection; containing, embodying and acknowledging tacit knowledge understood and shared between colleagues. It has provided a deeper understanding of the therapist's lived experience, using shared creative expression to open liminal spaces for discovery, communication and facilitate connectedness. Participating in the art therapy method with colleagues as a researcher has deepened both my learning about the quality and texture of relationship, the intimacy enabled by the art-making process, and respect for the power and potential of images to embody a different form of knowing.

> Four independent yet similar rivers form the 'head' of this odd-looking creature. It is concerned with thoughts and words; of communicating what is known. Flowing down, intertwining, connecting through line colour, form and texture. Warming through the art-making to find liminal and shared spaces, of something understood. One moves on prematurely, pushing away intimacy, disconnected and defended by words like self-reliance and independence, perhaps masking a need to belong. Strikingly similar, three others flow on and continue to dance around each other, sharing what is deeply understood: resilience and respect; strength and sadness; frustration and loneliness.

Figure 8 *Research response image: Painting a picture of art therapy in Australian cancer care.* Jody Thomson (2015). Pastels on paper.

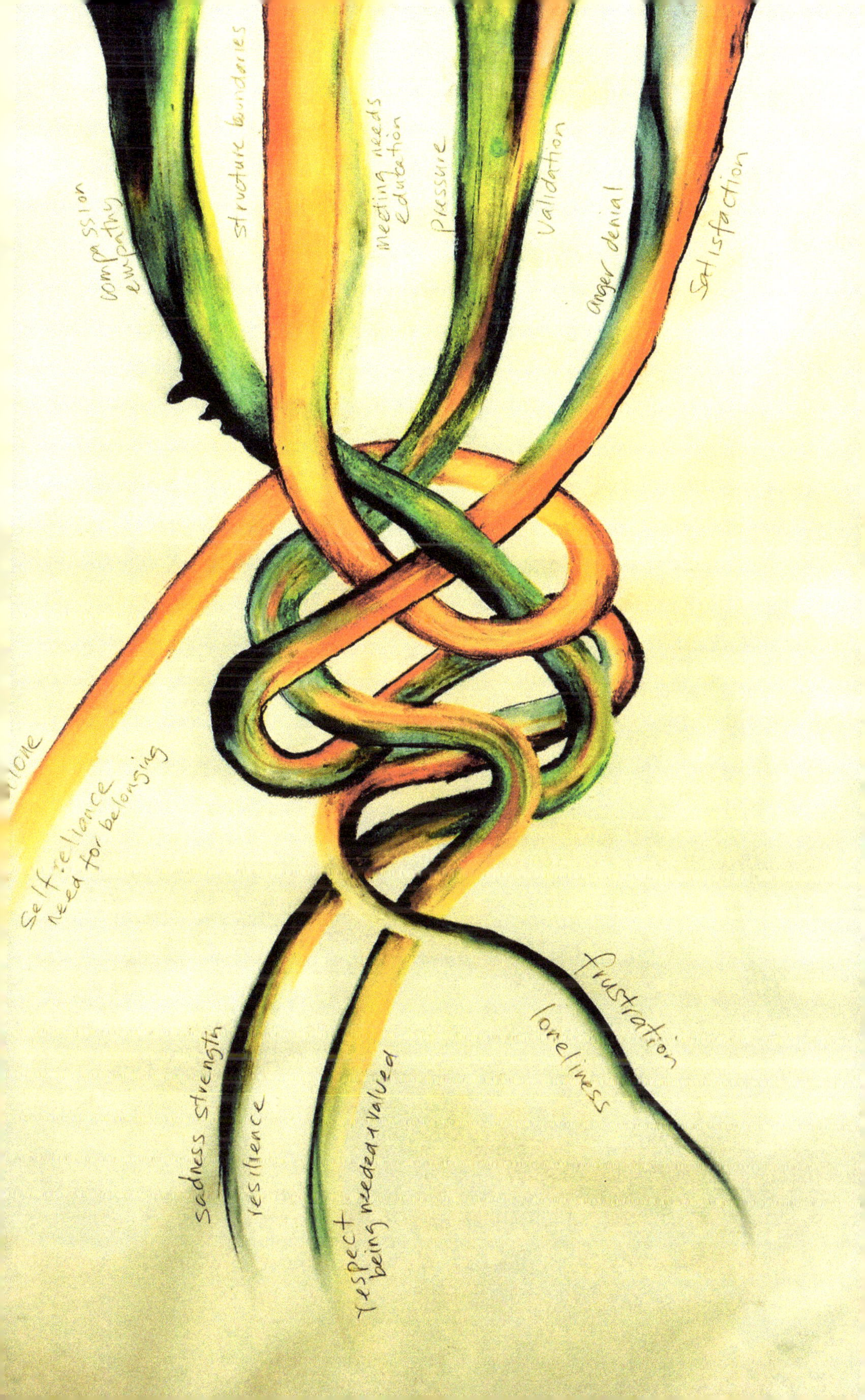
compassion
empathy
structure boundaries
meeting needs
education
pressure
validation
anger denial
satisfaction
self reliance
need for belonging
frustration
loneliness
sadness strength
resilience
respect
being needed + valued

References

Allen, P. (1995). *Art is a way of knowing*. Shambala, Boston and London.

Barone. T. and Eisner, E. (2012). *Arts based research*. Sage, Los Angeles and London.

Bocking, M. (2005). A 'don't know' story: Art therapy in an NHS medical oncology department. In: Waller, D. and Sibbett, C. (Eds.) (2005) *Art therapy and cancer care*. Open University Press, Maidenhead.

Connell C. (1998). *Something understood. Art therapy in cancer care.* Wrexham Publications, London.

Csikszentmihalyi, M. (2002). *Flow*. Rider, London.

Duesbury, T. (2005). Art therapy in the hospice: Rewards and frustrations. In: Waller, D. and Sibbett, C. (2005). (Eds.) *Art therapy and cancer care*. Open University Press, Berkshire, England and New York.

Finley, S. (2014). An Introduction to critical arts-based research: Demonstrating methodologies and practices of a radical ethical aesthetic. *Cultural Studies <-> Critical Methodologies*, 14(6): 531–532.

Fish, B. (2012). Response art: The art of the art therapist. *Art Therapy: Journal of the American Art Therapy Association*, 29(3): 138–143.

Hardy, D. (2005). Creating through loss: How art therapists sustain their practice. In: Waller, D. and Sibbett, C. (2005) (Eds.) *Art therapy and cancer care*. Open University Press, Berkshire, England and New York.

Heidegger, M. (1962). *Being and time* (Macquarrie, J. and Robinson, E. Trans.). Harper and Row, New York.

Hogan, S. and Pink, S. (2012). Visualising interior worlds: Interdisciplinary routes to knowing. In: Pink, S. (2012) (Ed.). *Advances in visual methodology*. Sage, London.

Kerr, I. (1998). Art therapy, psychological support and cancer care. In: Connell, C. (1998) *Something understood. Art therapy in cancer care*. Wrexham Publications, London.

Leavy, P. (2015). *Method meets art: Arts-based research practice* (2nd edition). Guilford Press, New York.

Liamputtong, P. and Rumbold, J. (2008) (Eds.) *Knowing differently. Arts-based and collaborative research methods*. Nova, New York.

McLeod, J. (2001). *Qualitative research in counselling and psychotherapy*. Sage, London and Thousand Oaks, CA.

McNiff, S. (1998). *Art-based research*. Jessica Kingsley Publications, London.

McNiff, S. (2008). Art-based research. In: Knowles, J. and Cole, A. *Handbook of the arts in qualitative research: Perspectives, methodologies, examples, and issues*. Sage, Thousand Oaks, CA.

McNiff, S. (2014). Art speaking for itself: Evidence that inspires and convinces. *Journal of Applied Arts and Health*, 5(2): 255–262.

Moustakas, C. (1994). *Phenomenological research methods*. Sage, Thousand Oaks CA.

Pink, S., Hogan, S. and Bird, J. (2011). Intersections and inroads: Art therapy's contribution to visual methods. *International Journal of Art Therapy:* formerly *Inscape*, 16(1): 14–19.

Pratt M. and Wood M. (1998). (Eds.) *Art therapy in palliative care: The creative response*. Routledge, London, Canada and New York.

Rose, G. (2012). *Visual methodologies: An introduction to researching with visual materials (3rd edn)*. Sage, London.

Rumbold, J., Fenner, P. and Brophy-Dixon, J. (2012). The risks of representation: dilemmas and opportunities in art-based research. *Journal of Applied Arts and Health* 3 (1): 67–78.

Sibbett, C. (2005). Liminal embodiment: embodied and sensory experience in cancer care and art therapy. In: Waller, D. and Sibbett, C. (2005) (Eds.) *Art therapy and cancer care*. Open University Press, Berkshire, England and New York.

Skaife, S. (1993). Sickness, health and the therapeutic relationship: Thoughts arising from the literature on art therapy and physical illness. *Inscape, Summer:* 24–29.

Thomson, J. (2016). Beneath the surface: The lived experience of the art therapist. *ANZJAT Australian and New Zealand Journal of Arts Therapy*, 11(1): 25–37.

Thorley, C. (2005). Illness, recovery and renewal – and the role of creative painting experiences. Unpublished MA Thesis, *University of South Australia*.

Wadeson, H. C. (2011). *Journaling cancer in words and images. Caught in the clutch of the crab*. Charles C. Thomas, Springfield USA.

Waller, D. and Sibbett, C. (2005). (Eds) *Art therapy in cancer care*. Open University Press, Maidenhead, UK.

Westwood, J. (2010). Hybrid creatures. Mapping the emerging shape of art therapy education in Australia. Unpublished PhD Thesis. University of Western Sydney, Research Centre for Social Justice and Social Change.

Wood, M. (2005). Shoreline: The realities of working in cancer care and palliative care. In: Waller, D. and Sibbett, C. (2005) (Eds.) *Art therapy and cancer care*. Open University Press, Berkshire, England and New York.

Yalom, I. (1980). *Existential psychotherapy*. Basic Books, New York.

Zammit, C. (1999). The art of healing: A journey through cancer, implications for art therapy. MA Art Therapy thesis, Edith Cowan University, Western Australia.

Zammit, C. (2001). The art of healing: A journey through cancer: Implications for art therapy. *Art Therapy: Journal of the American Art Therapy Association*, 18(1): 27–36.

Zammit, C. (2008). The experience of dying: A reflective topical autobiography. Unpublished PhD thesis, *Southern Cross University, Lismore, NSW.*

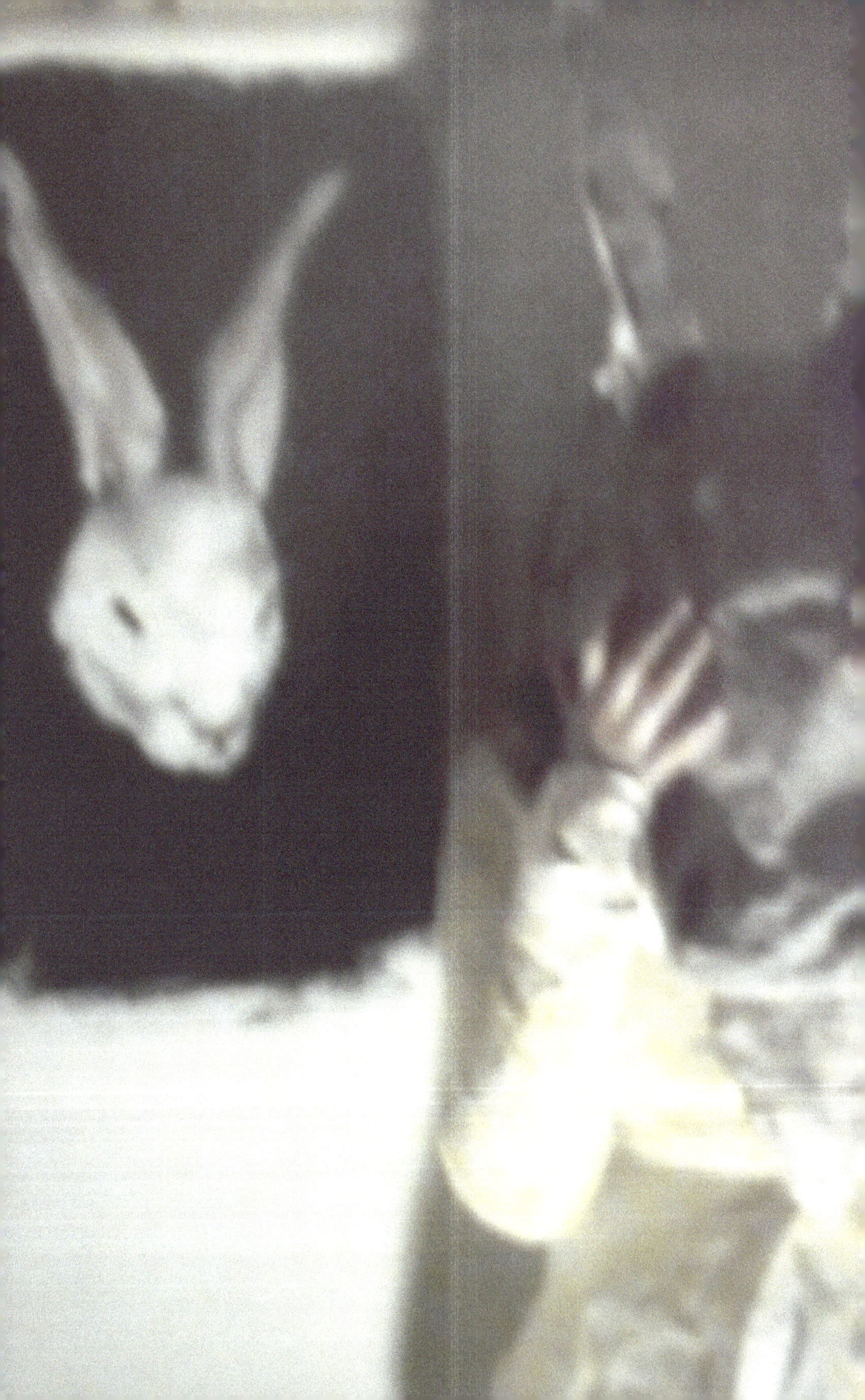

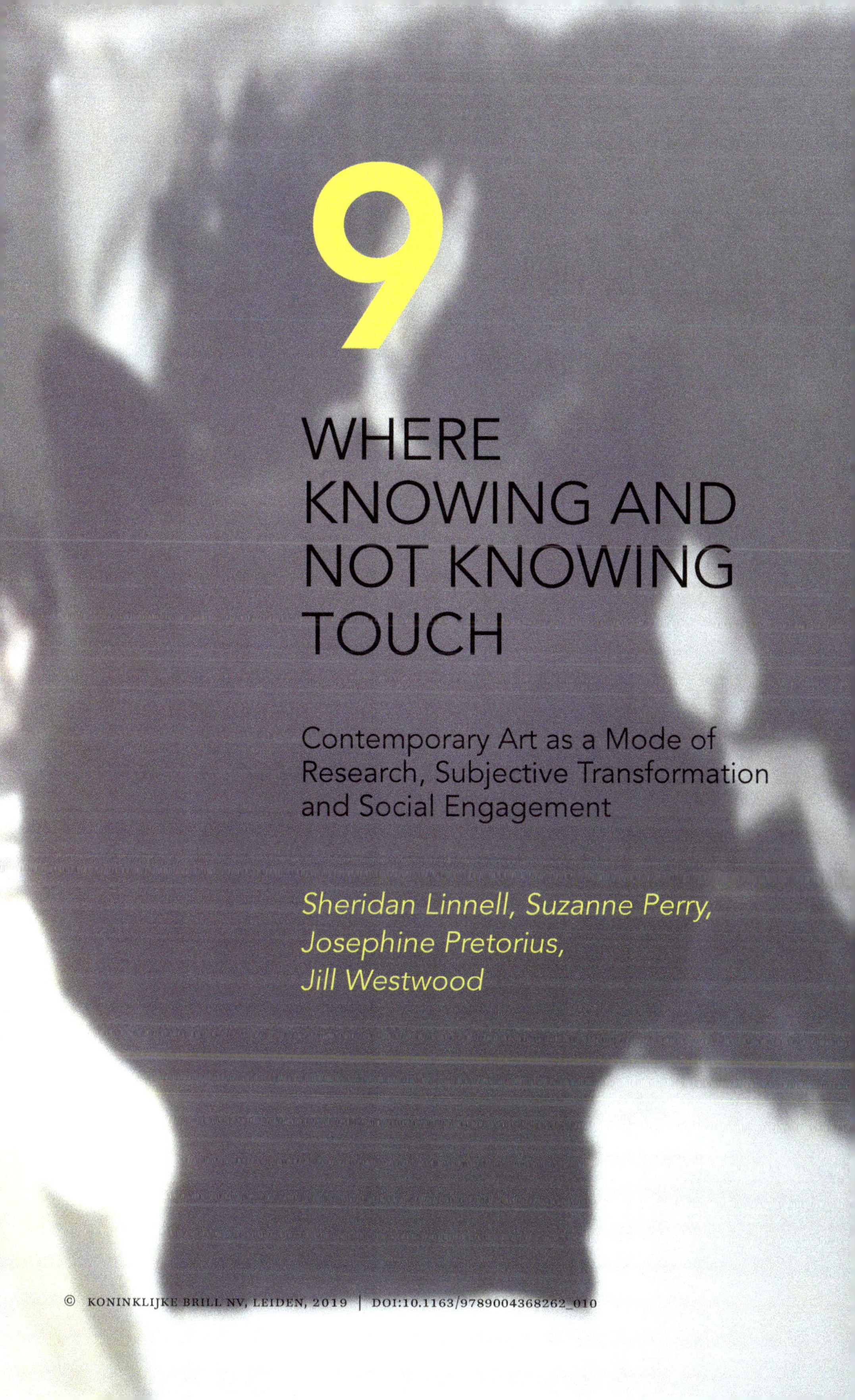

9

WHERE KNOWING AND NOT KNOWING TOUCH

Contemporary Art as a Mode of Research, Subjective Transformation and Social Engagement

Sheridan Linnell, Suzanne Perry, Josephine Pretorius, Jill Westwood

 | DOI:10.1163/9789004368262_010

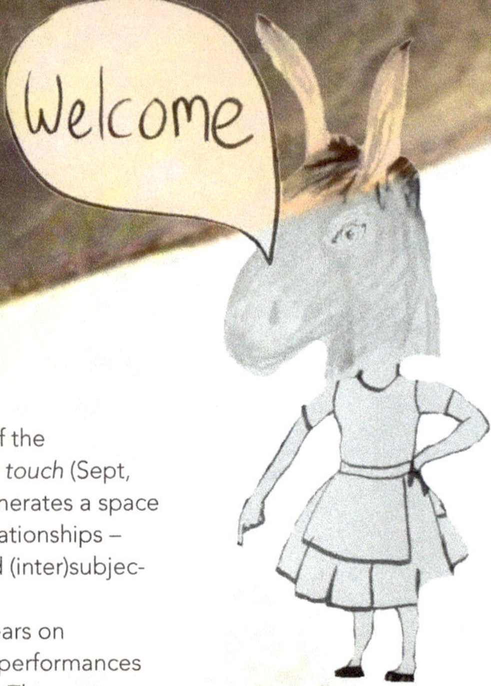

In this chapter we offer a creative account of the exhibition *Where knowing and not knowing touch* (Sept, 2007), as part of an ongoing project that generates a space for questioning binaries and researching relationships – between artist and audience, aesthetics and (inter)subjectivity, the psychic and the social.

We worked collaboratively for several years on site-specific art installations and interactive performances while teaching together in the Master of Art Therapy and Graduate Diploma in Expressive Therapies at the University of Western Sydney[1] (Linnell, Perry, Pretorius and Westwood, 2005, 2006, 2007; Perry and Westwood 2006, 2007; Westwood 2008). While we conceptualise our collaborations as contemporary art, our positioning across the domains of art, therapy and education challenges the separation of the aesthetic sphere.

As artists and art therapists we are primarily concerned with a *relational aesthetics* (Bourriaud, 1998/2002; Hyland Moon, 2002), with the subjective, relational and emotional resonances of art. In our work we aim to open up a critical site for moments of aesthetic experience that connect and resonate with our audiences in surprising and moving ways. Our work is at once theoretically informed and immediately accessible, a paradox that draws attention to the complex yet everyday character of becoming our 'selves'.

As educators and activists we aspire to a *pedagogy of hope* (Freire, 1994) that contributes to shaping creative possibilities for social change, although rather than 'raising consciousness', our work disturbs and arouses something at the edges of consciousness and intentionality. We attempt – and we also notice how we inevitably fail – "not to foreclose on the ethical resource that inheres in uncertainty" (Butler, 2001: 34).

1 Now known as Western Sydney University

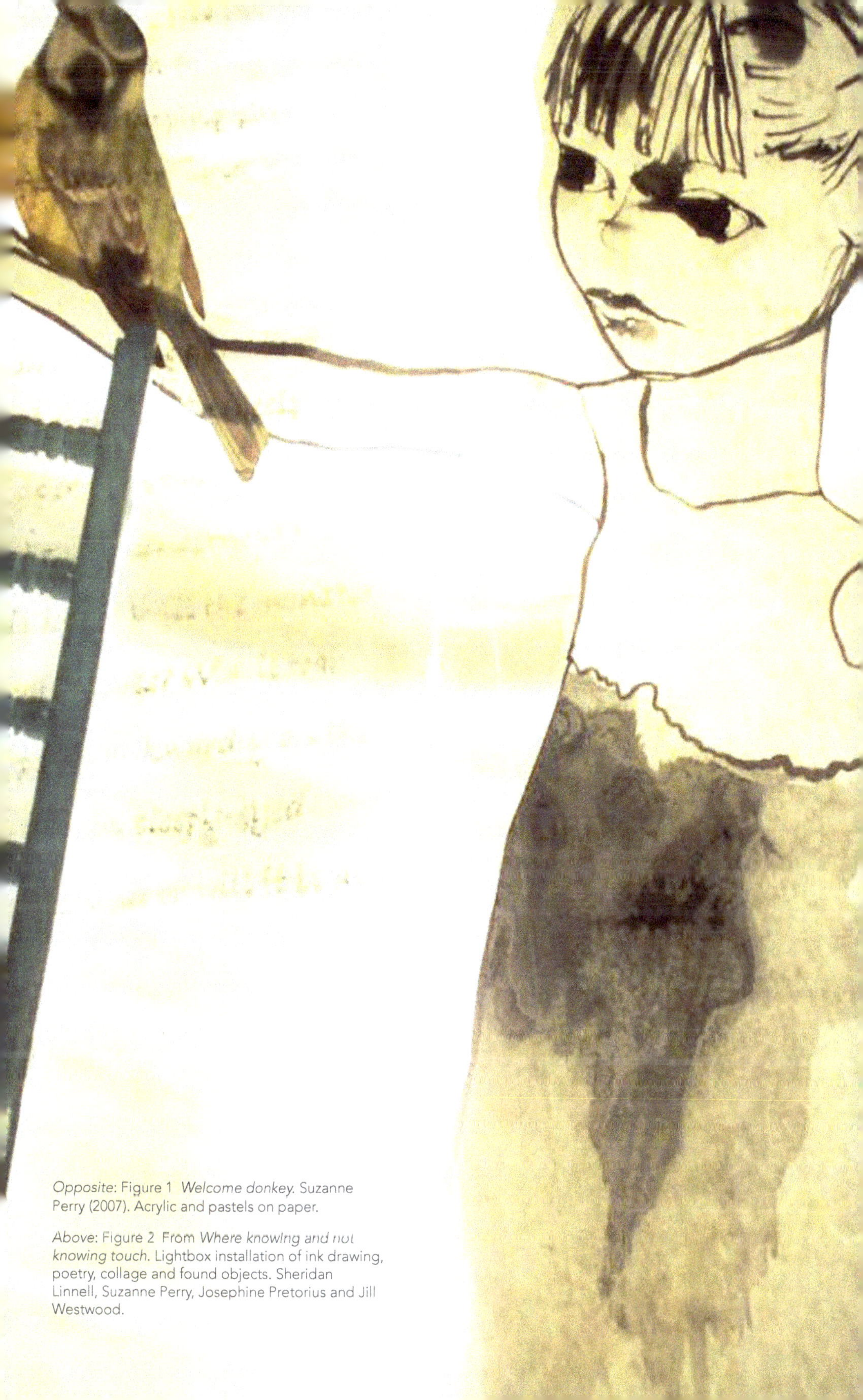

Opposite: Figure 1 *Welcome donkey*. Suzanne Perry (2007). Acrylic and pastels on paper.

Above: Figure 2 From *Where knowing and not knowing touch*. Lightbox installation of ink drawing, poetry, collage and found objects. Sheridan Linnell, Suzanne Perry, Josephine Pretorius and Jill Westwood.

Working with film, photography, drawing, painting, writing and installation, with made and found objects and memorabilia, we explore the intersections of memory and imagination. We bring spaces that are generally experienced as private and interior into a social and cultural domain, connecting and blurring our early biographies and re-collected images, creating memories and fictions of childhood that are somehow more resonant and 'true' than the story of any one of us alone. We create a play of ambiguities, a *hauntology* (Venn, 2002) of figures and shadows that play across a suggestive emotional landscape. We touch upon unspeakable moments of love and connectedness, of fear and loss.

We locate this work alongside that of other contemporary artists who "engage modes of embodied perception as a means of understanding mourning in a lived place" (Bennett, 2005: 70). Such art is haunted by our radical dependence on others, by ambivalent feelings of trust and fear, hinting at environments and experiences that may be sinister or sublime. We work on the borders of knowing and unknowing, attempting to make visible that which is hidden or inaccessible. Through processes of remembering that are shadowed by traces of what cannot be remembered, we research the powerful and ordinary intertwining of psychic and social life (c.f. Butler, 1997).

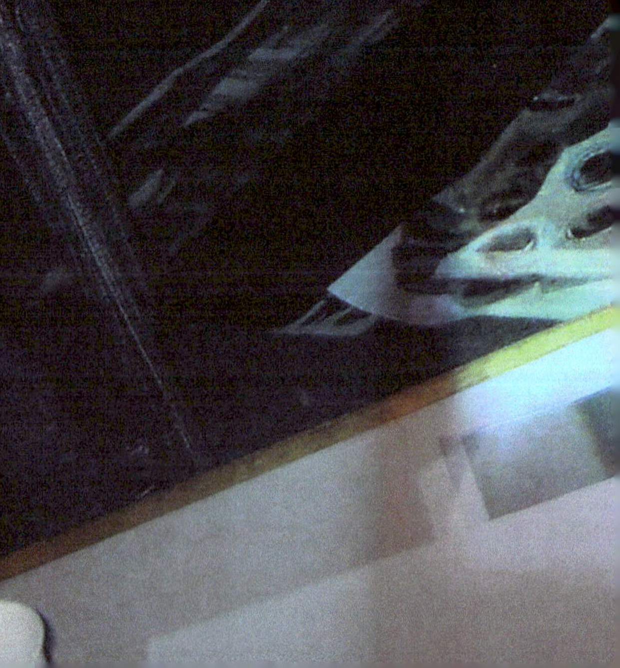

Figure 3 Where knowing and not knowing touch. Sheridan Linnell, Suzanne Perry, Josephine Pretorius and Jill Westwood (2007). Installation, lightbox and mixed media, ink, watercolour and collage.

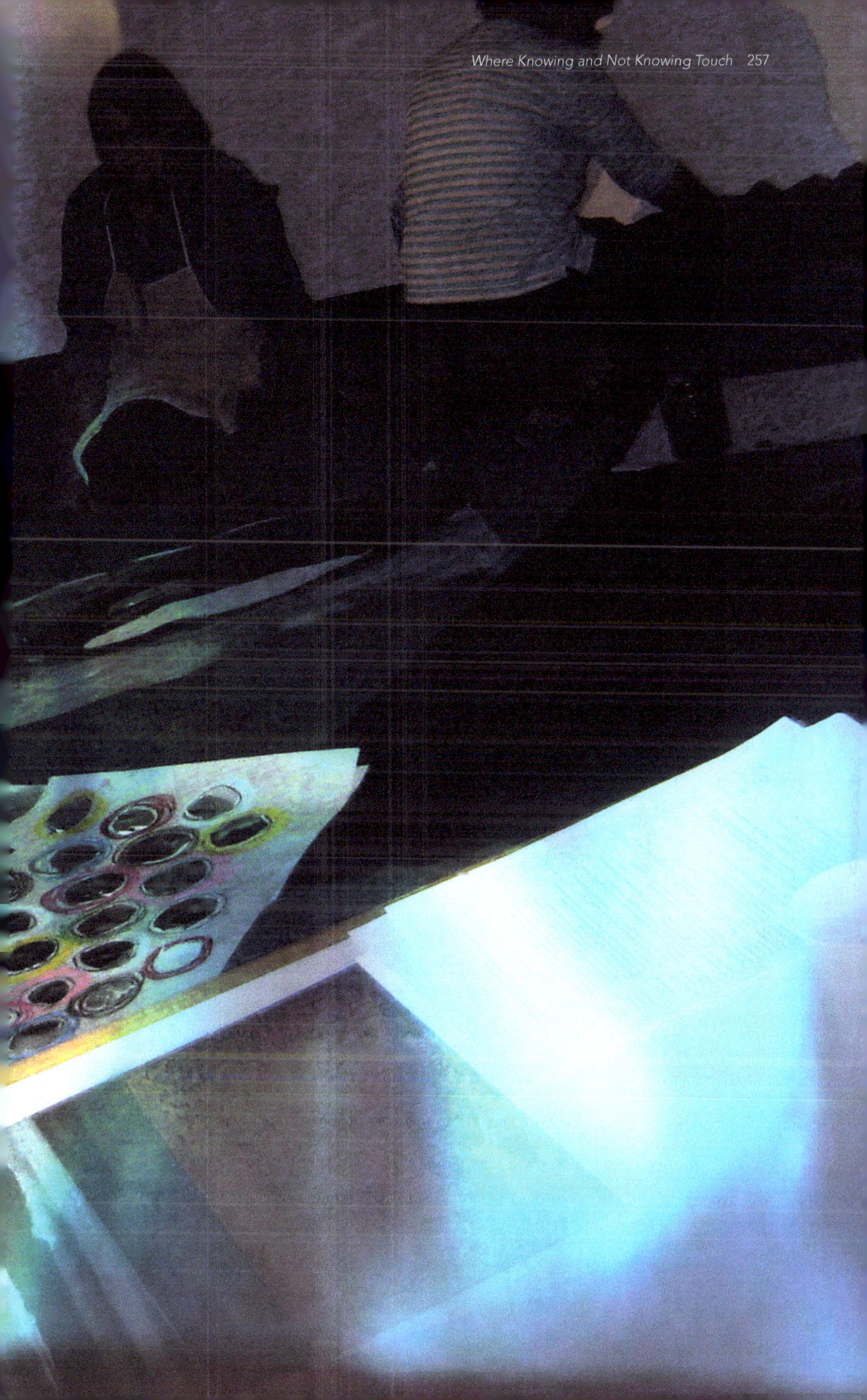

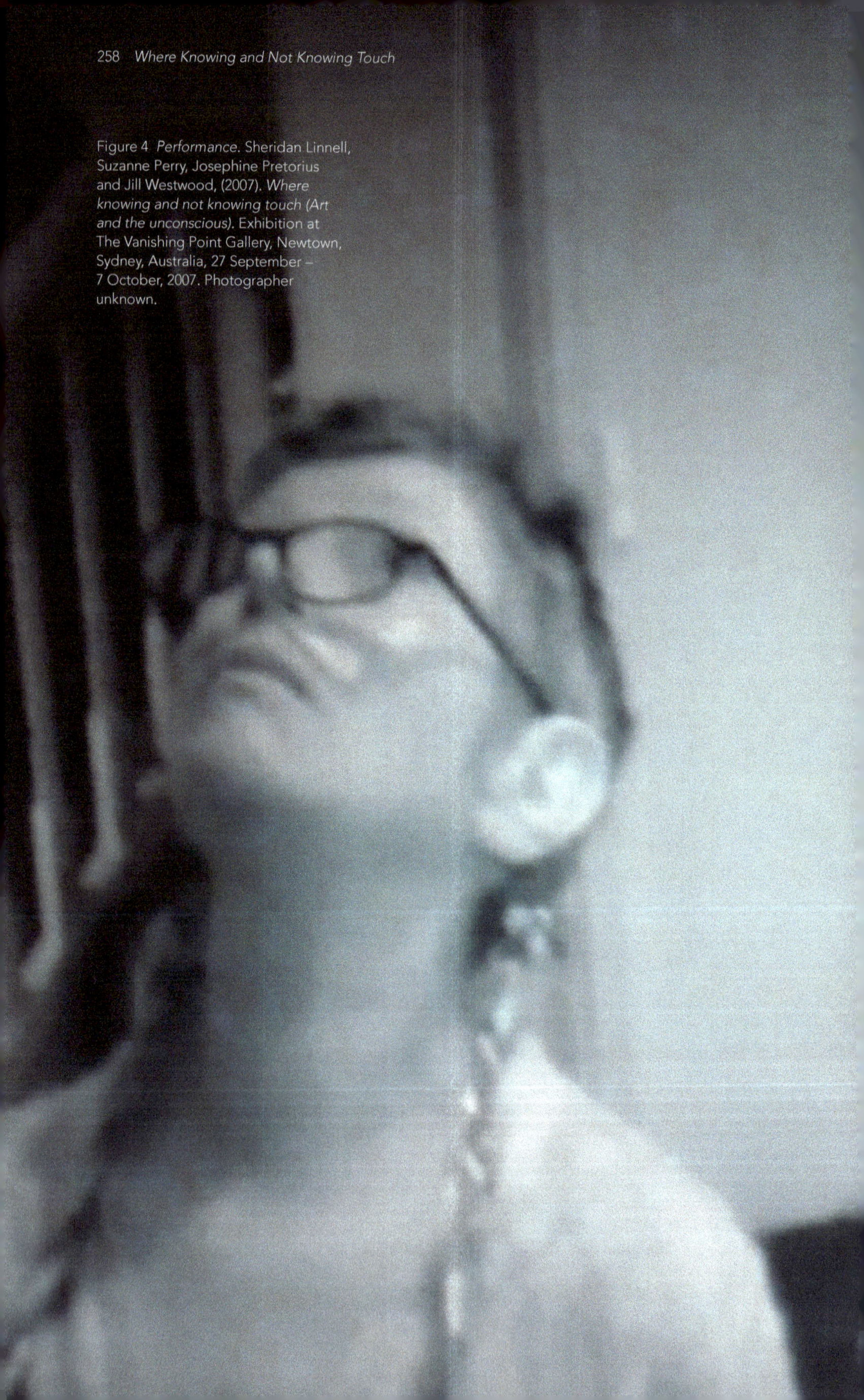

Figure 4 *Performance*. Sheridan Linnell, Suzanne Perry, Josephine Pretorius and Jill Westwood, (2007). *Where knowing and not knowing touch (Art and the unconscious)*. Exhibition at The Vanishing Point Gallery, Newtown, Sydney, Australia, 27 September – 7 October, 2007. Photographer unknown.

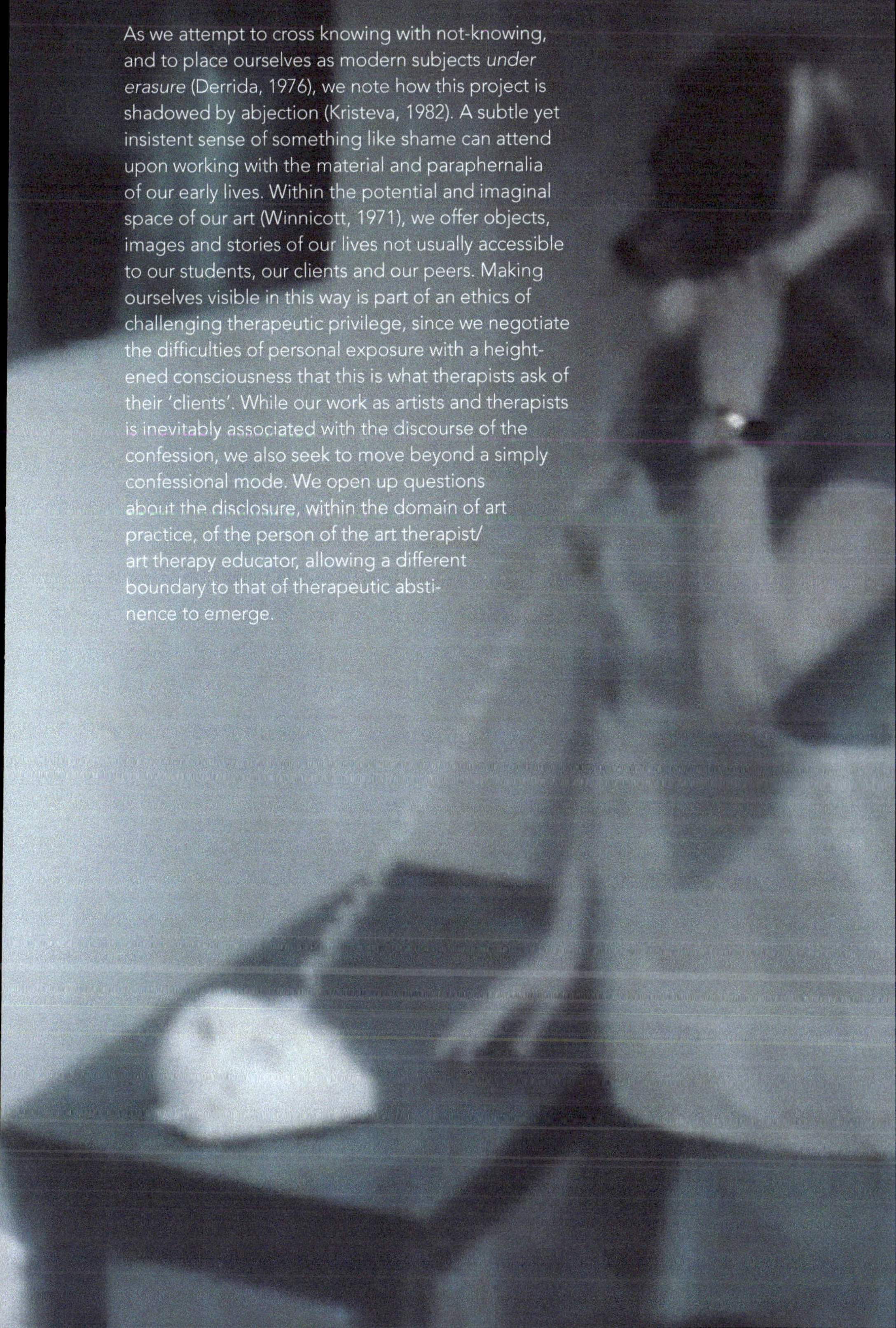

As we attempt to cross knowing with not-knowing, and to place ourselves as modern subjects *under erasure* (Derrida, 1976), we note how this project is shadowed by abjection (Kristeva, 1982). A subtle yet insistent sense of something like shame can attend upon working with the material and paraphernalia of our early lives. Within the potential and imaginal space of our art (Winnicott, 1971), we offer objects, images and stories of our lives not usually accessible to our students, our clients and our peers. Making ourselves visible in this way is part of an ethics of challenging therapeutic privilege, since we negotiate the difficulties of personal exposure with a heightened consciousness that this is what therapists ask of their 'clients'. While our work as artists and therapists is inevitably associated with the discourse of the confession, we also seek to move beyond a simply confessional mode. We open up questions about the disclosure, within the domain of art practice, of the person of the art therapist/ art therapy educator, allowing a different boundary to that of therapeutic abstinence to emerge.

Our audiences are invited to 'return the gaze'. They become our co-researchers through artist-facilitated sessions and performances that engage them in arts-based responses to the work. We regard the making and audiencing of our art as heuristic research into our ongoing formation as subjects (c.f. Davies and Gannon, 2006). As Sally Swartz has pointed out, "(t)o unlearn clinical privilege is not simply to replace one theory with another, but to move into a realm of negotiating subjectivity itself" (2005: 508).

We embrace, in this work, a contemporary feminist project – "the significance of women artists and their work in redressing exclusive versions of history, reconceiving female subjectivity in and through difference and renegotiating the very limits of aesthetics" (Meskimmon, 2003: 185).

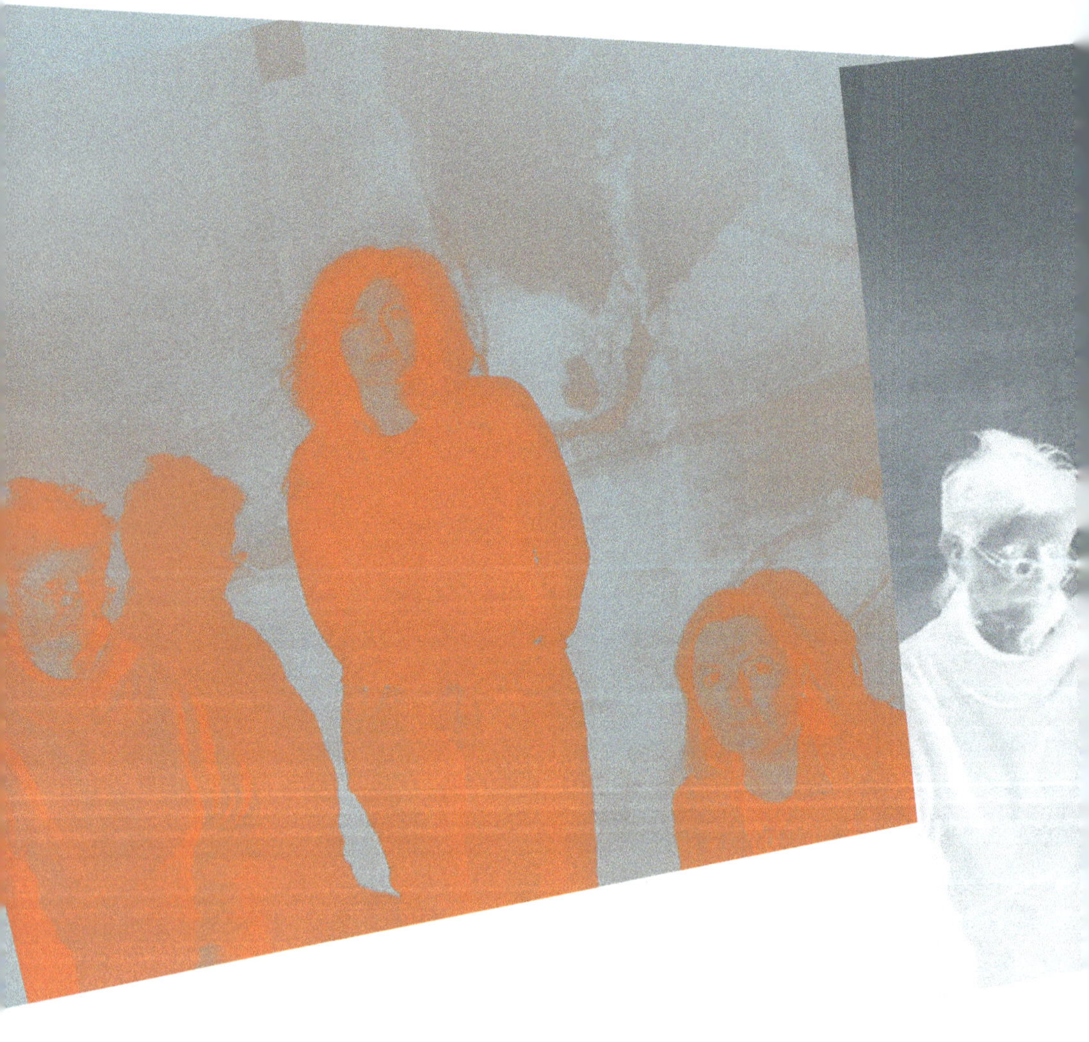

This assemblage of images and text embodies the complexity of our positioning and our relationships. As four white women committed to an ongoing recognition of the effects of colonisation and other forms of injustice, we do not wish to suggest that the particular experiences we document are exemplary, or that our fictions of a collectivised childhood can access the 'universal'. Rather, we are interested in an explanation of eloquent particulars that gesture towards our radical vulnerability and interdependence, shaping an aesthetic practice that supports an ethical relationship to the Other and the imagination of a more just and inclusive notion of the human (Butler, 2004).

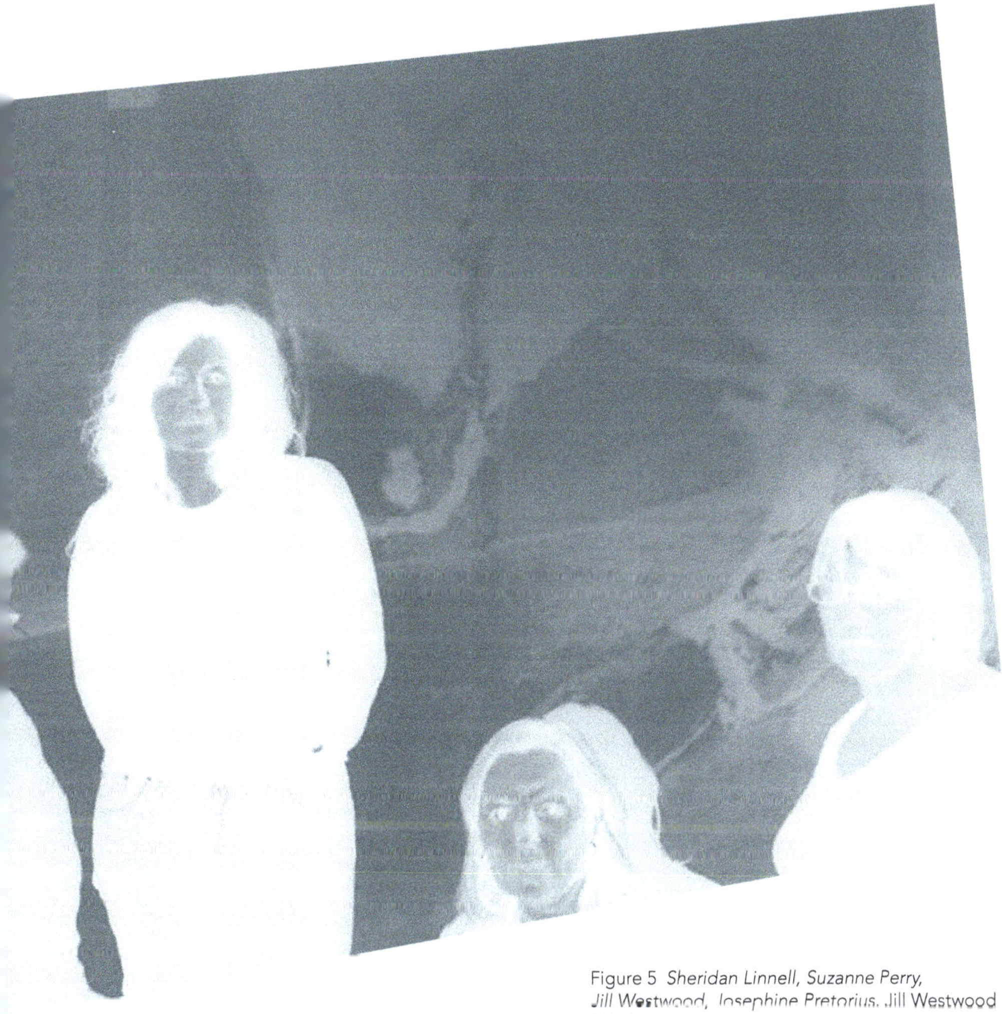

Figure 5 *Sheridan Linnell, Suzanne Perry, Jill Westwood, Josephine Pretorius*. Jill Westwood (2007). Photograph.

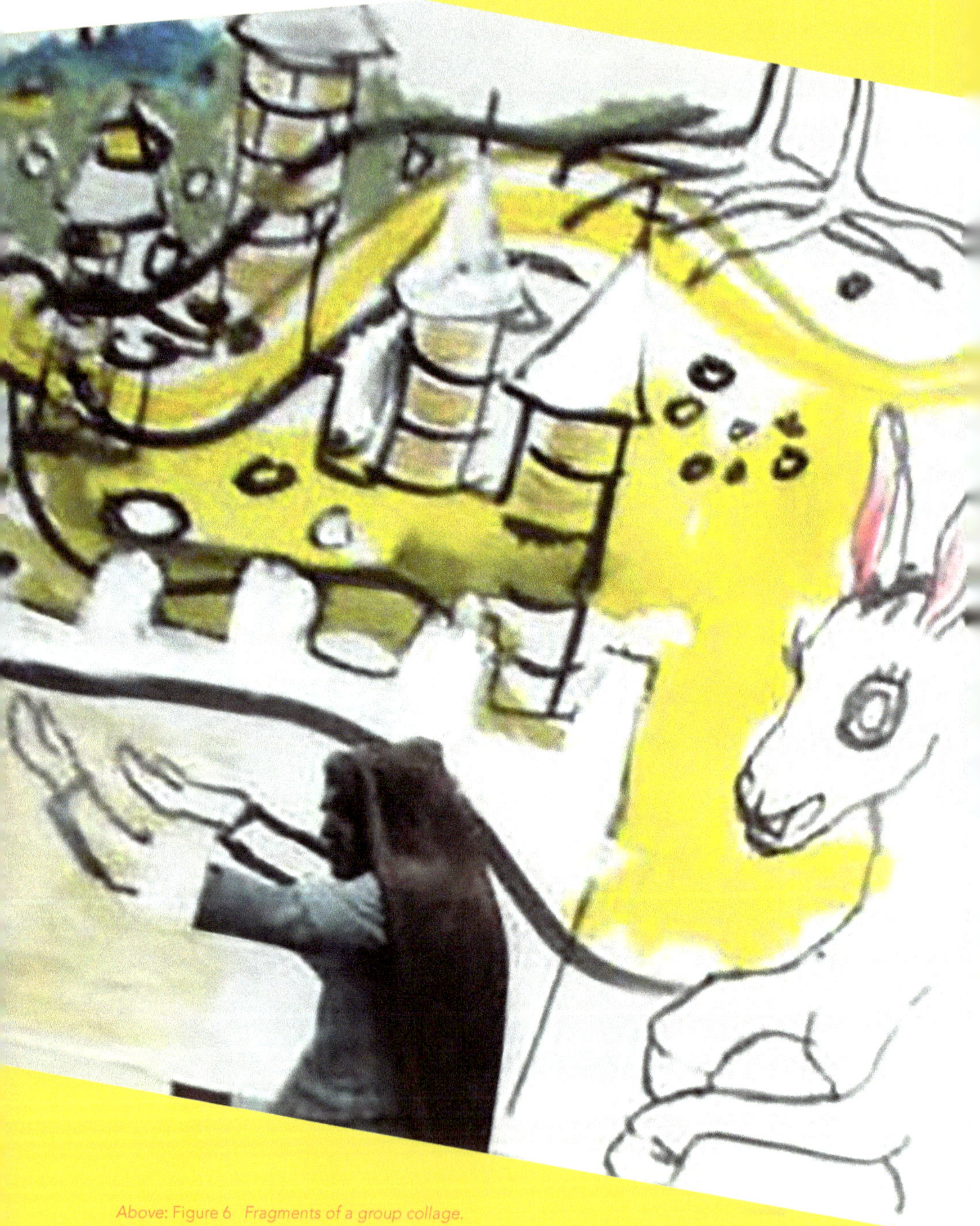

Above: Figure 6 *Fragments of a group collage.* Sheridan Linnell, Suzanne Perry, Josephine Pretorius and Jill Westwood, (2007). Collage, ink and watercolour on paper.

Opposite: Figure 7 *Cat-human.* Suzanne Perry, (2007). Ink and pastels on paper.

Sheridan

The sister I never had is holding a buttercup. Slender green stalk, yellow flower head bobbing under my chin. Do you like butter? she asks me. A loving interrogation. Blush of pale English sunshine spreading from my neck to my lips.

The sisters are laughing and talking around the kitchen table. We are playing at being grown-ups. The bright bossy one with her blond ponytail is already organising our next game. The big sister with the fringe sits back, nodding quietly. Our littlest sister is doodling on the table, drawing fairytale palaces, imaginary children and a bestiary of strange creatures – dead birds, gigantic insects, a floating cat's head and a being who is half-human, half beast.

When I grow up I want to be a writer. When my little sister grows up she wants to be an artist. I think that my middle sister wants to live in a country cottage and bake cakes for beautiful children with hair like corn and take photos of them playing, but probably she'll be the captain of a sailing boat and have to save us all from the pirates. I don't know what my big sister wants: she who dreams of wildebeests racing across the veldt, a stalking lioness behind her dreaming lids.

All of us wear bonnets and bows. We dribble milk. We take our first wobbly steps. We stretch our chubby arms up toward someone outside the frame.

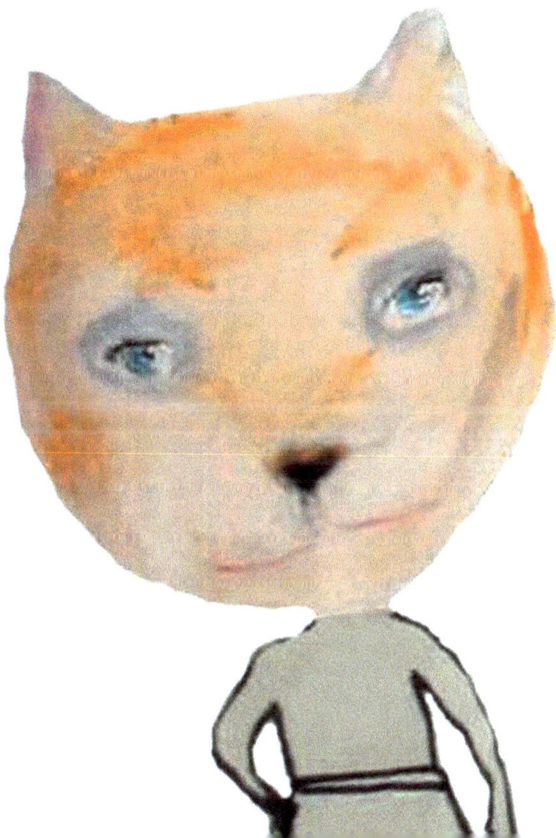

The traces of our dead are projected on the living room walls. My grandmother holds me again. I can feel her hands under my arms as I tilt forward, sleepy and full in my white woollen dress. My grandfather holds my hand as I skip along the path in my Sunday best. My mother's twin sisters lean back in deckchairs, shapely in their new swimming costumes, dark permed hair curling around their youthful, laughing faces as they watch my brother and I make sandcastles at the edge of the water.

We are making a castle. The wire armature is jagged and cuts our hands. We cover the sharp edges with white plaster bandages wound around towers and turrets; we open windows into dim interiors; we smooth over cracks. My sisters gather up their inks and paints, their cameras and books. We must do this again sometime, they say, and leaning forward, each of them holds me for a moment, a brushing of warm goodbyes on soft cheeks.

Do you like butter?

I hold the nodding flower head under my chin, mouthing the words. A faint yellow stain rises from my neck to my lips like a confession.

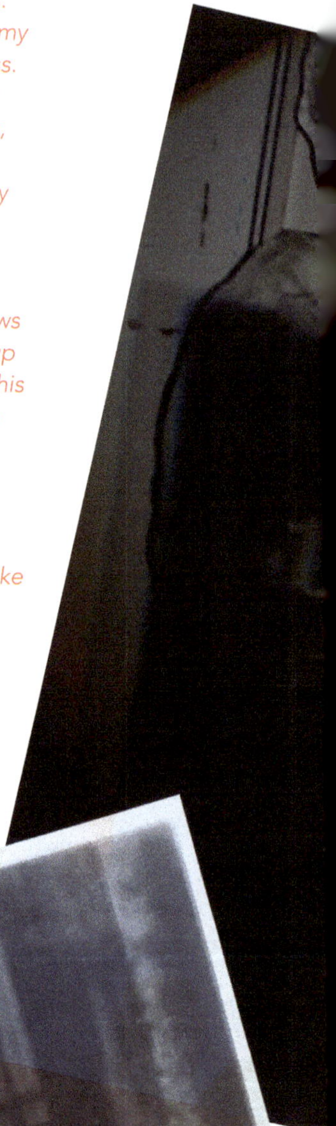

Right: Figure 8 *Castle and birthday party projection.* Sheridan Linnell, Suzanne Perry, Josephine Pretorius and Jill Westwood, (2007). Plaster, wire and slide projection construction.

Below: Figure 9 *First steps: Sheridan with her grandmother Grace and an unknown woman.* Edward Preece (1954). Photograph.

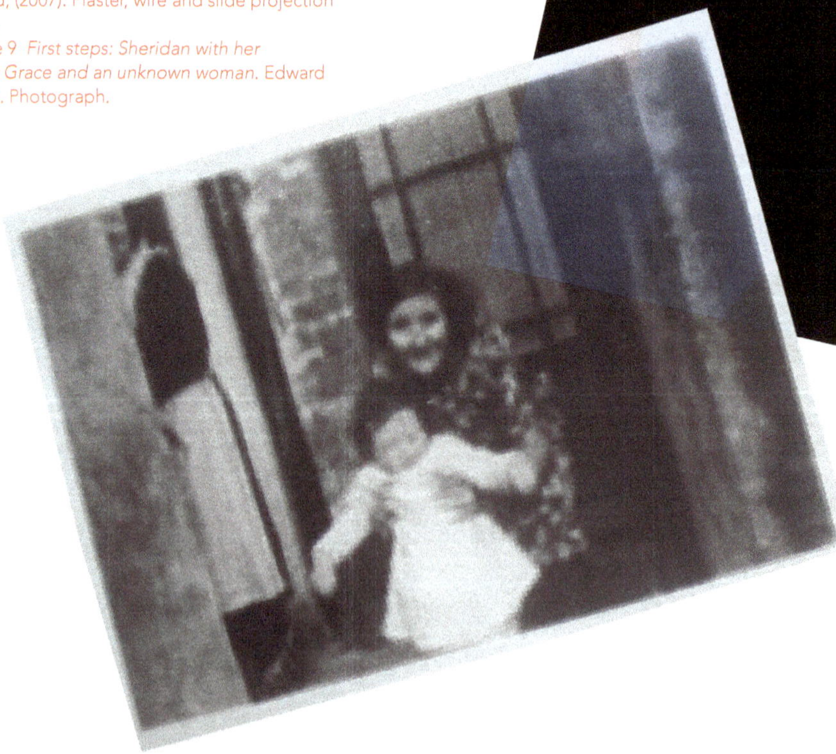

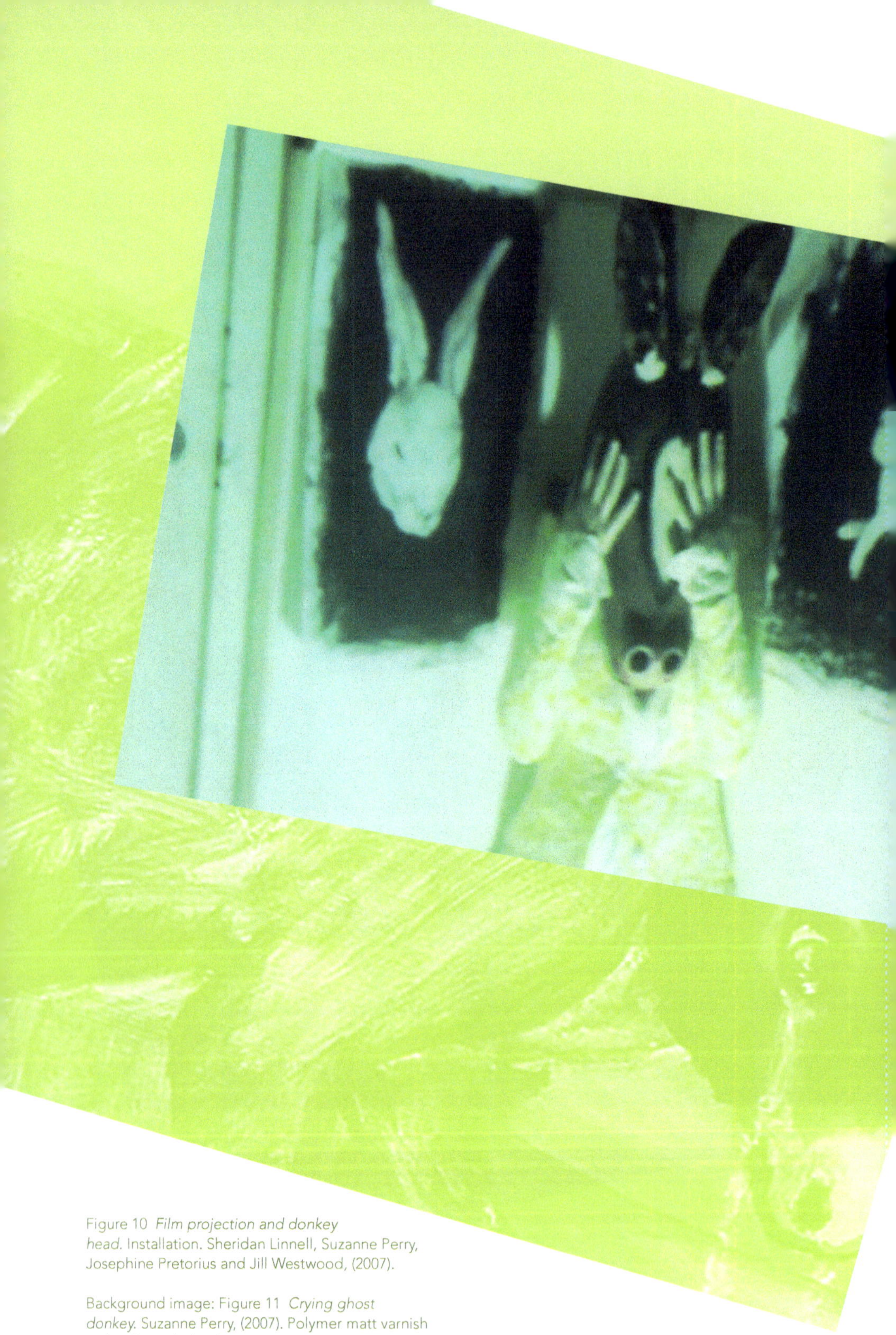

Figure 10 *Film projection and donkey head.* Installation. Sheridan Linnell, Suzanne Perry, Josephine Pretorius and Jill Westwood, (2007).

Background image: Figure 11 *Crying ghost donkey.* Suzanne Perry, (2007). Polymer matt varnish on hardboard, detail.

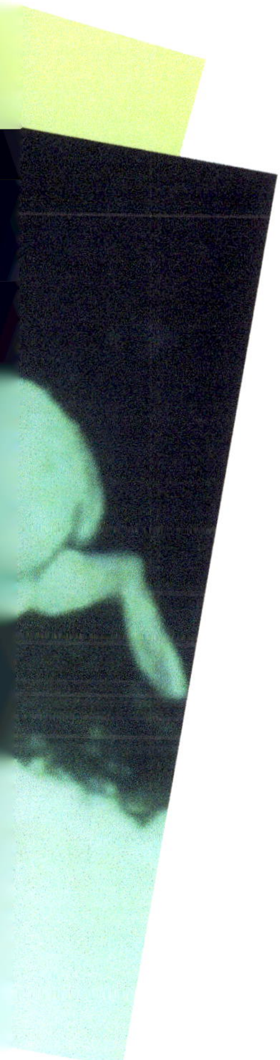

Suzanne

It only took eight ice cream containers, some rocks, tadpoles and the assistance of Chrissie Castle's brother to create a cascading palace of golden pools, where tadpoles lived like royalty and transformed into mythological creatures with uneven legs… that was my earlier work. Then I had my first conscious experience of art-making.

One day the teacher made a booming announcement across the room, "Who is a good drawer?" The children turned and pointed at the awkward shy child at the back of the room. "She can, sir" some of the children yelled out. She sat silently, and didn't say a word; maybe they meant someone else. The teacher, who had never really noticed this child, said "We need a large drawing of Mary and her baby". The awkward girl began to draw and she couldn't stop, she got to stay in the classroom on her own during lunch and just kept drawing.

I think one of the roles making art has held for me has been about retreating and being seen. These opposing experiences have at times created a tension within me and at the same time have offered me a way to live in both realities. One where I can disappear and the other where I can be noticed, and relate with others in a way that is only made possible through the art.

What's it like to be the artist in the family? You just keep looking and building up your own aesthetic memory that holds some of your family stories. These are the ones that are openly shared, as well as the stories that have no words; the latter only exist in fragmented and sometimes faded images inside me.

Some of these images I have chosen to work with evoke resonances within me, a remembering of place, of who I was then and who I still am now. These images hold generational narratives of connectedness and of separateness. They remind me of how important it is to belong and be loved; they also remind me of the pain and struggles in our attempts to do so. The donkey has become the imaginal vessel of our secrets and memories. He feels and contains the feelings that can never be fully spoken. He is like a large donkey ghost that hovers above the childhood home, witnessing and paying homage to all of those moments in our lives when knowing and not knowing touch.

Josephine

When I look at the old and curling photographs of my brother I know that my story is about having and losing, and about dying in the context of living. And perhaps that is what all our stories are about, in one way or another. Death is woven into and between and beneath the bright threads of our ordinary lives.

> *She remembers the front garden with orderly rows of Barberton daisies and brightly coloured pansies, the neat middle class home, the lounge room unused, smelling of floor polish, for receiving visitors and family celebrations, the ticking and chiming of the grandfather clock under the watchful eye of her grandmother as she sits quietly sewing in her frame on the wall.*

Theodore Maeder, 67, French farmer, marries Levena Maria Hiltze Wepener, 36, Dutch on 12 July 1913.

> *December 1913.*
>
> *My dear Papie*
>
> *Thank you for your nice letter which I got this morning. I was looking out for one. You say I must tell you about the people I know they are very few. All those we visited when we were here asked very kindly after you and wanted to know "of ek jou weg gegooi het." Old Mr Boynes is still very ill. I saw Mr Pieter von Maltitz this morning but he had not much to say for himself…It is much drier here than in Harrismith have had no rains lately. And yet there are nice apricots… The baby had to be circumcised yesterday so he is rather troublesome today. ...And now dear husband let me thank you for your kind wishes. I hope you will spend a happy xmas and new year. That God's richest blessings be yours and that we will be spared to live for many years together (for you know that I am happy with you) is the heartfelt wish of your wife*
> *Vinnie.*

They call their firstborn Du Plessis Delatte (Essa for short) to continue the family name.

> *Dear Papa*
>
> *The blessing of my good Lord be on the anniversary of your seventy seventh year.*
>
> *Your child*
> *Essa.*
> *Harrismith.*
> *21st November 1924.*

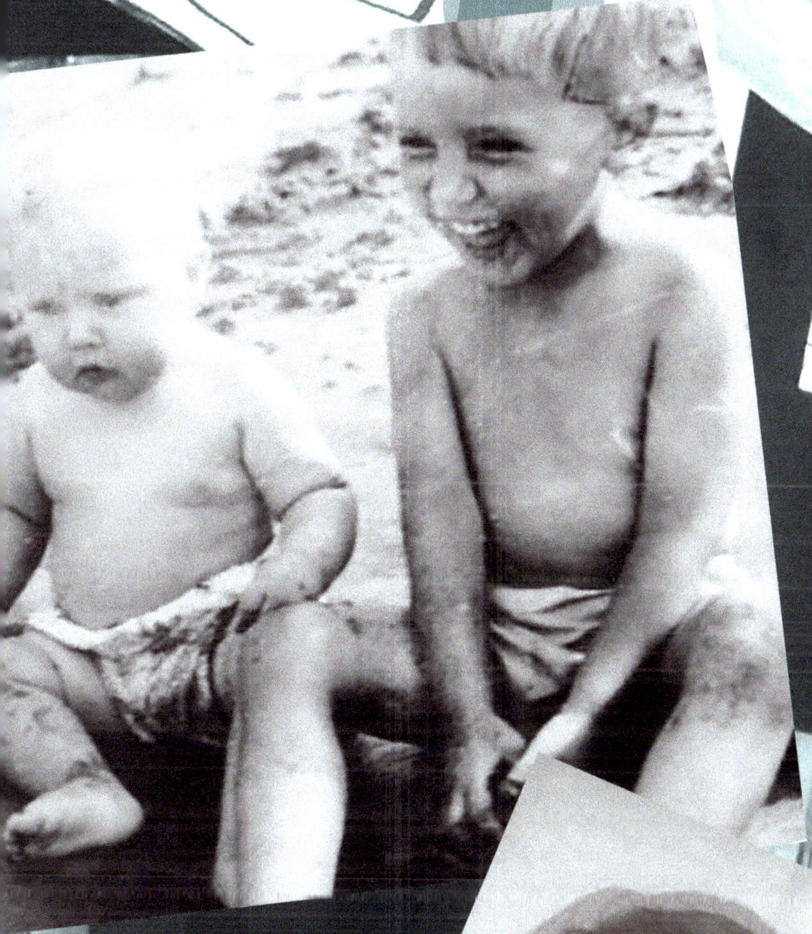

Left: Figure 12 *Josephine and her brother.* Hermanus Stephanus Pretorius, (1953). Photograph.

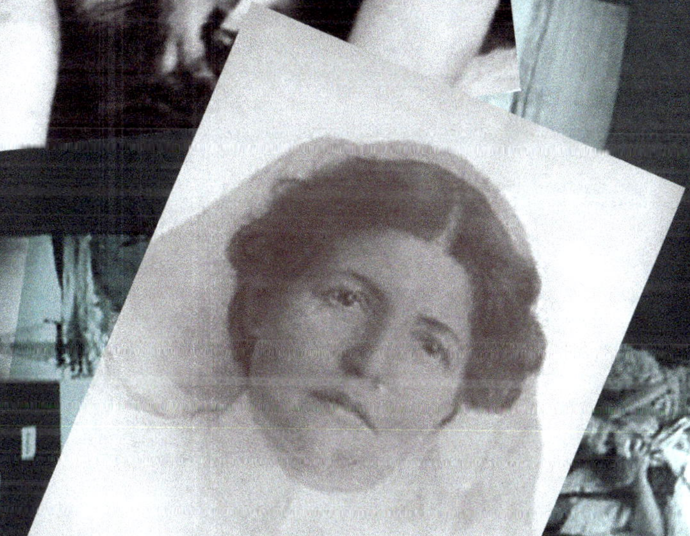

Figure 13 *Vinnie in her nurse's uniform.* Photographer unknown, (1930s). Photograph.

He dies that same year and Vinnie takes in lodgers and delivers babies.

> *My mother is 10 and the oldest of 5 children. They and their cousins from neighbouring farms ride horses bareback and play tricks on the lodgers whom they resent for eating the eggs they themselves cannot afford to. They play with the kraal children and teach each other Zulu and English. She learns to bury the resentment she feels at having to care for her younger siblings when her mother is away caring for other children.*

Du Plessis Delatte Maeder, 36, marries Hermanus Stephanus Pretorius, 29, in 1950. Herman is born in 1951, Josephine in 1953 and Theo in 1958 shortly before their grandmother dies.

She recalls feelings of shame that she feels nothing, that she cannot cry, when her mother takes her into the room and draws back the sheet covering her grandmother's face.

His pencil case releases a fragrance of wood shavings and pencils. A spare shirt button, just in case. A nice quality paintbrush with the tip broken off so that it would fit. A screwdriver. Two pairs of scissors, stored in his pencil case after he died – the first inscribed with Es and the second Josephine (named after his sister Josephine Louise who died of diphtheria at the age of two.) His hidden tenderness escaping infrequently from beneath a carapace of absent-mindedness and irritability. He never speaks of the war, or of his father who drowned in the mighty Fish River as he stood on the banks with his mother who could not swim, or of being fostered out and then going to boarding school at the age of 6. When my aunt tells me his family were horse breeders from Ficksburg a memory stirs of my father laughing uproariously in thigh-slapping fashion as he tells a story about horse thieves.

> *39, 21st Street, Parkhurst.*
>
> *A quick bowl of cornflakes and then straight outside to join the gang. There are Lorna and Clive Hazlehurst on their bicycles, he quietly in the shadows of she with the unruly, wild red hair with temper to match. Across the road, Jenny and Diane Nelson born on the same day and year as myself – 20th January 1953. Freshly arrived from Australia, that country miles beyond my childish reach. Australia, where strong and cheerful men fight each other and then gather at the pub for a beer. At least, that is what I gather from watching The Sundowners. Theresa, from that strange family, who is never allowed to play outside. That odd boy who reaches adolescence before I do and sings 'Joy Pretorius, happy and glorious' when he sees me. And my best friend Lucille Seaward, who has a bad older sister who goes out with the wrong kind of boys and gets a tattoo. And Herman, fetching me yet again from Lucy's house, because the shadows are lengthening across the veldt and dinner has been served and Dad is threatening to give me a hiding unless I return home right now.*

> *One Saturday my father said let us go for a picnic at my uncle's farm … we were so glad that we shouted three cheers for Dad. So that afternoon we started off, and when we got there we jumped out of the car. Mother set out the blankets and food. First we played hide and seek and then catches. Then we had the food, and went home at five o'clock and in the morning we did not get up till half past eight and our usual time was 7 o'clock. (Josephine, age 5)*

Another photograph, this time of the twins.

She holds their yet warm heads in her hands and in her gaze. Later they are wrapped in their great great grandmother's shawl before being lowered gently, tenderly, into the tiny white coffin.

She remembers his great peals of laughter, his quick wit, a skinny slip of fierce energy with bright brown eyes. She was puzzled by his struggles at school and hardly registered that he had failed 2 or 3 times. At 15, and he barely 17 but with the confidence of youth and a freshly granted licence, she clambers terrified into the cockpit of a two-seater Cessna for the flight from Johannesburg to Bulawayo in Zimbabwe …

> *She recalls his way with girls. Mary caught his eye and he married her. She did not last long either, first the bullet from the gun of a passing stranger which felled her metres from her children, only to succumb finally, a year later as she lay conscious, but impaled, on the steering column of her car purchased with her Tupperware earnings.*

I was unseeing as he was unravelling under the weight of it all when his time came.

> *They are asked to identify his body. She stands motionless with one brother, gazing through the viewing window with the curtains drawn to one side, at her other brother lying there staring up at the ceiling. She retrieves some glass fragments and a NSW Fire Brigade card from the front of the car.*

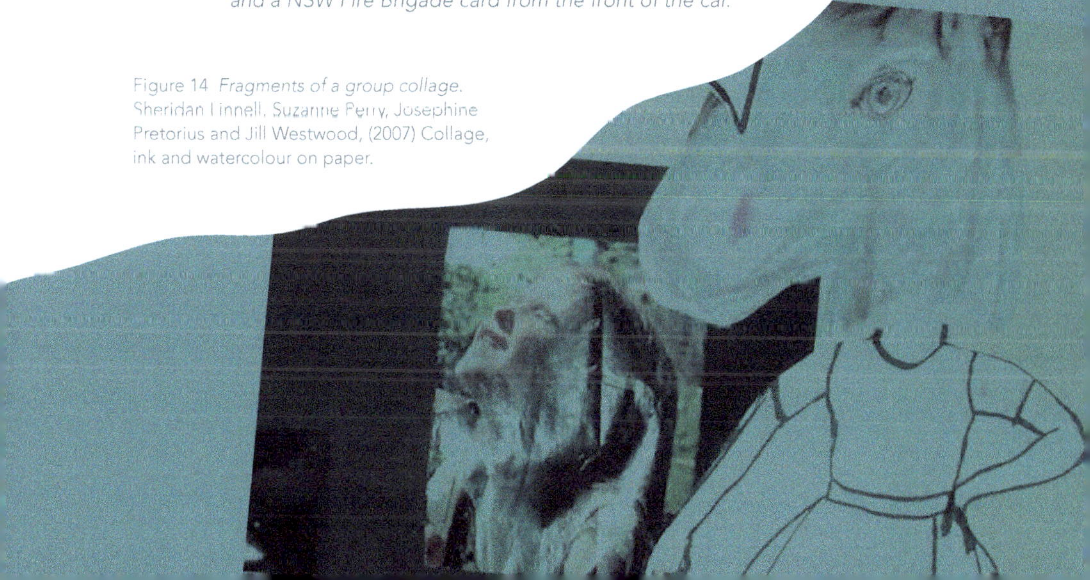

Figure 14 *Fragments of a group collage.* Sheridan Linnell, Suzanne Perry, Josephine Pretorius and Jill Westwood, (2007) Collage, ink and watercolour on paper.

Jill

Together we have built a sacred site in the cottage on the hill. It is an embodiment of a poetics of space (Bachelard, 1994). I wonder how the depth and love of the emotional transactions within and beyond its walls can be acknowledged and known? There is a delicate and awkward beauty in our uncertainty and our efforts to share and 'become' in this place.

We begin by bringing our images and objects to show each other and we start to play. Through these materials, stories, ideas and feelings are exchanged. The work develops. We become propelled by the significance of this deeper sharing and what is created…a dance unfolds that calls us to say "Come and see what we have found and made." It is as innocent and ordinary as a child showing a parent a picture they have made. It is simultaneously a profound and transformational act for humanity.

After hours, the cottage is transformed from education space to playscape. It becomes the alchemical vessel in which we collaborate and imagine into being the pantheon of odd and tender creatures at play in the interior landscape of who we are. We inevitably reveal ourselves in unexpected ways. We know, and yet know not who we are. We know and yet know not what we might become.

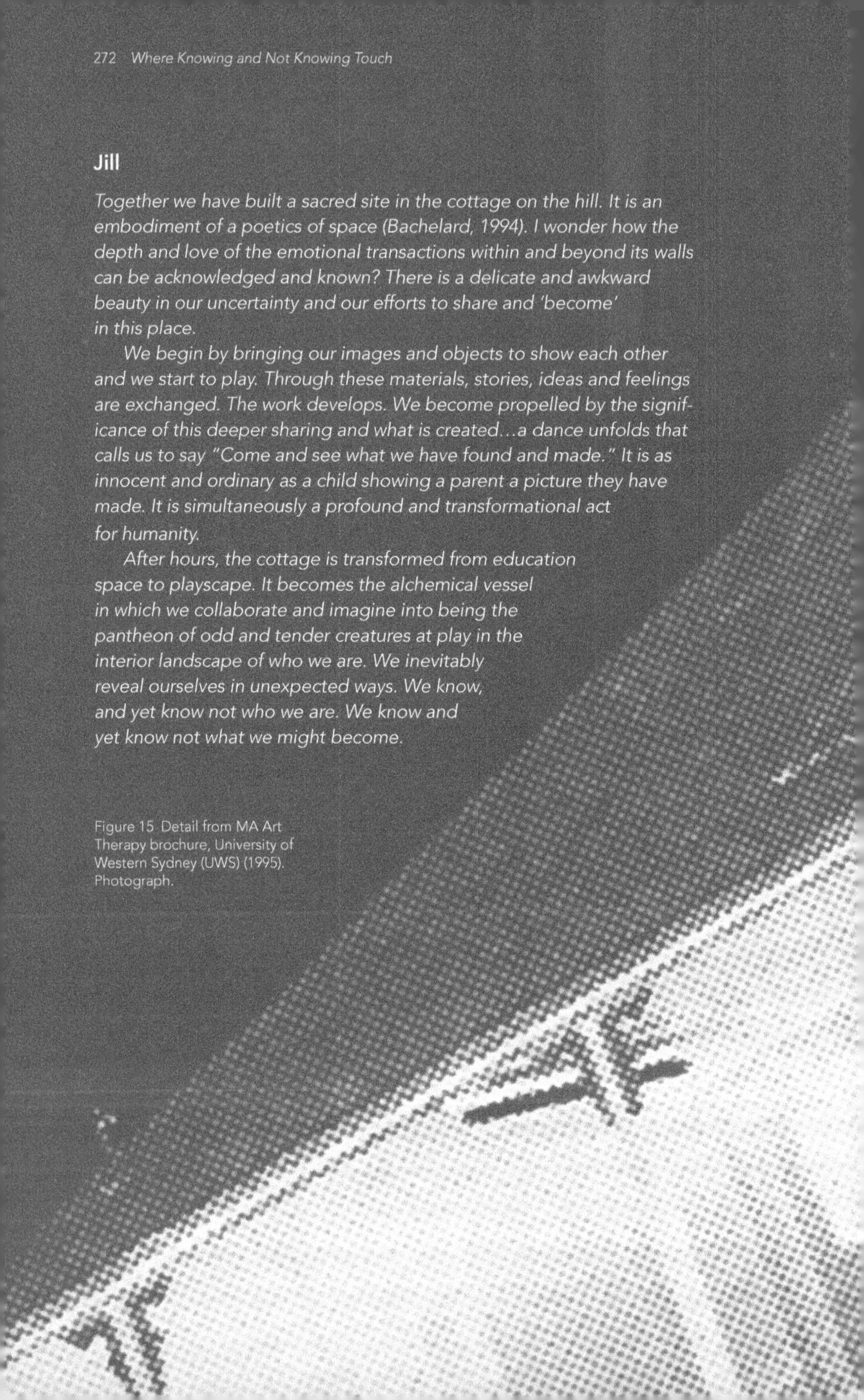

Figure 15 Detail from MA Art Therapy brochure, University of Western Sydney (UWS) (1995). Photograph.

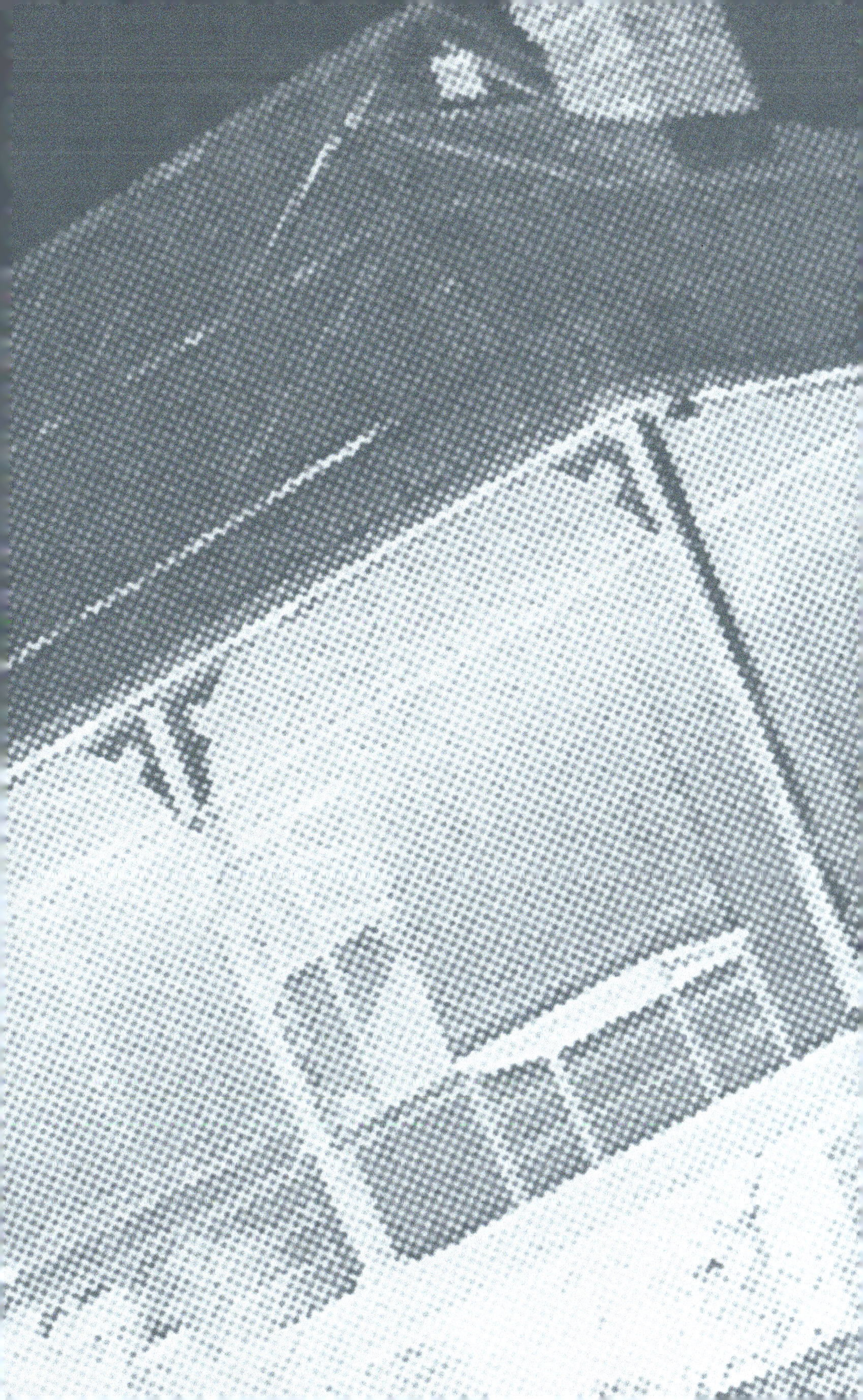

She is sitting with her brother. She can still recall the taste of the salty traces from the skin of the family ingrained in the fabric on the armrest. It is a place of beginning and safety. There is an uncertain expression on the little children's faces but also a holding and togetherness. Christmas 1963 – a department store in a big city in the middle of England. She and her brother have a photograph taken holding two monkeys. Her monkey snuggles into her winter coat. She cuddles the warm furry animal. Her brother's is more alert and doesn't settle so easily. As she reflects now she realises perhaps only a few weeks later he became seriously ill and his life in jeopardy. She does not recall much of that phase; she can only imagine what it might have been like from the distance of now.

She sits with her father at the foot of the slide on their annual holiday in North Wales. They go to the same guesthouse every year with Grandad. She is anxious because the children want to slide down. Her father doesn't seem to be concerned and holds her reassuringly. She wonders now, how or if she can be reassured?

The two little girls are in the living room of one of the fireman's houses. It is the first colour photograph she remembers seeing and it's an instant Polaroid one taken by a lady who is visiting from America. A family photograph sits on the TV in the background.

As I look at this picture I remembered how Jackie's Dad died when we were about 5 years old. Jackie was away at the time, as they must have known how ill he was. He was very young maybe under 30 years old. When Jackie returned she came over to see me. I was standing in our driveway; she said "My Daddy died". Neither of us was outwardly emotional but it was a very big moment. She said she wanted to go and tell Mrs Walters a lady down the road. I said "I think she already knows". I don't remember what happened next. I look back and reflect on the depth and complexity of such an event that is evoked powerfully from this little colour picture.

Above: Figure 16 *Jill and Graham with monkeys.* Photographer unknown (1962). Photograph.

Far right: Figure 17 *At the foot of the slide.* Margaret Westwood (1963). Photograph.

Right: Figure 18 Jill and Jackie. Photographer unknown (1964). Polaroid photograph.

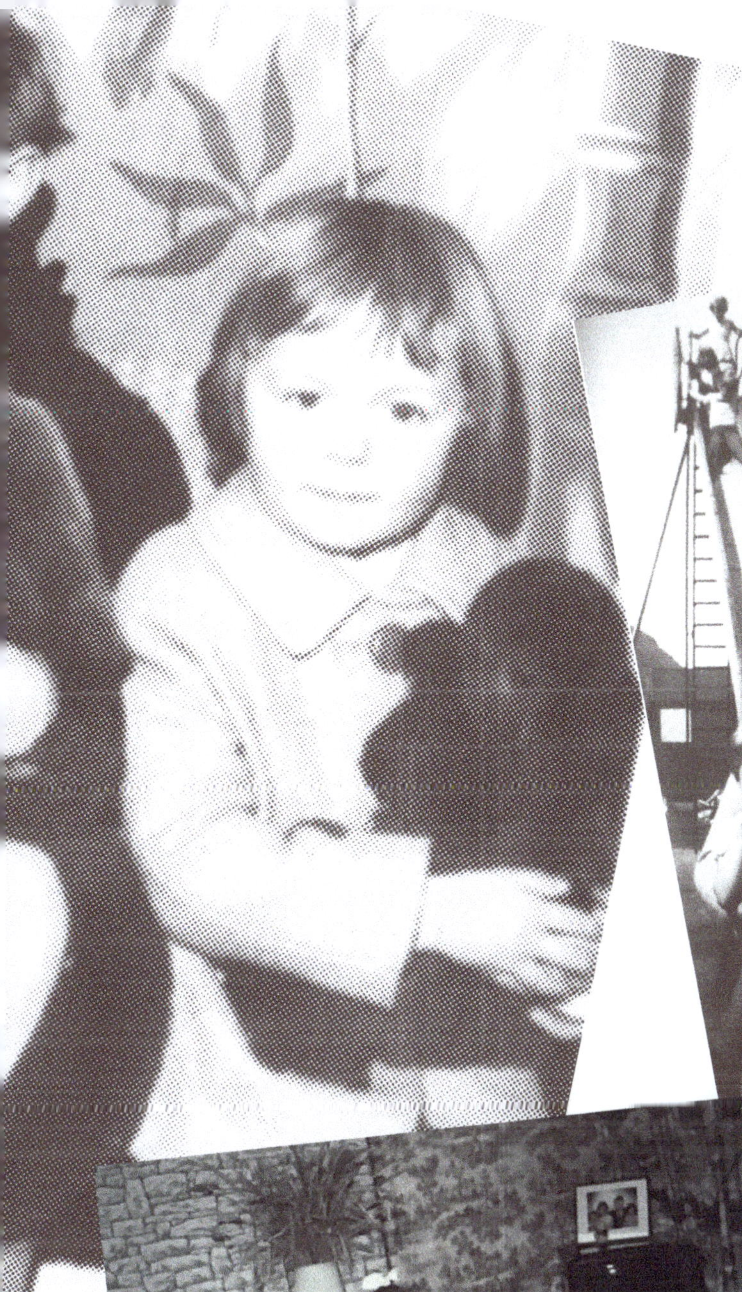
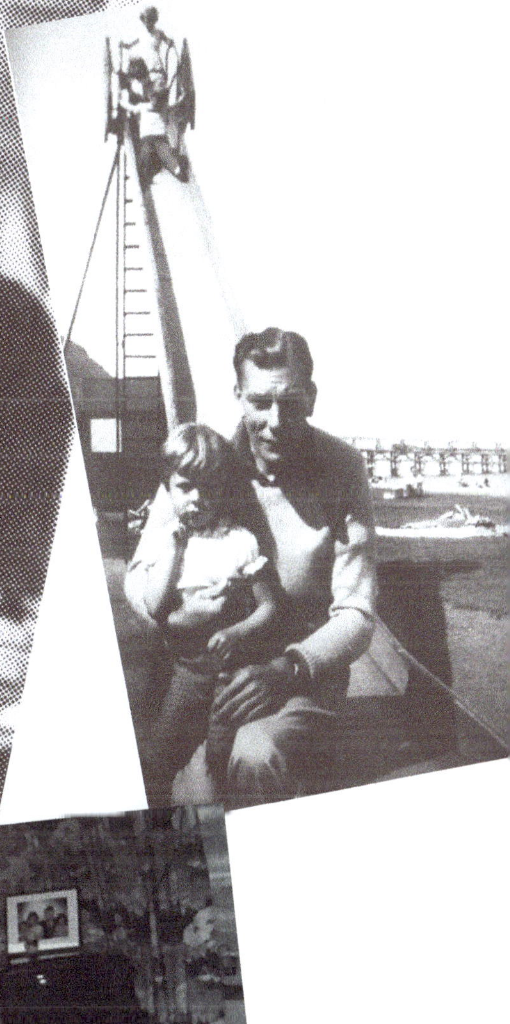
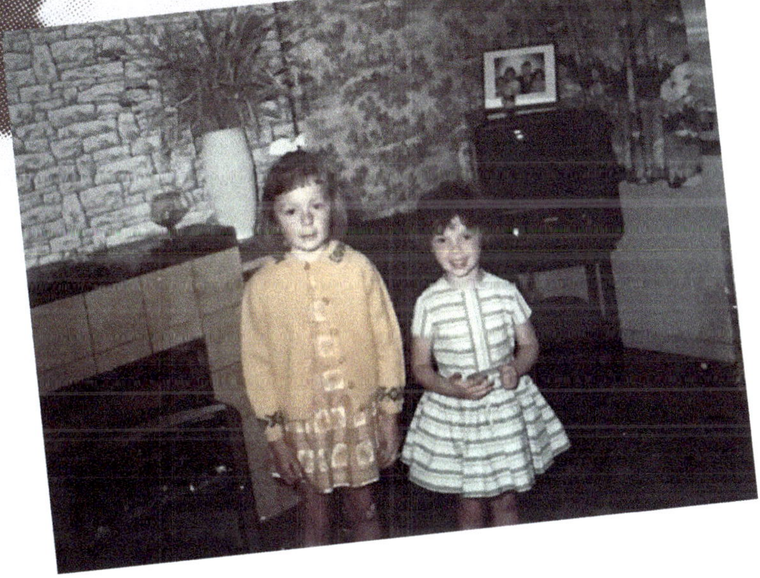

She keeps a penny made in 1917 in her purse. Earlier she was so very sure her father gave it to her because it was made in the year he was born. Now she is uncertain and she thinks she kept it because it was made in 1917 and it reminded her of her father and some moments she shared with him when she found the penny. She thinks she may have elaborated that he gave it to her not only to insulate her from the pain of his loss but because in many ways he did give it to her, as this is what is in her heart. She keeps it with her always. It is completely sacred and negligible.

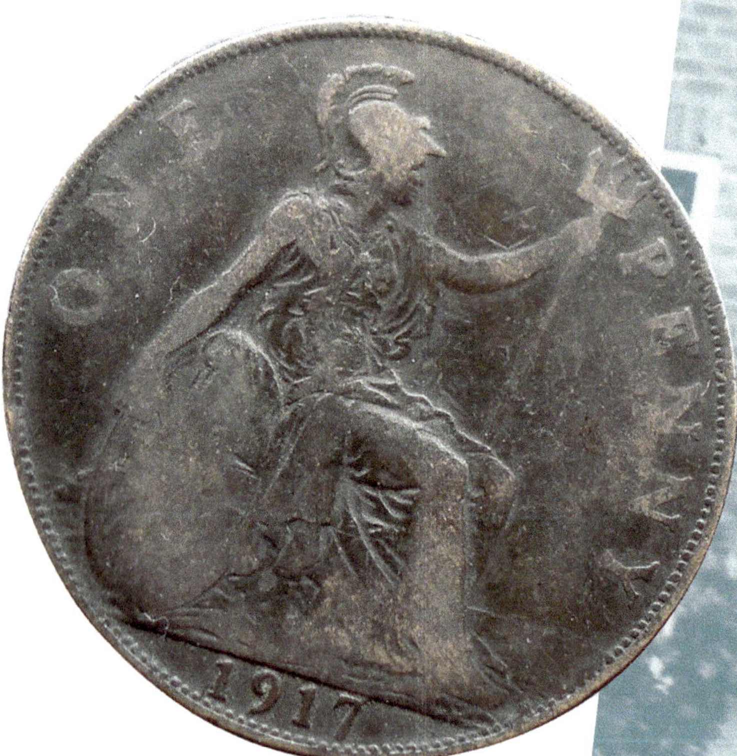

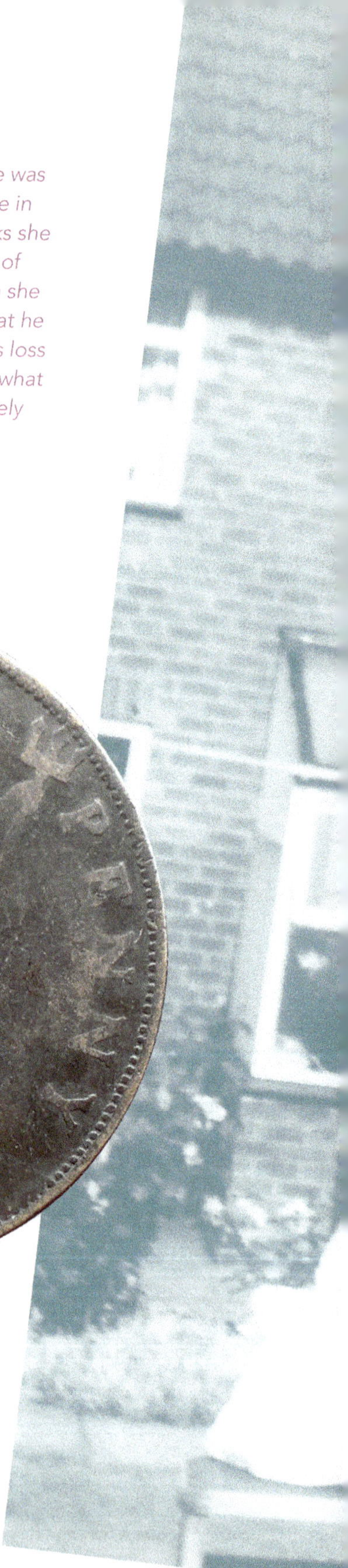

Above: Figure 19 *One penny, 1917*. Jill Westwood, (2007). Photograph.

Right: Figure 20 *My birthday party in the garden of my family home*. Margaret Westwood (1965). Photograph.

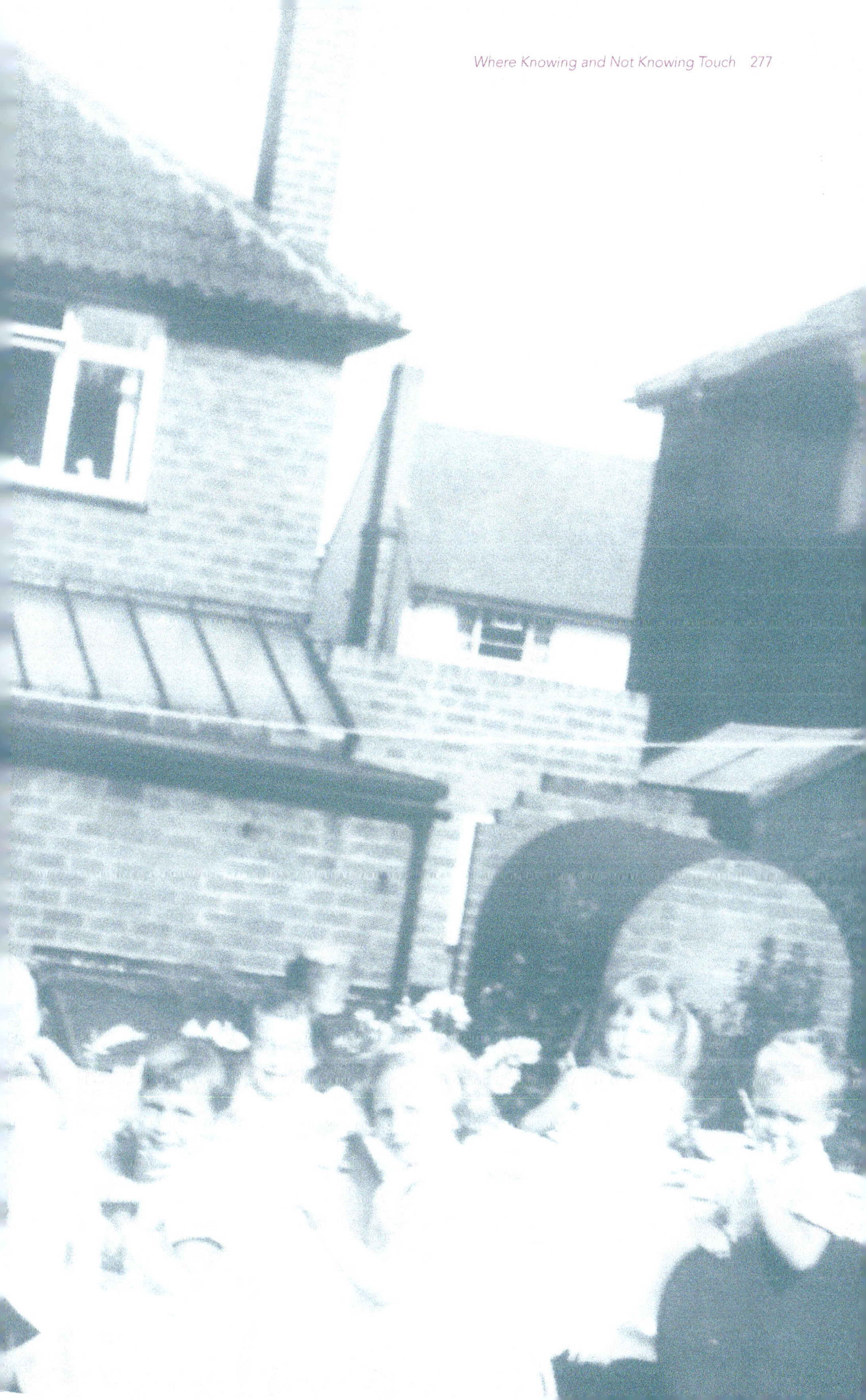

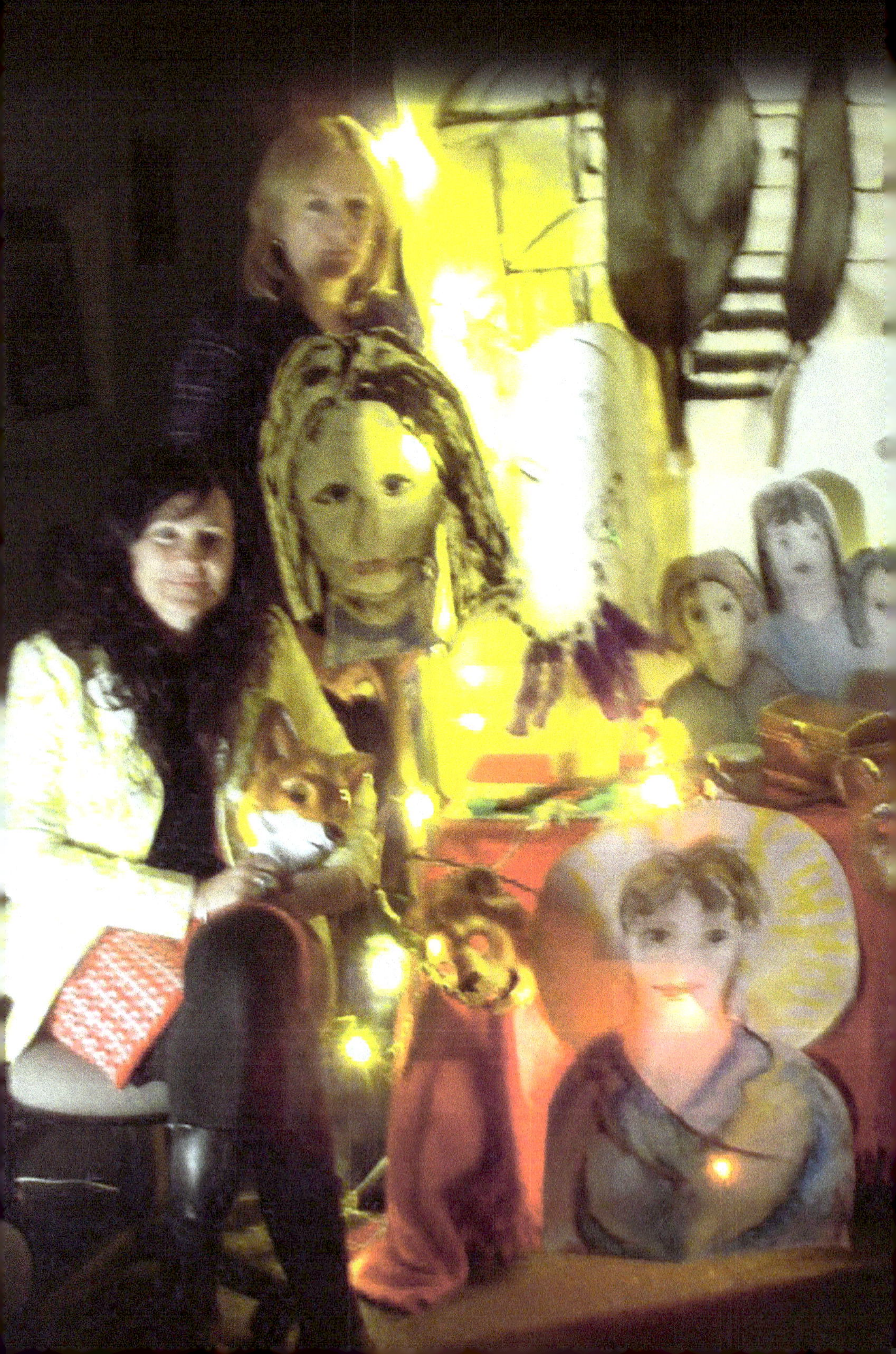

Fragments, moments and essences of the deep thick fabric of lives remembered and forgotten. Looking into the darkness our eyes become accustomed and we can begin to see into the shadows. Recognising we can only ever see fragments and aspects but in this act of looking and being receptive we can attempt to move beyond the surface.

Our work is about the emotional transactions between ourselves and others. This shapes our souls and that of others in known and unknown ways. Our vulnerability opens a portal to transformation and love. It is delicate and arduous work, but it is exquisite in its complexity and its intention to see and be seen.

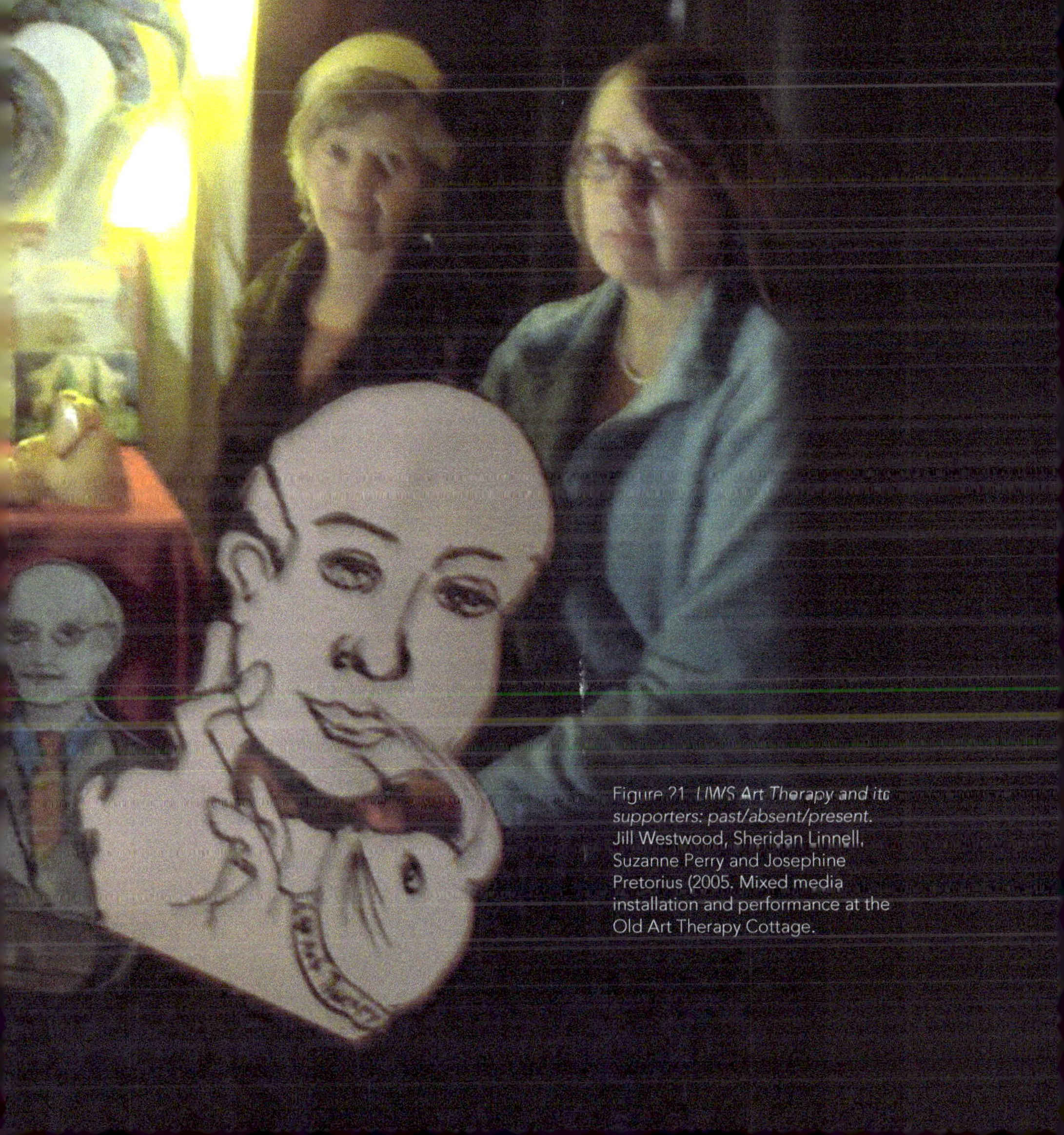

Figure 21 *UWS Art Therapy and its supporters: past/absent/present.* Jill Westwood, Sheridan Linnell, Suzanne Perry and Josephine Pretorius (2005. Mixed media installation and performance at the Old Art Therapy Cottage.

References

Bachelard, G. (1969/1994) *A poetics of space*. Trans. Jolas, M. Beacon Press, Boston.

Bennett, J. (2005) *Empathic vision; Affect, trauma and contemporary art*. Stanford University Press, California.

Bourriaud, N. (2002) *Relational aesthetics*. Trans. Pleasance, S. and Woods, F. Les Presses du Reel, France.

Butler, J. (2001) Giving an account of oneself. *Diacritics*, 31, (4): 22–40.

Butler, J. (2004) *Precarious life: the powers of mourning and violence*. Routledge, New York and London.

Davies, B. and Gannon, S. (2006) *Doing collective biography*. McGraw Hill/Open University Press, Maidenhead, Berkshire.

Derrida, J. (1976) *Of grammatology*. Trans. Spivak, G. John Hopkins University Press, Baltimore and London.

Freire, P. (1994) *Pedagogy of hope*. Trans. Barr, R. Continuum: London.

Hyland Moon, C. (2002) *Studio art therapy: Cultivating the artist identity in the art therapist*. Jessica Kingsley Publishers, USA.

Kristeva, J. (1982) *Powers of horror*. Trans. Roudiez, L. Columbia University Press, New York.

Linnell, S., Perry, S., Pretorius, J. and Westwood, J. (2005) *The work of art is the work of embodiment* (art/performance/film/installation). Australia National Art Therapy Association Conference, November. The Quakers School, Hobart, Tasmania, Australia.

Linnell, S., Perry, S., Pretorius, J. and Westwood, J. (2006) *The work of art is the work of embodiment* (art/performance/film/installation). The Art Therapy Cottage, Kingswood Campus, University of Western Sydney, New South Wales, Australia.

Linnell, S., Perry, S., Pretorius, J. and Westwood, J. (2007) Where knowing and not knowing touch. *Art and the unconscious,* exhibition at the Vanishing Point Contemporary Art Gallery, Newtown, Sydney, Australia.

Meskimmon, M. (2003). *Women making art: History, subjectivity and aesthetics*. Routledge, London and New York.

Perry, S. and Westwood, J. (2006) *The work of art is the work of embodiment* (art/performance/installation). Australian and New Zealand Art Therapy Association inaugural conference, Manly, New South Wales, Australia.

Perry, S. and Westwood, J. (2007) *The work of art is the work of embodiment* (art/performance/installation). American Art Therapy Association 38th Annual Conference, Albuquerque, New Mexico, USA.

Swartz, S. (2005). Can the clinical subject speak? Some thoughts on subaltern psychology. *Theory and Psychology*. 15 (4): 505–525.

Venn (2002). *Refiguring subjectivity after modernity*. In: Walkerdine, V. (Ed) (2002). *Challenging subjects: critical psychology for a new millennium*. Palgrave, Houndsmills, UK.

Westwood, J. (2008). *The work of art is the work of embodiment* (art/performance/film/installation). *Education in Art Therapy Conference*, Pedagogical University, Krakow, Poland.

Winnicott, D. (1971) *Playing and reality*. Penguin, Harmondsworth.

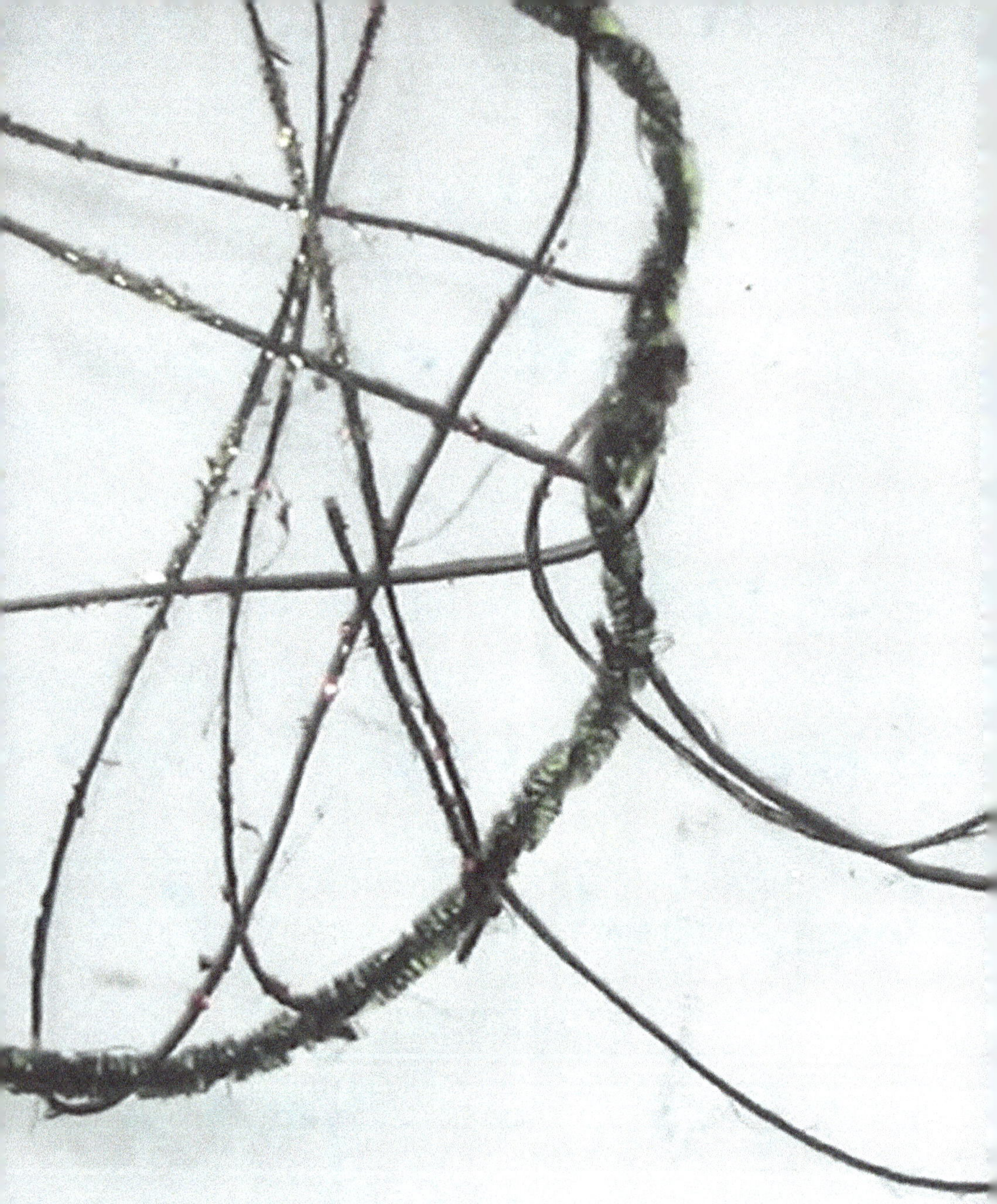

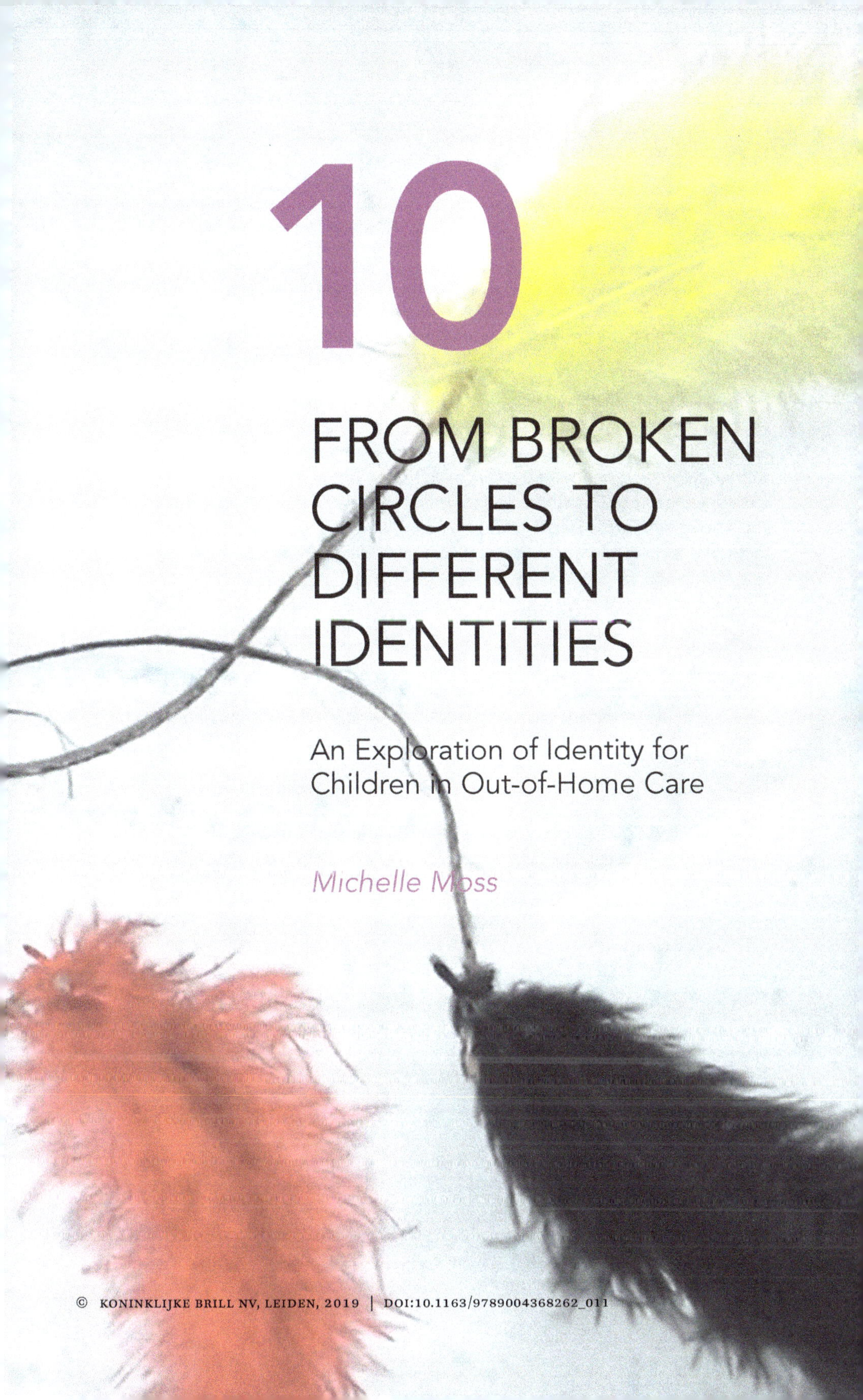

10

FROM BROKEN CIRCLES TO DIFFERENT IDENTITIES

An Exploration of Identity for Children in Out-of-Home Care

Michelle Moss

 | DOI:10.1163/9789004368262_011

Introduction: broken circles

The circle as a form:

> ... expresses the totality of the psyche in all its aspects, including the relationship between man and nature. Whether the symbol of the circle appears in primitive sun worship or modern religion, in myths or dreams, in the mandalas drawn by the Tibetan monks, in the ground plan of cities, or in the spherical concepts of early astronomers, it always points to the single most vital aspect of life – its ultimate wholeness.
>
> Jung, 1964: 66

If there is a symbolic form and related themes to arise out of this research it would be those attributable to the circle, for it appears here as a visual symbol that is shared across cultures. The circle represents wholeness, a space with no beginning or end. It is a space where the inside of the circle can be considered sacred. This is the case for many cultures, inclusive of the Australian Aboriginal, Torres Strait and South Sea Islander cultures, which are the focus of this research. Circles are symbolic in Aboriginal art and ceremony and speak of the connection to the land, the spirit and the community.

The circle can also be a symbol for identity, as evidenced by a number of Indigenous adult respondents in this research. For example:

> *The concept of the circle are absolute. The centre of everyone and everything. Throughout the different Aboriginal communities they each share the same concept, even though it may be in a different language or dialect, everything emanates from it and nothing exists outside the circle.*
>
> Aboriginal Elder, 2005

> *Identity, it's like a circle because it's how you fit in and it's where you fit in.*
>
> Bree, Indigenous worker, 2005

> You're in the clan, it's like a circle, if you take one piece out of it the circle breaks.
>
> Malcolm Walker, Indigenous Elder

It has been argued that the legacy of the Stolen Generation and past legislative practices has created many broken circles (Queensland Government, 1997; Haebich, 2001). This research seeks to explore what this means for children and young people in out-of-home care. Hence there is an assumption that kinship and family connection is important to identity to different degrees for different individuals.

This research started from an exploration of a technique for recording life experiences known in the literature as *Life Story Book* work. It has been used widely in Australian child protection by child protection workers with children in out-of-home care but, as will be illustrated here, has ended up being about something much larger. *Life Story Book* work is intrinsically about preserving and documenting a sense of identity for children who come into out-of-home care. This connection of *Life Story Book* work with identity led me on a journey to discover the historical context of Identity Theory and what this means for children in out-of-home care.

There is much written in western literature about identity formation with age-specific theories and stages mapping out 'normal' identity formation in a healthy individual. The context of my work environment and working with Indigenous people certainly led me to challenge the appropriateness of the *Life Story Book* models I was reviewing for Indigenous cultures, along with the theoretical assumptions underpinning the models that were Anglo-centric. Consideration needed to be given to other cultures but, perhaps arguably more important, the meaning of identity for Indigenous children and young people in out-of-home care needed further investigation. In Australia, Indigenous children are 8–9 times more likely to be in out-of-home care than non-Indigenous children. In 2013–14 some 39,716 Indigenous children received a child protection service, a rate of 137 per 1,000 (Australian Institute of Health and Welfare, 2015). Given this overrepresentation, this research had a particular focus on Aboriginal, Torres Strait Islander and Australian South Sea Islander children.

The community the research was undertaken in itself was relatively small. I was also one of the few child trauma counsellors and certainly the only art therapist in the region. Some of the children in the research were therefore known to me which helped to ensure that a level of trust already existed. Likewise, having worked in several positions in the Department of Child Protection and in an Indigenous organisation prior to conducting the research, I had close connections with Indigenous child protection workers and again trust had built up over time. I believe these relationships aided the research and the disclosure of narratives both professional and personal by the interviewees.

Ever present is the disclosing of specificity in terms of the respondents. An underlying assumption throughout the research was that individual specificity matters. That is, gender, culture, age cohort and family history all play a role in how we view the world and ourselves. That said, my specificity as a researcher, worker and resident in the field of the research at the time was undeniably present throughout the research.

Prior to becoming an academic, I worked in three states across Australia as a qualified arts therapist and in child protection. I have worked with traumatised children and families for over 20 years, both in Government and non-Government organisations and as a private practitioner and consultant. I believe that this depth of experience across the child protection sector put me in a unique position of being able to critique the sector from different positions. I am especially equipped to comment on the work as a child and family trauma counsellor/art therapist, a child protection worker, as a worker in the non-government sector (NGO) and as an academic.

More recently I had managed a new service in the Northern Territory that provided trauma counselling for Aboriginal children who live on over ninety remote communities across the Northern Territory. I worked in 35 of these communities. As a new service within an untried cultural context, the service utilised Action Learning and aimed to arrive at a transferable model of therapeutic practice, appropriate to the remote community and cultural context. For many of the children and families who live remotely, English is a second, third or even a fourth language. The use of creative therapies proved successful (according to feedback from the families and communities involved) in being both culturally appropriate and being able to transcend language barriers. The privilege of being able to work with Aboriginal people from so many different communities has undoubtedly increased my cultural understanding and knowledge.

Indigenous identity, as explored and illustrated in this research, is linked to the Indigenous Australian's sense of Spirit. Their Spirit is intrinsic to healing. What does this mean for western practice and our work with Indigenous children, families and communities? This research explores this question as it pertains to Indigenous children in out-of-home care. In terms of my own practice and being able to provide meaningful professional supervision, the necessity to continually question and critique the assumptions that underpin the western models of therapeutic engagement we were drawing from was paramount. This in itself proved to be a huge challenge for many of the workers.

Whilst the research represents a small cohort of children (20) from a small regional Queensland town, it does not discount its pertinence. One of the key findings to come out of the *Crime and Misconduct Commission Inquiry into Child Abuse in Foster Care* (Crime and Misconduct Commission, 2004) echoed the findings from a plethora of other, judicially-based enquiries into child protection, both in Australia and internationally, that found that the child in child protection is not viewed as the primary client (Lonne and Thomson, 2005). The research sought to address this by bringing the stories and artworks of individual children and young people to the fore.

The research site in itself was unique in the Indigenous interracial mix it represented. Only two participants in the research were from only one cultural group and only one of these was Anglo-Australian. The children in this study represented children from up to five cultures, ensuring a unique opportunity to explore how children negotiate several cultural identities simultaneously. It was also important to consider child protection work practices in terms of multi-cultural specificity and what this means for children in care.

The research uses a qualitative methodology and is in line with pragmatic research methods, concurrently utilising a variety of quantitative research tools. Methods such as triangulation, prolonged observation, thematic analysis and pattern-making, which can compensate for the generally ungeneralisable nature of pure qualitative data analysis, were used (Newman and Benz, 1998; Onwuegbuzie and Leech, 2005). As a non-Indigenous researcher, the selection of a qualitative approach helped to ensure that the voices of the children, young people and practitioners involved in the study would be at the centre of the findings.

In this research the word Indigenous is used to describe multi-cultural or inter-racial children and workers as a collective of all three cultures. This is because of the complexity of each child's and worker's cultural roots.

Research aims and methodology

The aim of the research was to ascertain how children and young people view and negotiate identity and, in so doing, explore identity from Aboriginal, Torres Strait, Australian South Sea Islander and interracial perspectives. Ultimately the research explored how young people in care from different cultural backgrounds negotiate essentialist and political notions of cultural identity and race. It provides insight into the images created by children and young people and explores identity, culture and sense of self from their own perspective.

Notions of identity for individual children within the care system in the central Queensland region were analysed by exploring not only the views of the children themselves but also addressed how the child protection system impacts upon children. In terms of the participants, this research included both children in and not in out-of-home care, some of whom were siblings. The research also looked at levels of self-esteem. Rosenberg (1979) defines self-esteem as 'the wish to think well of oneself' (cited in Sakinah et al 1994: 124). In exploring self-esteem, the research sought to analyse the linkage, if any, between self-esteem and identity.

The research sought to include children as young as four years of age and utilised narrative art therapy techniques to help ensure a child-friendly process. Special ethics requirements were needed in order for this to occur. The use of art in the interview process allowed for other dimensions to be explored as well as providing further insight into the young person's world. Although the focus of the interviews was on identity and perceptions of the self, the young person's stories were often disclosed when they began to discuss family and connectedness. The use of art therapy techniques to facilitate this process was incorporated into the research design. Art provided the vehicle by which children and young people were able to explore their own narratives more fully. In order to provide an Aboriginal perspective to the exploration of the images made by the children, Mr Anthony Duwun Lee, a Northern Territory Aboriginal artist and Traditional Healer was consulted.

Given the historical disempowerment experienced by children, young people and Indigenous community members generally an inclusive, empowerment-based methodology was used (Gibbs, 2001: 29). Participants were invited to contribute in order to promote improvements to the out-of-home care system. Pictorial tools and child and young people friendly forms and information sheets were developed. All of these tools were informed via consultation with a group of young people in care who were also members of CREATE[1]. The study utilised methods and techniques whereby all participants were respected and their strengths were reinforced. In line with 'strengths based practice' frameworks (Bernard, 2002), participants were recognised as being experts in their own lived experience.

The common fields used in the data analysis included gender, care status, age and cultural identification. Information that can have a big impact on self-esteem and sense of self, such as level of abuse, neglect and contact with family was also collected from

1 The CREATE foundation was formally known as the Australian Association of Young People in Care which was founded in 1993. It is the Peak Body that represents the voices of young people in care. 'It has developed into a small volunteer driven organisation with an office in every state and Territory around Australia' (CREATE Website).

a combination of Departmental files (both electronic and paper- based), the workers and the children themselves; this was in order to gain a fuller understanding of the vicissitudes of each young person's lived experience. This level of data collection enabled the interviews to be viewed within a context which in turn allowed for greater depth in comparative data collection and analysis. The data was triangulated and this is further explored later in the chapter.

Theoretical underpinnings

For Foucault, scientific truth is a product of the dominant discourse in society which reproduces sites of power and knowledge. Truth:

> … induces regular effects of power. Each society has its regime of truth, its 'general politics' of truth: that is, the types of discourse which it accepts and makes function as truth … (as well as) the status of those who are charged with saying what counts.
>
> Foucault, 1972: 131

How the dominant discourse impacts on child protection decision-making and workers' perceptions of childhood and Indigenous culture is particularly pertinent.

Underpinning much of social work practice in child protection is a particular model of childhood, steeped in developmental theory, which emphasises "… universal and invariant age–related developmental stages" (Winter, 2006: 56). Winter highlights the issues surrounding the current model of childhood utilised within social work child protection practice that is based on notions of passivity that disqualify children as active agents. He suggests that the framework for looked after children creates a paradigm that embodies the dominant adult view about children and childhood (Winter, 2006). This is particularly the case for younger children, and notably for Indigenous children.

Developmental theories in Australia have continued to inform child protection practice frameworks.[2] For Erikson (1968), ego identity is achieved through a process of 'identity crises'. Of eight stages, there are five developmental phases, each with its own identity crisis to be resolved. Working through a crisis leads to a resolution of an identity conflict. He argued that children need to emerge from childhood with a definite sense of who they are. Youth is viewed as a period in which 'role confusion' leads to clarity in one's identity.

Developmental theory and adult perceptions of childhood, it is argued, can "… create situations in which younger children, by virtue of their age alone, have their participation rights overlooked" (Winter, 2006: 57). Slee (1993) identified the fixed stages of development theory as sharing the following attributes:

2 Erikson's theory was one of the theories cited by non-Indigenous workers in the research as being influential to social work practice in child protection. Interestingly when Erikson's model was shown to the Indigenous participants they were surprised and commented that *"that boy's confused"* and *"Holy Hell! Someone should probe him and tell him a different story"* (Stella and Petra, Indigenous workers, 2005).

- the process is orderly, linear and lasts a reasonable time;
- the new state is judged as more desirable than the previous state;
- as an outcome, the organism is healthier and more organised.

Many theorists have criticised such developmentally-based theories by highlighting their perceived gendered, class and culturally based subjects. For example Slugoski and Ginsburg (1989) challenge Erikson, saying that his theory neglects:

> … the objective conditions of a large segment of human kind for whom the envisaging of alternative possible futures would be a futile, self-delusionary exercise. For a great many people, then, the notion of normative crisis and hence identity achievement may simply not apply; for such individuals there is no problem of identity.
>
> Slugoski and Ginsburg, 1989, cited in Shotter and Gergen, 1989: 37

Attachment Theory also played a central role in social work practice in Queensland at the time the research was undertaken. It has become "… one of the most influential models guiding parent–child relationship programs of prevention, treatment, and education, including programs for Aboriginal parents" (Neckaway, 2007: 65). A number of researchers have criticised attachment theories' underlying assumptions as being based on western ideologies regarding ideal dyadic relationships and preferred developmental outcomes based on the mother/infant bond (McShane and Hastings, 2004; Rothbaum, Weisz, Pott, Mikake and Morelli, 2000). For instance, not all cultures expect mothers to be the sole caregiver (Bournstien, 1992), nor do all cultures interpret the child's needs in the same way (Sagi, 1990), or have the same reactions to emotional expressions, such as the meaning of an infant's cry (Neckaway, 2007: 28). This is particularly pertinent in the context of child protection where level of attachment forms part of Risk Assessment.

It appears that this over-emphasis on Attachment Theory works to undervalue sociological, anthropological and culturally-based theories. It is also argued that the collective nature of Aboriginal family life that emphasises independence and autonomy in child-rearing, can influence how Aboriginal children express attachment (Lynch, 2001; Ralph, 1998). Ralph (1998) explores the notion of affiliation to Aboriginal families; Aboriginal child-rearing practices consider affiliation as very important. It is through these affiliations and family networks that attachment within the child's specific cultural context is expressed. It is therefore important to consider how universalised assumptions about attachment may influence decision-making in child protection and western-based counselling practices.

Myers (1991) explored the notion of identity among traditional Pintupi[3] society in Australia. He argues that:

3 'Pintupi' refers to an Aboriginal Group who originated from Western Australia and are now located in the Northern Territory, near Alice Springs

> … shared identity with others is a primary feature of selfhood … Their concept of shared identity represents a cultural appropriation of the significant relations of cooperation and exchange that lie at the heart of Pintupi social life.
>
> 1991: 104

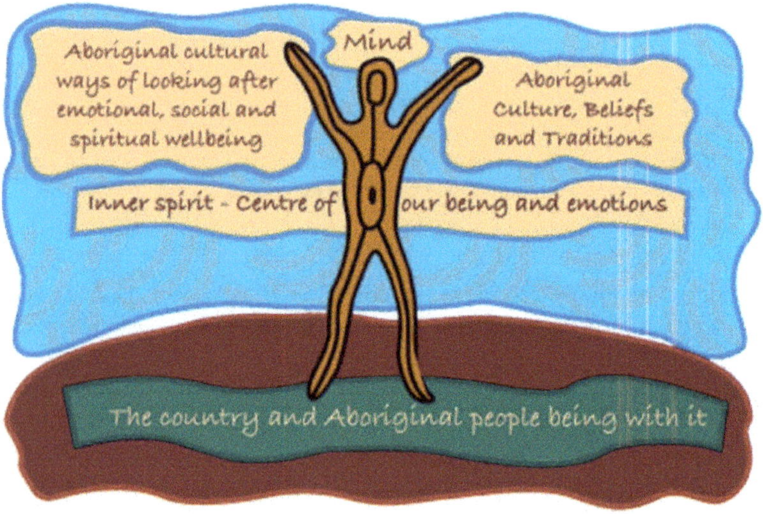

Figure 1 *Ngarlu Assessment Model*, Joe Roe, NWHS (Casey, 2014: 450).[4]

The term *walytja*, which is central to the Pintupi people, reflects a sense of belonging together or shared identity. Myers says:

> This critical notion of relatedness is rooted in the givenness of the individual, extended outwards from a spirit whose identity is derived from The Dreaming.
>
> Ibid: 105

> Fundamental to the Pintupi sense of identity is its extension to persons, place and things beyond the physical individual. Bilyurr is our spirit from within, which is in oneness with our physical body. Rai is our spirit from the country. The father dreams or sees the "child spirit" that wondered from the group dwelling place … He is now aware that his wife is or will be pregnant and that the child's spiritual connection in the form of an

4 Roe, (Purungu by skin name), is a Karajarri/Yawru man. His people are also from the Broome and Bidyadanga area. He completed a Bachelor of Applied Science in Indigenous Community Health (Mental Health Counselling Specialisation) in 1996. http://www.pallottine.org.au/waraja_ngarlu_wanduna.htm. Recent research specific to Queensland Aboriginal people in terms of spirituality and identity is currently unavailable. However, the model proposed by Roe is consistent with the findings in this and other research including models proposed by SNAICC reviewed later in this chapter.

> animal, fish, plant or a particular area in the land will coincide during the pregnancy, and be his/her Rai. The physical and spiritual conceptual place of birth becomes the central part of the identity of that person and he also becomes a protector/custodian. When we pass away our Rai (spirit from the country) goes back to the country where it pre-existed and becomes a 'child spirit' again, and remains in the group … awaiting another spiritual rebirth."
>
> Roe, 2000, cited in Casey, 2014: 450–451

The centrality of this concept of the spirit to identity and identity formation is particularly relevant in the child protection space.

The healing spirit

> When children become sick/sad, it is because their spirit has gone. If a child is hit or hurt, their spirit becomes misplaced and uncentred. They lose their sense of self.
>
> Peters, Tjilari and Ginger, SNAICC Conference, 2010

These Central Australian Aboriginal Elders, quoted above, who were also "Ngangkari" (traditional healers), spoke of being born with the spirit that holds itself in culture and language. Roe speaks of this approach as being about "Keeping the spirit strong" (cited in Casey, 2014: 450). Roe recognised that this concept of the spirit is a perspective shared across Aboriginal groups. The importance of the spirit was reiterated many times during this and other research. Of note is that it was to the spirit that participants continually referred when discussing wellbeing, for example:

> The key … the key for all of us, I think is the spiritual side of our black kids and that of all their brothers and sisters that are being … everything – you name it – that's happening to them … there's no space for the spiritual … Spirit is a healing thing.
>
> M1[5]

and:

> When a child goes through that (abuse) their spirit gets broken … their spirit gets broken and there is no one to support them … and a lot of young people commit suicide because their spirit is broken. (F2)
>
> McMahon, Reck and Walker, 2003: 5

5 Quotes marked with M or F are taken from research conducted by McMahon, Reck and Walker (2007).

Child protection: the historical context

It was also important to consider the historical context behind many local Indigenous people's lived experience as this may still be having an impact on young people, particularly those in out-of-home care. I refer here to the 'Stolen Generation' and the intergenerational impact of past policy and legislation within the child protection system in Queensland that involved the forced removal of Aboriginal children. As a consequence, the families of a large number of children in long-term foster care have experienced intergenerational involvement in the out-of-home care system. Duran (1990) refers to this 'soul wound' as being a consequence of colonisation and multiple losses across generations.

Part of *The Bringing Them Home Report* (1995) stories from Western Australian Aboriginal populations state that the effects of removal among others were:

- Feelings of alienation from their own people;
- Difficulties in imparting culture to their children;
- Breakdown of traditional family structures;
- Loss of cultural and spiritual identity;
- The loss of individual self-esteem, security and happiness.

Human Rights and Equal Opportunities Commission (HREOC), 1995: 73

It also states that: "Aboriginal people have universally complained of feeling that a part inside themselves has been forever removed, and lost to them." (HREOC, ibid).

Mal Walker, a Mackay Aboriginal Elder, described identity for young people as being "part of the circle out of which everything emanates and which contains the cyclical notion of life-death-life" (Moss, 2009, 2013, research transcript). The clan, land, elements, everything is connected within it and is interconnected. What these views represent is an entirely different paradigm surrounding the notion of childhood (Moss, 2009, 2013).

As highlighted earlier, the circle as metaphor was often used by Aboriginal, Torres Strait Islander and Australian South Sea Islander adults to describe childhood, identity development and connectedness. The Aboriginal model detailed on the next page proposes a continuum from pre-conception through to death within the life-death-life cycle. Table 1 (page 294) juxtaposes Karen Martin's Aboriginal model of childhood development (Secretariat of National Aboriginal and Islander Child Care, 2005a: 38) with Erikson's (1968) developmental model. It is important to acknowledge that due to the nature of the Aboriginal model, it does not sit well within the linear format of a table. Additionally it is pertinent to note that Torres and South Sea Islander child protection workers in this research considered that the Aboriginal model in the table did not "quite fit" their cultures. Martin's model is placed within its true circular context in Figure 2 opposite.

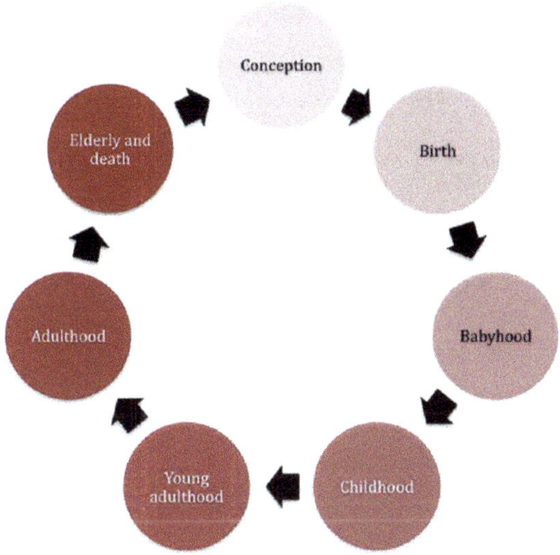

Figure 2 *Martin's model of Aboriginal child development*

Table 1 (page 294) compares Martin's model of Aboriginal child development with that of Erikson. Martin's model is a spiritual model, built on reciprocal responsibilities and relatedness. This relatedness extends further than the extended family as it incorporates everything that exists within the circle; everything is guided by the spirit. In contrast, the western model is linear and set within the medical model of normative development; this leads to detachment from the nuclear family during adolescence.

McMahon, Reck and Walker (2003) advocated extending the wellbeing indicators for Indigenous young people in out-of-home care to incorporate cultural identity and spirituality; these were identified as being particularly pertinent to Indigenous people when addressing their children's wellbeing. Their research highlighted the high level of concern among Indigenous community members for the one third of their children in care who are not placed with their families or communities. The research highlights the importance of gaining cultural knowledge of the wellbeing of young people in care, a knowledge that can only be obtained by the individual being immersed within their community and extended family, (McMahon, Reck and Walker, 2007).

Stage	Aboriginal Model	Age	Developmental Theory
Conception	Parents give function and service to the spirit of the child so that the spirit emerges. Parents prepare for the changes that will occur to 'grow-up' the child's spirit.	0–1	Trust versus mistrust. Awareness of self versus other.
Birth	Preparation for the arrival of the spirit of the child.	1–3	Autonomy versus shame and doubt. Growing separateness and individuation.
Babyhood	Introduction of the family to the child.	3–5	Initiative versus guilt. Increased differentiation and rivalry.
Childhood	Signified by physical maturation. Child viewed as capable, autonomous and an active contributor. Regulates own behaviour and building on reciprocating relatedness to others. Introduced to the elements such as the land, animals, spirits etc.	6–Puberty	Industry versus inferiority.
Young adulthood	Continuum from childhood. Experiences the world in ever- increasing sets of relatedness. Being guided by other people and other elements, especially the spirits.	Adolescence	Identity versus identity diffusion. Detachment from family.
Adulthood		Early Adulthood, 19–40	Intimacy versus isolation.
Adulthood		40–65	Generosity versus stagnation.
Elderly and death		65–death	Integrity versus despair.

Table 1 Martin versus Erikson

The research sample and setting

The initial stage of this research involved 20, in-depth, narrative art interviews with children and young people aged between 4 and 18 years. Two of the original participants participated in art-making but declined to take part in an in-depth interview. Participants were sourced from four age ranges: 4–7 years, 8–10 years, 11–14 years and 15–18 years. Each of these ranges contained a combination of male/female, Indigenous/non-Indigenous, and young people in and not in out-of-home care. The research was dependent upon the availability and suitability of potential participants for interview according to Aboriginal and Islander Foster Care agency workers, Department of Child Safety workers, carers and the children themselves. Hence the research sample contains a higher number of females, 13, or 65 per cent of the agency workers.

Of the young people interviewed, 65 per cent (13) were in out-of-home care while 35 per cent (7) had never been in care. Sixty-five per cent (13) were female, 35 per cent (7) male. Table 2 below outlines the cultural identity of participants.

Anglo/Australian	Aboriginal/TSI/ASSI	Indigenous/Anglo	Other
2	4	11	3

Table 2 Cultural identity of research participants

Three of the Indigenous/Anglo young people were unaware of their Aboriginal background at the time of the interviews. The 'other' grouping included Anglo/Afro, Anglo/Dutch and Chinese participants.

Different methods were utilised dependent on the cognitive ability of the individual to engage with the research. For those in the youngest age range, pictorial representations and storying were utilised in order to enhance understanding, informed consent and participation. For those in the older age ranges, a questionnaire was devised in order to provide in-depth information with regards to their identity and self-esteem. This information was also used to provide information for further discussion during the narrative interview. All the children and young people were invited to create an artwork during the interview and to speak to the narrative around the artwork. Some children created several pieces.

The particular qualities of image-making simultaneously allow for multiple meanings, timeframes and interrelationships for some experiences:

> … (We) simply do not understand what we are experiencing, either because the experiences aren't storyable, or because we lack the performative and narrative resources, or because vocabulary is lacking.
>
> White and Epston, 1990: 20

This is particularly the case with children who have experienced trauma; hence the image can be viewed as an extension of, as well as a vehicle for, the verbal narrative.

Interviews took place in a range of settings that included the young person's residence as well as a child friendly space. Participants were given a choice of their interview environment. This, along with other methodological decisions during the interview, helped to ensure that the young people involved felt that they had some agency and ownership of the process and thus felt more comfortable. Should there have been a disclosure of maltreatment during the interview process, ethical and mandated reporting was also undertaken to ensure the ultimate psychological safety of each young person. Given the nature of the artwork, disclosure is not uncommon. Participants also had the option of withdrawal and/or an opportunity to discuss the issue through an appropriate referral source.

Profiling and family history

In-depth profiling and family history were gathered utilising information provided by a combination of the young people themselves, out-of-home care agency staff, foster carers and departmental files. Information collected included the type and level of any abuse or neglect; family configuration including separation, divorce and death; number of schools attended; number of foster homes and departmental workers: all of these factors in combination can have an impact on a young person's life and self-esteem. Of the young people in the sample, 50 per cent (10 participants) had parents who were divorced or separated and 70 per cent (7 participants) were in out-of-home care. Five of those in care were in long-term, out-of-home care with two of these living with a relative carer. All of the young people in out-of-home care came from nuclear families that were no longer intact. As a consequence of family breakdown these young people had lost contact with some family members, three having little to no contact with their mother; all three were male. Ten had no contact with their father and four of these wanted to disown their family name. All of these children were in out-of-home care and cited the main perpetrator of abuse as being their father.

Several reasons were given for the loss of contact with parents. External factors included: father was the abuser so no contact allowed; there had never been any contact; father displayed inconsistency in contact; parent was deceased; and the young person choosing not to have contact. Reasons for loss of contact with the mother included: their mother being unavailable or highly mobile; deceased; or she did not want the child or for the child to have contact. In some instances the mother was basically unable to care for the child. This level of insecure connection, coupled with the child having experienced trauma due to abuse, can have a profound effect on a young person's sense of self and on future relationships. Findings indicate that the vast majority of children hold on to, or seek out, connection with their parents (Tucci, Mitchell and Goddard, 2006).

Of the types of abuse suffered by the young people in out-of-home care that were interviewed, 100 per cent had suffered some level of psychological abuse with 83 per cent also suffering neglect, 66 per cent domestic and family violence, 33 per cent child sexual assault and 16 per cent had been victims of severe, long-term sexual and physical abuse. In addition, the children in out-of-home care had all experienced the trauma of removal into care.

The artwork

Gilroy posits that "art-making can be a way of generating data" and that "different forms of display and audiencing can invite new understandings" (Gilroy, 2006: 96). It is important to consider the 'audiencing' of the image as a form of triangulation. Rose (2001) considers a simple structure for reading and interpreting the image in terms of its 'production', the 'image itself' and its 'audiencing'; that is, how something is made, what it looks like and how it is seen (cited in Gilroy, 2006: 97).

Gilroy also states that case study research that draws on visual methods enhances its validity because artworks can triangulate with texts of various kinds. "Triangulation refers to the use of data from different sources, gathered through different methods" (2006: 100). Triangulation is a powerful technique that facilitates the validation of data through cross verification from more than two sources. In particular, it refers to the application and combination of several research methodologies in the study of the same phenomenon. By combining multiple observers, theories, methods, and empirical materials, researchers overcome the weakness or intrinsic biases and the problems that come from single-method, single-observer and single-theory studies.

In the case of this research, triangulation occurred in several ways. The first was via the reading of images through the narratives surrounding the artworks, including the subconscious narrative such as body language, what we knew of the artist's story, and the verbal interviews. The second was the triangulation of audiencing, that is, how the art maker, the researcher and an Aboriginal Artist/Healer viewed the artwork. As stated earlier, Anthony Durwun Lee was invited to comment on the artworks and to choose his own process of doing so. In terms of process, he chose to first sit with the work and comment on the feelings they evoked for him. If there were more than one work by the same child, he would at first look at them separately and then 'read' them in sequence. He would then ask questions about the child, such as if they were in care or Indigenous. On numerous occasions he would state that by viewing the work he could ascertain that they were Aboriginal. At times he would shake his head at the sadness certain works evoked.

Data from the art-making process included subject matter, materials and colours chosen, what the individual decided to do with the artwork once completed along with the accompanying narrative which provided further insight. As Case and Dalley argue: "The image mediates between conscious and unconscious holding and symbolising past, present and future aspects of the client" (1992: 97). Of the 25 images that contained cultural symbols such as flags, Indigenous colours and totems, the majority were made by girls not in out-of-home care who were also Indigenous.

The two examples below make an interesting comparison.

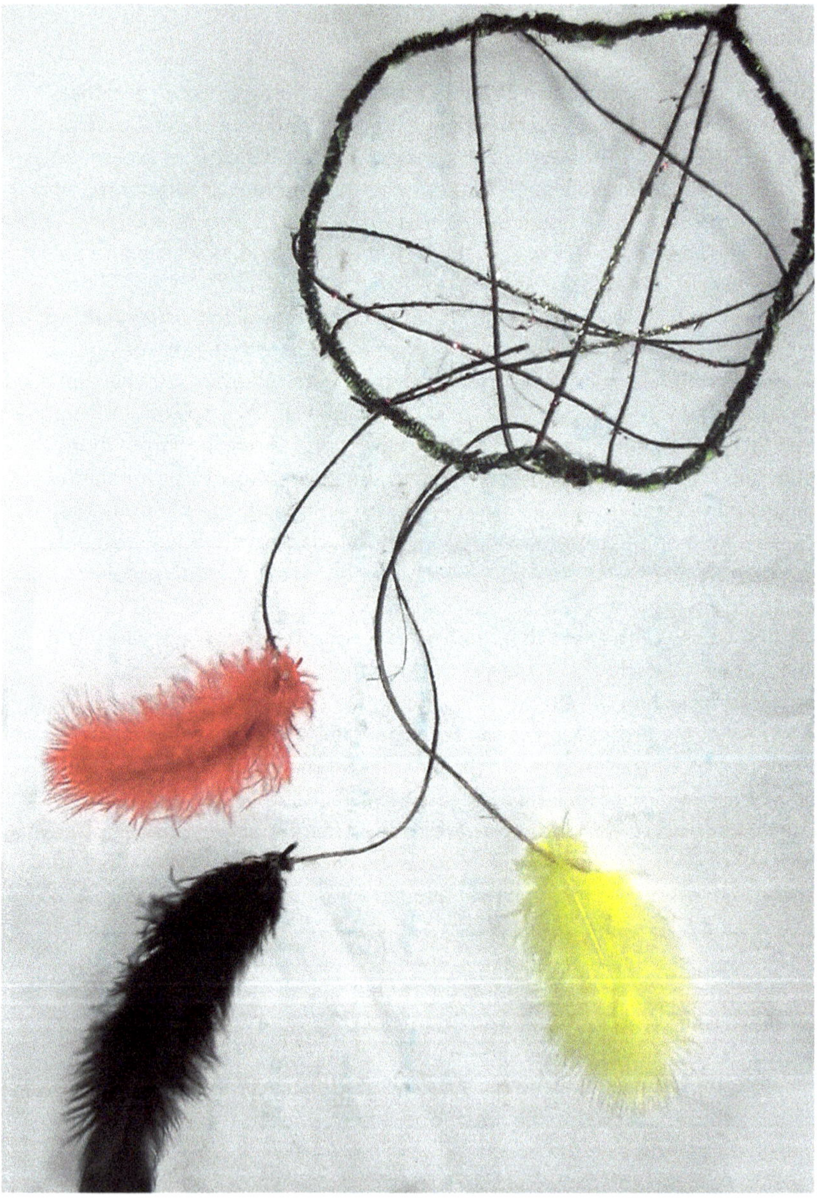

Figure 3 *Dream catcher.* Kate (2006). Mixed media.

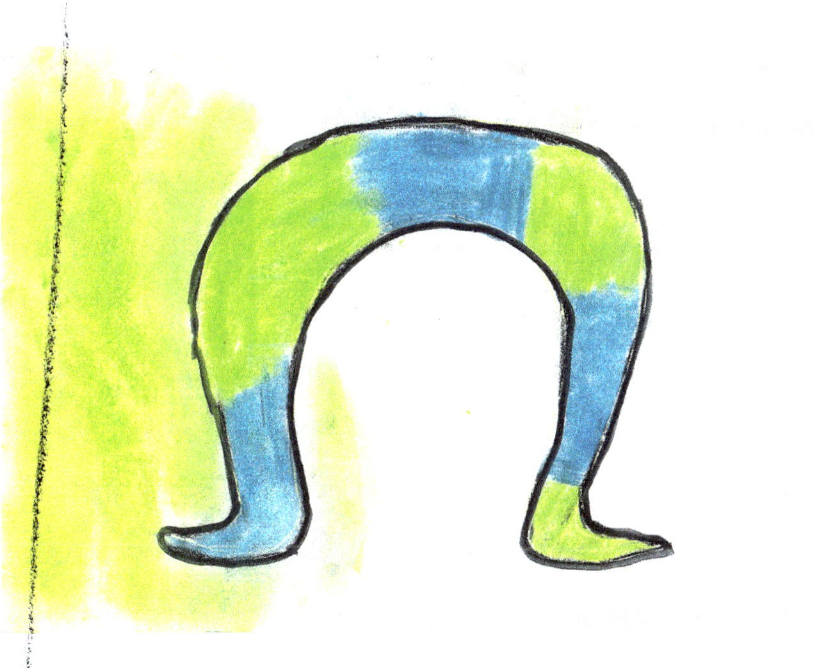

Figure 4 *Kangaroo-jack/Torres Strait Islander flag*. Dan (2006). Chalk pastel on paper

The first image (Figure 3) was created by an 11-year-old Indigenous girl, Kate, not in out-of-home care. She chose to use collage materials such as feathers and string and was very precise in her art-making process of a dream catcher created in Aboriginal flag colours. Her grandmother had taught her how to make it and although of Aboriginal/Torres Strait/South Sea Islander/ Malay and Anglo decent her father is Aboriginal. She was very proud of her creation and trusted the work would be returned to her once photographed.

On viewing Figure 3 Mr Lee stated: "This child was in a good place." I was most interested to know what he thought of Kate's cultural context. He simply stated that she had "cultural spirit." On viewing the photograph of Kate's Dream catcher his initial comment was: "Here is a child that is strong in wanting to know about culture." He went on: "It's about catching dreams and a spider's web was used. In Aboriginal culture, women would wrap their finger in spiders' webs to show status or level of law." Mr Lee was certain this child was Aboriginal and not in care, which was correct.

In contrast Figure 4 was created by a 14-year-old Aboriginal/South Sea Islander boy, Dan, in out-of-home care, who displayed little knowledge regarding his cultural heritage. He chose to copy parts of the Torres Strait Islander flag, was haphazard in his making of the drawing and the drawing remained unfinished and held little meaning for him. He stated during the interview that his mother did not want him and he would rather be on an island by himself as he could think of no significant person to include. He also showed me some dragon drawings he had drawn and kept but belittled himself and his artworks.

On sighting this work Mr Lee commented: "This child does not know his foundation." He asked for some details in how the work was made and said: "The Torres Strait Islander symbol of the headdress is incomplete. He is looking for his identity. He has issues with his identity; it is like he stopped half way and thought, 'it's not me!' This is an Indigenous boy I would say in care."

Mr Lee's comments certainly concur with what we know from other data sources about Dan's sense of identity. Dan was unable to articulate what culture he was from and remained confused as to why he could not return to his mother's home. His lack of knowing his foundation is visually demonstrated in the figure of the floating, unfinished headdress in Figure 4 that was renamed several times and discarded.

Some of the participants drew their family of origin. Figure 5 is an example from a 10-year-old Indigenous boy, Tony, in relative care. He chose red paper and red texta on which he drew stick figures, making the visibility of some

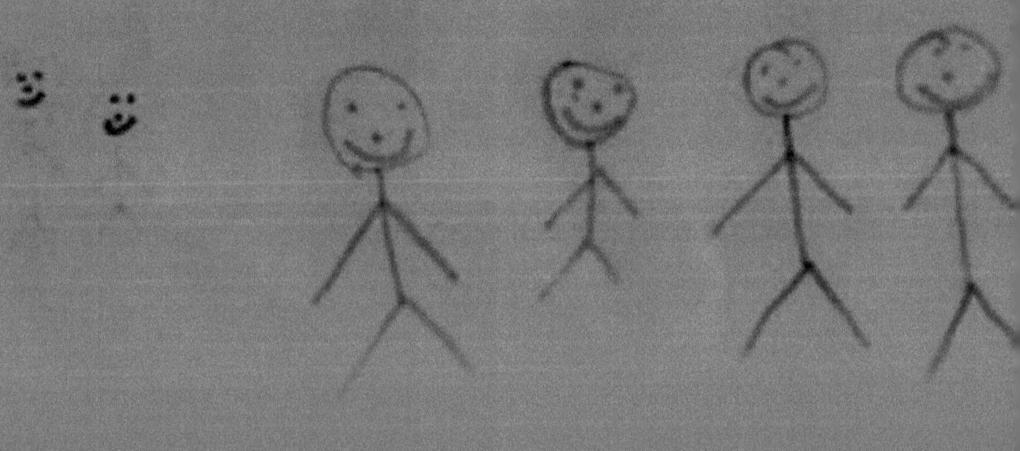

family members such as the parents difficult to see (this picture has been enhanced for clarity). He then proceeded to name all the characters (names are intentionally removed). It is noteworthy to attend to the groupings, the facial expressions and placement of the family. The parents have no faces at all and the floating legless figure of his baby brother appears at the top. This young person had been subject to severe physical and sexual abuse by his father, whilst his mother was highly mobile and mostly unavailable. The groupings in the picture are indicative of whom he felt closest to, in that he shared a placement with one other sibling and had some contact with his younger siblings. His older siblings were scattered geographically but it was clear from his narrative that he wanted regular contact with his older siblings.

Figure 5 *Untitled family drawing*. Tony (2006). Texta on paper.

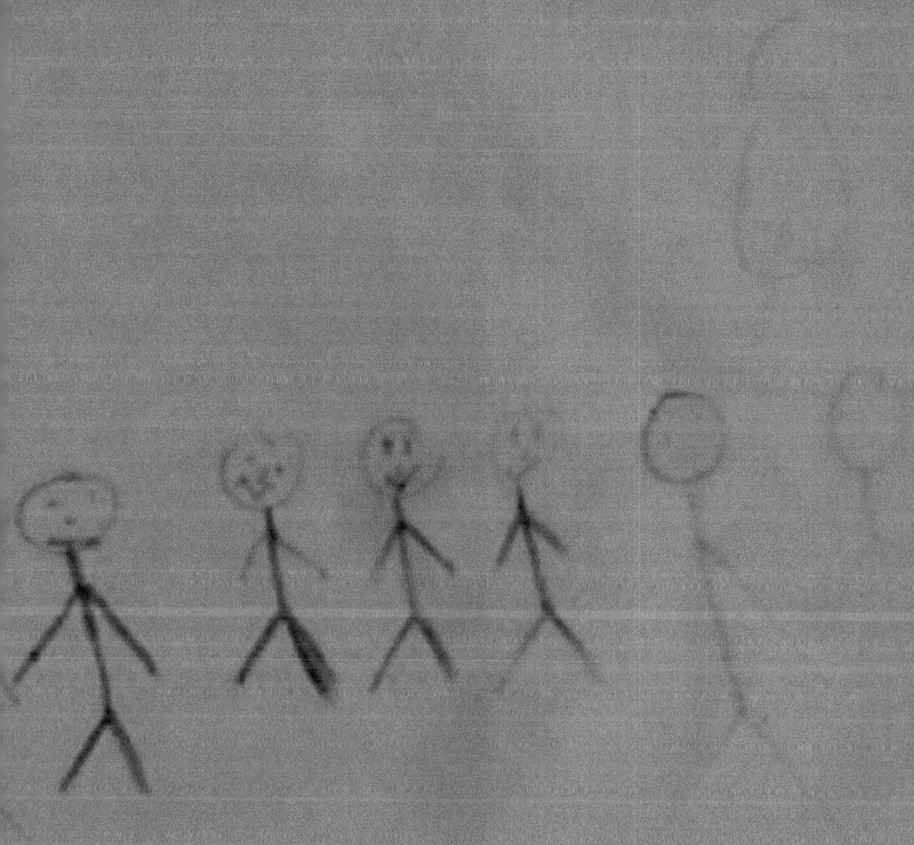

Tony also created the image shown in Figure 6. He began by using red and blue paint, straight from the palette, to paint diagonal lines that at times extended beyond the bounds of the plate. He then applied some black paint in the center of the plate and folded the plate in half, squashing the sides together. On opening up his plate, he proudly announced he was finished. Layering of a work can be indicative of something hidden.

Mr Lee's initial comment on sighting Figure 6 was "mirroring". He asked about the sequence of how the artwork was made and said:

> The energy of the artwork feels neglected and shunned. The self is hiding inside blackness. There is hope in that he used colours to express himself, then covered them up. He doesn't want to be seen or be known.

Mr Lee's initial impression of the family drawing in Figure 5 was "camouflage, red on red." Mr Lee went on to say that the artist sees the two siblings on the end differently, that they all seem happy except for the parents and that he has no relationship with the floating figure above. He thought that this child would be in care, which he is. This child also wanted to change his last name and made the following statement:

> I want to get out of this family situation. Change my name, cos I hate my dad … ! I don't want to live like my dad! I don't want to see his face!
>
> Tony, 10, Indigenous, in care

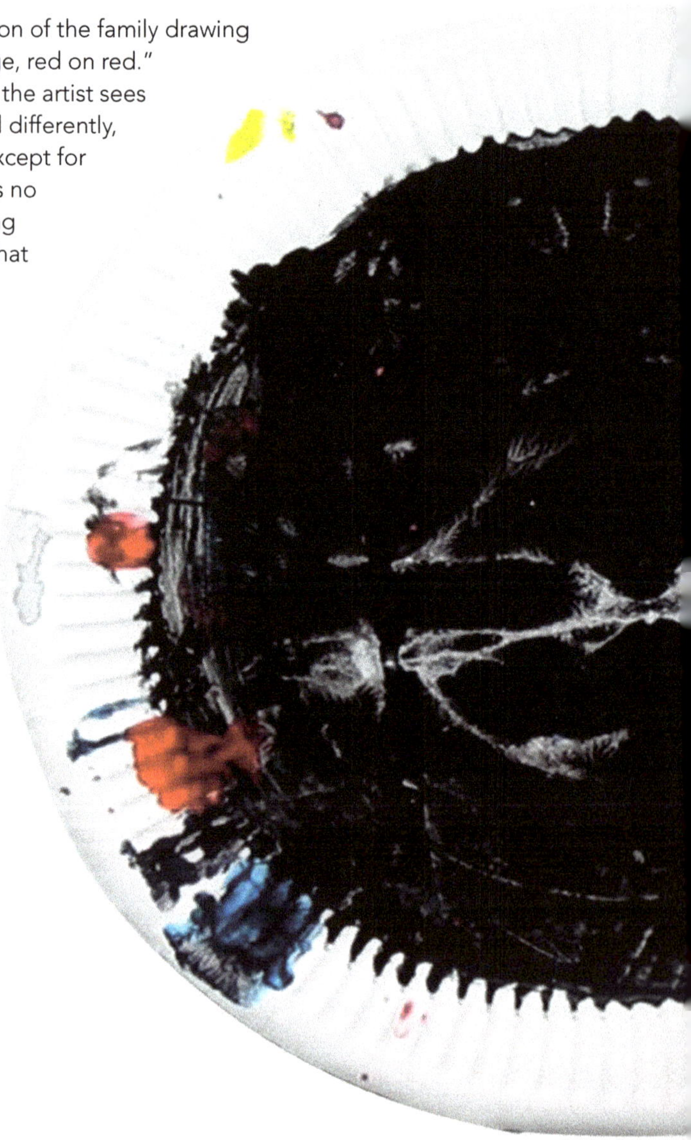

Figure 6 *Untitled*. Tony (2006). Paint on paper plate.

The image shown in Figure 6 is a typical example of the type of artwork created by a young person who has no contact with her father, ambivalent spasmodic contact with mother, separation from other siblings in care and a lack of knowledge about why she came into out of home care.

Both Figure 7 (below) and 8 (overleaf) were created by an Indigenous/ Anglo 15-year-old girl, Beth, who was in out-of-home care and who articulated a high level of anger, confusion and ambivalence towards her birth parents. She also was unable to trust and feared abandonment. Although aware of her Aboriginal heritage she chose to deny any cultural connectedness.

Figure 7 below, *Tear Drop 1*, shows the first 'tear-drop' that becomes a head that floats in the left-of-centre space amid a turbulent scribble in biro. The tear drop wears a smile which, although contradictory to the subject matter, is perhaps indicative of the smile Beth wears to cover her underlying sadness. The tear drop becomes a disembodied head with a beanie-like hat. It sits completely surrounded by turbulent marks. Such a scribble would have demanded a level of energy and an abandonment of control, although it is worth noting that the scribble in the main remains well contained within the page. Of note is that the smile becomes hidden with the imposition of the work on the other side of the page. This initial work remained unnamed, as attention was drawn to the second image (Figure 8, overleaf). This was drawn on the other side of the same page as Figure 7. That the image was flipped in order to overlay another image on the other side of the page would suggest that the initial 'tear drop' may represent those split-off feelings of anger and sadness.

When these works were shown to Mr Lee, he said: "Everything is done on the slant. It is unbalanced. There is a hidden smile, she blames herself, she needs to hide. There is lots of confusion. The smile isn't real."

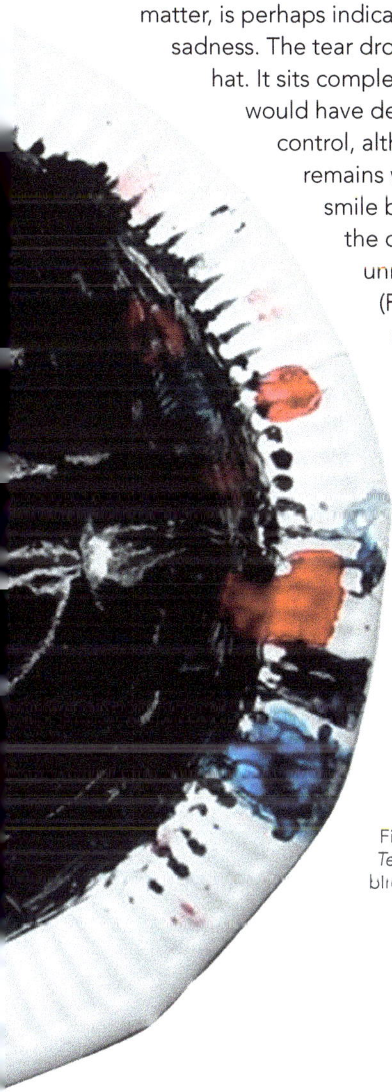

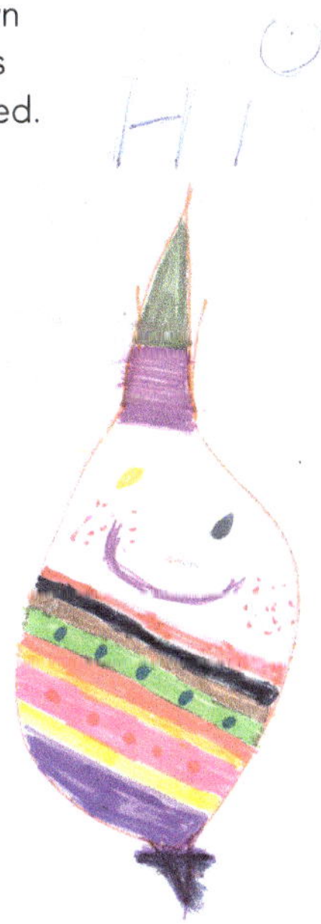

Figure 7 *"Spotty"*.
Tear Drop 1. Beth (2006). Texta and biro on paper.

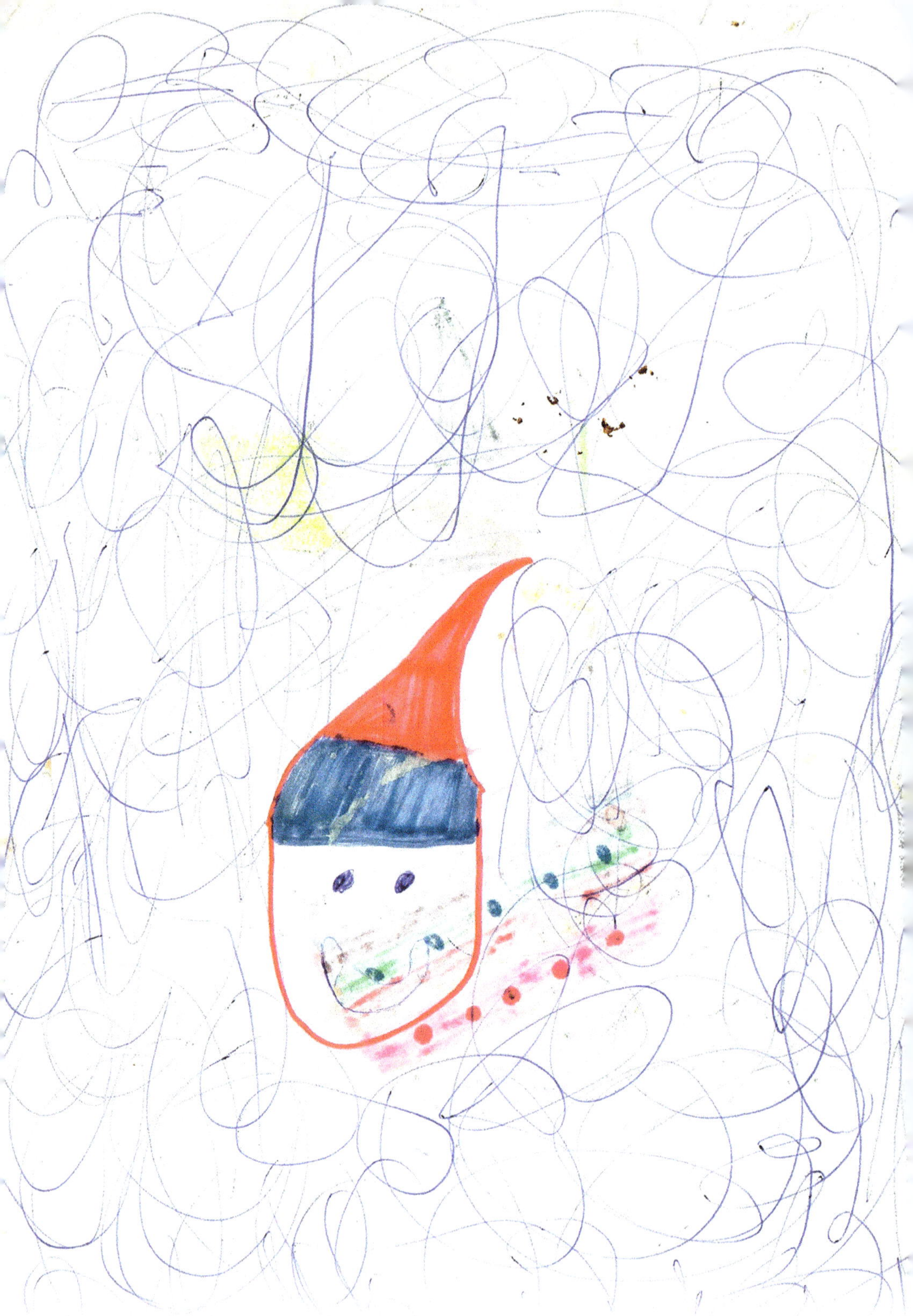

Figure 8 *"Spotty"*. *Tear Drop 1*. Beth (2006). Texta and biro on paper.

What young people had to say about identity and culture

Young people in the research were asked if they knew what identity meant. They were also asked questions in order to ascertain if they had an understanding of the concept as it applied to them if not the actual word. Thirty per cent (6 participants) knew what the word meant and 35 per cent (7 participants) displayed some level of identity confusion. Identity confusion was assessed during the interviews by analysing contradictions during the interview and being unable to answer any of the questions on identity, family and culture. For those 35 per cent of young people who did display identity confusion 5 were female, 2 were Indigenous and 4 were Indigenous/Anglo and 1 was Chinese; all were in out-of-home care. A typical example of this high level of identity confusion experienced by young people in out-of-home care was a 14-year-old Aboriginal/Australian South Sea Islander boy, Dan, who did not know his mother's or father's cultural background and cited the foster carer as being a blood uncle, even though they are not related and from a different cultural background. He showed little attachment to the carer and talked of running away and not needing anyone.

When asked about Australian culture it was very clear that the dominant culture is all-pervasive. For many of the young people it, "just is" or it is "the place that you live in". For one 13-year-old Aboriginal/Anglo boy, Andrew, who was in care and who identified solely as Anglo, it was viewed as being: "... rough and tough, guts and sporty". From the sample, children as young as seven and eight had a sense of the culture as 'other'. As one young person stated: "Culture is about someone from a different place". The majority of the interviewees were from a combination of cultures hence the research tried to ascertain whether negotiating multiple cultures was an issue for young people. All of the Indigenous girls not in out-of-home care spoke about being proud of being from different cultures, with girls from 8 years to 18 years being able to trace the cultures back through their family tree. Many were clear about their bloodline. Typical of the responses when asked if they ever felt they had to choose between cultures was one young woman's reply: "Yeah, well I see myself more Vanuatu because girls normally take their father's genes, so I think I am more Vanuatu than Torres Strait. So yeah" (Naomi, 17 years, not in care). This is in stark contrast to the majority of young people in care who were unable to articulate what cultures they were from and said that they felt disconnected from any culture.

One young woman Beth, in care, described her reaction when her mother informed her of her Aboriginality, the year before on an access visit: "It doesn't mean anything. I don't consider myself Aboriginal. To me Australia is just a country I was born in. I really don't care where I come from." This same young person mentioned finding some of her family history in a box her estranged father gave to his mother to give to her. "There was photos of when she (mum) was little and when mum was in foster care, stuff from the department. Her mother was in foster care so her background is nearly the same as mine". This was the first inkling of her family history that came to light when she began demanding answers at the age of 13. This example also raises the issue of intergenerational foster care and its effect on identity; this young person articulated deep-seated identity issues, felt unable to trust and had a history of depression.

Findings by Palmer suggest that: "[A] major issue for a few children (in care) was their real lack of family information" and "this along with other foster care experiences, could further limit family and child attachments leading to low self-esteem and identity confusion for the child." (1990:234). Sakinah et al (1994) also found that when youth are separated from their families without opportunities for personal contact or information, they may believe there is no familial or cultural heritage to relate to.

What was important to these young people?

When the young people were asked what is important to them, of the 30 per cent who cited their nuclear family none were in out-of-home care. This was in direct contrast to those children in care who more often cited friends. To Doyle (1997), relationships with same age peers, siblings, adults outside the abusive environment, organisational and religious groups, pets and toys can function as life-lines for children who have a history or who are currently victims of child maltreatment (cited in Iwaniec, Larkin and Higgins, 2006: 79). Siblings were rated as important by 75 per cent of the young people across the board. Of the 20 per cent who cited culture as important, none were in out-of-home care and all but one was female. For many of the Indigenous/Anglo young people in out-of-home care, culture was indelibly linked to the abuser; thus to deny their Indigeneity could also be a means, on an intra-psychic level, of severing their relational link to the abuser. This was particularly so for the 30 per cent of young people who wanted to change their family name and felt disconnected from their extended family.

Pets and art materials also rated highly in the research. The loss of a pet as a consequence of family violence and/or family breakdown coupled with departmental intervention, can have a huge impact on an already traumatised child. Abuse of and killing pets is often used by perpetrators of domestic violence as a part of their abusive behaviours (Tebault, 1999). Twenty per cent of the girls also named school as being important socially to them, in contrast to just 2 per cent of the boys.

Connection to family

Sense of connection to family was assessed in several ways including who the young person cited as being important to them, who they included in their family drawings and who they talked about during the interview regarding contact and wanting increased contact. Again siblings rated very highly with 75 per cent feeling connected to siblings; those in out-of-home care all wanted increased contact with siblings. Thirty-five per cent felt disconnected from their extended family with many of the children in care saying they did not know or have contact with extended family. Not surprisingly 50 per cent of the group showed signs of an overall lack of attachment, all of whom were in out-of-home care.

Many young people expressed emotions about their family of origin during the interviews. It was those young people in out-of-home care in the 8–15 years age range that expressed high levels of ambivalence towards their mother and talked of feeling betrayed by one or both parents. All but one of these young people identified as Indigenous.

A longitudinal American study found that adolescents who reported a "lower sense of connectedness to their families tend to engage in high risk taking behaviours" (Resnick et al, 1997, cited in Brindis, Park, Paul and Burg, 2002: 6). This was evidenced in this research via departmental files and information received from workers and interviews: those young people most disconnected from their families and cultural communities displayed a much higher level of risk-taking behaviours, were disconnected from the school system and were more likely to display depressive symptoms.

Self-esteem

The image in Figure 9 (overleaf) was created by an eight-year-old Indigenous girl, Abbey, in out-of-home, relative care. When asked who she would speak to if she had a worry she stated: "I keep it to myself, keep it inside me cos I just won't tell anyone and feel like running away." Abbey could not articulate her parents' cultural background, was unable to recognise emotions such as anger and fear, and identified strongly with her deceased father whilst displaying ambivalent attachment towards her mother. Abbey at times stopped contact with her mother and cited her mother's drinking behaviours as the issue.

Mr Lee spent a longer time analysing Figure 9 'Hello sun' when he noted that art-making was important to this child. He spoke of how sad and confused the figure was and that the border was drawn with a ruler. He noted: "She can draw a happy face but didn't. The swirling glitter and flower on her dress is messy like she's messed up inside and the word dog. She's emotionally confused. She wears the love hearts on the outside of the drawing behind the border."

Abbey's statement was typical of the 25 per cent of young people who talked about having issues with trust; all of these were in out-of-home care. Self-esteem was assessed in different ways. For younger respondents signs such as negative self-talk, self-conscious behaviours, ridiculing self and their artwork were analysed.

As highlighted earlier, for young people 11 years and over a questionnaire was devised in order to gain a fuller assessment that looked at culture, body image, self-esteem, drug-taking habits and a self-rating device that ascertained how they felt about different aspects of their physical self and their abilities. Other indicators included consistent or yo-yo dieting, binge drinking and/or regular drug abuse and self-harming behaviours. Of this age group, seven participants had a history of depression, of which five were Indigenous females. Four participants felt unequal to others and although there was an equal split in responses between male and female participants, three were Indigenous and all were in out-of-home care. One male and three of the females in this group

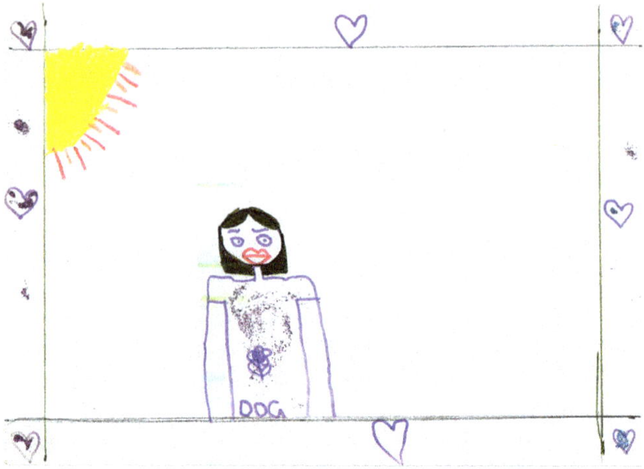

Figure 9 *Hello sun*. Abbey (2006) Texta on paper

described feelings of not liking their physical self and were highly critical of themselves with all but one of this group being Indigenous and in out-of-home care. These same young people feared abandonment.

All of the participants who did not identify as Anglo and were in care displayed self-esteem issues with a marked gender divide around body size and body image. Ninety per cent of the Indigenous girls in out-of-home care over 13 years had issues with body size and weight.

Interviews with workers

In order to ascertain how child protection workers viewed identity and how this translates into practice, workers were interviewed. These workers self-selected to participate. The table below provides a breakdown of the cultural specificity of the participants.

	Department of Child Safety Workers	AICCA Workers	Total
Indigenous	3	4	7
Non-Indigenous	4	–	4
Total	7	4	11

Table 3 Cultural specificity of child protection workers

The interviews comprised eight open-ended questions, utilised as a prompt within a conversational format in order to encourage narrative input. These questions were:

- What does identity mean to you?
- Do you think identity is important?
- How is identity formed?
- What influences identity?
- What's your view about identity and children in care?
- What theory bases do you use when dealing with identity issues?
- In practice how do you deal with these issues?
- Do you think different issues face Indigenous children and young people in regards to identity?

All of the workers interviewed could cite cases where the wrong cultural identity was attributed to a child and the negative effects this had on the child. Indigenous workers also spoke of a different value system; that is systemically, extended family were viewed by their non-Indigenous colleagues as not being part of the nuclear family and were not included as part of the case plan. This, coupled with the tendency to underrate the importance and cultural meaning of ceremonies such as funerals, likely contributed to this loss of connection to family and cultural identity:

> They should be having access every second or third week. Let the kids start seeing who their great grandmother is … you know, she's the black lady, she lives on a dirt floor … let them experience that … but then they are not given the opportunity.
>
> Stella, Indigenous child protection worker

Stella described children's attendance at ceremonies as being "The building block for the child's identity":

> The thing that hurt me the most was the Department stopping those children from attending their grandmother's funeral. See to me, that funeral was more than just putting to rest their grandmother because being there they get into that circle of family and how they are related and so it's you know, really important. Well they might think that's not important and we sort of can't really get that through that, yes it is because that's a building block for that child's identity.
>
> Stella, Indigenous child protection worker

> You know, I know how the Department thinks like … oh … a funeral that's morbid for a child, they will get traumatised. But for us it's part of that circle, the link, the spirituality. It's no use saying, oh grandma's gone to heaven and cry because you know this is what happens. This is where grandma is, this is grandma's grave. This ceremony is where the families will come, people will come from miles around, come to that funeral and that's their family expectations … it's more or less like a family reunion.
>
> Petra, Indigenous child protection worker

The majority of Indigenous worker respondents highlighted not only the differences between Aboriginal, Torres Strait and Australian South Sea Islander cultures but also spoke of the importance of knowing the differences between the numerous Aboriginal cultures:

> Look at this little one that a co-worker had to go and work with. Those little kids don't know who they are. They don't know their origin. You know we didn't know where to start with those kids and look and that big time Team Leader who said, oh take some books out show 'em some of this, show 'em that .... It's alright saying that but we gotta know where they are actually from. You know are they desert people or do they come from near the sea?
>
> Petra, Indigenous child protection worker

A participant from The Aboriginal and Islander Child Care Agency (Australia) [AICCA] referred to another case:

> It took a while for all the paperwork to be done. The family wasn't deemed suitable so we went outside the family and got an Aboriginal person as a carer for that child. The Department still wouldn't let it go. They said she was settled with a white carer.
>
> Bree, Indigenous child protection worker

Several Indigenous Departmental participants talked about non-Indigenous Department workers making judgments that they arrived at due to skin colour:

> There was a case where we didn't know the family name and the comment from the workers was: 'They are not Aboriginal they are too white'! This was from white workers. I found that really offensive, how dare they! If you passed my grandson on the street you wouldn't connect that he was my grandson.
>
> Stella, Indigenous child protection worker

Discussion

The broken circles were ever present in the narratives of both the young people in care and in the lives of some of the Indigenous workers interviewed. Dialogue from the Elders of the Central Desert who described illness and sadness in a child as a loss of spirit, was echoed in the narratives of the workers and children in this research. The legacy of the Stolen Generation and the cultural losses that ensued, in the eyes of the Indigenous workers in this research, continue to be recreated by a child protection system that refuses to acknowledge and incorporate other cultural ways of knowing and being into practice. This has consequences for identity formation for children in care.

Ever present in the research was the concept of the spirit and the spirit's link with identity and wellbeing. The sense of an Indigenous worker visiting a child occasionally so that the child will *"see a black face"* and thus identify with their Indigenous culture is highly problematic, as highlighted by a number of workers who spoke of a child needing to *"be"* in the culture and to live the culture via connected family, community members and through ceremony.

Lack of therapeutic engagement or access to appropriate counselling was also of concern. Training with specific applications for Indigenous therapeutic engagement with this cohort of children is not part of core training in a large number of social work and psychology courses. Being able to really engage with children and young people it appears is left to the individual skill set of the worker. Perhaps there is an assumption that by simply opting to work with children in child protection or counselling, that workers possess these skills, or that being trained to work with adults is transferable to working with children.

The theoretical divide between Indigenous and non-Indigenous workers came to the fore in the research; both are working with the same children and families yet they appear to be working from a different value base. In fact, they appear to be working from a different understanding of key concepts such as identity and identity formation.

The complexities of life for children in care were reflected in the children's narratives and artwork. Not only were these children dealing with removal into care, loss, the abuse itself, ongoing family issues and contact visits, but they also had to continuously negotiate their place in a foster family.

Findings from the research clearly demonstrate key differences in terms of connectedness, self-esteem, identity and psychological wellbeing for the young people in out-of-home care compared with those not in care. Young people not in care in all age ranges and both genders were much more connected to their family of origin and extended family and, as a result, identified culture and cultural practices as being important to their sense of self. Young people in care were much more likely to have lost contact with father, mother, siblings and extended family. They were also much more likely to display attachment issues, felt unable to trust, were unable to recognise emotions, had self-esteem issues and displayed a lack of cultural knowledge and a poor sense of self.

Many Indigenous young people in out-of-home care are not given opportunities to know their "country", be involved in ceremony and ritual or have knowledge of where they fit into the "circle". The key principle behind current frameworks of practice in social work, in line with developmental theory, is one of familial separation and autonomy in adolescence; this contrasts with the key principle of the Indigenous circle which advocates familial attachment and entrenchment. The few children in the research who were living with a relative carer and were linked into their extended family, cited the extended family and church as being very important to them. They also knew what culture they were from and, like the young people not in care, had little difficulty negotiating multicultural identity in that they knew and were proud of their heritage. This was in direct contrast to other young people who lived in relative care or with Indigenous carers who were not linked into their extended family.

Young Indigenous/Anglo females in care in this research were much more likely to suffer depression, identity confusion and develop self-esteem issues, particularly about body size. For young people in out-of-home care there was a definite correlation between self-esteem and identity confusion linked to their family of origin. As Bond describes:

> Most Aboriginal families right around Australia know the importance of identifying our 'mob' and where and who we are related to and where we fit in.
>
> cited in Secretariat of National Aboriginal and Islander Child Care, 2005b: 40

The majority of the young people viewed their siblings and regular contact with them as very important. Many children in care develop very close sibling bonds due to the sharing of trauma. Pets also rated highly and young people often loose pets and or access to pets as a result of coming into care.

The majority of young people, even those in the younger age groups, were able to articulate through a variety of ways their point of view. As one young person stated: Abbey, an eight-year-old in relative care but whose relative is not linked into the extended family said: "They should let me do respite with family, not white carers so I can see my other family more." This was also clear in some of the comments made by the young people about child protection workers, for example:

> They should listen to young people. Hear what they have to say, to ask them what they think and if they are safe.
>
> Beth, 15-year-old, Ind/Anglo girl, in care

> Not really happy with the department, there's not enough people and they are not around to listen to what you really want.
>
> Dan, 14-year-old, Indigenous boy in care

Paradigm shift

This research highlighted the need to reassess how workers deal with identity issues for children in care and the theory basis that underpins their work. Family Systems Theory might be reworked to incorporate context and specificity in order to better inform how to work with identity in child protection practice. There is potential in this model for adaptation to the child protection context in work with Indigenous children and families. It is vital that information about the child and his or her community – in terms of who the key players are in the circles surrounding the child – is attained at the onset of intervention. It is also important to understand that, as a child ages, the key players positioning in relation to the child are likely to move and change; practice and planning therefore needs to encompass a level of fluidity. Therapeutically this would involve including certain members of the family and community, at different times, into the therapeutic process. From the perspective of child protection agencies, such a model would rely on culturally informed and timely departmental case planning that considers the potential therapeutic impact of departmental intervention, along with utilising child friendly and culturally appropriate practices.

The proposed model demands that qualified child protection workers, work in true partnership with identified, appropriate Indigenous cultural advisor/s relative to a particular case. This entails including the Indigenous worker/s or advisors in all decision-making, assessments and case planning processes in regards to the child, with all stakeholders attending access visits and meetings as a team. Undoubtedly this model is more resource-intensive but I would argue that aside from modelling respectful behaviour, it also has the potential to help build trust and relationship with the family, which one could argue aids positive casework outcomes. The role of the Indigenous advisors is pivotal in providing the bridge between the family, their community and the state. In this way the importance of Indigenous knowledge is recognised.

In this model the child is in the centre. The model demands dialogue and mutual respect between stakeholders but most of all, it proposes that the rhetoric of 'being in the best interest of the child' be superseded by the inclusion of the child. Karen Martin's Aboriginal Model of identity formation, discussed earlier, highlights the differences in how Aboriginal people view childhood as compared with western/Anglo constructs such as Developmental Theory. Within Indigenous cultures, Aboriginal children are considered capable, autonomous and active contributors from an early age. Hence Aboriginal constructs of childhood and spirit could easily be incorporated into this model. The model also has the potential to be fluid enough to be relevant to Torres Strait and Australian South Sea Islander families, although further research needs to occur to ensure that this is the case.

The model would demand a systemic rethink that simplifies and streamlines processes. It would enable extended family to be involved from the onset of intervention. In contrast to the current child protection system in Queensland and elsewhere in Australia, the proposed systems approach is about flexibility within a framework of engagement with clear plans and goals that incorporates identity, connection and cultural knowledge at its core. The literature highlights that specific needs exist for Indigenous children as members of a minority community within an often racist society (Bamblett, Frederico, Harrison, Jackson and Lewis, 2009). A strong cultural identity can help counteract this racism. The therapeutic possibilities within child protection practice also need consideration. Healing for traumatised children does not just occur in isolation within the counselling space, it can also occur through a myriad of positive relationships.

Conclusion

From the research findings it is clear that Indigenous and Indigenous/Anglo young people in care fair badly in comparison to their not in care peers. For Indigenous young people in care, those who were with relative carers and who were connected to extended family and community fared best in terms of sense of self, self-esteem and a sense of connectedness, even when parents were unavailable and inconsistent. Those young people not in care were easily able to negotiate and trace their culture through their family lines and were proud of their cultural heritage. This was in direct contrast to the majority of Indigenous and Indigenous/Anglo young people in out-of-home care where negotiating hybridity was an issue. Girls in particular displayed high levels of identity confusion, often resulting in depression.

Further research is needed to articulate other models of childhood from an Aboriginal, Torres Strait Islander and Australian South Sea Islander viewpoint. These models need to be incorporated into child protection practice for it is clear from the research findings that for Indigenous cultures, identity is linked into the extended family, the land, ceremony and community.

Young people as young as five and six years of age were able to clearly articulate their thoughts and opinions; these should not be discounted during case planning. Contact with siblings and extended family was viewed as very important for these young people, with all participants stating that their department worker never asks them about this kind of contact.

Real and continuous participation with extended family and community in ceremony and tradition needs to be highlighted and incorporated into case planning practice for it is within this context that young people in care can find connection, belonging and pride in their cultural heritage and identity and thus can remain part of 'the circle'.

The utilisation of creative therapies and narrative was intrinsic to achieving both research and therapeutic outcomes and further research needs to be conducted to explore culturally appropriate models of practice when working with Indigenous children and families. It is imperative that we continue to question our own assumptions and theoretical underpinnings if we are to promote true healing within this context.

References

Ascione, F. and Arkow, P. (1999). *Child abuse, domestic violence and animal abuse. Linking the circles of compassion for prevention and intervention*. Purdue University Press, West Lafayette, Indiana.

Australian Institute of Health and Welfare (2015). *Australia's welfare 2015. Australia's welfare* series no. 12. Cat. no. AUS 189. Canberra.

Bernard, B. (2002). Turnaround people and places: moving from risk to resilience. In: Saleebey, D. (Ed) (2002). *The strengths perspective in social work practice*. Allyn Bacon, Boston.

Bornstein, M. (1992). Review of social influences and socialisation in infancy. *Journal of Developmental and Behavioral Pediatrics*, 24: 528–539.

Brindis, C., Park, M., Paul, J. and Burg, S (2002). A profile of adolescent health: the role of race, ethnicity and gender. *Journal of Ethnic and Cultural Diversity in Social Work*, 11 (1–2): 1–32.

Case, C. and Dalley, T. (1992). *The handbook of art therapy*. Routledge, London.

Casey, W. (2014). Strong spirit, strong mind model. Informing policy and practice. In: Dudgeon, P., Milroy, H. and Walker, R. (Eds) (2014). *Working together: Aboriginal and Torres Strait Islander mental health and wellbeing. Principles and practice*. Second edition. Commonwealth of Australia, ACT.

Commonwealth Government (1997). *Bringing them home. National inquiry into the separations of Aboriginal and Torres Strait Islander children from their families*. Commonwealth of Australia, Canberra.

Crime and Misconduct Commission, (2004). *Protecting children: an inquiry into abuse of children in foster care*. Crime and Misconduct Commission, Brisbane.

Doyle, C. (1997) Emotional abuse of children: issues for intervention. *Child Abuse Review*, 6: 330–342.

Dudgeon, P., Milroy, H. and Walker, R. (2014). *Working together: Aboriginal and Torres Strait Islander mental health and wellbeing. Principles and practice*. Second edition. Commonwealth of Australia, ACT.

Durán, E. (1990). *Transforming the soul wound: A theoretical/clinical approach to American Indian psychology*. Archana Publications, Canada.

Erikson, E. (1968) *Identity, youth and crisis*. Basic Books, New York.

Foucault, M. (1972). *The archaeology of knowledge*. Translator: Smith, S. Tavistock Publications, London.

Gibbs, A. (2001). Social work and empowerment–based research: possibilities, process and questions. *Australian Social Work*, 54 (1): 29–39.

Gilroy, A. (2006). *Art therapy, research and evidence-based practice*. Sage Publications, London.

Haebich, A. (2000). *Broken Circles*. Fremantle Arts Centre Press, WA.

Human Rights and Equal Opportunities Commission (1997). *Bringing them home: Report of the national inquiry into the separation of Aboriginal and Torres Strait Islander children from their families.* Commissioner: Ronald Wilson, Human Rights and Equal Opportunities Commission, Sydney.

Iwaniec, D., Larkin, E. and Higgins, S. (2006). Research review: risk and resilience in cases of emotional abuse. *Child and Family Social Work*, 2006, 11 (1): 73–82.

Jung, C. (1964). *Man and his symbols*. (2nd ed.) Pan Books, London.

Lonne, B, and Thomson, J (2005). Critical review of Queensland's Crime and Misconduct Commission Inquiry into abuse of children in foster care: Social work's contribution to reform. *Australian Social Work*, 58 (1): 86–99.

Lynch, P. (2001). Keeping them home: The best interests of Indigenous children and communities in Canada and Australia. *Sydney Law Review*, 23 (4): 501–542.

McMahon, A., Reck, L., and Walker, M. (2007). Defining well-being indicators for Indigenous children in care. Unpublished paper, James Cook University, Australia.

McMahon, A., Reck, L. and Walker, M. (2003). A fork in the road: Redefining the wellbeing of Indigenous children in foster care. Paper presented at *Our future generations: national Indigenous child welfare and development* seminar, Melbourne, Australia.

McShane, K. and Hastings, P. (2004). Culturally sensitive approaches to research on child development and family practices in First Peoples communities. *First Peoples Child and Family Review: A Journal on Innovation and Best Practices in Aboriginal Child Welfare Administration, Research, Policy and Practice*, 1 (1): 33–48.

Moss, M. (2013). Broken circles to a different identity: An exploration of identity for children in out of home care in Queensland, Australia. *Child and Family Social Work*, 14 (3). pp. 311–321.

Myers, F. (1991). *Pintupi Country, Pintupi Self.* Australian Institute of Aboriginal Studies. Smithsonian Institution Press, Canberra.

Neckaway, R. (2007). Is attachment theory consistent with Aboriginal parenting realities? *First Peoples Child and Family Review, 3* (2): 65–74.

Newman, I. and Benz, C. (1998). *Qualitative–quantitative research methodology: Exploring the interactive continuum*. Southern Illinois University Press, Carbondale, Il.

Onwueeguzie, A. and Leech, N. (2005). On becoming a pragmatic researcher: The importance of combining quantitative and qualitative research methodologies. *International Journal of Social Research Methodology*, 8 (5): 375–387.

Palmer, S. (1990) Group treatment of foster children to reduce separation conflicts associated with placement breakdown. *Child Welfare*, 69: 227–238.

Peters, R., Tjilari, A. and Ginger, T. (2010). Healing – traditional healing in Central Australia: Ngangkari work-Anangu way. Presentation at the Secretariat of National Aboriginal and Islander Child Care National Conference Healing in Practice, Alice Springs.

Ralph, S. (1998). The best interests of the Aboriginal child in family law proceedings. *Australian Journal of Family Law*, 12 (2): 140–149.

Resnik, M., Bearman, P., Blum, R., Bauman, K., Harris, K. and Jones, J. (1997) Protecting adolescents from harm: Findings from the National Longitudinal Study on Adolescent Health. *Journal of the American Medical Association*, 278 (10): 823–832.

Rose, G. (2001). *Visual methodologies: An introduction to the interpretation of visual materials.* Sage, London.

Rosenberg, M. (1979) *Conceiving the self.* Basic Books, University of Michigan.

Rothbaum, F., Weisz, J., Pott, M., Miyake, K. and Morelli, G. (2000). Attachment and culture: Security in the United States and Japan. *American Psychologist*, PubMed, 55 (10): 1093–1104.

Sagi, A. (1990). Attachment theory and research from a cross-cultural perspective, *Human Development*, 33 (1): 10–22.

Sakinah, N., Salahu-Din, S. and Bollman, S. (1994). Identity development and self-esteem of young adolescents in foster care. *Child and Adolescent Social Work Journal*, Springer, 11 (2): 123–135.

Slee, E. (1993). *Concepts of development in child, adolescent and family development.* Harcourt, Brace and Jovanovich, Sydney.

Slugoski, B. and Ginsberg, G. (1989) Ego identity and explanatory speech. In: Shotter, J. and Gergen, K. (Eds.) (1989) *Texts of identity.* Sage, London.

Secretariat of National Aboriginaland Islander Child Care (2005a). *Footprints to where we are; A resource manual for Aboriginal and Torres Strait Islander children's services.* SNAICC Publications, Victoria.

Secretariat of National Aboriginal and Islander Child Care (2005b). *Through young black eyes: A handbook to protect children from the impact of family violence and child abuse.* SNAICC Publications, Victoria.

Tehault, H. (1999). *Child abuse, domestic violence and animal abuse. Linking the circles of compassion for prevention and intervention.*

Tucci, J., Michelle, J. and Goddard, C. (2006). *Every child needs a hero.* Australian Childhood Foundation, Australia.

White, M. and Epston, D. (1990). *Literate means to therapeutic ends.* Dulwich Centre Publications, Adelaide.

Winter, K. (2006). Widening our knowledge concerning young looked-after children: The case for research using sociological models of childhood. *Child and Family Social Work*, 11 (1): 55–64

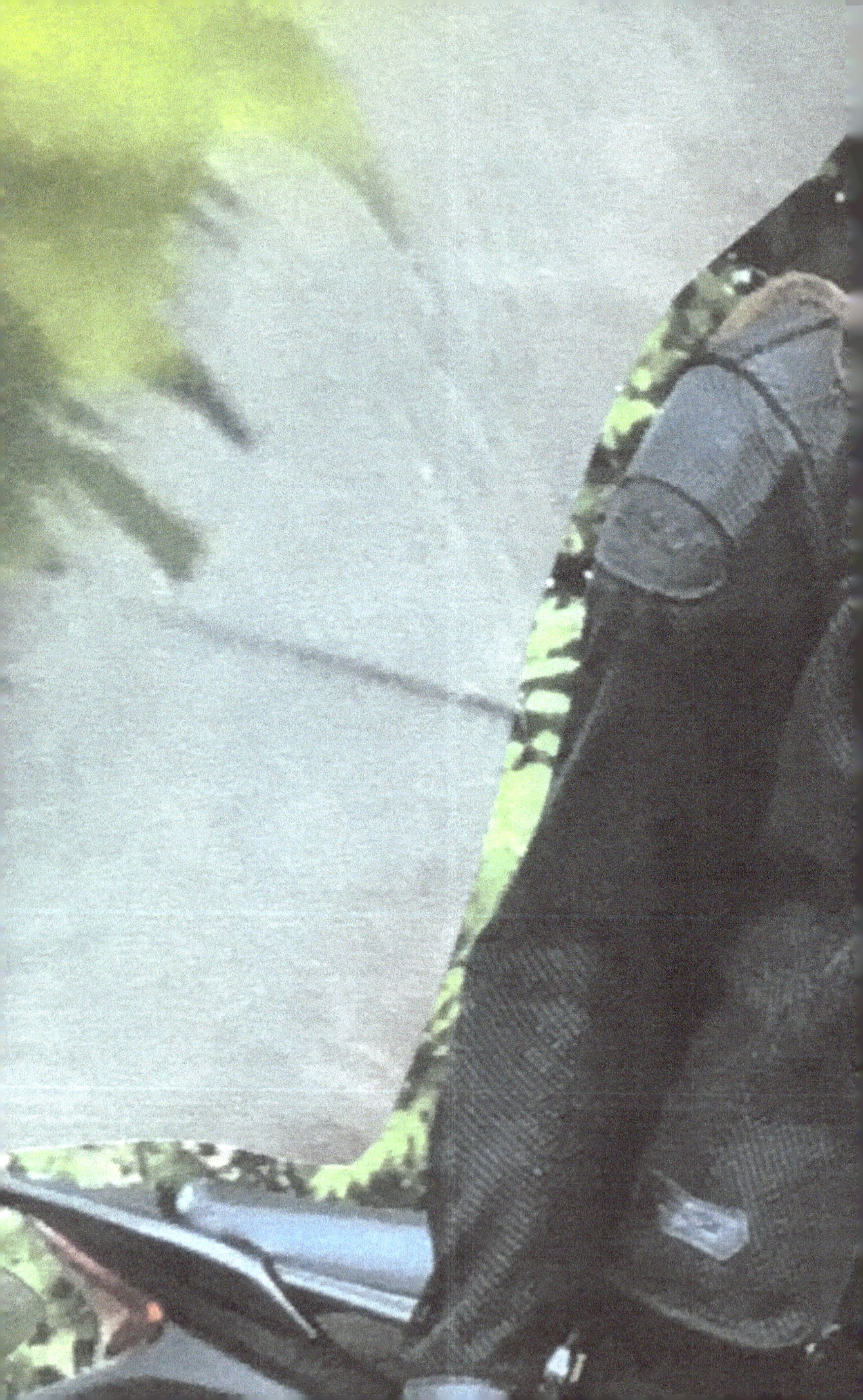

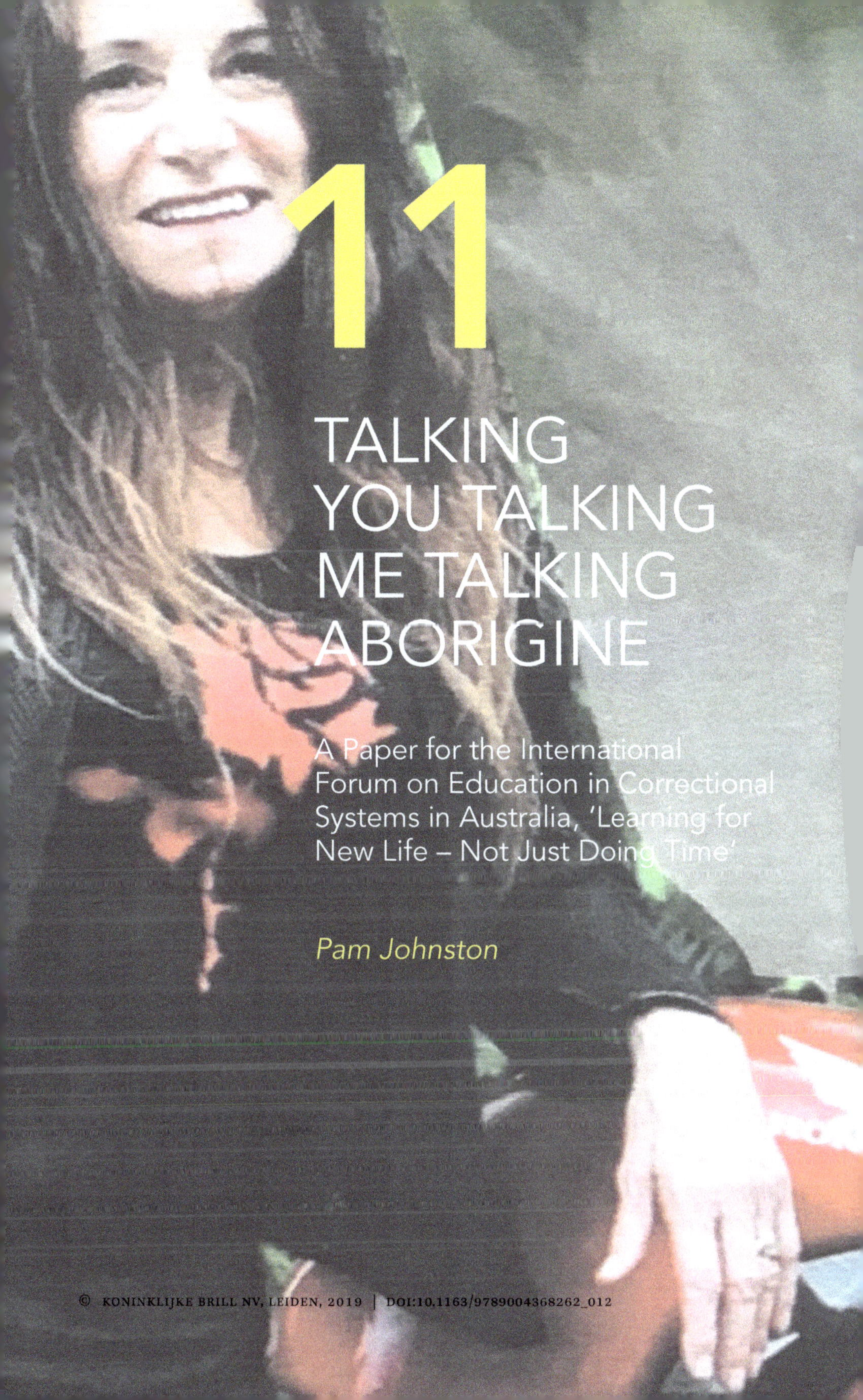

11

TALKING YOU TALKING ME TALKING ABORIGINE

A Paper for the International Forum on Education in Correctional Systems in Australia, 'Learning for New Life – Not Just Doing Time'

Pam Johnston

 | DOI:10.1163/9789004368262_012

This chapter was originally published as a conference paper and was presented to delegates, to countless students and to us by the author, our late co-editor, Pam Johnston. It is reproduced with permission from her family and from the Australasian Corrections Education Association (ACEA). We honour Pam's contribution to our learning, and to this book, by including it in its original, unedited form as a visual memoir of a seminal text that testifies to Pam's life and work.

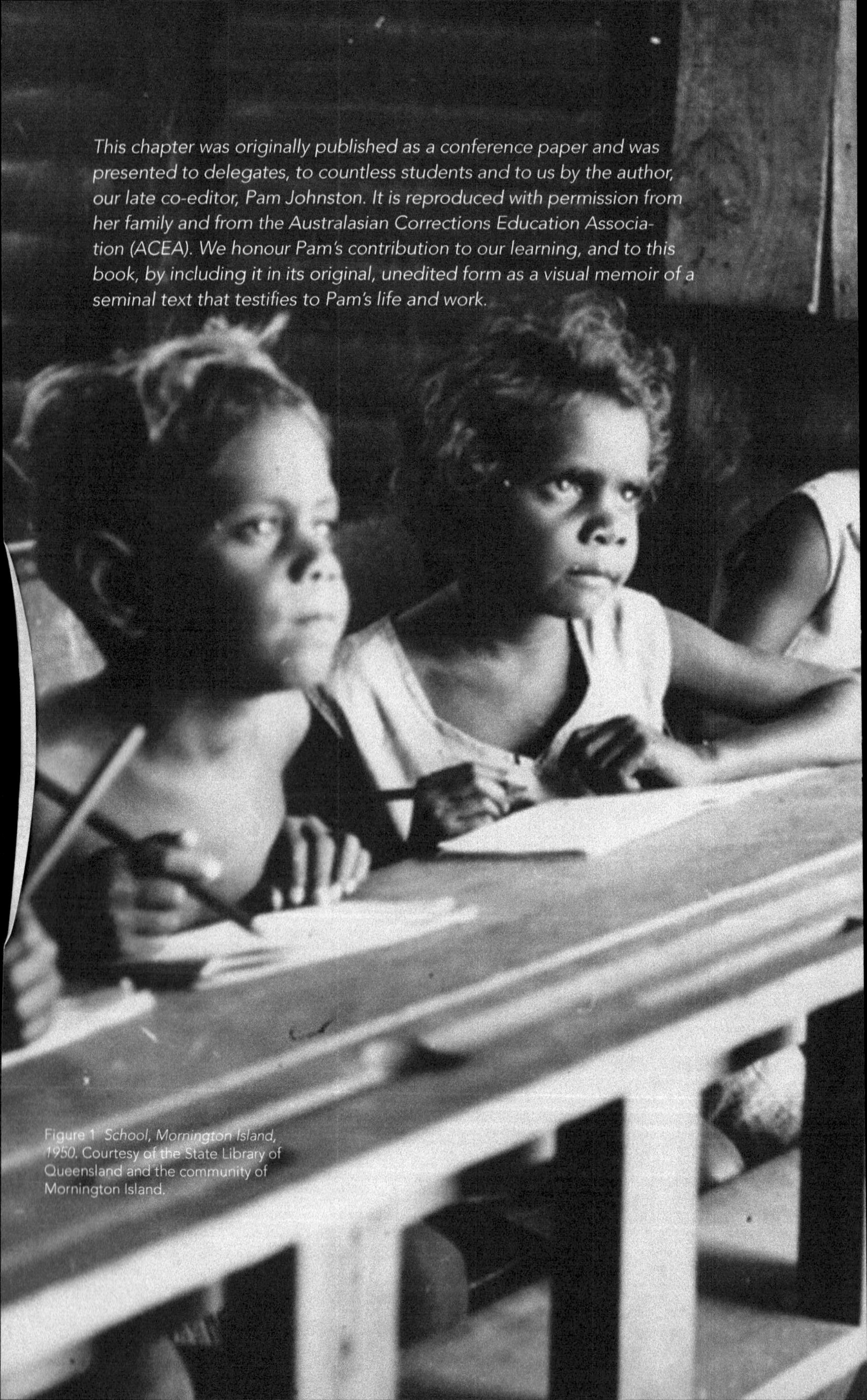

Figure 1 *School, Mornington Island, 1950.* Courtesy of the State Library of Queensland and the community of Mornington Island.

Letter to a Teacher[1]

Dear Sir/Madam,

Before you take charge of the classroom that contains my child, please ask yourself why you are going to teach Aboriginal children. What are your expectations? What rewards do you anticipate? What ego needs will our children have to meet?

Write down all the information and opinions you possess about Aborigines. What are the stereotypes and untested assumptions that you bring with you into the classroom? How many negative attitudes towards Aborigines will you put before my child?

What values, class prejudices and Norma principles do you take for granted as universal? Please remember that 'different from' is not the same as 'worse than' or 'better than' and the yardstick you use to measure your own life satisfactorily may not be appropriate for their lives.

The term 'culturally deprived' was invented by well-meaning middle-class whites to describe something they could not understand.

Too many teachers unfortunately, seem to see their role as rescuer. My child does not need to be rescued, he does not consider being Aboriginal a misfortune.

He has a culture probably older than yours, he has meaningful values and a rich and varied experimental background. However strange or incomprehensive it may seem to you, you have no right to do or say anything that implies to him that is less than satisfactory.

Our children's experiences have been different from those of the 'typical' white middle-class child for whom most school curricula seem to have been designed.

I suspect that this typical child does not exist except in the minds of curricula wishers. Nonetheless, my child's experiences have been as intense and meaningful to him as any child's.

Like most Aboriginal children his age, he is competent. He can dress himself, prepare a meal for himself, clean up afterwards, care for a younger child.

He knows his surrounds all of which is his home, like the back of his hand.

He is not accustomed to having to ask permission to do the ordinary things that are part of normal living.

He is seldom forbidden to do anything, more usually the consequence of an action are explained to him and he is allowed to decide for himself whether or not to act. This entire existence since he has been old enough to see and hear has been an experimental learning situation arranged to provide him with the opportunity to develop his skills and confidence in his own capabilities. Didactic teaching will be an alien experience to him.

---

1 *Koori Mail*, February, 2001, who say "While the author of this letter is unknown, and it has been reprinted before, the message that it seeks to convey is just as relevant today to the educators of our children and those whose job it is to plot the path for their future."

He is not self-conscious in the way many white children are. Nobody has ever told him his efforts towards independence are cute.

He is a young human being energetically doing his job, which is to get on with the process of learning to function as an adult human being.

He will respect you as a person, but he will expect you to do likewise to him.

He has been taught, by precept, that courtesy is an essential part of human conduct and rudeness is any action that makes another person feel stupid or foolish.

Do not mistake his patient courtesy for indifference or passivity.

He doesn't speak standard English but he is in no way 'linguistically handicapped'. If you will take the time and courtesy to listen and observe carefully, you will see that he and the other Aboriginal children communicate very well, both among themselves and with other Aborigines.

They speak 'functional' English, very effectively augmented by their fluency in the silent language, the subtle, unspoken communications of facial expressions, gestures, body movement and the use of personal space.

You will be advised to remember that our children are skillful interpreters of the silent language. They will know your feelings and attitudes with unerring precision, no matter how carefully you arrange your smile or modulate your voice.

They will learn in your classroom, because children learn involuntarily. What they learn will depend on you.

Will you help my child to learn to read, or will you teach him that he has a reading problem? Will you help him develop problem-solving skills, or will you teach him that school is where you try to guess what answers the teacher wants?

Will he learn that his sense of his own value and dignity is valid, or will he learn that he must forever be apologetic and 'try harder' because he isn't white"

Can you help him acquire the intellectual skills he needs without at the same time imposing your values on top of those he already has?

Respect my child. He is a person. He has a right to be himself.

An Aboriginal Parent

In an attempt to establish a picture of Indigenousness in Australia I will refer first of all to a number of statistics which I am sure have been heard and seen many times over the last few years in print and through the electronic media. I think these statistics are the most accessible way that I can illustrate what I want to present next. I am going to address first of all, the issue of the systematic discrimination of Aboriginal people since the time of colonisation, that is from the time of Captain Cook of England's arrival, to the present. I will also address the issue of the identity and the constructed identity and history of Aboriginal people since the time of colonisation. Finally I will talk about education and offer some strategies that I have developed, for comment.

In speaking of the education of Aboriginal people within prisons and beyond, my conceptual framework would be remiss if I did not explore these areas of discrimination and racism. By addressing issues of discrimination and identity I will hopefully, go some way towards illustrating an Aboriginal social reality and an Aboriginal perspective which impacts on Aboriginal receptivity to education as it is offered in a prison setting, and beyond.

The discrimination of Aboriginal people in our society is probably best reflected as I've already stated, in the statistics available through the Australian Bureau of Statistics in a number of comparative areas between Aboriginal and non-Aboriginal social realities. Estimates of the Indigenous population as at 30 June 2001[2] were:

State	Indigenous Population	Per cent of Total Population
New South Wales	121,142	28.4
Victoria	24,586	5.8
Queensland	118,749	27.8
South Australia	24,313	5.7
Western Australia	61,505	14.4
Tasmania	16,644	3.9
Northern Territory	56,364	13.2
Aust. Capital Territory	3,589	0.8

On 1 March 2000, there were 4,080 Indigenous prisoners in Australia (20 per cent of the Australian prison population). The national rate of imprisonment for indigenous persons was 1,755 per 100,000 adult indigenous population.

2 *Year Book Australia 2001*, Australian Bureau of Statistics, Number 83: pp.134–6.

New South Wales recorded 1,815 Indigenous person per 100,000 adult Indigenous population. Nationally, the Indigenous rate of imprisonment was 15 times the non-Indigenous rate. The highest ratios of Indigenous to non-Indigenous rates of imprisonment were recorded in Western Australia and New South Wales with Indigenous imprisonment rates 20 and 14 times the non-Indigenous rates respectively.[3] Some other statistics to absorb are:[4]

	Indigenous	Non-Indigenous
Life expectancy	56.9 years	75.2 years
Infant mortality	15.2 per 1000	5.0 per 1000
Total fertility	2.2 per 1000	1.8 per 1000
Under 30	68.1	43.7
Living in major urban areas	30.3	62.7
16 -year-old students	57.0	83.5
Bachelor degree	2.0	10.4
Unemployed	22.8	9.3
Employed as labourers	24.3	3.7
Household income per capita	158	310
One-parent family	29.6	14.5
Renting housing	63.8	27.1

As you are aware, these statistics are referred to again and again in many different areas, as already noted, and are depressing for their lack of variation from year to year. They are the sums that illustrate the day to day reality of possibility and hope for Aboriginal people and they are the sum of the experience and conclusions of many Aboriginal people who end up in the prison system. The statistics name a history of discrimination that appears to be accepted by non-Indigenous Australians and which is impacting on generations of Aboriginal people. I draw on the work of Philomena Essed for a definition of racial-ethnic prejudice and discrimination which is applicable in Australia:

3 *Year Book Australia 2001*, Australian Bureau of Statistics, Number 83: pp.473–4.
4 *Year Book Australia 2001*, Australian Bureau of Statistics, No.83 : Chapter 11, Crime and Justice, Australian Bureau of Statistics, Number 83, p.473. See also Draft Indigenous Education Policy, Adult Education and Vocational Training Institute (AEVTI) and Department of Corrective Services Aboriginal Policy

> Racial-ethnic prejudice is an attitude; an element of common sense, based on false generalisations of negatively valued properties attributed to racial-ethnic groups other than one's own. Common sense should not be understood as a product of deliberate, systematic, and consistent thought. It is derived from and designed to cope with the routine activities of everyday life. Common-sense notions about racial-ethnic groups and related issues enable an understanding of and communication about racial-ethnic matters in the ordinary flow of daily activities …
>
> Racism is transmitted through acts generated from a social attitude that takes the legitimacy of the racial-ethnic social order for granted. These acts, defined as discrimination, (re)produce the racial and ethnic inequalities of the social structure. Put another way, discrimination includes all acts, verbal, nonverbal, and paraverbal, that result in negative or unfavourable consequences for the dominated racial-ethnic groups, in particular. Thus, racial discrimination is defined in terms of acts and their consequences even when actors do not intend or realize, let alone pursue, the social consequences of their actions.[5]

Many Aboriginal people who end up in prison (although I don't say all) regardless of the crime/s they may have committed, believe that it is discrimination against them as Aboriginal people that is the reason for their being imprisoned. If we examine the statistics and the conclusions/inferences about Aboriginal people that have been drawn from the statistics presented, this Aboriginal viewpoint is not unreasonable.

Dispossession and despair have their own culture, their own theory and their own psychology. Colonisation has created its own myths,[6] and its own history for both Indigenous and non-Indigenous Australians. The myths surrounding Indigenousness were created by observer Europeans who also placed history, now, then, and pre-time, as European.[7]

By this systematic negation of the 'other person' and a determination to deny the other person all attributes of humanity, colonialism forces the people it dominates to ask themselves the question constantly: "In reality, who am I?" (Fanon, 1990, 200). [Editors' note: This citation, which was not footnoted in Pam's original paper, is from Fanon, F. (1961/1990). The Wretched of the Earth. (Trans. Constance Farrington, 1963), Penguin, Harmondsworth.]

---

5 Philomena Essed, *Diversity, Gender, Colour and Culture* translated by Rita Girgour, Amherst: University of Massachusetts Press, 1996, pp. 10–11. See especially Chapter 1, 'Common sense and the "other": From paternalistic to competitive racism'.

6 Roland Barthes, *Mythologies*, Noonday Press, New York, 1990. Myth, wrote Barthes, is a mechanism which produces a distorted, deformed knowledge, a knowledge "deprived of memory", "half-amputated", but still alive (122). This knowledge is presented as 'the real', as fact, as certain. But while it may have an element of truth, it is also a "dream". Mythical speed is "frozen speech" (125), a "magical object" from which history has been emptied out.

7 Paul Gilroy cites McGrane: "Beyond Europe was henceforth before Europe … differences residing in geographical space … became differences residing in developmental historical time … the simultaneity of geographical space was transformed into the successive linearity of evolutionary time' (90.cit. 329) What and who was out there beyond Europe was prior to Europe, before, not of or in Europe's time.

Each of us is surrounded by what we understand are "facts" which are interpreted via our areas of knowledge and learning. Facts cannot have shape without language.[8] As John Jackson says in his 'Hart and the Concept of Fact':

> These ascriptions do not come out there from the world, but from the conventions of the language that we have adopted to reflect the conceptual frameworks or frames of reference that makes sense to us. To determine whether something is to count as a fact, therefore, we do not dip into some linguistically naked reality, but instead we must ask whether it can be justified within the conventions of a language which are grounded in what Wittgenstein (Ludwig Wittgenstein, 'Philosophical Investigations') calls our *forms of life*.[9]

Facts themselves then, are interpreted according to many factors. Thus for a non-Aboriginal person who has been raised in a European-based education system, the linguistics of 'facts' can scientifically prove[10] that Aboriginals are 'less than' in relation to themselves. The 'facts' for an Aboriginal person who cannot see their own experiences of their lives reflected in any positive way, are that they are powerless and invisible. That their Aboriginality is the cause of everything that happens to them is confirmed by the statistical information that has already been presented, *and which is actually happening to them.* Is it then unreasonable for an Aboriginal person to assume that despite what they have done, they are imprisoned for their Aboriginality?

In 1996 the median age of the Indigenous population was 20 years compared with 34 years for the total population. With 40 per cent of the Indigenous population aged under 15 and 3 per cent over 65 the Indigenous population of 1996 had a younger age structure than that of the total Australian population at the beginning of this century.[11] 73,200 Indigenous children were attending primary school in 1999 and 33,400 Indigenous children were attending secondary school in 1999 compared to a non-Indigenous primary and secondary school population of 3.2 million students. 8,000 Indigenous students were attending institutes of higher education, with 479 of these doing post-graduate study, compared to a non-Indigenous higher education student body of 686,3000.[12]

---

8 Ngaire Naffine, *Feminism & Criminology*, Allen & Unwin Australia 1997, Ch. 6, "An Ethical Relation" p.139.

9 John Jackson, 'Hart and the Concept of fact', *The Jurisprudence of Orthodoxy: Queen's University Essays on H.L.A. Hart*, eds. P. Leith and P. Ingram, p. 72. John Jackson, 'Hart and the Concept of fact', *The Jurisprudence of Orthodoxy: Queen's University Essays on H.L.A. Hart*, eds. P. Leith and P. Ingram, p. 72.

10 Charles Darwin, 'On the Origins of Species by Means of Natural Selection: or the Preservation of Favoured Races in the Struggle for Life. New York University Press, New York, 1988 (1876), also Jean Jacques Rousseau, 'A Discourse on Inequality', Ed. And translated by Maurice Cranston, Penguin, London 1984 (1753).

11 *Year Book Australia 2001*, Chapter 5, Population, Australian Bureau of Statistics, Number 83, p.134.

12 *Year Book Australia 2001*: Chapter 10, Education and Training, Australian Bureau of Statistics, p. 403–427.

In all probability then, given the statistical information, there is a young Indigenous population some of whom will more likely than not, experience a prison education equally as likely as they will experience a non-prison education. It is also reasonable to presume that their understanding of why they are imprisoned is because of their Aboriginality. This conceptual relationship with the world is also a 'fact' for Aboriginal people in terms of education, employment, access to housing, health and so on, and it continues as a cultural normalcy with this younger generation growing up in the same world.

Thus discussions about Indigenous education which include the recognition of the social, historical and political realities of Aboriginal life will, indeed, reverberate through generations and will, indeed, impact on the survival of Indigenous people in this country.

The question of the definition and construction of Aboriginality in Australian society has been debated by generations of scholars and more recently by Aboriginal people themselves.[13] While I am aware of the extent of the depth and passion of this debate, I draw attention to it to highlight some of the influences that have impacted on the lives of Aboriginals and which have shaped the sense of identity of Aborigines in Australia.

The naming and classification of Aboriginal people have been an integral part of the colonising process. Michael (Mick) Dodson, the former Aboriginal and Torres Strait Islander Social Justice Commissioner, explored the purpose and function of *white* Australia's definition of the Indigenous people of Australia in the 1994 Wentworth Lecture, 'The end in the beginning,: Re(de) fining Aboriginality'. Dodson says:

> The definitions and constructions have not simply been for the control and management of Indigenous peoples. Our constructed identities have served a broader purpose of reflecting back to the colonising culture what it wanted or needed to see in itself. The constructions of Aboriginality, in all their variations, have marked the boundaries which define and evaluate the so-called modern world. Whether Indigenous peoples have been portrayed as 'noble' or 'ignoble', heroic or wretched had depended on what the colonising culture wanted to say or think about itself.[14]

13 Charles D. Rowley, 'Who is an Aboriginal? The answer is 1967', appendix A. in Charles D. Rowley, *Aboriginal Policy and Practice*, vol. 1, *The Destruction of Aboriginal Society*, Canberra: ANU Press, 1970: Athol Chase, 'Empty vessels and loud noises: Views About Aboriginality today', *Social Alternatives*, 2 (2), 1981, pp.23–7: Myrna E. Tonkinson 'Is it in the blood? Australian Aboriginal Identity, in Jocelyn Linnekin & Lin Poyer (eds.) *Cultural Identity and Ethnicity to the Pacific*, Honolulu University of Hawaii Press, 1990 pp. 191–218, Andrew Lattas, 'Nationalism, aesthetic redemption and Aboriginality', *The Australian Journal of Anthropology*, 2 (3), 1991, pp. 307-24, David Hollinsworth, 'Discourses on Aboriginality and the politics of identity in urban Australia', *Oceania* 63 (2) December 1992, pp. 137 55 and comments on Hollinsworth's paper (in the same volume) by Mudrooroo Nyoongah (pp. 156–7), Bain Attwood (pp.) 158–9), Andrew Lattas (pp. 160 4) and Jeremy Beckett (pp. 165 7, and a reply by Hollinsworth (pp. 168 71).

14 Michael Dodson, 'The end in the beginning: Re(de)fining Aboriginality', The Wentworth Lecture, *Australian Aboriginal Studies*, no. 1 1994, p.8.

This issue of constructed Aboriginal identity is very much at the forefront of my awareness – it hits me in the face with regular monotony each time I teach Aboriginal people in prisons. Dr Lorraine Johnson-Riordan comments in a significant soon to be published paper:[15]

> … education, along with other disciplines has a history. It is saturated in the grand master narratives of Modernity. That includes the privileging of rationality, genealogies of origins, universalising and homogenising narratives of 'the individual' and selfhood, narratives of identity formation, human progress and development, assumptions of sameness of culture and community, and the deployment of historical amnesia.[16]

Education's power then is embedded in its ability to make Aboriginal history invisible to 'knowledge' and in the process it makes Aboriginal life, Aboriginal day to day experiences, invisible to Aboriginal people as they are living it. Their lives *are* Aboriginal, yet 'education' does not tell them so. They are *Aboriginal* which lives internally and is experienced externally as a conflict and a confusion. This can perhaps be best illustrated by a recent experience of mine in a maximum security prison. It is my habit to introduce myself to inmates one by one within their living environment when starting, which most often requires a custodial officer to let me in and see me out again. In this example (which is not an unusual one) the officer introduced me as the new Aboriginal teacher *"come to teach you how to be Aboriginal"*. It was a serious introduction and by its existence causes considerable damage to the inmate in her/his relationship with the processes of institution/education by its denial of integral identity.

Another example is the reference to the idea of 'traditional' Aboriginality as opposed to most inmates not being 'proper' Aborigines. It is worth noting that Aboriginal culture is a living culture and that it is vital that this is asserted through every pore of Education's being. A living Aboriginal culture refers to a Traditional Aboriginal society, a Transitional Aboriginal society, and a Contemporary Aboriginal Society. Traditional Aboriginal society refers to Aboriginal societies and cultures developed over thousands of years with its foundations in the Dreaming. Transitional Aboriginal society is Aboriginal society since the arrival of Europeans in the 18th century. This includes the effects of cultural contact during the period from the first arrival of Europeans. Contemporary Aboriginal society refers to Aboriginal culture and communities as they exist in Australia to the present.

The variety of communities, rural, urban, and traditionally orientated, and the role of Aboriginal history, science and culture in the total Australian context; the disparities between Aboriginal and non Aboriginal societies in relation to socio-economic status, education success, health, housing and land ownership, and the prevailing attitudes and their causes between Aboriginal and non-Aboriginal people are portrayed by Aboriginal people in cultural expressions, particularly art.

---

15 Lorraine Johnson-Riordan, *Decolonising the 'white' nation: decolonising 'white' psychology*, International Journal of Critical Psychology, 2001 (currently unpublished).

16 See for example, Couze Venn, Occidentalism: Modernity and Subjectivity, Sage, London, 2000.

Professor Judith Atkinson, new Director of the College of Indigenous Australian Peoples, at Southern Cross University located in northern New South Wales, at Lismore, and also a Bundjalung woman of that region, said in relation to Indigenous education at the centre:

> I am vitally interested in the relationship between well being of people and well being of country. I am particularly interested in how traumatised groups and traumatised country results from natural disaster and human atrocity, and the natural and powerful human capacity to heal trauma. I want to know more about how people work together to help each other heal. I would like to document more, the cultural processes that Aboriginal peoples demonstrate in healing practice in our ceremonies song, art, story, and ritual and the links between so called 'traditional' cultural healing processes and the cultural knowledges and skills we utilise today in contemporary Indigenous healing practice.'[17]

Aboriginality is the only identity in the world defined legally. Aboriginality is as follows:

1 The person must identify as Aboriginal.
2 The person must have a mother or a father who identifies as an Aboriginal person.
3 The person must be accepted by their community as an Aboriginal person.

Aboriginal identity is amazing in its diversity and this has been the case since pre-European times. Aboriginal identity is based in a particular relationship to country. That relationship is clear and is identifiable through community relationships that go back to the Dreaming. Time is not static in this relationship so as much as the past will define Aboriginal relationship, so does the future, as well as the present. Mnemonics of place is reflected in the cultural practices of relationship to country and these cultural practices through song, art, story, and ritual, are vital to the continuing identity of Aboriginality. Dispossession has damaged both identity and relationship to country and for a healing to take place, Aboriginal education and healing as described by Professor Judith Atkinson, become one and the same.

The discipline of art making has had a confusing relationship to Aboriginal education which is worth talking about a little. Often the significant contribution of the processes of art making to the broader education of individuals through the development of an innate human creativity becomes the argument for a continuing programme of Aboriginal art education. These arguments can be more appropriately applied to the larger population both within a Corrective setting as well as within our education institutions in the society in which we live. The value and justification of art and culture in our society is ongoing, most recently in the tax debates in relation

17 *Koori Mail*, Wednesday, October 17th, 2001: 'New Director is Prepared for Challenge', Education Section p.29.

to the application of Australian Business Numbers and the definition of artists as small businesses in order to define the taxation process.[18]

Dr Margaret Seares at her National Press Club Address on 13 June 2001 notes that in the British government's recent Green Paper, *Culture & Creativity: The Next 10 Years,* there is clear recognition from the government as a whole of the value of immersing young people in creative pursuits including the arts. There appears to be a genuine conviction that such a move is vital if Britain is to generate a workforce which has, again, the communication skills, team work, problem solving, risk taking attributes that we understand are required in our new environment – and which are inherent in the arts experience. The foreword to the Green Paper by the Prime Minister, Tony Blair, proposes that the arts matter "because they can enrich all our lives" – standard fare. But he also says, "they also matter because creative talent will be crucial to our individual and national economic success in the economy of the future".

Dr Seares address is significant because it explains the importance of creativity to our overall quality of life as Australians. A creative life allows for a non-verbal development of a rich imaginative life, a rich spiritual life, and recognition, identification and naming of feelings and emotions, a self and identity based on a realistic self-concept, problem solving skills, team-building, risk-taking and structural skills, a safe path to literacy and numeracy, among many others. Dr Seares says:

> … there is potential for the arts to have significant impacts upon various areas of community life … Education, health, crime, social rehabilitation, community building, cultural identity – these are just a few of the areas where research exists showing the positive impact the arts can play in successful outcomes for the individuals and communities concerned.[19]

Dr Seares' significant comments are important in understanding the great contribution art education has made to our overall Australian community in all its diversity. Her comments cannot be applied specifically and particularly to Aboriginal people. Art has its own significance and its own arguments for the ongoing support of a focused art education within prisons and they are important arguments that apply also to Aboriginal people, as part of the family of humans. However, Aboriginal art programmes must have their own reasons, their own theory and justification which is different from the general art programmes as they apply, both within and outside prisons.

Indigenous identity is rooted deep in the land from where one comes as stated earlier. This relationship to land is not a relationship to 'nature' or the 'natural world', which is shared by all humanity. Aboriginal identity is affirmed through spirituality, through culture, and through history. Aboriginal spirituality is bound up in Creation Stories and a relationship to the flora and fauna of the country we belong to. Aboriginal spirituality is also expressed through our culture. Aboriginal culture is represented through our creativity

18 See National Association for the Visual Arts (N.A.V.A.) discussions papers on tax, 1999–200.

19 Dr Margaret Seares, former Chair of the Australia Council, at her National Press Club Address on 13 June 2001.

as human beings and *it is holistic*. By this I mean there is an interconnectedness of subjectivities rather than an objectivity of disciplines. A better way of explaining this is to explain a difference of culture between non-Indigenous and Indigenous people.

For non-Indigenous people, the assertion of individuality is an essential part of identity. In modernity, Individuality is easily lost. Thus authorship becomes an essential assertion of the individual. For Indigenousness, individuality is a given through relationship to land, community, and culture.

Community is of greater value and is therefore of greater assertive importance. The community one comes from, the people one is related to, the land one bears relationship to, has a greater social value.

These relationships are sacred and have traditionally been expressed in ceremony and in body painting. In very recent times, these markings have become "paintings" in the European way, as objects to be observed and explained, with a market value of their own. These paintings, be they from Yirrkala, Yuendemu, the Kimberleys, Yorta Yorta, wherever, have become an important (and I would suggest only) cultural signifier of a national identity. This is particularly so for many Indigenous people.

It is an acknowledged historical and political fact as stated earlier, that many, many Indigenous people were dispossessed from their language, their lands, their families, their spirituality, and their sacredness. Thus we have almost as a national reference, an understanding of the term "stolen generations" where governments and missionaries targeted Indigenous children for removal from their families from 1814 until the early 1970s.[20]

This disruption has impacted on Aboriginal life generationally. It has allowed for an ongoing discussion on Aboriginality including its culture, its history, and its identity, that has excluded Aboriginal people. It has disadvantaged them in such a way that official inquiries have had to be convened, legislation has had to be enacted and other processes set into place in order to redress some of the horrific disadvantages suffered by Aboriginal people.

In Modernity Indigenous people of Australia are a deeply traumatised people. Education, along with incarceration, has been a main signifier of disadvantage and alienation to Aboriginal people and a major contributor to this trauma. I refer yet again to the statistics that 73,200 Indigenous children were attending primary school in 1999 and 33,400 Indigenous children were attending secondary school in 1999 compared to a non-Indigenous primary and secondary school population of 3.2 million students. Eight thousand Indigenous students were attending institutes of higher education, with 479 of these doing post-graduate study, compared to a non-Indigenous higher education student body of 686,3000.[21]

---

20 *Bringing Them Home. Report of the National Inquiry into the Separation of Aboriginal and Torres Strait Islander Children from their Families*, convened on 2 August, 1995 and report handed down 5 April 1997 by Human Rights and Equal Opportunity Commission President Ronald Wilson, published by Sterling Press Pty. Ltd. Commonwealth of Australia, 1997.

21 Year Book Australia 2001: Chapter 10, Education and Training, Australian Bureau of Statistics, p. 403–427.

As well as the reasons outlined earlier, art education's significance to Aboriginal inmates can perhaps best be discussed in relation to my own experiences as an Aboriginal person teaching Aboriginal people in a prison setting. The underlying trauma of so many Aboriginal individuals and communities described in other sections demands acknowledgment if the educational process is to be successful. Acknowledgment also requires redress.

Through painting and the exploration of culture and identity my students have been led into a desire for a wider language. Given current recidivism rates many of my students have become quite skilled. It is a sad indictment that young Aboriginal people have more chance of being exposed to structured educational processes inside prison than they would outside prison. Given this, once again I assert the importance of what is actually offered, and how it is offered.

Aboriginal inmates by any disadvantage, are not unintelligent, unskilled or unmotivated. Without wishing to stereotype, Aboriginal social and communication skills are quite advanced. This is the result of the community culture in which they grew up, in many cases. Aboriginal history is traditionally an oral history. This does not mean that it is 'less than'. Oral history is held in a very structured way by being contained within individuals and clan groups, and within communities.

Many Aboriginal paintings that Australians are aware of, such as the "Honey Ant Dreamings"[22], and "Wakiripirri Dreamings"[23] are documentors of an oral history that contains very complex information on genealogy, geology, pharmacology, astrology, and other areas of science.

Traditional painting and ceremony document Aboriginal oral history. In many cases only certain people or certain groups have the right to produce particular parts of a whole story. Traditional Aboriginal art is meticulously retained and executed and to do other than to take care of it would mean for many of its traditional guardians a fate worse than death.[24] Art is central to Aboriginal life; it expresses the identity of individuals and family groups, and connects people to the land. It also comments on the contemporary realities of its makers.[25]

Where traditional European society is a literate society – by that I mean that written word is the predominant language of communication, documentation, and expression, for Aboriginal individuals and communities a visual language fulfills that role. Thus, in order of importance, oral skills and visual skills are primary and literacy and numeracy skills in the European educational framework, come after that. This is where Aboriginal art classes are so

22 Honey Ant Dreaming paintings from Yuendemu in the Northern Territory have been painted by the Napaljarri, Tjungarrayi, Tjupurrula clans.

23 The Wakiripirri Dreamings are owned by Napanangka, Napangardi, Japanangka, and Japangardi skins.

24 Colin Galvin, Aboriginal Art and the Protection of Indigenous Cultural Rights – a paper presented in the Australian Centre on Koori Issues: October 15, 1991, 228.

25 Avril Quail, *Marking our Times: Selected works of art from the Aboriginal and Torres Strait Islander Collection at the National Gallery of Australia,* Catalogue Introduction, National Gallery of Australia, 1996, 6

important, particularly in a Correctional setting and this is their difference from the non-Aboriginal art classes, which I emphasise here, also have a vital role to play in education and in society.

Within a prison setting how does an Aboriginal person work out who s/he is? What decides identity (not who)? What do you surround yourself with to say who you are? These questions demand an acknowledgment of Aboriginal life *under colonialism.* Without asking these questions and without seeking the answers the education we are presenting continues the problem.[26]

In answering these questions it is relevant to consider the Aboriginal images that Aboriginal people in prison are already surrounded by. I note that they constantly choose to do dot kangaroos, snakes, hands, goannas, and the sort of imagery that clearly fits a stereotypical Aboriginality in terms of presentation of art. The execution and presentation of these works is nearly always meticulous indicating a pride and care that often does not extend to other areas of their lives.

Despite great trauma in their lives, the Aboriginal students have continued to paint the images I have described, sometimes taking weeks to complete a work. It is important to realise that Aboriginal prisoners choose these images because of a relationship with the viewer as well as because of the meaning to the artist her/himself. The viewer could look at the work, which is observably Aboriginal and accept that it is Aboriginal art. Following from these observations, the viewer could conclude that it is done by an Aboriginal person. Or else they could query whether an Aboriginal person did it. Whichever way it happened, the artist's identity as an Aboriginal person is inevitably confirmed. In the production of the artwork that is produced, a first level of identity has been established, that of another person recognising Aboriginality.

The issues of education and dispossession form a complex background for the Aboriginal person in prison claiming identity through their artwork, a process unique to Aboriginality. It is reasonable to surmise that the artist's intended audience is both Aboriginal, but also non-Aboriginal, and that the imagery is deliberately confrontational in that the visual language elucidates and validates identity and therefore a history that is otherwise denied.

The artists who paint in prison describe again and again how it makes them feel "good" in their Aboriginality to have these pictures around them.

The Aboriginal students were doing these works for a different audience say, than those works which consciously research and process the imagery of Aboriginality. Nevertheless a clear function of the work was that the viewer understood by its imagery that it was Aboriginal art: therefore, the artist must be an Aboriginal artist.

---

26 See, for example, Kris Johnson: 'Learning to be White', in *Travelling Tracks: a collection of writing by Indigenous students of Goolangullia*, University of western Sydney, Macarthur, 1998, 29–32: also Lorraine Johnson-Riordan, 'Teaching/Cultural Studies (or Pedagogy for "World Travellers"/World-Travelling Pedagogy, in Joyce Canaan and Debbie Epstein, eds., *A Question of Discipline: Pedagogy, Power and the Teaching of Cultural Studies*, Westview Press, Boulder, Colorado, 1997, 117–130.

Since I first became aware of this particular process, whether I am teaching Aboriginal people in Technical and Further Education Centres, Universities, prisons, or communities, I meet the same responses. In simple terms, the process tells me how important it is to have cultural items that are perceived to be part of that culture and identifiable as part of the culture, in order to tell yourself who you are. The confirmation comes from within and without. Therefore to be surrounded by one's own being becomes a healing process and healing is a vital component of Aboriginal education.

It must also be observed that the imagery of the Aboriginal students was not imposed. It comes from and is informed by many Aboriginal communities. The hand, colours, goannas, snakes, lizards, turtles, and so on, come from somewhere. They are not accidents developed in a vacuum, just suddenly 'there'. They are images that have a discernible history and come from a specific culture. They *are* identifiable.

When I taught the Koori class at Mulawa Women's Correctional Centre from 1990 to 1996, I organised for these natural painting skills to be extended by establishing an ongoing mural project. This project wove itself around many of the buildings in the grounds and particularly established the identity of the 'Koori Room' in the education grounds. We talked, and we painted.

This is the traditional Aboriginal way and it is a comfortable way for students to become involved in a process of education.

Part of the process of developing imagery was to discuss the areas from which mothers and fathers came and the development, side by side with the murals, of their own sacred painting to be understood and explained only by the artist in each case. From these discussions we could research and establish appropriate imagery from the area. This process required a connection with culture and land, and an understanding of the students' relationship to that process as well as the end result which ensured that an inner dialogue was established in which their own lives and reality was the major narrative.

The development of both the imagery and the end result was holistic, by which I mean it allowed for a number of disciplines to both cross and interact: most importantly it addressed spiritual and cultural issues in a most personal way that allowed both ownership and healing. For Aboriginal people who continue to come into prison the murals will speak to them in a lonely and frightening setting. The murals will tell them that they are not invisible – for education to follow, students must feel visible, must feel they have a presence which is based in their reality. These murals, I am pleased to say, still exist today and hopefully will be for a long time into the future.

The development of the murals also allowed discussion on appropriate paints – the stability or otherwise of paint was a topic discussed, as was the impact of the sun, the chemical development of colour, and so on. In fact all the requirements of the technicalities of paint, fine art, and design were covered. I say that the most important part of this educational process was the spiritual healing that went on. I have sought in all my programmes to incorporate this Aboriginal perspective as an integral part of learning and teaching.

One could ask the question – given Aboriginal dispossession and the history of colonisation, how different then is the prison setting from Aboriginal inmates' experiences of education as they grew up? The answers would be varied but overall, I would have to say that the relationship to education was punitive and unproductive. Statistically, of course, Aboriginal people have less access and opportunity to education and this contributes to employment and other problems and may well be a contributor to their incarceration. For all the problems, both political and social, of their representation in prison, there is an opportunity within this setting to make education meaningful to Aboriginal people. There is an opportunity, through learning to empower, and to redress disadvantage – or we can continue the disadvantage.

An area of Aboriginal teaching in Corrective settings that cannot be avoided is that of literacy, or the lack of it. It is clear that it is an issue within prisons and it is an indicator of an alienation or disadvantage within our society. It is an issue that regularly confronts me within the classroom. I have sought to address it by recognising the primary cultural literacy skills of an Aboriginal traditional oral and visual culture. From this recognition there have been a number of strategies that I have developed that lead Aboriginal students to the written word.

I originally started teaching Aboriginal people in Long Bay Prison at Malabar, here in New South Wales. Many of the Aboriginal students were already enrolled in a number of programmes, all of which required a degree of literacy. In every case the literacy skills that the students had were far behind the requirements of the courses they were involved in. As many of these courses were being conducted by correspondence the students were, in a sense, set up for failure. And of course this was happening.

By setting aside a number of classes to simply sit and talk about the courses they were involved in, their experiences of schooling in the past, and their expectations, I was able to recognise some of the major problems that the students were confronting. The biggest single problem was that of writing an essay. Writing a paragraph was an insurmountable problem, let alone an essay. They had written before them all the processes and structures of essay writing and were being led through the process as well by committed teachers. Still it was a problem.

As I listened to the students 'speak' I realised that their literacy was contained in their language. I had a couple of small tape recorders which I brought into the prison (I did not realise at the time that this was NOT ON!) and encouraged the students to talk into the tape recorder. At first they were, of course, very self-conscious, not of the performance of the speaking, but of the sound of their voices played back to them. However, once used to the process, they went one by one to the chapel, which was a quiet and accessible place, and 'spoke' their essay into the tape. After they had done this, it was simply a matter of transcribing the tape to the written word. 'Correct English' was secondary to the integrity of voice although the basic structure of an essay was maintained.

By encouraging the students to trust what they were already skilled in, their oral ability, the students were no longer intimidated by the process of the written word. In the case I describe, the written word was another language and the strategy I used was that of translation skills from primary language – oral – to second language – written.

This strategy was developed again from 1994–1996 between the then Norma Parker Centre and Mulawa Women's Correctional Centre when I was teaching the Aboriginal classes in both these centres. In these classes, our primary focus was on painting and with the recidivism rate of the young Aboriginal women, over time the students became quite skilled and started to look for other language to assert their being.

Starting at the Norma Parker Centre for three hours a week initially, eight women I had known for many years started meeting and talking. I encouraged this round table talking as a recognition of a primary cultural skill and reference, that of an oral tradition. This talking started with working out what were common experiences and where those experiences and Aboriginality met. This important process helped to name a history that they had a place in. As Phillip Adams said in a recent article;

> History isn't was. History is. No matter how much we wipe our feet at the front door, we track history through the house. Leaving its muddy footprints all over the carpet.[27]

In owning these experiences and their history the women became quite powerful in their culture. It certainly contributed to an understanding of my assertion that they had a choice about whether they perceived themselves as victims or not. This did not deny the very real experiences of racism that they experience – what it did do by its owning was to put these experiences in a political, social, and historical context that made sense. This in turn gave them a control over the very real rage many felt at the events of their life. When this process was started there was a varying rate of literacy from illiterate to barely literate to quite literate.

Once we started these meetings (classes), I installed myself as the scribe by writing down particular narratives that came out. I did this with the group's permission and with the understanding that we would, first of all, learn to read and write, and secondly, aim towards a book of some sort. I would read my text back to the group at the end of our time and the women would observe spelling, structure, and so on. Over a period of time the role of scribe broadened as each woman became both confident and competent in this area. My focus was still on the idea of surrounding my students with their Aboriginality. With this in mind I taught them to write and to listen for the integrity of voice and language of each person. A 'correct' writing structure would come later I decided. The bigger test was to read individual texts to women who weren't part of the group, to see if they identified the voice of the writer. If there was the response "Oh that's so and so – it sounds just like her!" then I felt we had succeeded.

---

27 Phillip Adams, History is now, not later. The *Weekend Australian*, July 21–22, 2001, Review. p.36

By owning their own language and their own stories in this way, the skills base was expanded rapidly to the point where we had a number of stories that they felt were publishable. It had taken over a year to get from illiteracy to this point. I was concerned about the impact some of the stories might have. These stories spoke of incredible pain, suffering, and brutality, which, in the 'normal' course of events, would be considered private. In exposing these stories the women were very vulnerable I felt. In articulating these events as they had happened to the women, it seemed that there should be a follow-up process – perhaps counseling or psychological long- term support.

By this time I had obtained funding to publish. As a group, we talked through the issues that I raised, as well as other issues as they came up.

The final decision by the group was a resounding "publish!" The title of the work was to be *Free Spirit.*[28] I discussed with many professionals what I should do as a consequence of the revelations in the book. I was advised by Social Workers, Counselors and Psychologists that I was on dangerous ground and that professionally, I needed to put supports into place for those who might need them. However, within my own community, the discussion was very different.

Sorrow was expressed but also admiration that the women had achieved so much for themselves. I came to understand, as I already knew, that the healing language was already in the book and was already in the community. In naming their pain they owned it and that in itself was empowering. Learning the skills of naming through first of all, speaking (oral) of it, then painting (visual) it, and finally writing it down and publishing made visible what was invisible.

I wrote on the last page of this publication:

> The intention in both of the courses that produced this book was to understand history and culture and to develop literacy skills. The first teaching strategy of this course in both The Norma Parker centre, and at Mulawa Women's Detention Centre, involved extensive and casual round table discussions in order to establish where students came from, and what they understood to be 'Aboriginality'. It was a necessary definition in order to develop the discussions in terms of understanding history and culture. My interest in developing this strategy was two-fold. The first part was to put self and personal narrative into the context of a documented Aboriginal experience, and secondly to step over the endless stereotyping that goes on in relation to Aboriginal studies.
>
> Aboriginal people have been for so long observed and defined by the 'other' that their own studies of Aboriginality have become a part of their alienation from self – they observe the Aboriginal as the 'other', rarely connecting their own lives with Aboriginal history and culture. Thus the personal narrative, the 'telling' becomes a validation of identity and of existence. It's a way of saying "I am here: I lived in these times and this is what it was like for me." In the classes that produced this book, we picture a grandchild five generations to come, reading

28 The title comes from a section of a film *Blackfellas* where the main character says, "I'm free, I'm free". Many of the students were going home within the month of publication. They observed they would be "free spirits" just like the character in the film.

our stories. We asked the question, "where is the story of Aboriginal women's incarceration?" "Where are the stories that led to this point?" "What are the common themes?" "What are the differences?" We noted that we are hearing of the rise of the Aboriginal author, yet we are still seeing so few compared to non-Aboriginal authors observing the Aborigine, and contexting our lives and who we are.

Our discussion led through an analysis of Protection and how it informs us now. We found that our common acceptance from quite a young age, of police and institutional interference in our families led to an inability in many cases to effectively parent – which, it must be said, is not an inability to love. We noted that the institutionalisation of psyche continued in schooling where some students had completed up to Year 9 and Year 10 were still effectively illiterate. This did not mean that we were stupid but that the education system we had been through had failed us; that for most students further education was as realistic as a trip to Mars. We saw that our children were sometimes lost to us as we were lost to our mothers, and they to their mothers. We observed that addiction and suppressed rage, poverty and hopelessness, were a common personal experience; that the feelings of despair were all pervading, that the events that led to these feelings were still 'secret'.

The good things we had were the memories of close family and friends, of a culture that involved both the mystic and the pragmatic; that we could tell a good yarn, empathise, and laugh. Once again we noted the things untold and unspoken. These things started slipping out. These stories were written in personal diaries that I had supplied to the students. They also came through being dictated to me and read back once transcribed. They were stories told to each other and transcribed. We were careful not to lose the 'voice' – the individual stamp on language that makes 'telling' authentic.

There is a way each person speaks that belongs uniquely to them. That 'voice' gives the feeling and strength to any personal narrative. It moves the readers soul because it resounds with truth and integrity – call it what you will.

The teaching strategies as much as the curriculum application had to be necessarily different from standardised methods. Teaching in gaols requires different strategies from teaching anywhere else, I would venture to say. Teaching Aboriginal women in gaol has added challenges with no available references that are directly applicable. The strategies I have used in these courses have, as usual, led down unexpected and unexplained rivers and way out into oceans that we could have been lost upon. The writing becomes documentation and this book becomes a permanent record and insurance that we will never be lost if the stories are told. They are now part of that ever-expanding pool of Aboriginal history and culture as told by Aboriginal people. It is such a little drop but the ripples are huge. It says we are part of a living culture and that we have survived.[29]

29 Pam Johnston, *Free Spirit*, a book produced by Aboriginal women from Norma Parker Centre and Mulawa Women's Correctional Centre, funded by Blacktown Institute of TAFE, Granville Institute of TAFE. and the Department of Corrective Services, and published by Contemporary Women Artists Gallery Press, 1996, p.20.

The strategies used in the practice of education can help empower Aboriginal inmates, heal the ongoing effects of colonisation within Aboriginal communities. However, education must be relevant. Education must look both inward and outward, to its language, to its methodology, to its history, and to its understanding of both theory and knowledge. Education has to look at the implications of the practice of professional power on Aboriginal people and take responsibility for the effects of a power that in the past has discriminated against Aboriginal people by being part of the colonising process rather than being part of a solution.

Figure 2 *Pam Johnston*. Jill Westwood (2014). Collage assemblage featuring photograph of Pam Johnston. Original photographer unknown.

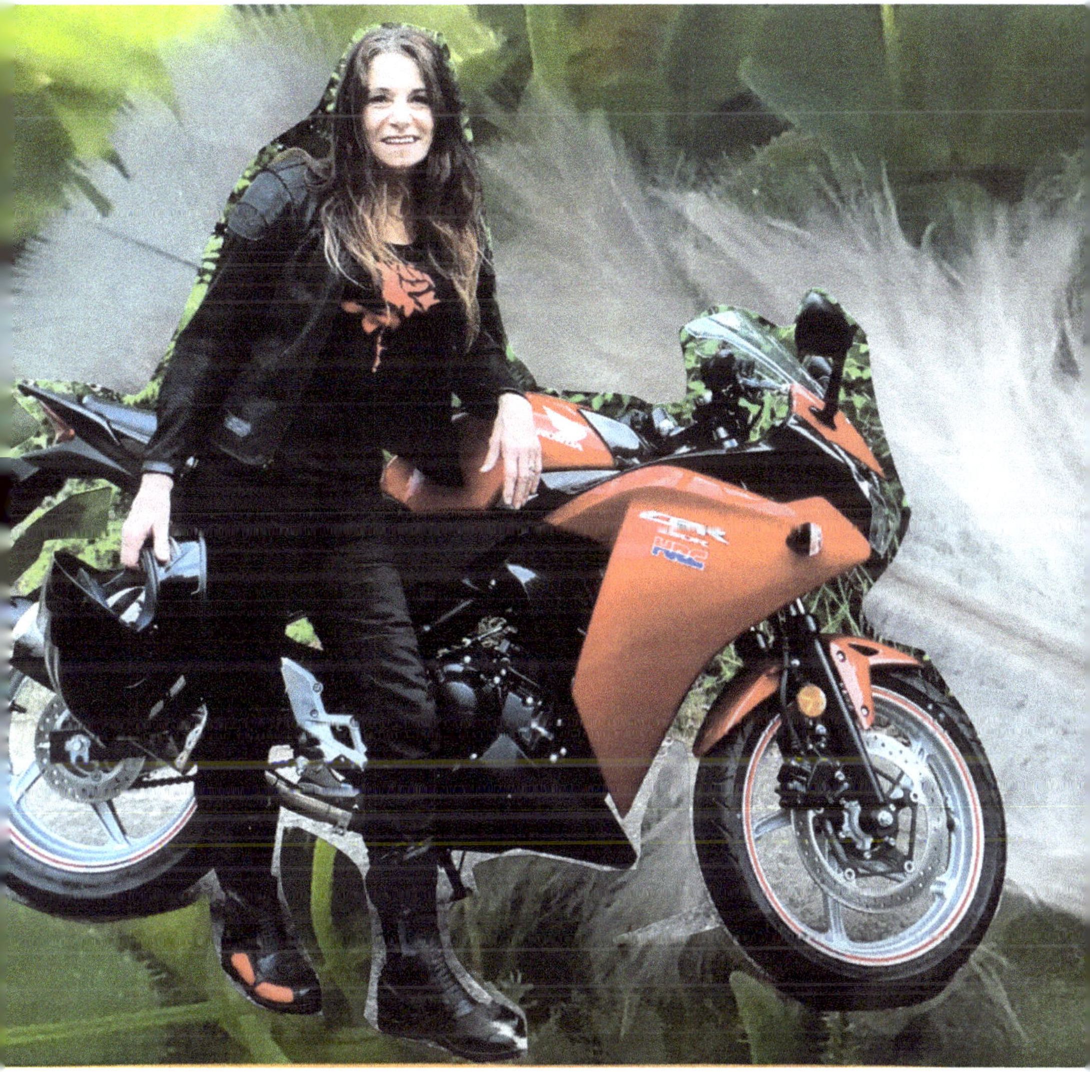

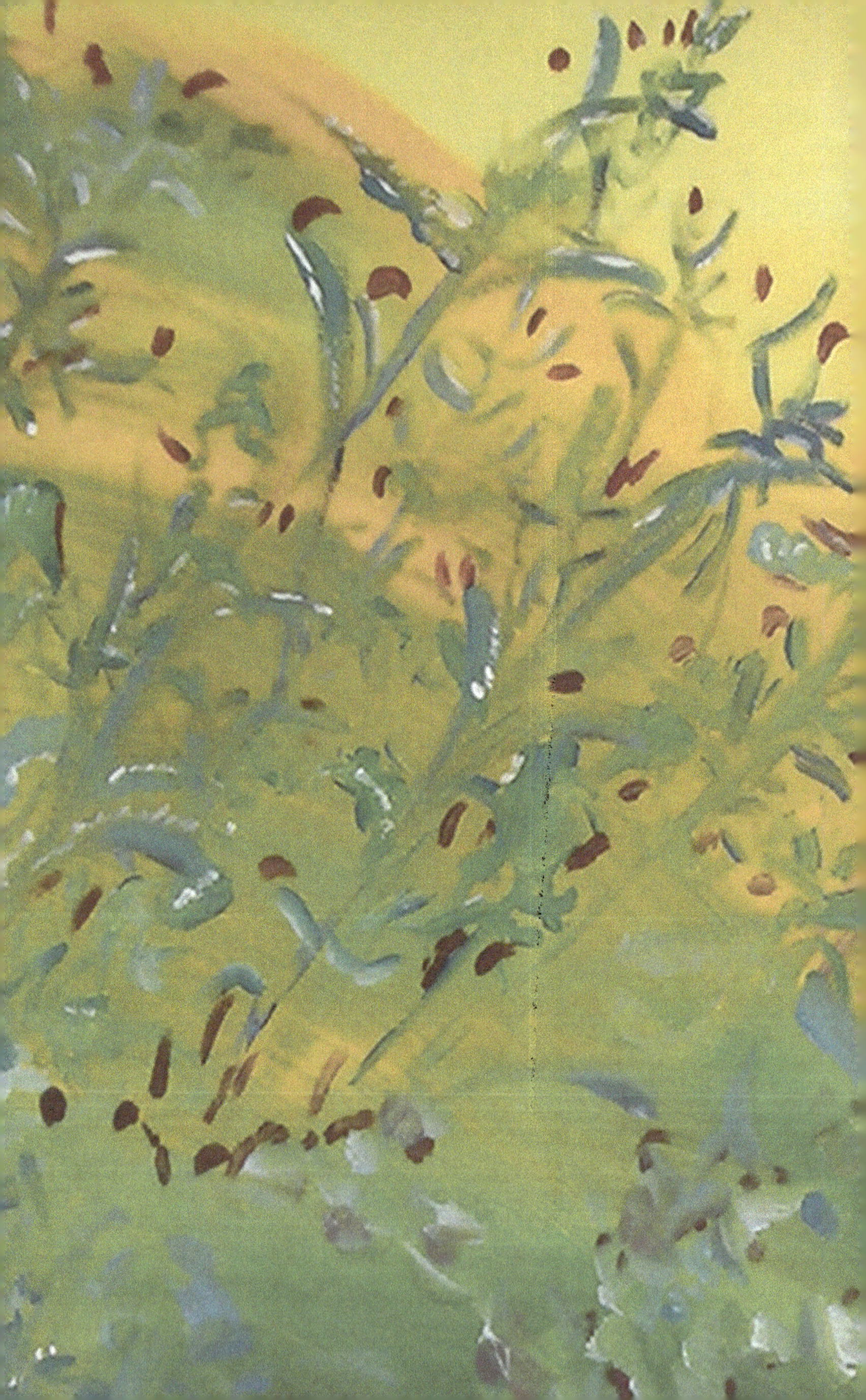

12

INTER-MISSION

An Enactment of How Art Psychotherapy and Narrative Therapy Shaped Teamwork and Therapeutic Practice in a Community-Based Counselling Service for Young People in Western Sydney

Sheridan Linnell

 | DOI:10.1163/9789004368262_013

Introduction

I wrote the short play or ethnographic drama (Richardson, 1997) that forms the centrepiece of this chapter from the edited transcripts of a videotaped conversation and email communications with members (workers, trainees and managers) of a counselling centre that is part of the Wesley Mission, one of Australia's largest non-government welfare organisations.[1] The centre, which is located in an area of outer Western Sydney marked by significant social and economic disadvantage, works from a social justice and 'strengths-based' perspective[2] with young people and their families. Over the three years prior to this conversation, the team had experimented with introducing some different approaches to working with young people, in particular, narrative therapy and art psychotherapy. This initiative was associated with an informal partnership between the counselling centre and the Master of Art Therapy at the University of Western Sydney (UWS), now Western Sydney University, with the centre offering placements to art therapists in training and employing several graduates of the course. The emphasis was not so much on taking up a narrative approach to art therapy (Freeman, Epston and Lebovits, 1997; Riley, 1999; Riley and Malchiodi, 2003; Hoshino and Cameron, 2008) as on seeing what emerged from bringing the differing frameworks of art psychotherapy and narrative therapy into a particular context for therapeutic practice. Moreover, narrative therapy and art therapy were brought into the team's ways of conceptualising and exploring their relationships with each other. For reasons that I will explain later in the chapter, the cultural influence of these therapies upon and within the team, rather than the specifics of therapeutic work with young people, is the major focus of this chapter.

The conversation was originally videotaped as the basis for a joint presentation at an international conference on narrative therapy and the arts (Linnell, Hanslow and Rummery, 2006). As my colleagues and I prepared for this conference, I was increasingly taken with the parallels between the recorded conversations and my own experiences as an art psychotherapist, narrative therapist, art therapy educator and doctoral researcher.

---

1 Wesley Mission, a church-based organisation with secular employment practices, offered art therapy placements each year to students on the Master of Art Therapy at UWS for many years. To date, the agency has employed at least seven of our art therapy graduates in various centres, on either an ongoing or project basis.

2 Some commentators within art therapy (e.g. Malchiodi and Riley, 2003) tend to group solution focussed, strengths-based and narrative approaches together, referring to them as 'post-modern' because these approaches move away from discourses of pathology and lack. However, I prefer to maintain a distinction between these approaches. Strengths-based therapy tends to locate strengths within the client, thereby inverting rather than exceeding the notion of the damaged self. Narrative therapy attempts to go beyond this inversion by deconstructing the humanist focus on the autonomous individual. Rather than 'looking for strengths', narrative therapists search out marginalised moments, and look for fissures within dominant accounts, that can be mapped into a revisioned narrative of self and relationship. In reflecting on the work at Wesley Mission, we discussed moving from a humanistic to a narrative construct by situating young people's stories of their 'strengths' within relational contexts (Linnell, Hanslow and Rummery, 2006).

When it came to writing something from the transcript of our conversations, however, I found myself hesitating to offer an analysis or an exposition of themes. I did not want to claim to truly 're-present' the views of others. Nor, as someone whose own artistic practice foregrounds writing, did I wish to write a rational account that would bolster the myth that visual images are intrinsically more 'creative' than words.

The interview itself was already a performance of meaning, conditioned by its purpose as the basis of a public presentation, and by my presence as someone outside of and unfamiliar to some of the team and yet very familiar to others. Although I had taken leave from my (then) part-time lecturing position in art therapy at UWS in order to resume full time study and complete my PhD, the art therapists and the trainee who were part of this discussion had at one time or another been my students. The team manager, whom I had known and worked with professionally for many years, was also a participant in the conversation. What could be said, and what was left unsaid, was inevitably shaped by a multiplicity of intersecting discourses, narratives, interests, relationships and hierarchies of which I was a part. My representation of this interview (or any other) could not be innocent and transparent.

Given this context, I wrote the ethnodrama that follows with a view to denaturalising assumptions of representation and truth, at the same time lending a dramatic urgency and weight to the expression of ideas, feelings, actions and relationships that shaped the team's practices and sense of themselves as therapists. Like the team painting that is the focus of its second act, the drama attempts to weave an artwork from multiple contributions, although in the writing, I am the one holding the brush. In this holding, I do not take up a Romantic position that artists and their art can tell an unconstrained truth. I am working within 'discourse' in Foucault's (1980) sense of the word: within a rich, messy landscape of intersecting relations of power and knowledge that shape what and whom become recognisable and acceptable. I am both enabled and limited by my obligations to the participants, and by my anticipation of the audiencing of the drama in its original live performance, and now in this chapter. However, I do take the position that, in offering a further iteration of meaning through an arts-based practice, I can open up an experiential/experimental space.[3]

I hope that this movement from 'transcript' to 'script' – and from interview to performance – will underline the making of meaning, and the meaning of making, that is inherent in the related projects of art, writing, therapy and research.[4]

3 It has been pointed out that some ethnodramas reinforce the researcher's claim to objectivity (Denzin, 2003; Snyder-Young, 2010): for instance, by privileging documentary theatre whether or not this is the most aesthetically appropriate form, or by insisting that sections of transcript must necessarily be reproduced exactly as they were spoken, without editing. I have kept this immanent critique in mind during the writing of this chapter.

4 There is not the space in this paper to explore the performative dimensions of art therapy and narrative therapy (Linnell, 2007, 2010). See Sally Skaife's (2008) brilliant deconstruction of the art psychotherapy/ art as therapy binary, in which Skaife turns radically toward a performative understanding of art therapy.

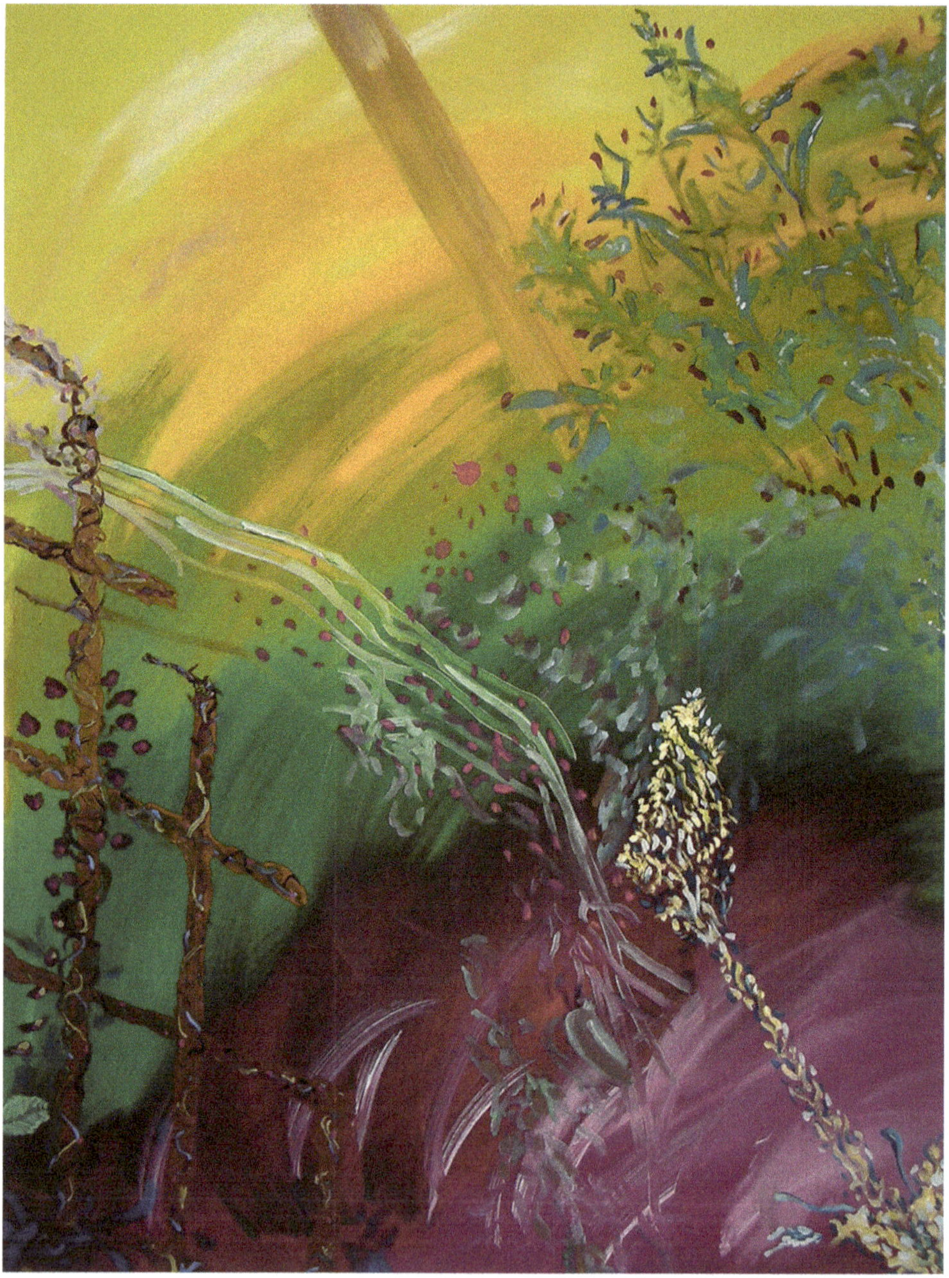

Figure 1 *Untitled (known as 'The team painting')*. Joanna Keyser, Nancy Aviah, Ian Hanslow, Josh Hinchcliffe, Liz Rummery, Fiona Tung and Sandy Weule-Warburton, (2005). Acrylic paint on canvas board.

A Yellow, Green and Burgundy Moment

A Short Ethnographic Drama in One Act, Two Scenes, Three Colours and Many Different Lines[5]

Scene 1

On one side of the stage, an actor costumed in dark red ('Burgundy') is sitting on the ground, working in a quiet and absorbed way with art materials. She occasionally leans over to write some words or to draw in a small journal with a collaged or hand-painted cover. On the other side of the stage, two actors costumed respectively in green and yellow ('Green' and 'Yellow') sit facing the audience. A photograph of the counselling team upon whose words this drama is based is projected onto the wall behind 'Green' and 'Yellow'.

GREEN *(looking around)*: When I first came here, it blew my mind. I was hearing stories that would break my heart. Narrative therapy helped me deal with that because I knew the young people who came here weren't going to be boxed – they were going to be embraced.

(addressing the audience)

It sounds weird … but you could almost see the narrative theories and ideas in the air here. When I went to team meetings there was this playfulness and movement – things were explored, whether it was in relation to the work with young people or to the team itself. You could just see this movement around the place. I went away thinking, "This is it! I just want to be a narrative therapist …"

YELLOW *(gesturing towards Burgundy, who continues to be absorbed in drawing)*: At first I asked, 'What *is* this?' *(Addressing the audience)* Coming from a psychology background where my training is predominantly to look for answers and a clear direction, I was initially confused. But I soon found my curiosity engaged by the emphasis in art therapy on creating a space in which to 'sit with uncertainty'. I started noticing how this practice allows space for thinking about what is happening. It's not as though art therapy has no 'outcomes'. I'm starting to notice what art therapy provides space for – capacities to imagine, to relate differently, to embody one's feelings in the language of art, unexpected skills of concentration and connection, the ability to create something …

GREEN: In the last couple of weeks I've entered into a different space, a place of struggling with how narrative therapy fits with me and how it fits with art therapy. I love that sense in art therapy of sitting in silence with someone making art. I'm asking where that 'sitting with' might be in narrative therapy.

5 The original cast consisted of the conference presenters: Liz Rummery as 'Burgundy', Ian Hanslow as 'Yellow' and Sheridan Linnell as 'Green'. Some aspects of the play and performance were influenced by pragmatics, such as there only being three of us, the time limit for the presentation, the need to restrict props to what we could carry on a plane, and even which of us could find or borrow the appropriately coloured clothing!

I've entered into this different space where I'm beginning to critique – it's been quite unsettling.

YELLOW: After the young people have left, the art pieces are still there. They are some kind of testimony, and yet I can't know about them in any definite or conclusive way.

BURGUNDY: How could you know what my art means for me? I could try to tell you, but it changes … often I'm not sure what it means, even if it means anything at all.

YELLOW: I often have really strong responses to the art pieces. What do I do with that? What do I do with my own responses to someone's work? I don't want to make interpretations or give my thoughts and feelings a truth status, but I don't want to ignore them either.

GREEN: I think about therapy not only as an art therapist, but from the position of being a client of art therapy, too. From that experience, I have come to really appreciate the value of sitting with feelings, as a testimony to what someone has been through.

YELLOW: I do want to acknowledge that. It worries me, though, when some therapists think you have to search out painful feelings or you aren't doing real therapy. That approach doesn't suit everyone and it certainly doesn't work for most of our young people.

BURGUNDY: As someone who has spent so much time practising as an artist, sitting with not knowing for years and years and years – and enjoying the knowing that comes from sitting with not knowing – I'm interested in what can come from the art-making process itself. I understand that narrative therapy is not about one story, but I think it's sometimes practised that way. Sometimes verbalising something narrows things.

GREEN: Does that mean we are narrowing things now?

YELLOW: What if narrative questions can open up space rather than close it down?

GREEN: And surely not all visualities are desirable. What about the clinical gaze, surveillance, or the Western technologies of point of view and perspective, all masquerading as the truth? Sorry, that was a bit of a rave. I've just been reading about critical visual methodology and it's gone to my head.

YELLOW *(smiling and looking at her/his own costume)*: And not all silences are golden.

BURGUNDY: All this talk about 'sitting with in silence' sounds a bit funny when most of the time in the young people's group they're playing their music and talking and I'm on my feet and trying to keep up! And yet, you know … just being with young people in whatever way, while we make art, not pushing them somewhere they maybe don't want to go, affirming that relationship, without filling up the space with words, and later you might see a story in the art …

GREEN: I wait for a time to ask narrative questions rather than jumping straight in. Questions that create a context where people might find words for the previously unspeakable.

YELLOW: It seems like there's a tension between some art therapy ideas and practices and some of the ideas and practices of narrative therapy – but perhaps it can be a useful tension? 'Sitting with' a tension around 'What is this?' and letting go of the idea that you have to have the answers, because lots of things will be there in the discovery.

BURGUNDY (*surprised*): When you name that tension, it feels like you've been reading my journal!

Scene 2

Yellow, Green and Burgundy sit on the side of the stage with the art materials. They are looking at a canvas, which is propped on a chair with its back to the audience so that the audience cannot see the image, and talking to each other.

Yellow: Did you notice how our conversation began to change when this painting was brought into the room?

GREEN: It even has its own chair …

BURGUNDY: I think I can remember the way that it happened. We had a large canvas on the ground. We were all sitting around. We were all sitting back.

YELLOW: I remember going across on the ferry to North Sydney with the blank canvas, wondering what it would look like when it came back.

GREEN: It was on the ground and there were shadows from things outside that were overlaying the canvas, so we decided to start with that.

BURGUNDY *(addressing Yellow):* And my memory of the way it happened was that you laid down the background with a big brush. *(A little teasingly)* You laid our foundation. Gold, green and burgundy – which we all thought was a bit odd, but then, why not …

YELLOW: And then we painted – we picked out the shadows that we wanted to respond to and added some colour to them.

GREEN: This almost lattice scaffolding type thing; I think we talked about that as our organisational structure.

BURGUNDY: Some of the meaning we gave to that was also about reaching out to our young people.

YELLOW: We were thinking of particular young people as we added these pink blobs.

GREEN: One of the pink blobs was larger than all the rest. It jumped out at us, and this provoked a particular meaning. A particular young person we remembered as having a very large influence on us all.

BURGUNDY: These white blobs that our chaplain added held a different sort of meaning for us, the kind of work she does and how that complements the work the rest of us do.

YELLOW: Adding a lightness to the work.

GREEN: We all added our bits and talked about what different aspects of it might mean for us …

BURGUNDY: … and talked about the process of doing it after we finished…

YELLOW: Why we did particular things …

GREEN: … what we were thinking of when we were doing them …

BURGUNDY: … and how it was to do it together.

YELLOW *(animatedly):* What stands out for me is my excitement and how I thought I just want to get cracking on it. And now when I come out with something at meetings, when I come out with one of my ideas about what we can do, people still comment, "Mmm. There's another yellow, green and burgundy moment!" Because people were thinking …

GREEN and BURGUNDY *(in unison): That* combination. How's it going to work?

YELLOW: I put it there and then the image just started to build on top of it.

GREEN: This painting got painted after it started with yellow, green and burgundy, and I know I was thinking, "What the heck am I going to do with this?"

BURGUNDY: We were all having our little freak-out – which I suppose is what teams sometimes do – where you feel everyone hit the wall. And yet it was in sitting with and acknowledging a difficulty that this painting got painted. And every time I look at it, I go 'Woooop' – it *is* possible! If I'm sitting here thinking where do I go with this, whether that's to do with a young person I'm working with or something in the team, I can look at this painting and know it's possible.

YELLOW: That moment was a really significant manifestation of the way this team works. How we make sense of art therapy – how we make sense *with* art therapy. How the narrative practices within the team make space for difference. How the people here are such remarkable individuals but we are also more than that, because we make up a team. And this painting sort of embodies that.

GREEN: It was within that richness that this painting got painted.

BURGUNDY: People come to the front door and see the painting and read what we have written. How this is about our team …

YELLOW: When the manager from head office saw this painting in the foyer she was really surprised. She thought it was a professional painting, not the artwork from the team day. She said that she had expected something more like a collage of individual parts put together.

GREEN: Some people have even suggested we sell it to raise funds. Next thing they'll be suggesting we sell off the young people's art too – that's economic rationalism for you!

BURGUNDY: It's interesting to hear people talking about the painting's value. Because it was a pretty powerful experience for me, doing this as a team. *(turning to Yellow)*

Was that your experience, too? I felt so touched by what you spoke to at the time …

YELLOW: I find it hard now to talk about what happened on the day. Certainly it was very strong. I can't really put it into words.

(While Yellow and Burgundy continue to look at the canvas, Green walks to the other side of the stage, sits, and mimes the action of typing a letter. An overhead of the team painting is projected on the wall behind her.)

GREEN: Subject: my reflection. Re: our team artwork.

Hi there! Looking back at when we were working on the artwork together, I remember first sitting back and letting others start off the work. I'm not sure why but it's ended up being executed as most of our projects do, with Sam[6] starting them off, either by laying down the groundwork, having the idea or delegating. So Sam was the first to go down on his hands and knees and put the background on. When he had explained his background idea, everyone sort of looked at him strangely, but when he started on his idea and the background was all done, everyone loved it; again this can be a reflection on how the team sometimes operates. We found that the canvas being on the ground in the living room fell under a beautiful shadow from the nearby window, so there was now lattice work, branches, leaves, even the shadow of a mug on the canvas. We all agreed to use these shadows as a base. When all the other staff had started a bit on it, I thought I would put my little bit on. I had kept to myself; I remember thinking a lot about this being the last time a particular team member was to be with us on a team-building day. The shadow of the mug reminded me of her,

6 A pseudonym

her cups of coffee and her warmth, so I decided that I would put the mug on the artwork to represent her, but at this point the sunlight had moved and there was no mug. I could just make out a mug handle, so I put that on, that's all that's left now, it doesn't look anything like a mug but as long as it's there, so is she, she's not exactly part of our team anymore, but she's still here, we still see her, we still talk to her. The other contribution I made was on the latticework and on the little leaves. The other staff members had already done most of the work, but I put on the finishing touches, a little bit of extra colour. I feel that's like my role at the centre too, I help with things here and there, an extra pair of hands, adding finishing touches and a bit of colour...

The End

A play of difference

Drama is classically a genre that allows for both the expression of conflict and the emergence of common themes. Writing in the form of a play allows for a play of difference. I found drama an appropriate form for embodying the differences, as well as the connections, between various participants' stories of their engagement with narrative and art therapies, with young people and with each other. The dramatic genre enabled me to give space to different discourses and to perspectives that I do not necessarily share. Creating three fictional voices from a larger number of contributing people's statements made it possible to notice how certain discourses traversed our conversation rather than remained the 'property' of individuals. The dramatic form is also suggestive of how ideas, rather than being fixed truths, are situated in changing realities and can vary across time and context. A repetition and variation of language and themes became apparent in my reading of the interview transcript, and this patterning inspired the structure and momentum of the drama. The preferred and/or taken-for-granted languages of both art therapy and narrative therapy were emphasised and 'made strange' by their juxtaposition with each other and by their inclusion in the genre of drama. Within a dramatic structure, the incommensurability of some art therapy language with the language practices of 'narrative' was given space, rather than the arguably more 'essentialist' art therapy talk being subjected to the discipline of rewriting within poststructural/narrative rhetorical conventions that would be more acceptable to a conference audience largely composed of narrative therapists.

What could be included in this play was limited by considerations of client confidentiality. Within our conference presentation, we firstly performed the play and then went on to include the voices and images of young people via an account of a cultural development project that utilised art therapy toward publicly reportable outcomes, including an exhibition. Consistent with our philosophies and practices, we wanted young people to 'have the last word' but that project is not 'my' story to tell and is not the focus of this chapter. Within the ethnodrama itself, I did not include specific stories of therapeutic work with young people because their counsellors and art therapists on the team considered it to be either impractical or untimely to seek permission from these particular young people and their families to include their stories. However, some of the counsellors participating in the interview said that holding these therapy stories in mind gave a depth to their more generalised responses. I drew instead on the stories that team members told of encountering art therapy and narrative therapy, and on how they described the effects of these practices of art and narrative on themselves and their team relationships. I was somewhat concerned that this shift away from stories of working with young people might dilute the dramatic intensity. As Johnny Saldaña (2003) emphasises, ethnodrama needs to entertain ideas and also entertain the audience.

The contrast between the more reified or abstracted tenor of the first scene and the more embodied and situated tenor of the second scene mirrored a very noticeable shift in the videotaped conversation on which the drama is predominantly based. This shift relates to and highlights a move from more abstracted dialogue, from which the specifics of therapy stories have been elided, to the dramatisation of particular team narratives. This shift also coincided with the decision to (literally) bring a painting, one that the team had made together on a team-building day, into the room where we were taping. The change in the conversation is amplified in the drama by the scene break, drawing attention to and provoking thought about the difference an art-making process and product can make to a therapeutic or research conversation.

Scene 1. Picturing art and narrative therapy

The first scene of the play opens with the words of an art therapy trainee practitioner who finds herself entranced by narrative ideas when she first comes into the team. Her words vividly picture the play of ideas, the 'dance' of narrative, as though the person's training and sensitivity as a visual artist enable her to make narrative visible. As the enchantment fades, critique becomes possible. The character begins to wonder where space, silence, and the quiet relation of 'sitting with', all powerfully defining experiences of art psychotherapy, are to be found in narrative therapy. Narrative therapy involves an active deconstruction of pathologising narratives and co-authoring of preferred stories, but people do not always want to talk about their lives and/or their art. The art therapy space legitimates the possibility of a productive silence that will not be negatively labelled as the client's 'resistance'.

This spirited appreciation and critique of narrative therapy is juxtaposed with dialogue adapted from the responses of a young psychologist, trained in a positivist psychological model, to being introduced to the aesthetics and psychodynamics of art psychotherapy. He describes a trajectory from doubt, through curiosity, to a cautious interest in which questions are kept alive. The critical qualities and openness of mind that typify the best of contemporary positivist thought are paradoxically engaged to move beyond the limits of the rational.

As the drama unfolds, more questions emerge – often unanswerable questions, but here given a productive space – in relation to the different discursive practices of art therapy and narrative therapy. How can one value silence alongside more active and conversational means of deconstruction? How can one listen to one's visceral, emotional and embodied responses, without giving these a privileged status 'outside' of discourse? What is the value of 'sitting with' pain and other intense emotions? Is this 'sitting with' a testimony to a person's resilience or a reinforcement of trauma? As a therapist, when should one speak and when be silent? Does silence also speak? What is held in an artwork through and beyond our intentions and attributions? If the visual is not unitary or innocent, what are the ethics pertaining to a therapy of multiple visualities? How can narrative therapy be critiqued from the space of the aesthetic, from that paradoxical connection of the irrational and the sensible? If, as practising artists, art therapists know about not knowing, what are the ethics pertaining to that uncertainty?

The drama is suggestive of therapeutic and discursive practices that allow incommensurability and uncertainty to play themselves out alongside a vigorous commitment to the ethics of social justice. In this view, therapists could 'provide assistance' and respect our clients' (and funding bodies') wishes for 'answers', 'outcomes' and 'solutions', without necessarily foreclosing on questions, on the indeterminacy of narratives and on processes of 'dis-solution' (White, 2004). Making art and not pressuring a person to talk about it may be 'therapeutic' although hard to quantify. In this view, therapy can be a space both inclusive and in excess of the desire for 'results'. The challenge is to acknowledge the gift inherent in that excess, while working within dominant cultures of rationality and control. Moving beyond binaries of process-oriented and outcome-oriented therapy, it becomes possible to acknowledge the subtle and powerful transformations in relationships and subjectivities that are paradoxically enabled by stepping away from expectations of specific behavioural outcomes.[7]

The play is not an attempt to resolve the differences between art psychotherapy and narrative therapy, since the notion of re-solution could be seen as part of the positivist and rationalist discourse that both art therapy and narrative therapy seek to challenge.

The drama poses the question of whether the tension between narrative therapy and art psychotherapy, between conversation and silence, between a narrative trajectory and an acknowledgement of the limits of what can be told, is a useful and productive tension (Linnell, 2008).

---

7 I am grateful to my colleague and co-presenter, Liz Rummery, for sharing thoughts that disrupt the binaries of directive and non-directive therapy, and of therapeutic process and outcome. For instance, in her section of our paper, on the young people's art-based action research project on the meanings and practices of community, Liz noted how the young people in the project were 'doing' community in their relations with each other, even when they were not obviously responding to the action research questions by 'talking' or making art about community (Linnell, Hanslow and Rummery, 2006).

While these questions and remarks are not framed within the logic of empirical enquiry, their co-existence within the aesthetic space of the ethnodrama enacts a possibility that contradictions and uncertainties in therapy and research may open up unexpected lines of flight, beyond the citation of known and legitimated theory and practice (Winslade, 2009).

The last few lines of the first scene mirror a therapeutic paradox, whereby recognition from another may act as an emotional 'surety' in the face of radical contradiction or uncertainty. Ironically, here it is the response of a committed narrative therapist that resonates with the other, an art psychotherapist.[8] A sense of connection and containment comes, in this context, from an embodied understanding of the tension between therapies, and more significantly, from attunement to the ethical and subjective tension for the therapist caught inbetween.

Scene 2. Bringing in the art: the team painting

In the second scene of the play, the externalising, projective and ineffable qualities of an art image (see Figure 1, page 344) are 'canvassed'. The three characters, Green, Yellow and Burgundy, are looking at an image that the audience cannot see.

The dialogue develops a dramatic narrative of how the painting is made, picturing in words the initiatives, conflicts, collaborations, intentions and accidents of its making. The painting has been collectively made as part of a team-building day.[9] The work of this art is thus the work of making connections and meanings: around the team's relationships with each other, with the young people, with preferred values and practices, and with the community, other agencies, and the wider organisation.

A moment of tension and conflict, hinting at the drama of power, emerges through an account of how the team manager lays down a strong background, much thicker than a conventional wash, in apparently clashing colours. (This is the moment, and these are the colours, from which the play and its three characters take their names.) Others in the team, particularly those with formal art training, are initially shocked. They wonder how they can make the painting work in the wake of this unusual and possibly naive move. Yet somehow they do. A person puts down these thick blocks of apparently clashing colour, and it paradoxically 'works'. But what is the work, relational and technical, that makes it work? This can be taken as a Foucauldian dynamic of power's mobility (Foucault, 1980). The authority of team leadership is enacted in the team leader making this first move, and yet there is a subtle

8 This dialogue was adapted from a part of the transcript where the art psychotherapist talked of feeling deeply understood by a response of the team manager in his role of clinical supervisor.

9 The art-making was facilitated by a beginning art therapy practitioner on the team, Joanna Keyser, who was unable to join us for the videotaped conversation. While she did email some comments that have been included at points in the drama, she did not comment on her facilitation of the painting. Neither did others in the team except to say that Keyser was skilful – a skill that is underlined by its lack of intrusiveness and capacity to bring the creativity and contribution of others to the fore.

play of power in the various responses to this – who is managing whom and what, here? Humour and camaraderie mark this moment with a certain reflexive self-consciousness. For the art therapists, the moment is emblematic of the fruitfulness of 'sitting with' a difficulty and allowing a process to unfold, rather than foreclosing on uncertainty by trying to 'fix' the 'problem'. For the manager and the team, this "yellow, green and burgundy moment" becomes a guiding metaphor of the importance of taking risks and of the wider relations of trust between them. Meanwhile, the painting, having hovered momentarily on the brink of an aesthetic disaster, becomes a 'success', to the extent that stories will circulate about how it is mistaken for a 'professional' painting and is ascribed a monetary value.

The other act that significantly shapes the painting is when the participants/ artists follow the wavering shadows that lay across the canvas, the momentary imprints of leaves and latticework, the negative of the sunlight that shines through this particular window, in this particular place and time. Thus the painting and its meanings are constituted between a centered authority and a decentered serendipity, between intention and surrender to chance, between a constituting agency and a constitutive 'outside'. It is tempting to attempt to capture and interpret these shadows, as indeed the drama soon does, and as this second *ekphrasis*[10] (my current writing) is about to do. Paradoxically, metaphysics can hold the specificity of the moment captive, much as Foucault (1991) thought that body is imprisoned by the soul, or that the erotics of multiple and specific pleasures are hollowed out into the hermeneutic depth of 'desire' (Foucault, 1980). Shortly, these shadows will be caught in the net of a psychological metaphor. Just for a moment though, I would like to hover with/in the shadows, to melt into them as into a syncope (Clement, 1987) in which intention disappears and emerges transformed. To be at one with their movement towards the fleeting possibility of selves, of my-self, becoming shadow, becoming lattice, becoming leaf (Deleuze and Guattari, 1977). These are 'mo(ve)ments' (Davies and Gannon, 2006) in, and out of, time, towards which theory can only gesture.

Multiple therapy discourses circulate around the painting and its meanings. Taking up the guiding narratives of a post-Romantic psychotherapy and aesthetics, the team members note the parallels between their team processes and their processes of making art. Questions of monetary value are mapped into questions of emotional and ethical value. The young people and the stories that cannot be spoken are displaced into the painting as pink blobs. One of these 'blobs', in its size and intensity, speaks of the challenges of the relationships between a particular young person and the team. The work of art allows for the acknowledgement of that which is forbidden to other forms of speech. In this particular counselling culture, care is taken not only to maintain confidentiality but also, when speaking of clients, to speak of them in ways that honour their implicit presence, rather than objectify and

10 A description in words of an artwork.

pathologise them. Art allows the counsellors to keep this ethical contract while displacing the difficulty of maintaining it into the artwork, in the form of a large and visceral blob of pink paint.

In the making of this painting, it is not clear, and cannot be made clear, whether thought, feeling or the making is prior. This painting is a dance, every bit as much as the art of narrative is a dance: of the symbolic with the referential, of the consciously intended with the surprise, even the intrusion of that of which one was not conscious until now, of the accidents of the surface with the surfacing of meaning, of condensation with displacement, of that which is intensely felt and believed with that which only comes into existence through the making. Here Foucault's point, that we must sometimes refuse to give 'proper names' in order to map the infinite relations of painting, is of relevance (Foucault, 1994). By not figuring the organisation and its relationships through a realist aesthetic, the painting allows, on the one hand, a symbolic intensification of meaning and emotion, and on the other hand the opening out of unexpected lines of flight.

The painting frames the team's narratives, and the team's narratives frame the painting. In effect, there are many paintings projected onto the canvas: by different members of the team, by a person viewing the painting differently at different times, by the viewers of the actual painting, and by the readers and audience of my constructions of the painting in the dramatic text, and now in this chapter. By the time the photographic image of the team painting is projected behind the players towards the conclusion of the play, one might even expect this to be an anticlimax. Although the painting is arguably compelling and well composed for a spontaneous collective and community work, so much meaning and description has been projected into the image at this point, so many potential team paintings made available, that I did wonder if introducing the material presence of one such painting would be a limiting move. In our performance of the drama, this was not our experience. A little gasp of admiration escaped from the mouths of many in the audience as the work was projected. Perhaps the painting was amplified and enlarged symbolically by the dramatic and narrative trajectory leading up to its display, just as it was physically enlarged and made luminescent by the technology of projection. Perhaps the charmed aesthetic contract of the drama acted in much the same way as art therapy, which often brings an image vividly to life within the ritualised space and time of the therapeutic relation. Perhaps the audience brought something powerful to their audiencing of the painting, enlivening it with all their deferred expectations and imaginings. At any rate, the audience's responses, during the performance and in the comments after our presentation, supported the team's sense that the coming together of different narratives of therapeutic practice, team relationship and organisational ethics was effectively embodied in their painting.

A chorus of one

The last speech of the play is taken almost in its entirety from an email message from an administrative worker who participated in the team painting but not in the videotaped conversation. The speech is rather like a classical chorus providing a commentary on the play's action, a trope taken up in narrative therapy, although in taking the form of a soliloquy, the speech also echoes the carving out, in art psychotherapy, of a space of interiority – a space that is embodied through the image and realised through a relation with the other.

In privileging this last speech, I do not wish to give it a truth status, but rather to signal the contingency of truth. I gave these words a privileged position in the play because I was impressed with their citational, poetic and critical potential to bring together the themes of the play and to embody a further deconstructive move. I also liked the subversive flavour of attempting to give a person at the bottom of the professional hierarchy, and someone who is not trained as a therapist, the last word. (This mirrored our intent in ending the actual conference presentation with the words of the young people.) At the same time, I want to acknowledge the limits of this intent. As a writer, there is a sense in which one always 'has the last word' – even if through privileging the words or images of others. There is also a sense in which one never has the last word on anything, since reading/ listening/ viewing always creates the text anew.

Rather than echoing how people take themselves up within the professional discourses of therapy, the email message evokes a subject who practices a (gendered) expertise of reconciling and smoothing over discomfort, of thinking the best of people and situations, of waiting while others take their turn, of remembering the small details and putting the finishing touches. The email message supports, in expected and unexpected ways, the anecdotal perspective that workers in administrative positions know a great deal about the character and dynamics of their managers and teams. At the beginning, the writer seems to minimise the more conflictual aspects of the team's response to how its leader began the painting, presenting this story in a way that smooths out its rough edges and makes things 'right'. Then, as the email progresses, the writer of the email brings into play her memory of another counsellor who was present for the last time on the occasion of the team painting and who is no longer in the team. While this development is consistent with the narrative of getting it right and remembering what others have overlooked, it also radically exceeds that narrative.

The writer recalls how she paints a trace of this particular person, present on the day but missing so far from the publicly narratable stories of that day, into the picture. The shadow of the ex-worker's mug casts a shadow of a doubt across the otherwise unitary narrative of teamhood, a narrative exemplified by expressions of unity built on a sufficient, rather than excessive, amount of dissent. Perhaps the shadow of the mug handle is, to the narrative of teamhood, what the large pink blob is to the narrative of clienthood, allowing for the displacement and expression of an intense emotionality that would otherwise threaten narrative and team coherence. Painting can portray a shadow of something (or someone) unacceptable, even unthinkable. Curiously, neither the email writer nor anyone else 're-marks' upon if and how the ex-worker painted herself or her perspective into the picture on the occasion of the team painting. What marks and remarks did *she* make? How has she left her mark on this occasion and on other occasions, and on the team? Within the narratives of the team painting, how are her (re)marks viewed, read, recalled, preserved, cherished, absorbed, appropriated, abjected, erased?

It is not only the painting itself, but the poetic words of the email, that embrace this shadowy (im)possibility, which might 'simply' be the ethical difficulty of speaking of/ for someone who is not there to speak for herself, or might be haunted by a more complex and specific unspeakability. In a gesture that is enabled by and yet exceeds the artwork that it cites/ describes, the writer recalls, with sadness and loving specificity, the present absence, and the absent presence of someone excluded for whatever reason from the dominant narrative. This absent presence, mediated by the email writer's understanding of the 'departed' person, emerges from the shadows. No longer a team member, she is thus 're-membered' (c.f. Meyerhoff, 1982).

A 'telling' obligation

For all that this artwork has strong and shifting meanings in the narratives within which this thoughtful and passionate team of colleagues constitute themselves, I cannot tell you the truth of the team painting, and neither could the team who painted it. This does not negate my attempts to paint for you an approximation of the painting's specificities and its multiplicities, to dramatise for you the contexts and processes of its creation, and to narrate for you some of the stories of its meanings, its audiencing, and its effects. From a poststructural ethical positioning, the contingency and multiplicity of truth heightens, rather than relieves, my responsibility as a narrator, entering me into an indefinite and passionate obligation.

Derrida (1987) writes an extended meditation upon Cezanne's statement that "I owe you the truth in painting and I will tell it to you" (Cezanne to Emile Bernard, 23 October 1905, in Derrida, 1987: 2). According to Derrida, Cezanne's promise is a performative that promises another performative. Cezanne's promise thus bears an infinite and deferred relation to the truth it promises. The 'truth' is that I am bound to attempt to tell or perform the truth even while this is impossible. Painting thus becomes an infinite response to a debt to the other, a debt that the promise of painting is always bringing into being.

To move, now, from the grand narrative of the 'Great Masters' to the modest contingencies of collective art-making within a community organisation – I cannot tell, show or give you a singular truth of the team painting. Similarly, I cannot offer a true story or representation of the ideas, practices and experiences discussed and enacted in this chapter. I am, however, obliged to stretch the conventions of practitioner research and writing, destabilise the notion of a singular truth and offer, to the best of my ability, an ethical, reflexive, vivid and nuanced account.

References

Clement, C. (1987). *The weary sons of Freud.* Verso, London. Original work published 1978.

Davies, B. and Gannon, S. (2006). *Doing collective biography.* McGraw Hill/ Open University Press, Maidenhead, Berkshire.

Deleuze, G. and Guattari, F. (1977). *Anti-Oedipus.* University of Minnesota Press, Minneapolis. Original work published 1972.

Denzin, N. (2003). *Performance ethnography: Critical pedagogy and the politics of culture.* Sage, Thousand Oaks,CA.

Derrida, J. (1987). *The truth in painting.* Chicago University Press, Chicago. Original work published 1978.

Foucault, M. (1980). *The history of sexuality, Volume 1: An introduction.* Vintage Books, New York. Original work published 1976.

Foucault, M. (1991). *Discipline and punish: The birth of the prison.* Penguin, London. Original work published 1975.

Foucault, M. (1994). *The order of things: An archaeology of the human sciences.* Vintage Books, New York. Original work published 1966.

Freeman, J., Epston D. and Lobovits, D. (1997). *Playful approaches to serious problems: Narrative therapy with children and their families.* W.W. Norton, New York.

Hoshino, J. and Cameron, D. (2008). Narrative art therapy within a multicultural framework. In: Kerr, C. and Hoshino, J. (Eds.) (2008). *Family art therapy: Foundations of theory and practice.* Routledge, London and New York.

Linnell, S. (2008). Found wanting and becoming undone: a response to Eva Bendix Petersen's 'Passionately attached: academic subjects of desire.' In: Davies, B. (Ed.) (2008). *Judith Butler in conversation: Analysing the texts and talk of everyday life.* Routledge, London and New York.

Linnell, S. (2010). *Art psychotherapy and narrative therapy: An account of practitioner research.* Bentham Science Publishers, UAE.

Linnell, S. Hanslow, I. and Rummery, L. (2006). Arts of connection: bringing together visual arts practice, art therapy training, and narrative therapy and community work. Conference paper and performance. Inaugural International Festive Conference. Working with the stories, songs, drama and poetry of people's lives: Linking narrative therapy and community work with the fields of drama, song, film, fiction, and poetry. Adelaide, Australia, March, 2006.

Myerhoff, B. (1986). "Life not death in Venice": Its second life. In: Turner, V. and Bruner, E. (Eds.) (1986) *The anthropology of experience.* University of Illinois Press, Chicago.

Richardson, L. (1997). *Fields of play: Constructing an academic life.* Rutgers University Press, New Brunswick.

Riley, S. (1999). *Contemporary art therapy with adolescents.* Jessica Kingsley Publications, London and Philadelphia.

Riley, S. and Malchiodi, C. (2003). Solution focussed and narrative approaches. In: Malchiodi, C. (Ed) (2003). *Handbook of art therapy.* The Guilford Press, New York and London.

Saldaña, J. (2003). Dramatising data: a primer. *Qualitative Inquiry*, 9(2): 218–233.

Skaife, S. (2008). Off-shore: A deconstruction of David Maclagan's and David Mann's 'Inscape' papers. *The International Journal of Art Therapy*, 13(2): 44–52.

Snyder-Young, D. (2010). Beyond 'an Aesthetic of Objectivity': Performance ethnography, performance texts and theatricality. *Qualitative Inquiry*, 16 (10): 883–893.

White, M. (2004). Narrative practice, couple therapy and conflict dissolution. In: White, M. (Ed) (2004) *Narrative practice and exotic lives: resurrecting diversity in everyday life*. Dulwich Centre Publications, Adelaide.

Winslade, J. (2009). Tracing lines of flight: Implications of the work of Gilles Deleuze for narrative practice. *Family Process*, 48 (3): 332–346.

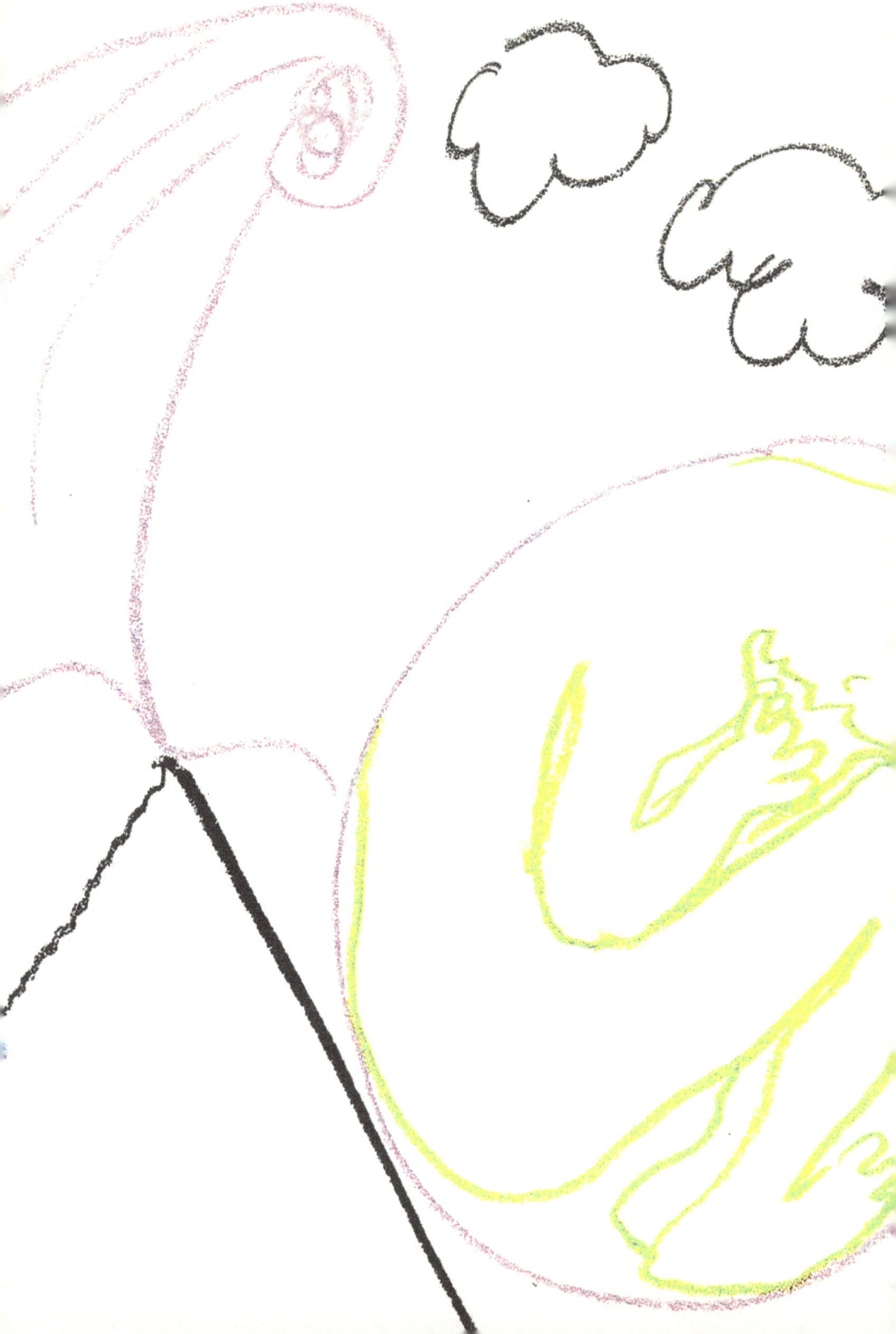

13

A Conversational Model of Art Therapy

Nicolette Eisdell

 | DOI:10.1163/9789004368262_014

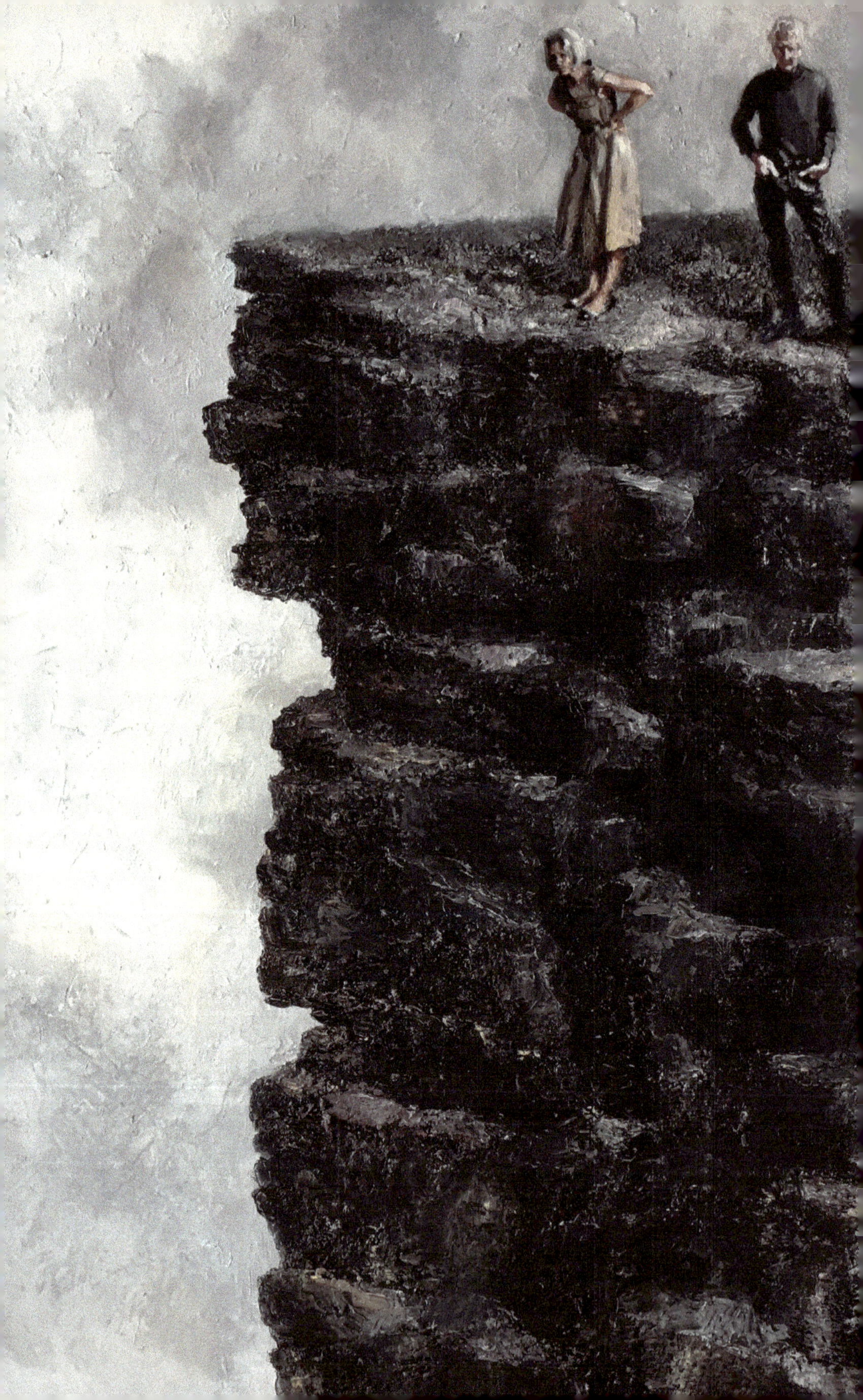

Opposite: Figure 1 *Professor Russell Meares and Dr Susanne Meares*. Nicolette Eisdell (2010). Oil on canvas.

Right: Figure 2 *Professor Russell Meares*. Nicolette Eisdell (2010). Oil on canvas.

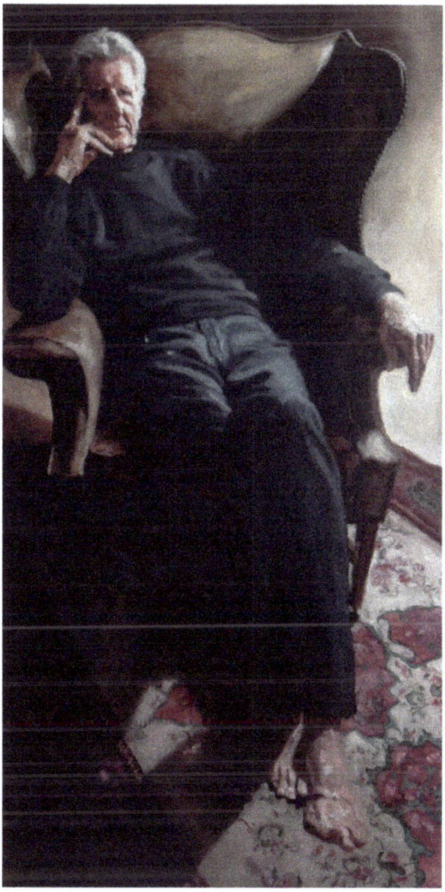

Nicolette Eisdell is an artist and was one of the first cohort from the University of Western Sydney MA Art Therapy program. She went on to further training in psychotherapy with Russell Meares, an Australian psychiatrist who developed an approach with British psychiatrist and Jungian analyst Robert Hobson called a Conversational Model. Russell's father was Ainslie Meares (1910–1986) a well-known psychiatrist and psychotherapist who wrote a seminal book The Door of Serenity *(1958) which discusses psychotherapy with a person who used art in the process. This is part of a background where art and psychotherapy came together in Australia. Thus drawing on the theoretical legacies through father and son Eisdell brings together the art therapy perspective with the Conversational Model, to form a marriage of theory and practice, distinctly of this context. First published in 2005,[1] this piece has a significant place in the field between art therapy and psychotherapy and the lineage of theoretical developments in Australia. As a renowned artist Nicolette's portraits of Russell Meares and his wife Dr Suzanne Meares speak another visual layer of knowledge. Russell is pictured barefoot in an interior (above) and together with Suzanne in the landscape of the cliffs in Sydney, NSW (opposite).*

1 *Psychology and Psychotherapy: Theory, Research and Practice* (Wiley, 2005), 78: 1–18. Reprinted with permission.

> What I say and do in therapy is aimed at promoting understanding: a 'conversation', a meeting between two experiencing subjects (an I and a Thou), here and now, in such a way that learning can be effective in other relationships. If, as I believe, psychotherapy is a matter of promoting a personal dialogue, then we need to know how to receive, express, and share feeling: how to learn a language of the heart in its minute particulars.
>
> Hobson, 1985: xiii

This chapter illustrates the 'minute particulars' of a 'Conversational Model' of art therapy that was used to engage an isolative, reluctant, incarcerated patient charged with a capital offence. The playful nature of the 'visual' conversations triggered poignant 'verbal' conversations. This enabled the patient to reflect on his disturbed early life which had led to destructive behaviour. Now he can begin to imagine an alternative future. The Conversational Model was jointly created by Australian psychiatrist Russell Meares and his mentor, British psychiatrist and Jungian analyst Robert Hobson. The model provided the theory to understand the patient. It is a developmental theory unique in its clinical application.

The focus of this chapter is two sessions that altered the course of therapy. The interventions illustrate the basic tenets of the Conversational Model. As therapist and patient began to engage in interactive visual games, symbols of alienation and persecution – at first predominant – faded. Rapport quickly developed, facilitating the beginnings of a self-reflective capacity. This resonated through the imagery.

To understand the journey, it is important also to understand the historical context. Art therapy emerged from a synthesis of art and psychoanalysis. This drew on the vastly different creative energy of both, but its unique genius derived from working on their complementary nature. It was out of this intellectual construct that the concept of using art as a therapeutic tool – that is, art therapy – emerged.

Art and psychoanalysis: a brief overview

From the earliest days of psychoanalysis, the making of art was viewed according to the analyst's theoretical stance. This is illustrated in the attitudes of the two giants of psychoanalysis – Sigmund Freud and Carl Jung. While the former was ambivalent, the latter was unequivocal. There is abundant literature on the connection between art and psychoanalysis, but I will limit my focus to those psychoanalytic theories of art and the artist[1] directly related to the theory and practice of art therapy[2] outlined in this chapter.

1 Due to space constraints, important historical works exploring psychoanalytic theories of art and creativity have been omitted, e.g. Ernst Kris's (1952) *Psychoanalytic explorations in art*; Marion Milner's (1957) *On not being able to paint*; Otto Rank's (1932) *Art and artist: Creative urge and personality development*; Hanna Segal's (1991) *Dream, phantasy and art*.

2 The following publications provide an overview of art therapy theory and practice: *Art as therapy: An introduction to the use of art as a therapeutic technique*, edited by Tessa Dalley

Freud's ambivalence is reflected in his view of the artist as 'not far removed from neurosis'. In Freud's view he/she is:

> … oppressed by excessively powerful instinctual needs [and] turns away from reality and transfers all his interest, and his libido too, to the wishful constructions of his life of phantasy, whence the path might lead to neurosis.

Freud described conflicting constitutional factors: 'a strong capacity for sublimation and a certain degree of laxity in the repressions'. But, in the same paragraph, Freud also wrote: "there is, in fact, a path that leads back from phantasy to reality – the path, that is, of art" (Freud, 1973: 423). The psychology of the 'true artist', he believed, was a convoluted journey from neurosis to ultimate fulfilment. The latter equated to "honour, power and the love of women" (ibid: 424).

Recognising the centrality of images in dream interpretation, Freud still did not incorporate art-making into his classical technique. This was despite the following observation, much quoted by art therapists (Dalley, 1984; Rubin, 1987):

> We experience it (a dream) predominantly in visual images; feelings may be present too, and thoughts interwoven in it as well; the other senses may also experience something, but nonetheless it is predominantly a question of images. Part of the difficulty of giving an account of dreams is due to our having to translate these images into words. 'I could draw it', a dreamer often says to us, 'but I don't know how to say it.
>
> Freud, 1973: 118

Freud's colleague and contemporary, Carl Jung (1964, 1966, 1967), was the forerunner of art therapy. He viewed art-making as a means of expressing the sacred and mysterious – an important element in the 'individuation' process. Jung used art in his own self analysis and encouraged his patients to express themselves *"by means of brush, pencil or pen"*, between sessions (1966: 48). Here Jung preempts the art therapy movement:

> It is not a question of art at all – or rather, it should not be a question of art – but of something more and other than mere art, namely the living effect upon the patient himself.
>
> Jung, 1966: 48

Extending the application of Freudian theory, Anna Freud and Melanie Klein (1959) incorporated art-making into their respective psychoanalytic techniques, to overcome a lack of free association, in their work with children.

(1984); *The handbook of art therapy by Caroline Case and Tessa Dalley* (1992); *Images of art therapy: New developments in theory and practice* by Tessa Dalley, Caroline Case, Joy Schaverien, Felicity Weir, Diana Halliday, Patricia Nowell Hall and Diane Waller (1987); *Development and diversity: new applications in art therapy*, edited by Doug Sandle (1998); and *Approaches to art therapy: theory and technique*, edited by Judith Rubin (1987).

Naumburg regarded art as 'symbolic speech'. A Freudian analyst, Naumburg published her findings on the therapeutic and diagnostic value of art-making in the treatment of neuroses (Naumburg, 1947) and psychoses (Naumburg, 1950). She paved the way to the central thesis of this paper – that symbolic 'visual' communication is for some patients less problematic than, and can facilitate the later development of, 'verbal' speech:

> Objectified picturisation acts then as an immediate symbolic communication which overcomes the difficulties inherent in verbal speech.
>
> Naumburg, 1958: 512

Developing a strategy on the use of art as symbolic speech, British analyst Donald Winnicott (1971) converted an existing drawing game into a 'technique' to engage his young patients at the start of therapy. He named it 'the squiggle-game', describing it as "a game with no rules" (1974: 141). The focus is on engaging his patient, rather than the creation of a product for interpretation:

> In this squiggle game I make some kind of an impulsive line-drawing and invite the child whom I am interviewing to turn it into something, and then he makes a squiggle for me to turn into something in my turn.
>
> (1974: 19)

Winnicott expands upon the theoretical aspects of the game:

> The squiggle game is simply one way of getting into contact with a child: An artificial link is made between the squiggle game and the psychotherapeutic consultation, and this arises out of the fact that from the drawings of the child and of the child and myself one can find one way of making the case come alive.
>
> (1971: 3)

Robert Hobson (1985) also adapted a pre-existing game, a 'party game', to psychotherapy. In work that has particular relevance to this paper, Hobson used this 'technique' to engage a withdrawn adolescent called 'Stephen'. Using a shared lead pencil and an old envelope, he invited the boy to play, the instructions being simply that "someone draws a line and then someone else goes on with the picture: Let's play together and see what comes out of it" (ibid: 10). He viewed the technique as "an invitation to explore the unknown, an adventure which calls for courage." (11).

Hobson refers to it as 'imaginative activity' as distinct from Jung's 'active imagination'[3]. The latter, Hobson (1985) defined as "a kind of colloquy, or dialogue, with the personalised fantasy images … an inner conversation with personal 'selves'" (102), a solitary activity. In contrast, "imaginative activity proceeded within a relationship – a verbal and non-verbal *dialogue*" (ibid). As

---

3 Marie-Louise von Franz (1964) described active imagination as *"a certain way of meditating imaginatively, by which one may deliberately enter into contact with the unconscious and make a conscious connection with psychic phenomena"*. But, unlike with 'guided imagery', *"the meditator remains completely devoid of any conscious goal or program. Thus the meditation becomes the solitary experiment of a free individual, which is the reverse of a guided attempt to master the unconscious"* (206–207).

exemplified by both Hobson's 'party game' and Winnicott's 'squiggle game', both analysts specifically utilised these techniques in their initial interviews with difficult-to-engage adolescent patients.

The Conversational Model

The Conversational Model is one of the best-validated of all currently employed psychotherapies. An abbreviated version of the model has been manualised as 'psychodynamic-interpersonal' (PI) psychotherapy (Shapiro and Firth, 1985; Shapiro and Startup, 1990). PI has proved to be effective in depression (Shapiro, Barkham, Rees, Hardy, Reynolds and Startup, 1994; Shapiro and Firth, 1987; Shapiro, Rees, and Barkham, 1995), in certain psychosomatic disorders (Guthrie, Creed, Dawson, and Tomenson, 1991), and to be cost-effective in treating repeated users of clinic services (Guthrie, Moorey, Margison, Barker, Palmer, Mcgrath, Tomenson and Creed, 1999). A brief form of PI is useful in reducing repeated episodes of self-harm (Guthrie, 2001). The conversational model also produces beneficial effects and is cost-effective in the treatment of personality disorders (Hall, Caleo, Stevenson and Meares, 2001; Meares, Stevenson and Comerford, 1999; Stevenson and Meares, 1992, 1999).

At the heart of the Conversational Model is the idea that "I can only find myself in and between me and my fellows in a human conversation" (Hobson, 1985: 135). To an outsider this may seem like an 'ordinary' conversation, but it is a "special kind of conversation" (ibid: 199) in which the therapeutic focus is on the mutual creation or discovery of a "language of the heart". Hobson explains that "in an intimate personal conversation we are sharing a feeling language" (ibid: 49).

Elaborating upon the idea of a 'feeling' language, Russell Meares (1998) identifies two kinds of conversation. One is connected to a particular use of words which becomes a "linguistic marker of 'self'" (ibid: 875). This conversation has a non-linear form – an aimless, meandering quality in which shifts and jumps occur according to associations and analogy. Importantly, it is characterised by a feeling of wellbeing or pleasure, a sense of 'aliveness' and an attitude of intimacy. Attention is focused on an inner world of personal meaning, which is connected to the world of symbolic play, the world of metaphor. Meares (1995) calls this the 'narrative of self'[4] (541).

In contrast, the 'linear' language – connected to the traumatic memory system – is characterised by anxiety, a lack of vitality, a sense of disconnectedness from self and other, and a diminished capacity to play or use metaphor. Attention is directed outward, towards the external world. Events are reported chronologically, sequentially, devoid of personal meaning (Meares, 1998).

Figure 3 Detail of *Professor Russell Meares*. Nicolette Eisdell (2010). Oil on canvas.

4 Meares (2000) devoted a chapter to a definition of 'self', extrapolating from the writings of William James, James Baldwin and Pierre Janet.

Developmental theory

Meares (2000) has further developed the model, providing a theory that supports the development of a non-linear 'feeling language'. Extrapolating from empirical studies, he proposes that soon after birth, mother and infant become involved in 'a proto-conversation', a 'form of conversational play, out of which will emerge the 'selfhood' of her child' (15). Meares suggests that it is "the resonance between the 'conversing'partners' which has 'a transformational effect" (17). Developmentally, it is this initial proto-conversation within the dyadic intersubjectivity of mother and baby, that makes 'symbolic play' possible (Meares, 2000: 138).

Meares (1993) focused extensively on the establishment of a therapeutic 'play space'[5] in which the sense of self can be generated, on the fragility of that play space, and on how and what may disrupt it. During symbolic play, the child transforms the objects in his environment into symbols of his own imagination – i.e. the leaf becomes a boat – whilst all the time chattering to himself in an inner-directed conversation, totally absorbed, seemingly oblivious to the presence of the care-giver.

It is through this process that the child begins to sense an 'inner world', a sense of selfhood. For the adult patient the process is similar. It is this symbolic play which is the precursor of the adult state of self-reflection or contemplation. But when a developmental disruption has occurred, as illustrated in the following clinical illustration, the therapist's task is to foster the emergence of the non-linear 'narrative of self'. Meares (2000) elaborates:

> In essence, the therapist's goal is to participate in the creation of a feeling of 'aliveness' in an individual whose sense of ordinary living is one of 'deadness'.[6] (125)

This is a fitting introduction to the patient, who was in such a state of 'deadness' when he first entered therapy.

Clinical illustration

Alex was an isolative, 25-year-old incarcerated psychotic patient convicted of murder. He approached me requesting individual, rather than group, sessions. Alex made it clear he would not talk about his feelings, his past, his family or his offence, but he would draw. Initial sessions were characterised by stilted

---

5 There are strong parallels between Meares' 'play space' and Winnicott's 'playground' – a 'potential space' – a space where play between mother and baby starts. And later, the space between therapist and patient, in which the artwork – synonymous with Winnicott's notion of the 'transitional object' – is created. However, a comparison of Winnicott's theories with those of Hobson and Meares would be well beyond the scope of this paper

6 Other analysts spoke of 'aliveness' and 'deadness': Winnicott (1971) interpreted a 'squiggle' as a picture of *"a coming alive 'inside', following a phase of deadness 'inside"* (109); regarding a lack of mirroring, Kohut (1976) wrote *"his craving to fill an inner void, to obtain a sense of aliveness, therefore became intense"* (809); and Thomas Ogden (1997) monitored his own sense of aliveness/deadness during 'reverie' to understand the analysand's unconscious communications.

disjunctive dialogue and long periods of silence. Note the linear quality of the image (Figure 4), the faceless disembodied stick figure pinned to the cross. Alex's suffering was palpable. My attempts to explore the artwork were met with monosyllabic responses and heavy sighs.

Disjunction and repair

Central to the Conversational Model is the concept of disruption and repair. Meares (1993) recognised that therapy generally begins in a state of disjunction. Thus the therapist's task is to make a connection in a manner that resonates with the patient's inner world (Meares, 2000: 124).

I clearly needed to connect with Alex. Aware that I am part of what may appear to Alex as an abusive autocratic system – a prison hospital – I mused aloud about how painful our therapy sessions must feel for him. And with regret stated 'I must seem like a torturer![7]'

For the first time Alex smiled and began to explain that if he didn't attend he was afraid he might never be discharged. What a terrible bind! Aligning myself with him I said, 'well, if you have to be here, you may as well enjoy it! How about we play some drawing games together?' Alex beamed. The idea that one could 'enjoy' therapy and 'play games', was new and appealing. It seemed we had finally connected and the process of repair had begun.

Early in therapy this faceless disembodied stick figure pinned to the cross emerged, perhaps reflecting Alex's own distress.

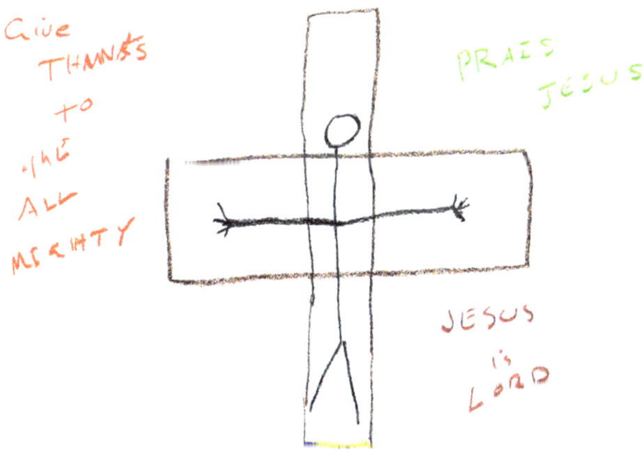

Figure 4 *Faceless figure.* Alex (undated). Crayon on paper.

7 Meares and Hobson (1977) elaborate on ways a therapist can damage a patient. Certain interventions can leave the patient feeling attacked and persecuted. The therapist may evade his/her part in a two-person psychology by inferring that all the patient's responses to the therapist are 'transference', denying the therapist's responsibility for empathic failures/the countertransference.

It was Donald Winnicott (1974) who first acknowledged the importance of 'play' in an 'adult' psychotherapeutic context, in relation to a sense of self:

> It is in playing and only in playing that the individual child or adult is able to be creative and to use the whole personality, and it is only in being creative that the individual discovers the self. (63).

Squiggle with a twist

Next session I suggested we play Winnicott's (1971) 'squiggle-game'[8]. However, when played with a range of art materials rather than a lead pencil – as in Winnicott's original version – the game took on a whole new dimension.

Choosing a pale blue crayon I made a scribble and invited Alex to 'make something out of it'. Alex drew a distressed face (Figure 5), and without prompting related it to recent frightening 'paranoid' thoughts – abusive 'foul-mouthed voices' in place of the usual comforting voice of his 'forgiving loving' God.

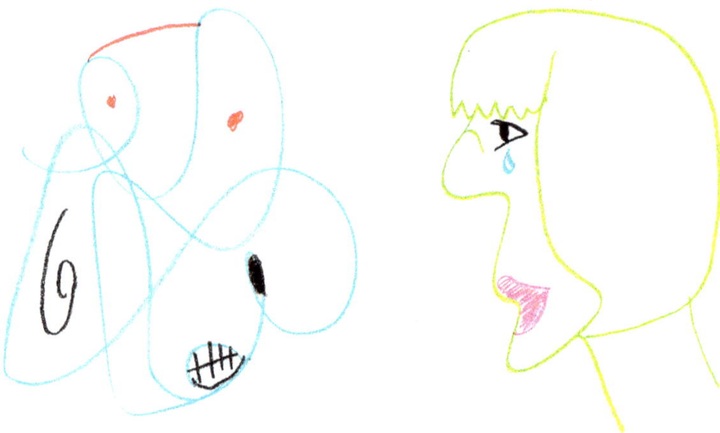

Figure 5 *The conversation begins.* Joint drawing (undated). Crayon on paper. A variation on Winnicott's 'squiggle-game'. Alex's distressed face (left) and the therapist's response at right – the start of a 'visual' conversation.

8 Thomas Ogden (1997) and his colleague Bryce Boyer (1997) used the phrase a 'verbal 'squiggle game'' to describe how their own internal dialogue informs their analytic work. Ogden interprets his periods of 'reverie' within the session as intersubjectively co-constructed, and subsequently interprets the analysand's material in accord with this 'reverie'. Boyer believes that, through *"projective identification…the analyst learns from the patient what the latter cannot think consciously"* (64–65). The Ogden/Boyer 'squiggle game' differs from Winnicott's (1971) version, which primarily aimed to facilitate the patient's free associations, interpretations rarely being given.

Reflecting on the formal qualities of Alex's artwork, I note a sense of distortion and fragmentation, with disparate parts precariously linked together. The image could well symbolise Alex's battle to hold together a fragmented self.

On the same sheet of paper, choosing green crayon Alex made a scribble. My intention was clear; I would respond to his image. After completing my drawing (Figure 5), instantly recognising that the images related to one another, Alex said, 'she's sad about him feeling so bad'. Undeniably, a visual conversation had begun. Judging by the image that followed, Alex experienced my pictorial response as empathic.[9]

My turn to draw the scribble. Choosing blue crayon, on a new sheet of paper I drew a shape. Alex responded. Using yellow crayon he drew an oval shape, eyes and a mouth showing teeth (Figure 6) – at this point he'd left out the ears, nose, eyebrows and hair. 'It's a smiling face', he said, before drawing a mauve coloured scribble for me to complete. With the same crayon, I completed my drawing in response to his (Figure 6). Delighted by his shift in mood I had 'amplified' his expression.

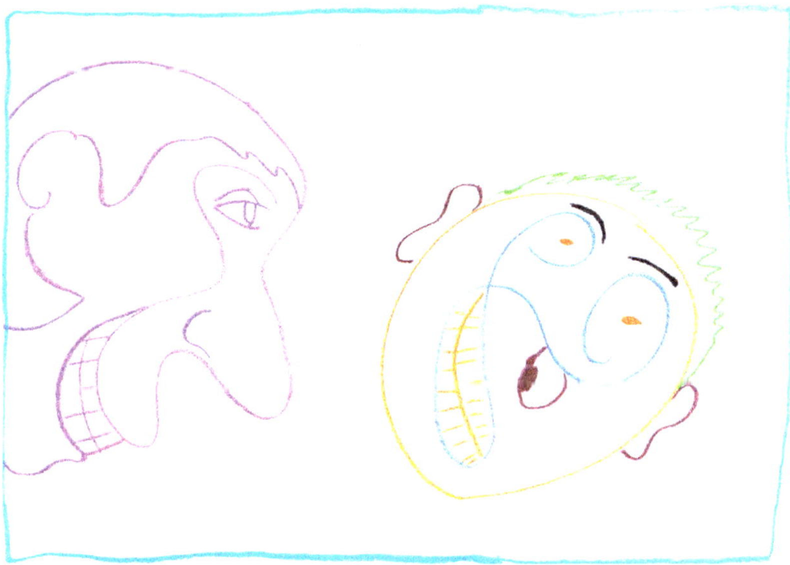

Figure 6 *The conversation develops*. Joint drawing (undated). Crayon on paper. As the squiggle-game proceeds, the conversation develops.

Amplification, a basic tenet within the conversational model, was originally a Jungian concept. It is beyond the scope of this paper to elaborate on this concept, but Hobson (1971) provided a detailed analysis of the genesis of Jung's complex theory of amplification, before later reinterpreting the concept in terms of the Conversational Model:

9 Unintentionally I drew the mouth as a pink heart – on its side – perhaps relating to my intention to respond with soothing comments.

> A single work … has many facets … It cannot be translated into unequivocal discursive language; but it can be extended, expanded, or amplified.
>
> Hobson, 1985: 54

Implicit within the Conversational Model is the 'amplification' of positive affect, based on the premise that positive affects – knocked out during repeated childhood traumas – are reactivated during the therapeutic process. Being the benchmark of a sense of self, positive affects are highly prized. Similar is the Self Psychological concept of 'mirroring', which relates to the patient's need to have their archaic grandiosity reflected back through the 'gleam in the mother's eye' (Kohut, 1966: 252). However, Hobson (1985) differentiates between the two, explaining that 'in responding, I am amplifying, not merely reflecting' (23). For Hobson the difference resided in the added 'inflection' provided by the therapist.

Explaining that he wanted to make his drawing 'more real … like yours' Alex went back to 'finish' his own, using an expanded colour range – ears and nose in deep red, hair in green and eyebrows in brown. Finally, I reached over and drew half a blue rectangular border enclosing his half of the page. Using the same blue crayon, he completed the blue border, mirroring my marks. The border acted as a frame to 'contain' the images, whilst drawing attention to the feelings – further 'amplifying' them.

For the art therapist, translation from the 'visual' to the 'verbal' may or may not occur. Either way the joint focus is on the artwork in which is embedded a metaphor, created within the dyadic intersubjectivity of therapist and patient. The artwork symbolises the 'triadic'[10] intersubjective dimension of the therapeutic relationship (Meares,1998). Analogous is Meares' concept of the 'metaphoric screen' upon which the patient projects associative thoughts – like a movie in the making – to be gazed upon by both patient and therapist. The therapist's task is to stay within the metaphor, remarking upon the artwork/movie, rather than the patient/co-observer (Meares, 1983: 76).

Hobson's 'party game' reinvented

In the following session I invited Alex to draw a picture 'together' – taking it in turns to draw something, or anything, using whatever colours we liked. Hobson (1985) described a variation of this technique.

Alex began, drawing a large mauve circle (Figure 7 opposite). No words were spoken. I saw the circle as an egg. Choosing green crayon – the patients wear green tracksuits – I drew a person curled up in it, a kind of embryo. Again using mauve crayon, Alex drew both the water and a huge wave. Now, it seemed, the embryo was threatened by the wave. I drew two flesh-coloured hands coming from outside the picture, symbolic of my rescue fantasy.[11]

---

10 Ogden's (1994) 'analytic third' is analogous to Meares' 'third element' (1993: 33), 'third term' and 'third zone' (2000: 138).

11 In relation to such transference, Stuart Perlman (1999) concluded that "a common dynamic for therapists involves a search to repair the deprivations and traumas of their own lives by curing

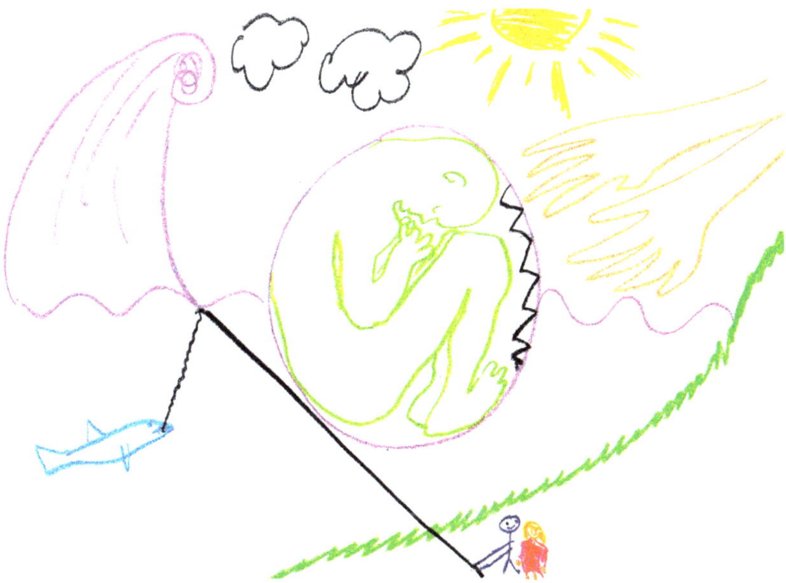

Figure 7. *Alex being saved by God.* Joint drawing (undated). Crayon on paper. A variation on Hobson's 'party game'. This joint drawing is embedded with meaning for Alex.

In response – using black crayon – Alex drew a thick crack on the egg near the hands. Next a thought flashed through me – 'I need some grounding' – so I drew the grass, a solid base. Alex then drew the shark – another threat, I thought, this time from below. In response, I drew a fishing rod with the hook in the shark's mouth. Alex took the bait, drawing a man, albeit a stick-figure, smiling, holding the rod. I drew a woman beside him, sharing his delight. Finally, he drew two clouds which I associated with lowered mood. In response I drew the sun, for me a hopeful symbol. He put his crayon down, saying 'it's finished'.

So what did the picture mean to him? Without hesitation he said it was a picture of himself 'being saved by God'. I note his positive interpretation, indicative of his sense of feeling valued by an idealised other. As Meares says:

> The child who feels good, attaches meaning to this feeling and to this valuation, so that people who are part of him or her, share this goodness and are idealised. On the other hand, experiences which are essentially traumatic involve a negative valuation. The traumatised child senses himself or herself as bad, even though the trauma was not his or her fault. The other people who are part of the experience are also bad, persecutory, and so on.
>
> Meares, 2000: 68

patients, who are seen as representing therapists' needy child parts" (60). In reality, Perlman recognised, it is the patient who has to make the changes. The best we can do is to remain open, point the way, and give encouragement.

Clearly, I was being idealised here, but I chose not to interpret the transference. A 'traditional' transference interpretation links together a current incident in the patient's life, the therapeutic relationship, and the patient's developmental history (Casement, 1985). Although several analysts have warned against 'premature' transference interpretations (Casement, 1985; Winnicott, 1974), few have questioned their ultimate therapeutic value. Meares (2000) however, actively discourages transference interpretation:

> More recent studies, which involve taped recordings, produce, in the main, opposite results. The studies, comprehensively reviewed by Henry et al. (1994), tend to show that transference interpretation correlates negatively with outcomes. One of the better known of the studies cited came from Piper et al. (1991). These and other findings cannot be ignored. Yet the management of transference phenomena … is central to the therapeutic process. (164)

Meares recommends that the therapist use the transference to monitor the patient's subjective experience of the therapeutic dyad[12], and their own countertransference, rather than as a tool to promote 'insight' in the patient. For, by passively accepting the therapist's 'expert' knowledge, the compliant patient forfeits any possible sense of agency, diminishing, rather than strengthening a sense of self (Hobson, 1985; Meares, 2000).

This serious but playful visual conversation allowed a joint yet separate exploration into the inner worlds of therapist and patient – as Hobson noted – bringing pleasure to both. Rather than a 'collusive avoidance of anxiety' (Hobson, 1971: 100), Hobson argues that such interactive therapeutic interventions exemplify the sharing of a 'symbolical attitude' (Hobson, 1985: 10). Hobson defined this important term as 'an openness to receive what is novel, a counteraction to the more usual tendency to confirm our assumptions and presuppositions' (142). Moreover, although a purposeless[13] activity in that one didn't know where one would end up, the Hobson's 'party game' seemed to serve the purpose of engaging a patient who, for one reason or other, had not been able to speak.

American art therapist Mildred Lachman-Chapin (1979, 1983, 1987) proposed a Self Psychological approach to art therapy. She devised a controversial 'interactive technique' which differs significantly from the Winnicottian and Hobsonian drawing games outlined in this paper. Essentially, art therapist and patient engage concurrently in separate artworks, neither looking at the other's artwork in progress:

12 Similar is Patrick Casement's 'interactional viewpoint to listening'. Casement attempts to gauge the impact of his therapeutic interventions from the patient's responses - as distinct from the more autonomous intrapsychic material which arises- as well as the patient's effects upon him in terms of countertransference (1985: 59).

13 Winnicott (1974) recognised the importance of 'relaxation' as a precursor to a sense of 'non-purposive being' in contrast to 'purposive activity'. In the former state, free-association becomes possible (64).

> When we have both finished, the patient shows me what he has done and we talk about what it means to him, what ideas it stimulates, how he feels about it. Then I tell him what responses his artwork evokes in me. Next I show the patient what I have done and ask him to respond to it. Finally, I talk about my work. (1983: 14)

Critics question the therapist's motives, suggesting that it may be the therapist's anxiety or exhibitionism which led him/her to create artwork along with the patient. It is considered unlikely that the therapist can be attentive to the patient if immersed in his/her own inner world. According to Meares, however, the effectiveness of any intervention – controversial or otherwise – can only be judged by what follows (Meares, 2001).

The family

Alex took another sheet and quietly began to draw (Figure 8). A child-like picture of his family emerged. There's Dad, his sister and himself. Mum is absent. He began to speak of his childhood dream to live with his father. Finally he began to tell his story.

When Alex was 10 months old his parents separated. His father took Alex's sister, who was 18 months older, back to Eastern Europe to live with her grand parents. Alex was left with his mother. He did not see his father again until he was 5 years old, and his sister until he was 10, when she returned to live with her father. At 12, Alex began using alcohol. At 15, Alex's mother moved back to Eastern Europe, leaving no forwarding address. Alex tried, but failed, to look

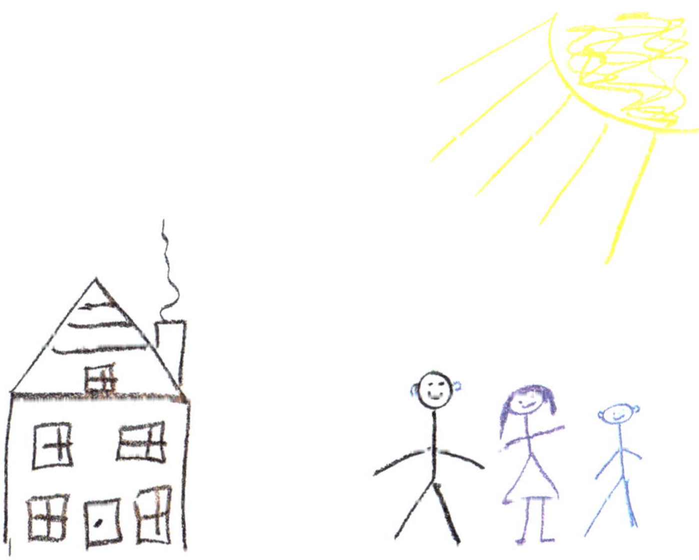

Figure 8 *Alex and his family.* Alex (undated). Crayon on paper. Alex's own drawing of a house with father, sister and himself. Mother is absent.

after himself, ending up in squats and on the streets. He began to drink heavily and abuse drugs. A short stint of living with his father ended disastrously. After an intense argument about leaving empty beer cans lying around, Alex was 'kicked out'; his father's last words being 'and don't come back'. Once more rejected and abandoned, Alex headed back to the streets, enraged.

With interest I noted that the large black 'Dad' stick-figure had no ears, and wondered aloud if it was something about Alex 'not being heard'. He didn't comment but drew on the ears in blue, the colour used to represent himself. Then, oscillating between the past and the future, memories began to flow. He recalls being quietly tearful while Dad was driving him home to Mum, wanting to stay with Dad but too afraid to ask. A huge sun fills the right hand side of the image. 'When I'm released we'll be together' he says, future hopes reactivated. On the left, a house is drawn. Commenting 'there's smoke coming out the chimney', I speculate that there's a sense of 'warmth' there. He tells me how he would 'muck around' with Dad. I note that the house has an attic, 'a place to put things' says Alex. In this way the stories began to flow. The form of conversational language associated with the 'sense of self' had began to emerge and an attitude of intimacy was developing (Meares, 2000).

The family revisited

Some months later Alex again drew the family (Figure 9). This time Mum is included. His (future) dog – previously identified with qualities of faithfulness, protection and playfulness – is beside him. Note the detail in this pencil drawing, particularly the ears, the smiling mouths and the hands. This is the 'happy family' that eluded him.

His was a deprived childhood. Mum worked long hours. No room of his own, he slept on a camp bed in the living room. A witness to violence perpetrated by various male callers left Alex feeling powerless and ashamed that he couldn't protect his mother. Mum 'beat' him for such misdemeanours as finding his sandwiches in 'the toy box'. Alex blames himself; he was 'bad' and deserved to be punished.

From a stylistic perspective, Alex explained that he liked the drawing in pencil because he 'can change things … and make it right'. I note that it looks faint, easily 'rubbed out'. He's drawn himself as extremely muscular, yet he tells me how 'skinny' he was at 15. He felt depressed, couldn't eat. He recalls saying goodbye to his mother at the airport. Overcome with grief and panic, Alex wept, but was told to stop. He felt ashamed.

In this drawing he's sixteen, which is interesting because this is a year *after* his mother left. His fantasy is clear. He wished his parents had stayed together, been a 'real' family. He's convinced he wouldn't be in this predicament today, wouldn't have been living on the streets, wouldn't have turned to drink, drugs and crime.

At eighteen, a drunk, drugged, angry and violent Alex, with a friend, without provocation, beat up and ultimately murdered a vagrant, before setting him alight. Mystified, Alex recollects his 'co-accused' having told him

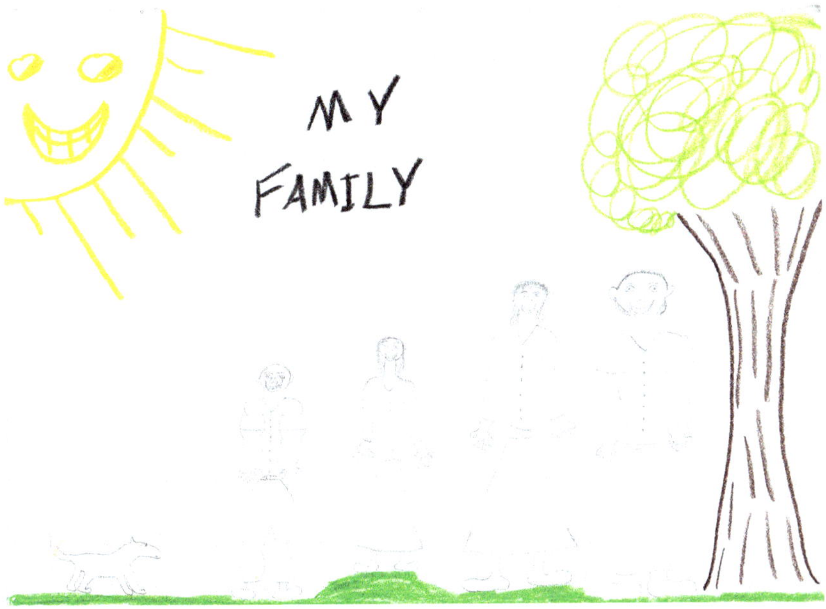

Figure 9 *My family.* Alex (undated). Crayon and pencil on paper. Seven months later, Alex drew the happy family that eluded him, complete with (future) dog.

that, as he hit the man, with every blow, he shouted 'Mum ... Mum ...' Alex recalls it like a nightmare, hazy, menacing, unreal, but with intense shame. Meares (1993) explains such acts of violence, where the victim becomes the victimiser, in terms of his theory of 'reversals'. During a trauma the precarious self and traumatiser are fused. At times of intense anxiety, an unassimilated traumatic state is triggered, knocking out any sense of self. With no 'sense of self' left, it is as though 'the other comes to inhabit the victim', resulting in a 'switch' or reversal (Meares, 2000: 87).

More recently, Alex didn't draw at all. He began to speak of the 'near disasters' suffered in childhood, corresponding to the various scars on his head and body. The conversation crescendos when, during various sporting activities, he has been able to make a 'come-back', 'winning against all odds'. Through this metaphor he was able to acknowledge how far he's come since the start of therapy seven months earlier, when he 'couldn't talk'. While pointing to the circular space above and between us I commented 'it's almost as if you've done the drawing up here today, rather than down there' pointing to the blank paper. He smiled, realising that he'd 'talked the whole session'! No longer dependent upon the artwork to facilitate expression of 'the third zone' (Meares, 2000), the process was becoming internalised.

Conclusion

The Conversational Model provides a sound theoretical basis from which to understand and explore the patient's inner world. Alex entered therapy with a disrupted sense of self, characterised by an impoverished ability to play. Trapped in a linear world, exemplified by his image of the disembodied faceless figure nailed to the cross, Alex struggled to overcome a sense of disconnectedness from himself and others. His rigid religious beliefs, although an attempt to find inner peace, further isolated him, creating an unbreachable schism between the saintly and despised aspects of himself. Through our joint participation in the modified Winnicottian and Hobsonian games, an atmosphere of connectedness developed between us, allowing symbolic play to begin.

Through the process of therapy, Alex was beginning to develop a self-reflective capacity and an emotional vocabulary; first visual, then verbally articulated. His repertoire of responses expanded, he could now both draw and talk. The images, reviewed over the course of therapy, provided ample opportunities for further expansion, elaboration and clarification. There was a chance to note repeated themes, recognise differences and similarities, whilst appreciating over time the subtle but noticeable shifts in style, content, colour and tone.

Clearly, this approach was successful with this patient, and may be successful with others. However, such interactive interventions have been discouraged from the general practice of psychoanalytic art therapy – particularly in Britain – despite precedents set by Winnicott and Hobson. It is important that any 'technique' be used with caution, with sound clinical judgment in accord with the therapist's training and expertise, and with each patient's specific developmental needs in mind. Some patients are clearly able to engage both visually and verbally without such a directive approach. Some may in fact find such interventions extraneous, or worse, intrusive or childish and thus insulting. However, in this particular case, Alex may have been deprived of the opportunity for a positive therapeutic experience without the art therapy 'conversations'. The journey undertaken suggests that, with some patients, working interactively with visual imagery may facilitate the development of a therapeutic relationship in which words can at last be spoken. This process could mean the difference between a patient becoming a member of the community, or remaining a threat to it.

References

Boyer, B. (1997). The verbal squiggle game in treating the seriously disturbed patient. *Psychoanalytic Quarterly,* 66: 62–81.

Case, C., and Dalley, T. (1992). *The handbook of art therapy.* Routledge, London.

Casement, P. (1985). *On learning from the patient.* Routledge, London.

Dalley, T. (Ed) (1984). *Art as therapy: aAn introduction to the use of art as a therapeutic technique.* Routledge, London.

Dalley, T., Case, C., Schaverien, J., Weir, F., Halliday, D., Nowell Hall, P., and Waller, D. (1987). *Images of art therapy: New developments in theory and practice.* Routledge, London.

Freud, S. (1973). *Part II. Dreams.* In *Introductory Lectures on Psychoanalysis.* The Pelican Freud Library, Vol. 1. Penguin Books, London.

Guthrie, E., Creed, F., Dawson, D., and Tomenson, B. (1991). A controlled trial of psychological treatment for the irritable bowel syndrome. *Gastroenterology,* 100: 450–457.

Guthrie, E., Kapur, N., Mackway-Jones, K., Chew-Graham, C., Moorey, J., Mendel, F., Marino-Francis, F., Sanderson, S., Turpin, C., Boddy, G. and Tomenson, B. (2001). Randomised controlled trial of brief psychological intervention after deliberate self poisoning. *British Medical Journal,* 323: 1–5.

Guthrie, E., Moorey, J., Margison, F., Barker, I. I., Palmer, S., Mcgrath, G., Tomenson, B. and Creed, F. (1999). Cost-effectiveness of brief psychodynamic-interpersonal therapy in high utilisers of psychiatric services. *Archives of General Psychiatry,* 56: 519–526.

Hall, J., Caleo, S., Stevenson, J. and Meares, R. (2001). An economic analysis of psychotherapy for borderline personality disorder patients. *Journal of Mental Health Policy Economics,* 4: 3–8.

Henry, W., Strupp, H., Schact, T. and Gaston, L. (1994). Psychodynamic approaches. In: Bergin, A and Garfield, S. (Eds), (1994) *Handbook of psychotherapy and behaviour change.* Wiley, New York.

Hobson, R. (1971). Imagination and amplification in psychotherapy. *Journal of Analytical Psychology,* 16: 79–105.

Hobson, R. (1985). *Forms of feeling: the heart of psychotherapy.* Tavistock, London.

Jung, C. (1964). *Man and his symbols.* Anchor Books, New York.

Jung, C. (1966). *The practice of psychotherapy. The collected works of C.G. Jung,* Vol 16 (2nd ed). Routledge and Kegan Paul, London.

Jung, C. (1967). *Memories, dreams, reflections.* Fontana, Fontana.

Klein, M. (1959). *The psychoanalysis of children.* Hogarth Press/Institute of Psychoanalysis, London.

Kohut, H. (1966). Forms and transformations of narcissism. *Monographs of the Journal of the American Psychoanalytic Association,* 14: 243–272.

Kohut, H. (1976). Creativeness, charisma, group psychology: reflections of the self-analysis of Freud. In: Ornstein, P. (Ed.) (1978) *The search for the self,* Vol. 2. International Universities Press, New York.

Kris, E. (1952). *Psychoanalytic explorations in art.* International Universities Press, New York.

Lachman-Chapin, M. (1979). Kohut's theories on narcissism: Implications for art therapy. *American Journal of Art Therapy,* 19 (October): 3–9.

Lachman-Chapin, M. (1983). The artist as clinician: An interactive technique in art therapy. *American Journal of Art Therapy,* 23 (October): 13–26.

Lachman-Chapin, M. (1987). A self psychology approach to art therapy. In: Rubin, J. (Ed.) (1987) *Approaches to art therapy: Theory and technique*. Brunner/Mazel, New York.

Meares, R. (1983). Keats and the 'impersonal' therapist: A note on empathy and the therapeutic screen. *Psychiatry,* 46: 73–82.

Meares, R. (1993). *The metaphor of play: Disruption and restoration in the borderline experience*. Jason Aronson, Northvale, NJ.

Meares, R. (1995). Episodic memory, trauma and the narrative of self. *Contemporary Psychoanalysis,* 31(4): 541–555.

Meares, R. (1998). The self in conversation: On narratives, chronicles, and scripts. *Psychoanalytic Dialogues,* 8(6): 875–891.

Meares, R. (2000). *Intimacy and alienation: memory, trauma and personal being.* London: Routledge.

Meares, R. (2001). What happens next? A developmental model of therapeutic spontaneity. *Psychoanalytic Dialogues,* 11, 755–769.

Meares, R., and Hobson, R. (1977). The persecutory therapist. *British Journal of Medical Psychology,* 50: 349–359.

Meares, R., Stevenson, J., and Comerford, A. (1999). Psychotherapy with borderline patients: 1. A comparison between treated and untreated cohorts. *Australian and New Zealand Journal of Psychiatry,* 33: 467–472.

Milner, M. (1957). *On not being able to paint.* Tarcher/Putnam, New York.

Naumburg, M. (1947). *An introduction to art therapy: Studies of the 'free' art expression of behaviour problem children and adolescents as a means of diagnosis and therapy* (2nd ed, 1973). Teachers College, Columbia University, New York and London.

Naumburg, M. (1950). *Schizophrenic art: its meaning in psychotherapy.* Heinemann, London.

Naumburg, M. (1958). Art therapy: Its scope and function. In: Hammer, E. (Ed). *The clinical application of projective drawings*. Charles C. Thomas, Springfield, Illinois.

Ogden, T. (1994). The analytic third: Working with intersubjective clinical facts. *International Journal of Psychoanalysis,* 75: 3–19.

Ogden, T. (1997). Reverie and metaphor: some thoughts on how I work as a psychoanalyst. *International Journal of Psychoanalysis,* 78: 719–732.

Perlman, S. (1999). *The therapist's emotional survival: dealing with the pain of exploring trauma.* Jason Aronson, New Jersey and London.

Piper, W., Azim, F., Joyce, S. and McCallum, M. (1991). Transference interpretations, therapeutic alliance and outcome in short-term individual psychotherapy. *Archives of General Psychiatry,* 48: 946–953.

Rank, O. (1932). *Art and artist: Creative urge and personality development.* Alfred Knopf, New York.

Rubin, J. (Ed) (1987). *Approaches to art therapy: Theory and technique.* Brunner/Mazel, New York.

Sandle, D. (Ed) (1998). *Development and diversity: New applications in art therapy.* Free Association Books, London.

Segal, H. (1991). *Dream, phantasy and art.* Tavistock/Routledge, London and New York.

Shapiro, D., Barkham, M., Rees, A., Hardy, G., Reynolds, S. and Startup, M. (1994). Effects of treatment duration and severity of depression on the effectiveness of cognitive-behavioural therapy and psychodynamic-interpersonal psychotherapy. *Journal of Consulting Clinical Psychology,* 62: 522–528.

Shapiro, D. and Firth, J. (1985). Exploratory therapy manual for the Sheffield psychotherapy project. Available from Psychological Therapies Research Centre, University of Leeds, UK. Memo 733.

Shapiro, D., and0 Firth, J. (1987). Prescriptive versus exploratory psychotherapy: outcomes of the Sheffield psychotherapy project. *British Journal of Psychiatry,* 151: 790–799.

Shapiro, D., Rees, A. and Barkham, M. (1995). Effects of treatment duration and severity of depression on the maintenance of gains following cognitive-behavioural therapy and psychodynamic-interpersonal psychotherapy. *Journal of Consulting Clinical Psychology,* 63: 378–387.

Shapiro, D. and Startup, M. (1990). Raters manual for the Sheffield psychotherapy rating scale. Available from MRC/ESRC Social and Applied Psychology Unit, University of Sheffield, Memo 1154.

Stevenson, J. and Meares, R. (1992). An outcome study of psychotherapy for patients with borderline personality disorder. *American Journal of Psychiatry,* 149: 358–362.

Stevenson, J. and Meares, R. (1999). Psychotherapy with borderline patients. Part II. A preliminary cost-benefit analysis. *Australian and New Zealand Journal of Psychiatry,* 33(3): 473–477.

von Franz, M.-L. (1964). The process of individuation. In: Jung, C. *Man and his symbols.* Anchor Books, New York.

Winnicott, D. (1971). *Therapeutic consultations in child psychiatry.* Hogarth Press/Institute of Psychoanalysis, London.

Winnicott, D. W. (1974). *Playing and reality.* Penguin Books, Harmondsworth, UK.

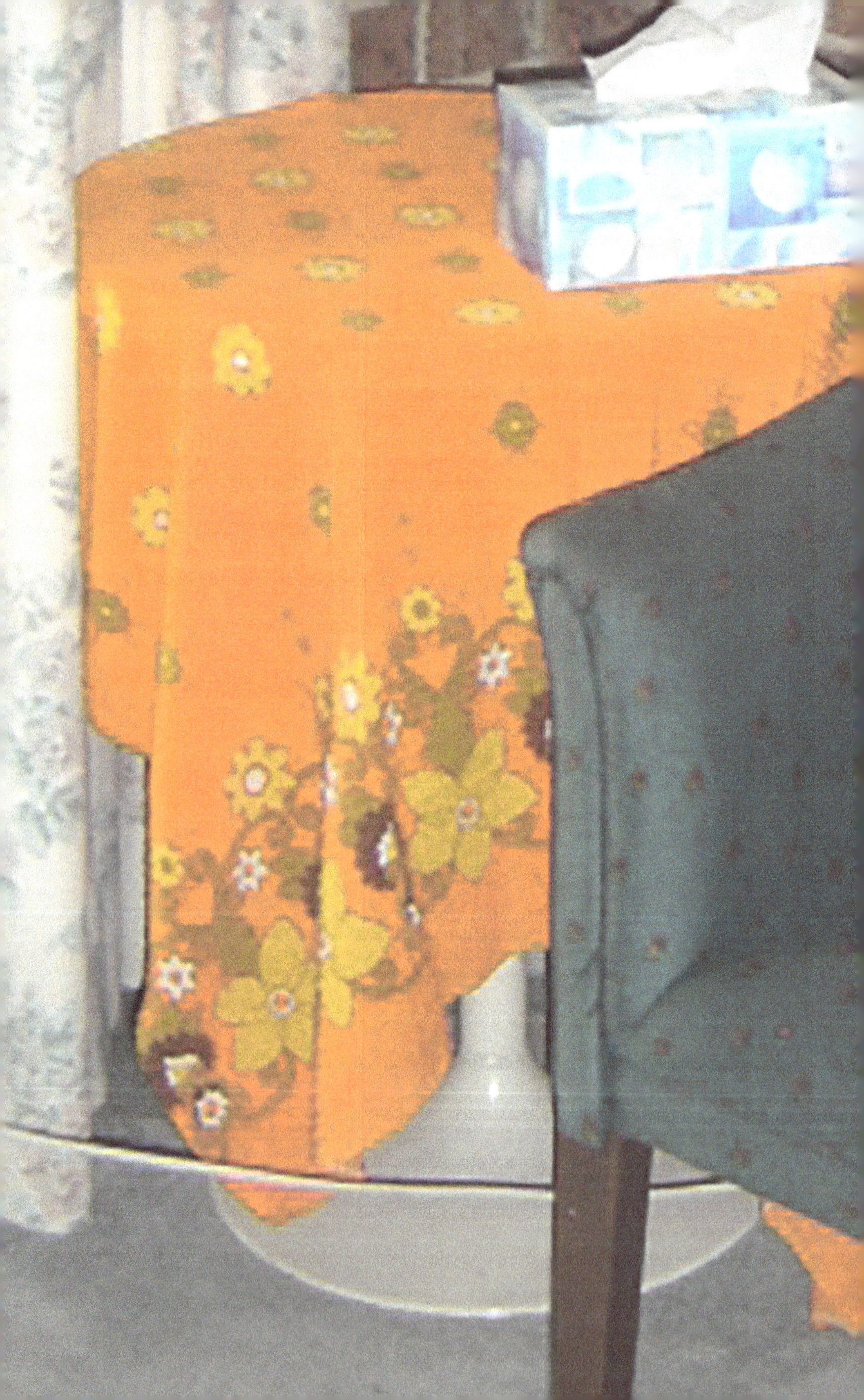

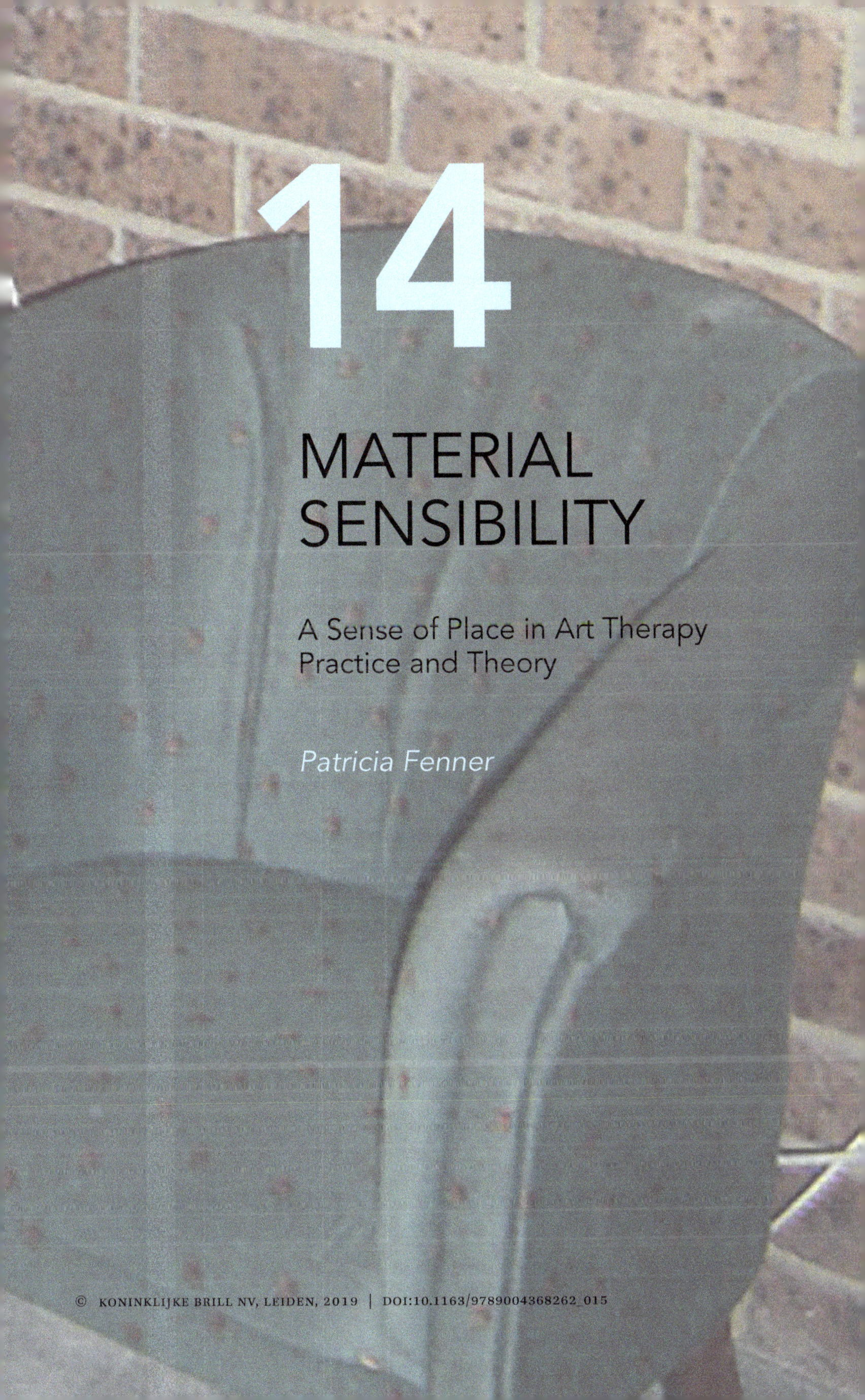

14

MATERIAL SENSIBILITY

A Sense of Place in Art Therapy Practice and Theory

Patricia Fenner

© KONINKLIJKE BRILL NV, LEIDEN, 2019 | DOI:10.1163/9789004368262_015

One foundational assumption in art therapy is that the nexus of therapeutic effect is facilitated via a three-way process comprising the client, the therapist and the image, a construct which emerged from the discourse. Much of our theory and practice is considered discourse-driven which, in the English-speaking world, has been built largely upon traditions emerging from the USA and Britain (traditions themselves indebted to other European contexts). It is rarely acknowledged that such discourse itself is always emplaced, that it arises from some *where*, and not from disembodied minds curiously dislocated from the contexts those minds physically inhabit. An appreciation of the role of place as constitutive to both therapy practice and to our discourses is unfamiliar in how we understand art therapy. Yet the subtle and permeating effects of place and space influence the traditions of those discourses, evident in the discipline-driven confines of our thinking.

The boundaries of these disciplines are increasingly being breached with studies inhabiting in-between zones, producing discourses such as those of feminism and postcolonialism (Gulson and Symes, 2007). Ideas have taken off both within disciplines and between them, "blurring or jumping" (ibid: 6) the boundaries. This paper has emerged from a *jumping* over of some of the boundaries of our habituated art therapy discourse which, historically, has been informed through the lens of psychology and constructs of the self. The larger study, from which the following discussion emerged, explored an understanding of art therapy wherein place and matter were identified as constitutive to theory and practice. By illuminating the experiences of both therapists and clients of the therapy setting, the vital role played by place and the material context of practice in the therapy process itself was identified. Such a focus redirects our gaze from *how* therapy occurs to *where*, and the meanings related to distinctive material features within those settings which are perceived via the senses. In this sense our construct of the dynamic triangular relationship might be expanded and reformed to include place and matter into its ambit.

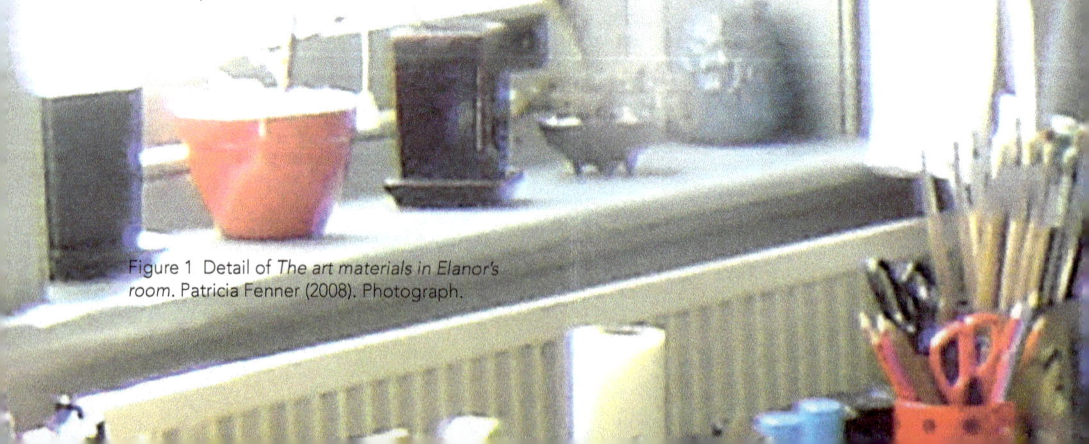

Figure 1 Detail of *The art materials in Elanor's room*. Patricia Fenner (2008). Photograph.

The art therapy room

The room of art therapy practice has been understood as providing functions beyond the practical and has been conceptualised as the symbolic expression of the psychological processes of therapy. Visual art is, by nature, matter bound and art therapy implicitly locates the psychological in the material. The reverse is also acknowledged, that the material insinuates itself into the psychological (Kagin and Lusebrink, 1978; Lusebrink, 1990; Malchiodi, 1998; McNiff, 1995, 1999; Robbins, 1987, 1994). However, it was not until approximately the last fifteen years that more thorough attention was paid to conceptualising and understanding the impact of setting qualities on practice (Bell, 1998; Case, 2000; Deco, 1998; Henley, 1995; Kalmanowitz and Lloyd, 1999, 2002, 2005; Killick, 1997, 2000; Malchiodi, 1995, 1998, 1999; McNiff, 2004; Moon, 2002, 2010; Wood, 1997, 2000). These more recent contributions could be said to implicitly embrace the notion of the room as constitutive of therapeutic effect, with much attention paid to the studio in art therapy practice.

An integral aspect defining a positive sense of place is its inherently containing qualities. Art therapists have utilised this concept of the room of therapy as a containing element (Brooker, Cullum, Gilroy, McCombe, Mahony, Ringrose, Russell, Smart, von Zweigberg, and Waldman, 2007; Brown, 2008; Case and Dalley, 1992; Deco, 1998; Edwards, 2010; Henley 1995; Kalmanowitz and Lloyd, 1999, 2005; Killick and Greenwood, 1995; Schaverien, 1989, 1992; Wood, 1997, 2000). The room, as psychological container, is argued to provide that function in concert with other material and psychological factors such as the art materials, therapist presence, and psychological practice.

The notion of containment is also implied in the concept of the frame or inner sanctum which is provided by the therapy setting and practice (Schaverien, 1992: 65). Schaverien put the case for a space set apart from the day to day, which can facilitate access to an internal space. Through their actual rigidity, a room's walls form a material frame which facilitates a kind of freedom. The contained art therapy setting offers a stability and reliability out of which potent creative responses can emerge (Wood, 2000). The studio provides security and caring (Korlin, Nyback and Goldberg, 2000), facilitates a creative state of reverie (Wood, 2000), is an expression of the therapist's presence (Brown, 2008; Case, 2000), and acts as a potential or transitional space (Case and Dalley, 1992; Kalmanowitz and Lloyd, 2005; Killick, 1997).

The notion of the space as an alchemic vessel reinforced the suggestion that clients walk into another world as they enter this heightened domain (Kalmanowitz and Lloyd, 2002; Malchiodi, 2002; McNiff, 2004). McNiff avowed that the mood or ambience of the studio is the foundation and driver of transformative art-making. The mix of people, materials and space, are protected by the studio which represents the integrity and heart of the activity. Seen in this light, the notion of environment means much more than a simple physicality, but includes mood, spirit, life blood and companion, as contemporary Australian artist Daws stated, "when I enter (the studio) in the morning I feel it wraps itself around me" (McDonald and Lloyd, 2007: 58).

Real world rooms

In Australia, we see hospital and community-based art therapy practices come and go. However, when a commitment is made to a discipline which argues for particular physical requirements, a conflict between interests can emerge. A hospital, for example, may prefer flexible, multipurpose rooms which are easily converted for diverse functions. The art therapist in private practice may face different challenges in availability and affordability of appropriate space when renting or sharing a room, and may be affected by hire-by-the-hour constraints. Wood (2000) saw art studio practice at risk, arguing that therapists should demand a contemporary form of studio accommodation suitable for psychotherapeutically informed art therapy set within physical conditions able to evoke the absorbed art-making of the studio experience.

As art therapy practice in Australia clamours for inclusion in the mainstream repertoire of healthcare, therapists here know the multi-purpose, generic and converted setting well. It has been argued that, where physical conditions are less than optimal, a studio approach, underpinned by the artist identity of the therapist, can be invoked (Moon, 2002). This is not an argument for the strength of the relational component in therapy but one highlighting the therapist as facilitator of the creative process. Moon described a setting where the dedicated physical space is replaced by the studio art therapy attitude and practice.

Understandings of the studio and studio attitude are centrally placed across a range of different orientations, from the psychoanalytic orientation of writers like Killick (2000), Case (2000) and Case and Dalley (1992) to the humanistic studio art therapy approaches of other therapists including Moon (2002) and Allen (1992, 2008). Practitioners also work in settings quite different from the studio however, working in small rooms and with more individual clients than groups. The reality of these practitioners' circumstances is less well-represented in this discussion, although Wood's (2000) discussion of a contemporary style studio may represent these practices best.

Research has not been available on the experience of these diverse kinds of rooms from either therapist or client perspectives, or on how ideas and theories about good setting arrangements actually convert into conditions people experience as useful for therapeutic change. It is likely that art therapists consider materiality in their therapy more than those psychotherapy practitioners who place weight in the relational and focus primarily on spoken narratives or transferences of their clients. However, even within the scope of art therapy literature there is still a heavy leaning towards a how-to-do discourse rather than one of a where-to-be, or a place-attentive practice. The reality of the room-as-experienced is either overlooked or seen to function largely in relation to art-making and the image. Questioning how clients and therapists experience and value the room, regardless of its arrangement or style, opened out the field of discourse to considering, on the one hand, the minutiae of furnishing, objects and other physical content in the room, and on the other, the overall sense of being there: the sense of place.

Place experience

In posing a question about this lived experience, the study breached the discipline boundaries of literature on the meaning of objects (psychology, consumer studies) as well as that of the study of place (philosophy, human geography, architecture). Places occur where people are connected to the world by webs of significance, and the constructs we use to make sense of these relationships span complex conceptual domains (Relph, 2008). Basso (1996) conceptualised subject/place interaction as a process of *interanimation*. As we create places, we are creating and apprehending purchase of ourselves. Our identities are formed through what we see and experience as we make material from the immaterial of ourselves. As Basso stated simply, places energise ideas and feelings in people and these ideas and feelings re animate those people's responses to those places, wedding each to the other. The reflexive process of interanimation involves creation and reflection back of self (in the material world) and operates on large and smaller scales, from the nature of our cities to the intimacy in the arrangement of a room. We perceive and modify places simultaneously. It is within place that subjectivity emerges and place is "*integral to the very structure and possibility of experience*" (Malpas, 1999: 32, emphasis in original). Rather than being founded on a backdrop of place, subjective experience is located in and experienced through, complex and energetic environments.

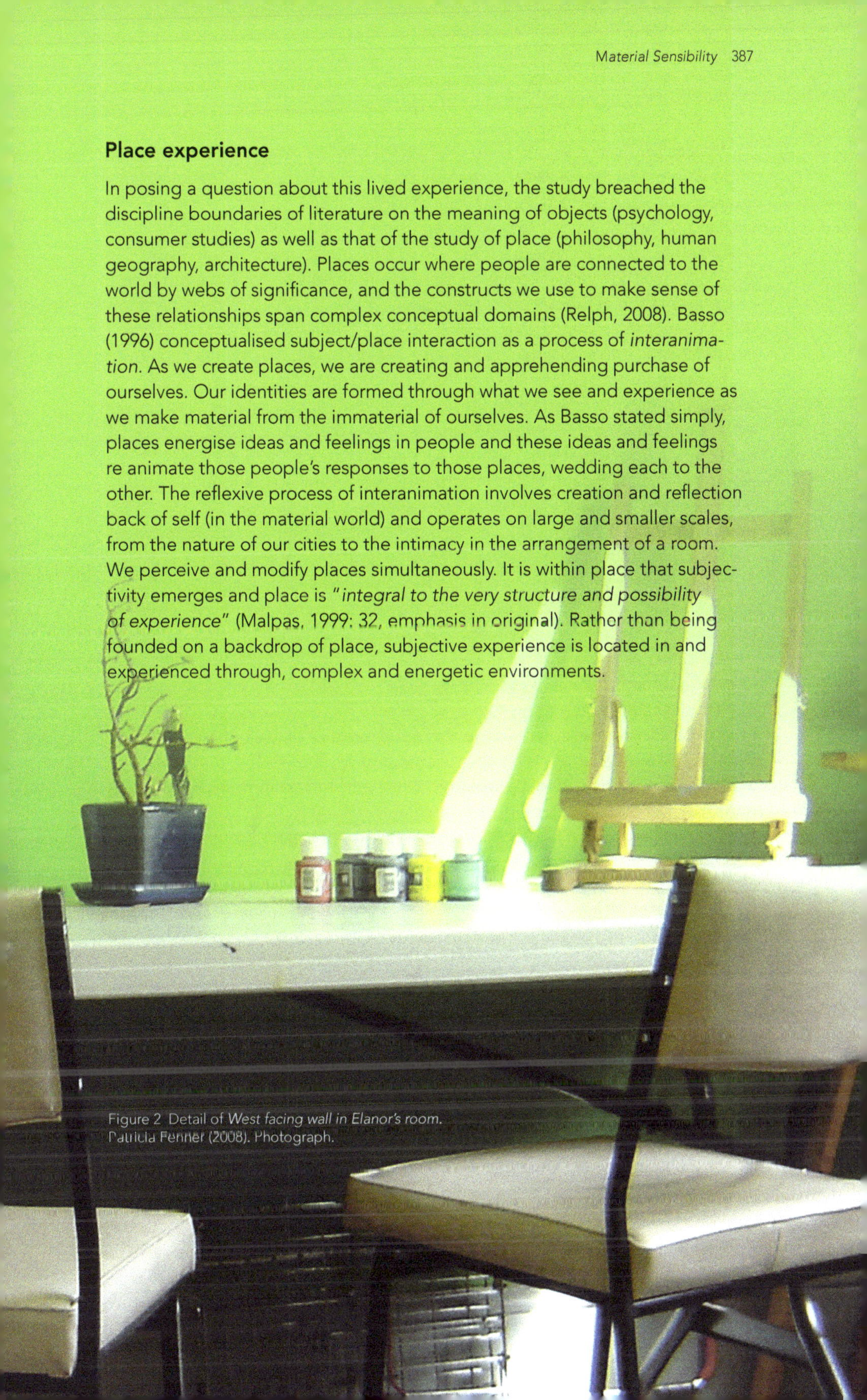

Figure 2 Detail of *West facing wall in Elanor's room.* Patricia Fenner (2008). Photograph.

Malpas (2008) also alerted us to the hazards of place. In its name, ownership and exclusion can be declared in the service of self, community or national interest. Boundaries which create zones of exclusion and depersonalisation such as on the psychiatric ward, where some art therapists work, have been described as *anti-place* where expression of individuality is prohibited (Casey, 2000; Stoller, 2003). Where control in these environments is loosened, the tone and presentation of the self becomes more fluid (Davies, 2007). Davies' account of the patient she referred to as Nirmal, illustrated the way even a small corner in a psychiatric building can be experienced as personally rich in meaning.

Places are what humans make of them, according to Gruenewald (2003), something which we often fail to see. It is incumbent upon us, he said, to apply a place consciousness to our world, lest we ignore dangerous possible consequences. Assuming that the "material cultural formations" (ibid: 628) we call places are somehow natural and inevitable leaves us vulnerable to ignoring our responsibilities as place-makers. Unintentionally we can legitimise the powerful ideologies embedded in much of place decision-making. This political dimension is integral to Gruenewald's argument: that large scale, place-making decisions are frequently held in the hands of a powerful few, resulting in loss and reduced control of public places. Art therapists can relate to these ideas as the places in which we are often required to practise in organisational settings fall short of ideal and are at times barely adequate. By becoming accountable to the places where we live and work we will enrich and empower our environments socially, materially and ecologically, according to Gruenewald (2003).

An inquiry into the lived experience of the room or place in the art therapy setting already challenges a basic convention of psychotherapy, that of a focus on the individual as separate from a place-based context. Typically it is the interpersonal which claims a particular focus. Whilst psychological in influence, the construct of place takes us beyond reification of the self and the individual psyche. Likewise the influence of psychoanalysis on the practice of art therapy also privileges the power of the unconscious over a phenomenological, here-and-now perception of a reality including, but also beyond, the self. Dialoguing with place is more than a process of projection, of the self talking with the self (MacWilliams, 2002), or an insistence on a purely human world (Berman, 1990).

Malpas (2008) reminded the reader of the Indigenous Australian concept of people belonging to the places they inhabit, where proprietorship is absent, and in its place there is a sense of a need to protect, preserve and provide guardianship for those places, not exploit them. Through a focus on the lived experience of therapists and their clients, reclaiming of the discourse of place can potentially extend and enrich an otherwise prospectively limited and discipline-restricted view of the setting of art therapy.

Central to this study was the work of place and architecture theorist Dovey (2010) who utilised the work of Deleuze and Guattari (1987) in proposing the concept of place as an assemblage rather than as something fixed and stable. The notion of assemblage places emphasis on the converging of material, social, and expressive elements as comprising and constituting a sense of

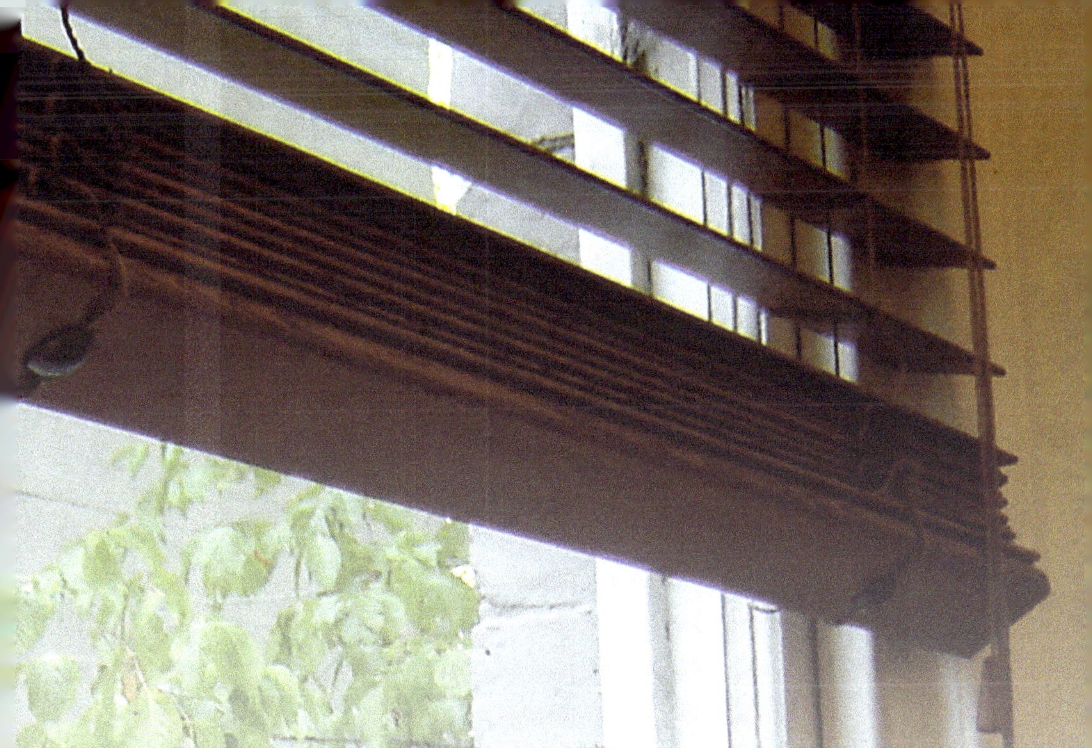

Figure 3 Detail of *The window view seen from client Melinda's chair*. Patricia Fenner (2008). Photograph.

place. This theoretical position encompasses the complexities of place as a structured, discursively constructed and experienced phenomenon (Dovey, 2010) wherein we embrace the lived dimensions of its irreducibly material, mental and meaning-filled nature (Cresswell, 1996; Know, 2005). Dovey (2010) developed the notion of mood as a point of intensity in the assemblage of place. A point of intensity refers to the effect of these social, material and expressive forces to evoke an intensity of mood. In this way, a sense of a place is linked to the affect of the encounter, which takes place prior to reflection, language or meaning-making.

Objects and meaning in the art therapy room

An encounter in the therapy room is not only situated in time and space but is embedded culturally and is replete with information and misinformation regarding art, artists, and psychotherapy. A room can be read as a psychological diagram of intimacy (Bachelard, 1958/1994). Such a reading is thought to commence with the whole, where ambience is received from the context before the particular (McCracken, 1988). Rapoport (1990) held that environmental meaning is affect driven rather than being the result of a detailed analysis of specific objects, at least initially. Within clinical literature, including art therapy literature, the psychiatric Mental State Exam (Rubin and Zorumski, 2005) includes the reading of physical aspects of a person including height and weight, dress and grooming. The same non-verbal, setting-driven readings are taking place in reverse, as clients note features of the setting, from the clothing of the therapist through to the impact of furnishing on a room's ambience (Gordon, 2000; Sands, 2000).

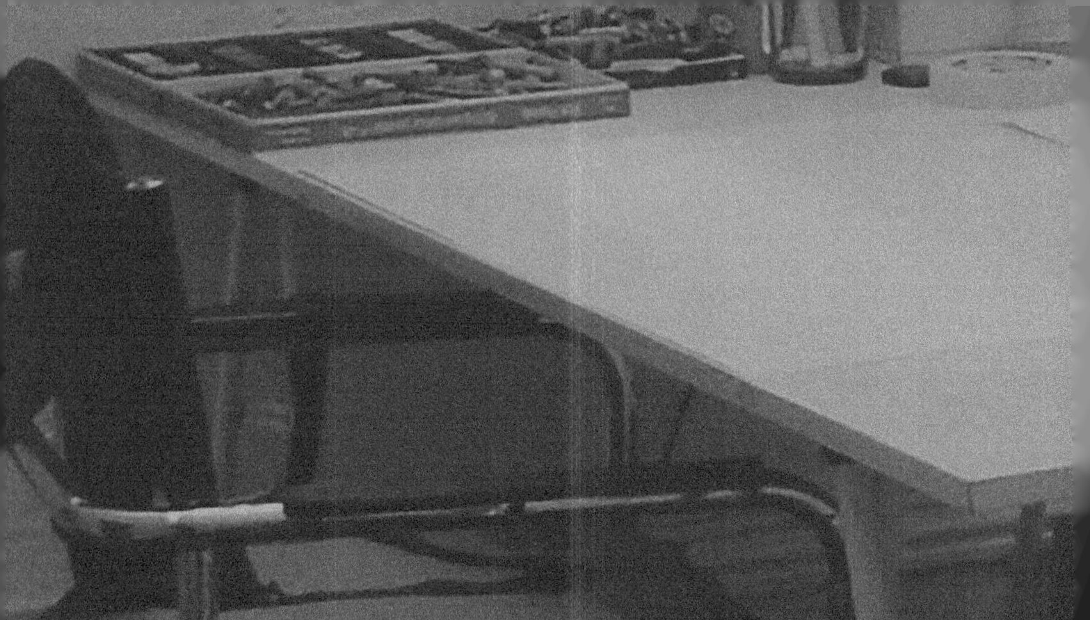

Figure 4 Detail of *Cate's therapy room.*
Patricia Fenner (2008). Photograph.

Gosling, Ko, Mannarelli and Morris (2002) claimed we craft physical environments out of objects to reflect and reinforce who we are, and likewise observe environments to form impressions of their occupants. Brunswik (1956) added that the elements of an environment serve as a kind of lens through which underlying constructs can be indirectly perceived. How reliable these cues may be, depends to some degree on how personal the content (Gosling et al., 2002). A discussion of object meaning reveals two interlinked themes: one, the meanings linked to the self and two, what objects symbolically communicate to others. Both these invariably assume the notion of things as inert and mute, and people as acting beings. This is however a feature of Western thinking whereas in some non-Western contexts life is attributed to things (Komter, 2001). Objects, after all, also comprise qualities entirely separate from our culturally invested meaning-making. Lawlor (1997) reminded us that wood is its hardness, texture, resistant nature, colour and smell, just as Buber stated the obvious that the tree before him is no imagination or projection; it is reality in active relationship with other living elements (Buber, 1970: 58). The immaterial aspect of place is emphasised in notions of place attachment, identity and having a sense of place; however, the material dimension of place is often neglected in the discussion (Cresswell, 1996). According perhaps to a different logic, Elkins (1996) described agency in the inanimate: "An image is not a piece of data in an information system. It is corrosive, something that has the potential to tunnel into me, to melt part of what I am and re-form it in another shape" (42).

Objects are integral aspects of places which are made figural by people for different reasons at different times. The notion of object assumes, more often than not, things made through low to high level human and industrial production. The world of nature, every bit as much matter and material, is largely ignored in this literature and seen to belong to other disciplines such

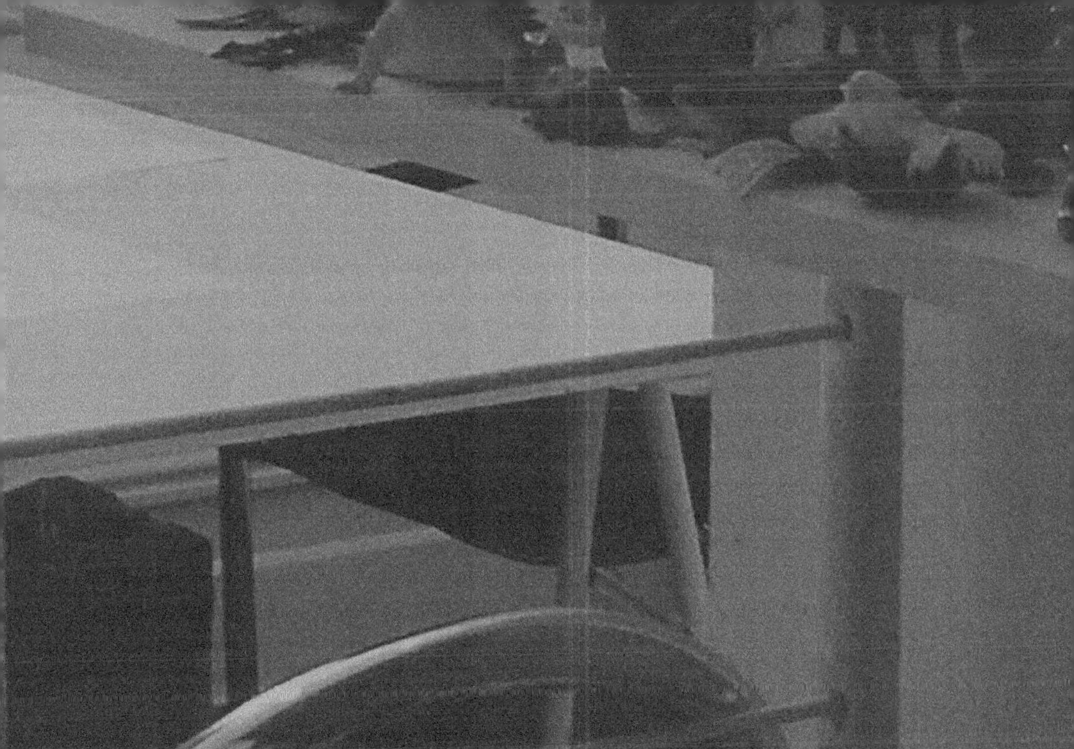

as botany, environmental science or geography. Yet in our lived experience all these elements coexist: the flower in my vase, the cat sleeping on the window sill, the curtain moving in the breeze. The division of the various integrated aspects of places into separate categories, packaged into discipline-specific discourses, falsifies what in lived experience is unified: one.

Overview of the study, method and procedures

Rather than approach this art-based inquiry from a top-down theory-driven perspective, the resulting understandings were informed from the viewpoint of phenomenological lived experience. Incorporating two phases, the experiences of the researcher as both client and therapist comprised the first heuristic phase. This subsequently informed the method of the second phase wherein five therapist–clients pairs explored experiences of their respective rooms of therapy. Participants were recruited according to an intensity sampling approach (Patton, 1990) with the intention to draw upon rich descriptions of the phenomenon under investigation. Therapist participants were recruited through the national register of art therapists through whom client participants were recruited.

Two of the rooms from phase two were from work settings in the public health context, namely the alcohol and drug rehabilitation sector and from a community-based relationship counselling service. The other three settings were located in private practice. A total of 14 experiences were utilised, four in the heuristic phase and 10 during the therapist–client phase. All participants, the majority of whom were female, were adults from the Melbourne area. University ethics requirements stipulated that only clients who had completed or were in the final phase of their therapy should participate. No additional ethical requirements were determined by management of the two agencies involved.

Data collection and analysis procedures

During phase one, as researcher, I explored my experience of four different settings where I had been either a client or therapist by creating visual representations of that experience. I explored the respective richness of data created through memory of a therapy setting which I then compared with the experience of making the art-based response *in situ*. It was evident from this process that images from the latter approach were more loaded with both affect and meaning. Utilising an art-based method, participants in phase two were invited to make visual representations of their experiences of their rooms of therapy. Each participant of a client–therapist pair made these art-based responses separately and at no point did I bring participants into discussion together about their experiences. Although this would have been interesting, it would however have answered a different question from the one I pursued.

Two and three dimensional art materials were made available to all participants. Some people preferred to use familiar materials from their rooms whilst others were keen to utilise media I supplied. The art-making procedures I proposed varied to some degree between the two cohorts due to art-making experience and expertise, differing roles in the therapy dyad, and also the quite different relationship to me as researcher. The procedure for data collection with clients, which in most cases took no more than one and half hours, was structured and involved my presence at all times. Following art-making I engaged with the participant in a dialogic immersion of the image which was audio recorded and later transcribed for analysis.

Therapist participants were invited to develop data in the manner they considered would produce the richest representation of their experience. In one case this produced a lengthy installation process made *in situ* which I video recorded. However most participants, pressed for time, followed a process quite similar to that of the clients, making art in a two dimensional form which was followed by an audio recorded, facilitated verbal immersion process with the researcher.

The transcripts were analysed thematically by the researcher and taken back to research participants for verification of accuracy. Individual themes were reduced to common themes, twelve of which emerged from the therapist data and ten from the client data. I did not undertake an expert-knower position in relation to the art works and limited my interpretive input to the thematic reduction process, privileging instead meaning to the maker. This was done in keeping with the empathic phenomenological methodology (Willis, 2001). The resulting conceptualisations were mine.

Results and discussion

A range of significant themes of the experience of the room evolved from this inquiry. For the purposes of this chapter I shall focus on how a sense of place, mediated via the material dimensions of, and affective responses to, the room play a role in the therapy process for both clients and therapists. I shall also propose the notion that art therapy practitioners and their clients may be especially predisposed and sensitised to these material and place-based aspects of therapy compared with, for example, those participating in talk-based therapies. This has implications for our understanding of the possible meanings and effects an environment may hold within the processes of therapy and why we should not neglect a place-based understanding of practice.

Thinking materially: The therapist optimises her own capacities

All therapist–participants referred to their rooms as impacting positively on therapeutic capacity. In one case, this enhancing quality was simultaneously experienced as a disempowering threat. In this case the therapist experienced her room as mirroring a conflict in her professional identity. The way the room provided for each therapist, however, was different. Three distinct, yet interlinked, aspects comprised the relationship therapists had with their rooms: as a place where a communicative exchange with certain special objects occurred; as an extension of the therapist or even as a separate entity; and the room as a reflection of the identity of the therapist. Thus, the room acted as both a tool in the service of the therapist (and client) and as an additional agentic factor with which the therapist collaborated. Broadly speaking, a parallel process can also be seen reflected within the practice of art therapy. The role of the image can be weighted in different possible directions: as either an object regarded with a life of its own, replete with communications about the art-maker (image as primary), or as a means (or tool) in the service of understanding its maker (maker as primary). The distinctions between these two approaches are fine, primarily attitudinal, and the approaches are not mutually exclusive. However these preferences can be seen reflected in therapists' engagement with the materiality of the room.

The room as collaborating entity or personification

Some participants expressly identified the room as a collaborator, a benevolent presence, and separate from the therapist with its own influence on both therapist and client. Here the room was seen as reflecting the values of the therapist. Therapist Elanor (a pseudonym, as are all names used in this chapter) was most forthcoming in her conceptualisation of the room as an entity and, whilst she advanced this sense of the room more than other participants, her descriptions reflected, to varying degrees, those of the others.

Elanor was strongly invested in honouring the material nature of her setting. Amidst her individual themes, are expressions such as 'the setting as live entity', 'the room behaves as a responsive person', 'is an active and benevolent presence.' Two views of Elanor's room are shown here (Figure 5 and Figure 6 overleaf) which she was explicit in thinking of as personified.

> … You know how you think as you talk, I have caught myself … like the way some art therapists advocate for the art work as a living and another entity, the third partner, the messenger … I have found myself describing the space in a similar way to a client or maybe when I've talked with my colleagues. I think of the space as communicating things symbolically … to the client but also to me.

This notion of room as personality or separate entity is resonant with Mathews' encounter with the world as manifest (Mathews, 2003, 2005). Mathews advocated a participatory relationship with the world, as she argued against the attitude of investigation in favour of one of encounter, where we embrace objects as subjects and consider the detail of these encounters with materiality. An object, she said, is matter "present-to-itself" occupying space from within as well as from without (Mathews, 2003: 32). A subjectivity sensitised to matter is an emplaced subjectivity, oriented to habitation, as opposed to domination and subjugation. The subjectival nature of the universe, she said, "renders it an arena not merely for causality but for communication" (14). She addressed what she saw as the Western antipathy for "personification, and (a) determination to empty the world of interiority" which is regarded as primitive and superstitious (76). An encounter with the room, permits a relational engagement with the nature of its matter, its substance, which she said, enables regard. This way we open ourselves to an experience of "mutuality" (78).

She reflected that, by personifying certain phenomena, we make the subjectival nature of that matter humanly accessible and create a "larger psychophysical field" through which to communicate (ibid: 82). Thus we engage in a subject–subject encounter, an intersubjective approach sensitive to differences and particulars. Elanor appreciated her room, using descriptions such as "responsive… as a living and another entity ... a space that can provide … the space speak(s) to the person, hear(s) the person … there (are) different moods … it just keeps moving and changing … like the space was helping."

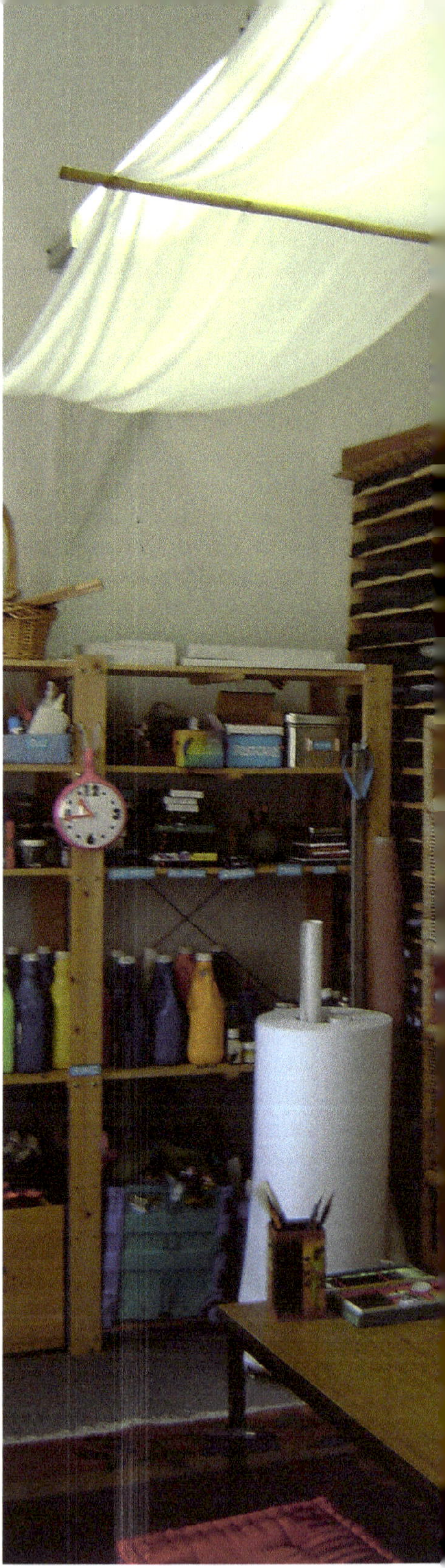

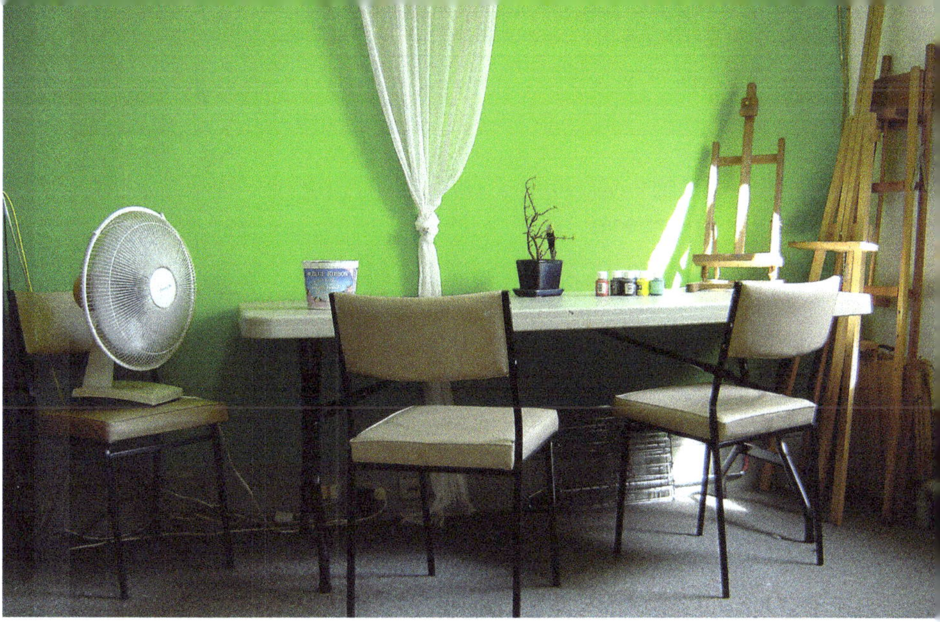

Opposite: Figure 5 *East facing wall in Elanor's room*. Patricia Fenner (2008). Photograph.
Above: Figure 6 *West facing wall in Elanor's room*. Patricia Fenner (2008). Photograph.

Different from, yet not in conflict with, Mathews' notion of personification, is that of Lakoff and Johnson (2003) who see personification as an aspect of metaphor in the structure of language. By considering objects as persons, Lakoff and Johnson argued we enable greater access to comprehending the world and our experiences in it more fully. We can relate to physical and non-physical phenomena in terms of human motivations and characteristics. Personification, they said, is not a single unified process, however. We understand certain types of characteristics to be present in objects as we impute human qualities to things non-human.

It is worth mentioning at this point that not all experiences of the entity or personality of the room were benevolent. Therapist Ruth's experience was a mix of benevolent critique and a harsher tone from a particular part which she titled the "dark side". The sense expressed of this aspect of the room was of a separate force or power threatening at times to unbalance the good-enough working environment of her 'functional' room side. When we sense something, the sense quality is not in the matter *per se* but is an event, an action bridge which connects the two dimensions of materiality and expressivity, the two sides of a sense of place (Dovey, 2010). In all cases the rooms evoked expressions of mood or intensity. The Deleuzian notion of intensity, according to Dovey, is the high degree of affect experienced in response to the interconnecting of points between the flows in the assemblage. In this study intense, affect-laden responses were expressed in relation to ambient, material and aesthetic qualities. Separately, therapists and clients found zones and objects in the room where meaningful encounters, or moments of intensity, occurred. This notion also relates to the kinds of responses individuals had to discrete objects and zones, which were loaded with affect and meaning.

A communicative exchange with special objects enhances therapeutic capacity

All five therapist–participants recruited for the study referred to an aspect of the room with which they had a particular, most often constructive, relationship which provided support to them in role. These objects acted as reminders of qualities or experiences which they used to summon capacity when challenged in the therapeutic process or relationship. These objects supported a way of being and acted as a statement of professional identity. All five objects provided access to something transcending the material, to the immaterial, via visual, textural and associative qualities deemed present in those objects. As Case (2000) utilised a painting as an imaginary supervisor, so too did therapist–participants in this study call on objects as guides and supports.

Epp and Price (2008) reminded us of the fluid nature of our attachments to particular objects over time whereby those of significance can be seen to move in and out of salience. Rochberg-Halton (1984) wrote that patterns in object meaning can be found according to age. Younger persons most often identify objects of action which require some physical manipulation, whereas older people most often hold dear objects of contemplation. Therapist–participants of this study most often cherished objects of contemplation.

Transitional objects

A consideration of objects of special interest as transitional in the participant cohorts created a further link in the web of understandings in this study. Winnicott (1969) discussed the transitional object as the first not-me possession of the infant. In adult life, transitional phenomena can be found in the intense experiences of the arts, religion and other areas of creative endeavour. Winnicott was quite clear that the essence of the transitional object was its illusory nature. As Gibson (2004) put it, the transitional object acts to fill a gap, an absence, in material form. It is through this experience that we learn a heightened sensitivity to material objects, and that objects of the external world can be loved. Turkle (2008) placed more emphasis on the object's material qualities, suggesting objects of this kind are not utilitarian but are affect-laden and become tools with which to think. She recalled Winnicott's assertion that our search for objects to love continues throughout all stages of life.

Participant Venus utilised a photograph of the couch of Freud in this manner (Figure 7). This image, though quite small, provided Venus with a gaze-based dose of self-nourishment. This visual interaction, prospectively contained Venus' anxieties in the face of a challenging and distressed client and gave her the inner capacity to bear the pains of others. She was reminded of the hard work entailed in being a therapist, a sense of the heritage of psychotherapy practice and the challenges endured in its development, as well as a kind of collegial reassurance. Venus described viewing this image as helping her to set an internal ambience.

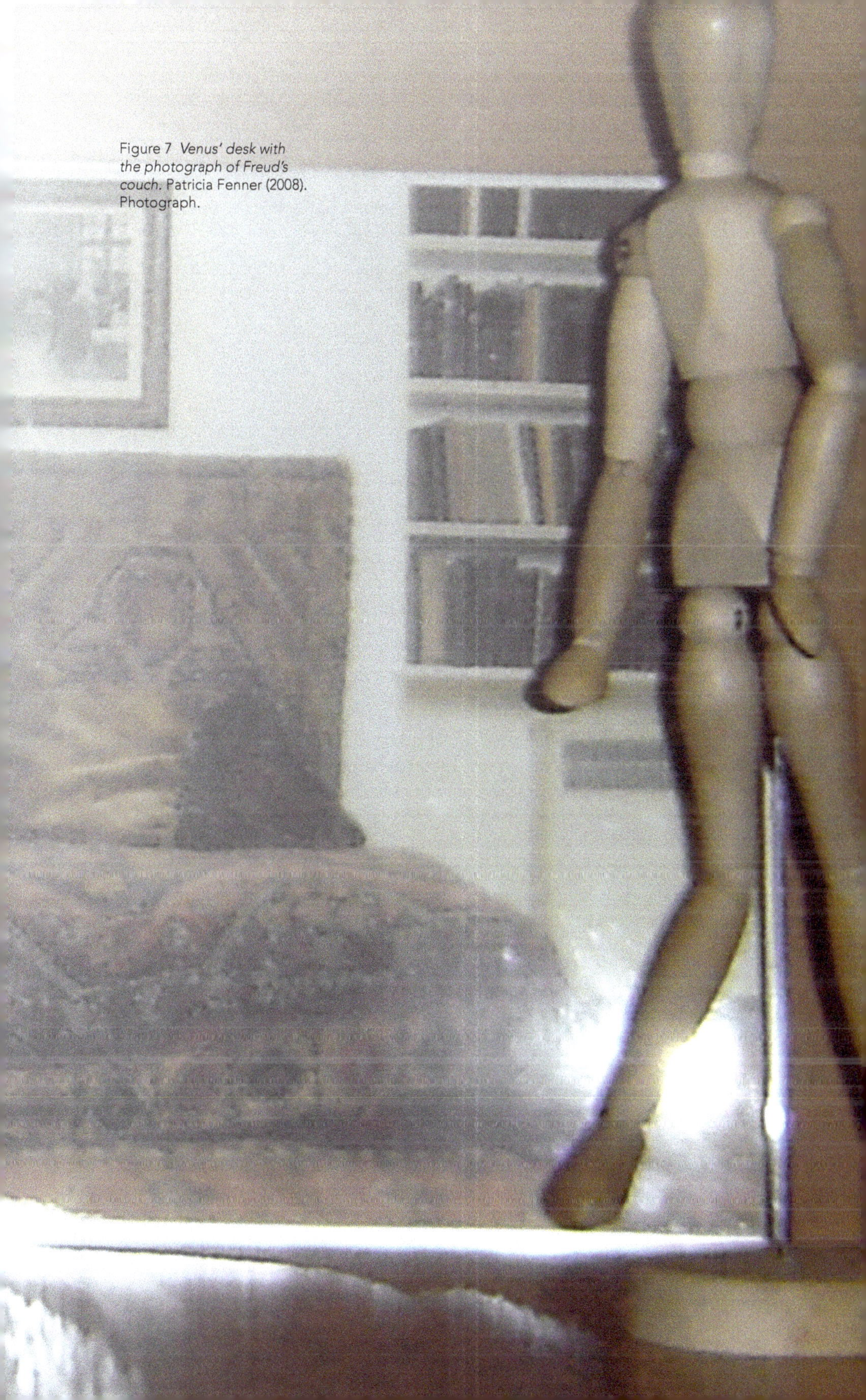

Figure 7 *Venus' desk with the photograph of Freud's couch.* Patricia Fenner (2008). Photograph.

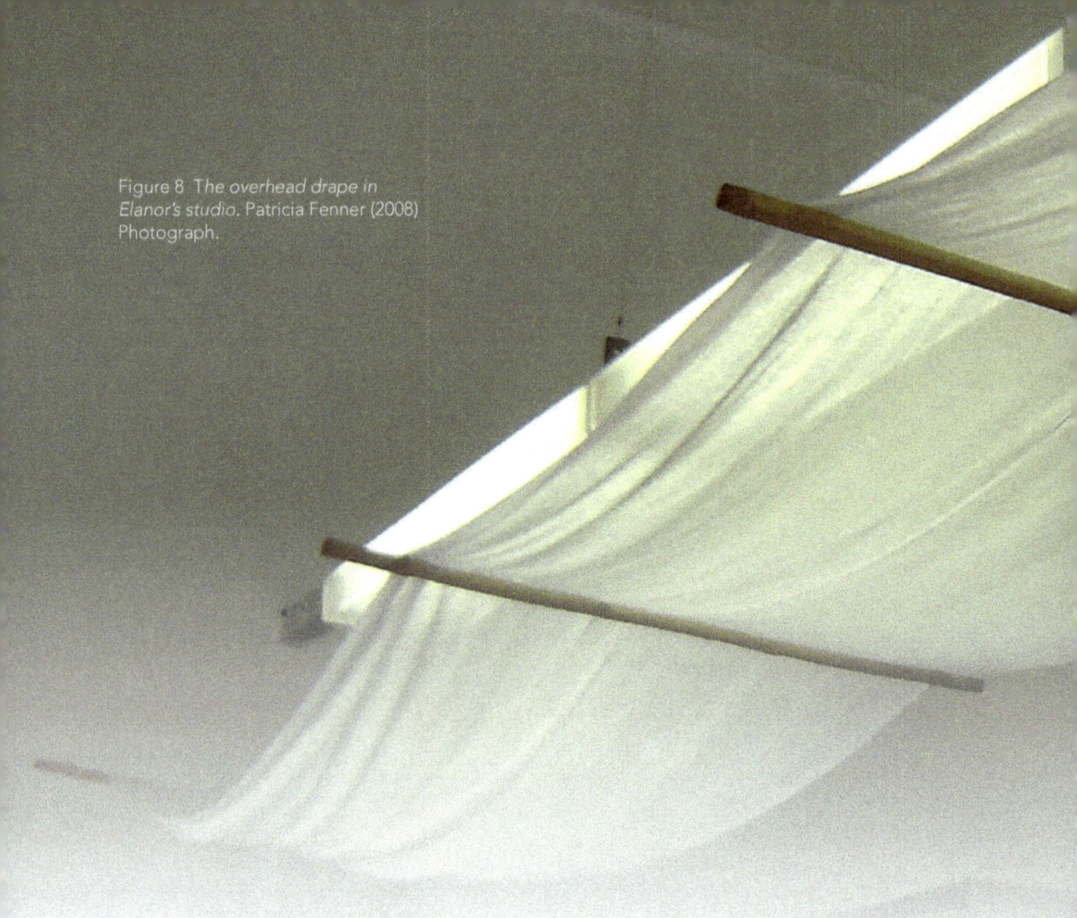

Figure 8 *The overhead drape in Elanor's studio*. Patricia Fenner (2008) Photograph.

Rochberg-Halton (1984) argued against seeing objects as transitional as this conceptualisation strips away the material nature of reality from the object itself. In doing this stripping we reduce our capacity for a communicative dialogue with "an objective web of meaning" (ibid: 364), where objects are both the vehicles for emotion and meaning and the medium of that emotion and, above all, embodied components of place.

Sacralisation

Elanor interacted intensively with the whole room as a unified entity or personality. Through her art-based response she drew particular attention to some elements within that whole, including a single material form, the white fabric drape hovering under the fluorescent lighting in the room (Figure 8). This she referred to as representing qualities of "another world". She referred to this drape as embodying a sense of "grace", a quality she wished to internalise, and a benevolent overview of her practice not dissimilar to the notion of the internalised supervisor (Casement, 1990).

The drape form represented an intention to silently bridge differences between people present in the room. Its hovering, integrating presence, reminded her to stay open to possibilities, to avoid becoming "tunnel-visioned" and to quietly and graciously remain fresh, above things while viscerally and relationally engaged. The meaning embedded in the drape emerged to Elanor through the inquiry process, as she spoke of its particular qualities.

Venus' photograph could be considered a "prosthetic possession", not one enacted in order to create an impression but as a professional support (Tian and Belk, 2005: 300). In her silent dialogue with this image, she created a narrative about "sticking (and) living with complexity", evoked by the visual quality of the luxurious Persian rugs shown in the photograph of Freud's consulting room. This she referenced in some of the patterning shown in two components of her three-part art response (Figure 9).

The notion of complexity in harmony and of luxury, represented in the fine, coloured weave of the rugs, acted as a metaphor representing an ideal state or capacity for herself and her clients. In this sense, the image acted to symbolically draw intra and interpersonal qualities to mind, in a companioning and supportive manner (Lett, 2001). Through being photographed, the image in Venus' office held the "contagious property of the sacred" (Belk, Wallendorf and Sherry, 1989: 29) acting as a symbolic reminder. This, the authors referred to as the creation of sacredness through "tangibilised contamination" (ibid: 29).

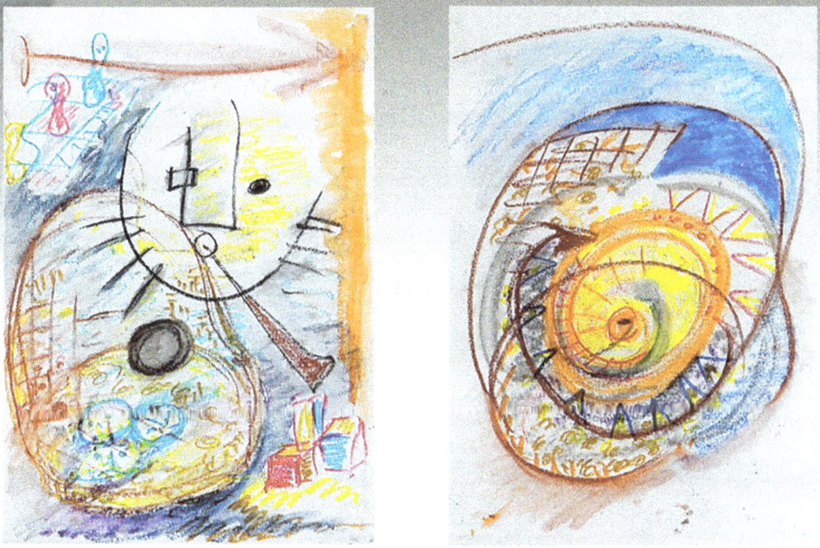

Figure 9 *Two components of Venus' three-part art response.* Venus (2008) Oil pastel on paper.

Therapist Cate affectionately, and somewhat ironically, referred to her room as a *"white brick box"*, a package complete in its own terms (Figure 10 overleaf). Cate only kept items in the room which served a facilitating, practical, aesthetic or metaphoric function. Although entirely unpretentious, this room showed there were no accidents of style, aesthetic or function.

A painting in Cate's direct line of vision when working (Figure 11 overleaf) provided her with a visual reminder and material sense of the desired transcendent space she sought to foster in the action of the therapy

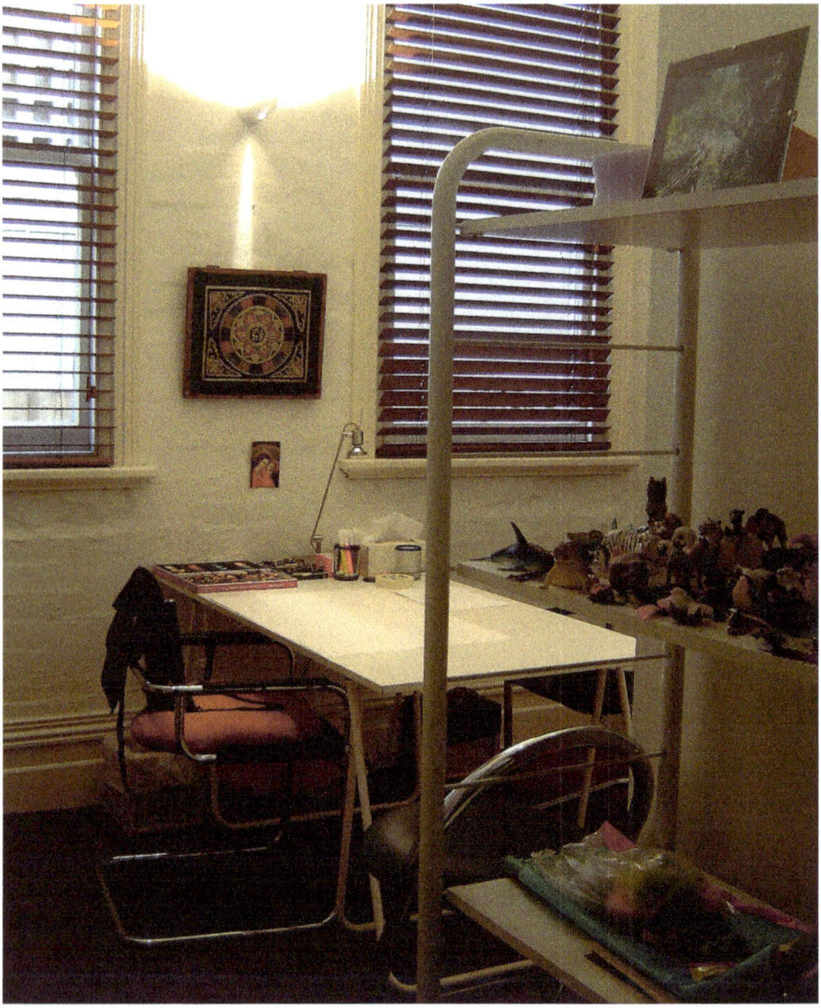

Figure 10 *Cate's therapy room.* Patricia Fenner (2008). Photograph.

process. Its meaning was manifest through its power to invoke, remind of and symbolise her belief structure, values and approach to therapy and in particular to recall an occasion when she had a powerful and embodied experience of these values. This central feature (the painting), was represented at the heart of Cate's art-based response (Figure 12, page 402), which she described as "the heart" with a precious "golden centre, whole and complete with an all-knowing capacity" which she referred to as a "transpersonal sense." This centre emanated healing. Cate explained that a three-way relationship was held through this golden centre between the client and herself (and) a third aspect or dimension which she referred to as a higher source of wisdom.

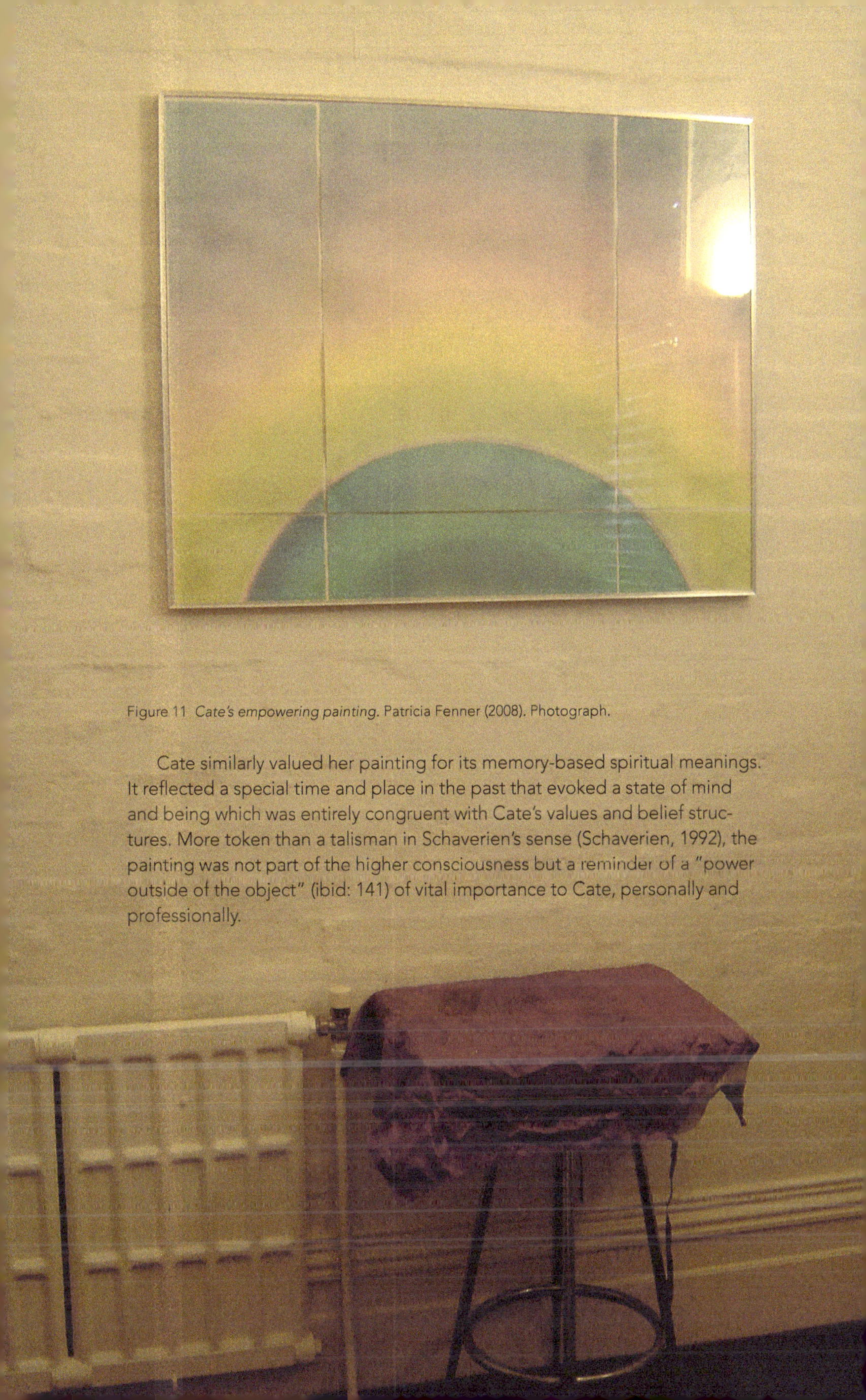

Figure 11 *Cate's empowering painting.* Patricia Fenner (2008). Photograph.

Cate similarly valued her painting for its memory-based spiritual meanings. It reflected a special time and place in the past that evoked a state of mind and being which was entirely congruent with Cate's values and belief structures. More token than a talisman in Schaverien's sense (Schaverien, 1992), the painting was not part of the higher consciousness but a reminder of a "power outside of the object" (ibid: 141) of vital importance to Cate, personally and professionally.

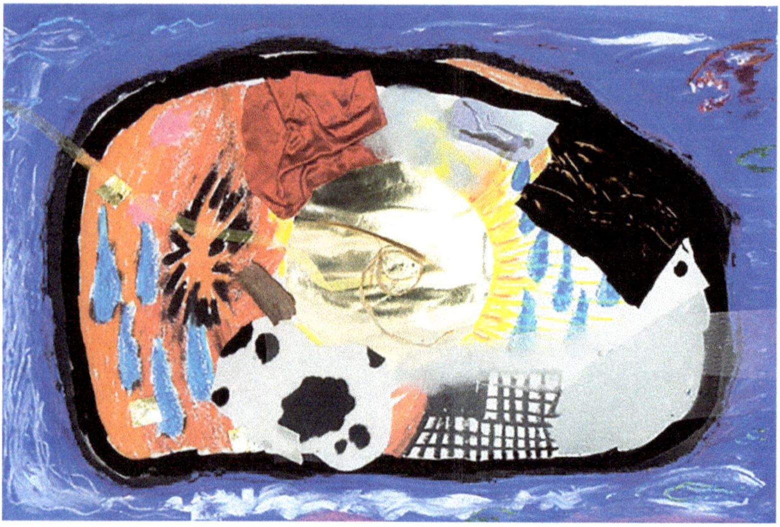

Figure 12 *Cate's art response to her experience including the 'golden centre'.* Cate (2008). Acrylic paint, oil pastel, collage on paper.

Belk, Wallendorf and Sherry (1989) referred to the work of Armstrong (1971) who wrote from a humanistic anthropological stance on "affecting presence" in order to illuminate the qualities of what they termed quintessence. Armstrong described this presence quality, found frequently though not exclusively in the arts, as elusive because of its threefold nature: the physical, social and affecting, the last of these being "undeniably intrinsic" (Armstrong, 1971: 34). The affecting event or thing, he said, bears a "perpetuating action, complete within itself" (24). It acts continuously, and is in many regards like a person with a sense of autonomy, acting as a subject. A transaction occurs, according to Armstrong, between the person and the object with an affecting presence. The transaction becomes mutually informative, of the person being informed by object and vice versa, which brings Armstrong's (1971) sense close to Mathews' (2003) philosophic position on the subjectival nature of matter.

Clients' experiences of place and meanings in matter

All client-participants expressed attachments to certain parts of the room in a way that indicated experiencing a sense of place. Several clients demonstrated how a single room can be mindfully 'subdivided' to create a zone over which a client feels she or he has temporary ' ownership', necessarily separate from their therapist. Some client participants gave explicit examples of this. Sandra found reassurance and comfort in being able to sit and orient herself from her zone comprising the chair, small round table with its colourful cloth, and the tissue box (Figure 13) which she represented in her art response (Figure 14, page 404).

When Parr (2000) referred to the way patients made "self expressive use of microspaces" (232) within mental health-care settings, she could have been referring to these experiences of 'own place' zones.

Dovey's (1999) distinction between power to (empowerment) and power over (domination), were subtle particularities to which these two clients were sensitised. Sandra was unequivocal that beyond this zone, things did not belong to her. She read the organisation of the room as signifying power relations between herself and her therapist (Godkin, 1978). Malpas (2008) stated that embedded in a relationship to place is always a claim of ownership which, at times, is disguised. Cresswell (1996) similarly argued that the effect of place goes well beyond its spatial geographic elements, always in fact intersecting with "sociocultural expectations" (8).

Clara, like Sandra, was acutely aware that in order to do the introspective and demanding work of therapy, and in order to feel personally authorised, she required a sense of sanctuary, of security and intimacy. She needed a sense of a place of her own which, for her, depended upon the physical and sensory attributes in the room. Altman and Low (1992) wrote of the defining

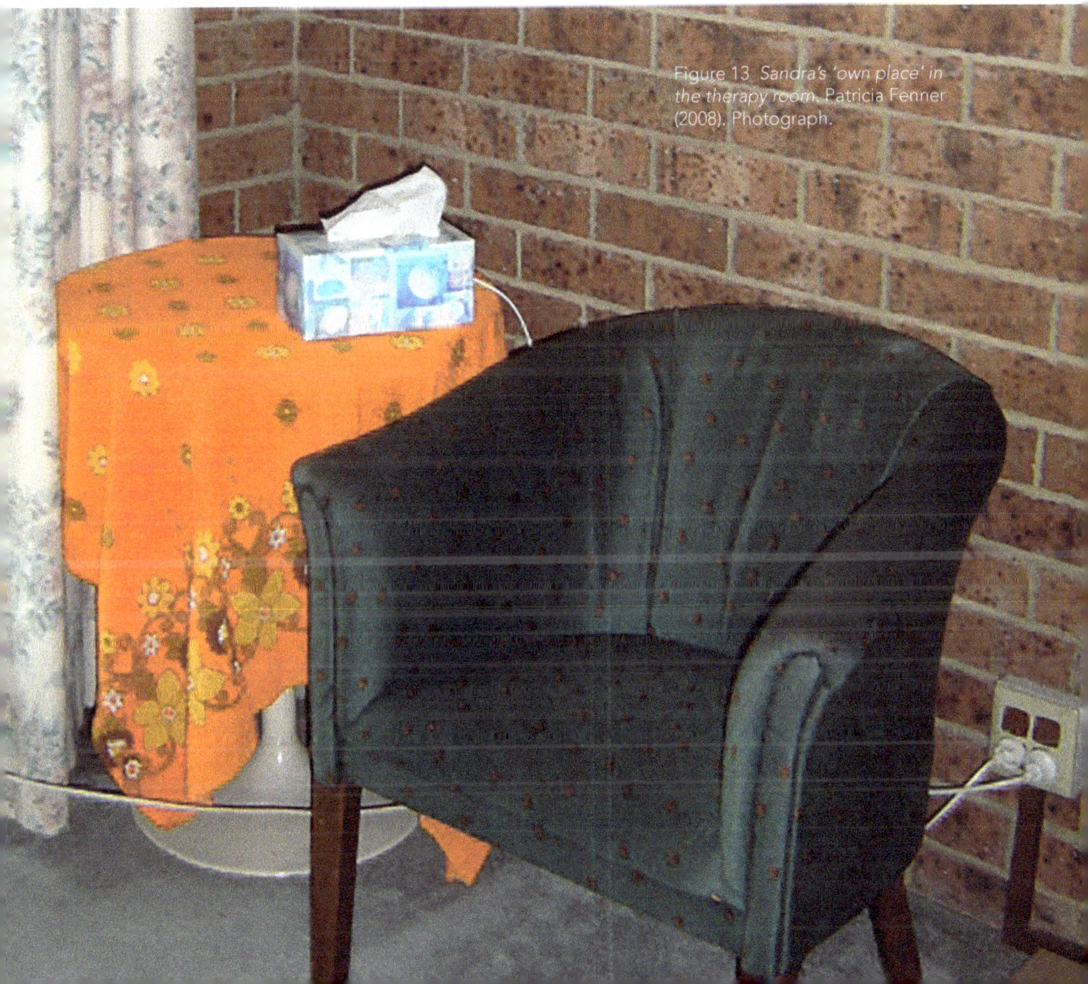

Figure 13 *Sandra's 'own place' in the therapy room.* Patricia Fenner (2008). Photograph.

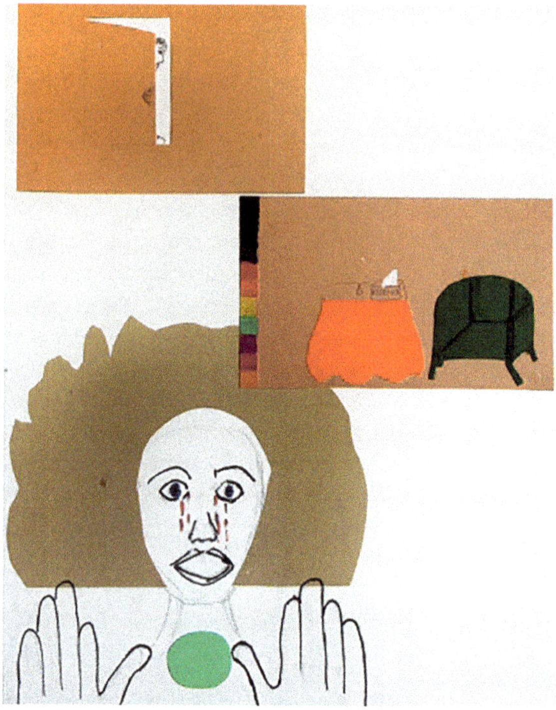

Figure14 *Sandra's representation of her experience including her 'own place'*. Patricia Fenner (2008). Collage, pencil felt on board.

characteristics of place, attachment and emotion. One becomes attached to place because it provides satisfaction as it "permit(s) control, creativity, and mastery, and (it) provides opportunities for privacy, personal displays, security and serenity" (7). In having a sense of place, the client finds his or her identity bolstered.

As a person with a long history of mental illness, client Raygan may have been reassured that his therapist Elanor's room was a place where he could be understood and belong. He experienced the room as both a gift and an invitation to play and take new risks. In this room, he found new capacities including the stilling of his medication-induced hand shaking. The visual and resource-rich qualities of being in this place were appreciated:

> I love that corner (the art materials corner)… just like (they say) 'come and try me' … it's like being a kid in a lolly shop … and all the materials that are available, and Elanor, if you haven't got something she'll get it for you.
>
> Raygan

Although Raygan referred here to a specific end of the room (Figure 15), he indicated a generalised experience of freedom in the studio through both his art response (Figure 16, page 406) and verbal expressions. He experienced no need for a special zone for himself and instead felt authorised throughout the entire area.

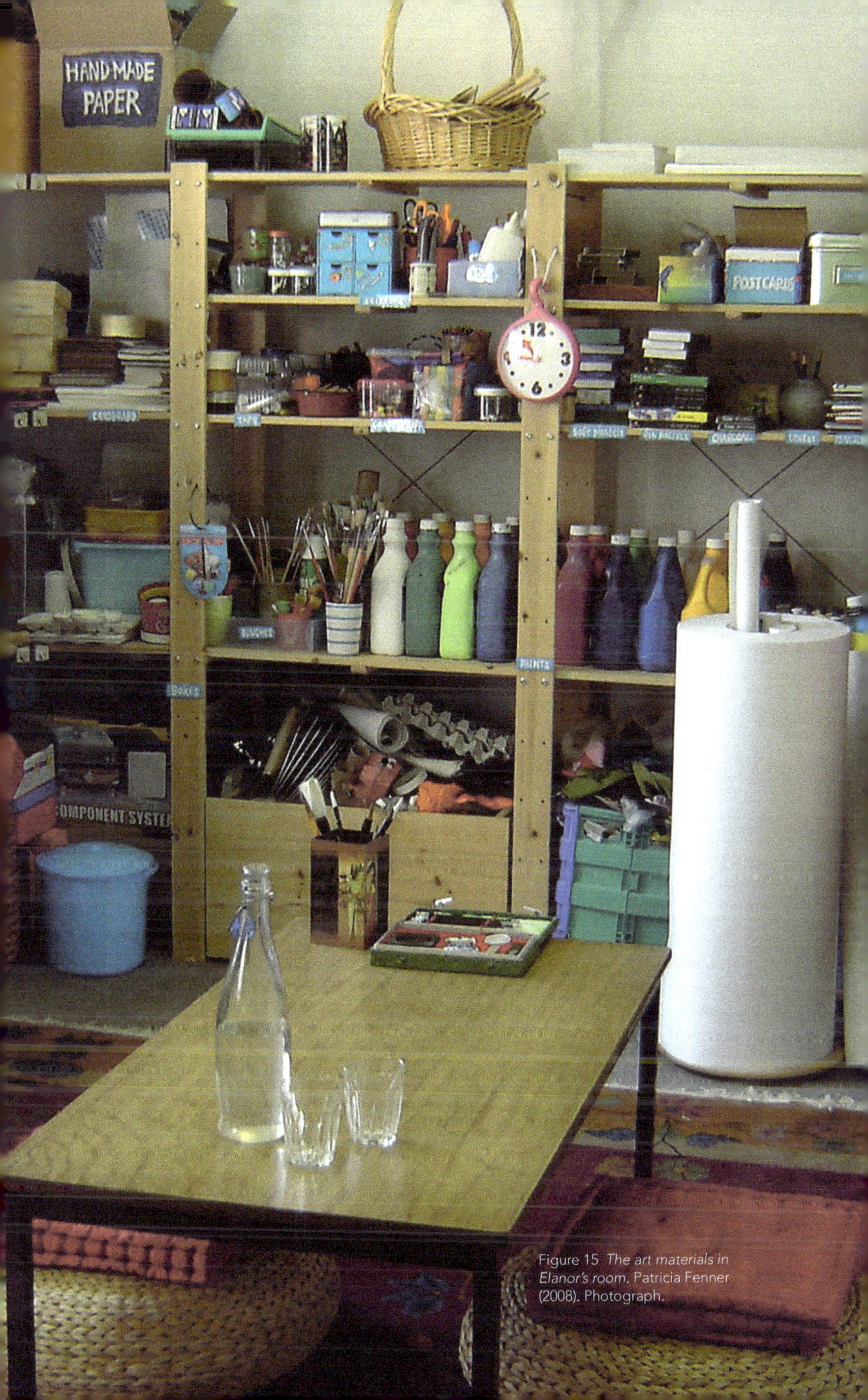

Figure 15 *The art materials in Elanor's room*. Patricia Fenner (2008). Photograph.

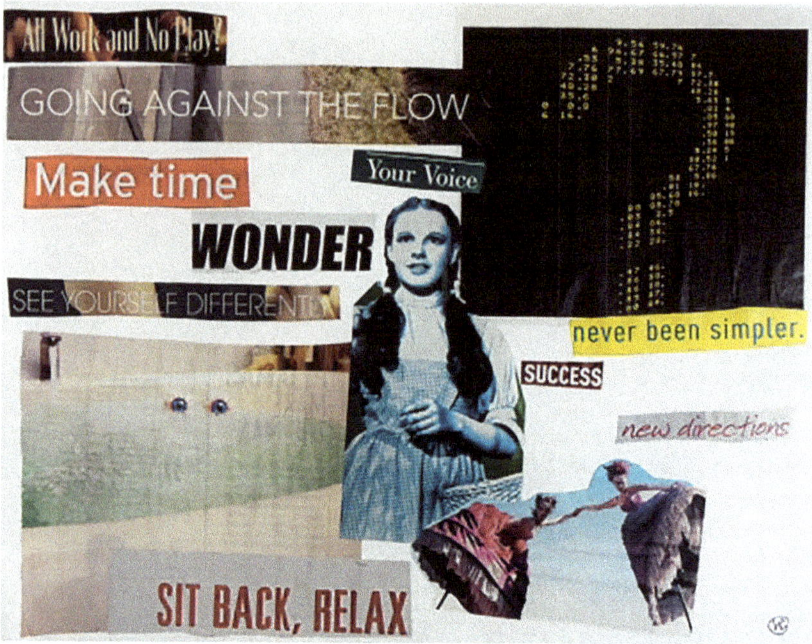

Figure 16 Raygan's art response. Raygan (2008). Collage on board.

It was Elanor's usual practice to vary the furniture constellation in the room and, except for fixed items such as the art materials shelving, she altered the room arrangement according to group and individual client requirements. No specific area was designated as 'her's' and art-making took place on walls, the floor, easels and different tables from time to time. This flexible approach created an extended zone wherein her client Raygan felt authorised and which he looked forward to with delight, arriving to a room which in some ways was unpredictable.

> Elanor's such a lovely person, very understanding and I love her room. It's so flexible. Sometimes I come in and I don't know how it's going to be ... sometimes the table is in the centre and sometimes we work on the wall ... There's another table in there...and it gets rearranged and it's nice not knowing quite how you are going to come into the room and find it, you know.

This environment provided for him, perhaps better than he might have dreamed possible. A quality of abundance exudes: "I love those boxes of cut outs. I sometimes feel I'd like to do a whole wall in that." Raygan spoke with a love for the place of his therapy which enveloped him in possibilities and benevolence (Mathews, 2005).

Objects and images in the room – differing functions, differing readings

Therapists varied in their attentiveness to the visual appearance and practical functioning of the room; some paid attention to the whole whilst others attended more to specific aspects, such as whether any images were displayed on walls, and less to other components. However, clients responded independently to features or objects in ways which were unintended by their therapists which sometimes fell within the perceived zone of ownership.

In a similar manner, clients Clara, Melinda and Deena emphasised the important role played by the view to nature out the window which was possible from their seats, as limited as it often was (Figure 17). In two of these cases the therapists involved were unaware of the value their clients placed on this aspect of the room.

However therapist Cate intentionally kept one of the white walls in her room unadorned in the manner of a 'blank canvas'. This way, her client could gaze and create or discover aspects of his or her inner self. Her client Melinda created a reference to this in her art response and expressed the importance

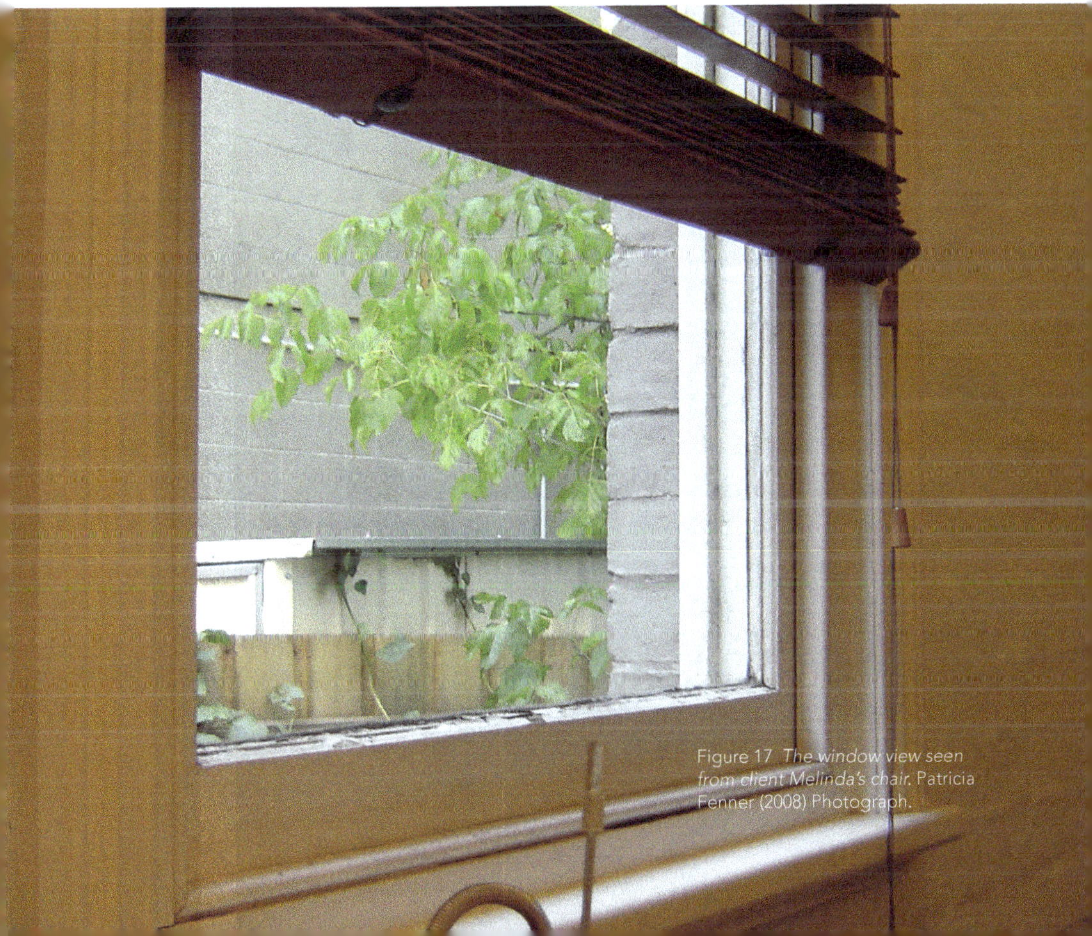

Figure 17 *The window view seen from client Melinda's chair.* Patricia Fenner (2008) Photograph.

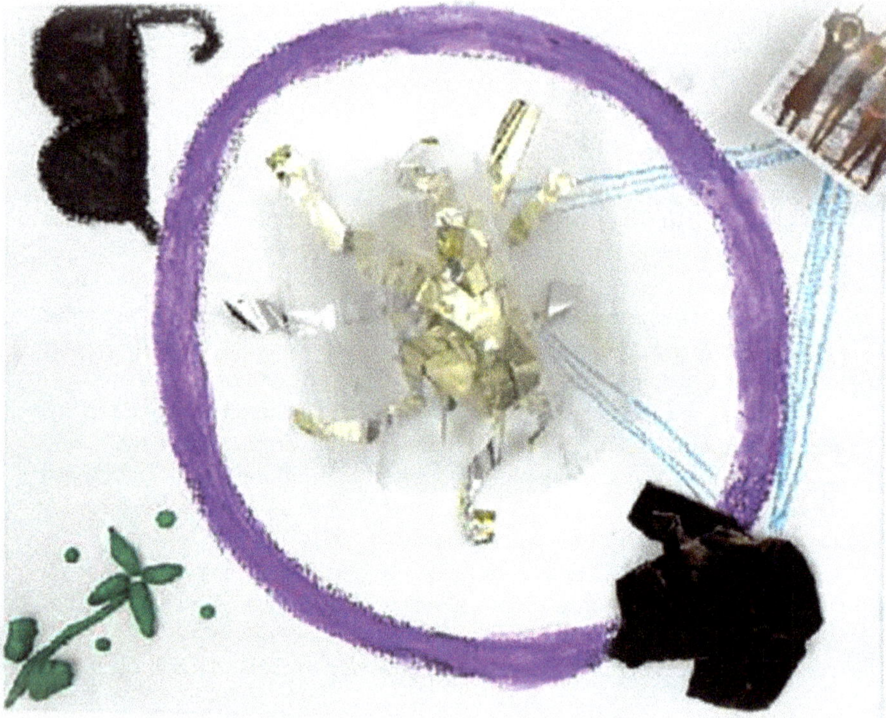

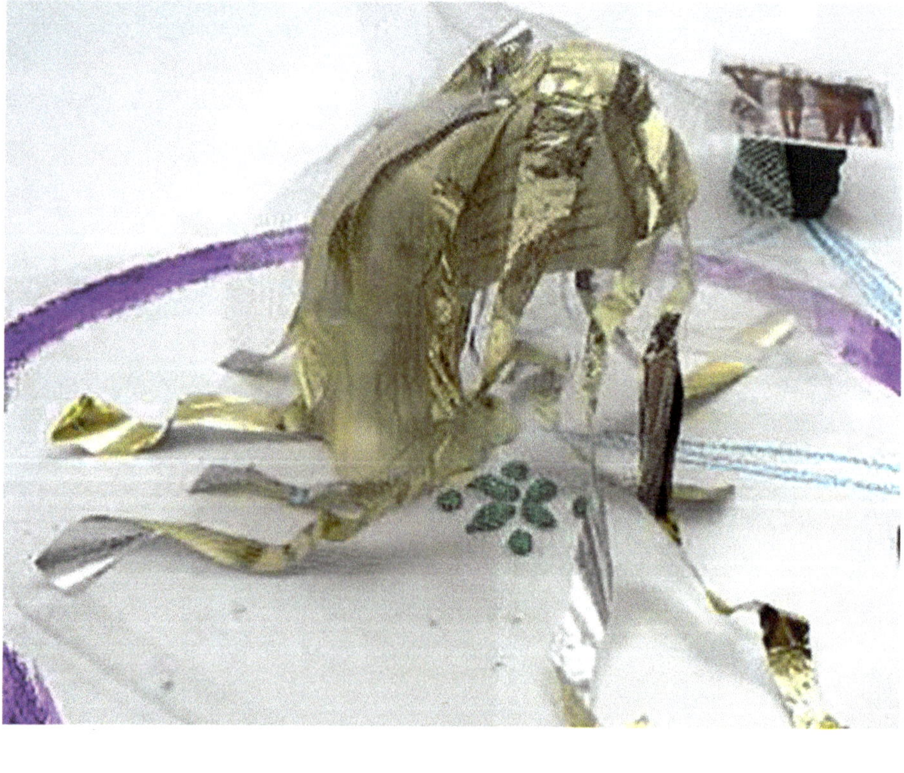

of this whiteness in her dialogic exploration with me afterwards (Figures 18 and 19). This whiteness represented qualities of openness, of possibility and a freedom to create without the imposition of a predetermined agenda or influence. Her choice of the hard white canvas board for her visual work, rather than paper, was a direct reference, she said, to her positive experience of these walls. Rather than feeling confined in this small 'white box', as Cate called it, the dominance of the white extended Melinda's experience of inner possibility. Its physical solidity stood as a metaphor for its reliability. She compared this with the opportunity created by the blank sheet of paper "where all or nothing is possible." Here the mind could rest or project according to the client's determining alone.

Art therapy and material/expressive elements in the assemblage

Two interconnected dimensions of the practice of art therapy relate to this enhanced experience of place which transcend the interpersonal. Firstly, art therapy brings an appreciation for materials through the physical act of manipulating media in the therapy process. Secondly the therapy can create an expanded appreciation of the object world, which results from both the making experience and attaching affect and meaning to completed images and three dimensional forms in therapy. What might it be that predisposes art therapists to think about the experience of their rooms, that is, beyond their practical requirements?

Art therapists are very often also practising visual artists. There are also those who practise their art-making in periods rather than continuously, and others whose art practice has reduced over time, as they maintain an engaged therapeutic practice. All, however, have made art a lot.

When an art work is completed in art therapy, the relationship developed in the making process continues as the form is contemplated, looked at over time. Art made in therapy is imbued with emotion, compounding the potential depth in the relationship. Informed by the process of art-making, both therapists and their clients, regardless of skill levels, extend their relational experience beyond the person-to-person. This art practice enhances an affinity with, or sensitivity to, matter and the completed tangible form is present in the world, there to be seen, part of the visual and aesthetic make up of the environment. Its meaning and form take up space, and become a part of place.

Making art involves an intrinsic engagement with media, with materials, with matter. Art therapy cannot exist without materials. Other forms of psychotherapy may use imagery from time to time, or engage in dialogue about paintings and meaning. Art therapy is the therapy type where images (including sculptures, installations and so on) are made. Art-making in therapy,

Opposite, top: Figure 18 *Melinda's art response* (seen from above). Melinda (2008). Paint, plasticine and collage on board.
Opposite, below: Figure 19 *Detail of Melinda's art work*. Melinda (2008). Paint, plasticine and collage on board.

means potentially using a diverse range of materials: from soft media like charcoal through to resistive kinds, such as stone, wood or metal and on both small and large scales. Some art therapists do not feel comfortable with a very broad range of media, preferring to offer those where their expertise best lies (Moon, 2010). However, irrespective of how active an art practice the therapist has, art therapy is inherently dependent on matter. (I am aware the recent interest in digital art-making may radicalise this in the future and that some of the current software imitates various sensory features of physical media).

Concomitantly, art therapists have a developed appreciation for matter. How does this appreciation and sensibility for physical materials affect their understanding of the experience of the room? I would suggest it does, through its congruence with the experience of place, whereby the material and expressive dimensions of experience are intensified.

From a phenomenological perspective, art-making entails working directly with matter, followed by looking at the developing form, back and forth, in a repeating manner. In working this way the art-maker develops a rich appreciation and regard for how materials behave, their feel, diversity, idiosyncrasies, and the rules they inherently impose. Art-makers understand the authority of matter, how materials exert themselves, not just symbolically but existentially. They know that a relationship exists between making with matter and cognition, referred to in a different context by Carter (2004) as *material thinking*. Art-makers are sensitised to this agency in matter, their stuff of trade; substances to them are both magical and familiar, "paint is water and stone, and it is also liquid thought" (Elkins, 2000: 5).

Creating form requires a communication process – a gesture into or with a medium is followed by a response, some gestures working more effectively than others on the way to creating the desired effect. The final form is the embodiment of that expressive exchange. The "creative intelligence of materials" can only be grasped through the experience of making in the locale of its production (Carter, 2004: xiii). This kind of "plastic intelligence" (Carter, 2004: 185) was also theorised by art therapists Kagin and Lusebrink (1978) and further developed by Lusebrink (1990). More recently Moon (2010) conceptualised art materials and other media from a social constructivist perspective.

Kagin and Lusebrink (1978) categorised two- and three-dimensional media according to their influence on the experience of image-formation and information processing in therapy. They constructed a scale of media properties according to media type, ranging from fluid to resistive qualities where, for example, a fluid material such as watercolour may stimulate an affective response, and a harder material, such as stone, may induce a more cognitive response (Hinz, 2009; Kagin and Lusebrink, 1978). In addition to the fluid resistive scale, Kagin and Lusebrink pointed to those materials which have boundary-setting qualities, and the impact these can have on art-making in therapy.

Figure 20 Detail of *Venus' three-part art response*.
Venus (2008). Oil pastel on paper.

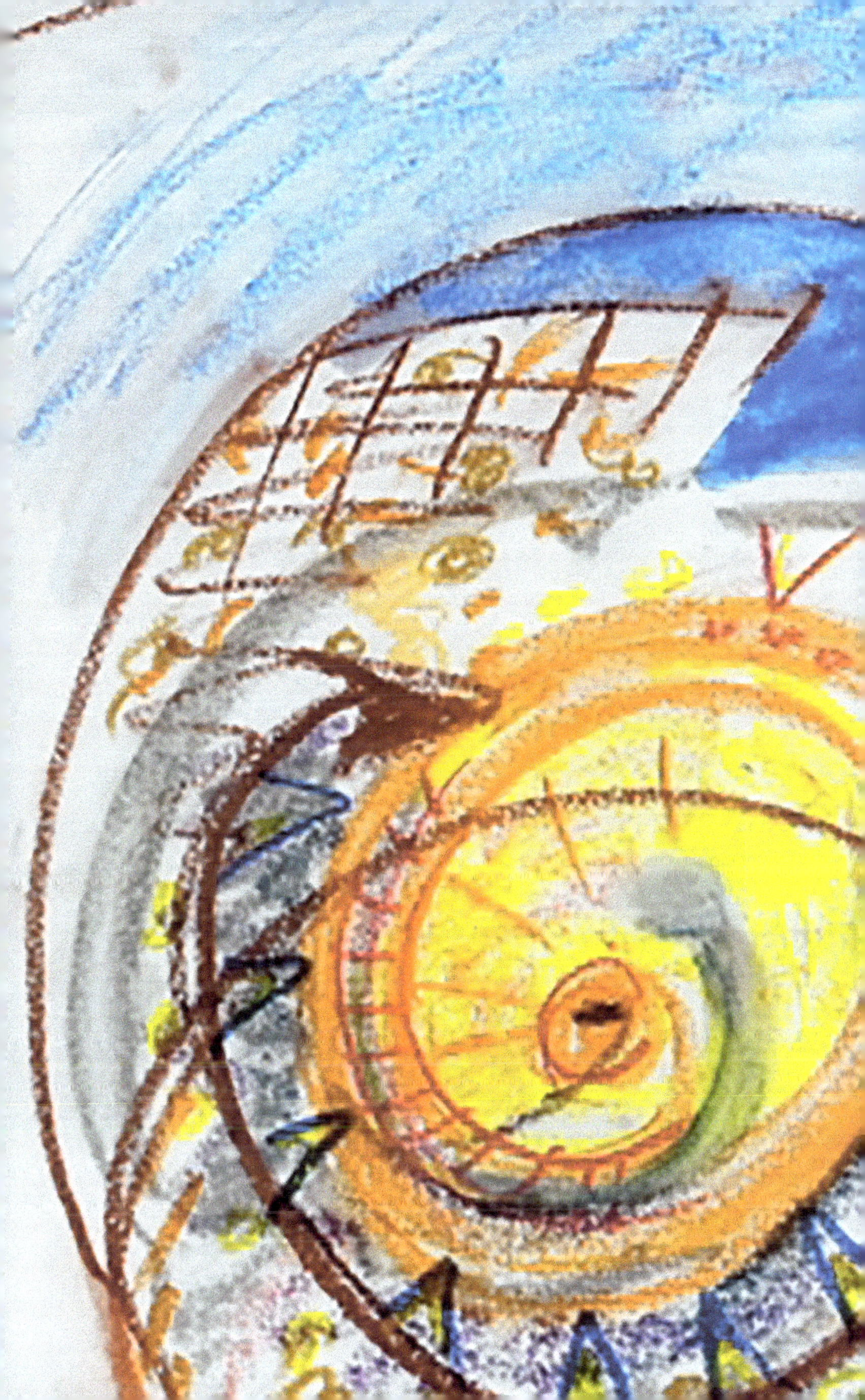

Materials inherently hold a boundary potential to greater or lesser degrees. Boundary-determined materials are those which impose a limit on expressive potential.

The use of mediators (art tools) such as painting with a palette knife or blowing paint through a straw, also influence expressive potential. The concept of the *media properties scale* was further advanced into the Expressive Therapies Continuum of Lusebrink (1990), a materials-based theory on image formation, cognition and expression in therapy.

The basis of its structure lies in the qualities of materials used in art-making and the kinds of thinking and emoting induced through contact and manipulation. Participants in this study, had varying levels of experience in using materials. Few clients of art therapy would necessarily be aware of this media-properties schema, but would have a more or less substantial body of experientially-derived knowledge. As such these were two cohorts sensitised to matter of various kinds and qualities and with a regard for the evocations of the material. The reality of the participants' being sensitised in this manner cannot be separated from the findings of this inquiry – nor should it be. Rather, by being aware of these factors, we can further our understanding of the overall experience of the room.

Art expression utilises materials or media which heighten experiences of touch, sight, hearing, smell, the kinesthetic and the haptic sense in therapy. As well as such heightening of experiences, we sense subtleties in our feeling responses to images. These diverse versions of 'sense' are incorporated into Dovey's discussion of assemblage, along with notions of 'common sense' and 'good sense.' All, he said, operate at the experiential, or pre-reflective, level. Sensing forms the connection between the material and expressive poles of assemblage. It is here that the intensity of affective experience of place occurs: "Intensity is a word we use to describe temperature, colour, activity, encounter, character or place where there is a high degree of some quality" (Dovey, 2010: 26).

Participants of this study demonstrated responses such as engendering support from material features of the room, and personified relationships to certain objects. Not only were these objects acknowledged for their agency, they were often loved, some primarily for their material nature, others for the information they communicated, many for both.

A relational orientation to objects is not the sole preserve of art therapy. However, it may be that in art therapy an openness to this attitude is particularly prevalent. Indeed, at the very heart of its practice, regardless of theoretical orientation, is a relational dynamic to the object of the image. This relationship has been much theorised. Foundational to most, is the idea of the triangular relationship of client, therapist and image, or in some formulations, artist, therapist and image (Case, 2000; Schaverien, 1990, 1992; Wood, 1990).

Just what is classified art material and what not, has been challenged by Moon (2010), who advocated a broadening or softening of what we understand to be the dividing line between non-art and art-related materials, or matter. But what of other objects in the room, those not created by client (or therapist) as part of the therapy process and usually considered more peripheral? Case (2000), writing from a psychoanalytic perspective, discussed a print on the wall of her consulting room and its impact on therapy with children. It is difficult to find literature on how art therapists themselves relate to objects in the room beyond the images made by the client. Through a phenomenological inquiry, this study found there are objects and environmental features with which these clients and therapists sustained a silent communication during therapy.

This form of communication is more likely to be something therapists are, to some degree, aware of and intentionally utilise. For the clients of this study however, this communication was more subtle and not entirely at the surface of awareness. However, by asking about the experience of the room, each client-participant nominated objects, views or ambient qualities which held meaning and helped sustain their engagement in therapy. Because these experiences are not necessarily brought into the therapeutic conversation, the function and nature of these relationships are normally considered outliers.

Conclusion

This study demonstrated how our clients' responses to our rooms can constitute a form of relationship and that for some therapists, the room, likewise, constitutes a partner relationship, one with layered meanings and functions. These relationships go beyond the interpersonal domain of the therapeutic relationship, engaging other aspects usually unrecognised in the therapy event. Indeed, this study demonstrated how the experience of the room forms an extended relationship and that the triangular relationship particular to art therapy formed by the therapist, client and image is not the only relational dynamic in the room.

However, by orienting our perspective to that of the lived experience of the room, the traditional way of understanding practice shifted. Dovey's description of the assemblage reconfigured the room (or studio) as a whole material and expressive event. Such a construction can include the interpersonal relationships, the material solidity of the walls, the rich encounters made with objects and zones in the room and the meaning made of these encounters as well as the sensory experiences of smells and sounds beyond the window. Considering the therapy room with these qualities as assembled place offers a dynamic context through which we can more fully appreciate the richness of our clients' experience as well as the extent of our own and conclude that, where the therapy encounter takes place becomes an inseparable dimension of the therapy itself.

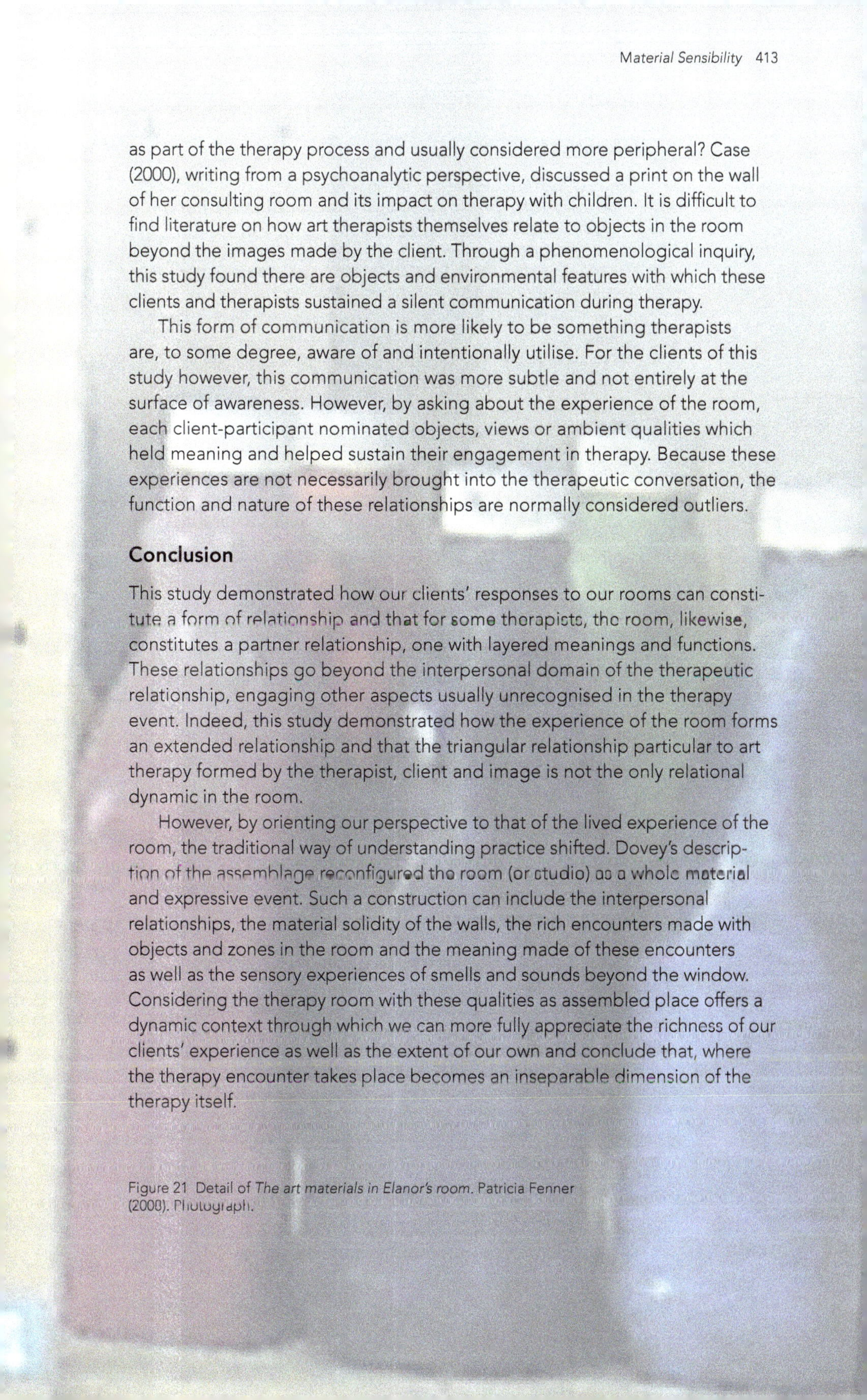

Figure 21 Detail of *The art materials in Elanor's room*. Patricia Fenner (2008). Photograph.

References

Allen, P. (1992). Artist in Residence: An alternative to "clinification" for art therapists. *Art Therapy: Journal of the American Art Therapy Association*, 9(1): 22–29.

Allen, P. (2008). Commentary on community-based art studios' underlying principles. *Art Therapy: Journal of the American Art Therapy Association*, 25(1): 11–12.

Altman, I. and Low, S. (Eds.). (1992). *Place attachment*. Plenum Press, New York.

Armstrong, R. (1971). *The affecting presence: An essay in humanistic anthropology*. University of Illinois Press, Urbana.

Bachelard, G. (1994). *The poetics of space*. Beacon Press, Boston (original work published 1958).

Basso, K. (1996). Wisdom sits in places. In: Feld, S. and Basso, K. (Eds.) (1996). *Senses of place*. School of American Research Press, Santa Fe.

Belk, R., Wallendorf, M., and Sherry, J. (1989). The sacred and the profane in consumer behaviour: Theodicy on the odyssey. *Journal of Consumer Research*, 16, (June): 1–38.

Bell, S. (1998). Will the kitchen table do? In: Pratt, M. and Wood, M. (Eds.) (1998). *Art therapy in palliative care*. Routledge, London.

Berman, M. (1990). *Coming to our senses: Body and spirit in the hidden history of the West*. Seattle Writers' Guild, Seattle, WA.

Brooker, T., Cullum, M., Gilroy, A., McCombe, B., Mahony, J., Ringrose, K., Russell, D., Smart, L., von Zweigberg, B. & Waldman, J. (2007). *The use of art work in art psychotherapy with people who are prone to psychotic states: An evidence based clinical practice guideline*. London: Oxleas NHS Foundation Trust and Goldsmiths, University of London, London.

Brown, C. (2008). Very toxic – handle with care. Some aspects of the maternal function in art therapy. *International Journal of Art Therapy*, 13(1): 13–24.

Brunswik, E. (1956). *Perception and the representative design of psychological experiments*. University of California Press, Berkeley.

Buber, M. (1970). *I and thou*. Touchstone, New York (original work published 1937).

Carter, P. (2004). *Material thinking*. Melbourne University Press, Melbourne.

Case, C. (2000). 'Our Lady of the Queen': Journeys around the Maternal Object. In: Gilroy, A. and McNeilly, G. (Eds.) (2000). *The changing shape of art therapy: New developments in theory and practice*. Jessica Kingsley, London and Philadelphia.

Case, C. and Dalley, T. (1992). *The handbook of art therapy*. Routledge, London.

Casement, P. (1990). *On learning from the patient*. Routledge, London and New York.

Casey, E. (2000). *Place*. University of California Humanities Center: UC Irvine.

Cresswell, T. (1996). *In place/out of place: Geography, ideology and transgression*. University of Minnesota Press, Minneapolis.

Davies, K. (2007). 'A small corner that's for myself': space, place, and patients' experiences of mental health care, 1948–98. In: Topp, L., Moran, J. and Andrews, J. (Eds.) (2007). *Madness, architecture and the built environment.* Routledge, New York and London.

Deco, S. (1998). Return to the open studio group: Art therapy groups in acute psychiatry. In: Skaife, S. and Huet, V. (Eds.) (1998). *Art psychotherapy groups: Between pictures and words.* Routledge, London and New York.

Deleuze, G. and Guattari, F. (1987). *A thousand plateaus.* Athlone, London.

Dovey, K. (1999). *Framing places.* Routledge, London.

Dovey, K. (2010). *Becoming places: Urbanism/architecture/identity/power.* Routledge, London and New York.

Edwards, D. (2010). Art therapies studio's project. *Art Therapy OnLine: ATOL,* 1(1). Retrieved 16.06.10, from http://eprints-gojo.gold.ac.uk/atol/home.html

Elkins, J. (1996). *The object stares back.* Simon and Schuster, New York.

Elkins, J. (2000). *What painting is.* Routledge, New York.

Epp, A. and Price, L. (2008). Family identity: A framework of identity interplay in consumption practices. *Journal of Consumer Research,* 35 (June): 50 – 70.

Gibson, M. (2004). Melancholy objects. *Mortality,* 9(4): 285–299.

Godkin, M. (1978). Space, time and place in the human experience of stress. Unpublished PhD thesis, Worcester, Clark University.

Gordon, E. (2000). *Mockingbird years.* Basic Books, New York.

Gosling, S., Ko, S., Mannarelli, T. and Morris, M. (2002). Personality processes and individual differences. *Journal of Personality and Social Psychology,* 82(3): 379–398.

Gruenewald, D. (2003). Foundations of place: A multidisciplinary framework for place-conscious education. *American Educational Research Journal,* 40(3): 619–654.

Gulson, K. and Symes, C. (2007). Knowing one's place. In: Gulson, K. and Symes, C. (Eds.) (2007). *Spatial theories of education.* Routledge, New York and London.

Henley, D. (1995). A consideration of the studio as therapeutic intervention. *Art Therapy: Journal of the American Art Therapy Association,* 12(3): 188–190.

Hinz, L. (2009). *Expressive Therapies Continuum: A framework for using art in therapy.* Routledge, New York and London.

Kagin, S. and Lusebrink, V. (1978). The Expressive Therapies Continuum. *Art Psychotherapy,* 5(4): 171–180.

Kalmanowitz, D. and Lloyd, B. (1999). Fragments of art at work: art therapy in the former Yugoslavia. *The Arts in Psychotherapy,* 26(1): 15–25.

Kalmanowitz, D. and Lloyd, B. (2002). Inhabiting the uninhabitable: The use of artmaking with teachers in Southwest Kosovo. *The Arts in Psychotherapy,* 29(1): 41–52.

Kalmanowitz, D. and Lloyd, B. (2005). Inside the portable studio: Art therapy in the former Yugoslavia 1994–2002. In: Kalmanowitz, D. and Lloyd, B. (Eds.) (2005). *Art therapy and political violence: With art without illusion.* Routledge, London and New York.

Killick, K. (1997). Unintegration and containment in acute psychosis. In: Killick, K. and Schaverien, J. (Eds.) (1997). *Art, psychotherapy and psychosis*. Routledge, London and New York.

Killick, K. (2000). The art room as container in analytic art psychotherapy with patients in psychotic states. In: Gilroy, A. and McNeilly, G. (Eds.) (2000). *The changing shape of art therapy.* Jessica Kingsley, London.

Killick, K. and Greenwood, H. (1995). Research in art therapy with people who have psychotic illnesses. In: Gilroy, A. and Lee, C. (Eds.) (1995) *Art and music: Therapy and research*. Routledge, London.

Know, P. (2005). Creating ordinary places: Slow cities in a fast world. *Journal of Urban Design*, 10(1): 1–11.

Komter, A. (2001). Heirlooms, Nikes and bribes: Towards a sociology of things. *Sociology*, 35(1): 59–75.

Korlin, D., Nyback, H. and Goldberg, F. (2000). Creative arts groups in psychiatric care: dDevelopment and evaluation of a therapeutic alternative. *Nordic Journal of Psychiatry*, 54 (5): 333–340.

Lakoff, G. and Johnson, M. (2003). *Metaphors we live by* (2nd ed.). University of Chicago Press, Chicago.

Lawlor, A. (1997). *A home for the soul*. Clarkson Potter, New York.

Lett, W. (2001). *Intersubjective and multimodal inquiry: The arts of resonance*. Melbourne Institute for Experiential and Creative Arts Therapy, Melbourne.

Lusebrink, V. (1990). *Imagery and visual expression in therapy.* Plenum Press, New York.

MacWilliams, D. (2002). Embodied dialogue with place: Intentional engagement of the world. Unpublished doctoral thesis, Pacifica Graduate Institute.

Malchiodi, C. (1995). Studio approaches to art therapy. *Art Therapy: Journal of the American Art Therapy Association,* 12(3): 154–156.

Malchiodi, C. (1998). *The art therapy sourcebook*. Lowell House. Los Angeles.

Malchiodi, C. (Ed.). (1999). *Medical art therapy with children*. Jessica Kingsley, London.

Malchiodi, C. (2002). *The soul's palette: drawing on art's transformative powers for health and well-being.* Shambhala, Boston.

Malpas, J. (1999). *Place and experience*. Cambridge University Press, Cambridge.

Malpas, J. (2008). Place and human being. In: Vanclay, F., Higgins, M. and Blackshaw, A. (Eds.) (2008). *Making sense of place*. National Museum of Australia, Canberra.

Mathews, F. (2003). *For love of matter: A contemporary panpsychism.* State University of New York Press, Albany.

Mathews, F. (2005). *Reinhabiting reality: Towards a recovery of culture.* University of New South Wales Press, Sydney.

McCracken, G. (1988). *Culture and consumption: New approaches to the symbolic character of consumer goods and activities*. Indiana University Press, Bloomington.

McDonald, J. and Lloyd, R. (2007). *Studio: Australian painters on the nature of creativity.* R. Lloyd Productions, Singapore.

McNiff, S. (1995). Keeping the studio. *Art Therapy: Journal of the*

American Art Therapy Association, 12(3): 179–183.

McNiff, S. (1999). The virtual art therapy studio. *Art Therapy: Journal of the American Art Therapy Association,* 16(4): 197–200.

McNiff, S. (2004). *Art heals*. Shambhala, Boston and London.

Moon, C. H. (2002). *Studio art therapy.* Jessica Kingsley, London and New York.

Moon, C. H. (2010). *Materials and media in art therapy: Critical understandings of diverse artistic vocabularies*. Routledge, New York.

Parr, H. (2000). Interpreting the 'hidden social geographies' of mental health: Ethnographies of inclusion and exclusion in semi-institutional places. *Health and Place* 6: 225–237.

Patton, M. (1990). *Qualitative evaluation and research methods* (2nd ed). Sage, Newbury Park, CA.

Rapoport, A. (1990). *The meaning of the built environment.* The University of Arizona Press, London.

Relph, E. (2008). A pragmatic sense of place. In: Vanclay, F., Higgins, M. and Blackshaw, A. (Eds.) (2008). *Making sense of place*. National Museum of Australia, Canberra.

Robbins, A. (1987). *The artist as therapist*. Jessica Kingsley, London and Philadelphia.

Robbins, A. (1994). *A multi-modal approach to creative art therapy.* Jessica Kingsley, London.

Rochberg-Halton, E. (1984). Object relations, role models, and cultivation of the self. *Environment and Behaviour,* 16(3): 335–368.

Rubin, E. and Zorumski, C. (2005). *Adult psychiatry.* Blackwell Publishing, Malden, MA.

Sands, A. (2000). *Falling for therapy.* Macmillan, London.

Schaverien, J. (1989). The picture within the frame. In: Gilroy, A. and McNeilly. G. (Eds.) (1989). *Pictures at an exhibition*. Routledge, London.

Schaverien, J. (1992). *The revealing image: Analytical art psychotherapy in theory and practice*. Routledge. London and New York.

Stoller, N. (2003). Space, place and movement as aspects of health care in three women's prisons. *Social Science and Medicine,* 56: 2263–2275.

Tian, K. and Belk, R. (2005). Extended self and possessions in the workplace. *Journal of Consumer Research,* 32(2): 297–310.

Turkle, S. (Ed.). (2008). *Falling for science: objects in mind.* MIT Press, Cambridge, MA and London.

Willis, P. (2001). The 'things in themselves' in phenomenology *Indo-Pacific Journal of Phenomenology* 1(1): no page nos., see *www.ipjp.org*

Winnicott, D. (1969). Transitional objects and transitional phenomena: a study of the first not-me possession. *Psyche,* 23 (9): 666–682.

Wood, C. (1990). The triangular relationship (1): The beginnings and endings of art therapy. *Inscape: Journal of Art Therapy,* Winter. 7–13.

Wood, C. (1997). The history of art therapy and psychosis (1938–95). In: Killick, K. and Schaverien, J. (Eds.) (1997) *Art, psychotherapy and psychosis*. Routledge, London and New York.

Wood, C. (2000). The significance of studios. *Inscape,* 5(2): 40–53.

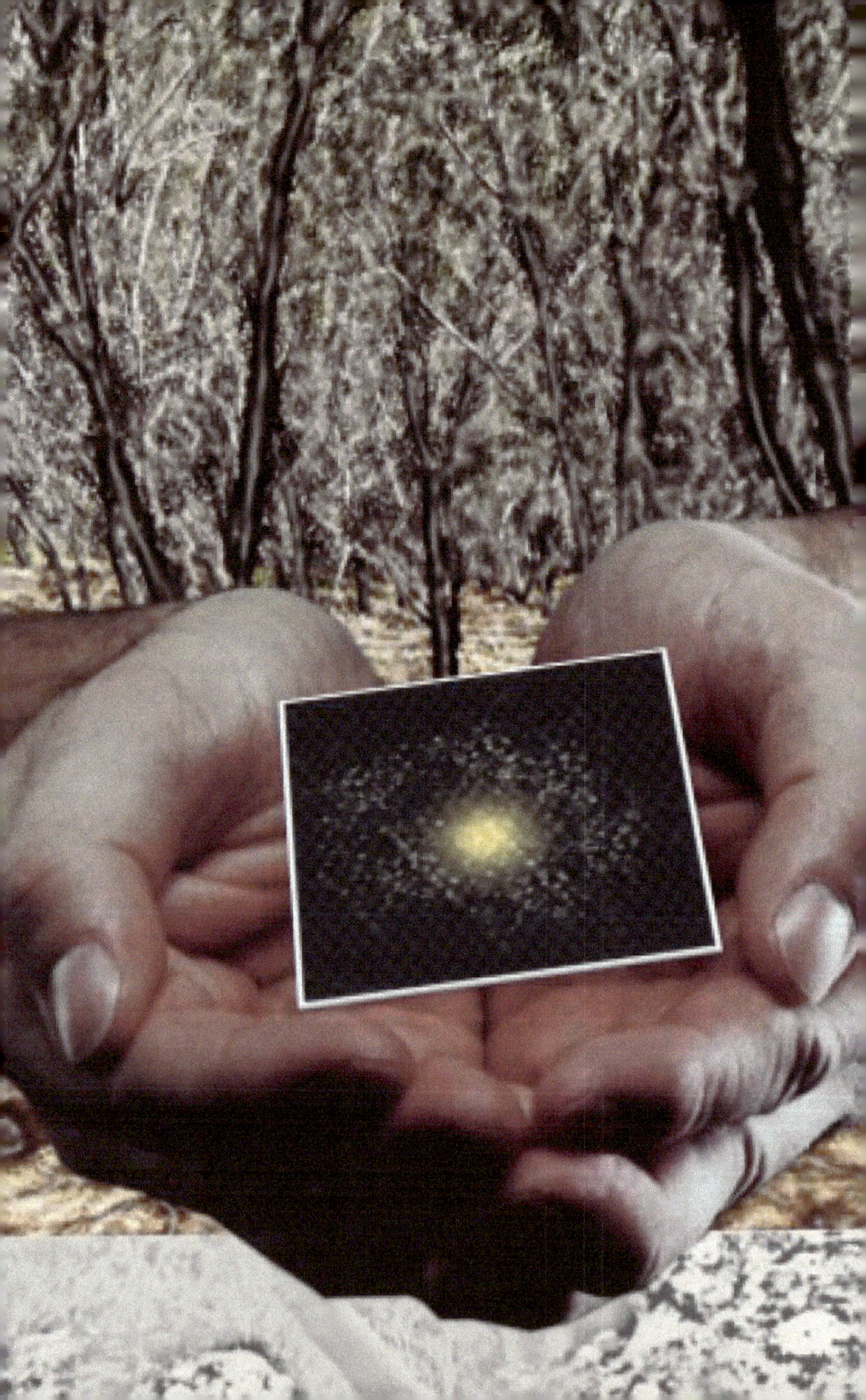

EPILOGUE: A LETTER TO ART THERAPISTS OF THE FUTURE

Lynn Kapitan

You probably don't remember me, but I have always dreamed of you. You carry my deep desire that art therapists are thriving in communities the world over, like the spark of many campfires along the shore on a dark and starry night. I see you gathering in the borderlands, the overlaps and intersections of art therapy's many different histories. Connected by the vast river of human knowledge, you are re-claiming its eddies, flotsam, and safe landings. You move with ease, your work valued and practiced in countless diverse communities – but it was not always so. Toss another log on the fire and I will share the visions I've had of you, glimpsed from many years of journeying.

I am an art therapist of what I think of as the second generation, taught by the art therapy "pioneers" – that small but feisty band, mostly in the USA and UK, who named and defined art therapy, and then announced its birth. I honoured them as elders and mentors, and told their stories of having discovered a whole new field. Their times were tumultuous: living through the Cold War, the USA Civil Rights Movement, and the Vietnam War, when institutions that once had seemed so solid began to crack from all the clamouring for freedom and change. Art therapy, they said, arose from a search for common ground in a world no longer unified in belief.

Trailblazers, they were. Their pioneer legacy gave my generation – and indeed all art therapists to come – a path forward, bushwhacked through dense thickets of bias that so often kept art therapy from being taken seriously. They sojourned with psychoanalysts, Jungians, social scientists, modernist painters, and art diagnosticians. If, like me, you had been an art therapist back then, you'd have studied the "art of madness" from psychiatrists and learned to analyse drawings for graphic signs of schizophrenia, personality disorders, abuse, addiction, and suicidal ideation. You'd have created scribble drawings, bridge drawings, family drawings, and human figure drawings, and then moved on to create mandalas, yes, and later still

Opposite: Figure 1 Detail of *Dreaming Australia, into art therapy's future*. Lynn Kapitan (2018). Digital collage.

 | DOI:10.1163/9789004368262_016

to retreat from the clinic entirely. Seeking validation, you might have been persuaded by the idea that art therapists were a modern resurrection of long-lost shamans – buying into a mainstream mythology that shamanism is an ancient archetype rather than a living cultural reality for Indigenous peoples (Napoli, 2018). It must seem unbelievable to you now; even for me it is painful to look only a short distance back and see my own inability to recognise these harmful views.

In my times, enormous energy was needed to keep the spark of art therapy alive within those well defined, clearly named, legally protected, and scientifically sanctioned structures known as a profession. I learned to see with disciplinary filters, to appraise new knowledge in relationship to sanctioned knowledge, new people or practices relative to established practices (Kapitan, 2015). I put aside my crafty, sensuous, howling ways of making art – that is, of making life, as so many women do – in exchange for access and for the science that would enhance art therapy's worth. The reflective dimension that made us empathically human felt as though it might slip away. As new priorities and complex needs competed for attention, my profession became vulnerable to fracture. In the constant struggle to gain a valid foothold in the patriarchal commerce of healing, somewhere in me I knew that something was not right with this configuration of things.

When I imagine you, future art therapists, I see you practicing in the vast fullness of human knowledge, freely shared like smooth pebbles released into the river's constantly moving flow. In your time you no longer have to choose whether to claim legitimacy by embracing science or to claim authenticity by embracing art. Art is expansively defined and practiced as an integral part of living, what people simply do to connect, to participate, and to share their lives with others. Freed from the false binaries of art and therapy, I envision you forever creating new approaches based on where and with whom you practice. You are skilled in "third space thinking" that attends to reciprocity and exchange, of the hybrid and the transcultural. If my generation's old identity question was "who are we?" I imagine yours will be "how do we all find home in this interconnected world?"

Art therapists of the future, more than anything, I see you living the truth that diversity is essential to your communities' survival, and not simply because different voices are present. To take up the daunting challenges you face, a multitude of talents and perspectives are plainly needed. You would find it unacceptably limiting to believe that biology determines health or that art always transcends culture. Quite the contrary – you understand that "transcending" culture is neither possible nor valuable; rather, art illuminates and communicates culture. Your experience affirms that people understand and express their distress in vastly diverse, culturally particular terms – as selves inseparable from their environments or kinship bonds, often intertwined with unsayable stories and the permeable spirit world (Watters, 2011).

Opposite: Figure 2 Detail of *Morialta Conservation Park, South Australia.* Eddee Daniel (2015). Photograph.

But it was not always so. Your profession was named in the West, in centres of influence that exerted an inescapable gravitational pull. Then, with the forces of globalisation and technology, art therapy began to travel – from the centre to the periphery. Global migration followed pathways worn deep from the carriage wheels, military boots, and shipping lanes of earlier colonising conquests, although this was barely noticed by most of us at first. Taking itself to be normal, superior and good, the West had long painted the Other as people without civilisation, without history, proper laws, or a proper God (Grosfoguel, 2011) – and later, in need of science and modern medicine to save them. I joined and help grow an art therapy field that had bought into this narrative – that art as healing was a new discovery rather than a practice as old as humankind. I wish that I, and others of my times, had seen through these violent myths from the beginning.

When did a critical mass of art therapists finally realise that the world-view of this profession had been too white and too Western for too long, excluding other colours and voices from mattering? I cannot say. But I remember well my own blinkered complicity. We lived and worked within a world system that stigmatised, marginalised, and oppressed; I, and so many other art therapists, could not always recognise how the lives and fates of all people were affected by our own. Art would bring order out of chaos, or so I was taught. But I see now how this belief was marked by the colonising past and present. Throughout history those who bring "order" to others always presume to know it best (Biko, 1978).

I imagine you, art therapists of the future, telling the stories of how the old colonising hierarchies of domination were interrupted, the creed of conquest and territory finally transformed. How you never had to buy into the idea of the DSM as a field guide to the whole world's illness and suffering (Watters, 2011) or take biomedical explanations as scientific fact. Gone are the whispers of supremacy that once nestled in the question of how best to heal a community's brokenness and despair. You heeded the call to transgress, aware of your capacity to either liberate or oppress. You have let go of taking responsibility for healing others and believe, instead, in a difference-centered responsibility. Each of you practices as a cultural being in dialogue with each other cultural being. Acutely aware that all are related to one another, no one is left behind and without full participation in their self-determination.

The world so very much needs the resilient communities you are committed to creating. Your artistry strengthens their social immune systems; your therapy is a collaborative partnership committed to healthy, free, and creative minds in a free, dynamic, and just social body (Martin-Baro, 1994). You are rooted in local authority, far beyond the colonising drift of art therapy's past. Because the community – and not art therapy – is the central force of change, your power as an art therapist is elastic enough to shift and be transformed as well (Kapitan, 2015). In the openings of these spaces, you call forth multi-vocal, synchronic, mixed, and hybrid perspectives and visions for the work at hand. Disorienting complexity and ambivalence arise as well, and they are accepted as sources of creativity, energy, and transformation.

Future art therapists, I imagine you converting walls of fear into far-reaching corridors of creativity and exchange. Shaped by a living landscape of practice, you create entanglements with kindred others to generate new skills, identities, and knowledge that can only be found by journeying together. With ever more linkages, the greater are your widening circles of impact. Art therapy is shared from person to person, community to community, such that no one lays territorial claim to it. As a result thousands and thousands of people are benefitting from this vital resource. This, I believe, is what a *re-claimative* art therapy (Lawson, Wood and McKenna, this volume) must look like.

I am inspired by your commitment to break away from the too-narrow ledges and ways of the past to achieve the unfinished dream of de-colonisation. You have learned to reach out to those who do not share your same history and discovered how the perspective of each art therapist is relevant to that of every other. I close my eyes and listen to you tell your own hard-won stories of working within the margins and borderlands. I listen to the yarning (ibid): those of you with privileged identities telling of how you strayed from the dominant path, shed your old habits and lost your way, and heard the deep murmurings of the earth when you took finally root. And those of you with marginalised identities telling of how you held on tight against the force of strong currents, staying steadfast and true to your

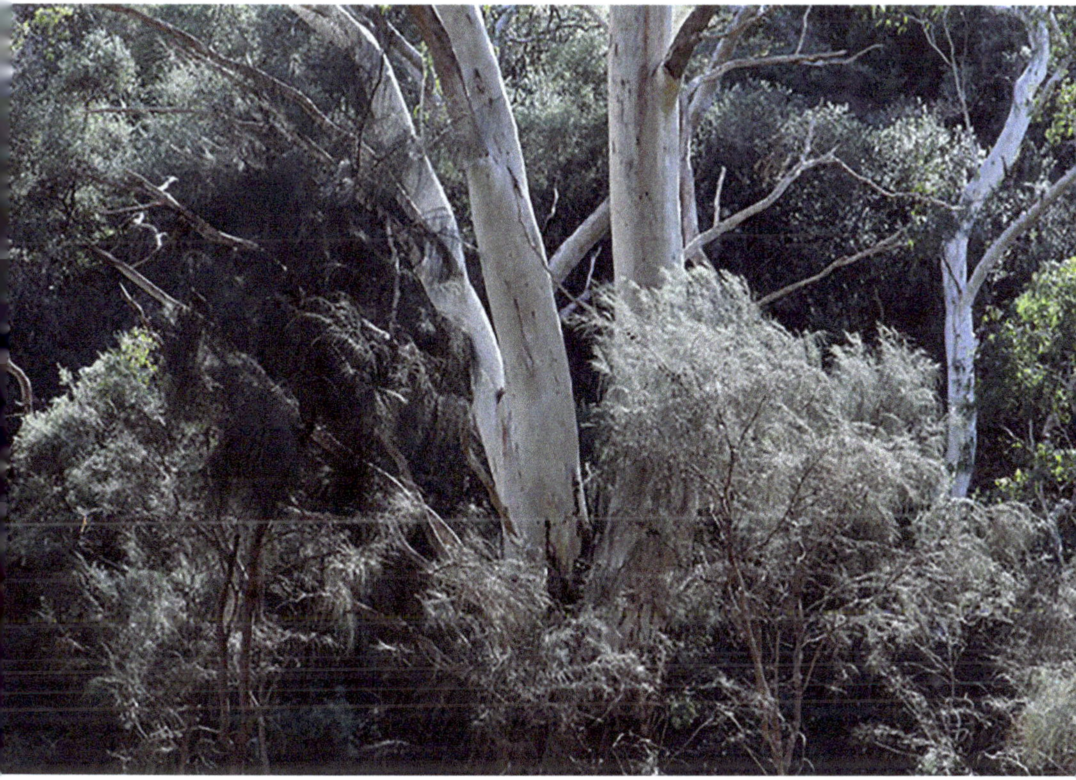

Figure 3 *Morialta Conservation Park, South Australia*. Eddee Daniel (2015). Photograph.

authentic ways of knowing. All of you sharing how, together in communities, you learned to think from your intimacy with all these places, to sit with the unnamed and follow its shadows (Akomolafe, 2016).

As I listen deeply with my heart, the ground beneath my feet shifts and cracks open. The colours of art therapy take on the reds and ochre of the Australian soil, the sage and sepias of the bush, and dusty charcoals of the campfires. "Where is *here*?" (Westwood, this volume) you ask. You are always asking this profound question, as it guides your knowing that the world is a web. My dreams are linked with you across time and space; our boundaries are porous and ever changing. We are in constant touch, thoroughly tangled up in each other's realities and histories. I imagine you theorising, hierarchising, interrogating, celebrating, deconstructing, and re constructing your work as many others have before you. But what I love and celebrate most is how much further you are able to take art therapy – far more expansively and beyond anything I could ever conceive or even imagine.

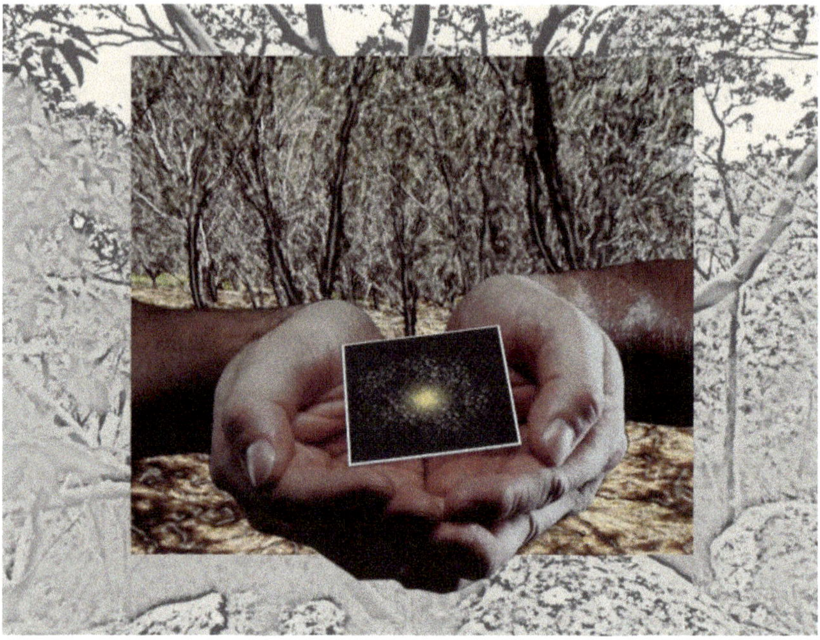

Figure 4 *Dreaming Australia, into art therapy's future.* Lynn Kapitan (2018). Digital collage.

I cup my hands reverently and imagine holding infinite images of you as the future of art therapy. But I do not think for a minute that when art therapy took its de-colonising, aesthetic turn, it was an easy embrace. Accountable to the 2,400 generations who were here before you, (Lawson et al, this volume) you would have had to help each other change the perceptual habits of so many art therapists in their lifetimes to be able to really see what is before your eyes (Henzell, this volume). What did you surround yourself with to say who you are? (Johnston, this volume). What myriad ways are you taking action on the knowledge that all oppression is interconnected? I dream of you heeding the call for liberation, courageously beginning the work of a different tomorrow.

Art therapists of the future, you inspire me by revealing what is possible. We cannot continue to live on this fragile earth without awareness of our interconnection to each other and to all beings. We must change. You carry my profound hope that thousands of years hence, though others may not know it, this work of healing will continue – in the movement of light and shadows across the landscape, in the rich and varied currents of creation ever flowing.

References

Akomolafe, B. (2016, June 20). *Dear white people – An open letter.* Retrieved from https://upliftconnect.com/dear-white-people/.

Biko, S. (1978). *I write what I like: Selected writings.* Bowerdean Press, London, England.

Grosfoguel, R. (2011). Decolonising post-colonial studies and paradigms of political-economy: transmodernity, decolonial thinking, and global coloniality. *Transmodernity: Journal of Peripheral Cultural Production of the Luso-Hispanic World,* 1(1). Retrieved from https://escholarship.org/uc/item/21k6t3fq.

Henzell, J. (2019). Psyche nullius: Reflections on art psychotherapy and psychiatry down under. In: A. Gilroy, S. Linnell, T. McKenna, and J. Westwood (Eds.). *Art therapy in Australia: Taking a postcolonial, aesthetic turn.* Brill Sense, Leiden and Boston, MA.

Johnston, P. (2019). Talking you talking me talking Aborigine. In: A. Gilroy, S. Linnell, T. McKenna, and J. Westwood (Eds.). *Art therapy in Australia: Taking a postcolonial, aesthetic turn.* Brill Sense, Leiden and Boston MA.

Kapitan, L. (2015). *Arts therapies in the ecotone: Contact, collaboration, and creative entanglement.* Keynote address to the Joint Conference of the Australian and New Zealand Arts Therapy Association and the Australian Creative Arts Therapy Association, Adelaide, Australia. October 2015.

Lawson, C., Woods, C., and McKenna, T. (2019). Towards Indigenous Australian knowing. In: A. Gilroy, S. Linnell, T. McKenna, and J. Westwood (Eds.). *Art therapy in Australia: Taking a postcolonial, aesthetic turn.* Brill Sense, Leiden and Boston, MA.

Martín-Baró, I. (1994). *Writings for a liberation psychology.* Harvard University Press, Boston, MA.

Napoli, M. (2018). *Ma tallepo 'opu ma 'akkala kennetto / We are waking up our story together. Arts-based Indigenous methodology.* Unpublished doctoral dissertation. Mount Mary University, Milwaukee, WI.

Watters, E. (2011). *Crazy like us: The globalisation of the American psyche.* The Free Press, New York, NY.

Westwood, J. (2019). Hybrid creatures: Art therapy education in Australia. In: A. Gilroy, S. Linnell, T. McKenna, and J. Westwood (Eds.). *Art therapy in Australia: Taking a postcolonial, aesthetic turn.* Brill Sense, Leiden and Boston MA.

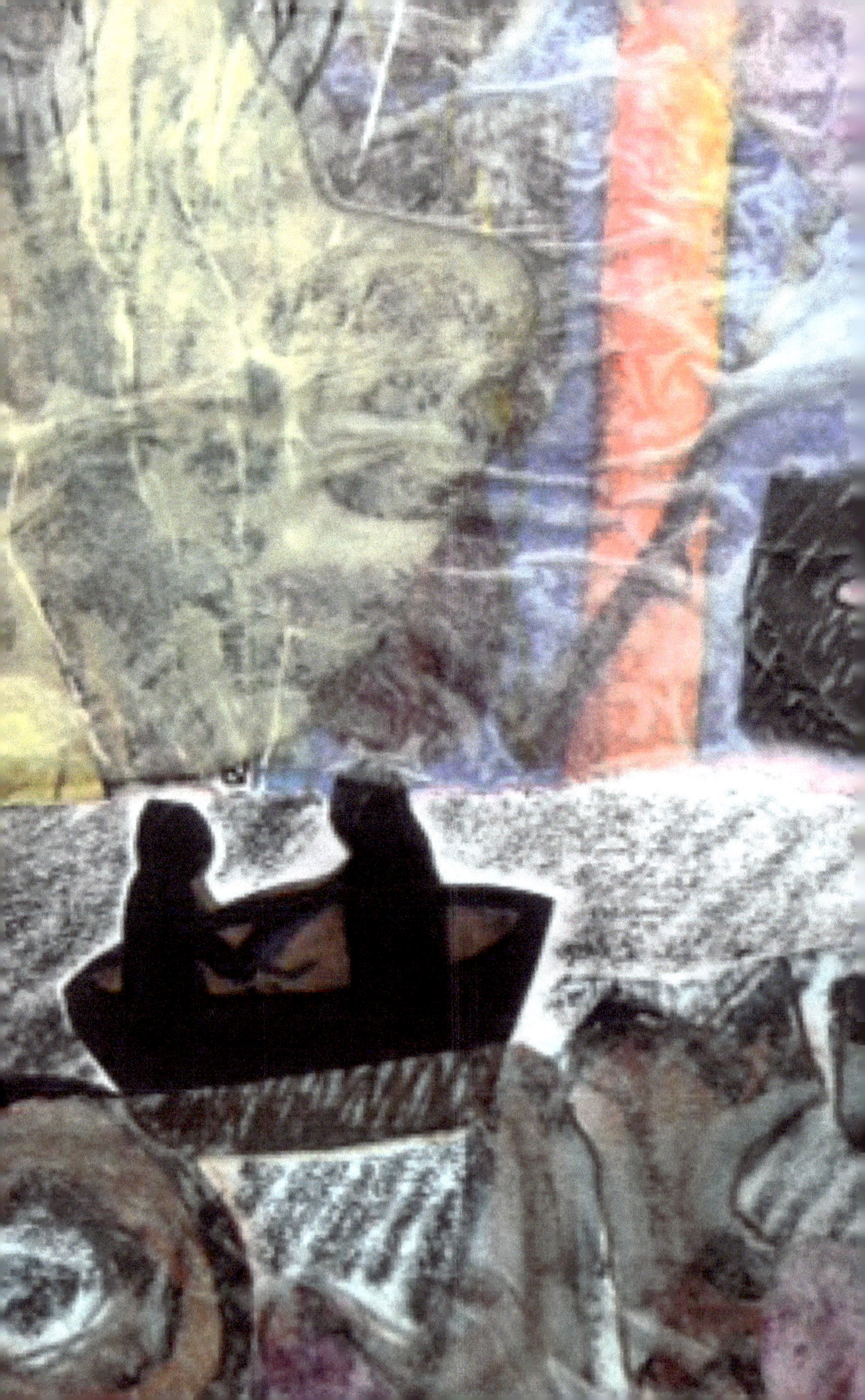

ABOUT THE CONTRIBUTORS

Jan Allen is the academic director at MIECAT and helped establish The MIECAT Institute (previously Melbourne Institute for Experiential and Creative Arts Therapy) more than 19 years ago. Jan teaches in the graduate program and supervises doctoral students at MIECAT, as well as collaborating in publications related to arts-based research, postcard dialogues and arts and intersubjectivity. Jan is a photographer and is currently undertaking daily practice of posting a photo a day on social media. This project called Fifty/2 has been going for four years.

Claire Edwards has a Postgraduate Diploma in Art Therapy from Goldsmiths, University of London and a Research Masters (art therapy and eating issues) from the University of Western Sydney. Claire has worked in child and youth mental health for 16 years and is currently in private practice at the innovative Kooky Clinic in Springwood, Queensland. Claire also has experience in adult mental health, trauma and alcohol and drug rehabilitation. In 2004 Claire helped establish the Masters of Mental Health – Art Therapy at University of Queensland where she now lectures. Claire has several publications focusing on clinical practice and art therapy outcomes.

Nicolette Eisdell's qualifications include a Diploma in Painting and Drawing from the Julian Ashton Art School; MA Art Therapy from the University of Western Sydney; and a Diploma of Adult Psychotherapy from Australia and New Zealand Association of Psychotherapists. For 14 years she was the sole art therapist at Long Bay Psychiatric Hospital, which later became the Forensic Hospital. Nicolette has been a finalist in several public exhibitions in Australia: the Salon des Refusés, The Portia Geach Women's Portrait Award, the New South Wales Parliament Plein Air Painting Prize and Eutick Memorial Still Life Award.

Patricia Fenner is Senior Lecturer and Course Coordinator of the Master of Art Therapy at La Trobe University, Melbourne. She is a researcher with diverse interests in art-based research, art-making and mental health recovery, and in particular, how the everyday material settings of our work play a role in what occurs in practice. Prior to working in the university sector, she worked in diverse contexts including public mental health and school education, as well as, as a community artist in both Melbourne and Berlin.

Andrea Gilroy is Emeritus at Goldsmiths, University of London, having spent 35 years as an art therapy educator and researcher and, latterly, a senior manager at the college. Between 1994 and 2007 she maintained an occasional role as an art therapy educator and researcher at the (then) University of Western Sydney. She has published widely, e.g. *Art Therapy, Research and Evidence-Based Practice* (2006), *Art Therapy Research in Practice* (2010), *Assessment in Art Therapy* (2012). Andy's 'encore' career has seen her returning to her practice as an artist.

Opposite: Detail of *It's been a long time*. Andy Gilroy (2016/17).
Collage, pencil, oil pastels and tissue paper on paper.

Julie Graves is a practising artist who uses a range of materials and experimental techniques to produce drawings, paintings and textiles. After graduating from Goldsmiths with a First in Textiles, she was appointed research assistant and digital archivist to The Constance Howard Resource and Research Centre in Textiles in London where she was approached by Andy Gilroy to create the original designs on which this book is based. She now lives and works in Portsmouth, creating work to commission and for exhibitions and taking part in community arts projects.

John Henzell was born in Manchester in 1938 but after his family emigrated to Western Australia in 1941 was educated and went to art school in Perth. He returned to Britain in 1959 and began working with psychiatric patients in NHS psychiatric hospitals. He became one of a small group who pioneered the use of image-making in psychotherapy and published their ideas in the journal they created and called *Inscape* – a word coined by Gerard Manley Hopkins to indicate the psychological force of vivid perception. He has worked in several universities in the UK and other countries as a lecturer, course leader, visiting speaker and examiner.

Pam Johnston was a visual artist, represented in collections in Australia and overseas before her untimely death in 2013 in a motorbike accident (Diana Wood Conroy's paper about Pam and her work *Pam Johnston Dahl Helm: Lost to our mothers* (2014) can be found here: http://ro.uow.edu.au/cgi/viewcontent.cgi?article=2376&context=lha papers). Pam, a Gomileroi woman, obtained her Doctorate at Wollongong University in New South Wales and wrote on education theory and cultural theory, particularly postcolonial theory. She lectured at several universities across Australia and in Britain and, beginning in 1989, taught in a number of Australian prisons including Long Bay Prison and the former Norma Parker Centre. At the time of writing this chapter she was a visual arts teacher and the Aboriginal programmes teacher at Emu Plains minimum security women's prison and Mulawa Women's Correctional Centre.

Lynn Kapitan is a Professor at Mount Mary University in Milwaukee. She is a former executive editor of *Art Therapy: Journal of the American Art Therapy Association* for which she has served for the past 25 years as peer reviewer, advisor, editor and publisher. Lynn is past president of the American Art Therapy Association and was awarded AATA's highest honour for her contributions to the advancement of art therapy. She currently practices community-based, cross-cultural art therapy in consultation with non-governmental organisations in Latin America. She has published widely on social action in art therapy, multicultural issues, research, strategic policy development, professional issues and leadership.

Carmen Lawson is a Murri woman from Queensland who, until retirement, worked as a counsellor/advocate and art therapist at Yorgum Aboriginal Family Counselling Service in Western Australia. She graduated with a BFA at Edith Cowan University, Perth in Western Australia and went on to complete her MA in Art Therapy. Carmen has a commitment to social justice for all people. She has an active interest in the combined use of the arts and in the use of performance art as a way of bringing meaning to the communities she lives in.

Sheridan Linnell is Associate Professor of Art Therapy at Western Sydney University, Australia, where she is also the Director of Academic Program for Clinical Psychology and Therapy Studies in the School of Social Sciences and Psychology. Her work encompasses teaching in the Master of Art Therapy and Master of Psychotherapy and Counselling, advising research students, and collaborative, arts-based and narrative research partnerships. Sheridan is a practising poet and occasionally collaborates on installation and performance art with colleagues and friends. She is passionate about socially just art therapy for a postcolonial, diverse world.

Paul Manning works in book publishing as a freelance editor and designer. He specialises in the design and production of educational and academic books and has overseen large-scale publishing projects including the Oxford History of Art and the Oxford University Press *Very Short Introductions* series. He currently works from a studio in his home on the edge of the Forest of Dean in the west of England.

Tarquam McKenna is a Professor at Deakin University, Melbourne, Australia. He has been active as an arts psychotherapist for thirty years and is past president and an honorary life member of ANZATA – the Australian and New Zealand Art Therapy Association. He is keenly interested in research methods and especially their applicability to Indigenous stories. Tarquam has taught, researched and supervised widely in the area of the arts, gender and sexuality. He is a founding member of the Asia Critical Ensemble, which examines social justice and the legacies of Paulo Freire in particular, and how colonisation has impacted on multiple lives around the world.

Michelle Moss is a lecturer in Health Sciences and Sociology at Charles Darwin University and a qualified Art Therapist, who has worked for many years as a child and family counsellor and in child protection with Indigenous children, families, and communities. Her research interests include arts therapy, working therapeutically with Indigenous people, critical pedagogy and child protection. She is currently researching the transferability of the TeaH (Turn 'em around Healing) model to Indigenous communities. The model has the potential to radically change how therapeutic work is conducted with Indigenous children who live in remote communities and as a result improve mental health outcomes.

Suzanne Perry is a practising artist and art psychotherapist; she has a Masters in Art Therapy and a Bachelor of Visual Arts. For the past 16 years she has been lecturing and providing clinical supervision at Western Sydney University for trainees undertaking their Masters in Art Therapy. She specialises in working with adults, children and their families who have experienced complex trauma and mental health conditions through the impact of family violence and interpersonal abuse. Suzanne's art practice explores the abject and the unconscious through painting, film and digital media.

Josephine Pretorius worked as a counsellor in child protection and domestic violence before training as an art therapist at the University of Western Sydney. Since qualifying she has worked in hospitals and community settings as well as in private practice. She taught for some years on the Masters Art Therapy program at the University of Western Sydney. She is currently working as a pastoral carer for the Sisters of Saint Joseph. She has a particular interest in the resonances between contemplative traditions and art therapy.

Jean Rumbold is a lecturer in the Department of Public Health at La Trobe University, supervising doctoral research, and has worked in private practice as a counselling psychologist and family therapist, and in leadership development with a range of business, educational and welfare groups. Her background is in education, and, like Jan Allen, she helped establish MIECAT and supervises in the professional doctorate there. Her research interests focus on arts and health, reflective practice, and arts-based and co-operative forms of inquiry. She co-edited *Knowing differently: Experiential and arts-based research methods* with Pranee Liamputtong.

Victoria Schnaedelbach is an Arts Psychotherapist, Arts Educator and Artist, practising in Melbourne. Late in her undergraduate medical education, she departed to pursue her special interest in the healing arts; the role of creativity in health and well-being. With a Masters in Experiential and Creative Arts in Therapy and a Bachelor of Medical Science, major research arenas include medical training about child sexual abuse, 'new ways of being with' mood disorders and chronic illness, and social and emotional learning. She was in private practice and also delivered arts programs in primary and secondary schools and community settings for numerous years and has now chosen to pursue a full-time personal arts practice whilst she attends to some health concerns.

Lilian Tann has completed the Masters in Experiential and Creative Arts Therapy at MIECAT. She has worked with children, adults and the elderly in community and institutional settings using the creative arts. Her background is in organisational work and she is currently working at MIECAT.

Jody Thomson is a visual art therapist in private practice, specialising in oncology since 2009. She is also a practising artist, a casual lecturer on the MA Art Therapy and a Social Sciences PhD candidate at Western Sydney University. She facilitates group psychotherapy for not-for-profit community organisations, a major hospital cancer support centre in Sydney, and is the founder and facilitator of an arts-based psychosocial cancer support charity. Her PhD research focuses on collaborative, ethnographic art-based inquiry into the experience of the therapist working with terminally diagnosed clients and cancer support service providers in allied health.

Jill Westwood is an artist, researcher, HCPC-registered Art Psychotherapist and Programme Convenor of the MA Art Psychotherapy, Goldsmiths, University of London. From 1995 to 2007 Jill was Course Coordinator of the MA Art Therapy and GD Expressive Therapies at Western Sydney University, NSW, Australia. Her art practice encompasses film, installation and performance and is concerned with the emotional and relational aspects of human experience. This draws on and is influenced by her experience as an art psychotherapist–educator. Her research interests include art-based approaches, art therapy education and the interface between art therapy and contemporary art.

Amanda Woodford is currently a Professional Doctorate candidate at MIECAT. An artist, arts therapist (MA CAT, AThR) and academic (MIECAT), she lives in Melbourne, Australia but was born and bred in Dunedin, New Zealand/Aotearoa. With both European and Middle Eastern heritage, she is interested in how therapeutic arts-based processes may assist in supporting community integration and a greater understanding of self.

Davina B. Woods, an Indigenous Australian, was a lecturer and PhD candidate in the School of Education at Victoria University. She wrote on colonisation and retracing her own family stories using 'artful autoethnography' which over time transformed into Creative Healing Inquiry. Her research and teaching had as one of its main objects to contribute to the paradigm shift regarding attitudinal and behavioural decolonisation as discussed in her co-authored chapter with Carmen Lawson and Tarquam McKenna.

INDEX

www.ingramcontent.com/pod-product-compliance
Ingram Content Group UK Ltd.
Pitfield, Milton Keynes, MK11 3LW, UK
UKHW022208051026
15624UKWH00001B/60

9 789004 315181